Proven[illegible]
the Côte d'Azur

3rd Edition

Benoit Éthier
Hans Jörg Mettler
François Hénault
Howard Rombough

Travel better, enjoy more

ULYSSES

Travel Guides

Authors
Benoit Éthier
Hans Jörg Mettler
François Hénault
Howard Rombough

Publisher
Pascale Couture

Editor
Stéphane G. Marceau

Project Coordinator
Jacqueline Grekin

Copy Editing
Anne Joyce
Eileen Connolly

Artistic Director
Patrick Farei (Atoll)

Page Layout
Typesetting
Isabelle Lalonde
Visuals
Anne Joyce
Isabelle Lalonde

Translation
Stephanie Heidenreich
Natalie Philpot
Christina Poole
Tracy Kendrick
Sarah Kresh
Danielle Gauthier
Andrea Szakos

Cartographers
André Duchesne
Yanik Landreville
Patrick Thivierge
Bradley Fenton

Computer Graphics
Stéphanie Routhier

Illustrations
Marie-Annick Viatour
Josée Perreault
Richard Serrao
Vincent Desruisseaux
Jenny Jasper

Photography
Cover Page
Bernard Van Berg
The Image Bank
Inside Pages
M. Raget/Megapress
Mauritus-Vidler/Reflexion
Tibor Bognár/Reflexion
Mehlig/Reflexion
Hinous/Megapress
E. Luider/Megapress
C. Sappa/Megapress

Acknowledgements: Many thanks to our friends in the region for their support and encouragement, in particular to Danièle Bérard, without whose help creating the Provençal French lexicon would have been much more arduous; thanks also to Bertrand Pierson, Christian Dussac, Sandra Hélie (CRT PACA), Francine Riou (office de tourisme d'Arles), Katia Zeitlin (office de tourisme Marseille), Natalie Steinberg and Carole Amy (CDT Bouches du Rhône), Gaël Jean (Gattière, France) and François Guindon.

OFFICES
CANADA: Ulysses Travel Guides, 4176 Saint-Denis, Montréal, Québec, H2W 2M5,
☎ (514) 843-9447 or 1-877-542-7247, ≠(514) 843-9448, info@ulysses.ca, www.ulyssesguides.com

EUROPE: Les Guides de Voyage Ulysse SARL, BP 159, 75523 Paris Cedex 11, France,
☎ 01 43 38 89 50, ≠01 43 38 89 52, voyage@ulysse.ca, www.ulyssesguides.com

U.S.A.: Ulysses Travel Guides, 305 Madison Avenue, Suite 1166, New York, NY 10165,
☎ 1-877-542-7247, info@ulysses.ca, www.ulyssesguides.com

DISTRIBUTORS
CANADA: Ulysses Books & Maps, 4176 Saint-Denis, Montréal, Québec, H2W 2M5,
☎ (514) 843-9882, ext.2232, 800-748-9171, Fax: 514-843-9448, info@ulysses.ca,
www.ulyssesguides.com

GREAT BRITAIN AND IRELAND: World Leisure Marketing, Unit 11, Newmarket Court, Newmartket Drive, Derby DE24 8NW, ☎ 1 332 57 37 37, Fax: 1 332 57 33 99
office@wlmsales.co.uk

SCANDINAVIA: Scanvik, Esplanaden 8B, 1263 Copenhagen K, DK, ☎ (45) 33.12.77.66,
Fax: (45) 33.91.28.82

SPAIN: Altaïr, Balmes 69, E-08007 Barcelona, ☎ 454 29 66, Fax: 451 25 59,
altair@globalcom.es

SWITZERLAND: OLF, P.O. Box 1061, CH-1701 Fribourg, ☎ (026) 467.51.11,
Fax: (026) 467.54.66

U.S.A.: The Globe Pequot Press, 246 Goose Lane, Guilford, CT 06437 - 0480,
☎1-800-243-0495, Fax: 800-820-2329, sales@globe-pequot.com

Other countries, contact Ulysses Books & Maps, 4176 Saint-Denis, Montréal, Québec, H2W 2M5,
☎ (514) 843-9882, ext.2232, 800-748-9171, Fax: 514-843-9448, info@ulysses.ca, www.ulyssesguides.com

Canadian Cataloguing-in-Publication Data (see page 7)

Printed in Canada
ISBN 2-89464-327-6

Everything is full-blooded. The food is full of strong earthy flavors... There is nothing bland about Provence...

Peter Mayle *A Year in Provence*

Table of Contents

Symbols

(ship symbol)	Ulysses's favourite
☎	Telephone number
⇄	Fax number
≡	Air conditioning
⊗	Fan
≈	Pool
ℜ	Restaurant
⊛	Whirlpool
ℝ	Refrigerator
K	Kitchenette
⌂	Sauna
⊘	Fitness centre
tv	Colour television
pb	Private bathroom
sb	Shared bathroom
s	Shower
ps	Private shower
fb	Full board (lodging + 3 meals)
½ b	Half board (lodging + 2 meals)
bkfst incl.	Breakfast included

ATTRACTION CLASSIFICATION

★	Interesting
★★	Worth a visit
★★★	Not to be missed

The prices listed in this guide are for the admission of one adult.

HOTEL CLASSIFICATION

The prices in this guide are for one standard room, double occupancy in high season.

RESTAURANT CLASSIFICATION

$	75F or less
$$	75F to 150F
$$$	150F to 225F
$$$$	225F or more

The prices in the guide are for a meal for one person, not including drinks and tip.

All prices in this guide are in French Francs.

Write to Us

The information contained in this guide was correct at press time. However, mistakes can slip in, omissions are always possible, places can disappear, etc. The authors and publisher hereby disclaim any liability for loss or damage resulting from omissions or errors.

We value your comments, corrections and suggestions, as they allow us to keep each guide up to date. The best contributions will be rewarded with a free book from Ulysses Travel Guides. All you have to do is write us at the following address and indicate which title you would be interested in receiving (see the list at the end of guide).

Ulysses Travel Guides
4176 Saint-Denis
Montréal, Québec
Canada H2W 2M5
www.ulyssesguides.com
E-mail: text@ulysses.ca

We acknowledge the financial support of the Government of Canada through the Book Publishing Industry Development Program (BPIDP) for our publishing activities.

We would also like to thank SODEC (Québec) for its financial support.

Cataloguing

Canadian Cataloguing-in-Publication Data

Main entry under title:

Provence & the Côte d'Azur

(Ulysses travel guide)

ISSN 1486-2646
ISBN 2-89464-327-6

1. Provence (France) - Guidebooks. 2. Riviera (France) - Guidebooks. I. Series

DC611.P958P7613 914.4'90484 C00-301881-5

List of Maps

Map Symbols

	Tourist information		Bird Sanctuary
	Train station		Mountain
	Bus station		Ruins
	Airport		Fortifications
	Parking		Lookout
	Beach		Church

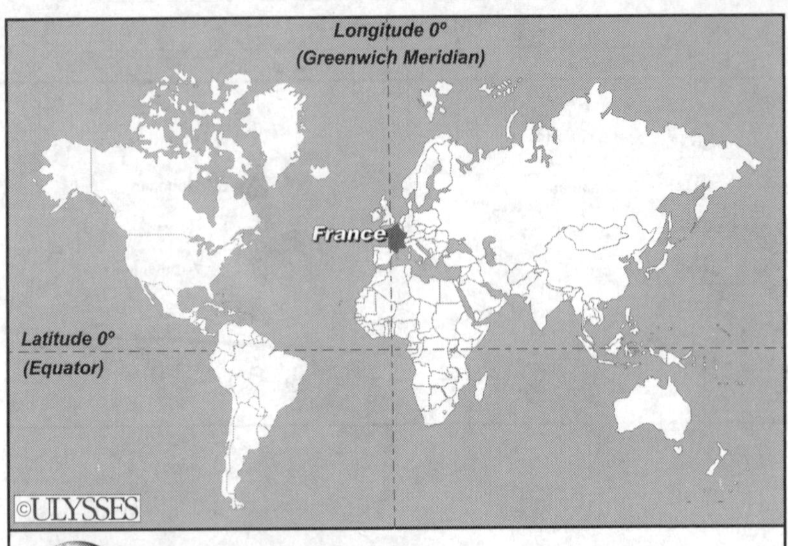

Where are Provence and the Côte d'Azur?

FRANCE	Provence-Alpes-Côte d'Azur
Capital: Paris Language: French Population: 58,333,000 inhab. Area: 547,026 km² (211,152 sq mi)	Population: 4,257,000 inhab. Area: 31,400 km² (12,120 sq mi)

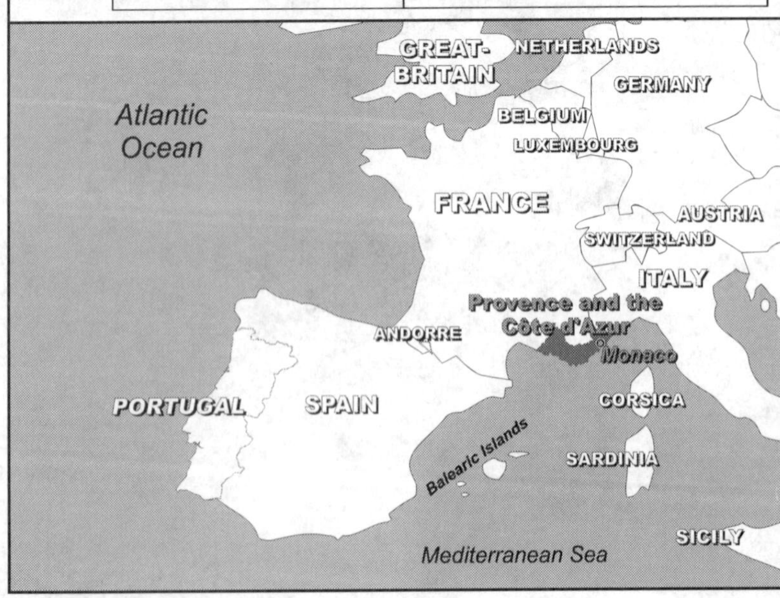

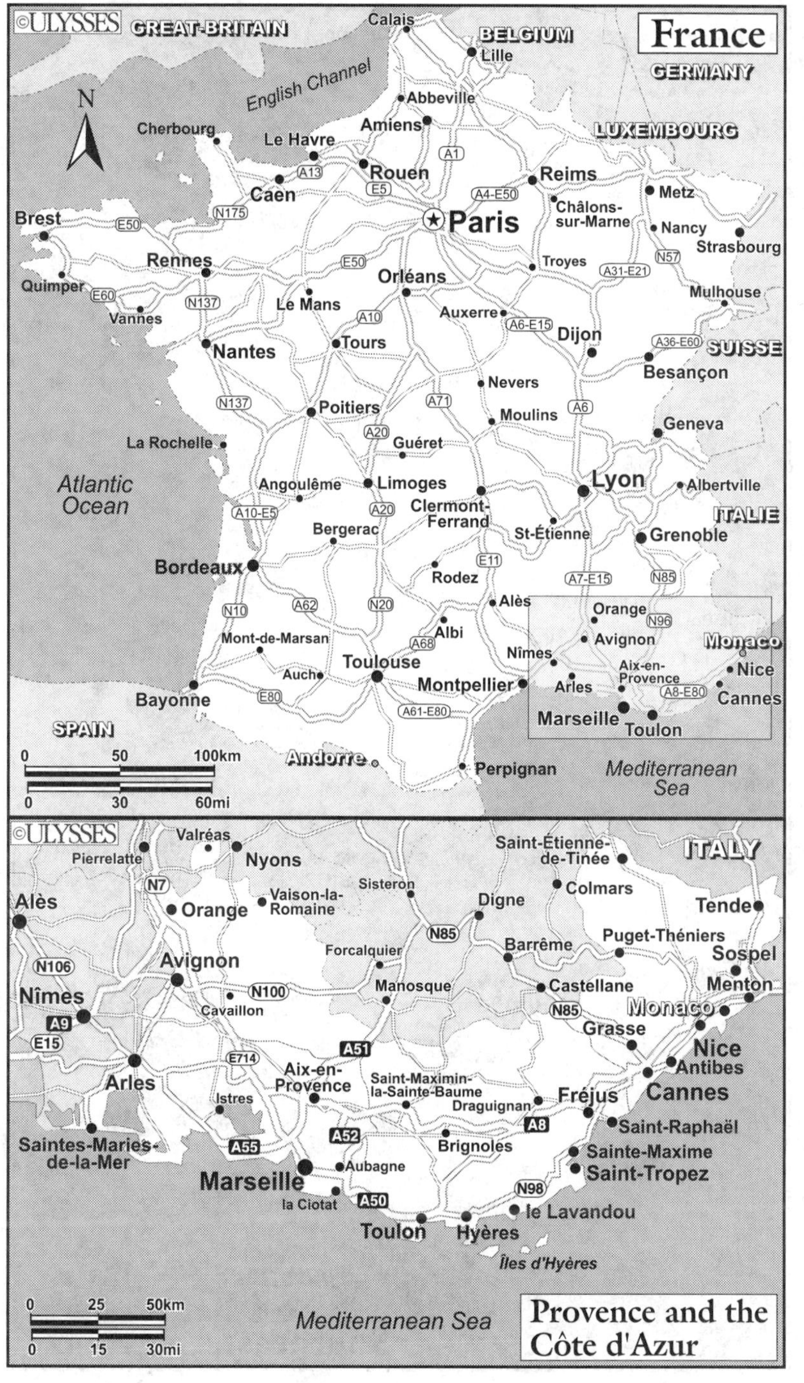
©ULYSSES
France
GREAT-BRITAIN
BELGIUM
GERMANY
LUXEMBOURG
SUISSE
ITALIE
SPAIN
Andorre
Monaco
English Channel
Atlantic Ocean
Mediterranean Sea
Calais
Lille
Abbeville
Amiens
Cherbourg
Le Havre
Rouen
Caen
Reims
Metz
Châlons-sur-Marne
Nancy
Strasbourg
Paris
Brest
Rennes
Quimper
Vannes
Troyes
Orléans
Le Mans
Auxerre
Mulhouse
Dijon
Besançon
Tours
Nantes
Nevers
Moulins
Poitiers
Geneva
La Rochelle
Guéret
Lyon
Limoges
Angoulême
Albertville
Clermont-Ferrand
St-Étienne
Grenoble
Bergerac
Bordeaux
Rodez
Alès
Orange
Avignon
Albi
Mont-de-Marsan
Nîmes
Toulouse
Aix-en-Provence
Nice
Auch
Montpellier
Arles
Cannes
Bayonne
Marseille
Toulon
Perpignan
A1
A13
E5
A4-E50
N175
E50
N57
A31-E21
N137
A10
E60
A6-E15
A36-E60
A71
A6
N137
A20
A10-E5
A20
E11
A7-E15
N85
N10
A62
N20
N96
A68
A8-E80
E80
A61-E80
0 50 100km
0 30 60mi
©ULYSSES
ITALY
Valréas
Pierrelatte
Nyons
Saint-Étienne-de-Tinée
Colmars
Sisteron
N7
Alès
Orange
Vaison-la-Romaine
Digne
Tende
N85
Puget-Théniers
Forcalquier
Barrême
Sospel
N106
Avignon
Castellane
Menton
Manosque
Nîmes
N100
Cavaillon
Monaco
A9
N85
Grasse
E15
A51
Nice
Antibes
E714
Arles
Aix-en-Provence
Saint-Maximin-la-Sainte-Baume
Fréjus
Cannes
Istres
Draguignan
A8
Saint-Raphaël
Saintes-Maries-de-la-Mer
A52
Brignoles
A55
Sainte-Maxime
Aubagne
Saint-Tropez
Marseille
N98
la Ciotat
A50
le Lavandou
Toulon
Hyères
Îles d'Hyères
0 25 50km
0 15 30mi
Mediterranean Sea
Provence and the Côte d'Azur

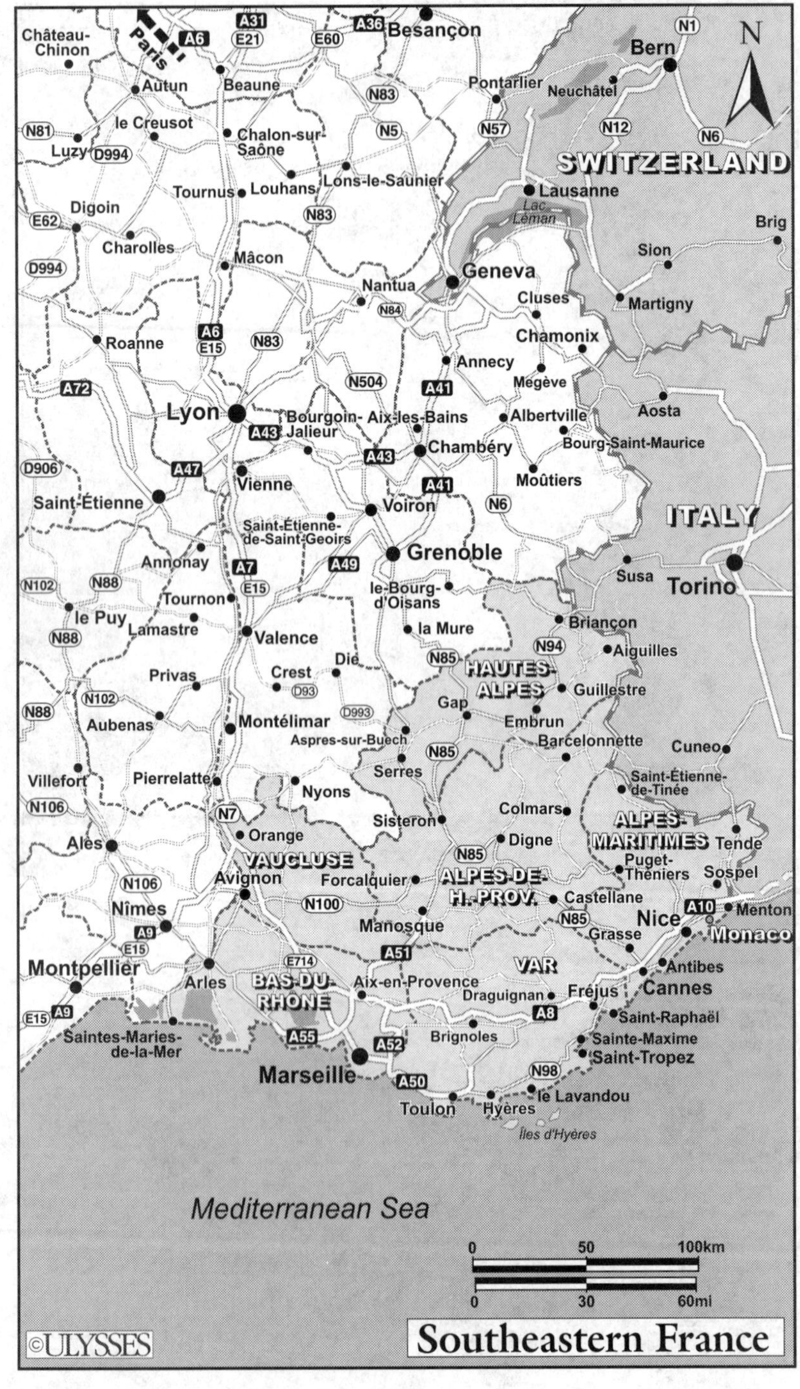

Southeastern France

Provence and the Côte d'Azur is a land of contrasts.

Its sunny climate and Mediterranean way of life offer something for everyone, no matter what your interests may be. Visitors will find sandy beaches on the Riviera, low plains in the Camargue, gently rolling hills in the Luberon and Vaucluse and steeper territory in the southern Alps. The lively metropolitan centres on the coast differ sharply from the traditional villages, hidden paths and panoramic landscapes of the interior. There are an infinite variety of treasures to discover in Provence and the Côte d'Azur. Around every corner there seems to be another Roman monument, field of beautiful lavender or delicious meal of *bouillabaisse* or *ratatouille* just waiting to be claimed, inhaled and devoured.

Geography

The region is bordered by four distinct geographical features: the Rivière Rhône to the west, the Comtat Venaissin and southern part of the Alps to the north, the Italian border to the east and the Mediterranean Sea to the south. The administrative and economic region known as of Provence-Alpes-Côte d'Azur as a whole counts 31,436m^2 (338,385 sq ft) and over four million inhabitants.

Provence and the Côte d'Azur is the most visited region in France, due to its fine weather, variety of natural beauty and historic sites, and of course, its Riviera attractions. Typically dry, hot summers are contrasted with unpredictable weather the remainder of the year. Winters can be harsh and cloudy in the mountainous areas, and mild along the coast. The Rhône Valley and part of the coast are frequently hit by the mistral, the cold, violent wind coming from the north at speeds of up to 290km/hr (108mph).

In general, the land is characterized by an undulating topographical surface and a magnificent luminosity, as it is an area that receives a great deal of year-round sunshine. Provence and the Côte d'Azur is distinguished by three geographical areas: the **low plains** of the Comtat, Crau and Camargue at the mouth of the Rhône basin; the **interior** with the calcareous plains of Provence, the hills of Provence and the mountains of the *Préalpes du Sud*; and finally, the rocky **coastline**, including the cliffs east of Marseille.

Low Plains of the Comtat, Camargue and Crau

These low regions next to the Rhône, (less than 250m (820ft) above sea level), are essentially alluvial plains. The Comtat and Camargue are muddy lands, while the Crau is pebbly. The narrow coastal plain is equally low and forms a ribbon the length of the Mediterranean.

Interior

The homogeneous, yet puzzle-like series of hills, plateaus and basins (250 to 500m or 820 to 1,640ft) is dominated by a great limestone chain stretching east-west. The hills of Provence include the Alpilles, Lubéron, Sainte-Victoire and Sainte-Baume, and are primarily of sedimentary rock. The Maures and Estérel range near the coast is of crystalline soil. From Mont Ventoux (1,909m or 6,263ft) passing by the Préalpes and reaching the Mercantour, the mountainous region rarely surpasses 3,500m (11,482ft). They are strongly marked by rough mountain ridges and deep limestone valleys.

Coastline

The varied Mediterranean coast is distinguished by the low, sandy riverbanks of the west, and the rocky cliffs of the east. Among these are the impressive white coves around Marseille (the highest cliffs in Europe) and the red porphyry ledges of the Esterel.

Flora

The sunshine and favourable climate of Provence and the Côte d'Azur allow many interesting trees and flowers to grow in the region. Olive and oak trees are predominant in the lower regions, as both enjoy the limestone soil under altitudes of 700m (2,297ft). The olive tree was introduced to the region by the Greeks 3,000 years ago, who called it "the tree of wisdom, abundance and glory."

Nowadays there are more than 50 varieties of olive trees; they grow to between 5 and 8m (16.4 and 26.2ft) and some reach 20m (65.6ft). Although they have a long life span, (centuries or even thousands of years), the olive tree's fruit is only suitable for picking for the first 15 years. The harvest is between November and January, depending on whether the ripe green olives or the mature black ones are desired. One thousand kilograms (2,205lbs) of olives give 10 to 15L (2.6 to 4gal) of oil. The first pressing yields the most sought-after virgin olive oil.

The holm oak (*chêne vert)* and the scrub oak (*chêne kermès*), both stubby trees, are seen throughout the region, including on hillsides slightly higher than those tolerated by the olive groves. Trees found on the plains or hillsides of the interior include pine (maritime, parasol and aleppo), the tall, distinctively shaped Cypress in their neat rows, plane, lotus, lime/linden (*tilleul*) sycamore and almond. Fields of lavender, displaying their violet flowers all summer long, are found in the hilly areas above 1,000m (3,281ft).

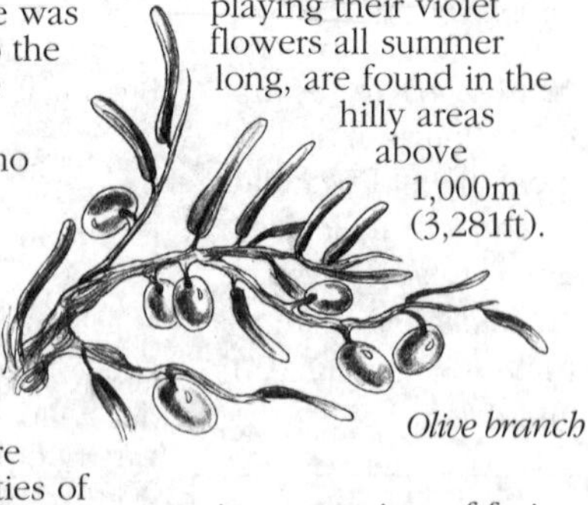

Olive branch

A great variety of fruit trees grow locally, principally peach, cherry, apricot, apple, pear and lemon. Carpentras and

Cavaillon are renowned for their tasty melons. Asparagus, new potatoes, strawberries, mushrooms and dessert grapes are found as well. Vineyards, either in the Côtes de Provence area northeast of Marseille or Côtes du Rhône in the southern Rhône valley near Orange produce fine drinking wines, including fruity rosés, dry whites and the famous reds, Gigondas and Châteauneuf-du-Pape.

Herbs are abundant throughout the area, especially rosemary, thyme and savoury which grow wild. Basil, marjoram, summer savoury (*sarriette*) and tarragon are popular. A selection of these, called *herbes de Provence* are sold in markets, and used in cooking to enhance meat, fish and sauces. Many of these plants are used traditionally as herbal remedies or for medicinal purposes. Sage is supposed to be good for fatigue and liver problems, rosemary helps the respiratory system and thyme is said to be an aphrodisiac. Herbal teas or *infusions* from thyme, rosemary or laurel are reputed to

Lavender Country

"La lavande est l'âme de la haute Provence." (Lavender is the soul of Upper Provence.)
- Jean Giono

Lavender is more than a symbol of Provence: it is the hallmark of this wild, secluded region with wonderful discoveries hidden around each bend in the road. It is impossible to imagine this region, stretching from the Vaucluse to the Alpes-de-Hautes-Provence and from the Hautes-Alpes to the border of the Drôme, without conjuring up images of the infinite, rolling expanses of mauve that stretch to the horizon and whose scent wafts through the villages and enchanting landscapes. An integral part of Provençal culture, the magic of lavender can be found everywhere, including distilleries, museums and gardens. Visitors, charmed by its scent, follow it through villages and picturesque landscapes, and discover it in the markets and fairs, which reveal the myriad lavender products available, from bouquets to lavender essence and honey. Lavender is harvested when it is in full bloom, from mid-July to mid-August, and will deeply move those with an eye for beauty in nature. Since the 1950s, the traditional lavender has been almost completely replaced by its cousin, lavandine, which produces five times as much oil. Today this new species accounts for approximately 80% of the lavender produced in Provence, while the original variety is found only in the highlands. Tourism offices can help you find the most beautiful spots and also provide you with *Les Routes de la Lavande*, a free brochure that guides you through lavender country. Among the loveliest fields of the Vaucluse, we recommend those by the Abbaye de Sénaque near Gordes, the Musée de la Lavande at Coustellet and around Sault, east of Nont-Ventoux on the Vaucluse plateau.

aid digestion. The Camargue is famous for its salt production, collected from the sea, pumped across huge salt tables, left to dry, then raked, washed and dried each September. It will later be ready for the dinner table.

Flowers feature largely in the countryside, markets and gardens of Provence Côte d'Azur. Roses, jasmin and carnations are also cultivated professionally for the perfume market, traditionally centred in Grasse. An estimated 10,000 tonnes of flowers are treated there every year and it is said that for every four bottles of perfume which circulate throughout the world, three use the floral essences originating in Provence.

Worth seeing are the regional natural parks, like that of Camargue. Since 1970, the Camargue park protects 500km^2 (193 sq mi) of fragile ecosystem, one which is unique to France because of its position at the mouth of the Rhône and the Mediterranean.

Fauna

Hot, sunny weather, grassy fields and the sweet perfume of wild flowers are the perfect conditions for insect life in Provence Côte d'Azur. It's hard to mistake the music of the grasshoppers and crickets when night falls. Mosquitoes and blackflies are abundant in the Camargue and the Rhône Valley. Toads, frogs and river bugs are found next to the rivers and streams, as are herons and even flamingoes.

The river banks in the Maures, Estérel and Rhône Valley are popular spots for amateur fishermen. Commercial fishing is centred on the seacoast, where crayfish, red mullet, John Dory, gilthead (*daurade*), monkfish, gurnard and scorpionfish are prized. Over-fishing of the sea has destroyed a large part of the marine-life, and pollution has killed off important marine plants. It is thought that a number of places in the Mediterranean will soon be a new kind of dead sea.

The Camargue is also the only place in France where wild horses can be seen. They are small, but hardy, and are thought to have originallly arrived from Asia. They are born with a grey or berry-coloured coat—only later does it turn characteristically white. Beavers, otters, ducks, buzzards, game and as many as 400 species of rare birds are found in the protected regional parklands.

In the Luberon regional park, created in 1977, you'll find wild boar, Bonelli eagles, and Grand Duke owls. Coastal conservation areas with an interesting variety of wildlife are located at Giens, Caraueiranne, Pradet, Bandol, Cassis and Estaque.

History

The history of the Provence-Alpes-Côte d'Azur (PACA) region is the story of a mosaic of territories that today is administratively unified but which over the course of its evolution experienced numerous fractures and jolts.

Prehistory

The existence of human beings in this region as far back as the Palaeolithic age (the period from three million to ten thousand years BC) has been confirmed by the discovery of 950,000-year-old stone tools near Roquebrune-Cap-Martin and of the 200,000-year-old remains of a man near Nice, in the cave of Lazaret.

The oldest traces of the way of life of prehistoric people go back to the Neolithic age (beginning in the 5th millennium BC). In addition to hunting and fishing, which were already commonly practised in the Palaeolithic age, agriculture, centred around the cultivation of wheat and barley, and animal husbandry developed in this period. With the adoption of a non-nomadic lifestyle and the arrival of the Iron Age, early villages began to appear, composed of stone huts and protected from external attack by ramparts.

A great number of vestiges from the Palaeolithic era have yet to be dredged from the floor of the Mediterranean. The water level of the sea has risen 100 to 120m (328 to 393ft) in that last few million years, so many artifacts from that era are now submerged. The recent find at Cosquer (named for its discoverer), an underwater cave in a rocky inlet of the Mediterranean near Cassis, the walls of which are covered in paintings that are as much as 15,000 years old, has renewed hope that there may be even more prehistoric treasures hidden in the region.

The Greeks and the Romans

The arrival of the Greeks in about 600 BC and the founding of Massalia (Marseille), which rapidly became an important commercial port, led to troubles with the Celto-Ligurian tribes that occupied the region. In addition to Marseille, the nexus of development, the Greeks established themselves in other coastal colonies, in particular Nikaia (Nice), Antipolis (Antibes), Athenopolis (Saint-Tropez), Kitharista (La Ciotat) and Olbia (Hyères). Wars were numerous between the Celto-Ligurians and the Greeks.

When Marseille was threatened by the Celto-Ligurian tribes in 125 BC, the Romans arrived in force and took advantage of the opportunity to stay, conscious of the strategic position of Marseille between Italy and Spain.

Relations between Marseille and Rome developed fairly quickly, to the point that Cicero (106-43 BC) considered the Marseillais to be "loyal allies." The war lasted from 125 to 121 BC and, once the Celto-Ligurian peoples were vanquished, the Romans had at their disposal a secure land route between the Alps and the Pyrenees.

The Romans rapidly conquered the entire southern part of Gaul, driven by proconsul Sextius Calvinus, who established himself near the thermal springs of Aix-en-Provence. This region became known as "Provencia" (hence "Provence"), with Narbonne, founded in 118 BC, as its capital (hence its other moniker, "Narbonnaise").

This was the beginning of the period of the Pax Romana, which lasted almost four centuries and which permitted the region to develop and to build an exceptional and complex network of roads, of which the Via Agrippa (present-day Nationale 7) and the Via Domitia, were part, crossing the country to the Pyrenees and on to Spain. The Roman roads generally retraced ancient Ligurian routes; they followed them so closely in fact that today it is possible to distinguish many villages that date from this earlier era simply by their name endings—"asque", "osque" and "esque", for example Vénasque, Manosque and Bresque. Roman thermal baths, theatres (those of Orange, Arles and Vaison-La-Romaine, among others), arenas (Arles, Fréjus, Cimiez, Nîmes), triumphal arches (Orange), aqueducts (Pont du Gard) and monuments are abundant in the area, and most of the larger structures are still in existence.

Arles began to flourish, especially after Caesar made it the new capital of the province in 49 BC, after conquering Marseille, which up until then had been independent. However, Narbonnaise was exploited by the Roman Empire, and the local population suffered from elevated taxes and very high duties and tolls, all the while living under the thumb of corrupt politicians and administrators.

The region began to decline in about 250 AD, with the first of a series of barbarian invasions. The territory was split; Arles held out the longest, until the Visigoth invasion of 476 (in the same period as the fall of the Roman Empire). Christianity, which had only made small inroads under Roman rule, began to play an increasingly important role in political and daily life. The monasteries of Saint-Victor (413), in Marseille, and of the Îles de Lérins, facing Cannes, began to enjoy prosperous times. However, the innumerable barbarian invasions did not abate, and, after the Visigoths, the Burgundians and the Ostrogoths, Provence was finally annexed to the kingdom of the Franks in 536, although it managed to preserve some measure of autonomy.

The Middle Ages

After six centuries of unification in the bosom of the Roman Empire, Provence was surrounded to the north by the mighty Germanic Empire, which desired to expand to the Mediterranean to reach Italy and the Orient, and to the south by the powerful Moors, who began to spread out in force in the seventh century.

The Moors, Muslim conquerors of North Africa and Spain, represented a constant maritime threat to the region from 830 to 1000. Before the end of the ninth century, they had established themselves in Fraxinetum, near Saint-Tropez, where they pillaged travellers and passing pilgrims.

The Christian community defended itself vigorously in the 970s and 980s, and their troops even sacked Fraxinetum in 973. Although peace was restored in the back country shortly after this victory, the coast remained vulnerable to unremitting Moorish raids over the next 200 years (especially the monastery at Lérins, on an island in the waters off Cannes, as well as Toulon, Îles d'Hyères and Camargue). All in all, the Moors' acts of piracy against Nice, Antibes, Toulon and Marseille caused more damage than their incursions inland, which certainly were a serious nuisance, but which did not constitute a continual threat.

During this period, the region officially fell into the hands of many different monarchs, including Charles le Gros (the Fat), Charles III (839-888), who declared himself king of Provence for a short while in 884. However, local power was held by the counts of Arles and Avignon, and the ultimate fall of the Moorish fortress at Fraxinetum (973) was credited to William, Count of Avignon, known as Le Libérateur (the Liberator). It was precisely this type of authority and independence that permitted the development of an agricultural feudal economy in Provence. The region's population was on the rise, Christianity was increasingly important and, with the renewal of commerce, the area saw the birth of a local nobility and the emergence of a bourgeoisie.

The Counts of Provence

Provence was ruled by various counts of Barcelona (Catalonia), beginning in 1112. This came about when the heiress of Provence, Douce, married Raymond Bérenger III, a count of Barcelona. Catalonia and Provence had previously been fast partners in the seafaring trade, and this new administrative alliance proved mutually profitable. In fact, the marriage created one of the most powerful maritime forces in the Mediterranean, and the economic prosperity that resulted permitted some towns to become independent municipalities, called consulates, including Arles (1130), Avignon (1136), Nice (1144), Tarascon (1150) and Marseille (1178).

The most famous of all of these Catalan counts was Raymond Bérenger V (1209-1245). He was renowned for his legislative measures and cultural refinement, but his greatest legacy was the reorganization of the region, executed in about 1235, which divided Provence into distinct administrative jurisdictions to strengthen his control over the area and extend his power over the entire territory. Once again Provence was at the head of European civilizations, its influence felt throughout the rest of France and reaching as far as Italy and Spain.

In 1388, a new chapter was opened with the annexation of Nice by the county of Savoie, which marked a radical rupture in the Alpes-Maritimes region: Provençals became Savoyards.

Relations with the Kingdom of France

During the first half of the 16th century, Provence was very much affected by the power plays of Francis I, King of France, and Charles V, the Hapsburg ruler of the Holy Roman Empire. The Swiss and German armies of Francis I introduced Protestant Lutheranism to the region, which proved to be a new catalyst of conflict in the second half of the 16th century, a period dominated by the Religious Wars.

The 17th century was much quieter in the area of Nice than it was in Provence, which belonged to France, the latter being continuously involved in battles to recapture its independence. However, toward the end of the century, Nice was once again the arena of conflict between Savoie and France, ultimately falling to the French who have occupied the entire region ever since. A raging outbreak of the plague in 1720 claimed 100,000 victims, with loss of life particularly heavy in Marseille.

The local economy benefited from the remarkable diversity of this era, with agriculture (mainly olives and grapes) complemented by a fruitful manufacturing industry (leather, paper, soap and fabric). The shores of Provence profited most thanks to their strategic position between the interior of the country and its Mediterranean neighbours. Marseille became the largest commercial port in France.

The French Revolution

France seemed to be in good shape when Louis XVI took the throne in 1774. Its economy was prosperous, its cities were mushrooming and its culture dominated all of Europe. But in the 1780s, the country experienced an economic crisis: the corrupt nobility was bent on preserving its privileges, the populace was taxed heavy-handedly, and the nation's finances were squandered in foreign wars. As a result the notion of the "divine right of kings" was seriously contested, and the citizens of Provence, encouraged by the other French provinces, demonstrated in favour of equality and a voice in the governance of the country.

On July 14, 1789, the bourgeoisie and the people of Paris revolted and captured the Bastille, a prison-fortress, by force. In August, the privileges of the nobility were revoked and on the 26th day of that same month a vote was held enacting the Déclaration des Droits de l'Homme (Declaration of the Rights of Man), which espoused liberty, equality and fraternity. Toward the end of December, France was divided into 83 departments (these in turn were subdivided into districts, cantons and commons), a structure that would be modified in 1800, the number of departments eventually stabilized at 98. Provence was split into three departments (Bouches-du-Rhône, Var and Basses-Alpes) in 1791. Then in 1793, Nice (including Monaco) was annexed to France.

Provence continued to oscillate between revolutionary and counter-revolutionary forces following the execution of Louis XVI in 1793, but in the meantime a new political figure was on the rise: Napoleon Bonaparte. The first military victory of this ambitious young Corsican lieutenant was wrought in the region: he recaptured Toulon from the English in 1793.

In 1804, Bonaparte crowned himself emperor of France, Napoleon I. He achieved a series of heroic conquests throughout Europe, including sieges of Austria and Prussia, but then underestimated the strength of the national resistances in Spain (1808), Russia (1812) and Germany (1813). Power-hungry, his judgement clouded by sheer ambition, Napoleon could no longer stop himself; following crushing political and military defeats, he abdicated the throne on April 6, 1814. Nice was returned to the Kingdom of Piedmont-Sardinia that same year.

While in exile on the island of Elba, Napoleon was preparing his return to power. He disembarked at Golfe-Juan in March 1815, but was pushed back from Antibes toward Grasse by royalist troops. He then attempted to cross the Alps on foot over a fearsome, snow-covered route—the famous "Route Napoléon," that crosses the territory to this day—which took him through Séranon and Castellane, after crossing Durance at Sisteron. His route to Paris was nicknamed "the flight of the eagle." These were Napoleon's Hundred Days, during which he recaptured power and the Bourbons were temporarily exiled to Belgium. However, his disastrous defeat at the Battle of Waterloo, June 8, 1815, definitively put an end to his aspirations, and he was banished again, this time to the island of Saint Helena.

After the end the second period of Napoleonic rule, the Restoration (the reinstatement of the Bourbons) brought long-sought stability to Provence. The bourgeoisie conducted their business unhindered. The authority of the Catholic Church visibly diminished. Industry experienced rapid expansion, largely due to the invention of the steam engine, as witnessed in the soap factory of Marseille, the coal mines around Aix, the spinning mills of Manosque, the tanneries of Barjols, the perfumeries of Grasse and the paper mills of the Vaucluse. Industrialization, however, did not penetrate the interior of Provence, where most residents continued to subsist as farmers.

In 1830, the duke of Orleans, Louis Philippe, a member of the liberal branch of the royal family, formed a new government. He lowered the legal voting age and considerably enhanced the powers of the middle classes. The nobility and the clergy saw their influence dwindling steadily. With the country in a period of unfettered industrialization, a new political class emerged in France: the socialists, whose purpose was to defend popular interests. The workers' movement began to make itself increasingly visible in the municipalities of Provence, especially in Toulon.

Shortly after 1850, Frédéric Mistral (1830-1914), Nobel laureate for literature, founded the Félibrige, a movement to revitalize use of the *langue d'oc* (a form of medieval French) and to promote Provençal literature, which was on the verge of disappearance. While economic, social and demographic pressures proved too strong for his project to be realized, Mistral nonetheless succeeded in preserving the region's traditional celebrations.

In 1860, Napoleon III allied himself with Piedmont and reclaimed the region of Nice through the Treaty of Turin. A carefully planned transportation network was built in Provence, with railroads linking Marseille to Avignon in the west and Cannes and Nice in the east. The Suez Canal, inaugurated in 1869, opened up new markets to Marseillais merchants. Nice became the tourist capital of Provence, a title that had belonged to Cannes and Hyères in the 1830s. Cosmopolitan crowds (especially wealthy English and Russian tourists) invaded the town's new Promenade des Anglais, eager to soak up its winter sunshine and its lavish nightlife.

From a Region in Crisis...

Until the outbreak of the First World War, France experienced vigorous economic development thanks in part to its colonization of North and West Africa and of Indochina. But despite thriving commerce, stimulated by trade between France and its African colonies, and the great number of passenger ships that left Marseille for Africa and Asia, the region's decline began and Marseille's status as the most important port in Europe was supplanted by Anvers, Hamburg and Rotterdam. Northern Europe was profiting from more rapid and efficient industrialization, which allowed it to offer better conditions for commercial shipping.

The final blow, however, fell in 1914 with the beginning of the First World War. The Great War sank Provence to a level of misery that it would not overcome until the end of the Second World War. Small-scale industry in the interior deteriorated, the work force was decimated by conscription and, following the October Revolution (1917), Russians no longer had disposable income to spend on travel. American tourists stepped into the role the Russians had played, vacationing on the Côte d'Azur in the 1920s, but the Wall Street stock market Crash of 1929 grounded them in their turn.

During the Second World War, Provence enjoyed the official status of a non-occupied territory up until 1942, despite continuous invasions by the Germans and Italians. In August 1944, while under German occupation, Provence was liberated by allied troops who disembarked on the shores of the Maures and Esterel.

The political life of Provence following the war reflected the 19th-century model: powerful factions emerged on both ends of the spectrum, and Marseille continued to project a strong image of independence from the central government in Paris. The far-left successfully recruited loyal followers, particularly in the interior.

The people, businesses and political institutions of Provence were heavily influenced by the return to power of French nationalists in 1962, at the end of the Algerian war. Provençals had made a habit of electing socialist representatives to the Assemblée Nationale, but they were no less inclined to turn radically to the right in elections in the 1980s and the early 1990s. Hence the extreme-right-wing Front National party of Jean-Marie Le Pen, which promotes a fierce anti-immigration platform, has gained ground since the late 1980s. But a split in the Front National in 1997 contributed to the party's weakening, as well as the return of a more vigorous belief in the region.

... To a Thriving Region

Today the region still makes the most of its climatic advantages and its geographic position at the heart of one of southern Europe's main routes of communication, to attract more and more high-tech industries. It is betting on manpower and tourism in the hope that these sectors will finally relegate the crises caused by the decline of port activity and heavy industry (now only visible at the refineries around Marseille) to the past. The more favourable economical conditions of the last few years are visible all over.

What can be garnered from this rich, long history, from this architectural and artistic heritage, from these incessant battles for autonomy, is the pride of a people who have fiercely protected a land. This land, thanks to its climate, its landscapes and the quality of life that it still enjoys today, is the living explanation of its place at the centre of so many historic rivalries.

Politics and Administration

Provence and Côte d'Azur are terms commonly used in tourism. However, they don't actually have a political or administrative significance, per se.

In 1790, one year after the French Revolution, the nation was divided into 95 *départements* which included about 36,000 districts (cities, villages, etc.). In 1960, President Charles de Gaulle divided France into 22 administrative regions in order to run the country more effectively. The administrative region **Provence-Alpes-Côte d'Azur (PACA)**, as it exists today, was established in 1972 during the presidency of Georges Pompidou. PACA comprises six *départements*: Alpes-de-Hautes-Provence (04), Hautes-Alpes (05), Alpes-Maritimes (06), Bouches-du-Rhône (13), Var (83) and Vaucluse (84).

This guide covers just four of the departments which form PACA: the Vaucluse, the Bouches-du-Rhône, the Var and the Alpes-Maritimes. However, the portraits which follow concern the six departments making up PACA.

In 1982, President Mitterand of the Socialist Party (elected in 1981 and re-elected in 1988 for another seven-year term, which he completed upon his death in 1996) reinforced an existing law permitting regional power by introducing a new law decentralizing existing administrative structures. At the moment, regional power is divided among three political bodies:

• ***préfets*** (prefects proposed by the Prime Minister but appointed by the President of the Republic), who are representatives of the national government and are responsible for applying its laws; ***conseillers généraux*** (general councillors elected by popular vote for a six-year period) who are members of the *conseil régional* (regional council) and represent their departments;

• ***maires*** (mayors) and ***conseillers municipaux*** (muncipal councillors), both elected by popular vote for a period of six years, who are responsible for the administration of each commune (collection of property and housing taxes, local development, etc.).

• ***présidents des régions*** (regional presidents) and ***conseillers régionaux*** (regional councillors) who are responsible for the interests and well-being of their region.

Despite this structure, real political power lies in the hands of the departments and the communes. Generally, the mayor represents the political majority of the commune. Regional bodies only receive a share of land taxes, property taxes, business taxes and car licensing fees. Their budget mainly goes towards spending on regional investments. Therefore, regions have some power, but nowhere near the political autonomy enjoyed by Swiss cantons, for example. France, has made efforts to decentralize towards the regions, but has not become a federation.

The importance of each commune can be highlighted by an interesting phenomenon: candidates for the mayors' seats in large cities might be politicians who already play important roles in national politics in Paris, but who don't have any previous attachment to the area in which they are running. Local electors often vote for these political personalities out of patronage, and the hopes that their city will later obtain operating budgets which are higher than the norm.

PACA is a region mainly led by the conservative right-wing (RPR—*Rassemblement Pour la République*) and conservative centre-right (UDF—*Union de la Démocratie Française* and the PR—*Parti Républicain*). Nevertheless, the Bouches-du-Rhône and especially its principal city Marseille, support the Socialist party as well as the Communist party.

During the late 1980s, the extreme right gained popularity in the area. The campaign platform of Jean-Marie le Pen and his Front National party campaigned on what many considered a racist platform, telling voters that their region was invaded by Arab foreigners. Four of the region's municipalities are presently run by the Front National.

Federal elections in May 1995 saw Chirac of the Gaulist RPR party become president for a seven-year term (replacing the Socialist François Mitterand, who died later the same year). France has had a coalition government since elections in 1997 when the rightist Chirac was forced to share power with the incoming Socialist Prime Minister, Lionel Jospin. Jospin's electoral priorities included lowering unemployment, and channeling resources to education, justice, regional development and culture.

Throughout 1998, tens of thousands of jobless demonstrated throughout France. It is no accident that the movement started in Marseilles, where one in five of the workforce is without a job since the city lost much of its heavy industry in the 1980s. Another 125,000 jobs have gone since 1992 with the decline of the Marseilles port. In early 1998, Jospin introduced a law that will reduce the working week to 35 hours from 39 hours by the end of the century in an attempt to force employers to hire more people.

Elections in 22 French regions in the spring of 1998 saw the Socialists making big gains against the traditional right due to the left-wing party's coalition with the Communist and Green parties. The extreme right National Front party led by Jean-Marie Le Pen gathered 15.3 per cent of the vote. In some areas around Marseilles, Paris and in Alsace, it reached as high as 30 per cent.

The *Parti Vert*, with only 8% of the popular vote, are concerned with protecting the countryside between Avignon and Aix-en-Provence, landscapes of which were immortalised by the painter Paul Cézanne. Currently they are monitoring the development of the Lyon-Nice line of the TGV, which threatens to disturb the area's natural beauty.

Now, with a conservative president at its head, France is governed by a social democracy with power shared by both the left and right wings. The country now awaits the election of a new leader in 2002.

Economy

Provence-Alpes-Côte d'Azur is one of France's major tourist regions, due particularly to the cachet of the Cannes-Nice-Monaco-Menton coastline. The area is also extremely fertile: agriculture and flower production is particularly important. Additionally, the region exploits its industrial, business and technological research capabilities, though industry is less-developed here in comparison to the national average.

The region is an important transportation crossroads with the port of Marseille (the most important in the Mediterranean) and two airports at Marseille and Nice. Over the centuries, the region developed important relations with the Middle East, Africa and Asia: 20% of its imports come from these three areas and 10 % of its exports end up there. Otherwise, the region maintains solid relations with its European Union member nations. Trade is particularly buoyant with Italy, PACA's most important trading partner. Italy represents 20% of its exports and 17% of its imports.

Agriculture

With more than 660,000ha (1,630,838 acres), PACA encompasses 2.3 % of the national agricultural surface area. The agricultural lands are quite diversified, for the region experiences different climates and types of soil. Arable land is in short supply along the seacoast, but it is nevertheless fertile and perfect for growing fruits and vegetables. This area is also known for its greenhouses and their flower cultivation. The excellent irrigation that characterizes the Bouches-du-Rhône provides the right conditions for vegetable farms and fruit orchards. The marshy wetlands of the Camargue produce a significant quantity of rice.

Vineyards producing grapes for wine-making and eating, plus orchards (olive, cherry, apricot, peach, fig trees) dominate a large region forming a band stretching from the Bouches-du-Rhône/Vaucluse border along the Durance Valley all the way to the eastern limit of the Var department. In the heart of the region, particularly in the area historically known as the Comtat Venaissin, is a vast plain where cereals, fodder and vegetables are cultivated. The territories of the Alpes du Sud, the Rhône delta and the Estérel are not suitable for agricultural production. However, they are ideal for growing herbs and aromatic plants (lavender, sage, thyme, rosemary, basil) which has made Provence famous the world over. Herb production represents 1,500 businesses spread over a territory of nearly 12,000ha (29,652 acres). Fragrant fields of lavender and its derivative lavandin are characteristic of this region.

The region grows the largest amount of flowers in all of France. Over 1,200 businesses occupying 1,800ha (4,448 acres) of land cover the coastal areas of the Var and the Alpes-Maritimes.

The number of people employed in the agricultural business fell by two-thirds over the last 40 years. At the start of the 1980s, a little more than 60,000 worked in this sector. Agricultural businesses tend to be smaller here than in the rest of France: the average holding is 15ha (37 acres) compared to 29ha (71.7 acres) elsewhere. Farming properties are particularly small in the Alpes-Maritimes, with an average of 11.2ha (27.7 acres) and even more so in the Var, with an average of 7.7ha (19 acres). However, these businesses generally benefit from high revenues, particularly those growing flowers, fruits and vegetables.

With the exception of the Alpes-Martimes and the Var, the PACA territory benefits from large irrigable areas.

Viticulture

For more than two thousand years, vines and olive trees have marked the Provençal landscape. Vines occupy more than 100,000ha (247,097 acres) in Provence, meaning 16 % of the region's agricultural area and 11 % of France's vineyards. Twenty thousand people are employed in the wine business, and the average vineyard measures 6ha (14.8 acres), which is close to the national average of 5.5ha (13.6 acres). The majority of the vineyard owners are members of one of the region's 174 cooperative caves (associations).

The dynamic Provençal wine industry is trying to become more specialized in order to offer consistently better wines. Despite the constant reduction in surface area devoted to growing grapes, the number of vineyards carrying the coveted "*appellation d'origine contrôlée*" (A.O.C.) tag has actually grown. Wines with this label must be made solely from grapes harvested in the designated domains. They are subject to specific quality controls, including the composition of different varieties of grapes that make up each particular cellar's unique wine.

Over the last 25 years, the number of A.O.C. wines has increased to the point where it now represents two-thirds of the overall production. Meanwhile, the output of so-called *vins de table* (table wines; most are perfectly drinkable for everyday purposes) has decreased. At the moment, sixteen *appellation d'origine contrôlée* wines exist, thus assuring the deserved acclaim of Provençal wines.

Fresh, young Provençal rosés are much admired and they perfectly complement the region's Mediterranean cuisine; of course quality reds and whites are abundant. Amongst the many fine wines in this region, two reds from the Côtes du Rhône area in the Vaucluse are justly renowned throughout the world: Châteuneuf-du-Pape and Gigondas. Also in the Vaucluse, Côtes du Ventoux and Côtes du Luberon wines are easily found and just as easily quaffed! Four A.O.C. wines are produced in the Bouches-du-Rhone: Côtes de Provence, Côteaux dAix, Palette and Cassis. The Var produces the very good Bandol, Côtes de Provence and Côteaux Varois wines. There are just a few small winemakers in the Alpes-Maritimes, a number with fine reputations such as the Bellet wines.

Livestock Farming

The vast grassy areas found in the alpine departments, the Vauclusian hills, the Alpilles and the large marshlands of the Camargue are used principally for sheep farming. Raising sheep is one part of the agricultural triumvirate (along with olives and wine) that has existed in the Mediterranean area for more than 2,000 years. Currently, 3,600 enterprises share of 60,000 ewe mothers for breeding.

Cattle raising takes up a large part of the mountainous region of the Hautes-Alpes and the lowlands of the Crau and Camargue. Pig farming is concentrated in the Bouches-du-Rhône. This industry is currently in decline, due to European overproduction causing the drop in prices. Game farming is handled mainly by large enterprises that produce primarily heavy fowl and chickens.

Much More Than Rosés!

Côtes de Provence wines are often mistakenly regarded as minor wines. The saying goes that this southern region only produces rosé wines. On the contrary: the rosés are exceptional, but there are also excellent whites that are completely unknown. As for the reds, many are marvellous wines that improve with age and lack none of the qualities of good Bordeaux and Bourgogne wines.

Admittedly, this success has not been effortless: it's the fruit of the labours of Provençal wine-growers who implemented more rigorous methods and applied better quality controls in order to obtain the label *appellation d'origine contrôlée* Côtes de Provence. Their territory covers 18,000ha (44,478 acres), extending from Aix-en-Provence to Nice.

First you must learn to know these wines, familiarize yourself with them and, above all, know how to drink them. The good reds are strong in tannin, so they need to breathe, and even require decanting ahead of time. Otherwise, they can be harsh and hard to take. It's best to visit the cellars to taste them on the premises. You'll notice that they never stop improving once they are poured. Often you'll have to wait until the third sip before discovering their full scope. It's then that the pleasure begins!

You'll be amazed by the number and diversity of the estates that produce these wines. You could easily spend your entire vacation visiting wine cellars. However, there are many other things to do in the region, so here a few suggested addresses.

La Maison des Vins Côtes de Provence
closed Sun in winter
Route Nationale 7
Les-Arcs-sur-Argens
☎04.94.99.50.20
This establishment was created to promote Côtes de Provence wines. Each estate can present three different vintages from their output, and you will find a collection of 650 bottles here. Moreover, each week, 12 different wines are presented for tasting. The wines are sold at estate prices. While the employees can give you sound advice, you can also take a wine-tasting course. Specialty foods from Provence are also on sale here and the site includes a gourmet restaurant.

La Maison des Vins Côteaux Varois
Abbaye de La Celle
La Celle
☎04.94.69.33.18
☎04.94.59.04.47
This establishment operates on the same principle as the one above, but introduces *appellation d'origine contrôlée* Côteaux Varois wines. This category brings together a large family: 400 wine-producers distributed in 12 cooperative cellars and 65 estates spread across 28 districts, centred around Brignoles in west-central Var or "Provence Verte". The Maison offers wine-tastings, organizes special events combining gastronomy and wine and has an educational sector focussed on grapevines and wine. It occupies one of the buildings of the exceptional historic monument, the Abbaye Royale de La Celle, which also houses the luxury hotel of the same name.

Visiting these two establishments can help you identify the cellars that you'd enjoy touring personally. Here are a few estates that produce quality wines.

Château de Cabran
closed Sun
Puget-sur-Argens
☎**04.94.40.80.32**
⇌**04.94.40.75.21**
Located near Fréjus, this estate features very likeable wines at good prices: the rosé is outstanding. The owner, a *bon vivant*, gives new meaning to the word "*sympathique*."

Château Saint-Maur
closed Sun year-round and Sat in winter
Route de Collobrières
Cogolin
☎**04.94.54.63.12**
⇌**04.94.54.00.63**
A small vineyard that borders on the Massif des Maures and the Péninsule de Saint-Tropez.

Château Minuty
closed Sat and Sun in winter
Gassin
☎**04.94.56.12.09**
⇌**04.94.56.18.38**
Located on the Péninsule de Saint-Tropez, Château Minuty welcomes you to its early 19th-century Provençal farmhouse. A very well-known estate.

Château Sainte-Roseline
Les-Arcs-sur-Argens
☎**04.94.99.50.30**
⇌**04.94.47.53.06**
Château Sainte-Roseline is located on the site of a former abbey. The chapel is open to visitors and its wine is distributed in Québec. Its unique and elegant bottles are immediately recognizable.

Domaine de L'Aumérade
every day 8am to noon and 1:30pm to 7pm (5:30pm in winter) closed Sun in winter
Château de l'Aumérade
Pierrefeu-du-Var
☎**04.94.28.20.31**
⇌**04.94.48.23.09**
This marvellous estate, shaded by numerous giant 400-year-old plane trees, is nestled on the plain near the Massif des Maures, slightly west of Collobrières in the Hyères backcountry. One of 18 holders of the title Cru Classé en Provence, its superior wine is enhanced by a unique presentation in incomparably elegant bottles. Their elegance is equalled only by that of the charming owner Madame Grimaldi who, along with her brother, carries on a 400-year-old tradition (King Henri IV enjoyed this wine in the 16th century). Madame Grimaldi speaks French with a charming Midi accent coupled with Provençal enthusiasm. The estate also houses a museum with an impressive display of more than 1,700 *santons* figures (clay figurines typical to Marseille), collectors's pieces from as early at the 18th century that come from a multitude of countries.

Château Saint-Julien d'Aille
9am to 12:30pm and 2pm to 6:30pm (7:30pm in summer) closed Sun in winter
Route de La-Garde-Freinet
Vidauban
☎**04.94.73.02.89**
⇌**04.94.73.61.31**
This property, which originated during the Middle Ages, is located in the foothills of the Massif des Maures. It produces a very good red wine, La Cuvée des Rimbauds. A truly delightful discovery!

Lastly, here are some white wines from the region of Arcs-sur-Argens that are highly recommended: **Château Roubine** (*☎04.94.85.94.94*), **Château La Font du Broc** (*☎04.94.47.48.20, Les Arcs-sur-Argens*), **Château Barbeiranne** (*☎04.94.78.84.46, Pignans*) and **Château du Rouët**'s Cuvée Belle Poule (*☎04.94.99.21.10, Le Muy*), less expensive than the preceding ones, but delicious!

Portrait

Fishing

Fishing is not an important economic activity in the region, as is commonly thought. In one year, the 1,500 fishers between Marseille and Menton produce on average 20,000 tons of fish. Around 90% of this catch comes from the Bouches-du-Rhône, the rest is from the Var and Alpes-Maritimes. Sardines represent half of this production; the rest is divided among bass, mullet, rascasse and octopus. These fish are commonly found on restaurant menus in the region. Other types of fish come from the Atlantic where the catch is much more varied.

Industrial Sector

Over the years, the industrial sector has developed around two different spheres. The first forms a strong, technologically-advanced sector of French and international groups including Exxon, British Petroleum, Arco, IBM and Texas Instruments. These businesses are involved in petroleum, ship building, aeronautics, steel manufacturing and electronics.

The second spheres includes a multitude of small and middle-sized businesses producing goods ranging from hand-crafted items to consumer goods such as food items, clothes, leather goods, furniture and construction materials.

Such development is the result of an important burst of industrial activity in the region between 1950 and 1974. Port industries including ship building, oil refining, petrochemical development and upgrading port services in Marseille (the Étang de Barre area) and Toulon, enjoyed the greatest growth. Since this time, this sector is in decline due to aging installations and failure to keep up with new research. Certain countries have rapidly industrialized and grabbed PACA's share of the market, notably in the oil refining, petrochemical, ship building and aeronautics sectors. The secondary sector has lost 100,000 jobs since 1975.

Many shipyards closed their doors in the 1980s. The disused sites were transformed with governmental assistance into industrial zones. Despite their growth, the number of jobs have diminished. Today, the region counts 100 industrial zones, of which 40 % are in the Bouches-du-Rhône.

PACA suffered significant job losses between 1975 and 1990. The situation was further aggravated in the early 1990s when the worldwide economic recession hit the region, and the rest of France.

Housing

Building construction has played an important part in the local economy. In 1974, it employed 166,000 people. From 1990, this number fell to 124,000, which is 8.4% of the total number of the region's employed, and 38% of the secondary sector jobs. Today, the sector has declined once more and suffered considerable losses of profit and jobs. The reasons are twofold: the economic recession of 1991-1993 and the saturation point for new building construction along the coast. The construction sector exploded during the 1980s along the Riveria, where every available piece of land was bought by speculators and prices skyrocketed. Inevitably, sites where too built-up, overpopulated and not always aesthetically pleasing. The end result is that many places along the coast have unfortunately lost their charm.

Energy Sector

The energy sector involves 19,000 jobs of which more than half work in the Bouches-du-Rhône. Jobs are found in coal mining (the Houillères de

Provence mine feeds a thermal power station producing 2.5 billion kilowatt hours of power), oil refining and natural gas. Nearly one third of the yearly natural gas production in France, 27 megatons, comes from the Fos and Étang de Berre refineries in the Bouches-du-Rhône. Hydro-electric power is supplied by a number of stations concentrated in the Alpine area which produce nearly seven billion kilowatt hours.

High-Tech Industries

A vast network of high-tech industries cover the region and are often complementary enterprises serving one another. Several technological zones establish the structure of the economic development of the region and are its driving force. Six of these link the territory. They are, from west to east:

- "l'Agroparc" Avignon-Montfavet, site of the Institut National de la Recherche Agronomique (INRA), which is concerned with agricultural and food production and research;

- the Manosque-Cadarache area, specializing in nuclear energy;

- "l'Europôle" in Aix-en-Provence, occupying 8,000ha (19,768 acres) on the Arbois plateau, and specializing in electronics;

- the multi-purpose Marseille-Provence area;

- the Toulon-Var area, specializing in instrumentation and weapons manufacturing;

- the multi-purpose Nice-Sophia-Antipolis area, a French version of California's Silicon Valley.

These technological zones share a common goal: research and innovation. They participate in realizing the region's great technological potential and are an important source of jobs. Additionally, they attempt to attract large business investments, thereby enforcing the strength of the Mediterranean arc, stretching from Valence in the west to Lombardy, Italy in the east. Plans are to enlarge this arc so as to include the technological areas of Gênes in Italy and Barcelona in Spain.

The region is the second most important in France in terms of research. Around 9,000 researchers work here, which is 10% of the country's total.

In just 25 years, the Sophia-Antipolis technological park in the Alpes-Maritimes has become the largest in Europe with over 700 firms represented.

People

Provence-Alpes-Côte d'Azur has around 4.5 million people. The region is the most urbanized in France after the Paris area. Nearly 90% of its inhabitants, around four million, live in large cities and their suburbs.

Before 1840, the population was spread reasonably uniformly across the six departments making up the PACA region. This equilibrium changed dramatically from 1936 onwards with industrialization, the strong growth of the tourist industry and the massive influx of retired people lured here by the favourable climate. Thus today the greatest population densities are found in communities along the Mediterranean coast: people have left the *arrière-pays* (back-country) for the pleasant conditions next to the sea.

However, there are exceptions to this. Some large coastal cities have suffered a population exodus from the centre towards the suburbs. An example is Marseille, which has lost nearly 100,000 inhabitants since 1975. An improved road network, a better quality environment and in particular, more affordable housing and land prices contribute to this effect.

The number of people choosing the sunny Provençal climate in which to have second homes has skyrocketed. Their number has more than quadrupled since 1962, jumping from 97,000 to 400,000 in 1994. The most sought after area for Parisians and wealthy Europeans looking for a comfortable vacation home is the Lubéron in the Vaucluse. Since the 1990s, the Alpilles area around St-Rémy-de-Provence and Les Baux has become increasingly popular. Elsewhere in the PACA region, certain pockets of the Alpes-Maritime region are favoured by the same crowd. Housing prices in Cannes and in neighbouring Côte d'Azur villages are unbelievably elevated. However, real estate is most expensive in Monaco, due to lack of space and its allure as a tax haven.

For a long time, the Provence-Alpes-Côte d'Azur was the most coveted region in France by property seekers. Now however, it is in second place after the Languedoc-Roussillon (southwest France) because of housing costs. In 1962, after Algeria achieved independence from France, PACA's population increased dramatically: hundreds of thousands of *pied-noirs* (French nationals working in the former north-African colony) returned and settled in the area. As well, during the period of strong economic growth in the 60s and 70s, tens of thousands of north-African workers (Algerians, Moroccans and Tunisians) found work in local industry and construction. Following the wave of Islamic fundamentalism in North Africa in the mid-90s, the pressure to immigrate to this region of France is even stronger. This is despite tough new French legislation restricting entry into the country.

The region has also welcomed immigrants from other Mediterranean cultures: Italians, Spaniards and Portuguese. Well-off northern Europeans (primarily Dutch, Belgian, German and Swiss) have also made the region their place of permanent residency, as well as many from the east and from Russia. At the moment, around 400,000 foreigners reside in the region. This is 9% of the population and comparable to the average found in other French regions. This group is found primarily in the Bouches-du-Rhône and the Alpes-Maritimes.

Culture

The region's varied culture is a colourful tapestry weaving together its rich heritage, language, traditions, customs and folklore.

Great artists have recorded its natural beauty for centuries, perhaps none more famously than the post-Impressionist painter Cézanne. Though critical opinion varies, Cézanne is considered by many as the precursor to Cubism. Braque, Derain and Dufy were enchanted by the strange volumes of the cliffs and viaducts of the Estaque coastline north of Marseille. Their colourful, fragmented interpretations on canvas spawned the Fauve movement.

As early as the 15th century, the county of Nice gave rise to a new school of painting influenced by the Italian Renaissance. Ludovico Brea was at the forefront of this movement, and he is sometimes referred to as Provence's Frau Angeliu. His works can be found in many chapels and small churches throughout the region.

Early 20th century painting turned darker and fractured as social and political troubles struck world-wide: Cubism was born. Simultaneously, a number of artists have made their mark on the region—great painters such as Matisse, Picasso, Chagall and Léger moved here to take advantage of the extraordinary light, landscapes and favourable climate.

The region is also home to *l'École de Nice* (School of Nice), with such artists as Klein, Arman and César. The movement is now in its third generation. Today, Nice and the surrounding area has become an important centre for artistic creation. Countless museums, small and large, attest to this vibrant artistic activity.

However, PACA has established an international reputation for its marvellous arts festivals. The Avignon theatre and dance festival and the Aix-en-Provence music and opera festival are two well-established annual events.

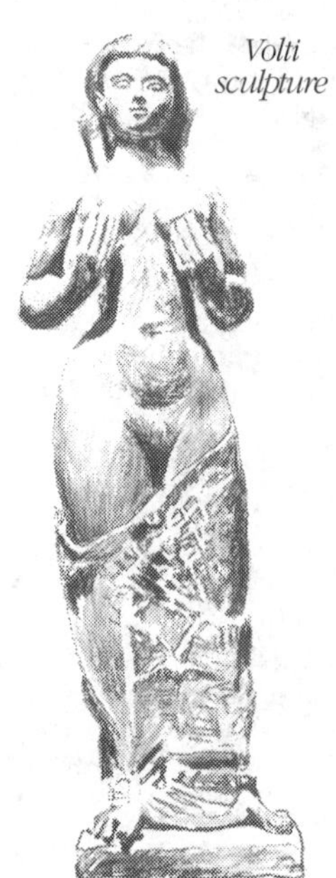

Volti sculpture

Both take place in the summertime and attract performers and avid spectators from around the world. See the list of major festivals on p 56.

The most famous festival of all must surely be the Cannes Film Festival, held every May. Now more than 50 years old, the Cannes festival is internationally recognized as the place for industry insiders to buy new films for their domestic markets, while an excited public can get in some good star-gazing. During the two-week festival period, the famous seaside boardwalk known as the Croisette and the beach below become awash with producers, directors, actors and actresses of various levels of talent and fame.

Clearly, culture is strongly anchored in this region and plays an unparalleled importance in its development. Now, more than ever, PACA's artistic life is flourishing despite real and threatened budget cut-backs due to the economic recession of the early 1990s.

Architecture

The Provence-Alpes-Côte d'Azur region possesses a monumental heritage and its history is extremely rich. Architecture in particular is exceptional. Architectural sites dating back to prehistoric times are to be found here. Amateur art historians can easily make a voyage back in time to discover a splendid variety of monuments, archaeological collections and museums to thrill the imagination. Their travels will take them from prehistory to present-day, passing by Antiquity, the Middle Ages and the Renaissance.

Happily, since the beginning of the 20th century, France deploys greater and greater efforts to protect its heritage, which was damaged by numerous wars and years of neglect. A law was passed in 1913, then a decree in 1924, which enforced the protection and respect for the nation's cultural heritage. This welcome vigilance means that today over 30,000 sites are protected in France. PACA contains 1,500.

Recent efforts have further strengthened - this national policy. In 1983, an urban code was adopted in order to assure greater protection of those sites already under the watchful eyes of conservationists. For example, special authorization must be granted to build around the perimeters of listed sites, so as to protect the historic and aesthetic character of the entire area. Conservationists regret that more wasn't

Tire or Pointe?

In keeping with southern French people's taste for lively conversation, the game of boules has become a symbol of Provence and seems to be played everywhere in cities and villages, nearly all of which have a *boulodrome.* The Provençal game of *longue* was more popular at one time, but has given way to pétanque (derived from "*pieds tanqués,*" meaning immobile feet) since the beginning of the 20th century. It was at this time that Jules "Le Noir" and Ernest Pitiot, both champions who were handicapped by rheumatism and lost a leg respectively, adapted the game of longue to their particular needs. This is how pétanque originated in 1910 in La Ciotat, a city that actually has a whole street reserved for playing boules.

Whether it's a game of *longue,* still preferred by purists and athletic players, or pétanque, the rules and object of the game are essentially the same. Players take turns throwing a metal ball weighing 650 to 800gr (23 to 28 oz) as close as possible to the *bouchon* or *cochonnet,* (a wooden ball 25 to 35mm or 0.98 to 1.4in in diameter). Whether a player chooses to *pointe* (throw the ball so that it lands as close as possible to the *bouchon)* or *tire* (forcefully throw the ball in an arch so that it knocks an adversary's ball out of the way), the game always elicits strong passions and long discussions that end over a well-chilled pastis. The game of boules has acquired devotees around the globe, and nearly 40 countries belong to the international federation of pétanque and the Provençal games. The separate French federation has more than half a million members, 80,000 of which are from the Provence-Alpes-Côte d'Azur region.

done sooner in order to prevent hideous building sites from going up in the past few decades, many of which have blighted PACA's natural beauty.

The main architectural sites in the region are:

Prehistoric and Antiquity Sites: Found in the Haut-Pays of Nice (Mont Bego, Fontanalba, Vallée des Merveilles) and along the coast (Terra Amata, the Lazaret grotto in Nice); the Triumphal arch and mausoleum near Saint-Rémy de Provence; and the Salien d'Entremont site near Aix-en-Provence. Other areas include the megalithic sites of the Haut-Var, Estérel, Grasse and Vence.

Roman Sites: The amphitheatre and triumphal arch in Orange; the agglomeration of monuments in Arles (including amphitheatre, arena, thermal baths and Cryptoportiques Arcade beneath the Forum); the Puymin and Villasse sites in Vaison-la-Romaine; the "trophy" of Turbie; the thermal baths of Cimiez near Nice; the monuments of Fréjus (arena, theatre, aqueduc and Gilded Gate).

Middle Ages: sites and ruins are found all over the region, including the Medieval villages of Antibes, Eze, Villedfranche, Menton, Vence, Saint-Paul, le Castellet, etc.; monuments include Saint-Honorat on the Îles de Lérins, the Verne in Colobrières. Ecclesiastical sites from this period are remarkable and include the Cistercian Abbeys known as the "trois soeurs" (three sisters): Sénanque (near Gordes), Silvercane (near la Roque d'Antheron) and Thoronet, innumerable churches and cathedrals existing in the villages and cities of the region (Saorge, Moustiers-Sainte-Marie, Digne, Saint Maximin-la-Sainte-Baume, latter parts of the Venasque Baptistry, Saint-Victor Abbey in Marseille) plus château-fortresses including Brignoles and Tarascon.

Renaissance: countless remarkable monuments from this period include grand private mansions called *hôtels particuliers*, châteaus at Gordes, Entaigues, etc.; residences known as bastides in the coastal region of Toulon and La Ciotat; homes in the city centres of major communities such as Avignon, Aix-en-Provence, Marseille, Toulon and Nice; military installations such as Fort Carré in Antibes, the Arsenal in Toulon, Fort Saint Nicholas in Marseille. Churches in the baroque style, showing a Genoese influence, are found in the Nice area around Menton, Sospel, la Turbie, etc.

The *belle époque*: this style took hold in the second half of the 19th century, leaving sumptous villas all along the Mediterranean coastline: Hyères, Cannes, Menton, Maures, Marseille. These charming villas capture a variety of styles: eastern (neo-Moorish), English (Gothic Revival) or Italian (neo-baroque).

Twentieth Century: Passing by influences of Art Nouveau and Art Deco, a number of striking contemporary structures have been built in our era, among them the Palais des Festivals in Cannes, the Chagall museum, the Acropolis cultural complex in Nice, Le Corbusier's high-rise neighbourhood in Marseille, and most recently the headquarters for the Bouches-du-Rhône in the outskirts of Marseille, completed in 1994.

The beginning of the 21st century is mainly marked by an effort to restore existing heritage sites and nature preservation.

Medieval Art

The Middle Ages gave us two important architectural movements: Romanesque and Gothic.

Romanesque Art in the PACA region was influenced by two sources. The first came from Arles (the ecclesiastical centre at the time), which was the birthplace for Art Provençal (sometimes called *Art Rhodanien* in French, after the Rhône river nearby). The second came from Lombardy, Italy, and was known as Art Alpine.

In the 12th century, Arles experienced an economic, legal and cultural renaissance. From this point on, artists of the period were influenced by art of Roman times. Their style became known as *art roman provençal* or Provençal Romanesque. This meant in church architecture, the predominant layout was a simple crucifix shape, usually with just a single nave, broken barrel-vaulted ceiling and balanced with tall double arches resting on pillars. Windows were rare; their tops were simple half-circle shapes.

Art Roman Alpine is more evident in the areas bordering Italy—the eastern part of Provence-Alpes-Côte d'Azur, and was developed from a base in the former ecclesiastical province of Embrun (still the best place to see this style today). However, this style was often adapted to the Provençal Romanesque form, particularly in architecture found farther west. So, in Fréjus, Grasse and Vence, cathedrals have a basilica design, with three naves and Lombardy arches. Finally, the Haute-Provence represents an area mixing these two artistic styles: *Art Rhodanien* predominates, but mixes with a number of other native influences.

Gothic Art is not well represented because of the duration and the strong presence of Romanesque architecture in the region. It arrived here much later—first thanks to the Angevins French dynasty and later by the Popes in Avignon. On top of that, it appeared in a simplified form: *Gothique Méridional* (Southern Gothic), characterized by churches with wide and low single-naves, choirs without ambulatories, and walls resting on supports. The finest example of this unique Gothic style is found in the Dominican basilica of Saint-Maximin-la-Sainte Baume.

Language and its Dialects

The historical language of this region is called *langue d'oc* (or *langue d'occitan*). It is a language with different dialects and modifications according to the area where it is spoken. *Langue d'oc* is a blend of neo-Latin tongues. It has less in common with French than with Catalan (which it merged with before the 15th century), Italian, Spanish and even Portuguese. The geographic boundaries amongst these dialects never coincided with the political-administrative boundaries. In general, two zones exist: the *sud-occitan* (southern occident) or *rhodano-méditerranéen* (*Rhone-Mediterranean*) and the *nord-occitan* (northern occident) or *rhodano-alpin* (Rhone-Alpine).

Today, the *langue d'oc* is spoken only by older citizens of the region, although it is not uncommon to see names of villages or of streets written in both French and Provençal, especially in the back-country. Throughout its history, the language has always been threatened. In 1539, François I made French the country's official language. Afterwards, in 1561, Italian became the official language of the county of Nice. In the middle of the 16th century, French spelling was used for the *langue d'oc*. Such incidents meant the language became little more than a patois or regional dialect, less and less used in the 20th century. However, for the past few years, there seems to be a new interest in the *langue d'oc*. Some regions are reclaiming its use in daily life: on radio and television, as well as on street and place names.

Occitan literature has known two periods of glory during its history: the troubadour period (between the 11th and 13th century) and in the 19th century. The work of the troubadours was marked by Christian, Jewish, Arab and Oriental influences. Their subject matter was infused with either eroticism or religion. In the 19th century, the *occitan* language experienced a renaissance with the publication of a Provençal-French dictionary. Most importantly however, the new passion of the *langue d'oc* was due to the poetry and prose of Frédéric Mistral. He founded the Félibrige literary movement, which promoted the use of the local dialect, and many poets followed in his footsteps. Mistral himself was a champion of the celebration of Provençal traditions and culture. He received the Nobel Prize for Literature and he became not only a local, but national hero.

The Provençal Dialect

Visitors to Provence will remark that the local population speak in a manner which is particular to the region.

Consulate General
29 Rue Wulfran Puget, 13008
Marseille
☎***04.91.76.12.82***

SPAIN
Spanish Embassy
22 Avenue Marceau,
75008 Paris
☎***01.44.43.18.00***
⇄***01.47.20.56.69***

Consulate General
38 Rue Edouard Delanglade
13006 Marseille
☎***04.91.37.60.07***

SWEDEN
Swedish Embassy
17 Rue Barbet de Jouy,
75007 Paris
☎***01.44.18.88.00***
⇄***01.44.18.88.40***

Consulate General
2 Rue Henri Barbusse,
13205 Marseille
☎***04.91.90.80.23***
⇄***04.91.91.35.00***

Consulate
27-29 Avenue Jean Médecin
06000 Nice
☎***04.93.88.14.40***

SWITZERLAND
Swiss Embassy
142 Rue de Grenelle,
75007 Paris
☎***01.49.55.67.00***

Swiss Consulate
13 Rue Alphonse Karf
06000 Nice
☎***04.93.88.85.09***
⇄***04.93.88.52.47***

UNITED STATES
American Embassy
2 Avenue Gabriel, 75008 Paris
☎***01.43.12.22.22***
⇄***01.42.66.97.83***

Consulate General
12 Boulevard Paul-Peytral
13286 Marseille, Cedex 06
☎***04.91.54.92.00***
⇄***01.91.55.09.47***

French Embassies Abroad

AUSTRALIA
6 Perth Avenue, Yarralumla
A.C.T. 2600
☎***(6) 270-5111***
⇄***(6) 273-3193***

BELGIUM
65 Rue du Cale, 1000 Bruxelles
☎***(2) 548 87 11***
⇄***(2) 513 68 71***

CANADA
42 Sussex Drive, Ottawa, Ont.
K1M 2C9
☎***(613) 789-1795***
☎***(613) 789-3480***
⇄***(613) 789-0279***

DENMARK
Kongens Nytorv 4,
1050 Copenhague K.
☎***(33) 325 090***
⇄***(33) 939 752***

FINLAND
Itaïnen Puistotie 13
00140 Helsinki
☎***(0) 171 521***
⇄***(0) 174 440***

GERMANY
An der Marienakapelle 3, D-53179 Bonn
☎***(228) 955 6000***
⇄***(228) 955 6160***

GREAT BRITAIN
58 Knightsbridge, London
SW1X-7JT
☎***(171) 201 1000***
⇄***(171) 201 1004***

ITALY
Piazza Farnese 67, 00186 Rome
☎***(6) 68.60.11***
⇄***(6) 68.60.13.60***

NETHERLANDS
1 Smidsplein, La Haye 2514 BT
☎***(70) 356 0606***
⇄***(70) 356 2047***

NORWAY
Drammensveien 69, 0271 Oslo
☎***(22) 441 820***
⇄***(22) 563 221***

PORTUGAL
Rua Santos o Velho n°5,
1293 Lisbonne Cedex
☎***(1) 608 121***
⇄***(1) 397 8327***

SPAIN
Calle de Salustiano Olozaga 9,
28001 Madrid
☎***(1) 435 5560 or 435 5697***
⇄***(1) 435 6655***

SWEDEN
Narvavägen 28, Box 10241
10055 Stockholm
☎***(8) 663 0270***
⇄***(8) 660 6290***

SWITZERLAND
46 Schosshaldenstrasse,
B.P. 3000, Berne 3006
☎***(31) 351 2424***
⇄***(31) 352 0526***

UNITED STATES
4101 Reservoir Road NW, Washington D.C. 20007
☎***(202) 944-6000***
⇄***(202) 944-6000***
⇄***(202) 944-6175***

Tourist Information

Tourist Offices Abroad

AUSTRALIA
Maison de la France
BNP Building - 12th Floor, Castlereagh Street, Sydney, NSW 2000
☎ ***(2) 231 52 44***
⇄ ***(2) 221 86 82***

BELGIUM
Maison de la France
21 Avenue de la Toison-d'Or, 1060 Brussels
☎ ***(2) 513 66 23***
⇄ ***(2) 514 33 75***

CANADA
Maison de la France
1981 Avenue McGill College, Bureau 490, Montréal, Québec, H3A 2W9
☎ ***(514) 288-4264***
⇄ ***(514) 845-4868***

DENMARK
Maison de la France
Ny Ostergade 3-3,
DK 1101 Copenhagen
☎ ***(33) 11.46.41***
⇄ ***(33) 14.20.48***

FINLAND
Maison de la France
c/o Ambassade de France
Service Economique & Commercial
Mannerheimintie 14 B,
0100 Helsinki
☎ ***(0) 60.36.55***
⇄ ***(0) 60.20.81***

GERMANY
Maison de la France
Keithstrabe 2-4, 10787 Berlin 15
☎ ***(30) 218.20.64***
⇄ ***(30) 214.12.38***

Maison de la France
Westendstrasse 47, Postfach 2927, D 60325 Francfort Main 1
☎ ***(69) 75.60.83.30***
⇄ ***(69) 75.21.87***

GREAT BRITAIN
Maison de la France
178 Picadilly, London W1V 0Al
☎ ***(171) 493 5576***
⇄ ***(171) 493 6594***

ITALY
Maison de la France
Via Larga 7, 20122 Milan
☎ ***(2) 58.31.64.71***
⇄ ***(2) 58.31.65.79***

NETHERLANDS
Maison de la France
Prinsengracht 670-1017 KX Amsterdam
☎ ***(20) 627.33.18***
⇄ ***(20) 62.03.33.39***

NORWAY
Maison de la France
Storgaten 10 A, 0155 Oslo
☎ ***(22) 42.33.87***
⇄ ***(22) 42.29.44***

PORTUGAL
Maison de la France
c/o Air France
Avenida de Liberdade 244 A
1200 Lisbon
☎/⇄ ***(1) 52.61.19***

SPAIN
Maison de la France
Gran Via 59, 28013 Madrid
☎ ***(1) 541.88.08***
⇄ ***(1) 541.24.12***

Maison de la France
Gran Via Corts Catalanes 656
08010 Barcelona,
☎ ***(3) 302.05.82***
⇄ ***(3) 317.29.71***

SWEDEN
Maison de la France
Normalmstorg 1 Av.,
S 11146 Stockholm
☎ ***(8) 679.79.75***
⇄ ***(8) 611.30.75***

SWITZERLAND
Maison de la France
2 Rue Thalberg, 1201 Geneva
☎ ***(22) 731.34.80***
⇄ ***(22) 909.89.77***

Maison de la France
Löwenstr 59, Postfach 7226, 8023 Zurich
☎ ***(1) 221.35.61***
⇄ ***(1) 212.16.44***

UNITED STATES
Maison de la France
9454 Wilshire Boulevard, Suite 975, Beverly Hills, CA 90212-2967
☎ ***(310) 271-7838***
⇄ ***(310) 276-2835***

Maison de la France
676 North Michigan Avenue, Suite 3360, Chicago, IL 60611-2836
☎ ***(312) 751-7800***
⇄ ***(312) 337-6339***

Maison de la France
444 Madison Avenue, New York NY 10020-2452
☎ ***(212) 838-7800***
⇄ ***(212) 838-7855***

Tourist Offices in Provence and the Côte d'Azur

You will have no trouble finding all the tourist information you need in Provence and the Côte d'Azur. Most villages and towns have a *syndicat d'initiative* (tourist office) to provide visitors with information. Throughout the guide the telephone numbers and addresses of the tourist offices in each area are provided.

Getting to Provence and the Côte d'Azur

By Plane

Most overseas visitors to Provence either arrive in Paris and continue their voyage south by plane or by high-speed train (TGV), or fly directly to the airports in Marseille or Nice.

International flights land at Paris Roissy Charles de Gaulle Airport, though a few charter flights may land at Paris Orly Airport. Several charter airlines also use Lyon Satolas Airport—overseas visitors may pick up the TGV to Avignon-Marseille from the SNCF train station connected to the terminal.

Airports

Charles de Gaulle Airport
Information
☎03.28.62.22.80
www.airfrance.fr

Orly Airport
Information
☎05.49.75.15.15

To reach the centre of Paris from Charles de Gaulle or Orly airports, a number of transportation options are available:

1) Car Rental

2) Taxi *(from 40min to 75min, depending on traffic; between 180F and 250F from Charles de Gaulle and between 120F and 180F from Orly)*

3) Rapid transit system (**RER**) to the city centre, then continue by the RATP-run Métro underground transportation system or by taxi. RER tickets cost between 40F and 50F, take about 45min, and leave every 15min throughout the day. **RATP** also provides a direct Roissybus service between Charles de Gaulle and Place de l'Opéra, *(35F)* and an Orlybus service between Orly and Denfert Rochereau Métro station *(30F)*. Both run every 15min throughout the day.

4) Air France bus service, direct to Étoile-Arc de Tiomphe *(from Charles de Gaulle Airport, 45F)* or Invalides and Montparnasse *(from Orly Airport, 35F)*.

Flights to Provence and the Côte d'Azur from Paris leave from Orly Airport, situated south of the capital. This is a bit of an inconvenience for passengers arriving from abroad at Roissy Charles de Gaulle Airport north of the city. Expect either a long journey on the RER and Métro across town or a very expensive taxi ride. Many visitors prefer to spend a day or more in Paris.

French airlines Air France, Air Inter, AOM and TAT offer regular daily flights to Avignon, Marseille and Nice. Flights last about 1hr 10min. Contact your travel agent or the airlines for details.

Avignon-Caumont Airport
Information
☎04.66.70.08.59

Marseille-Marigane Airport
Information
☎04.42.89.09.74
Reservations
☎04.91.91.90.90

Once in Avignon, Marseille or Nice, a number of **car rental** agencies offer a variety of automobiles and package rates. Prices for car rental vary considerably—some of the best deals are available only if booked from abroad, a week or more ahead of time. However, some local agencies offer better prices than the big international companies, and are worth investigating. Listings of car rental agencies are located at the beginning of each chapter.

Nice-Côte d'Azur Airport
General information
☎04.93.21.30.30
Flight information
☎08.36.69.55.55
≠04.93.21.30.29

There are several **car-rental** companies at the airport, including Avis, Hertz, Budget and Europcar.

Keep in mind, however, that prices asked at the airport are usually higher than those at the SNCF train station in the centre of Nice.

ADA *(☎04.93.14.31.44)*, an agency located in Cagnes-sur-Mer, offers the best car-rental rates. This agency will deliver the car to you at the airport.

The airport also has a few exchange offices, including the B.P.C.A., open everyday from 8:30am to 7pm (summer, until 8:45pm).

Certain international airlines, including British Airways, KLM and Lufthansa, offer several flights a week, with connecting flights for Nice, from Canada and the United States. Moreover, several American airlines provide direct flights from major American cities.

North Americans can also enter France via Paris, then take one of the many daily flights to Nice offered by the French airlines, Air France, Air Inter, AOM and TAT.

European travellers will have no trouble getting here, of course, as European airlines fly to Nice on a regular basis.

You can also get to Corsica from Nice. There are several flights a day between the major cities. Reaching Corsica by boat from the port of Nice is also an option.

There are many bus links from the airport to a number of destinations, including the SNCF train station in Nice. There is also helicopter service to Monaco.

Another airport, besides the one in Nice, serves the western part of the Côte d'Azur:

Toulon-Hyères Airport
☎04.94.22.81.60

This airport, however, is only used for domestic flights. It is 18km (11.1mi) east of Toulon. You can reach Toulon by bus or by train.

By Train

The region boasts an excellent railway network. There are several rail links a day offered by the TGV from Paris *(information: ☎01.45.82.50.50)*, Lyons or Marseilles. However, those who wish to reach Nice by travelling through Italy will have to summon up their patience: the trains are usually late and stop very frequently (even express trains). Fortunately, the scenery compensates fot this inconvenience.

By Car

A major network of highways links Nice to Paris, Italy and Spain. Taking these roads, however, means spending a lot of money. Moreover, gasoline is more expensive in France than in North America: 1L (0.3gal) of *essence* (gasoline/car petrol) costs about 6F (about double the Canadian price and triple the American price).

Be sure to carry some French currency with you for the toll booths (*péages*) on the larger expressways. French roads are in great condition but you pay for them! Credit cards are accepted.

Health

No vaccinations are necessary before entering France. Health services are excellent.

Illnesses

There are a significant number of AIDS cases—the region is the second most affected area in France after Paris. As in other places, cases of venereal diseases are known. It is therefore wise to take the necessary precautions.

The Sun

In spite of its benefits, the sun can cause numerous problems. Always wear sunscreen to protect youself from the sun's harmful rays. Many of the sunscreens available on the market do not provide adequate protection, so before setting off on your trip, ask your pharmacist which ones are the most effective against ultraviolet rays. Overexposure to the sun can cause sunstroke, symptoms of which include dizziness, vomitting and fever. Cover yourself well and avoid prolonged exposure, especially for the first few days of your trip, as it takes a while to get used to the sun. Even once you are used to the sun's intensity, moderate exposure is best. Wearing a hat and sunglasses can help shield you from the harmful effects of the sun. Lastly, don't forget that sunscreens are most effective when applied 20 to 30min before sun exposure.

First-Aid Kit

A small first aid kit can help you avoid many difficulties. It is best to prepare it carefully before setting off on your trip. Make sure you take along a sufficient supply of all prescription medicines you take regularly, as well as a valid prescription in case you lose them. Other medicines, such as Imodium or its equivalent (for intestinal disorders and diarrhea) may be purchased before leaving, but are also available in local pharmacies. In addition, adhesive and non-adhesive bandages, disinfectant, pain relievers, antihistamines, condoms and medicine for stomach upsets may be purchased before leaving but they are also readily available throughout Provence and the Côte d'Azur.

Insurance

Cancellation

Your travel agent will usually offer you cancellation insurance upon purchasing your airplane ticket or vacation package. This insurance guarantees reimbursement for the cost of the ticket or package in case the trip has to be cancelled due to serious illness or death. Travellers with no health problems are unlikely to require such protection, and should weigh its advantages carefully.

Theft

Most homeowner's insurance policies in North America cover some personal possessions, even if they are stolen abroad. In order to file a claim, you must have the police report. Depending on what is covered in your policy, it is not always necessary to take out additional insurance. European travellers, on the other hand, should make sure their policies protect their belongings in foreign countries, as this is generally not the case.

Health

This is without question the most useful kind of insurance for travellers, and should be purchased before leaving. Look for the most complete coverage possible because health care costs in foreign countries can add up quickly. When you buy your policy, make sure it provides adequate coverage for all types of potentially costly medical expenses, such as hospitalization, nursing services and doctor's fees. It should also include a repatriation clause in case the necessary care connot be admisistered on site. In addition, as you may have to pay upon leaving the clinic, you should check your policy to see what provisions it includes for such cases. During your stay in Provence, you should always keep proof that you are insured on your person, as it will save you a lot of trouble if you are unlucky enough to require health care.

Climate

Provence

Provence has a Mediterranean climate, characterized by a hot, dry summer period, very little rain (less than 60 rainy days) and therefore lots of sunshine.

Temperatures reach as high as 35°C in the summer, though 30°C is more common. In the winter, the climate is mild along the coastline and temperatures rarely dip below 10°C. However, the villages of the *arrière-pays* (inland countryside) are often cooler in the winter, especially those on exposed areas around the Vaucluse and Luberon hills. April and October tend to be the wettest months, with short, heavy outbursts of rain as well as lighter showers lasting a few days.

Conditions are ideal in late May and throughout June, when temperatures of around 26°C and abundant sunshine predominate. Plants, flowers and fruit trees are in full bloom and the roads are generally clear of vacationers. September is pleasant, with a favorable climate. The sea water is still warm at this time for those holidaying by the coast. In contrast, July and August are the high tourist season in Provence. Europeans are on vacation at this time and it is necessary to reserve well in advance for accommodation. Some of the more popular towns are over-crowded and getting around by car takes more time and patience.

The famous mistral wind hits Provence throughout the year. This ferocious wind lasts for a day or even days at a time, and can blow up to 100km/h (62mi/h).

Côte d'Azur

The Côte d'Azur also has a climate characterized by a period of summer drought, few rainy days throughout the year (fewer than 120), and consequently, a great deal of sunshine. As you move away from the coast and towards higher elevations, climatic conditions gradually change as is evidenced by temperatures (frost) and precipitation (rain cycles and levels). Thus, the back country has a more mountainous climate with Mediterranean nuances. Indeed, it can often be sunny on the coast, yet cloudy, foggy and rainy only a dozen kilometres away.

Temperatures rarely exceed 30°C (86°F) in summer. In winter, the climate is mild on the coast and temperatures rarely plummet below 10°C (50°F). On the other hand, the temperature in the back country is sometimes lower on account of the altitude. Then again, this means you can enjoy skiing only an hour from the sea, on mountains that reach up to 3,000m (9,843ft).

In April and October, the region is often subject to heavy rains that can last several days.

The mistral, the famous Provence wind, generally affects the part of the Côte d'Azur west of Fréjus. This wind can gust to 100km/h (62mi/h). Cannes, which lies east of Fréjus, suffers its last effects, with about thirty days of unflagging winds every year.

In summer, the heat is never unbearable on the Côte d'Azur, as steady ocean breezes temper the climate. Moreover, in winter, certain places such as Monaco are sheltered by the rocks surrounding them.

The Côte d'Azur is a very popular spot in July and August, when most Europeans are on holiday. June and September are even more pleasant, however: temperatures are lower and there are fewer people. September is also a must for swimming buffs, as the sea is still warm.

Packing

Much depends on the type of trip planned and during which season you travel. In winter, when temperatures are coler, be sure to bring a wool sweater, raincoat, jacket or overcoat and appropriate footwear. For the hot summers, pack loose, light cotton clothing. A sweater for air-conditioned rooms and high altitudes, plus a light windbreaker or raincoat might also prove useful. For active types, a bathing suit, solid walking shoes and appropriate hiking apparel (backpack for supplies, plus a sun hat) are advised. Of course, sunglasses, sun block and hat are necessary to prevent sunstroke.

Casual wear is acceptable in most cafés and restaurants, although good standards of dress are observed everywhere. During the warmer months, it is acceptable to wear shorts and T-shirts in outdoor cafés and fast-food places. However, they are not appropriate in fancier restaurants for the evening, when gentlemen wear trousers and perhaps a light-weight sports-jacket and women wear pants, skirts or dresses. Casinos and the top, chicest restaurants require a jacket and tie for men, and appropriate dress for women.

Safety and Security

You should take the same precautions in Provence as you would elsewhere. Keep your passport, traveller's checks and credit cards with you at all times. avoid bringing valuables to the beach, but if you must, keep an eye on them. Store valuable objects and papers in your hotel room if it is equipped with a small safe or at the hotel reception.

You should pack a copy of your passport and your intinerary, as well as a list of the serial numbers of your traveller's checks. If ever the originals are lost or stolen, knowing their reference numbers will make it much easier to replace them.

Although Provence and the Côte d'Azur is not a dangerous region, it has its share of thieves, especially in the places most frequented by tourists. A certain degree of caution can save you a lot of trouble. Don't keep your luggage or bags on the seat of your parked car in clear view; avoid showing the contents of your wallet when paying for a purchase; conceal your traveller's checks, passport and some of your cash in a money belt. Remember, the less attention you attract, the less risk of being robbed.

Car Theft

It may be hard for a North American to imagine the huge risk that exists in Southern France of having objects stolen from your car. Drivers would be wise to take the following precautions:

- Never leave your luggage in an unsupervised car. Thieves need only 5min to get what they want without any trace. Car door locks are no secret to these professional pilferers.

- Above all, do not leave anything visible that may be of value: bags, jackets, etc. The lock might be picked in hopes that the jacket contains a wallet.

- If you must keep your luggage in your car, be careful when stopping for gas or for fast-food. Park the car where you can see it constantly. In the city, pay for a parking lot, and choose a spot near the attendant.

- Always leave the glove box wide open to avoid the supposition that your camera might be inside.

In general, leave your bags at the hotel while you are sightseeing, even if you have checked out. The reception desk will usually keep them for you. Finally, always remember that whatever precautions you've taken, you could still be robbed and avoid carrying too many valuables with you.

Mail and Telecommunications

Stamps are sold at any post office, and also at the major hotels. Airmail is collected on a daily basis.

You'll have no trouble finding public telephones. Some still operate with coins but most use cards; these cards, known as *télécartes*, are available at the post office and *tabacs* (tobacco shops) and cost 40F for 50 units.

To call Provence and the Côte d'Azur from Canada and the United States, dial 011 33, then the local number. (For Paris-Île-de-France region, dial 011 33 1, then the local number.) From most European countries, dial 00 33, then the local number.

Discount rates are available at certain times of the day. In Canada, the cheapest time to call is between 6pm and 8am EST; in Switzerland and Belgium, between 8pm and 8am and all day Sunday.

Calling Long Distance

To call these places from Provence and the Côte d'Azur dial the code followed by the area code and local number:

- Canada and the United States: 001
- Belgium: 00 32
- Great Britain: 00 44
- Netherlands: 00 31
- Switzerland: 00 41
- Paris: 01

In addition, most hotels offer fax and telex services, as do all post offices.

Transportation

Roads

Besides the highways, there is a plexus of main, secondary and local roads, which leads to the smallest villages in the farthest reaches of the back country. Remember, however, that even the main roads do not necessarily have wide lanes. Roads are rather narrow and road-stops are a rare commodity. In any case, they are generally unpleasant, so finding a good picnicking spot is difficult, but not impossible!

Village roads in the back country are exceedingly tortuous and often very narrow. This often takes visitors by surprise, especially since the locals, accustomed to these conditions, frequently travel at high speeds.

As such, you are better off leaving your car in one of the public parking lots at the villages' entrances.

Watch out for speed bumps (*dos d'âne*, or donkey's backs) scattered here and there on the roadway both near and in the cities. Their purpose, of course, is laudable: to curtail speeding for the protection of pedestrians. However, if you do not look out for them—signs pointing them out are often only noticeable after having run over them—your car could suffer a nasty jolt. At best, drivers have just enough time to slow down at the last second by braking abruptly.

We must also point out that on the Côte d'Azur, drivers are somewhat rude: they are even rather reckless, are quick to lean on the horn, only rarely give way and do not hesitate to pass others as the road twists and turns. Also take note of motorcyclists, who nip dangerously in and out of traffic.

A Few Tips

Drivers License: North American and European drivers licenses are valid in France.

The Highway Code: North Americans are advised that at intersections, priority is given to cars arriving on the right, regardless of which driver stopped first. Stop signs and traffic lights are rare; however, major roads are served by round-abouts and cars within them always have priority. Therefore, wait for the way to completely clear before entering the round-about.

The use of seat belts is mandatory in France.

Maximum speed limit on highways is 130km/h (81mi/h).

Gas Stations: those on the highways are open 24 hours a day, others are usually closed at night. The former charge more, however. In general, the cheapest gas can be found at service stations located in shopping centre parking lots. Almost all gas stations and toll-booths accept credit cards.

A road map will make it easier for you to find your way around Provence. The detailed maps published by either Michelin or Institut Géographique National (IGN) are recommended. They identify even the smallest back-roads in the Vaucluse and Luberon hills, and will prove very useful.

Car Rentals

All international car rental agencies have branches in the region. Most are represented in the airports and around the main train stations. Throughout this guide, we'll do our best to provide you with the names and addresses of car rental agencies in the region. You'll find this information in the Finding Your Way Around section of each chapter. In addition to regular vehicles, many auto-leasers rent convertible cars, which makes driving more pleasurable along coastal roads.

All you need to rent a car in Provence is your driver's license. You must, however, be 21 years of age or older.

Consider the *"achat - rachat"* system for a car, which has advantages over renting on site. Find out more through a travel agent.

If you rent a car upon arrival, expect to pay around 250F per day (unlimited mileage) for a compact car. Better value deals are always offered for periods of a few days or a week. If you rent a car for a longer period, check with your travel agent before departing to find out if discount rental packages are available.

Motorcycle and Scooter Rentals

The idea of travelling the region's roads on a motorcycle or a scooter appeals to many people. A number of agencies specializing in the rental of this type of vehicle exist and are found in the Finding Your Way Around section of each chapter. Helmets are mandatory by law.

Public Transportation

The cities and towns of Provence are served by a growing network of buses and mini-buses. Local tourist offices will provide up-to-date schedules and details.

Hitchhiking

Hitchhiking is a popular means of transportation, especially for young people. It is a pleasant way to get around and meet people. Follow the same safety measures that you would anywhere else in the world if you choose to hitchhike. However, this type of transportation is becoming less and less popular and more difficult and dangerous.

Taxis

Private taxis are another way to get around the area, and

are practical for short journeys. However, it is an expensive mode of transportation if you are trying to get from one area to the next. Expect to pay around 13 F per kilometre, low fare. There are additional charges for luggage.

Taxis are easily found at airports and near train stations and hotels. Taxi stands are located throughout the larger cities like Avignon, Aix-en-Provence, Marseille and Nice.

Boats

Many private operators offer ferry services regularly between the coastline and neighbouring islands. One in particular is the service linking Nice to Corsica (see p 260). In all cases, check prices before boarding.

Pleasure boat rental, with or without skipper, is also possible.

Money and Banking

The local currency is the French Franc (F), equal to 100 centimes. There are 5, 10 and 20 centime pieces in circulation, as well as the ½, 1, 2, 5, 10 and 20F coins (be careful not to confuse the last two!) and 20, 50, 100, 200 and 500F bills.

Exchange Rates*

1 FF	= $0.21 CAN	$1 CAN	= 4.83 FF
1 FF	= $0.13 US	$1 US	= 7.47 FF
1 FF	= £0.09	£1	= 10.75 FF
1 FF	= $0.25 AUS	$1 AUS	= 4.01 FF
1 FF	= $0.32 NZ	$1 NZ	= 3.11 FF
1 FF	= 0.23 SF	1 SF	= 4.33 FF
1 FF	= 0.15 € (Euro)	1 € (Euro)	= 6.56 FF
1 FF	= 6.15 BF	10 FB	= 1.62 FF
1 FF	= 0.30 DM	1 DM	= 3.35 FF
1 FF	= 25.35 PTA	100 PTA	= 3.94 FF
1 FF	= 295.05 ITL	1000 ITL	= 3.39 FF
1 FF	= 0.34 fl	1 fl	= 2.97 FF

* Samples only—Rates Fluctuate

After January 1, 2001, you will generally be able to pay in Euros.

For easier on-the-spot reference, all prices in this guide are quoted in French francs.

Banks

Banks usually offer the best exchange rates for converting foreign currency into francs. Most banks in Provence and the Côte d'Azur are open Monday to Friday from 8:30am to noon and from 2pm to 4:30pm.

Exchange

You can also exchange money at foreign exchange offices. In the larger centres, some are open late at night and on weekends. Be sure to check both the exchange rate and the commission charge, before accepting a transaction (banks usually offer a better deal).

If banks and foreign exchange offices are all closed, you can always exchange money at one of the major hotels, though the rates won't be nearly as good.

Credit Cards and Traveller's Cheques

Visa and Mastercard are the most accepted. Even in large tourist centres, many places don't accept American Express and Diners Club cards. Shops, restaurants and hotels in small towns and villages don't always accept credit cards, so check ahead. You will usually have no trouble paying by traveller's cheque.

Exploring

Each chapter in this guide leads you through a region, town, city or village of Provence and the Côte d'Azur, including major tourist attractions followed by an historical and cultural description. Attractions are classified according to a star-rating system, allowing you to quickly spot the must-sees:

Interesting
Worth a visit
Not to be missed

The name of each attraction is followed by its address and phone number. Prices included are admission fees for one adult. It is best to make inquiries, for several places offer discounts for children and during low season.

Accommodations

There is no shortage of good accommodations in Provence, no matter what your budget and taste. From vacation villages and *gîtes ruraux* (rental houses) to inviting *chambres d'hôtes* (bed and breakfasts) and luxury hotels, the choice is large and varied.

In this guide, we have listed what we believe to be the best accommodations in each category. The prices quoted were in effect when this guide went to press, and are clearly subject to change at any time. Unless otherwise indicated, these rates apply to one double room for two people per night. Each listing also includes a complete address, telephone number and fax in order to assist you in making reservations from home. It is strongly advised to reserve accommodations ahead of time, especially during the summer season. The best places, particularly those with a unique location or special charm, should be booked well in advance.

Luxury Hotels

There are several luxury hotels in the region, plus a number of manor-style establishments in the countryside. These three- and four-star hotels meet all the international standards of comfort and convenience. Some have that little added plus—local character.

Small and Medium-Sized Hotels

There are a large number of small and medium-sized hotels and inns scattered throughout Provence and the Côte d'Azur. Most are independently owned, so the welcome and service are highly personalized. These are often as well-located as the luxury hotels (near important places of interest, with lovely views, etc.), but are more of a bargain.

Furnished Lodgings and Residential Hotels

These are two very similar options. In both instances, guests stay in fully-equipped (kitchenette, refrigerator, dishwasher, etc.) studios or apartments. Residential hotels have some of the characteristics of traditional hotels, such as private bathrooms, televisions and telephones, but are usually located in large, private homes. Local tourist offices supply comprehensive listings of these types of accommodations. Inquire about reservations, as some of these places are only available by the week.

Gîtes Ruraux and *Chambres d'Hôtes*

The *Gîtes de France* association proposes hundreds of *gîtes* and *chambres d'hôte* in Provence. This type of accommodation enables visitors to get to know local people; it is common in villages and practically non-existent in the larger city centres.

Some *gîtes* are independent units, while others adjoin the owner's residence. They are completely furnished and equipped with appliances. As a general rule, *gîtes* are rented by the week, but a few also offer weekend rates. *Chambres d'hôtes* are bed and breakfast accommodations in the owner's home, breakfast included.

All of these establishments must meet certain specific standards of quality before being listed in the association's annually-updated listings book *Gîtes Ruraux de France*, available in travel bookshops along with *French Country Welcome*. Some of France's most prestigious guesthouses are listed here.

Pierre et Vacances

In the Côte d'Azur area, this organization encompasses about fifteen establishments offering a range of services and activities, from simple hotels (Les Résidences) to more elaborate resort-type places (Les Villages). They are all admirably situated in places that take full advantage of the beauty of their surroundings.

Pierre et vacances provide apartments, equipped with a kitchen, ranging from small studios (for two to three people) to three-bedroom flats (for seven people). The latter establishment is ideal for families travelling with children. Certain locations even offer special activities for children.

These lodgings are rented on a weekly basis only. For more information, contact:

Espace Pierre et vacances
94 Boulevard du Montparnasse,
75014 Paris
☎***01.41.26.22.22***

Camping

There are loads of campgrounds throughout the region, and the variety of services offered is staggering. Camping is illegal on unauthorized terrain (wilderness camping).

Restaurants and Fine Food

Provence and the Côte d'Azur is overflowing with good places to eat, so you can enjoy excellent food wherever you go. Provençale cuisine is famous throughout the world, making this one of the best reasons to visit the area. In addition, international cuisine is represented (Oriental, African, Arabic) for visitors searching for something exotic.

As a general rule, restaurants are open from noon to 3pm and from 7pm to 10pm. In the large city centres, you can eat even later, especially during the high season. A few serve dinner only, starting at 7pm, and most are closed one day a week. We strongly recommend therefore, that you make reservations, especially at the height of the tourist season. At the same time, ask if the restaurant accepts credit cards, as this is not always the case.

In this guide, we have tried to provide you with the best possible selection of restaurants, for all budgets. Each listing includes the restaurant's telephone number, which will make it easy for you to call for reservations. The prices quoted are intended to give you an idea of the cost of a meal for one person, tax and tip included, but without drinks. Please note that, throughout France, tax and service are included in the prices on the menus.

Provençale and Niçoise Cuisine

During your stay on the Côte d'Azur, you will have the opportunity to familiarize yourselves with the local gastronomy—a varied and altogether delicious cuisine. A few good restaurants specialize in **traditional Provençale cuisine**, a mix of French and Italian influences, where olives and herbs

Gastronomical Glossary

Aïoli: Garlic mayonnaise, rather heavy and flavourful, with olive oil.

Anchoïade: Anchovy paste with olive oil and capers.

Boeuf en daube: Braised beef cooked with olive oil, lard, garlic and herbs. Served with a red-wine sauce.

Gnocchis: Potato-based pasta. Note that they are of Niçoise origin—not Italian.

Porchetta Niçoise: Suckling pig stuffed with garlic, onions and herbs. Also made with rabbit.

Lapin à la Provençale: Rabbit simmered in white wine, with garlic, mustard, herbs and tomatoes.

Loup au fenouil: Sea perch, also known as bass, which figures prominently on restaurant menus here.

Pan bagnat: Big Niçois sandwich made of anchovies, tomatoes and capers, sprinkled with olive oil.

Pissaladière: Onion tart (quiche) with anchovies and olives. A Niçoise specialty, without question.

Soupe au pistou: Vegetable soup seasoned with pistou (a kind of paste made from basil, garlic and olive oil), known as *pesto* in Italy.

Ratatouille Niçoise: Zucchini, eggplant and tomatoes enhanced with Provençale herbs, garlic, onions and olive oil. Can be enjoyed hot or cold.

Ravioles: Another Niçoise specialty. Pasta stuffed with meat or vegetables. Home-made is much tastier, of course.

Rouille: Served with fish soup and bouillabaisse. Made with mashed red peppers, garlic, olive oil, breadcrumbs and a bit of soup broth.

Salade Niçoise: Lettuce garnished with green peppers, tomatoes, anchovy fillets, radishes and eggs. There seem to be several versions; green beans and even beets are sometimes added. The whole salad is then seasoned with olive oil, of course.

Tapenade: Puréed black or green olives with capers, olive oil and a few anchovies.

reign supreme. The essence of this cuisine lies in the use of consistently fresh local products. Curiously, there are very few indiginous fish, despite the fact that the bouillabaisse de Marseille is famous the world over. Sea-bass (*loup*) and rascasse are local fish, and figure predominantley amongst the six or seven types necessary for an authentic bouillabaisse. But as there are restrictions on the amount of fish which may be caught (and water pollution seems to have killed off the rest), the price of bouillabaisse is consequently high. Many fish served on menus (particularly shell-fish) come from the Atlantic coast of France.

Anyone for Pastis?

Absinthe, which contains hallucinogenic substances and products considered to have narcotic properties, became a banned substance in 1915. The sale and consumption of this aniseed-flavoured beverage, which ravaged those who loved to drink it, is officially prohibited in France. In the Midi, where this beverage's refreshing qualities have been known for centuries, the ban did not signal the end of this drink, and owners continued to brew their own with the greatest of skill. After seven years of prohibition, the public authorities finally permitted the consumption of other aniseed-flavoured beverages. Since 1922, Provence has seen the development of a real craze for the "*petit jaune*." Thirst-quenching and cheap, pastis became a big hit. The number of brands multiplied, and pastis quickly became synonymous with sunshine and the seaside. In 1932, the ingenious Paul Ricard of Marseille developed his own pastis. Efficient sales and distribution networks ensured that the new *Ricard* pastis quickly rose to the top of a fabulously successful market that soon expanded beyond the southern region. Since the 1950s, after the prohibitions that followed WWII, pastis crossed international borders and now has fans on almost every continent.

Pricing in Cafés

Cafés, pubs, and sometimes restaurants as well, apply different rates depending on whether you consume something while standing at the bar, seated at a table or on the terrace. What seems entirely natural to Southerners proves altogether surprising to North Europeans and even more so to North Americans. If all you want is a coffee to wake up quickly, take it standing at the bar; this will cost you a little over 5F. Doing so, by the way, is very much in the Latin tradition. Drinking it at a table will cost you a little over 10F, and as much as 15F on the terrace. Whatever you do, do not make the mistake of ordering your coffee at the bar so as to drink it on the terrace!

Drinks

The licorice-flavoured alcohol **pastis** is one of the most famous local apéritifs. The two well-known brands are Pernod and Ricard and you will no doubt hear the expression in bars "*Donnez-moi un Pernod*" (Give me a Pernod).

Another popular apéritif is a kir—a glass of white wine with a touch of cassis (black currant) liqueur. A kir royale substitutes champagne for white wine.

There is no locally-made beer. The most common beers served in the area are Heineken, Carlsburg and Kronenberg. They are often available on tap. A **panaché** is a mix of beer and fizzy lemon soft drink.

Wine is privileged in the region, particularly the Côtes-de-Provence and Bandol wines. The latter are stamped with an A.O.C. label, which guarantees their quality, and grow better with age. Moreover, local vintages of decent, if not amazing, quality can be found virtually everywhere.

The region produces a significant quantity of rosé wine. It is served chilled and often as an apéritif.

In restaurants, it is wise to order local wines by the *pichet* (small clay pitcher). They are usually light and fresh and offer good value. Most restaurants offer a wide selection of French wines from other regions (Bordeaux, Burgundy, Alsace, Loire), but often at relatively elevated prices.

Restaurant Prices

Prices in this guide are for a meal for one person, including tax and tip, but not including drinks:

$ less than 75F
$$ between 75 and 150F
$$$ more than 150F

Entertainment

Nightlife

All sorts of nocturnal activities exist in the region. Larger city centres, notably Avignon, Marseille, Aix-en-Provence, Nice and Monaco offer theatres, concerts, nightclubs and dance clubs. Otherwise, the smaller towns and villages are very quiet at night. In these areas, the liveliest evening event can be a drink in a local café or impromptu concert in a village square.

Two weekly publications provide information about everything going on in the region: *L'Officiel des Loisirs* and *La Semaine des Spectacles*, both sold for 3F in newsstands. These weeklies also provide readers with information about exhibitions, museums, restaurants and films.

We have provided a list of Provence and the Côte d'Azur's major festivals and events on the following pages. These are also found in the Entertainment section of each chapter.

Shopping

If you love shopping and beautiful boutiques, you'll be in heaven in the Provençal cities of Avignon, Aix-en-Provence and Marseille, and on the Côte d'Azur in Nice, Monte-Carlo and Cannes. Leading French and European names in perfume, crystal, watches, haute couture and leather goods are found here. The major department store Galeries Lafayette has a branch in Marseille and in Nice.

These cities are popular tourist destinations, and some prices might be higher than elsewhere. Of course, bargains can always be found.

Shops are generally open Monday through Friday from 9am to 1pm and from 3pm to 7pm, and on Saturday from 9am to 5pm In addition to the major shopping streets, there are shopping centres in the suburbs of larger cities.

Tourists can be reimbursed for the French sales tax paid on articles sold in most large shops. The system, called *détaxe*, is only available if you spend more than 2,000F in one shop, on the same day. Forms are available from shops and travellers are reimbursed only after leaving the country. This tax refund only applies

Festivals and Cultural Events

January
Salon des Antiquaires *(Cannes)*. Antique show.
Célébration de la Fête de Sainte Dévote *(Monaco)*
Festival du Cirque *(Monte-Carlo, Jan to Feb)*. Circus.

February
Carnaval *(Nice, deuxième quinzaine)*. Carnival.
Fête du Citron (last two weeks). Lemon festival.
Corsos du Mimosa et Corsos Fleuris *(Sainte-Maxime, Borme-les-Mimosas and Saint-Raphaël; continues through Jul)*.
Féria de Primavera *(Nîmes)*. Spring fair.

March
Fête des Violettes *(Tourettes-sur-Loup)*. Violet Festival.
Concours de Boules dans tout le Var *(se continue jusqu'en Septembre)*. Boules contest.

April
Exposition Florale Internationale *(Cagnes-sur-Mer; early Apr)*. Flower festival.
Salon des Antiquaires *(Antibes)*. Antique show.
Foire des Vins *(Brignoles)*. Wine fair.
Festival du Printemps des Arts *(Monte-Carlo; Apr to May)*. Art exhibitions.

May
Cannes International Film Festival
Fête de la Rose *(Grasse)*. Rose Festival.
Foire Artisanale et Produits Artisanax *(Aups)*. Craft fair.
Floralies *(Sanary-sur-Mer)*. Flower show.
Festival des Arts et de la Poésie *(Seyne-sur-Mer)*. Art and poetry festival.
Grand Prix Automobile de Monaco (Formula 1 car-race)

June
Triathlon de Nice
Fêtes Médiévales *(Coaraze)*. Medieval festival.
Foire d'Olive *(Draguinan)*. Olive festival.
Festival de Musique *(Toulon; Jun to Jul)*. Music festival.
Fête des Fleurs *(Bormes-les-Mimosas)*. Flower festival.
Exposition du Prix International d'Art Contemporain (International contemporary art contest.)
Féria de Pentecôte *(Nîmes)*. Pentecost fair.

July
Festival International de Jazz *(Antibes-Juan-les-Pins)*. International jazz festival.

Festival d'Art Lyrique "Musiques au cœr d'Antibes" *(Jul to Aug)*. Opera and music festival.
Festival de Jazz *(Cannes)*. Jazz Festival.*Festival International de Folklore *(Lavandou)*
Rencontres Internationales de Musique Médiévale à l'Abbaye *(Thoronet, mid-July)*
Jazz *(Ramatuelle, mid-July)*
Festival de Provence *(Sanary-sur-Mer, all summer)*
Fête des Pêcheurs *(Saint-Tropez, early July)*. Fisherman's festival.
Festival International des Feux d'Artifice de Monte-Carlo *(Jul to Aug)*. Fireworks.

August
Festival de Musique *(Menton)*. Music.
Fête du Jasmin *(Grasse)*. Jasmin festival.
Foire Vinicole et Artisanale *(Vidauban)*. Art and wine fair.
Fête du Cuir *(Barjols)*. Leather fair.
Festival de Jazz au Fort Napoléon *(Seyne-sur-Mer)*. Jazz.
Festival de Théâtre *(Ramatuelle)*
Festival International de Musique de Chambre *(Entrecasteux)*
Festival National de Pétanque *(Arcs-sur-Argens)*.
Festival de Folklore Mondial *(Le Beausset)*. International folk festival.

September
Salon des Antiquaires, Brocanteurs et Métiers d'Art *(Cagnes)*. Antiques, thrift and crafts show.
Foire aux Potiers *(Fayence)*. Pottery fair.
Féria des Vendanges *(Nîmes)*. Grape harvest festival.

October
Festival International des Marionettes *(Cannes)*. Pupet shows.
Floralies Fleurs Séchées *(Entrecasteaux)*. Dried flower show.
Festival de la Bande Dessinée *(Hyères)*. Comic book convention.
Festival des Quatuors à Cordes *(Fayence)*
Coupe du Monde de Triathlon *(Monaco)*. Triathlon world cup.
Foire Internationale de Monaco (FICOMIAS). Fair.

November
Festival International de Danse *(Cannes)*. Dance.
Festival International de Jazz d'Hiver *(Cannes)*. Winter jazz-fest.
Festival MANCA *(Nice)*. Contemporary music.
Foire au Châtaignes *(La Garde-Freinet)*. Fair.

December
Foires aux Santons *(Fréjus, Aups, Draguignan, Bormes-les-Mimosas, La Garde-Freinet; Nov to Dec)*. Clay figurine fairs.
Fête du Millésime des Vins de Bandol *(Dec 5)*. Vintage wine festival.

to those who reside outside the European Community. Visitors must present their purchase invoices and goods at French customs upon leaving the country. A reimbursement cheque is then sent by mail. Moreover, several establishments that sell perfume charge what are said to be "duty-free" prices.

Typical souvenirs from the region include *Savon Marseillais* (soap), sachets of *Herbes de Provence*, olive oil, *santons de Provence* (small painted clay figurines representing Provençal daily life), pottery, and of course, wine. There are outdoor markets in most towns each week. These are great places to people-watch and pick up some souvenirs.

Fans of secondhand goods and antiques won't want to miss the big "flea market" on Cours Saleya, in Nice, held every Monday. Nice also boasts a great number of antique shops, mainly grouped together around the Acropolis and the Negresco Hotel. Finally, two major antique fairs are held in the region: in early January in Cannes and around Easter in Antibes. The small weekly magazine, *La Semaine des Spectacles*, usually provides a few details.

Also worth keeping in mind are all the handcrafted products to be acquired in the back country's small centres and villages, such as Tourettes-sur-Loup, Gourdon and Moustiers-Sainte-Marie.

Public Holidays

1 January
New Years Day

Variable
Good Friday

Variable
Easter

1 May
Labour Day

8 May
Armistice Day 1945

Variable
Ascension Day

Variable
Pentecost (Pentecôte)

14 July
Fête Nationale

15 August
Assumption Day

1 November
All Saints Day

25 December
Christmas Day

General Information

Time Difference

Provence follows Central European time, which is one or two hours ahead of Greenwich Mean Time (GMT), depending on the season. There is six hours difference between Canada and the Eastern United States. The farther west you go, the greater the time difference. This means Western Canada and the United States, are nine hours behind.

Electricity

Local electrictiy operates at 220 volts AC (50 cycles), so tourists from North America will need to bring along an adaptor with two round pins and a converter for their appliances.

Visitors from Great Britain will only need an adapter with two round pins.

Women Travellers

Women travelling alone should not encounter any problems. On the whole, women are treated with respect and harassment is relatively rare. Off course, a certain amount of caution is required; for example, women should avoid walking alone through poorly lit areas late at night.

Gay and Lesbian Life

In France, the public perception of homosexuality is not as liberal as it is in North America. This is particularly true of the southern part of the country, due to the values espoused by Mediterranean culture, which are based on the traditional idea of the family and are often inherently chauvinistic. What is more, there is a strong far-right presence in the Provence and the Côte d'Azur region, a movement that not only sows hatred against foreigners, but toward the gay population as well. Within this context, there are gay associations known as "SOS Homophobie" in the cities. These organizations denounce violent acts perpetrated against the community and come to the aid of victims of these acts.

Weights and Measures

France uses the metric system.

Weights

1 pound (lb) = 454 grams (g)

1 kilogram (kg) = 2.2 pounds (lbs)

Linear Measure

1 inch (in) = 2.2 centimetres (cm)

1 foot (ft) = 30 centimetres (cm)

1 mile (mi) = 1.6 kilometres (km)

1 kilometres (km) = 0.63 miles (mi)

1 metre (m) = 39.37inches (in)

Land Measure

1 acre = 0.4 hectare (ha)

1 hectare (ha) = 2.471 acres

Volume Measure

1 U.S. gallon (gal) = 3.79 litres

1 U.S. gallon (gal) = 0.83 imperial gallons

Temperature

To convert F into C:
subtract 32, divide by 9, multiply by 5

To convert C into F:
multiply by 9, divide by 5, add 32.

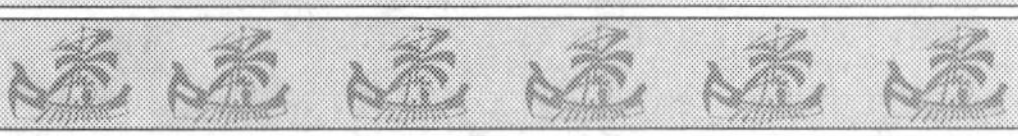

Moreover, other gay associations fight against AIDS and help those stricken by the disease. In other respects, the gay community in major centres is largely flourishing and has its own meeting places, such as bars, dance clubs, sports arenas and sometimes even saunas, though these are rather clandestine. You will find a few such places in the "Entertainment" sections.

Tabacs

Cigarettes, postage stamps and phonecards are sold in *tabacs* (tobacco shops) and in *bar-tabac* (tobacco-store bars). They are easily spotted by their illuminated signs, generally supplemented with the word "Tabac."

Emergencies

In case of an accident, here are some emergency telephone numbers:

Ambulance or Medical Emergency
(SAMU/Service Aide Médicale d'Urgence):
☎ ***15***

Police
☎ ***17***

Fire
☎ ***18***

Befitting its exceptional climate and varied landscape, Provence and the Côte d'Azur offer active types a vast selection of outdoor activities.

Provence and the Côte d'Azur rises from sea-level along the mighty Mediterranean coast to more than 1,900m (6,232ft) at the top of Mont Ventoux. With such extraordinary geographical differences, all types of activities are possible, from swimming and windsurfing to downhill skiing and hang-gliding.

In order to give you an overall idea of what is available, we have included below a summary of the most popular outdoor activites. In subsequent chapters, each of which is devoted to a specific region, the addresses listed in the Outdoor Acitivities section will enable you to obtain further information.

Two useful addresses will provide specific information about your favourite sport:

Chambre Départementale de Tourisme (Sports et Loisirs de Vaucluse)
La Balance-Place Campana, P.B. 147, 84008 Avignon Cedex
☎04.90.86.43.42
⇄04.90.86.86.08

Comité Départmental du Tourisme (Sports et Loisirs de Bouches-du-Rhône)
6 Rue du Jeune Anacharsis, 13001 Marseille
☎04.91.54.92.66
⇄04.91.33.01.82

Parks

Provence

Provence benefits from the Parc Naturel Régional du Luberon (120,000ha or 296,516 acres) across the Vaucluse and Alpes-de-Hautes-Provence departments and the Parc Naturel Régional de la Camargue (72,000ha or 177,910 acres) in the Bouches-du-Rhône. The organizations managing these two parks are responsible for preserving and, at the same time, promoting the natural surroundings. They also organize all sorts of activities ranging from guided walking tours, environmental festivals and museum visits.

The Season of Flowers

Do you love flowers? Then take note: the season begins in January with the mimosas...

Mimosas
(January to March)

Violets of Tourrettes-sur-Loup
(March to April)

Orange Blossoms
(April to May)

The "Centifolia" **Rose** of Grasse
(May)

Jasmine
(April to June)

Wild Narcissus on the Plain of Valderoure
(end of May)

Lavender
(summer)

Tuberoses
(July to August)

Centre de Ginès
Centre d'Information du Parc Naturel
Pont de Gau, 13460 Les Saintes Maries de la Mer
Information only
☎***04.90.97.86.32***

Mas du Pont de Rousty
Pont de Rousty, 13200 Arles
☎***04.90.97.10.40***
Camargue park museum and marked nature trail, 12km (7.5mi) southwest of Arles on the D570.

Maison du Parc du Lubéron
information, museum and shop
1 Place Jean Jaurès, 84400 Apt
☎***04.90.74.08.55***

Côte d'Azur

A group of high mountains peppered with many small lakes and valleys, the **Vallée des Merveilles** affords magnificent scenery. The site is unique, primarily on account of the many prehistoric rock engravings that can be seen here.

Mercantour National Park (created in 1973) is one of the seven national parks in France. It comprises 68,000ha (168,026 acres) of preserved land.

The place is also a mecca for hiking enthusiasts. It is advisable to bring some good walking shoes and a woolen garment in case you encounter bad weather, due to the altitude. There is a detailed description of this park in the "From Nice to Tende" chapter (see p 380).

Information
Destination Merveilles
☎***04.93.73.09.07***
Desination Nature
☎***04.93.33.06.93***

Summer Activities

Swimming

Provence

Provence isn't just villages perched on the sides of cliffs and wonderful hiking trails. It's also a region with streams, rivers and crystal-clear ponds worthy of a refreshing dip on a warm day. More than 20 spots are officially available for *baignade* (swimming) in the Vaucluse and are tested annually for water quality (A for good, B for average, C for water that may be occassionally polluted). Telephone the DDASS (Direction Départementale des Affaires Sanitaires et Social) health department for an up-to-date water quality report: ☎***04.90.27.70.00***. Lifeguards are not on duty at every swimming site; safety is therefore the responsibility of each swimmer.

In the Bouches-du-Rhône, the sand and pebble beaches of the Camargue next to the Mediterranean, including the Saintes-Maries-de-la-Mer area, offer an extensive choice of swimming spots. In Marseille, the municipality carefully reclaimed land from the sea in the late 1980s, so that today the Prado Beaches are one of the most popular summer desitinations for locals and visitors. A full range of water activities are available, though sun-tanning and swimming are still the favourites here (see p 238).

Nudist beaches (*plages naturistes*) are found at Martigues (Plage de Bonnieu), Salin de Giraud in the Camargue (Plage de Piemanson, known as Plage d'Arles) and at the Sugiton Calanque near Marseille (1hr walk from the Luminy parking area).

Côte d'Azur

The Côte d'Azur is literally teeming with beaches! Though often small and rocky, with the exception of major seaside resorts, such as Saint-Tropez, Cannes and Antibes–Juan-les-Pins, they are nonetheless varied. Nice and Menton are recognized for their pebbled beaches. Others are a little "wilder" due to the rocks: Saint-Jean-Cap-Ferrat, Cap-Martin, Îles de Lérins and Îles d'Hyères.

Antibes, Golfe-Juan and Cannes boast "classic" sandy beaches, but the most beautiful are unquestionably those in the Saint-Tropez area, on its peninsula. These are extensive and dot the coast for several kilometres. Do not expect to have them all to yourselves, however, especially in July and August. Moreover, because they attract many visitors, these beaches are inevitably more polluted than the calmer, more pleasant ones found between the Lavandou and Hyères.

Besides the sea, there are few places in which to practise water sports, save for Lac de Saint-Cassien and the sizeable Lac de Saint-Croix, a beautifully emerald-coloured artificial lake.

The colour of the water varies from one place to another, ranging from deep blue to turquoise, also characteristic of Caribbean waters. Indeed, on disembarking at Île de Porquerolles, one gets the impression of having reached the Caribbean. In Nice, the water bears a whole spectrum of colours.

The sea is generally calm or only slightly choppy in stormy weather, and there are real waves as a result.

Gardens

Provence and the Côte d'Azur are a paradise when it comes to their numerous botanical gardens (see "Exploring" section). These gardens and the favourable climate have resulted in numerous special festivals and celebrations. Here are the most important.

Monaco:
Salon Décoration et Jardin *(March)*

Nice:
Fêtes des Plantes *(March)*

Sophia-Antipolis:
Les Journées Jardins de Sophia *(March)*

Antibes:
Journées Exflora *(April)*

Vence:
Les Jardins de la Cité *(April)*

Monaco:
Monaco Expo Cactus/ Salon du Jardin Méditerranéen *(May)*

Menton:
month of gardens *(June)*

The quality of the water is usually good. The cleanest waters are on the Saint-Tropez peninsula and the islands. Certain other places are are not suitable for swimming, however, as they are littered with seaweed and all kinds of rubbish.

The water temperature is ideal for swimming between June and early October. During the month of June, the water rises from 16°C to 21°C, and can reach as high as 25°C in July and August. It is usually pleasant in September, as well.

There are two things bathers should watch out for: sea urchins, typically globular spiny bodies clinging to rocks in shallow marine waters, and jellyfish, which stick to the skin and burn.

Ile du Levant boasts the only "official" nudist beach. Indeed, the small part (10%) that is not taken up by the French navy, Héliopolis, is entirely reserved for nudists. Naturism is also practised in less accessible places, particularly Île Saint-Marguerite (off Cannes) and the west side of Saint-Jean-Cap-Ferrat. Regardless, it is common practice for women to go topless.

Boating and Cruises

Provence

Visitors are offered various programs of activities involving excursions at sea and rentals of all sorts of boats. Based obviously on the Mediterranean coast, a number of places in major sailing harbours offer the budding sailor an entire range of possibilities. Inquire at local tourist offices for details about local water-oriented events, including races and regattas. Otherwise, contact:

Comité Départemental de Voile
Base de Tholon, 18 Boulevard de Vallier, 13500 Martigues
☎ ***04.42.80.12.94***

Côte d'Azur

Association des Portes de Plaisance de la Méditerranée, du Littoral et des Voies Navigable Françaises
83700 Saint-Raphaël
☎ ***04.94.95.34.30***

Canoeing and Kayaking

Though most water ways in Provence aren't suitable for this sport, there is one exception. The scenic Sorgue River in the Vaucluse is a favourite spot for canoeing and kayaking enthusiasts.

For an exciting accompanied trip down the Sorgue from Fontaine-de-Vaucluse to Isle-Sur-la-Sorgue, including lively commentary, contact:

Michel Melani, Kayak Vert
84800 Fontaine-de-Vaucluse
☎ ***04.90.20.35.44***

For individual and group lessons contact:

Club de Canoë-Kayak Islois
La Cigalette, 84000 Isle-Sur-La-Sorgue
☎ ***04.90.38.33.22***
☎ ***04.90.20.64.70***

Other details can be obtained from:

Comité Départemental de Canoë-Kayak
Jean-Pierre Claveyrolle, HLM Les Comtamines 3, No 106 EGI, Route d'Avignon, 84300 Cavaillon
☎ ***04.90.71.32.53***

Côte d'Azur

Aéro-Aventures
☎ ***04.93.83.37.33***

Azur Canyoning
☎ ***04.93.29.36.34***

Espaces Sauvages
☎ ***04.93.08.15.18***

Water Sports

Côte d'Azur

You can enjoy every kind of water sport along the coast, from scuba diving (Île des Embiez specializes in it), sailboarding and sailing, to water skiing, etc. Because these sports activities require renting equipment, they are generally practised on beaches in the biggest centres. For more information, consult the Outdoor Activities sections of different chapters.

Visitors are also offered several options in connection with organized cruises and boat rentals of all kinds.

Boat renters offer budding sailors a whole range of possibilities, as do water-sports clubs.

Scuba Diving and Spelunking

The hidden water gorges of the Vaucluse, particularly along the Albion river (linking to terrestrial sites Fontaine de Vaucluse, Canyon de la Nesque and Plateau d'Albion), are unique diving spots for scuba divers. They are dangerous and only professionals have access to them. Contact:

Comité Départemental de Spéléologie du Vaucluse
Musée Requien, 67 Rue Joseph-Vernet, 84000 Avignon

The limestone basins with colourful plant and marine life along the Mediterranean attract professional divers from around the world. The coast offers scuba divers some of the finest conditions in Europe. Underwater prehistoric caves have been found, notably the Grotte Cosquer in July 1991. Here, 37m (121ft) below the surface, Henri Cosquer discovered a cave with paintings in charcoal or magnesium oxide dating back from 10,000 to 20,000 years. Divers must be experienced and licensed, otherwise a number of groups offer day and half-day lessons (including a first dive). Details from:

Comité Régional des Sports Sous-Marins
24 Quai de Rive Neuve, 13007 Marseille
☎04.91.09.36.31

Côte d'Azur

Comité Départemental des Plongeurs
☎04.93.61.26.07
Scuba diving.

Aero Aventures
☎04.93.83.37.33
This organization offers spelunking excursions in all areas.

Fishing

Provence

The region's rivers and ponds are favourite spots for those who love *la pêche* (fishing). Trout, salmon and eel are the most common species. Sea-fishing is possible along the Mediterranean coast, from ports such as Cassis, La Ciotat and Marseille (tourist offices provide details). Local regulations must be observed, so contact the associations before casting off.

A third type of fishing, called *pêche à pied* (literally: fishing by foot) takes place in Provence along the sandy rivers of the marshy Camargue region, where tiny mollusks known as tellines (like mussels but much smaller) are gathered by hand. Prepared with garlic and parsley, these tasty critters are served as an hors d'œuvre in the area.

In the Vaucluse contact:

Fédération Départementale de Pêche
5 Boulevard Champfleury
84000 Avignon
☎04.90.86.62.68

In the Bouches-du-Rhône contact:

Fédération Départementale de Pêche
Espace La Beauvallée - Hall B
Rue M. Gandhi, 13084 Aix-en-Provence
☎ ***04.42.26.59.15***

Hang-Gliding

Suspended by an airfoil at 2,500m (8,202ft) in the sky, hang-gliding is an exciting alternative to land-locked sports. In the Vaucluse, the most popular organisations arranging flights are centred around Mont Ventoux and in the Luberon. In the Bouches-du-Rhône, the Montagne Sainte Victoire and Sainte-Baume Massif area are favoured.

For detailed information regarding sites and their conditions, training courses and hang-gliding schools, contact:

Ligue de Vol Libre de Provence
c/o A. Keller
2 Rue Émile Guigues,
03200 Embrun
☎/≠ ***04.92.43.53.71***

Association Vaucluse Parapente
Maison IV de Chiffre, 26 Rue des Teinturiers, 84000 Avignon
☎ ***04.90.85.67.82***

Handgliding and paragliding information can also be obtained from the following:

Fédération Française de Vol Libre
☎ ***04.97.03.82.82***

Hiking

Provence

The region is ideal for everything from gentle walks along country paths to serious hiking through steep, rugged terrain. No matter your level of fitness, one thing is certain: the scenery is always remarkable and the chance to see countless unusual species of plant and wildlife awaits you.

Professional hikers and Sunday strollers will be spoiled in the Vaucluse and Bouches-du-Rhône. In the Vaucluse, for example, a number of marked trails are available for varying levels of expertise. Easy hikes are found in the plains of the Enclave des Papes (Papal Enclave) around Valréas, around the wine centre of Châteauneuf-du-Pape, and through low-lying fields and along rivulets of the Comtat Venaissin area. Only slightly more challenging are the well-marked trails through the glorious hills of the Dentelles de Montmirail. As in most areas, tourist offices here in the charming villages of Séguret, Gigondas, and Sablet provide specially prepared maps for visitors wishing to discover their region on foot. The tourist office in Vaison-la-Romaine is particularly well equipped to answer questions and provide maps.

For many visitors, Provence means one thing: the cliffside villages and fields of lavender in the Luberon. Countless pathways, backroads and expert hiking trails make their way throughout this most beautiful of areas. Much of the Luberon is a regional natural park and is carefully managed by professionals who have published numerous guides for visitors about its trails, flora and fauna.

The Bouches-du-Rhône benefits from its position facing the sea. Here, amateur explorers are invited to discover the Camargue region at the delta of the Rhone River. Nature lovers are spoiled here too—most of the Camargue is also a regional natural park where unusual wildlife (most famously, pink flamingoes) roam at will. Along the coast east of Marseille, the rugged fjords known as les Calanques offer serious hikers some trails worthy of an all-day outing. Inland, hikers may choose from the lovely Alpilles around the tourist centres of Saint-Rémy and les Baux (relatively easy, though rugged trails looking over the sun-drenched countryside), or better yet, the exceptional variety of trails in Cézanne's beloved area: Montagne Sainte-Victoire and the Saint-Baume Massif area southeast of Aix-en-Provence.

Due to the risk of forest fires, certain trails are systematically closed during the summer, so ask at the local tourist office before heading out.

The Vaucluse regional government publishes an excellent brochure with a map and details of hiking trails in the area. Though written in French, the map and suggested routes are easy to understand. Write ahead for a copy of the *Memento de la Randonnée Pédestre en Vaucluse* from the Chambre Départementale de Tourisme de Vaucluse (see p 61).

Specific information on hiking in the Vaucluse can be obtained from:

Comité Départemental de la Randonnée Pédestre
63 Rue César Frank, 84000 Avignon

In the Bouches-du-Rhône, contact:

Comité Départmental de la Randonnée Pédestre
La Batarelle Haute - Bât. D1, I Impasse des Agaces, 13013 Marseille

Côte d'Azur

Hiking is probably the best organized outdoor activity and one for which the greatest development efforts have been made in the back-country of the Côte d'Azur. It goes without saying that this is the best way to explore a few of the region's greatest natural resources.

As such, a plexus of well-maintained and marked out footpaths runs through the region. Moreover, there is a network of "Grande Randonnée" (or GR) trails, which can lead you all the way to Northern Europe.

Detailed maps will enable you to better prepare your excursions. With this in mind, we suggest those of the Institut Géographique National (IGN)'s blue series (1:25,000), available in travel bookshops.

Several hikes are briefly described in each of the chapters' "Outdoor Activities" sections. In addition, guides and books offering more detailed descriptions are readily available throughout the region.

As a general rule, most trails are open to everyone. However, hikers will still be exposed to certain "dangers": risk of sunstroke, sudden changes in temperature and risk of fog in the mountains.

Comité Départemental de la Randonnée Pédestre
☎/⇄ *04.93.09.91.27*

Snakes

Watch out for vipers in this region. Actually, though you may encounter them in the hills of the back-country, the only possibly dangerous ones are those in the Bouches-du-Rhône area; those found in other parts are harmless. Nevertheless, seeing a doctor is advised should one of these vipers bite you.

The slightest noise generally makes them flee, however. The likelihood of encountering one is therefore slim.

Rain

Showers are more frequent in spring and autumn. As such, if you plan on taking a walk in the mountains, it is wise to make inquiries about the weather forecast before setting out.

Clothing

Pack a long-sleeved sweater if you plan on exploring the mountain trails. If you are following the coastline, bring a bathing suit and a hat to protect you from the sun.

In winter, bring warm clothing. Once the sun has set, temperatures are much cooler, and all the more so in villages at high altitudes.

Sunstroke

Long sections of some trails are exposed to the sun, with no shady spots in which to take refuge. The risk of sunstroke is therefore considerable and threatens all hikers enjoying their favourite outdoor activity. Cramps, goose bumps, nausea and loss of balance are the initial syptoms. If these symptoms arise, the victim should be moved quickly into the shade, fanned and given something to drink.

To avoid this problem, always wear a hat and arm yourself with a good sunscreen. It is also stongly advised to go hiking early in the morning during the particularly hot summer days. No matter what season, wear thick and sturdy shoes and dress appropriately.

What to Bring

On each excursion, your backpack should contain the following objects: a water bottle, a pocket knife, an antiseptic, bandages (both adhesive and non-adhesive), scissors, aspirin, enough food for the trip and, during the summer, sunblock and insect repellent.

Camping

Côte d'Azur

There are cleared campgrounds throughout the area. On the other hand, it must be noted that camping in the wild is generally forbidden.

Prices vary greatly according to services offered.

Furthermore, trailer or camping gear outfitters offer their services in several places. Their addresses and phone numbers are listed throughout this book, in the "Accommodations" sections.

Cycling

Provence

A good way to discover the villages and countryside is by bicycle. This mode of transportation (called *cyclotourisme* or *randonnées à velo* in French) permits visitors to take their time to appreciate the history, sights and smells of Provence and to create personalized tours according to taste and whim. Often, hotels, inns and bed and breakfasts have bicycles for guests' use, so don't hesitate to ask. For serious exploring, especially along difficult routes, a mountain bike is recommended.

Ulysses publishes an authoritative guide to cycling in France called *Cycling in France.* This pocket-sized, ring-bound guide divides France into eight areas, from Alsace to Burgundy and from the Périgord and Quercy to the Loire Valley. The largest chapter covers Provence. Seven cycling tours are recommended in the region, making it the perfect companion to this Provence guide. *Cycling in France* provides a colour atlas with 32 pages of maps from the Institut Géographique National de France (IGN), plus 30 detailed routes. Special sections highlight the principal attractions, sites , tourist offices, population, market days and local specialities. Available wherever Ullyses travel guides are sold.

Professional cyclists from around the world take part in the annual Tour de France in July. Visitors to Provence and the Côte d'Azur can watch this passionate event, as the nationwide route runs through the region (tourist offices and the local press will announce where and when the cyclists are expected).

For a calender of cycling events and list of local organizations, contact:

Ligue de Provence de Cyclotourisme
Jacques Maillet, 15 La Trévaresse, 13540 Puyricard
☎***04.42.92.13.41***

For the Vaucluse, contact:

Comité Départemental du Vaucluse de Cyclotourisme
Roland Gabert, 4 chemin des Passadoires, 84220 Piolnec
☎***04.60.29.62.10***

For the Bouches-du-Rhône, contact:

Comité Départemental des Bouches-du-Rhône de Cyclotourisme
Pierre Flecher, Les Prevenches B 12, 36 Avenue de Saint Barnabé, 13012 Marseille
☎***04.91.34.89.92***

Côte d'Azur

The many winding roads through magnificent landscapes, be they by the sea or in the hills of the back-country, will delight cyclists. In the high season, however, cyclists must share these roads with drivers, which can become rather trying. Moreover, the heat, the pollution from cars and the many hills to climb will make conditions harder for some. Finally, cyclists must be in good physical shape to practise this activity in the back-country, on account of the numerous passes, valleys and winding roads.

Mountain Biking

Provence

What better way to discover Provence's hidden treasures than by mountain bike (known as VTT or *vélo tout terrain*)? The summer heat and many hills to climb in the Vaucluse, Luberon, Alpilles and Montange Saint-Victoire areas are bound to discourage some, however. You must be in good physical condition to enjoy this sport in these area.

The Vaucluse regional government publishes an excellent brochure with a detailed map of routes and their level of difficulty throughout the department. Portions of some of the routes are easy enough for bicyclists as well as mountain bikers. Write ahead for the *Memento de la Promenade et Randonnée Cyclotouriste/VTT en Vaucluse* from the Chambre Départementale de Tourisme de Vaucluse (address on the first page of this chapter).

For further information about mountain biking in the entire Provence region, contact:

Comité Départemental de VTT
Chez Stanis Kowalczyk, 5 rue de Bretagne, 13117 Lavéra
☎***04.42.81.59.05***

Côte d'Azur

Several places rent out these bicycles. The topography is ideal for this sport.

Fédération Française de Cyclisme (Comité régional Côte d'Azur)
☎***04.94.38.50.55***

Rock Climbing

Provence

With so many clliffs and sheer rocky surfaces in the region, Provence is ideal rock climbing (*escalade*) territory. This can be a dangerous sport and is therefore for professionals only. It shouldn't be attempted without the right equipment nor proper training.

In the Vaucluse, the main sites are at Buoux, the Dentelles de Montmirail and the Colline Saint-Jacques (Cavaillon). Contact:

Comité Départmental de la Montagne et Escalade
7 Rue Saint-Michel, 84000 Avignon
☎***04.90.25.40.48***

In the Bouches-du-Rhône, the number of sites, of varying difficulty is astounding. The favourite spots are Sainte-Victoire, the Calanques (a vertiginous climb above the turquoise sea), Sainte-

Baume and the Alpilles. Contact the very helpful Daniel Gorgeon at:

Comité Départemental Mont-Alp- Escalade
5 Impasse du Figuier, 13114 Puylobier
☎*04.42.66.35.05*

Côte d'Azur

Comité Départemental de la Montagne et de l'Escalade
☎*04.93.96.17.43*

Horseback Riding

Provence

There are numerous stables scattered throughout Provence. Horses with or without guides are available for visitors from some of the more than 50 *centres équestres* (equestrian centres) in the region. Riders often spend a few days exploring the hills and plains of Provence, but please note, only those with experience at high altitudes, on isolated terrain, and in variable climatic conditions (storms, fog, heat and cold) should attempt this sort of holiday.

The Vaucluse regional government publishes an excellent brochure for horseback riders, including a map with suggested trails, addresses of stables, and useful information. To receive the *Memento de la Randonnée Equestre en Vaucluse* or for more information about this sport in the area, contact:

Comité Départemental d'Equitation
René François, Chemin Saint Julien, 30133 Les Angles
☎*04.90.25.38.91*

In the Bouches-du-Rhone contact:

Comité Départemental des Sports Equestres
M. Girard - Les Décanis, Chemin de Collaver, 13760 Saint-Collaver
☎*04.42.57.35.42*

Côte d'Azur

Horseback riding is practised throughout the region. However, there are more riding centres in the back-country (even nearby), where there are more open spaces.

Comité Départemental d'Equitation Randonnée
☎*04.93.42.62.98*

Golf

Provence

Why not combine sight-seeing with a few rounds on a local golf course? Numerous 18-hole courses cover Provence, plus a choice of 9-hole and practise grounds are offered. The Comité Départemental du Tourisme Bouches-du-Rhône publishes an excellent colour guide to the 11 courses in its department (in French but easy to understand, free, address at the beginning of this chapter).

Côte d'Azur

The region boasts several golf courses, particularly in Var. Moreover, the Club Med in Opio, near Grasse, prioritizes golfing. The most appealing places are listed in the Outdoor Activities sections of the various chapters.

Ligue de Golf P.A.C.A
☎*04.42.39.86.83*

Tennis

Many hotels as well as public sports complexes have tennis courts. Equipment is usually supplied or can be rented in most instances.

Flying

If you want to enjoy some paragliding or flying in a deltaplane, there's quite a number of places that offer both activities.

Fédération Française de Vol Libre
☎*04.97.03.82.82*

where he reinstated it as the Pope's official residence the following year. He died in 1378, at which time the Great Schism erupted. Bowing to public pressure, the Vatican elected Urbain VI, the first Italian Pope in over a century. A number of cardinals rebelled against the decision and fled to Avignon. They voted Clément VII (1378-1394), followed by Benoît XIII (1394-1408) as their popes. The population dropped from 100,000 to 5,000 during this time. Supported by France, Spain and Naples, the pair would be known as *les anti-papes*, or anti-popes. Afterwards, Avignon was ruled by papal administrators up until the Revolution (1790).

12th century, Provence was split in two and ruled by the Count of Toulouse and the Catalan Count of Barcelona. However, from 1136 Avignon was impartial—it had its own governing council, *le consulat* and a military force, much like an Italian city-state of the period.

Avignon's greatest glory was from 1309 to 1417, when it became the Cité des Papes, the popes' city, a name which has stuck to this day. Avoiding feuds in Rome, the Pope Clement V decided that Avignon would become the centre of the Christian world. It was a natural choice, as the Papal rulers had already designated a large portion of Provence as their territory in 1274, called the Comtat Venaissin. Additionally, at the time of Clément V's arrival, Avignon was geographically closer to the heart of the Christian world than Rome. In all, seven popes lived in Avignon. The town prospered remarkably for over one hundred years, as kings, princes, intellectuals, artists, papal administrators and families of cardinals all made Avignon their home.

In 1481, at the death of Charles III, the nephew and sole inheritor of the *bon roi* René d'Anjou who died a year earlier, Louis XI of France, became Count of Provence. He annexed Provence once and for all to the kingdom of France in 1486 as the absolute monarchy based in Paris had no use for an independent southern partner.

Thus, for a century and a half local institutions were removed, and with them Provence's right to self-government. However, Rome continued to administer Avignon. The prosperous town therefore remained a foreign parcel of land within the French kingdom (and stayed that way until the Revolution).

The French monarchy coveted Avignon, and tried to take control of this precious jewel—Louis XIV occupied the town from 1663-67 and again in 1689-90, then Louis XV took hold of it from

1768-74. Avignon finally submitted and became part of France (along with the Comtat Venaissin) by a decree in the Assemblé National on September 14, 1791. However, it wasn't until February 19, 1797 that Pope Pious VI consented to give Avignon away in the Treaty of Tolentino.

The town continued to prosper during the 19th century, thanks to its role as an important agricultural and artistic centre. It became the leading area for ceramic manufacturing and silk and fabric weaving. The famous Provençal printed fabrics, heavily commercialized today, are local reproductions of the lovely, so-called Indian prints imported from the east during this period. Architecture of a religious, administrative and private nature, which flourished in the 17th and 18th centuries, continued, though at a slower pace. Many remarkable mansions *hôtels particuliers* are of particular interest. Although Avignon's population stands at 87,011 today, the greater metropolitan region holds 170,000.

Finding Your Way Around

By Plane

Avignon is served by the Avignon-Caumont Airport handling daily flights (one hour from Paris, for example) from across the country. Contact Air Inter for details. Certain international flights arrive in Nice or Marseille, although most are destined for Roissy-Charles-de-Gaulle Airport in Paris.

By Train

Avignon is conveniently just four-and-a-half hours away from Paris by the high speed TGV train. TGV trains leave twice daily, seven days a week, from Paris's Gare du Lyon and Charles de Gaulle airport. Reservations are not necessary in off-peak times, though reductions, called Joker fares, are available to all who book two weeks or one month in advance. Reservations for Joker fares can only be made in France, and you are obliged to stick to the day and time indicated on the ticket once it is purchased. Timetables are available at French SNCF train stations, SNCF boutiques and travel agents.

By Car

Avignon is at least eight hours drive from Paris (722 km or 449mi) by the **Autoroute du Soleil A7 - E15** expressway. However, traffic is quite heavy during holiday periods (July and August weekends, February school break, for example), and can add another couple of hours to your journey. Arriving from the north on the A7 - E15, carry on the A7 after Orange (the E15 veers towards Nîmes), and follow the signs for Avignon by taking the D225 or N100, both of which lead directly into the city centre. From Côte-d'Azur and the south-east, the N7 leads directly into Avignon. From Marseille take the A7 north and connect with the N7 north into the city. Be sure to carry some French currency with you for the toll booths (*péages*) on the larger expressways. French roads are in great condition but you have to pay for them!

Car Rental

The major car rental agencies are located next to the main SNCF train station, to the right upon leaving the station.

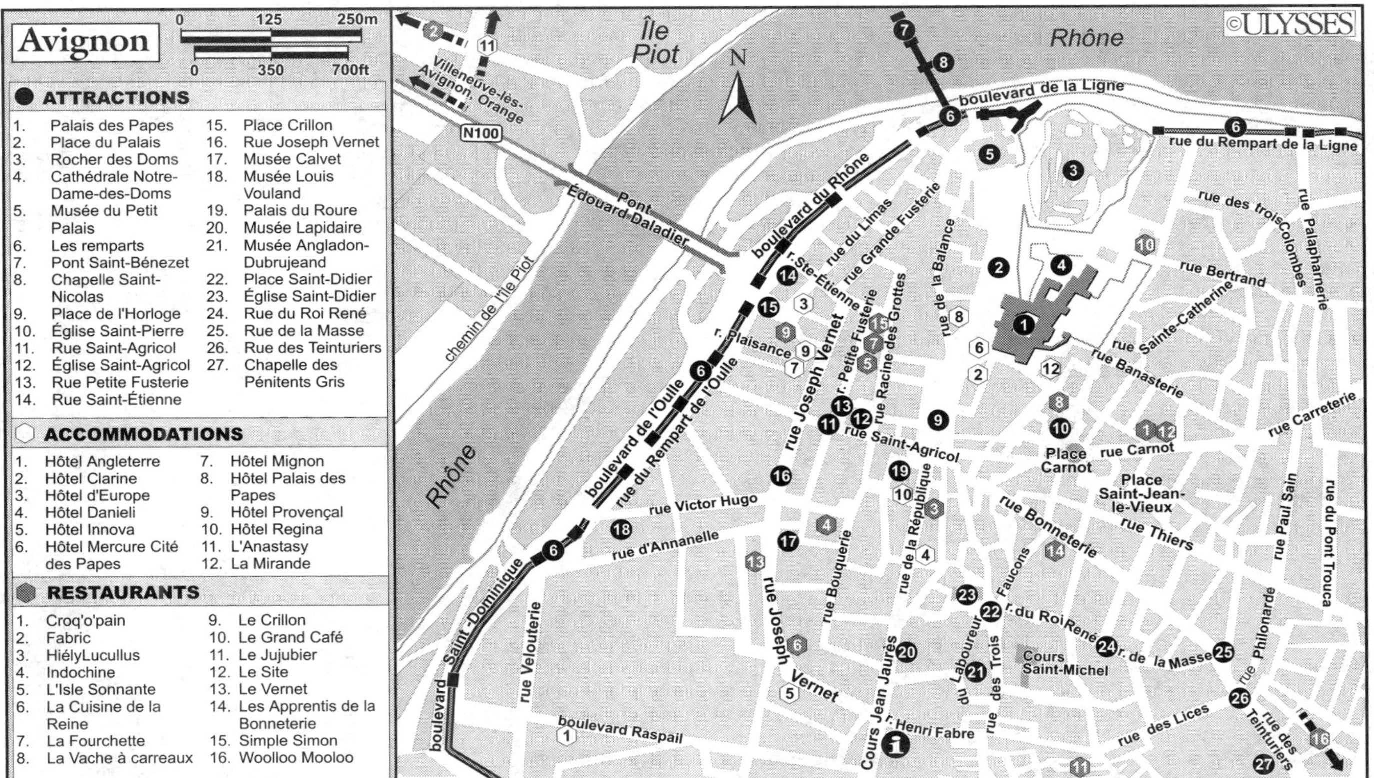
Avignon
0 125 250m
0 350 700ft
ATTRACTIONS
1. Palais des Papes
2. Place du Palais
3. Rocher des Doms
4. Cathédrale Notre-Dame-des-Doms
5. Musée du Petit Palais
6. Les remparts
7. Pont Saint-Bénezet
8. Chapelle Saint-Nicolas
9. Place de l'Horloge
10. Église Saint-Pierre
11. Rue Saint-Agricol
12. Église Saint-Agricol
13. Rue Petite Fusterie
14. Rue Saint-Étienne
15. Place Crillon
16. Rue Joseph Vernet
17. Musée Calvet
18. Musée Louis Vouland
19. Palais du Roure
20. Musée Lapidaire
21. Musée Angladon-Dubrujeand
22. Place Saint-Didier
23. Église Saint-Didier
24. Rue du Roi René
25. Rue de la Masse
26. Rue des Teinturiers
27. Chapelle des Pénitents Gris
ACCOMMODATIONS
1. Hôtel Angleterre
2. Hôtel Clarine
3. Hôtel d'Europe
4. Hôtel Danieli
5. Hôtel Innova
6. Hôtel Mercure Cité des Papes
7. Hôtel Mignon
8. Hôtel Palais des Papes
9. Hôtel Provençal
10. Hôtel Regina
11. L'Anastasy
12. La Mirande
RESTAURANTS
1. Croq'o'pain
2. Fabric
3. HiélyLucullus
4. Indochine
5. L'Isle Sonnante
6. La Cuisine de la Reine
7. La Fourchette
8. La Vache à carreaux
9. Le Crillon
10. Le Grand Café
11. Le Jujubier
12. Le Site
13. Le Vernet
14. Les Apprentis de la Bonneterie
15. Simple Simon
16. Woolloo Mooloo
©ULYSSES
Rhône
Île Piot
N
Villeneuve-lès-Avignon, Orange
N100
Pont Édouard Daladier
chemin de l'Île Piot
boulevard de la Ligne
rue du Rempart de la Ligne
boulevard du Rhône
boulevard de l'Oulle
rue du Rempart de l'Oulle
boulevard Saint-Dominique
rue Velouterie
boulevard Raspail
rue Victor Hugo
rue d'Annanelle
rue du Limas
rue Grande Fusterie
r. Ste-Étienne
r. Plaisance
rue Joseph Vernet
r. Petite Fusterie
rue Racine des Grottes
rue de la Balance
rue Saint-Agricol
rue Bouquerie
rue de la République
Cours Jean Jaurès
r. Henri Fabre
rue du Laboureur
rue des Trois Faucons
r. du Roi René
r. de la Masse
Cours Saint-Michel
rue Bonneterie
rue Thiers
Place Carnot
rue Carnot
Place Saint-Jean-le-Vieux
rue Banasterie
rue Sainte-Catherine
rue Bertrand
rue des troisColombes
rue Palapharnerie
rue Carreterie
rue Paul Sain
rue du Pont Trouca
rue Philonarde
rue des Lices
rue des Teinturiers

Avis
34 Bd St Roch
☎***04.90.82.26.33***

Budget
2A Av Monclar
☎***04.90.87.03.00***

Europcar
2A Av Monclar
☎***04.90.82.49.85***

Hertz
4 Bd Saint Michel
☎***04.90.82.37.67***

Practical Information

Tourist Offices

Office de tourisem d'Avignon
41 Cours Jean Jaurès
☎***04.32.74.32.74***
⇄***04.90.82.95.03***
www.ot-avignon.fr
A good starting point to pick up free maps, information and details about special events, including the theatre festival.

Opening Hours:
Mon to Fri 9am to 1pm and 2pm to 6pm
Sat 9am to 1pm and 2pm to 5pm
Sun (from Apr 1 to Sep 30 only) 9am to 1pm and 2pm to 5pm

During the performing arts festival:
Mon to Fri 10am to 7pm
Sat, Sun and holidays 10am to 5pm

There is a tourist office outlet near the Pont d'Avignon
Oct 1 to Mar 31, Tue to Sat 9am to 5pm
Apr 1 to Sep 30, every day 9am to 6:30pm

Office de tourisme de Villeneuve-les-Avignon
4 Rue des Récollets (near Place Charles David)
☎***04.90.25.61.33***
⇄***04.90.25.91.55***

Parking

Avignon is a historic city with winding streets, many of which are narrow or pedestrian only, so parking can be a problem within the walled city centre. Paying for underground parking lots alleviates some of the problem—the most convenient one is next to the Palais des Papes *(access by following signs from Rue de la République and Place de l'Horloge; 900 places; open 24 hours a day).* Otherwise, it is advised to park just outside the ramparts, along its perimeter, or in the parking lot on Avenue Monclar, situated between the Gare SNCF and Gare Routière train stations.

Banks

All the major French banks are found in the city centre, most along the Rue de la République *(Opening hours: Mon to Fri 8:30am to noon, 2pm to 4pm).* Most have foreign exchange desks, often offering a better deal than the independent exchange offices. Check both the exchange rate and the commission fee charged.

Post Offices

Cours Kennedy
Mon to Fri 8am to 7pm
Sat 8am to noon
☎***04.90.86.78.00***

Exploring

Avignon

The residence of seven popes and two anti-popes during the 14th century, the **Palais des Papes** ★★ *(45F with audio guide, last ticket sold 1hr before closing; every day except Dec 25 and Jan 1; Jan to end of Mar and Nov and Dec, 9am to 1:45pm and 2pm to 6pm; Apr to mid-Aug and Oct, 9am to 7pm; mid-Aug to end of Sep, 9am to 8pm; Place du Palais, ☎04.90.27.50.74)*, or popes' palace, dominates Avignon with its majestic towers and façade. The *vieux palais*, or old palace, was built by local architect Pierre Poisson for Pope Benoît XII (1334-1352) with a distinctly Cistercian soberness. Clément VI (1342-1352) seamlessly added his *nouveau palais*, or new palace, in a similar

Gothic, though more luxurious, manner (architect: Jean de Louvres).

Nowadays, visitors follow a map and discover cloisters, chapels, public reception rooms, private apartments, kitchens and even prisoners' chambers. Be sure to see the remarkable frescoes by Matteo Giovanetti in the Chapelle du Consistoire representing the lives of Saint John the Baptist and Saint John the Evangelist.

Provençal "Indiennes"

Well before they learned to print on cotton, the people of Provence were weaving wool, hemp, linen and silk, which they also knew how to dye. The creation of the Compagnie des Indes in the 17th century saw the first boats bring incredible Asian fabrics to Marseille, including taffeta, satin, wadding and especially printed cotton from India. The refined motifs and their striking colours caused a frenzy among the upper middle classes and the aristocracy. Very quickly, "indiennes," as these printed cotton materials from the East were called, graced the sofas, beds and windows of high society. With such success, many workers from the wool and silk industry left Paris and Lyon to establish themselves in Provence and produce cotton fabrics. The manufacturers took refuge in Marseille, protected by a customs border, and especially Avignon, a papal territory and thus not under the king's control. Naturally, they reproduced on the fabrics everything about Provence that inspired them: flowers, vines, herbs and olive trees. Later, more stylized, almost contemporary geometric patterns came into fashion, dominated by mauve and olive green tones. Cotton lost its appeal in the middle of the 19th century when factories mechanized, but this style has gained a renewed popularity today. It is appreciated around the world for its warm, shimmering colours depicting the earth, sky, sun, sea, the vines and flowers. The tradition endures thanks to the know-how of establishments like Souleïado, based in Tarascon.

The palace fell into disrepair following the popes' departure for Rome. It was at one point used as a barracks for Napoleon's armies, and it would have been demolished had it not been for the intervention of the French state's historical monuments service. Part of the palace has been used as a convention centre, and since 1947, the main courtyard is used by the theatre festival in the summer. The palace interiors are sparse and are of most interest to those fascinated by the popes' reign in France. Otherwise, admire this historic monument from the vantage point of the **Place du Palais ★** in front, created in 1404, or from the marvellous panorama of **Rocher des Doms ★**.

The **Cathédrale Notre-Dame des Doms ★★** *(Place du Palais, Rocher des Doms, ☎04.90.86.81.01)* is a simple, 12th century, Romanesque church where the popes officiated. Originally constructed between 1140 and 1160, with later additions (14th and 15th centuries primarily), the cathedral holds the tomb of Jean XXII and one thought to belong to Benoît XII. Note the 13th-century stone altar, and the chancel with its 12th-century marble pontiff's chair and superb painted cupola above.

Musée du Petit Palais *(30F; every day except Tue 9:30am to 11:50am and 2pm to 6pm; Place du Palais, ☎04.90.86.44.58)* houses an impressive collection of Italian paintings spanning from the Middle Ages to the Renaissance, most of them procured from the private collection of the marquess Campana di Cavelli Gian Pietro (19th century), as well as some canvases from the Avignon School (15th century) and a few Romanesque and Gothic sculptures. This museum will appeal only to admirers of 14th- and 15th-century art. The superbly renovated building was the palace of a cardinal in the 14th century.

The **Remparts**, or ramparts, 4.3km (2.7mi) stone walls circling the city were completed in 1370, and were designed to protect Avignon from invaders during papal times. Twelve towered gates lead into the city, including the Porte de la République (the entrance for Cours de Jean Jaurès, Rue de la République, Place de l'Horloge and the Palais des Papes).

The **Pont Saint-Bénezet** ★★ *(19F, bridge and palace 55F; Oct to Mar, every day 9:30am to 5:30pm; Apr to Sep, everyday 9am to 6:30pm; closed Dec 25, Jan 1 and May 1, ☎04.90.85.60.16)*, otherwise known as the Pont d'Avignon bridge, was constructed of wood from 1177 to 1185, and rebuilt in 1226 in stone.

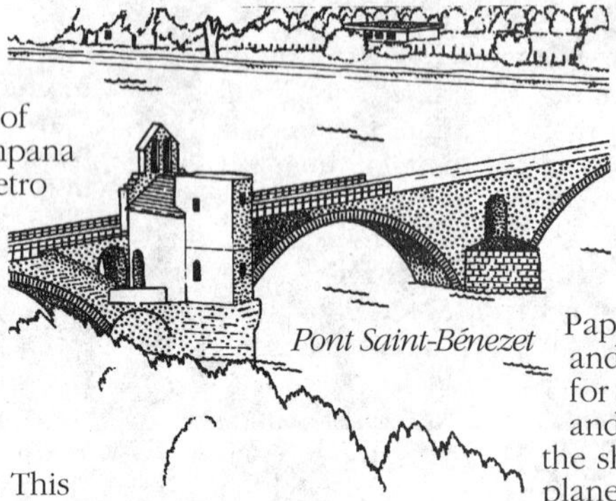

Pont Saint-Bénezet

Legend recalls that in 1177, a young shepherd, Bénézet, was instructed by an angel to build a bridge on the Rivière Rhône. The bishop of Avignon agreed to provide the money necessary if the boy could lift a stone so heavy that 30 men couldn't move it. Bénézet miraculously carried the stone all the way to the banks of the Rhône, on the site of the first arch. Needless to say, the community supported Bénézet's ambitious project with money and manpower. The bridge stretched across to the Île de la Barthelasse, though now just four of the original 22 arches remain, and the bridge ends in the middle of the river.

You can alos visit the little **Chapelle Saint-Nicolas**, a two-storey building dedicated to the patron saint of boatman. The lower level displays a Gothic-style architecture, dating from the 13th century, while the upper level, added in 1513, is in a Roman style.

The **Place de l'Horloge**, at the top of Rue de la République leading to the Palais des Papes, is a touristy and a popular spot for street musicians and beggars. Under the shade of large plane trees, you'll find a row of mediocre restaurants with boards advertising multilingual menus. Young waiters and waitresses stand in front of these terraces trying to entice passersby. The Hotel de Ville, or city hall, and municipal theatre are here, both solid examples of mid-19th-century architecture, plus, of course, a 14th-century clock tower.

The most interesting streets are found in the **Vieille Ville** (old town), on either side of the Rue de la République and the Place de l'Horloge (pick up a free Avignon map from the tourist office). Much of this labyrinth area of roads is pedestrian only, and a number of architectural wonders can be found amongst the commercial hustle and bustle.

The **Église Saint-Pierre** ★ *(Sat 10am to noon, Sun 8:30am to noon; Place Saint Pierre, ☎04.90.82.25.02)* is a 14th-and 15th-century church with amazing 16th-century carved wooden doors depicting the Virgin Mary, the Angel of Annunciation, Saint-Michel and Saint-Jérome. The interior includes paintings and floral scenes set in gilded wood panelling typical of the 17th century, a sculpted stone pulpit from the 15th century, and a stone retable in the small south chapel dating from early 1500.

It is also possible to make an interesting excursion to the east of Place de l'Horloge. Walk down **Rue Saint-Agricol** *(Rue Collège du Roure and Palais du Roure are on the left)*, past **Église Saint-Agricol** *(closed Sun afternoon)*, which was founded in the 12th century by the patron saint of Avignon and restored in the 14th century. From there, explore **Rue Petite-Fusterie**, **Rue Saint-Étienne** and **Place Crillon**, overlooked by the Hôtel d'Europe with its lovely courtyard and fountain, and **Rue Joseph Vernet** ★. The three streets are lined with elegant 18th-century mansions that today have been transformed into stylish shops, restaurants and antique stores.

Reopened in 1996 after extensive renovation, **Musée Calvet** ★★ *(30F; closed public holidays; Wed to Mon 10am to 1pm and 2pm to 6pm, closed Tue and public holidays; 65 Rue Joseph Vernet, ☎04.90.86.33.84)* is one of France's finest small public museums and is situated in the pretty 18th century mansion, l'Hôtel de Villeneuve-Martignan. It presents a mix of prehistoric, Greek and Roman antiquities with paintings, sculpture and *objets d'art* from the Renaissance to this century. French, and in particular, Avignonnais paintings are well represented. As well, there is a large and important collection of wrought-iron dating from the Middle Ages.

The **Musée Louis Vouland** *(20F; Jun to Sep, 10am to noon and 2pm to 6pm; Oct to May, Tue to Sat 2pm to 6pm; 17 Rue Victor Hugo, ☎04.90.86.03.79, ⇄04.90.85.12.04)* contains decorative arts from the 17th and 18th century in a grand *hôtel particulier*.

The **Palais du Roure** *(20F; Museum visit upon request or free guided tour Tue 3pm; 3 Rue Collège du Roure, ☎04.90.80.80.88)* provides an interesting inside look at bourgeois Provençal life while visiting the private residence (beautiful furniture and fabrics, local oil paintings) of the last owner, Jeanne de Flandreysy-Espérandieu, who lived here from 1909 until 1944. The building, l'Hôtel de Baroncelli-Javon, constructed in 1469, is the former mansion of a wealthy Florentine banker. Nowadays, it also houses a library devoted to the history and literature of Provence. The interior courtyard, with its Gothic door, fig trees, a curious collection of iron bells hanging on the walls and four authentic *pots d'Anduze* (wonderful, glazed clay pots made locally for over a century), is an oasis of calm in the centre of Avignon. According to a commemorative plaque, Jeanne de Flandreysy-Espérandieu saved the building, "gave it a soul and welcomed illustrious hosts".

Walking along the narrow streets in Avignon's historic neighbourhoods is one of the city's greatest pleasures. The city is divided by the north-south axis, Cours Jean-Jaurès and the Rue de la République, which date from the 1850s. Unfortunately, these are busy commercial streets with little charm. However, the stunning baroque façade of the **Musée Lapidaire** *(10F; Nov to Apr; Tue to Sun 10am to 1pm and 2pm to 6pm; 27 Rue de la République, ☎04.90.85.75.38)* is worth noting. Once a 17th-century Jesuit chapel, it now houses a collection of precious stones and archaeological artifacts.

Musée Angladon-Dubrujeaud ★★ *(30F; Nov to Apr, Wed to Sun 1pm to 6pm; May to Oct, 1pm to 7pm; 5 Rue Laboureur, ☎04.90.82.29.03, ≠04.90.85.78.07)*, housed in a magnificent restored mansion and open since 1996, offers a double pleasure: the ground floor displays paintings by Manet, Degas, Picasso, Modigliani, Cezanne and Van Gogh, while Chinese salons on the floor above display treasures from the Far East.

Start at the peaceful **Place Saint Didier**, by exploring the **Église Saint Didier** ★ *(open during services only)*, a simple church in the Provençal Gothic style built in the 1350s. A large nave contains late 14th-century frescoes and a charming stone altarpiece depicting the Carrying of the Cross, yet it is popularly known as Notre-Dame du Spasme (Our Lady of the Spasm). You'll understand why when you see the figures' shocked expressions.

Next, head east, along **Rue du Roi René** ★ for a look at a trio of superb 17th-and 18th- century *hôtel particuliers* or mansions. The austere Hôtel d'Honnorate de Jonquerettes at number 12 dates from the 18th century, and faces the pretty Hôtel de Fortia de Montréal, built a century earlier. A masterpiece awaits you on the corner at number seven: the elaborate Hotel de Berton de Crillon (1649), now an office building.

Still continuing eastwards, Rue du Roi René leads into the narrower, winding **Rue de la Messe** and a pair of beautiful *hôtel particuliers*. Turn right onto **Rue des Teinturiers** ★★. You'll find yourself in the neighbourhood once used by manufacturers of the famous Provençal prints called *indiennes* in the 18th century. The road is lined with plane trees and follows the meandering Rivière Sorgue—even a few of the abandoned water-wheels used by the *teinturiers* (clothdyers) can still be seen. This relaxed area has a couple of bar-cafés, two boutiques and a print shop and is frequented by artsy laid-back locals. It is pretty at night and not crowded. At number eight, you'll find the charming, 16th-century **Chapelle des Pénitents Gris** ★ *(Wed to Mon, 8am to noon and 2:30pm to 6pm, closed Sun pm, - Tue and public holidays)*.

Villeneuve-les-Avignon

During the reign of the popes of Avignon in the 14th century, Villeneuve counted many sumptuous cardinals' residences. The town's prosperity lasted up until the Revolution and it is still possible to admire its wide boulevards and its remarkable 17th-century mansions. Sitting high atop the right bank of the Rhône, Villeneuve is worth a few days' visit to explore its historical sites (medieval Fort Saint-André, Chartreuse du Val de Bénédiction, a Charterhouse which dates from the 14th century and conceals beautiful cloisters, Tour Philippe le Bel, and more). The tourist office offers a "Passeport pour l'Art" ("passport to art") at a cost of 45F, which entitles the bearer to discounts such as free admission to five sites including those mentioned above, Église Notre-Dame and Musée Municipal Pierre-de-Luxembourg (which houses a famous painting by Enguerrand Quarton of the crowning of the Virgin that dates from 1453-54).

Impressive **panoramic views** ★★ of Avignon, Mont Ventoux, the Luberon and of the Alpilles mountain ranges can be had from both Fort Saint-André and the Tour Philippe le Bel. A good flea market is held every Saturday, in the parking lot next to Place Charles David and Avenue Charles de Gaulle. From Avignon, cross the Pont Daladier bridge and follow the signs for Villeneuve, then turn right onto Avenue Gabriel Peri to reach the city centre.

Please see the following chapters for details about other excursions which can be started from Avignon:

Orange, see p 106.
Hills and villages of the Luberon, see p 141.
Camargue, see p 177.
Vaison-la-Romaine, see p 110.
Arles, see p 169.
St-Rémy-de-Provence, see p 163.

Outdoor Activities

For details about golf, swimming pools, tennis, squash, or even ice-skating, call Avignon sports hot line, better known as the Municipal Sports Service ☎***04.90.85.22.58***.

Mountain Biking and Hiking

The Vaucluse department tourist office, located outside of the city centre, provides maps and information about walking tours, mountain biking and hiking. (Avignon's tourist office will point you in the right direction too.)

Comité départmental de Tourisme
La Balance, place Campana,
B.P. 147, 84008 Avignon Cédex
☎***04.90.86.43.42***

Transhumance
B.P. 9, 84004 Avignon
☎***04.90.95.57.81***

By mountain bike (VTT—*vélo tout terrain*) or by foot, this group organizes tours of the Avignon area. Initiation tours, full-day or several-day tours (around the Dentelles de Montmirail, Vaucluse Mountains or Luberon Park) are also arranged. Equipment can be rented.

Two businesses offering bicycle rentals by the hour or the day:

Velomania
1 Rue de l'Amelier
☎***04.90.82.06.98***

Alain Blache
11 Avenue Monclar
☎***04.90.85.56.63***

Horseback Riding

Equestion Centre and **Avignon Pony Club**
Île de la Barthelasse
Chemin du Mont Blanc
☎***04.90.85.83.48***

Accommodations

Avignon

Hôtel Innova
160F-340F
pb, ps, tv
100 Rue Joseph Vernet
☎***04.90.82.54.10***
⇄***04.90.82.52.39***
Cheap, simple and centrally located. At this price, one tends to overlook the tired wallpaper and furnishings of this one-star hotel and appreciate the friendly welcome.

Hôtel Mignon
200F-280F
ps, tv
17 Rue Joseph-Vernet
☎***04.90.82.17.30***
⇄***04.90.85.78.46***
Cute hotel with character and basic rooms but considering the central location, good value. Breakfast room.

Hôtel Provençal
310F
ps
13 Rue Joseph-Vernet
☎***04.90.85.25.24***
⇄***04.90.82.75.81***
Simple, clean rooms (a few need refreshing)

with small bathrooms. No elevator. Good location.

Hôtel Regina
310F-330F
pb, ps, tv
6 Rue de la République
☎**04.90.86.49.45**
⇌**04.90.86.49.78**
Located above a corner café on one of Avignon's busiest roads, the Regina has three things going for it: it's inexpensive, central and near the SNCF train station. The 30 bedrooms have all the basic amenities but their decor is old-fashioned and some need freshening up. The reception doubles up as a breakfast room.

Hôtel Angleterre
310F-410F
tv
29 Boulevard Raspail
☎**04.90.86.34.31**
⇌**04.90.86.86.74**
The Hôtel Angleterre is an excellent choice among the more affordable hotels in Avignon. Located within the city walls near the very centre of town, it is still in a fairly quiet area, removed from the hustle and bustle. The hotel has 40 rooms that have no particular charm but are clean and well maintained. There is private parking behind the hotel.

Hôtel Clarine
320F-450F
≡, *pb, tv*
26 Place de l'Horloge
☎**04.90.82.21.45**
⇌**04.90.82.90.92**
A good-value hotel in the heart of Avignon, just steps away from the Palais des Papes. The 33 rooms lack character but are clean, decorated in fresh colours and perfectly adequate for a night or two. Despite overlooking the busy Place de l'Horloge, the rooms are soundproof.

Hôtel Palais des Papes
320F-600F
closed Jan to early Mar
ℜ, *pb, tv*
1 Rue Gérard-Philippe
☎**04.90.86.04.13**
⇌**04.90.27.91.17**
Comfortable hotel with Gothic interior, recommended more for its ideal location next to the Palais des Papes than for the somewhat cold welcome from the front desk staff.

Hôtel Danieli
390F-490F
closed Christmas and New Year's Day
pb, tv
17 Rue de la Républic
☎**04.90.86.46.82**
⇌**04.90.27.09.24**
Cheery rooms (though lacking local charm) and friendly reception staff in this centrally located hotel on the city's bustling commercial street. Breakfast room, bar, parking in paid public underground car park 200m (656ft) away.

Hôtel Mercure Cité des Papes
630F
≡, *tv*
1 Rue Jean Vilar
☎**04.90.80.93.00**
⇌**04.90.27.39.21**
H1952@accor-hotels.com
This large, six-storey hotel has 73 rooms without much character but that are nevertheless very comfortable. Guests don't stay here for the charm or pastoral ambiance, which can't be found, but for the location, in the shadow of the Palais des Papes. Breakfast is served on the sixth-floor terrace, which offers a breathtaking panoramic view of the city.

Hôtel d'Europe
690F-3,300F
≡, ℜ, *pb, tv*
12 Place Crillon
☎**04.90.14.76.76**
⇌**04.90.85.43.66**
Beautiful old 17th-century *hôtel particulier* belonging to Provençal nobility, converted into a hotel in the 18th century. Noted personalities, from Napoléon to Charles Dickens have stayed here. Friendly service and 50 good-sized, renovated rooms. The hotel's restaurant, La Vielle Fontaine, recently received a Michelin star.

La Mirande
1,800F-2,600F
≡, ℜ, ⊙, *pb, tv*
4 Place de l'Amirande
☎**04.90.85.93.93**
⇌**04.90.86.26.85**
A stunning former cardinal's palace, La Mirande was transformed in the

18th century into a mansion (one of 100,000 castles in France that are registered historical monuments), by the celebrated architect Mignard. It has recently been entirely restored by architect Gilles Grégoire and interior decorator François-Joseph Graff. IT is considered one of the most beautiful hotels in France: the 19 bedrooms and one suite, restaurant, breakfast salon, bar, covered inner courtyard and terrace are all impeccably designed with a harmony of colours, fabrics and antiques, befitting a *hôtel particulier* of the period. The owners, the Stein family, are considered '*mecenats*' (patrons) by the Avignonnais for their work. Situated at the foot of the Palais des Papes, this is relaxed luxury at its finest. Worth visiting if only to enjoy afternoon tea. Cooking workshops (from half-a-day to a week-long) take place in the hotel's renovated vaulted cellars.

Île de la Barthelasse

L'Anastasy
350F-450F, bkfst incl.
4rooms, sb or pb, ≈
Île de la Barthelasse, 5km (3.1mi) north, turn immediately right off the Pont Daladier bridge from Avignon
☎04.90.85.55.94
⇄04.90.82.94.49

A warm welcome awaits you at this attractive *chambre d'hôte* (bed and breakfast) run by local personality Olga Manguin, the former owner/chef of an Avignon café and her husband, Biquet, grandson of the influential Fauvre artist Henri Manguin. In summer, a copious breakfast is served on a shaded garden patio, in this peaceful country atmosphere (though it is just 15min from the centre of Avignon). Olga prepares evening meals upon request *(150F)* and offers one-week Provençal cooking courses several times a year (accommodation included, call or write for details). Tricky to find—follow Chemin des Poiriers and l'Anastasy is on your left 50m (164ft) after Distillerie Manguin. No credit cards.

Villeneuve-les-Avignon

Foyer International YCJG - YMCA
80F-120F, bkfst incl.
closed Dec 25 to Jan 2
7 bis, Ch. de la Justice
☎04.90.25.46.20

Two hundred beds, in a dormitory, shared rooms and individual accommodation. Half and full board available.

Restaurants

Avignon

Le Crillon
$
15 Place Crillon
☎04.90.27.17.01

A typical French café where the food is good though not exceptional and no one minds if customers linger over their espresso. Pasta dishes are 45F, omelettes 30F, a choice of ten salads between 40F and 50F. A trio of fixed-price menus called *Formules Bières* offer a main course, dessert and beer for 60F, 75F and 80F. In warm weather, a dozen tables are set out on a terrace, on charming Place Crillon. Menu at 110F.

Croq'o'pain Sandwicherie
$
23 Rue Carnot
no ☎

A popular student spot for its contemporary

design (metal café tables and sleek wood chairs) and low prices. Go for the Menu Croq'o—salad or a sandwich, plus drink and coffee for 32F.

La Vache à Carreaux
$
14 Rue Peyrollerie
☎04.90.80.09.05
This place is *vachement bon* (bloody good) as the French like to say. Here, cheese is the name of the game. The chef specializes in preparing original dishes that are cheese-based. Honey, nut, herb and cherry or even anise-flavoured cheeses, as well as *Pélardons de Cévennes* (goat cheese), *banons* (blue cheeses), and *brebis de Béarn* will delight cheese-lovers. The small restaurant has a warm decor with stone walls and low ceilings. It is located in a quiet street near the Place Saint-Pierre.

Simple Simon
$
Tue to Sat, 11:45am to 7pm
26 Rue Petite Fusterie
☎04.90.86.62.70
An authentic British flavour in the heart of Provence. Not such a bad idea when the savoury tartes, salads and English treats such as scones, lemon-curd tart or trifle (summertime only) are so well-prepared. Cosy interior, small outside terrace, smiling waitresses.

Le Site
$
Mon to Fri noon to midnight, Sat 4pm to 1am
23 Rue Carnot
☎04.90.27.12.00
In a bright vaulted stone cellar, this "Restaurant Internet" serves salads, sandwiches and hot dishes, plus a fixed-price, three-course menu at 95F. A number of tables have computers so you can surf while you eat.

Woolloo Mooloo
$
Tue to Sat
16bis Rue des Teituriers
☎04.90.85.28.44
Long and narrow café, with old tables and rough cement walls, attracting an arty crowd. A curious mix of Caribbean and American cuisine (trout with curried vegetables and white rice, apple crumble). Menus at 67F and 89F.

Le Grand Café
$-$$
closed Sun lunch and Mon
4 Rue Escaliers Sainte Anne
☎04.90.86.86.77
A great atmosphere (wood tables, five huge baroque mirrors, tall ceiling and stone floor), an arty crowd and good food make the Grand Café a favourite for lunch or dinner. Recent dishes include rabbit with rosemary, a lemony fish tajine and a green vegetable risotto. Menus at 95F and 160F; excellent desserts. Very good wine list with a number of items sold by the glass *(15-19F)*. Directly behind the Palais des Papes by the Manutention cinema.

Les Apprentis de la Bonneterie
$$
28 Rue de la Bonneterie
☎04.90.27.37.97
A small bistro with a relaxed atmosphere in the pedestrian zone southwest of the Place de l'Horloge, Les Apprentis de la Bonneterie serves generous portions of unpretentious food that highlights local ingredients and culinary traditions. From lamb to scorpion fish and duck, the chef prepares all dishes with a knowing touch. The front room has a pleasant, casually retro feel with its curios and old glass-paned cupboards, and welcomes a very mixed clientele comprised of locals and visitors.

La Cuisine de la Reine
$$
closed Sun
Le Cloitre des Arts
83 Rue Joseph Vernet
☎04.90.85.99.04
The Cloitre des Arts is a renovated, 19th-century mansion housing a tearoom, bar, boutique and restaurant, La Cuisine de la Reine. The latter is smartly decorated with dark wood floors, mustard-coloured walls and velvet armchairs in plum, deep rose and gold. The modern menu includes a good choice of meat, fish and pasta; desserts are home-made. Lunch menu is 110F, dinner menu

165F. Brunch is served every Saturday, 11:30am to 2:30pm.

La Fourchette
$$
Mon to Fri
17 Rue Racine
☎04.90.85.20.93
Forks on the wall and ceiling set the scene for this smart restaurant styled like a country inn and much enjoyed by locals. Fish is the house specialty, while the beef *daube* with macaroni gratin and grilled saumon with puréed potates and sorrel are also excellent.

Indochine
$$
3bis Rue Petite Calade
☎04.90.86.20.74
An aquarium with exotic fish near the bar, colourful oriental decor and waiters in pressed white jackets set the tone for this restaurant. Dishes derive from Laos, Cambodia and Tonkin—lunch menus at 49F to 69F offer variety and value, as does the 89F dinner menu. Smooth, somewhat formal service.

Le Jujubier
$$
Mon to Fri lunch only
24 Rue des Lices
☎04.90.86.64.08
As the sign promises, here you'll find Provençal cuisine as it used to be. Marylin and Marie-Christine spent six months studying old Provençal recipes, which they now follow down to the smallest detail in their pleasant restaurant, decorated in soothing yellow and olive-green tones. Cold zucchini soup with basil, ox cheek with carrots and anchovies, aïoli (Fridays) and blood sausage with leeks are only a few of the delights that await you here. The meat dishes, priced at 85F to 110F, and the fish at 90F are excellent value for the price, as are the rest of the menu items. Guests are warmly welcomed. No credit cards.

Le Vernet
$$
Easter to Oct
58 Rue Joseph Vernet
☎04.90.86.64.53
A charming restaurant, Le Vernet has acquired a most enviable reputation over the years, to the point where it is considered one of Avignon's finest dining establishments. Opened by chef Claude Clareton, the restaurant certainly has one of the most attractive terraces in town, shaded by majestic trees and sheltered from the noise of the street by a stone wall and a wrought iron fence. Today Anne-Marie, Claude's wife, and their son Laurent continue the rich tradition of the late chef Clareton. Among the dishes are the sublime house specialty, *agnolade d'Avignon,* tender beef entrecote steak, and the daily fish special, always fresh, all prepared with the greatest skill. The fixed-price menu for 120F includes three courses, and you can order a small carafe of Côtes-du-Rhône for an additional 25F. It is essential to reserve in advance if you want a table on the terrace, but you can also enjoy your meal in the attractive dining room set up in an old pharmacy. To thoroughly please the owner, just mention Montréal, where her daughter, dancer and choreographer Estelle Clareton, settled several years ago to pursue her successful career.

Hiély-Lucullus
$$-$$$
closed Tue and Wed at lunch, one week at the end of Jun and two weeks in Jan
5 Rue de la République
☎04.90.86.17.07
This very popular Avignon restaurant, located upstairs in a building neighbouring Place de l'Horloge, reveals a discreet elegance. The great classics of French cuisine are prepared here with a great deal of care and offered in three set-menus *(130F, 160F and 220F)*. For example, the roast rabbit liver in a pastry puff and the dill-scented grilled cod served with an eggplant purée are simply delicious. The only disappointing note of this fantastic meal was the dessert platter, which could at best be described as banal; this restaurant really needs a good pastry chef.

L'Isle Sonnante
$$$
Tue to Sat
7 Rue Racine
☎***04.90.82.56.01***
Menu at 160F (lunch) and 285F (dinner) only. Fresh room with pretty porcelain and oak bar with brass fittings. One of the best restaurants in Avignon, and the creative menu says it all: red fish terrine with tomato *coulis*, rabbit filet with a Nyons olive purée stuffing; *dorade* filet in puff pastry with mint-flavoured *fervettes*. Excellent cheese and desserts. Highly recom mended.

Villeneuve-les-Avignon

Fabrice
$$
Closed Sun pm and Mon
3 Boulevard Pasteur
☎***04.90.25.52.79***
Worth crossing the Pont Daladier into historic Villeneuve (follow Avenue General Leclerc, turn right at Avenue Pasteur), for a fresh, modern twist to Provençal cuisine. Young chef Fabrice Guisset did his military service in Paris, cooking for Edouard Balladour, Finance Minister at the time. He works wonders with local produce such as courgettes, eggplant and flavourful tomatoes in his deliciously simple vegetable terrine with tapenade vinaigrette, pistou soup with chèvre croutons, or smoked tuna with crispy artichokes and asparagus. The dining room, with a subtle coral-coloured nautical look, is in the house where his grandfather once lived. Friendly, attentive service; pleasant patio.

Entertainment

Avignon

Bars and Nightclubs

Le Bistrot d'Utopia
Mon to Sat 11:45am to midnight, Sun 2pm to 11pm
4 Rue Escaliers Sainte Anne
☎***04.90.27.04.96***
A laid-back bar and café, next to the La Manutention Cinema and Le Grand Café, with a young crowd. There's a good choice of coffee, tea, hot chocolate and fruit juices, plus a selection of tartine grillée (toasted sandwiches), a charcuterie plate and cakes. Beers priced at between 12F and 22F include Adelscott, Chimay Rouge and Pietra. Terrace in good weather.

Le Blues
25 Rue Carnot
☎***04.90.85.79.71***
Live music and DJs attracting a quieter, somewhat older crowd than at Red Zone next door.

L'Esclave Bar
every day 10pm to 5am
12 Rue du Limas
☎***04.90.85.14.91***
L'Esclave Bar is a gay nightclub.

Le Liverpool
every day
23 Rue de la République
☎***04.90.82.17.78***
This hangout for Avignon's billiard-playing youth is run by a friendly chap. Open quite late every evening.

Le Red Zone
25 Rue Carnot
☎***04.90.27.02.44***
A pub-like atmosphere with a number of draught beers and a young crowd make this a good spot to hear live music (Latin, rock, blues, salsa) and DJs playing hip hop, jungle and house music. Check local press for details.

Theatres

Avignon has a lively and varied theatre scene, so it is worth checking the local press or asking at your hotel for details on productions. The following are worth checking out:

Théâtre du Balcon
38 Rue Guillaume-Puy
☎***04.90.85.00.80***

Théâtre du Belier
53 Rue Portail Magnanen
☎***04.90.82.51.83***

Théâtre du Cabestan
11 Rue Collège de la Croix
☎***04.90.86.11.74***

Théatre des Carmes
6 Place des Carmes
☎*04.90.82.20.47*

Théâte du Chêne Noir
8bis Rue Sainte-Catharine
☎*04.90.86.58.11*

Théâtre du Chien Qui Fume
75 Rue des Teinturiers
☎*04.90.85.25.87*
Artistic director Gérard Vantaggioli's theatre is always producing something of interest, including a new-talent night "Les Amoureux de la Scene" (last Friday of every month) with semi-professional and amteur actors, comedians, poets, rock or opera singers and an improv "Ce Soir on Improvise au Chien" (one Friday every month) with stand-up comedians. In French.

Movie Theatres

Le Capitale
3 Rue de Pourquery de Boisserin
information/booking:
☎*08.36.68.20.22*
The latest releases on four screens.

Pathé Palace
38 Cours Jean Jaurès
information/booking:
☎*08.36.68.20.22*
The latest releases on five screens.

Le Vox
Place de l'Horloge
information/booking:
☎*08.36.68.03.70*
The latest releases on two screens.

La Manutention Utopia Cinema
4 Rue des Escaliers Sainte Anne
☎*04.90.82.65.36*
The best art house cinema around, showing international films, plus a great bar and café.

Île de la Barthelasse

Bars and Nightclubs

Le Bistroquet
6pm to 3:30am
☎*04.90.82.25.83*
Rock, reggae, rhythm and blues—its all found here at this long-established nightclub a short drive across the Rhône (take the Pont d'Aladier). Check the local press for details of visiting bands and precise times. Parking is not a problem.

Shopping

Avignon

Cafés au Brésil
10am to noon and 2pm to 7pm, closed Sun
24 Rue des Fourbisseurs
☎*04.90.82.49.71*
Cafés au Brésil sells nothing but the best teas, coffees and fine delicacies, including locally produced honeys.

Droguerie—Vannerie
10am to noon and 2pm to 7pm
closed Sun, Mon AM
33 Rue Bonneterie
☎*04.90.86.13.66*
Bargain shop which sells Savon de Marseille from the only real soap manufacturer left producing this body and laundry shop. Beware of expensive imposters in trendy tourist shops elsewhere!

Fontaine de Bacchus
Tue to Sun 8am to 1:30pm
Les Halles, Place Pie
☎*04.90.82.74.84*
Former Montrealers Nicole, a jovial Quebecer, and her French husband, Alain Bellec, offer a good selection of Côtes du Rhône wines and can also suggest the best wineries to visit. This little market stall is worth a stop, if only to meet this friendly young couple.

Foto Eclair
closed Sun
4 Rue Saint Agricol
☎*04.90.85.15.72* One-hour photo developing: 2,80F per photo plus 18F for 24 exposures.

FNAC
closed Sun
19 Rue de la République
84000 Avignon
☎*04.90.14.35.35/43*
Enormous choice of CDs and huge selection of books (from fiction to fine art and technology to travel).

Galeries Lafayette
closed Sun
22 Rue de la République
☎ ***04.90.86.59.13***
One-stop shopping for life's necessities and the rest—clothes, sportswear, cosmetics, houseware, small appliances. Due to be redeveloped on the same site as part of a shopping complex.

Les Halles
Tue to Sun, 6am to 1pm
Place Pie
Modern, covered farmers market with local produce, meats and fish. Wonderful selection of seasonal fruits—cherries, apricots, plums and peaches freshly picked in the region. The perfect place to prepare a picnic—sliced meats, breads, cheeses, olives and wines are all available.

Hervé Baum
Tue to Sat
19 Rue Petite Fusterie
☎ ***04.90.86.37.66***
⇄ ***04.90.27.05.97***
Long-established antiques shop, one of the best in Avignon, includes objects for the garden and decorative items. A wonderful, personal selection by Baum, includes pieces from a few francs to a few thousand francs. The owner also displays at Isle-sur-la Sorgue on weekends. Other antiques shops are found on Rue Petite Fusterie, parallel to Rue Joseph Vernet (for smart fashion shops).

La Memoire du Monde
Mon to Sat 9am to 7pm
26 Rue Carnot and 16 Rue de la Bonneterie
☎ ***04.90.82.47.93***
Good selection of literature, theatre and travel books.

Monoprix
closed Sun
24 Rue de la République
☎ ***04.90.82.60.14***
Everything your heart desires in France's answer to Woolworth's.

Mouret Chapelier
Tue to Sun 9:30am to noon and 2:30pm to 7pm, Mon 2:30pm to 7pm
20 Rue des Marchands
☎ ***04.90.85.39.38***
The only hat-maker in France classed as a Historical Monument for the Louis XVIth shop design.

Pharmacie Gregoire
closed Sun
7 Rue de la République
☎ ***04.90.80.79.79***
Helpful pharmacy, centrally located.

Sports Montagne
closed Sun
50 Rue Carnot
☎ ***04.90.85.61.45***
Specialist sports shop with everything needed to hit the mountains in all four seasons, including equipment and gear for hiking, skiing and mountain climbing.

Seret Sports
closed Sun
29 Rue Saint-Agricol
☎ ***04.90.82.57.73***
Large selection of sports equipment and clothes.

La Trapézienne
Tue to Sun 7:30am to 8pm
22 Rue Saint Agricole
☎ ***04.90.86.24.72***
Good quality pastry shop selling local candy specialities, including *cailloux*, *calisson d'Aix*, plus savoury items including *fougasse crattelons*. Its speciality is *Gateau Trapézienne* (mousseline cream in a fine brioche).

Veronique Pichon
closed Sun
21 Place Crillon
☎ ***04.90.85.89.00***
Beautiful pottery in luscious colours manufactured nearby at Uzès by the same family for nearly 200 years.

Nîmes

Reserved and nonchalant yet animated, the city of Nîmes stands at the crossroads of Provençal and Languedoc culture.

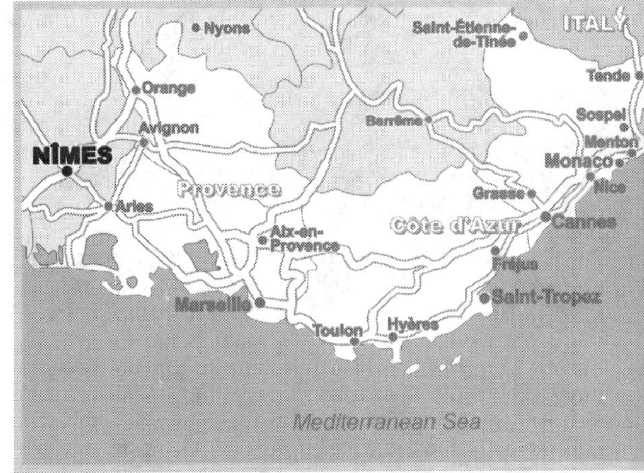

What would elsewhere be cause for an identity crisis, has been turned into an asset in Nîmes: this city, more than any other place, has learned to make the most of its unique geographical location. Influenced by a bullfighting culture that reaches a frenzy during the colourful *férias* (see p 101), the city's history dates back to the dawn of time.

Founded by Roman emperor Augustus, the colony of Nemausus reached its peak during the second century AD. An impressive network of aqueducts supplied the city with water and the famous Pont du Gard still proudly stands today, 23km (14mi) northeast of the city. During this period, Nîmes, along with Lyon and Narbonne, was one of the most important cities of Roman-occupied Gaul.

The invasion of the Vandals three centuries later marked the beginning of the old colony's decline. During the Middle Ages, the city dwindled to the areas around Cathédral Saint-Castor and the Arènes, a fortress that served as a haven for the people during times of conflict. As of the 17th century, at the end of the religious wars, Nîmes experienced a rebirth thanks to its textile industry. This new prosperity manifested itself in town planning, with the creation of new residential areas and the construction of numerous private and public buildings. The destruction of the city's rampart walls at the end of the 18th century and the arrival of the railway 100 years later gave the city its present layout.

Boulevards that surround the old centre have replaced the ditches where the walls used to be. They have been listed as a *Secteur Sauvegardé* (protected area) since 1985. The construction of the train

From Nîmes to Genoa to San Francisco

A Jewish immigrant from Bavaria, Levi Strauss arrived in San Francisco in 1847 with a batch of serge from Nîmes in his bags. This very strong and waterproof cloth was used to cover merchandise and to make trousers for sailors and fishers. The material originated in Nîmes, but was exported via Genoa and was used to make the sails of Christopher Columbus's caravels that sailed to conquer the Americas. Unable to find buyers for his cloth, Levi Strauss decided to try making pants from it. He wasn't particular about details and made the clothes very sturdy, reinforcing the seams with rivets.

Like all successful entrepreneurs, he owed his success to the fateful role of chance. The gold rush struck in 1849 and miners needed extremely rugged clothing. The trousers produced by this lucky tailor came at just the right time and enjoyed instant success among the prospectors. Such are the beginnings of the great empire of "*bleu de Gênes*," or blue jeans, as the Americans pronounced it, now one of the symbols of that nation. The name "denim" continues to bear witness to the fact that the textiles originally came from Nîmes ("*de Nîmes*" in French).

The success was phenomenal. Today, millions of young and not-so-young people across the planet wear this simple type of miners' pants.

station and Avenue Feuchères has now pushed Nîmes's development toward the south.

Fortunately, many antique and historical treasures have magnificently survived the passage of time and bear witness to a glorious past. Nîmes (its name derived from Roman Nemausensis, then Nesmes and Nismes) is home to some of the best-preserved Roman ruins in Europe.

The Departement du Gard sector, while preserving its history, has nevertheless kept up with the times and harbours some real gems of contemporary art and architecture. The superb Carré d'Art (see p 96), in particular, blends beautifully into its surroundings and draws attention to its neighbouring Roman counterpart, the Maison Carrée (see p 96). Without question, this city of 130,000 shows itself to be a modern and dynamic city that has succeeded in integrating its rich heritage.

Finding Your Way Around

By Plane

The Nîmes-Arles-Camargue Airport, in Garons, is located about 10km (6mi) southeast of the town centre (*☎04.66.70.49.49*). There are four daily flights from Paris (1hr). An airport shuttle leaves from the town centre (*☎04.66.29.27.29*).

By Train

The Nîmes train station is just a few minutes from the town centre at the end of Avenue Feuchères (*☎08.36.35.35.35*). The TGV has five or six links to Paris that take only 4hrs, 15min. Other frequent destinations include Arles (30min), Avignon (30min) and Marseille (1hr, 15min).

By Bus

The bus station is located right behind the train station (*Rue Ste-Félicité, ☎04.66.29.52.00*). You can take a bus to Pont du Gard (35min), Avignon (1hr, 15min) and Arles (1hr).

By Car

It is at least an 8hr drive from Paris to Nîmes (725km or 451mi) on the A7 and A9. The A54 takes you to Arles (30km or 19mi) and the A9 followed by the N100 to Avignon (43km or 27mi).

Car Rental

Avis
1800 Avenue du Maréchal Juin
☎04.66.29.05.33

Europcar
1bis Rue de la République
☎04.66.21.31.35

Hertz
5 Boulevard de Prague Centre Atria
☎04.66.76.25.91

At the Airport

Avis
☎04.66.70.49.26

Budget
☎04.66.70.49.42

Europcar
☎04.66.70.49.22

Hertz
☎04.66.70.19.96

Parking

There is a total of six public (paying) parking lots. The parking lot at the Arènes (Esplanande Charles de Gaulle) is the most central and therefore the most convenient for tourists.

Practical Information

Tourist Office
6 Rue Auguste
30000 Nîmes
☎04.66.67.29.11
≠04.66.21.81.04
Info@ot-nimes.fr
www.ot-nimes.fr

Post Office
There is a post office at 1 Boulevard Bruxelles (Esplanade Charles de Gaulle) as well as at the corner of Boulevard Gambetta and Rue Robert.

Exploring

Nîmes

For 60F, you can purchase a three-day pass that allows you to visit all the monuments, museums and the Amphithéâtre. These passes are sold at various ticket counters.

Built at the end of the first century AD, the Roman **Amphithéâtre** ★★★ in Nîmes (*28F, 34F includes Tour Magne; Jun to Sep 9am to 7pm, Oct to May 9am to noon and 2pm to 5pm; at the end of Rue de l'Aspic, ☎04.66.76.72.77*) is considered the best-preserved amphitheatre

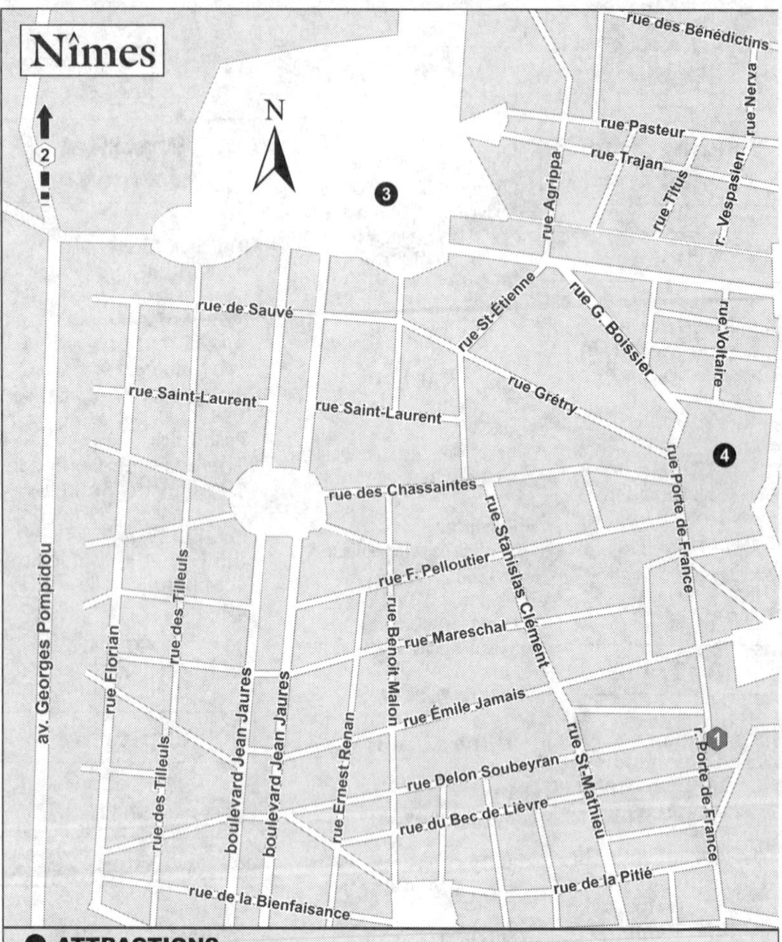

ATTRACTIONS

1. Amphithéâtre
2. Maison Carrée
3. Jardins de la Fontaine / Temple de Diane / Tour Magne
4. Carré d'Art / Musée d'art contemporain
5. Musée archéologique / Musée d`histoire naturelle
6. Chapelle des Jésuites

ACCOMMODATIONS

1. Atria Novotel
2. Auberge de Jeunesse
3. Hôtel Amphithéâtre
4. Hôtel Central
5. Hôtel de la Maison Carrée
6. Hôtel de Milan
7. Hôtel Plazza Clarine
8. New Hôtel La Baume

RESTAURANTS

1. Au Chapon Fin
2. Chez Jacotte
3. Dragon d'Orient
4. La Truie du Filhe
5. Le Jardin d'Hadrien
6. Le Paseo
7. Les Alizés
8. Marco Polo
9. Pétrus
10. Restaurant Nicolas

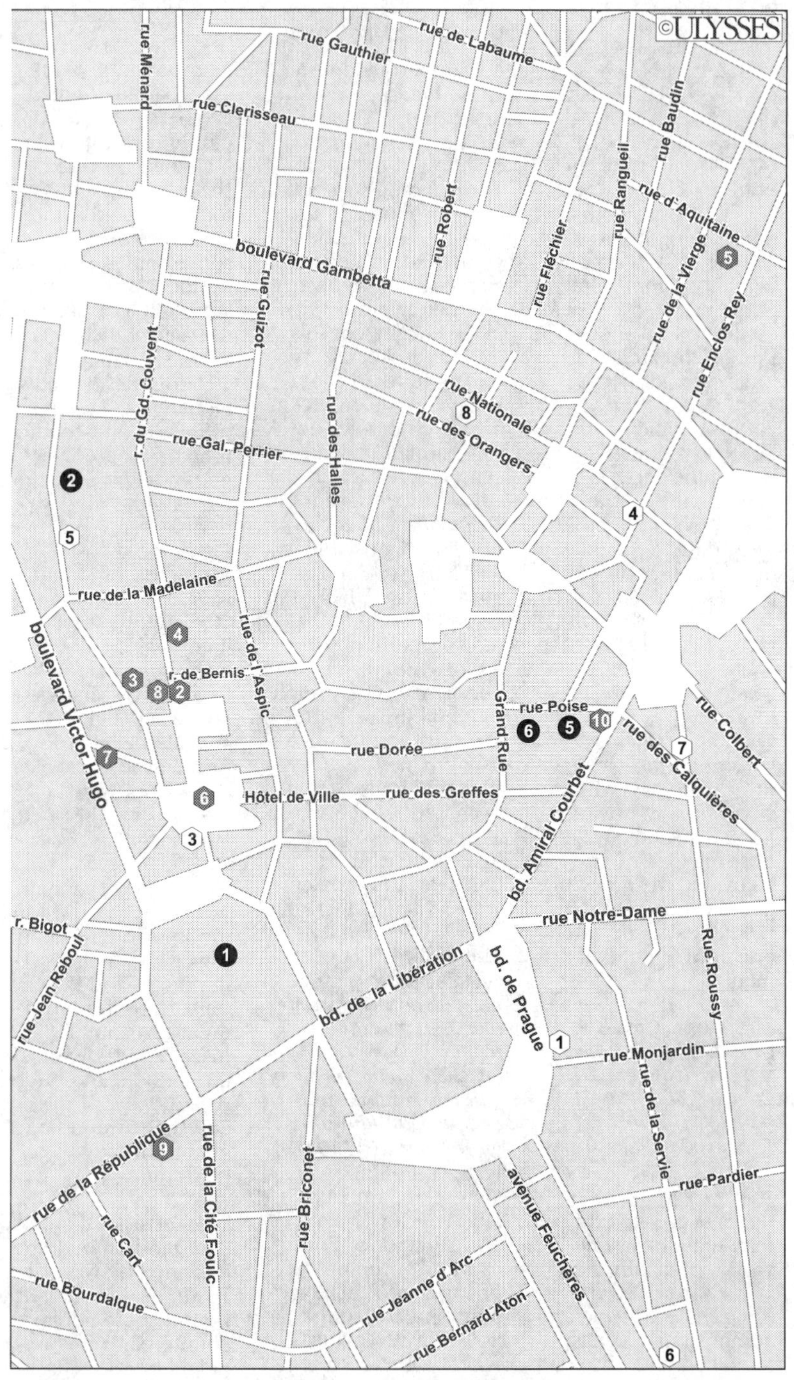
©ULYSSES
rue de Labaume
rue Gauthier
rue Ménard
rue Clerisseau
rue Baudin
rue Ranqueil
rue d'Aquitaine
rue Robert
rue Fléchier
boulevard Gambetta
rue de la Vierge
rue Guizot
rue Enclos Rey
r. du Gd. Couvent
rue Nationale
rue des Orangers
rue des Halles
rue Gal. Perrier
rue de la Madelaine
boulevard Victor Hugo
rue de l'Aspic
r. de Bernis
Grand Rue
rue Poise
rue Dorée
rue des Calquières
rue Colbert
Hôtel de Ville
rue des Greffes
bd. Amiral Courbet
rue Notre-Dame
r. Bigot
rue Jean Reboul
bd. de la Libération
bd. de Prague
Rue Roussy
rue Monjardin
rue de la Servie
rue de la République
rue de la Cité Foulc
rue Briconet
avenue Feuchères
rue Pardier
rue Cart
rue Bourdalque
rue Jeanne d'Arc
rue Bernard Aton

in the world. Almost exactly the same as the one in Arles, it measures 133m by 101m (436ft by 331ft) and can hold up to 24,000 spectators. The Visigoths transformed it into a fortress in AD 404 after gladiator fights were outlawed. A viscount's castle was subsequently built in the arched building and by the 18th century, it became a village which was home to some 700 people. In the early 19th century, the amphitheatre was cleared and restored to be used once again as an exhibition arena. As of 1853, Camargue bull races were organized as well as bullfights. Although this ancient monument is now the abode of *torreros*, athletes and artists instead of gladiators, it will always remind us of Roman society and how they loved and cultivated the art of the grandiose, which would leave spectators quivering with excitement.

The **Maison Carrée ★★** *(free admission; Jun to Sep 9am to noon and 2pm to 7pm, Oct to May 9am to 12:30pm and 2pm to 6pm; Place de le Maison Carrée, ☎04.66.36.26.76),* one of the best-preserved Roman temples in the world, originally stood at the forum square, the city's economic and administrative centre. Modelled after the Temple of Apollo in Rome, it was built under Emperor Augustus at the beginning of the first century AD and is the only remaining building of the forum. The building's smooth lines, proportions and elegant columns bear witness to an undeniable Greek influence. Alternately a meeting place for city consuls during the Middle Ages, stables for Sieur de Brueys in the 16th century, a church for an Augustinian convent a century later, an archive office for the *département* after the Revolution and a Fine Arts and Archeology museum until 1875, this splendid building has rediscovered its sobriety of yore. Inside, people can visit a modest exhibition on the site's history. Its unusual name (the "Square House") comes from Old French when all rectangles (the actual shape of the building) with four angles were called "squares."

The **Jardins de la Fontaine ★★** *(free admission; every day summer 7:30am to 10pm, winter 7:30am to 6:30pm; entrance on the corner of Quai de Fontaine and Avenue Jean-Jaurès)* were built in 1745 by Jacques-Philippe Mareschal, a military engineer for Louis XV and Director of Fortifications for the province of Languedoc. The gardens spread around the Source de Nemausus where a theare, a temple and thermal baths stood during the Roman period in Gaul. This extended green area *à la française* is utterly romantic with its majestic iron gate, shady paths, statues, fountain, ponds and the gardens, which hide some Roman remains. To the left of the fountain stands the **Temple de Diane**, which was seriously damaged in 1577 during the religious wars. The ruins of this second-century monument are overgrown with vegetation, creating the most wonderful effect.

At the top of Mont Cavalier, after climbing 10min along a path lined with Mediterranean trees, you will find one of Nîmes's renowned sights, the **Tour Magne ★** *(15F, 34F includes the Amphithéâtre; Jun to Sep 9am to 7pm, Oct to May 9am to 5pm; ☎04.66.67.65.56).* Of the 7km (4mi) of rampart walls that stood during the Roman period, this tower was the most important and is the only one still remaining. This 34m (112ft) many-sided tower has three floors and offers a superb view of the city and the surrounding area from the top of its platform.

The **Carré d'Art**, a decidedly modern building designed by Norman Foster, is considered to be the contemporary counterpart of its neighbour, the Maison Carrée, and houses the multimedia library and

A magnificent sailboat heads for harbour, with Saint-Tropez, one of the most celebrated resorts on the Côte d'Azur, visible in the background. - *M. Raget*

Nestled along the edge of a field of lavender, the Abbey of Sénanque is among the most impressive landmarks of Provence. - *Mauritus-Vidler*

teurs) and offers regional cuisine that includes bull and lamb specialties. The setting, classic and unpretentious, is as reserved as the menu is traditional and authentic. Whether you choose the *menu saveur*, *détente* or *gourmand*, you will be assured a delectable meal carefully prepared using the finest local products.

Le Jardin d'Hadrien
$$
11 Rue Enclos Rey
☎04.66.21.86.65
Another member of the renowned Confrérie de Restaurateurs de Métier du Gard (Gard association of professional restauranteurs), Le Jardin d'Hadrien offers excellent regional cuisine in a very pleasant, congenial setting. The dining room has stone walls and the restaurant's splendidly green inner courtyard is beautifully designed. Besides the à la carte dishes, the chef offers a delicious fixed-price menu.

Pétrus
$$$
closed Sun
7 Rue de la République
☎04.66.76.04.81
Recognized as the best food in Nîmes, the chic Pétrus guarantees its guests healthy, fresh, authentic and fragrant regional cuisine of the highest quality. Whether it be an appetizer of foie gras or lobster salad, or a main dish of savoury fish or tender grilled meats, the entire menu is the epitome of culinary art. The decor, which is classy and tasteful, doesn't fall prey to ostentation.

Entertainment

Nîmes

Espace Pablo-Romero
closed Sun
12 Rue Émile-Jamais
The Espace Pablo-Romero is a Spanish-style café with a bullfighting motif: the bars are mounted on impressive bulls's heads and are arranged around a patio where guests can savour some very Spanish *tapas.*

La Cantina
closed Sun in summer, Sun to Tue 6:30pm to 1am, Wed and Thu 6:30pm to 2am, Fri and Sat 6:30pm to 3am
4 Rue Graverol
☎04.66.21.65.10
La Cantina is a Latin bar with an informal setting and a modest, bric-a-brac decor. With a laid-back atmosphere, this is the ideal place to sip an imported beer or a glass of vine while dining on a light, Mexican-style meal. Here, Latin music such as *salsa* takes precedence. Stage shows are also presented.

The Féria
Every year in June, during Pentecost, a exciting fervour of drinking, singing and dancing takes over the streets of Nîmes. During the Féria, a virtual five-day party, you can watch bullfights in the Arènes, *abrivados* or *encierros* (running of the bulls in the streets), see musical troupes called *peñas* stroll down the boulevards, or dance a few *sevillanas* in a *bodega*, those infamous caves where wine flows like water. You can watch jousts on the canals of the Fontaine, take part in the Pégoulade (the carnival-type parade along the boulevards on Wednesday evenings) or boogie to your heart's content at one of the many balls and concerts. The Féria has been evolving since its inception in 1952 and has even been increased to three times per year: in addition to the traditional June celebrations, Nîmes now has a Féria des Vendanges in September and a Féria de Primavera in February. You can reserve a spot for the various events at the Bureau de Location des Arènes (*One Rue Alexandre Ducros, ☎04.66.67.28.02).* You're required to put aside between 100F and 500F to watch a bullfight.

Shopping

Nîmes

The charming **Rue de la Madelaine**, where the oldest house in Nîmes is located (not to be missed!), is the most important shopping street in the city.

The textile industry in Nîmes was born under Louis XI and was, for many centuries, the driving force of the city's economy. Although still in existence, the weaving tradition in Nîmes is struggling and there are but a few rare spots where you can still buy quality cloth. The Indiennes de Nîmes *(2 Place des Arènes)* constitutes a fine little boutique for fabric lovers.

A large **market** is held on Mondays on the Boulevard Gambetta. An **organic foods market** is held on Fridays on Avenue Jean-Jaurès. Saturday mornings is reserved for the **flea market** on the parking lot at the Stade des Costières.

The Haut Comtat Venaissin

The Haut Comtat Venaissin includes Orange, Vaison-la-Romaine, les Dentelles de Montmirail, l'Enclave des Papes and Carpentras.

The area once known as the Comtat Venaissin covered most of the present-day Vaucluse department. The northern part of this scenic area is highly enjoyable for many visitors to Provence, for it provides a rich history, a varied landscape and many small towns to explore without the crowds of tourists.

The Comtat Venaissin grew during the popes' installation in Avignon, from 1305 to 1376, and during the reign of the anti-popes, known as the Great Schism, 1378 to 1409. Carpentras was purchased in 1320 and made capital of the county, a distinction held by Pernes-les-Fontaines since 968. Carpentras was later made the seat of the *États du Comtat,* similar to the *États de Provence,* which were local administrative assemblies.

Pope Jean XXII bought the rights to the town of Valréas with Richerences in 1344, and the towns of Visan (1344) and Grillon (1451) were added later. This explains why a small part of the northern Vaucluse, surrounded on all sides by the Drôme department, exists today as a small enclave.

In 1348, Pope Clément VI bought Avignon from Queen Jeanne, but the city remained independent from the Comtat Venaissin. Much later, Louis XIV in 1662-1663 and in 1688-1689 and Louis XV between 1768 and 1774 occupied the region and tried to annex the Comtat Venaissin to France. It finally surrendered, along with Avignon, on September 14, 1791.

The area surrounding the town of Orange has its own unique history. Known as Arausio, the town was a Roman military colony following Caesar's conquest of Provence in 50 BC. From 35 BC, a typical Roman city took shape, including roads, houses, shops, and monuments. Today, visitors can still marvel at Orange's famous amphitheatre, triumphal arch and temple.

During the 15th century, this small enclave within the Comtat Venaissin became the Principauté d'Orange, or principality, after passing from the houses of Baux, to Chalon, to William of Nassau and finally to Stathouder of the Netherlands in 1529. The principality enjoyed a number of privileges. It had an important university, and due to its liberal spirit, it harboured many Protestants during the Religious Wars. During the war with Holland and its leader William III of Nassau, Louis XIV occupied Orange (1662) and destroyed the citadel along with its fortifications and ramparts. Today the Dutch Royal Family retains its historical name of Orange-Nassau.

Finding Your Way Around

By Car

The Upper Comtat Venaissin is serviced by a good road network. From Paris in the north and Avignon or Marseille in the south, the N7 Highway passes through **Orange**, while the A7-E15 Autoroute du Soleil freeway passes right next to it.

Vaison-la-Romaine is a good-sized town with a number of accommodations and dining options, and is a practical starting point from which to discover this entire area.

The scenic Dentelles de Montmirail hills (including villages such as Séguret and le Barroux) and Mont Ventoux are easy drives away. Vaison-la-Romaine is at the crossroads of the D975 and D977 (from Orange) and the D938 from Carpentras. SNCF trains connect these cities to the larger centres, though renting a car in Avignon or Marseille is the most practical way to explore the smaller villages which are inaccessible by rail.

Practical Information

Tourist Offices

The tourists offices mentioned here will provide you with all kinds of maps, and precise, detailed information. The staff are competent and pleasant. The Vaison-la-Romaine office has a good selection of books for sale, dealing with such topics as regional cuisine and handicrafts. They even offer wine tasting, and have wine for sale as well.

Orange
5 Cours Aristide Briand,
☎ ***04.90.34.70.88***
⇄ ***04.90.34.99.62***
A tourist office annex is open Apr to Sep at Place des Frères Mounet.

Vaison-la-Romaine
Place du Chanoine Sautel
☎ ***04.90.36.02.11***

Carpentras
170 Allée Jean-Jaurés
☎ ***04.90.63.00.78***
⇄ ***04.90.60.41.02***

Entrechaux
Place du Marché

Grignan
☎ ***04.75.46.56.75***

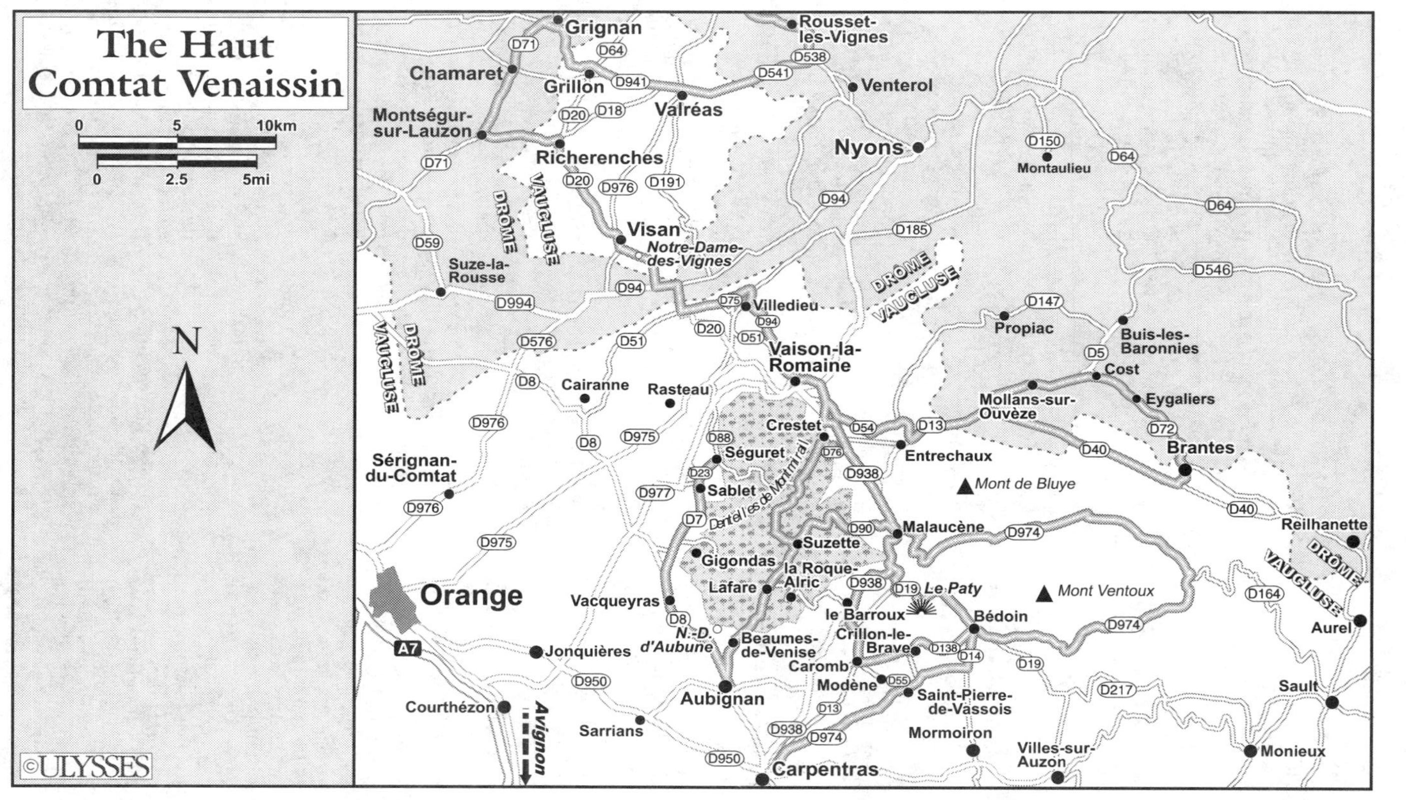
The Haut
Comtat Venaissin
0
5
10km
0
2.5
5mi
N
©ULYSSES
Grignan
Rousset-les-Vignes
Chamaret
Grillon
Valréas
Venterol
Montségur-sur-Lauzon
Richerenches
Nyons
Montaulieu
Visan
Notre-Dame-des-Vignes
Suze-la-Rousse
Villedieu
Propiac
Buis-les-Baronnies
Cost
Eygaliers
Vaison-la-Romaine
Mollans-sur-Ouvèze
Brantes
Cairanne
Rasteau
Crestet
Entrechaux
Séguret
Mont de Bluye
Sablet
Dentelles de Montmirail
Sérignan-du-Comtat
Malaucène
Reilhanette
Suzette
Gigondas
la Roque-Alric
Lafare
Le Paty
Mont Ventoux
Orange
Vacqueyras
le Barroux
Bédoin
Aurel
N.-D. d'Aubune
Beaumes-de-Venise
Crillon-le-Brave
Jonquières
Caromb
Modène
Saint-Pierre-de-Vassois
Sault
Courthézon
Aubignan
Sarrians
Mormoiron
Villes-sur-Auzon
Monieux
Carpentras
Avignon
DRÔME
VAUCLUSE
A7
D71
D64
D941
D538
D541
D20
D18
D150
D976
D191
D94
D185
D59
D546
D994
D75
D147
D20
D51
D5
D576
D8
D54
D13
D72
D88
D76
D40
D23
D938
D977
D7
D90
D974
D975
D19
D164
D14
D138
D55
D950
D217
D13
D938
D974
D950

Valréas
Place Aristide-Briand
☎*04.90.35.04.71*

Exploring

Orange

Faced with so many interesting sites and villages to explore in Provence, Orange is sometimes pushed aside. A couple of hours are usually all that are awarded to this town of 28,000 inhabitants—a glimpse of the Roman Théâtre Antique and a drive past the Arc de Triomphe and then on to more exciting things.

While Orange admittedly lacks the elegance of Avignon and Aix, the character of Marseille or the breathtaking scenery of the Luberon hills, the town does hold unexpected pleasures and a longer visit is merited. It possesses charming small squares, with animated cafés under the leafy shade of tall plane trees, a pleasant old town with narrow streets and a lively Provençal market every Thursday. Live musical performances (opera, recitals, jazz and rock), and giant-screen films take place all summer long at the open-air Théâtre Antique and should not be missed.

The **Théâtre Antique** ★★★ *(30F, reduced rate 25F, includes admission to the Musée d'Orange; Apr 1 to Oct 4, everyday 9am to 6:30pm; Oct 5 to Mar 31 open everyday 9 am to noon and 1:30pm to 5pm; closed Dec 25 and Jan 1)*, Orange's most famous monument, is the only Roman theatre in Europe with its stage wall intact. It dates from the early first century AD, when a great variety of performances took place, uniquely during the daytime. From the exterior, the great wall is 103m-long (338ft) and 37m-high (121ft). Inside, the stage wall has five tiers, with supports on the upper two levels and decoration on the others.

If you think the statue of the Emperor Augustus above the Porte Royale, or royal doorway, looks reconstructed, you're right. It was unearthed during excavations of the theatre in 1931, and though all its bits and pieces were stuck together it somehow looks off-balance. The stage, 61.2m-long (201ft) and 13.2m-wide (433ft), was made of wood and once had a decorated roof.

During Roman times, the privileged class sat on movable seats on either side of the stage in an area known as the *parascenia*. Behind them, 9,000 spectators sat on the stone tiers (the *cavea*) that are divided into three parts and are linked by underground galleries with large entrances. The ruins of a temple and one of the only three existing Roman gymnasiums in the world are found to one side of the theatre.

Nowadays, when visiting Orange during the summer months, try to catch one of the evening performances in the theatre and hear how fine the acoustics really are. Thank goodness Louis XIV was sensitive enough to preserve the stage wall, which he called "the prettiest wall in my kingdom", when he gave orders to destroy Orange's citadel and ramparts nearby, in the 17th century. Films are shown throughout July and August *(for further information contact the tourist office ☎04.90.34.70.88)*; an international opera and classical music festival The Chorégies d'Orange, is held in July *(for details contact the Chorégie d'Orange, P.O. Box 205, ☎04.90.51.83.83, ⇄04.90.34.87.67; reservations ☎04.90.34.24.24)* and an international music festival, featuring theatre and dance called Les Nuits d'Été is held every August *(for information contact Les Nuits d'Été ☎04.90.51.89.58 in Orange or ☎01.44.68.69.00 in Paris)*.

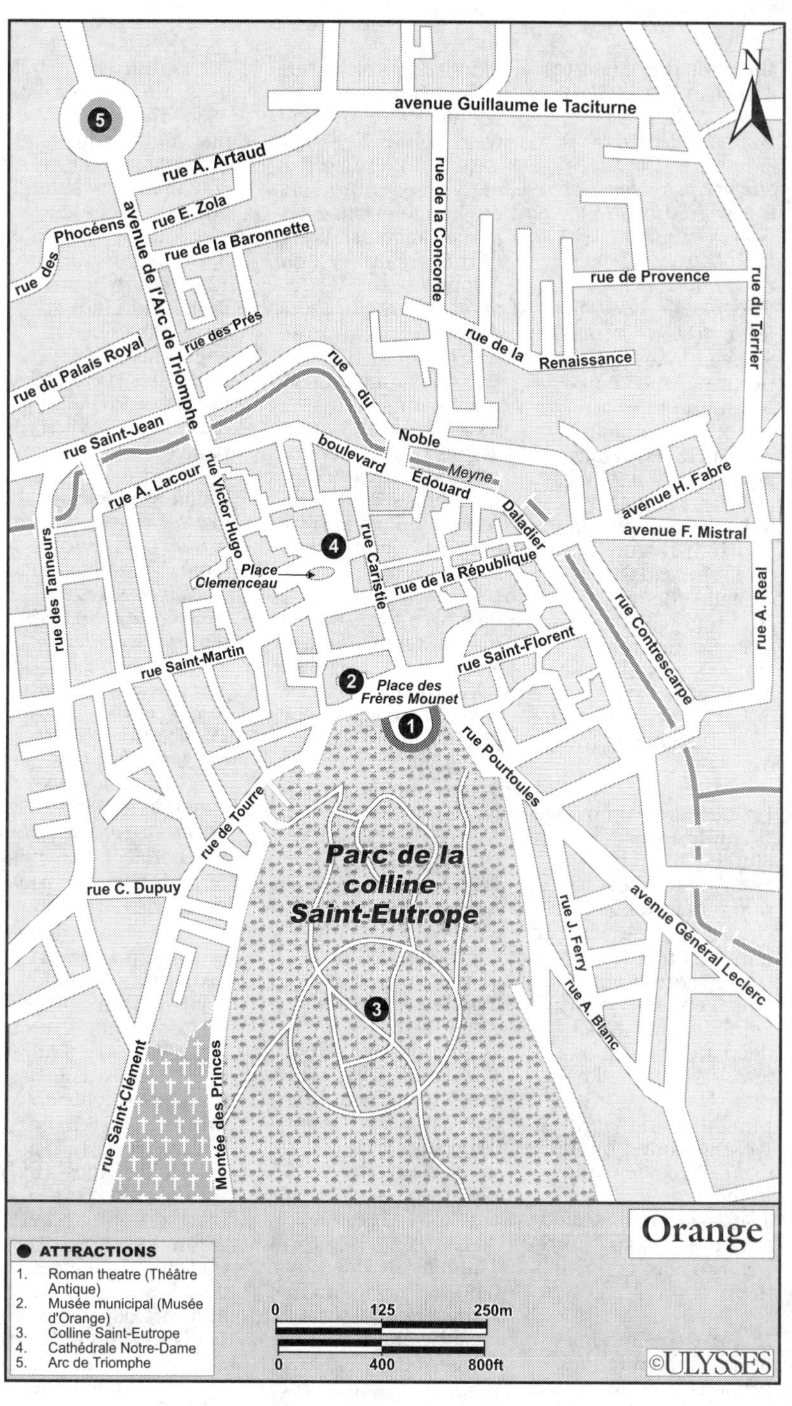
avenue Guillaume le Taciturne
rue A. Artaud
rue E. Zola
rue des Phocéens
rue de la Baronnette
avenue de l'Arc de Triomphe
rue de la Concorde
rue de Provence
rue du Terrier
rue des Prés
rue du Palais Royal
rue de la Renaissance
rue du Noble
rue Saint-Jean
boulevard Édouard Daladier
Meyne
rue A. Lacour
rue Victor Hugo
avenue H. Fabre
avenue F. Mistral
rue des Tanneurs
rue Caristie
Place Clemenceau
rue de la République
rue A. Real
rue Contrescarpe
rue Saint-Martin
rue Saint-Florent
Place des Frères Mounet
rue Pourtoules
rue de Tourre
Parc de la colline Saint-Eutrope
rue C. Dupuy
avenue Général Leclerc
rue J. Ferry
rue A. Blanc
rue Saint-Clément
Montée des Princes
Orange
ATTRACTIONS
1. Roman theatre (Théâtre Antique)
2. Musée municipal (Musée d'Orange)
3. Colline Saint-Eutrope
4. Cathédrale Notre-Dame
5. Arc de Triomphe
0 125 250m
0 400 800ft
©ULYSSES

Musée Municipal (Musée d'Orange) *(30F, 25F for access to the Théâtre Romain; Apr 1 to Oct 4, Mon to Sat 9am to 7pm, Sun 10am to 6pm; Oct 5 to Mar 30, Mon to Sat 9am to noon and 1:30pm to 5:30pm, Sun 9am to noon and 2pm to 5:30pm; Rue Madeleine-Roch, ☎04.90.51.18.24).* Situated in an old, 17th-century manor house, this museum explains the origins of Orange and encloses statues, pottery, old maps of the city, painted portraits of local dignitaries and 18th-century furniture. The cadastre room contains the original land register of Orange, which dates from 100 AD, as well as segments of the exceptional friezes that decorated the ancient theatre.

Upstairs, a room named "L'Art de Faire l'Indienne" ("l'Indienne" here refers to a printed fabric) will fascinate all those who are intrigued by the history of Provençale prints, which are sold in marketplaces and which decorate many rooms in hotels and bed and breakfasts. The first printed cotton fabrics were imported by the Compagnie des Indes in the 17th century. They were immediately very popular and Europeans began copying them.

In 1686, the importation of Indian fabrics was restricted to protect the local wool and silk industries, which were mainly concentrated around Lyon. The ban was lifted in 1759, and local factories like that of the Wetter brothers of Orange became important manufacturers of "indiennes." A large painting of the Wetters depicting one of them dressed in an impressive jacket in crimson set off by a green leaf motif hangs in this room, as do photographs of production methods employed, including some that show workers applying large printing blocks to bare canvases.

Pick up a free street map of Orange at the tourist office and discover the city on foot. Leave from any of the pretty squares in the **Vieille Ville** (old city) behind the theatre and Place des Frères-Mounet – Place aux Herbes, Place de Langues or Place de la République. From Place Saint-Martin, many charming 17th- and 18th-century houses may be seen, as may the walls of a convent along Rue Millet and Rue Condorcet. Livelier Rue Victor-Hugo, for its part, shows off some interesting façades and inner courtyards, notably at numbers 43, 39 and 25.

The **Hôtel de Ville** (town hall) has occupied the former residence of the wealthy and noble De Langes family since 1714. Its characteristic wrought-iron belfry dates from 1711, while its façade was rebuilt in 1880. The Musée Municipal d'Orange has reconstituted a tomb containing the skull and bones of a corpse that was discovered on these premises in the 12th century! Rue du Pont-Neuf (14th century) was once Orange's main artery, a role it has since ceded to Rue de la République, which runs parallel to it.

Colline Saint-Eutrope *(On foot: take the Princes de Nassau passageway or the more difficult Philibert de Chalon passageway, which both leave from the southern end of Cours Aristide-Briand, or walk past the east side of the theatre, leaving from Rue Pourtoules, to the steps of the A. Lambert passageway. By car: take the one-way Montée des Princes de Nassau and park near the entrance).* This hill offers a beautiful **panoramic view** of the city and is recommended to photographers who want to capture the Roman theatre, Plaine de Comtat and even Mont Ventoux on film. The hilltop was first home to a Celtic colony, then to a Roman encampment and, in the Middle Ages, Bishop Saint-Eutrope erected a church here. A fortified castle was built on the summit by the House of Nassau and was destroyed by Louis XIV in the 17th century during a period of conflicts with the Netherlands. Today the hilltop harbours a peaceful park lined with paths and laid out with an observation deck, a statue of the Virgin Mary and a public outdoor pool set in a grove of conifers. *(Piscine des Cèdres, summer, every day 10am to 7pm; snack bar with patio).*

Cathédrale Notre-Dame *(mass at 10:30am, summer only; Rue Notre-Dame).* This cathedral was consecrated on the 26th of October, 1208, on a site originally occupied by a Roman temple, and was then rebuilt many times over. It was destroyed by the Huguenots in 1561, rebuilt in the 17th century and then restored again in the 18th century by the last bishop of Orange, Monseigneur du Tillet. In the 19th century, the neo-classical eastern door was added, and frescoes and stained-glass windows were commissioned. Ravishing, although sober, Chapelle Saint-Joseph was recently restored in the Provençal style, leaving fragments of the murals that were painted on its walls in various periods from the 17th to 19th century.

Along with the theatre, the **Arc de Triomphe** ★★, or triumphal arch, built between 21 and 26 AD, is classed by UNESCO as a historical monument. It does not actually commemorate any military triumph, but instead once marked the entrance to the Roman town of Arausio (now Orange) and testifies to the great deeds of the soldiers of the 2nd legion who founded it in 36 BC. The north side of the three-arched monument is the best preserved—on it can be found panels of weapons, naval spoils, objects of worship and engraved inscriptions. The rectangular mass is 19.57m x 8.5m x 19.21m (64.2ft x 27.9ft x 63ft) and the central arch is 8m-high (26.2ft). Underneath the vaulted roof, notice the ceiling decorated with hexagonal boxes.

Arc de Triomphe

Sérignan-du-Comtat

Sérignan is 8km (5mi) north of Orange, at the intersection of the D43 and the D976.

This charming little village possesses a beautiful 17th-century mansion, just next to **Église Saint-Étienne** (18th century) and its wrought-iron campanile-style bell tower that holds three bells dating from three different eras.

Châteauneuf-du-Pape

Everyone appreciates a summer home, even popes. During his stay in Avignon in the 14th century, Pope Jean XXII had a château built in this community which henceforward was called Châteauneuf. Subsequent popes had vines planted in the pebbly land surrounding their getaway residence and a quite drinkable wine was made. Due to the popes' and their prelates' demanding tastes, a great wine was born. The area's wine first received attention outside of the area in the 18th century. It has been regarded as one of the world's great wines since 1929, when it was granted the title *appellation d'origine controllée* Châteauneuf-du-Pape, enforces rigorous standards on growing and production.

Nowadays, nearly seven million bottles, about half of the total production, are exported. Châteauneuf-du-Pape is the only French wine authorized to be made from 13 different types of grapes *(for wine festivals* *see p 129;* *details about Châteauneuf-du-Pape vineyards, visits and tastings, contact the Comité de Promotion des Vins de Châteauneuf-du-Pape, 12 Avenue Louis Pasteur, 84230 Châteauneuf-du-Pape, ☎04.90.83.72.21, ⇄04.90.83.70.01).*

The village of Châteauneuf-du-Pape is crisscrossed by many tiny streets punctuated by fountains (notably **Fontaine de Souspiron**, which dates back to the 14th century), harbours the vestiges of ancient ramparts and possesses lovely houses as well as two chapels (Saint-Pierre-de-Luxembourg, from the 18th century, and Saint-Théodoric, from the 11th century). The Provençal Romanesque **Église Notre-Dame-de-l'Assomption** presents but a few ornaments; however, its simplicity lends it a candid beauty. All that remains of the castle of the popes is a guard tower and a part of the outer wall of the residential quarters; the rest of it was ravaged by fire during the Religious Wars and then seriously damaged in 1944. Nonetheless, it offers a splendid view over the Vallée du Rhône, Avignon, the Dentelles de Montmirail and the Luberon. Finally, **Musée des Outils de Vignerons du Père Anselme** *(free; every day 9am to noon and 2pm to 6pm; Route d'Avignon, ☎04.90.83.70.07)* houses a collection of instruments and accessories that date back to the 16th century, including a wine press, barrels and corkscrews.

Vaison-la-Romaine

Visitors get three towns for the price of one when visiting Vaison-la-Romaine. This charming place of great archaeological importance is divided by the Ouvèze River—on the right bank lies the old Roman site as well as modern-day Vaison, while on the left bank, built up against a rocky hillside, is the Haute Ville, or upper town, dating from the Middle Ages.

The Celt tribe known as the Voconces inhabited the area since the Iron Age, and a settlement called Vasio on the spot of present day Vaison became an administrative and political capital. Following the occupation of Provence by the Romans in the first century BC, the Voconces became their allies after local wars (58-51 BC). During the first century AD, Vaison became a well-structured Roman town, with shops, a theatre, residential streets, and water arriving from a nearby aqueduct.

After Provence was divided in 1125, Vaison belonged to Raymond V, Count of Toulouse. He promptly built a château on the right bank hillside overlooking the Ouvèze. During the 13th century, following the Religious Wars, the population abandoned the plain and moved to the Haute-Ville (just below the château), where they were protected from invaders. By the 17th century, times became relatively more peaceful, and Vaison's citizens returned to the lower plain across the Ouvèze. Although records of Vaison-la-Romaine's reconstruction date as far back as the 15th century, it wasn't until 1848 that the town received state financing for archaeological work. Serious excavations began in 1907 (the Puymin area) and in 1934 (the Villasse area).

The Pont Romain (Roman bridge) was reopened in 1994 after having been closed for repairs following the disastrous flooding of the Ouvèze on September 22, 1992. During the course of a violent thunderstorm, the river inflicted 150 million francs of damage and, tragically, caused 37 deaths.

In the sumptuous, sweet-smelling setting of the Dentelles de Montmirail, the 5,700 Vaisonnais prove to be as friendly as ever and take the time to welcome visitors. If only for this reason, it is worth stopping a spell here to soak up some local history before setting out on excursions to the sights in the surrounding area.

Remarkably the archaeological sites of the **Roman Cities–Puymin ★★ and Villasse ★** *(41F, combined ticket for both sites, plus the Musée d'Archéologie and the Cathédrale and Cloître; Jun to Aug, open everyday 9am to 12:30pm and 2pm to 6:45pm; Mar to May, Sep and Oct, open everyday 9:30am to 12:30pm and 2pm to 5:45pm; Nov to Feb, Wed to Mon 10am to noon and 2pm to 4:30pm, closed Tue, closed Dec 25 and Jan 1)* were only discovered this century. They provide a clue as to why the Roman town of Vasio was nicknamed *urbs opulentissima*, or very opulent city. As these two areas are ruins, it is important to pick up a descriptive map at the tourist office beforehand in order to fully explore the area. Puymin *(opposite the tourist office, entrance at the corner of Rue Burrhus and Rue Bernard Noël)* is more interesting since the remains of the buildings are in better shape allowing the complexity of Roman life to unfold before your eyes.

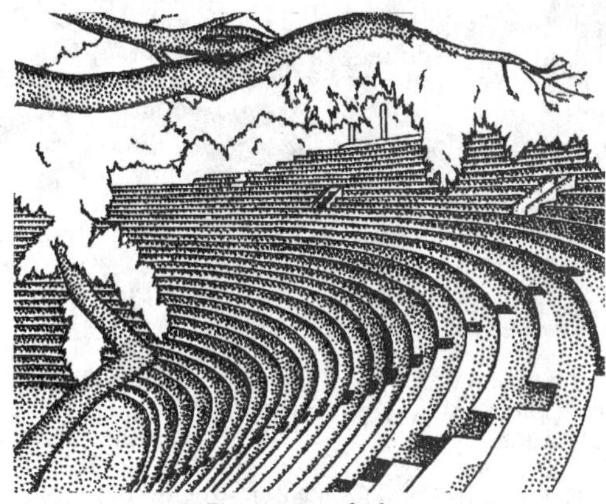

Roman amphitheatre

The first area after entering Puymin is the villa of the wealthy Massii family, note the inner courtyard, reception rooms, kitchen and lavatories. A large part of the house is still buried underneath the modern city—it is thought to have covered 2,000m². Following this was a colonnaded promenade, called Pompeii's Portico, leading to a series of narrow houses that were rented at the time. Behind the wooded area is the **Musée d'Archéologie**, an archaeological museum containing many objects (jewellery, tools, ceramics), friezes and most noteworthy, marble statues of the emperors Claude, Domitien, Hadrian, and the latter's wife, Sabine, all found on the site.

Beyond the museum, along a rising pathway, is the first century AD **Roman amphitheatre.** Similar in design to the theatre at Orange, this one is smaller and has lost its stage wall. About 7,000 spectators could sit here, on 32 rows of seating, split by three principal stairways. It has been heavily reconstructed, and is now the site of theatrical and musical performances in the evening during the summer months (contact the tourist office for a *Les Nuits d'Été* program).

The **Villasse area** *(entrance opposite the Place Burrhus parking lot, by the tourist office)* consists of the ruins of two large residences (**House of the Dolphin**, **House of the Silver Bust**) divided by the so-called Colonnade Road and Road of Shops, and a public hot-springs bath.

Cathédrale Notre-Dame-de-Nazareth and **Cloître ★** *(same hours as the Roman ruins, except closed Oct to Apr, noon to 2pm)*. The cathedral and cloister were completely rebuilt in the 12th and 13th centuries on the site of a 6th-century church. Vaison's cathedral is a marvellous example of Provençal Romanesque architecture. From the exterior, standing in front of the east apse, you'll notice the monument actually rests upon remains (column drums, pieces of entablature) of an original Gallo-Roman basilica. The square bell-tower is oddly off-centre. Inside, six bays and aisles are supported by square pillars. The nave's cylindrical vaulted ceiling and cupola above the last bay were 12th century additions. Note the marble altars—the one in the north apse is thought to be from the 6th century.

Through a separate entrance on the north side, visit the pretty barrel-vaulted cloister. Like the cathedral, it too was completed between 1150-1160 and restored at the end of the 14th century. The columns supporting the arches facing the interior courtyard are remarkably sculpted; interesting artifacts (sarcophagus, inscriptions in stone, statues) line the surrounding galleries.

People intrigued by ecclesiastical architecture will want to take the extra trouble to visit the **Chapelle Saint-Quenin** *(visit only by prior arrangement with the tourist office; from Avenue Général de Gaulle, turn left onto Avenue Saint-Quenin, 500m or 1,640ft on the left).* Built during the second half of the 12th century in the Provençal Romanesque style, the nave was reconstructed between 1630 and 1636. Its curious feature is the unusual triangular apse and its fine decoration (fluted half columns with Corinthian capitals), notably the joyful frieze. Saint-Quenin was a Vaison bishop in the 6th century.

The **Pont Romain** is a Roman bridge linking the Grand Rue to the upper town. Nearly 2,000 years old, the modest bridge is 17m-wide (55.8ft) and 7m-high (23ft). Its parapet was ripped apart during a flash flood in 1616, and rebuilt afterwards. The embankment was destroyed by a German bomb in 1944, and the bridge's vault shaken. The flood of September 1992 destroyed the parapet a second time. Following renovations costing 2.5 million francs, the bridge has now reopened. Locals remark that it is narrower—the architects followed the bridge's original design.

The **Haute Ville ★★**, or upper town can be reached by turning right after crossing the Roman bridge and by entering via a ramp on the left. By car, cross the Ouvèze by the Pont Neuf, and follow signs indicating the parking lot for the Château. The *Vaissonnais* moved from the right bank of the Ouvèze to the upper town next to the Château during the 13th century, when they were threatened by ruthless invaders. A walk through the narrow, cobble-stone streets (most prohibited to cars), is like stepping back in time. Coming from the Roman bridge, look for the **Place des Poids**. The only real remains of 14th-century architecture are sections of rampart walls and two arched gates. Note the beautiful façades of the houses, which date from the 16th to the 18th centuries and the belfry with the 17th-century wrought-iron cage.

The pretty **Place du Vieux Marché** with its plane trees, fountain and small café, was the location for a weekly market that lasted from 1483 through to the 19th century. Along the Rue de l'Eveché is the deteriorating Palais Épiscopale, Hôtel de Taulignan, the Chapelle

Pénitents-Blancs and the Hôtel Fabre de Saint-Véran. The church at the end of the Rue de l'Église (the interior is not open to the public) was built in 1464, with later additions. Good views can be had from the tiny, attractive square in front of the church.

The Upper Town is dominated by the ruins of the château built by the Count of Toulouse, Raymond V, in the late 12th century (access by foot only, a steep climb). It became a papal fortress when the Comtat Venaissin passed into the hands of the popes in 1274. From the 16th century onwards, its was restored for comfort, yet was abandoned in 1791 during the Revolution. The château's prime interest today are the fine views over Vaison-la-Romaine and the region from the foot of the crumbling monument (visitors are not permitted inside.)

The Dentelles de Montmirail

This pretty hill range with deep valleys southeast of Vaison-la-Romain provides some of the best scenery in all of Provence, equal in beauty to the Luberon. The jagged, limestone rock formations with pointed peaks indeed resemble lace fabric (hence the name in French, *dentelle* means lace). Many charming villages appear to miraculously hang from the sides of rocky cliffs, and the narrow roads are perfumed with the sweet smells of the yellow *genêt* (gorse or woodwaxen), aromatic plants and fresh pine trees. Late spring and early summer are particularly enjoyable when fruit trees and flowers blossom. An entire day or more could be spent simply touring the back-roads, stopping at a few of the picturesque villages. Alternatively, the Dentelles de Montmirail is a walker's paradise (the Vaison-la-Romaine tourist office will supply information and maps for hikers). The highest point is Mont Saint-Amand (734m or 2,408ft), and most of the many signposted pathways are not too taxing.

Suggested Route:

From Vaison-la-Romaine, head south on the D938 (direction Carpentras) for about 5km (3,1mi). Turn right onto the D76 to visit the charming, untouched village of **Crestet** ★. Here you'll find the pretty **Église Saint-Sauveur** dating back to the 11th century (with a working fountain dating from 1787 in front), a private château (belonging to the bishops of Vaison-la-Romaine until the Revolution), and some wonderful views. Near the spot where you leave your car is an old, municipal, covered wash basin, with a tinkling drainage gutter running past stone steps and beautiful wild flowers. Higher up, a few pedestrian streets twist and turn. The front doors of homes, some seem abandoned, open directly onto the road. There are no shops, cafés or businesses. A local historian, Charley Schmitt, has written a guide about the village's history *Mieux Connaitre Crestet, Village Vauclusien* which is available for 45 F in local bookshops and from the author's home which is signposted on the road.

You might want to inquire about the exhibits offered at the **Centre d'art de Crestet** *(opening hours vary; chemin de la Verrière, Crestet, ☎04.90.36.34.85, ≠04.90.36.36.20)*. Administered in conjunction with the Ministère Français de la Culture, this contemporary art museum features both temporary and permanent exhibits, and offers workshops. Art and nature are in harmony here, as the museum is beautifully situated in a thick forest atop a hill.

Return to the D938, and turn right onto the D90 at **Malaucène** (10km or 6.2mi), whose busy main road is bordered with plane trees. The stretch of the D90 between Malaucène and

Beaumes-de-Venise, passing by Suzette, as well as the very narrow D90A to La Roque Alric, must be one of the most beautiful routes in Provence. Wonderful views of the Dentelles and its vineyards greet you at every turn (as does the heady citrus perfume of wild thyme, and more *genêt* and pine trees). At **Suzette** you'll find an attractive church and fine views over the rolling hills. If you've braved the twisted D90A, you'll discover the small community of

Herbes de Provence

A great diversity of aromatic plants grow in the fertile, sun-drenched alpine and Mediterranean soils of Provence, offering a magnificent palette of colours and scents associated with the joy of life. Since antiquity, the people of Provence have placed much emphasis on plants, which grow so abundantly in the region. Whether used as a valued commodity for barter, for medicinal purposes or as a cooking ingredient, aromatic plants have always been closely tied to Provence's history and traditions.

Today, hundreds of different plant varieties grow in Provence, some of which are very popular and well known; certain varieties are domesticated while others simply grow wild. Over the years, aromatic plants known as "herbes de Provence" have become an indispensable part of Provençal cuisine and have contributed to the region's renown in both their fresh and dried forms.

But what exactly are these pungent plants that have become so dear to Provence? Most will be familiar and indispensable seasonings in your kitchen. First, there is garlic, or *ail*, which has given its name to the famous aioli. Then there are onions, which, used in soup, are said to aid digestion. And finally there is a whole array of really well-known plants such as estragon, ideal for preserves nad *sauce scarlée*, (which is used to make essential oils), parsley (eaten raw), fennel, with its strong anise flavour, savory, with numerous usages and basil, called "pistou" in southern France, which gained its reputation from the famous soup in which it is the essential ingredient.

We end this almost inexhaustible list with the herbs of the most typical landscape of Provence, the *garrigue* (scrubland), where the aromas of the Midi are most pungent. This chalky, stony region with its dry thickets and gentle slopes grows fragrant lavender, rosemary, whose flowers attract bees, sweet bay shrubs, the leaves of which are used in ratatouilles and marinades, thyme, a powerful antiseptic that grows everywhere in the scrubland, and marjoram, also known as oregano, which often grows along the side of the roads and is delicious on pizza. It's difficult to imagine cooking without these sublime flavours!

La Roque Alric perched on the cliff-side, with a wooden cross high up on the top of the hill. Back on the D90, you'll pass by **Beaumes-de-Venise**. The excellent sweet Muscat *vin doux* or dessert wine is produced from grapes grown in the neighbouring sun-blessed vineyards.

Now follow the D81, leading onto the D8 north towards **Vacqueyras**. Here you will pass the **Chapelle Notre-Dame d'Aubune** constructed in the 9th and 10th centuries. Past Vacqueyras, turn right onto the D7 for **Gigondas**. The area produces the celebrated red Côtes du Rhône Cru or vintage Gigondas wine, considered the finest in the area. Numerous properties as well as a co-operative are open for tasting *(information from the tourist office, Place du Portail, ☎04.90.65.85.46)*. The town dates from the Middle Ages. It has the ruins of a château and lovely views from the church terrace overlooking the impressive landscape. Inside the **Église Saint-Catherine** (11th century) are three interesting statues in gilded wood—the parish patron saints Cosme and Damien, and the Notre Dame des Pallières.

Carrying on the D7 north, you'll hit the village of **Sablet**, calm and peaceful, and taking the road on the right, (D23) the popular town of **Séguret ★**. A centre for craftsmen and artists, its pretty narrow cobbled streets, 12th-century church, belfry (14th century) and Mascarons Fountain are well looked after. However, its official designation (along with a number of other towns) as "the prettiest village in France" means it is crowded on weekends and during the summer. A number of tourist shops and a special parking lot for cars and buses below the town attest to Séguret's popularity with visitors, so it is best to visit during the week. From Séguret take the D88 north, and connect with the D977 back to Vaison-la-Romaine.

Mont Ventoux

A day trip by car to the top of this mountain (the highest in Provence, 1,912m or 6,273ft) is for all those who enjoy spectacular views. From Vaison-la-Romaine, take the D938 south (direction Carpentras) to Malaucène. In the village, turn left at the road indicating D974 Mont Ventoux. The D974 is a well-kept, scenic (naturally it is steep and twisted at times!) road (26km or 16.2mi) leading directly to the summit from the north face. **Commanding views ★★★** as far as the Alps to the north-east and Marseille to the south can be had from the top. Two viewing tables explain the important geographical sites, and a weather station, observatory, ugly television antenna and small chapel are nearby. Please note: fog and heat haze can diminish the view, plus heavy winds mean it can be quite cool at the summit. The upper part of the D974 is closed in bad weather, such as when there is heavy snow in the winter.

Continuing on the D974 from the summit, the pine-bordered road is dotted with a few picnic tables and a **ski station** *(for information about ski conditions, rentals and prices, telephone the Chalet d'Accueil du Mont Ventoux ☎04.90.63.49.44)*. Near the bottom, scenes of civilization reappear—restaurants, cafes and inns. **Bédoin** is a pretty village with tree-shaded roads and a Jesuit church from the early 18th century.

The D19 from Bédoin passes a panoramic stop called Le Paty and connects with the D938 taking you north to Vaison-la-Romaine or south to Carpentras. An alternative route which is worth taking is the small D138, which can be reached by passing through the centre of Bédoin and turning right, in a westwards direction, towards the hilltop town of **Crillon-le-Brave**. This village is named after a soldier who served under Henri IV, who was born at Murs, lived in Avignon and had a château here. Nowadays the village has come alive thanks to a four-star country inn, the Hostellerie de Crillon-le-Brave (see p 123), owned by a Canadian group, and a very good simple restaurant at its base. Remains of ramparts and the Église Saint-Romain (12th to 14th centuries) are the sole interest here, apart from the wonderful views.

A confusing series of roads leads back to the D938 and the town of **Le Barroux**. Try following the D138 south from Crillon-le-Brave, and turn right onto the D55 to the hamlets of St-Pierre-de-Vassols, Modène and then Caromb. The D55, D21 and better yet D13 (north) lead to the D938. The massive fortress-like **Le Barroux Château** *(20F; May, Jun and Oct, open everyday 2:30pm to 7pm; Jul to Sep, open everyday 10am to 7pm; ☎04.90.62.35.21)* dominates the landscape. Built in the 12th century and rebuilt in the 16th, the château fell into ruins after the Revolution. After restoration work began in 1929, it was burnt by the German army in 1944. The view and the château's interesting design are worth noting, though as it is under restoration again, there is little in the way of furniture or objects inside.

Mont Bluye

A second excursion from Vaison-la-Romaine, around scenic Mont Bluye and the Toulourenc River Valley is recommended, as it is an area of great natural beauty. Unspoilt by man, it is a chance to visit more charming villages perched on hillsides amongst a rugged landscape. Three kilometres (1.9mi) south of Vaison on the D938 (direction Carpentras), turn left onto the D54 to **Entrechaux** where you will find the 10th-century **Chapelle Notre-Dame-de-Nazareth**, ninth-century **Chapelle Saint-André** and 11th-century **Chapelle Saint-Laurent** *(tourist office in Place du Marché, ☎04.90.65.63.95)*.

Take the D13 through Entrechaux, and take note that the road becomes the D5 as you cross the Toulourenc River and into the Drôme department. Continue through Mollans-sur-Ouvèze, following the D5 for 6km (3.7mi) in the direction of Buis-les-Barronies, then turn right on the smaller D72 road at the tiny hamlet of **Cost**. The scenic D72 leads eastward past **Eygaliers**, a village known for its production of *tilleul*, (lime/linden), and rises sharply, as you approach Brantes.

Perched 600m-high (1,969ft) on a craggy cliff, **Brantes ★★** seems like a village forgotten by time. One basic hostelry greets visitors, otherwise there are no businesses. A couple of narrow streets (accessible by foot only) lead to a small **chapel ★** facing the valley. Like a hidden treasure, it is adorned with freshly painted trompe-l'oeil arches, oil paintings, three hanging copper candelabrum and statuary. Nearby, is the pottery workshop of Jaap Wieman and Martine Gilles. This husband and wife team have produced lovely earthenware (floral and fruit patterns in pink, yellow and pale blue, for example) here for 20 years and they now supply a shop in Paris. A small showroom *(call ahead: ☎04.72.28.03.37, ⇄04.75.28.18.61)* is open to the public where a simple dessert plate couls easily cost you 160F!

Twist down the D136 from Brantes and turn right onto the D40 west. This is a delightful **16km (9.9mi) valley drive ★** along the winding tree-lined banks of the Toulourenc. Locals swim and fish for trout in the river; the peace and quiet of the area is perfect for cycling, walking and horseback riding. You have now circled back and will pick up the D5 again. Turn left, towards Entrechaux and the D938 for Vaison-la-Romaine or Carpentras.

The Enclave des Papes

This small parcel of land seemingly inserted in the Drôme north of Vaison-la-Romaine is in fact part of the Vaucluse. The principal city of Valréas was bought from the king of France by Pope Jean XXII in the 14th century. The area remained papal territory, part of the Comtat Venaissin, until the formation of departments during the Revolution in 1791. The four communities of Valréas, Richerences, Visan and Grillon agreed to remain loyal to their Provençal origins and joined the Vaucluse. Today, the area's economy is supported by light industry, sheep farming, agriculture (notably tomatoes, melons, and asparagus), very good Côtes-du-Rhône wine and, in certain wooded areas, that typically French delicacy—truffles.

From Vaison-la-Romaine, take the D51 north and after 2km (1.2mi) turn right onto the D94 for **Villedieu** (another 4km or 2.4mi). This sleepy village of 550 people has a pretty, shaded square with large plane trees and a fountain (drinks and coffee from the Bar du Centre are served here). On foot, cross through the impressive stone gate in the old rampart wall and walk up to the 12th-century church. Its simple interior features a small, circular glass window above the altar with a luminescent red cross, and a couple of oil paintings (one from the 17th century portrays a particularly menacing devil).

The inhabitants of the region head to Villedieu on Sunday evenings, for a "pizza night" in the square. Arrive early (starting at 7pm) to order your slice from the restaurant-truck, and join in the festivities. The square is also very lively on Saturday nights in the summertime *(Jun 1 to Aug 15)*, when groups of locals serve up a dinner *à la provençale* (brochettes and *pistou*), for approximately 60F, Villedieu wine included.

Driving through Villedieu, take the D75 which becomes the D51 to the D20. Follow the D20 into the Enclave des Papes (the road turns left and for a few hundred metres becomes the D94, then take the first right to regain the D20). Just before the town of Visan, turn right down a small road which is signposted Notre-Dame des Vignes. Hidden amongst fir trees stands a remarkable chapel – an oasis of ecclesiastical tranquillity in the middle of nature. Fully-restored and classified as a historical monument by the French state, **Chapelle Notre-Dame des Vignes** ★ dates from the 13th century. The vaults were restored in the 17th century with painted *trompe-l'oeil* florettes, and the newly-restored wood-panels of the altar glisten with gold leaf. The chapel has been a site of hermitage for nuns since 1490. It was closed earlier this century, but is now maintained by two nuns. Mass is held every Friday at 6pm during the summer, and a popular retreat takes place every Sep. 8. *(Tue, Thu to Sat, 10am to 11:30am and 3pm to 6pm, Wed 3pm to 5:30pm, Sun 3pm to 6pm, closed Mon, closes at 5pm in winter).*

Carry on the D20 for 10km (6.2mi), passing through Visan, until you reach **Richerenches**. Note the stone ramparts which still surround the old part of the city, and particularly the heavy gate studded with iron nails and the interesting square clock tower that overlooks the town. An important truffle market takes place here Saturday mornings from November to March.

At the end of the town, turn left onto the D18

(which becomes D71B) for **Montségur-sur-Lauzon.** Officially located in the Drôme, this village of 800 people is mentioned here because on the hilltop in the centre of Montségur-sur-Luzon is a curious primitive **chapel** (dating from 958), next to the ruins of a 12th-century château. The square belfry is topped by an unusual feature—a small cupola in stone. Inside, note the strange tank-like structure discovered in the wall on the west side of the original 10th century nave. Historians are not sure whether it was a druid altar, sacrificial tomb or primitive baptismal font. Skeletons were found under the heavy stones covering the floor—a reminder that up until the Revolution, parishioners were buried in the church upon request. The Montségur-sur-Lauzon chapel is open for exhibitions, concerts and visits throughout the year, generally in the afternoons *(check first with the tourist office at Grignan, ☎04.75.46.56.75).*

Take the D71 north, past Chamaret to **Grignan**. Again, we're officially in the Drôme, but you should not miss a chance to visit one of the finest chateaux in Provence. Grignan is a lively town with a bank, post office, cafés and businesses which encircle the elevated château and 16th-century church (note the 17th-century retable and organ). Unlike so many chateaux in the region, the **Château de Grignan** has been beautifully restored and possesses a fine collection of period furniture, paintings and *objets d'art (30F, includes obligatory guided visit; everyday 9:30am to 11:30am and 2pm to 5:30pm; Jul and Aug until 6pm; Nov to Mar closed Tue; closed Dec 25 and Jan 1; ☎04.75.46.51.56).*

This Renaissance château dates back to the 11th century, but was entirely restored in the 1600s when it belonged to Comte François de Grignan, the son-in-law of the Marquise de Sévigné, a celebrated woman of letters. From her residence at the Hôtel Carnavalet, in the Marais district of Paris, the Marquise de Sévigné travelled three times to the palace for prolonged stays with her daughter and eventually died here in 1696. Apparently, she found Provence too cold and referred to it as "the land of goats." Isabelle Schuimer, who holds the position of permanent palace guide, has a true talent for storytelling; a tour with her is sure to be entertaining and interesting.

From Grignan, take the D941 to Grillon and Valréas. The former capital of the Enclave des Papes, **Valréas** is today its principal city. Housing the Hôtel de Ville, or city hall, the **Château de Simiane ★** is the former residence of the grandchild of Madame Sévigné. It was restored by her husband, Louis de Simiane, in the early 18th century, and today you may visit the reception rooms, library and archives and admire its paintings and furniture *(free admission, Sep to Jun with guided visit, Mon to Sat 3pm to 5pm; 20F, Jul and Aug, including 2hr guided visit of the town and its monuments; Wed to Mon 10am to noon and 3pm to 7pm; Place A. Briand, ☎04.90.35.00.45).*

The **Église Notre Dame de Nazareth ★** *(open everyday 10am to noon and 2pm to 6pm)* appears to have been built upon an 11th-century church and transformed in the 15th century. The **Musée du Cartonnage et de l'Imprimerie** *(10F; Apr to Sep 10am to noon and 3pm to 6pm; Oct to Mar 10am to noon and 2pm to 5pm; 3 Avenue Maréchal-Foch, ☎04.90.35.58.75)* is a rather curious spot. During a tour of the city, take a look at the 16th-century **Chapelle des Pénitents Blancs** *(free; Jul and Aug, two days a week; the schedule varies, inquire at the tourist office; next to the church)*, which supports a coloured ceiling encrusted with rosettes. Also take note of the elegant

17th- and 18th-century manor houses along Grande-Rue, Rue de l'Horloge and Rue de l'Hôtel-de-Ville. Every year, on the 23rd of June, **Nuit de Petit Saint-Jean** is celebrated in the streets of Valréas with a parade of 350 costumed revellers from among whom a young boy is chosen to be protector of the city. A free sound and light show begins at 10pm.

A visit to **Rousset-les-Vignes** *(Route D538, 6km or 3.7mi from Valréas)* is another must since the entire village is registered as a historic monument, not to mention the beautiful views it offers over the whole of the plain of the Enclave des Papes.

Carpentras

Carpentras lies in the flat, fertile land known as the Comtat plain, equidistant from Vaison-la-Romaine (28km or 17.4mi), Orange (24km or 14.9mi) and Avignon (23km or 14.3mi). It has always been a market town, and has suffered numerous invasions and occupations. Greeks and Phocaeans came here to buy local products including wheat, honey, sheep and goats. It was a colony under Julius Caesar (the Roman commemorative arch at the south end of the city still remains intact). Ramparts were constructed during the period of invasions and bishops sought refuge on the high ground at Venasque. Burgundians, Ostrogoths and Franks successively occupied Carpentras until the 12th century when the region was controlled by the Count of Toulouse.

It became part of the newly created papal territory Comtat Venaissin in 1229. For one hundred years, local unions and bishops disputed for control of the city. Finally, it became the capital of the Comtat in 1320, and a second ring of ramparts was built to keep out pillagers. Capentras had a period of relative prosperity during the 17th and 18th centuries, during which time many public buildings were restored and private *hôtels particuliers* were built. A sizeable ghetto harbouring Jews who fled to this papal land following persecution in France in the 14th century existed until the 19th century.

The **Porte d'Orange** ★, or Orange Gate was built when Pope Innocent VI, realising that the old Roman ramparts were too slender, called for a new stone defensive wall to surround Carpentras (1357 to 1379). Most of it was destroyed in the 19th century, but the heavy gate still remains.

Cathédrale Saint-Siffrein ★ *(Place Générale de Gaulle, ☎04.90.63.08.33)* was built on the site of a 12th-century Romanesque cathedral, and shows a diversity of architectural influences owing to the fact that it was built over a span of 100 years (1405-1519). The ensemble is essentially late southern Gothic. Some striking ornamentation in gilded wood by famous local sculptor Jacques Bernus (1650-1728) is located in the chancel. Note the delicate wrought-iron railing with eight candle braces on the nave balcony, which leads to the bishops' apartments. The elaborate and flamboyant Gothic sculpted south entrance is called the *Porte Juive*, or Jewish door, because it was used by Jews who had converted to Catholicism.

The **Arc Romain** ★ *(Place d'Inguimbert)*, or Roman arch, was built during Augustus' reign in the first century AD to commemorate the Roman victory over the barbarians. The east side facing the Palais de Justice (courthouse) represents two chained prisoners. It is the only Roman ruin left in Carpentras.

The **Aqueduc de Carpentras** *(along the D974 going toward Bédoin)*, entirely built of remarkable ochre stone, was erected in the 15th century by Antoine d'Allemand and was restored 300 years later. The aqueduct numbers 48 arches and is 631.5m-long (2,072ft) and 23m-wide (75.5ft).

The **Musée Comtadin-Duplessis** ★ *(30 F, includes all four museums; Nov to Mar 10am to noon and 2pm to 4pm; Apr to Oct 10am to noon and 2pm to 6 p.m; enter by the Bibliothèque Inguimbertine 234 Boulevard Albin-Durand, ☎04.90.63.04.92)* houses two inviting museum collections in a pleasant 18th-century *hôtel particulier*, with a garden. The Comtadin museum (ground floor) presents an important collection of local folklore, including furniture and unusual items such as bird decoys, cattle bells and figures. The Duplessis museum (first floor) has oil paintings (14th to 16th century) of local figures, including canvases by Carpentras native Joseph Duplessis (painter to Louis XIV) as well as some period furniture.

Musée Victor de Sobirat *(same hours as Musée Comtadin-Duplessis; Rue du Collège; ☎04.90.63.04.92)* presents an interesting collection of decorative art—furniture, pottery and assorted objects—in an attractive 18th-century residence. Take note in passing of the rare Moustiers ceramic bidet, which dates from the 1700s.

For its part, **Musée Lapidaire** *(same hours as Musée Comtadin-Duplessis; Rue des Saintes-Maries, ☎04.90.63.04.92)* offers a collection of prehistoric artefacts and objects related to natural history that highlights archeological discoveries made in the region.

Though the Place de la Juiverie was almost entirely destroyed in the 19th century, the **Synagogue** ★★ *(Mon to Thu 10am to noon and 3pm to 5pm, Fri 10am to noon and 3pm to 4pm, closed during holidays; Place de la Mairie, ☎04.90.63.39.97)* has kept most of its original components. Located in the centre of the old *carrière*, the synagogue was built between 1741 and 1743 by architect Antoine d'Allemand. Its facade does not differ from those of neighbouring houses because of a very strict regulation that prohibited all exterior decoration and dimensions that were too large. The lower medieval part where the *mikva* and the bakehouse are situated has a monumental staircase leading to the prayer hall. This place of worship has two levels, the assembly hall with its tabernacle, and the platform gallery with the *tebah*, or officiant's gallery.

Inside the 18th-century **Hôtel-Dieu** ★ *(10 F; Mon, Wed and Thu 9am to 11:30am; Place Aristide-Briand, ☎04.90.63.10.72)*, or hospital, hides a pharmacy dating from 1762 which is still completely intact. Note the painted panelling by Duplessis, the remarkable collection of earthenware jars (from Italy, Montpellier and Moustiers), and some brass and glass containers. Also visit the chapel and grand staircase. Let's hope that this is the only hospital visit during your trip to Provence.

Outdoor Activities

Hiking

The Comtat Venaissin region is ideal terrain for walking and hiking. The most remarkable walks are found in the beautiful hills of the Dentelles de Montmirail. Serious hikers will be thrilled with the well-marked trail GR 4 which winds through this area, past Crestet, Séguret and Gigondas. At least three days is suggested to complete the entire circuit of 55km (34.2mi). For a guidebook and details, contact the hiking association:

Cîmes et Sentiers
Vaison-la-Romaine
☎04.90.36.02.11

Vaison-la-Romaine

The tourist office in Vaison-la-Romaine publishes a very good guide in French called *Inventaire des Chemins et Drailles du Massif des Dentelles de Montmirail* which describes the trails of the Dentelles de Montmirail.

Rando-Ventoux, Centre Régional de la Randonnée
Buisson
☎04.90.28.95.61
This group arranges guided walks through the hills of the Dentelles de Montmirail, as well as in the Mont Ventoux area.

Rasteau

Centre Laïque d'Accueil et d'Éducation Populaire
Jun to Sep only, Thu only
☎04.90.46.15.48
The Centre Laïque d'Accueil et d'Éducation Populaire, located near Séguret, publishes a guide to two interesting, clearly-marked trails that allow you to discover the flowers, the fields and the vines of the region. It also organizes instructive guided hikes with specific themes such as "Villages et Panoramas," "La Flore Méditerranéenne et la Vie des Abeilles" (Mediterranean flora and the life of bees), and "L'Ouvèze."

Well-marked trails, between four and 12km (7.5mi) in length, also exist within the Enclave des Papes, starting from Richerenches, Valréas and Visan. For more information about these contact the tourist offices of these localities.

Finally, a 16km-long (9.9mi) marked trail circles Châteauneuf-du-Pape; the city's tourist information office distributes an explanatory pamphlet.

Horseback Riding

Orange

École du 1er REC
Route du Parc
☎04.90.51.63.85
École du 1er REC riding school arranges accompanied horseback-riding tours of the area.

Vaison-la-Romaine

Rando-Ventoux Centre Régional de la Randonnée
Buisson
☎04.90.28.95.61
The Rando-Ventoux Centre Régional de la Randonnée group arranges guided tours on horseback through the hills of the Dentelles de Montmirail, as well as in the Mont Ventoux area.

Le Crestet

Centre Équestre "Les Voconces"
☎04.75.23.42.05

Carpentras

Ranch de l'Etalon Blan
Chemin de Sève, Entraigues
☎04.90.83.17.68
Tours on horseback are arranged at this ranch, which is also a pony-breeding centre.

Mountain Biking

Gigondas

Détroit Evasion Sportive
Eric Neuville
☎04.90.36.03.57
This association rents mountain bikes and, upon demand, organizes guided bike tours of the Dentelles de Montmirail.

Accommodations

Orange

Hôtel Arcotel
150F without shower
230F with shower
pb in some rooms
8 Place aux Herbes
☎04.90.34.09.23
⇄04.90.51.61.12
Jor8225@aol.com
Excellent location on a charming square with a large plane tree. The 19 rooms in this old building are modern, though basic; each is well-equipped and clean. Parking is in the hotel's private courtyard.

Hôtel Saint-Florent
200F-350F
pb
4 Rue du Mazeau
☎04.90.34.18.53
⇄04.90.51.17.25
Many of this hotel's 18 rooms, which are decorated in Provençal fabrics, are large and therefore appropriate for families and couples. This is fairly simple accommodation, and some of the rooms could use a bit of brightening up. The location is central, near the Théâtre Antique and Place aux Herbes, but there is no parking.

Hôtel Clarinne Orange-Centre
250F-450F
tv
4 Rue Caristie
☎04.90.34.10.07
⇄04.90.34.89.76
acigalounhotel@gulliver.fr
A small hotel slightly removed from the hub of activity around the Arènes, the Hôtel Clarinne Orange-Centre has 29 modern, comfortable rooms renovated in a simple, minimalist style. This clean, well-maintained establishment is certainly a good place to stay, located a few minutes from Orange's main attractions.

Hôtel Le Glacier
285F-400F
pb, ≡, tv
46 Cours Aristide Briand
☎04.90.34.02.01
⇄04.90.51.13.80
hotelgla@aol.com
The 30 tasteful, good-sized rooms are regularly renovated and each has a modern bathroom. Although the hotel is on a noisy road, all but two rooms face the back and look onto rooftops and neighbouring terraces. Le Glacier has been in the Cunha family for three generations and a friendly, warm welcome awaits everyone.

Hôtel Arène
360F with shower
600F with bath
pb or ps, ≡, tv
47 Place de Langes
☎04.90.34.10.95
⇄04.90.34.91.62
Considered by many as the best hotel in Orange, each of the 30 rooms is eclectically furnished. Some have small balconies overlooking the pretty square (directly behind the Hôtel de Ville, city hall). The helpful owner, Danielle Coutel, offers personal advice on the best restaurants in the area and is attentive to such details as home-made jams with breakfast and flowering window boxes outside. Private parking garage.

Sérignan-du-Comtat

Hostellerie du Vieux Château
360F-800F
closed one week in late Dec and one week in Feb
pb
Route de Sainte-Cécile les Vignes
☎04.90.70.05.58
⇄04.90.70.05.62
With large, fresh, individually decorated rooms, each with a modern bathroom, this inn is more expensive than similar establishments. Madame Truchot is very friendly and takes care of all your requirements. The excellent restaurant is popular at lunch and dinner-time with locals. This pretty village has a handsome 17th-century *hôtel particulier* next to the 18th-century Église Saint-Etienne, with a typical wrought-iron cage belfry housing three bells, each dating from different periods. Serignan is 8km (5mi) north of Orange, at the crossroads of the D43 and the D976.

Châteauneuf-du-Pape

La Garbure
320F-380F
pb, ≡, tv
3 Rue Joseph Ducos
☎04.90.83.75.08
Opposite the handsome Hotel de Ville sits this pleasant hotel, with comfortable rooms and a central location. The hotel dining room offers local cuisine at reasonable prices (set menus at 98F, 130F and 150F).

Vaison-la-Romaine

Hôtel Burrhus
240F-320F
closed Nov 15 to Dec 15
ps or pb
2 Place Montfort, B.P. 93
☎04.90.36.00.11
⇄04.90.36.39.05
24 simple and cheery rooms (10 at 250F are

brand new). A few look onto the square that can be noisy during the summer, but they have wonderful views of the Haute Ville, or upper town, and of its château. In good weather, breakfast is taken outside on a shaded terrace. Excellent value and highly recommended for the friendly welcome and down-to-earth charm of hosts Jean-Baptiste and Laurence Gurly.

Hôtel de Lis
350F-450F
pb, tv
2 Place Montfort, B.P. 93
☎04.90.36.00.11
⇄04.90.36.39.05
The more elegant sister hotel next to Hôtel Burrus (check-in there first) has 8 large, newly-refurbished rooms decorated in understated good taste. Breakfast in your room or at the Burrus.

Le Logis du Château
360F-470F
closed from late Oct to late Mar
pb, tv, ≈, ℜ
Les Hauts de Vaison
☎04.90.36.09.98
⇄04.90.36.10.95
The striking view, quiet setting and friendly staff constitute three good reasons to choose this establishment, even though its decor has not been updated since the 1970s and the breakfast is to be avoided (tasteless orange juice, vile coffee...). The hotel's main clientele is a bit older, but it also welcomes groups. There is covered parking.

L'Éveché
400F-440F bkfst incl.
no credit cards
ps, one room with pb
Rue de l'Éveché
☎04.90.36.13.46
⇄04.90.36.32.43
In a restored 16th-century house in the heart of the medieval Haute Ville, or upper town, this charming *chambres d'hôte* (bed and breakfast) has four comfortable rooms decorated in Provençal fabrics, with cool clay-tile floors, white walls and some antiques. The bathrooms are small and modern. Breakfast is served on a private terrace full of flowers and plants, that overlooks the town. Fine touches include thick towels and locally made perfumed soap. Pleasant welcome from the owners, Aude Verdier and her architect husband Jean-Loup. Popular with foreign tourists, so book early.

Hostellerie Le Beffroi
465F-655F
closed late Jan to late Mar
tv, ≈, ℜ
Rue de l'Évêché, Medieval City
☎04.90.36.04.71
⇄04.90.36.24.78
beffroi@wanadoo.fr
This medieval-character hotel in the historic part of the Hostellerie Le Beffroi has 22 rooms with a historic decor. Well-located at the heart of the old town, it offers fabulous panoramic views of Vaison-la-Romaine and the surrounding area from its magnificent garden. The hotel has parking spaces available, a point worth noting in this old city with narrow pedestrian streets.

Crillon-le-Brave

Clos St. Vincent
340F-430F, one cottage 700F for two people, 800F for four
no credit cards
bkfst incl.; ≈
☎04.90.65.93.36
⇄04.90.12.81.46
Highly-rated bed and breakfast with five tasteful rooms with wood beams in a fresh Provençal style. Thick feather duvets are provided in the winter, and cool cotton quilts in the summer. The smell of fresh rosemary prevails throughout the house. The owner, Françoise Vazquez, serves a delicious breakfast of home-made jams and breads on a long table. Evening meals are available if Françoise is notified a day ahead *(130F, wine and apéritif included)*. The high season is often booked months in advance.

Hostellerie de Crillon-le-Brave
750F-1150 F
½b add 260 F per person
closed Jan to Mar
≈, ℜ, pb, tv
Place de l'Eglise
☎04.90.65.61.61
⇄04.90.65.62.86
This hotel, owned by Canadians is entirely decorated in Provençal prints (everything from

the waiters' waistcoats to the wall coverings). It features pretty reading rooms, professional service, and an unstuffy attention to detail. Remarkable views can be had of Mont Ventoux and the Dentelles de Montmirail. There are 20 rooms, plus apartment suites, in four different buildings. The very good but pricey restaurant has a wood-burning fireplace for the cooler months and a lovely stone terrace surrounding a small fountain in the summer (popular with smartly-dressed locals for Sunday lunch). Here you'll savour the wonderful charm of an English country-inn.

Villedieu

Château de la Baude
580F bkfst incl.
≈, tennis, tv, billiard room
La Baude
☎04.90.28.95.18
⇌04.90.28.91.05
After spending over two years restoring a 12th-century fortress, Chantal and Gérard Monin opened this luxury bed and breakfast in 1994. Three rooms and two two-bedroom duplex suites *(880F for four people)* are designed in a fresh Provençal style. Peaceful natural setting with a friendly welcome. No credit cards.

Brantes

L'Auberge
120F-150F
☎04.75.28.01.68
Very basic rooms with wash basin only, (shower and toilet in the hall). Chosen for its friendly atmosphere, in an out-of-the-way setting, this charming cliff-side village is perched 600m (1,969ft) above the Rivière Toulourenc valley. Lunch and dinner available for an unbeatable 55F and a special Sunday lunch for 110F.

Carpentras

Hôtel du Fiacre
250F-480F
ps or pb, tv
153 Rue Vigne
☎04.90.63.03.15
⇌04.90.60.49.73
Hôtel du Fiacre is a serene, 18th-century *hôtel particulier* with a calm inner courtyard where breakfast is served. Helpful, smiling staff. Despite the old-fashioned decoration in the bedrooms, this is a good place to stay in a town which otherwise doesn't have much reliable accommodation away from busy roads.

Bastide Sainte-Agnès
450F-520F, suite up to 700F bkfst incl.
closed mid-Nov to mid-Mar
≈
1043 Chemin de la Fourtrouse, take the Route de Bédouin, then the Route de Caromb
☎04.90.60.03.01
⇌04.90.60.02.53
gerlinde@infornie.fr
If Carpentras is not bursting with remarkable places to stay, the Bastide Sainte-Agnès is surely the exception. The charming owners Jacques and Gerlinde cordially welcome their guests in this inviting old 18th-century farmhouse, which has been renovated to suit modern tastes. The decor in the four guestrooms and 70m² (753 sq ft) suite, as well as the common rooms, is exuberant and undeniably tasteful, while the verdant garden provides a wonderful sense of tranquility. A cooking area has been installed near the pool so that guests can barbecue or prepare other meals outdoors on their own. What's more, the owners can recommend the best restaurants and suggest itineraries that will let you discover the region's marvels.

Crestet

Le Mas de Magali
350F-375F
closed mid-Oct to early Apr
tv, ≈, ℜ
Chante Coucou district
☎04.90.36.39.91
⇄04.90.28.73.40
Le Mas de Magali has nine excellent rooms in a rural setting, offering calm, greenery and serenity on its 3ha (7.4 acre) property. The rooms are spacious, and all have a private bathroom, while some also have a terrace. All provide a comfortable and cozy atmosphere. The garden and terrace of this family-run hotel offer panoramic views of Mont Ventoux and the surrounding area. At night, finely prepared Provençal food seasoned with local herbs and spices is served beneath the stars.

La Respelido
350F-450F bkfst incl.
33 Rue de l'Hospice
☎/⇄04.90.36.03.10
Owners of La Respelido since 1998, Jacques and Gi Veit love Le Crestet, the delightful village they have adopted as their own. Located in an old oil mill, the two pleasant guest rooms, one large and one small, blend perfectly with the rest of the place, which exudes a sense of history, charm and good taste. The friendly couple serves hearty breakfasts in the walled-in courtyard filled with greenery and flowers. The breakfast consists of seasonal fruits, homemade jams, farm eggs and organic bread. Those who love wine and truffles should note that Jacques has a list of some good producers and will gladly pass on his knowledge about the village and the region's history and wines. On request, he'll plan your stay to focus on themes like wine, olive oil and Provençal cuisine. In winter, the owners will plan itineraries that introduce guests to fresh black truffles: how to find them, where you can buy them and how to prepare them. This is an excellent place to stay at the centre of one of the most authentic little medieval villages in Provence.

Mastignac
350F-450F bkfst incl.
closed Nov 1 to May 15
≈
Route de Taulignan
☎04.90.35.01.82
Madame de Précigout, a very elegant hostess, has received visitors in her magnificent 19th-century residence since 1991. She bought this venerable country home in 1967 and completely renovated it. Located 4km (2.5 mi) from Valréas, this was the family residence before the lady of the house began renting out its five bedrooms. Guests will appreciate the carefully decorated guest rooms and common rooms, as well as the peaceful garden that borders on the vineyards. This guest-house definitely has charm to spare.

Ferme La Ribaude
1,000F
early Apr to late Oct
≈, pb
☎04.90.36.36.11
⇄04.90.28.81.29
An exceptional bed and breakfast—seven huge suites with cool stone floors, stylish bedrooms with minimalist furnishings decorated by the host, Renata Luhmann. Built on the site of a former wine estate, La Ribaude offers seclusion, silence, peace, comfort and unparalleled views over the scenic hills of the Dentelles de Montmirail.

Restaurants

Orange

La Roselière
$
closed Wed and Thu evening
4 Rue du Renoyer
☎04.90.34.50.42
La Roselière is a rustic restaurant with a small shaded terrace on a quiet street corner, near the Cathédrale Notre-Dame and the Hôtel de Ville (city hall). Items are market fresh—grilled eggplant, fillet of fresh cod and roasted rabbit, for example. Casual and friendly.

La Claire Fontaine
$-$$
4 Place des Cordeliers
☎04.90.34.55.44
La Claire Fontaine is a restaurant, café and ice cream shop, and stands on the picturesque Place des Cordeliers with its giant plane trees that provide a cool respite on hot summer afternoons. The small establishment is 2min from Les Arènes, visible in the background, and has an inviting terrace right by the fountain from which the place derives its name. The honest, unpretentious food is listed in the form of various specials.

L'Aïgo Boulido
$-$$
20 Place Sylvain
☎04.90.34.18.19
Attractive Provençal decor complements this popular restaurant specializing in regional cuisine, such as chicken breast stuffed with *tapenade* (olive paste), half baby chicken prepared with an onion and orange-zest chutney, roast sea bass with macerated garlic cloves. Try to book a table in the front room, or on the terrace if you don't mind the noise of cars passing by on the street next to it.

Le Garden
$$
6 Place de Langes
☎04.90.34.64.47
This well-situated restaurant on a peaceful square offers a variety of local dishes, including rabbit terrine, salmon on a bed of fennel with a dill sauce, and fillet of pork seasoned with rosemary. Warm *amuse-gueules*, or tongue-teasers, start the meal, while home-made *tuilles* (curled wafer-thin almond cookies) accompany some desserts. Although the young waitresses try hard, the serviece is not very professional.

Le Parvis
$$
3 Cours Pourtoules
☎04.90.34.82.00
One of Orange's fanciest restaurants serving updated Provençal classics from its chef J. M. Berengier. Most dishes succeed, such as snails in filo-pastry pockets with a tomato *coulis*, grilled red mullet and nougat with fresh strawberries, though portions are small and the sauces unexciting. Service is efficient though reserved.

Sérignan-du-Comtat

Le Pré du Moulin
$$-$$$
From Easter to Oct
Route de Sainte-Cécile-les-Vignes
☎04.90.70.05.58
Le Pré du Moulin is the Hostellerie du Vieux-Château's superb restaurant, and needs no further introduction. Matching the high quality of the guestrooms, the place serves sophisticated food that is very popular with locals and visitors who are prepared to spend some money. A splendid, idyllic terrace, protected and cool beneath the plane trees, adjoins the venerable inn. Among the dishes we recommend is the delicious pressed veal and crisp sea bream with pig's feet and marrow.

Châteauneuf-du-Pape

Le Pistou
$$
closed Sun pm and Mon
15 Rue Joseph Ducos
☎04.90.83.71.75
Good Provençal cuisine and a wine list strong on local bottles (eight types of Chateauneuf-du-Pape priced between 150F and 250F). Yellow and orange decor with framed prints of the 13 varieties of grapes that make the Chateauneuf-du-Pape so unique.

Vaison-la-Romaine

Du Vieux Vaison
$
every day noon to 3:30pm and 7pm to midnight closed Wed from Sep to Jun
Rue du Château, Haute Ville
☎04.90.36.19.45
Du Vieux Vaison is the place to go for delicious wood-oven pizzas and other pizzeria-style fare. Meals are served on a pleasant patio right by the ramparts or in a panoramic

dining room. The service is cordial.

Le Batleur
$-$$
closed Sun evening, Mon and Oct
One Place Théodore Aubanel
☎*04.90.36.28.04*
Tasty family cooking, including its specialty rack of lamb with almond stuffing. Completely renovated after closed for six months following the tragic flooding of the nearby Rivière Ouvèze in 1992. Reasonably-priced wine list.

Le Cigalou
$$
closed Tue evening and Wed
45 Cours Taulignan
☎*04.90.36.04.67*
Le Cigalou is a pleasant little Provençal restaurant, located on a street lined with plane trees, along with a number of other establishments of varying quality. It stands out from these other places due to its authentic food and welcoming, friendly service. Whether you dine in the bright dining room decorated in warm hues or on the outdoor terrace, you'll enjoy the Provençal rennet stomach, rabbit legs with tapenade, leg of lamb with garlic puree and lark. On Saturday evenings a guitarist creates a little ambiance with classic French *chansons*. Guests can choose among three options: the menu for 120F, an appetizer and main dish for 100F or a main dish and dessert for 90F.

Le Tournesol
$$
closed Tue evening and Wed
30 Cours Taulignan
☎*04.90.36.09.18*
The food at Le Tournesol is inspired by basic, unadorned Provençal cuisine. This small restaurant with a dozen tables set up inside and three out on the terrace draws a varied clientele. Younger and older people, locals and visitors alike appreciate the courteous, attentive service. Although the selection is limited, the menu lists enough specialties that it is an adequate representation of what Provençal cuisine has to offer, and guests can choose among different fixed-price menus. Like the dishes themselves, the atmosphere is simple and without artifice.

Auberge de la Bartavelle
$$-$$$
closed Mon
Place-sur-Auze
☎*04.90.36.02.16*
Chef Richard Cayrol's creative menu takes its inspiration from southwest France. The menu includes ravioli in truffle juices, cod in a light saffron-flavoured cream sauce and warm chocolate terrine. Fresh herbs are used liberally, and dishes are presented as a festival of colours.

Le Brin d'Olivier
$$-$$$
closed Wed and Sat lunch
4 Rue du Ventoux
☎*04.90.28.74.79*
Very good Provençal food prepared with flair. Popular with locals; best in warm months when dining on the terrace is a real pleasure (and the restaurant interior is rather bland).

Les Jardins du Beffroi
$$-$$$
Rue de l'Évêché, Medieval Town
☎*04.90.36.04.71*
The restaurant of the Hostellerie Le Beffroi, Les Jardins du Beffroi, serves excellent food from the southwest part of Provence in an enchanting setting. The splendid gardens will delight guests, who can enjoy a magnificent view of the surrounding region. Several different fixed-price menus are available.

La Fête en Provence
$$$
closed Wed
Upper Town, Place du Vieux Marché
☎*04.90.36.16.05*
You couldn't ask for a more intimate, peaceful and picturesque terrace than that of the wonderful restaurant La Fête en Provence. Surrounded by stone walls and the old buildings of the medieval city, and graced with pretty gardens, it represents a culinary highlight of Provence and southwestern France. The chef skilfully prepares imaginative cuisine. We recommend the sub-

lime salmon steak, the divine garlic cod and the extraordinary truffles baked in pastry. The fixed-price menu is definitely worthwhile. The wine selection includes some good Côtes-du-Rhône, Côtes-du-Ventoux and some exceptional Châteauneuf-du-Pape.

Séguret

Le Mesclun
$$
Apr to Sep open everyday, closed Mon in the off-season
Rue des Poternes
☎04.90.46.93.43
≠04.90.46.93.48

A cosy restaurant down a pretty stone road in the village, serving delicious meals made from local products such as linguini pasta with herbs and chèvre, roast lamb with almonds and prunes and, for dessert, cheesecake with red berries. Outdoor terrace with magnificent panoramic views.

Crillon-le-Brave

Restaurant du Vieux Four
$-$$
fixed-price menu only
closed Mon and Jan to mid-Feb
70F weekday lunch, 120F evenings and Sunday lunch
located in the village below the hotel
☎04.90.12.81.39

This country-style restaurant opened in 1993, replacing the village's bakery. Wonderful Provençal specialties include salmon fillet with leek and basil sauce, thyme-scented lamb, and grilled eggplant with a tomato *coulis*. Fresh desserts. Popular with locals who know good food and good value, so reserve ahead. No credit cards.

Brantes

L'Auberge
$
☎04.75.28.01.68

The restaurant at L'Auberge offers lunches and dinners at the unbeatable price of 75F, and the Sunday lunch special costs only 130F. For a description of the rooms see p 124.

Carpentras

Le Marijo
$
closed Sun and Tue at lunch
73 Rue Raspail
☎04.90.60.42.65

A cheery place welcoming locals, students and tourists who come for the reliable if unremarkable Provençal dishes such as fish soup, followed by either *pieds et paquets à la Marseille* (sheep tripe) or steak with tapenade (olive paste) plus cheese or dessert, all for 95F. Regional menu for 132F.

Les Halles
$-$$
closed Sun
41 Rue Galonne
☎04.90.63.24.11

A pleasant little restaurant that serves simple family fare at very reasonable prices, Les Halles seems to be a congenial spot that is popular with the people of Carpentras. The small, lively bistro sports bright, colourful modern paintings on its walls. Its terrace, at the far end of a spacious, quiet courtyard near the town hall, is relaxing. The service is attentive and the fixed-price menus are extremely affordable given the quality of the unpretentious yet delicious food.

Le Vert Galant
$$
closed Sat and Mon at lunch, Sun evening
12 Rue Clapies
☎04.90.67.15.50

A pleasant rustic decor (candles and dried flowers on the tables, oil paintings by local artists on the walls) greets customers at one of Carpentras' better restaurants. Elaborate selections include filet of roast duckling, kale stuffed with *escargots*, good cheeses and a sublime citrus fruit pie for dessert.

Le Poème
$$
closed Tue and Wed at noon
Montée du Tricot
☎04.75.91.10.90

A tiny, congenial restaurant with a dozen

tables at the centre of the charming village of Grignan, Le Poème is a good place to stop for its tranquility and mouthwatering food. Guests will rave at the fixed-price menus, with dishes that are simple but authentic and flawlessly presented. This small restaurant has no terrace but an airy interior. It is located a few minutes below the château, and overlooks the town hall.

Au Délice de Provence
$$-$$$
closed Tue evenings and Wed
6 La Placetta
☎***04.90.28.16.91***
Without a doubt the best dining establishment in Valréas, Au Délice de Provence serves, as one would expect, fixed-price menus of authentic Provençal cuisine in generous portions. This renowned establishment has an airy interior, but no terrace, and draws on the best of traditional recipes and local ingredients for dishes like their delicious scorpion fish filet, perfectly roasted coquerel and delicately prepared white cabbage stuffed with three kinds of fish.

Entertainment

Sorry night-hawks, but the Upper Comtat Venaissin is a quiet place and visitors are hard-pressed to find evening entertainment in the area. Young revellers looking for nightclubs and cosmopolitan bars with the latest music will have to check out larger centres.

Evenings in this area are spent in restaurants and local cafes. Indeed, in most of the towns and villages, the liveliest event at night is a performance by a local musician in a bar or café. In these cases, flyers posted in the area announce dates and times.

There are exceptions, however, as many local **festivals of culture and tradition** are held every year, particularly in the summertime. The best-known take place in the spectacular 2,000-year-old outdoor Roman amphitheatre in Orange: **Les Nuits d'Été du Théâtre Antique** *(opera and ballet, plus classical and popular music; Aug; ☎04.90.51.89.58)* and the **Chorégies d'Orange** *(classical music and opera; Jul-Aug; ☎04.90.34.24.24).*

Theatre de la Haute Ville
Rue des Fours, upper Town
☎***04.90.28.71.85***
Theatre lovers will be interested in the Theatre de la Haute Ville in Vaison-la-Romaine. Actor-director Bernard Jancou presents a variety of theatre productions throughout the year that are widely appreciated. For the latest program, check local papers or with your hotel.

Cinéma El Florian
54 Avenue Jules Ferry, Vaison-la-Romaine
☎***08.36.68.69.22***
Film buffs should check out the Cinéma El Florian, which shows a good mix of recent French releases, popular American movies and art-house films on two screens.

Wine-lovers will enjoy the colourful festivities in Châteauneuf-du-Pape:

Le Saint-Marc
late April
Le Saint-Marc, named after the wine-makers' protector, includes celebrations such as a street procession, tastings and a dinner.

La Fête de la Véraison
first weekend of Aug
Weekend-long activities draw thousands of people to celebrate the moment when the grapes turn red and mature— features tastings, local crafts, open-air entertainment, and a mass in Saint-Théordoric chapel.

Le Ban des Vendages
The first day of the grape harvest, is announced publicly during a big supper.

Among the other festivals and special events worth mentioning are the **Festival de la Sorgue**, held at Isle-sur-la-Sorgue, at Lagnes and at Le Thor *(Jul to Aug; music and theatre)*; the

Fête d'Été de Malaucène *(Aug; music)*; the **Estivales de Carpentras** *(Jul; music, dance, theatre)*; the **Fête Votive de Châteauneuf-du-Pape** *(first week of Jul; folk music and dancing, pétanque competition)*; the **Grand Prix de la Chanson Française et les Nuits de la Nesque de Pernes-les-Fontaines** *(Aug; music and theatre)*; the **Foire d'Art et de Poterie de Gigondas** *(Jul to Aug; art and pottery fair)*; the **Foire Artisanale et la Grande Fête des Vins d'Acqueyras** *(Jul. craft fair and wine festival)*; and the **Festival de Musique et la Foire Artistique de Beaumes-de-Venise** *(Aug; music festival and art fair)*.

Villedieu

Bar du Centre
$
Jul and Aug, every day 7:30am to midnight
closed Mon rest of the year
☎04.90.28.91.64
A bar like any other where the likeable Yvelise Clerand serves up cool drinks across from the town square in the shade of tall plane trees.

Shopping

Orange

Le César
47 Rue Caristie
☎04.90.34.99.88
Le César is a bakery and pastry shop recommended for its excellent custom-garnished baguette sandwiches (smoked ham, sausage, tuna...). This is the perfect place to stock up for a picnic, which you can take on the neighbouring steps of Théâtre Antique, while admiring this restored attraction.

Vaison-la-Romaine

Lanchier-Avias
Tue to Sun 7:30am to 8pm, closed 1pm to 1:30pm in off-season
Place Montet
☎04.90.36.09.25
Good pastry shop run by the same family for three generations. Specialties are *pavé* (fruit tart with almond paste and local honey), and *croquantes* (crunchy almond biscuits). Pastries are made with freshly-picked local fruits.

Lou Canesteou
closed Sun pm and Mon
10 Rue Raspail
☎04.90.36.31.30
Vaison's finest cheese shop offers a good selection of locally-made chèvre including *banon* (wrapped in oak leaves), *picadon* and *cachat*.

Photo Video
Avenue General de Gaulle
☎04.90.36.02.09
One hour photo developing.

Pharmacie Lecerf
closed Sun and Mon
32 Place Montfort
☎04.90.36.37.88
This drugstore has extended opening hours.

Carpentras

Jouvaud
Rue de l'Évêché
☎04.90.63.15.38
⇄04.90.63.21.62
Classy pastry and gift shop. A few tables for tea and cake are provided in case you can't resist the extraordinary cakes, pastries and chocolate. Nougat made with lavender honey is its specialty. The store also sells unique gift items.

R. Clavel
Rue Porte d'Orange
☎04.90.63.07.59
Fifth-generation chocolate and sweet shop that claims the world record for making the largest *berlingot* candy.

The Plateau du Vaucluse and the Luberon

For many visitors and residents alike, the Plateau du Vaucluse and the Luberon represents the heart of Provence. This region is blessed with an unparalleled and varied natural beauty: gentle rolling hills, impressive gorges and fertile plains.

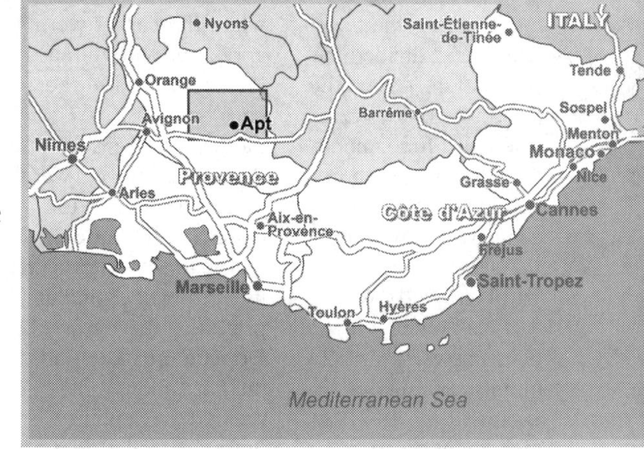

Human presence here goes back to the Palaeolithic period (10,000 BC). The Celt and Ligurian peoples occupied the territory from the 4th century BC onwards—the ruins of their communities (known as *oppida*) have been discovered in the area. It was a time when druid priests were respected religious leaders, preaching immortality and reincarnation.

The Celts were superstitious and believed that certain shepherds possessed supernatural powers, such as the ability to read signals and hear voices from the earth and the sky. According to them, their interpretation of natural phenomena protected their flocks of sheep and helped crops to thrive. They prepared magic potions from plants and herbs to ward off sickness and evil forces, and believed witches (male and female) existed to wreak havoc on the world.

The Romans settled here following the creation of their new colony in 118 BC, but little is known of their stay. The region was greatly influenced by a fervent wave of Christianity from the late

Middle Ages through to the 10th century, and religion played an essential role for hundreds of years. Churches and priories were erected, as were the three masterpieces of Cistercian architecture: the Sénanque, Silvacane and Thoronet abbeys (each built during the 12th century). During the same time, the Vaudois religious movement gained popularity and divided the population. Today, the Vaudois would be classified as a fundamentalist religious sect. It began in the late 12th century by a wealthy Lyon merchant, Pierre Vaud (or Vald), who fled his hometown after his sect's was excommunicated by Pope Lucius III in 1184. The movement's leaders, Barbes or Beards, were lay preachers whose members renounced material possessions and strictly followed the Gospels. They retaliated against organized religion and congregated in secret in members' homes. Most were peaceful farmers, though some historians note that there were Vaudois who went so far as to raze churches.

Many Vaudois settled in the Luberon region in the 15th century, which had been devastated by the plague and pillaging. Wealthy landowning nobles and the priories and abbeys welcomed the opportunity to see the area resettled and cultivated again. However, the Vaudois were persecuted during the Reformation movement, when Inquisitors were appointed throughout France to capture "heretics," mainly Lutherans. In 1545, François I's troops were sent to the region to eliminate the Vaudois who had settled primarily in the Luberon. Supported by the Baron of Oppède, president of the Parliament of Aix and led by Captain Polin, forces left Pertuis on April 16 of that year and destroyed 11 villages in six days. Nearly 3,000 were murdered, hanged or burned at the stake. Thousands sought refuge in the hills and isolated areas of the Vaucluse plateau or escaped to Italy.

The following centuries were relatively more peaceful, yet still marked by violence. As elsewhere, the 19th century saw economic growth. The importance of the region's agriculture was recognized, and an infrastructure (artisans, small commerce) emerged that supported the needs of the local population.

Nowadays, this region is untouched by the industrialization common in areas with towns and cities of greater importance. Agriculture is the main economic activity. Here, the noble professions of farming and sheep-herding continue to reign. Farmers work independently and rarely possess more than 30 hectares (74 acres) of land each. While driving or walking through the area, you will notice the variety of things grown. Two items predominate: vineyards in the valleys and lavender fields in the drier, higher areas.

Some villages seem to have been undisturbed for centuries. They are typically perched on the sides of limestone cliffs. As in the past, houses and activity now appear to centre around each village's church and château. However, both the Vaucluse plateau and the Luberon have changed since the 1970s when wealthy Parisians and Europeans bought second homes here. The residences and swimming pools of actors, politicians and industrialists are discretely hidden down silent paths, behind cyprus trees and protected gates. The invasion has had a positive effect—in 1977, the Parc Naturel Régional du Lubéron

The Olive Tree, Existent Since the Dawn of Time

The olive tree is so characteristic of the landscape of Provence that it is difficult to imagine that it did not always grow there. Although it had long existed as a wild species, it only began to be cultivated under the Phocaean colonists in the 6th century BC. Olive oil was commonly traded in antiquity, and had many different uses: as fuel for lamps, as an ointment, as a therapeutic balm and as a cooking ingredient. Its health benefits, known to the ancients, have been rediscovered today through pharmaceutical and dietary studies.

The olives used to make the oil are brought to the mill no more than three or four days after being picked so as to preserve their freshness. To obtain oil after the first cold pressing, the olives are ground into a thick paste. This paste is then spread out in thick layers on round mats piled on top of each other and pressed hard. A dark green, gold-tinged juice is extracted and placed directly into a centrifuge where the oil is separated from the water. Virgin olive oil is obtained directly from the fruit itself by a mechanical or physical process, with no chemical procedures, and falls into several categories. Only extra-virgin (an absolutely flawless flavour with an acidity level of no more than 1%) and virgin olive oil (a flawless flavour with an acidity level of no more than 2%) are obtained through cold pressing and are designated both as "virgin oil" and as a "natural product."

As with wine, many aspire to the prestigious designation of "Appellation d'Origine Contrôlée." There is an infinitely nuanced vocabulary to describe the various flavours and aromas of all these oils, each of which has a distinctive character derived by blending different types of olives at different stages of ripeness. There are about 630 different kinds of olives, some of which are destined for use in making sweets. Olives, in some form, are thus found on every table.

A small question to end with: are green and black olives two different varieties? In fact, they are not. The only difference is how long they have ripened, with black olives obviously being the riper of the two.

Plateau du Vaucluse and the Luberon

was created. The 120,000ha (296,400-acre) park became a conservation area where strict building regulations are imposed with the goal of preserving its fragile ecology and natural beauty.

Many of the newcomers are writers, artists or artisans who respect the land and want to keep the area undeveloped. Tourism now plays an important role in the local economy and is the sole livelihood for many owners of hotels, restaurants and shops. This particular region of Provence has been in the news so much since the 1980s that it has drawn hoards of tourists from as far as Australia and Japan. If at all possible, we suggest you travel in the early autumn, or best of all in May or June. Though you might miss the violet splendour of the fields of lavender in July and August, the fruit trees and flowers in bloom make for fantastic scenery, and accommodation is easier to find.

Finding Your Way Around

By Car

Due to the number of interesting small villages in relatively isolated spots, a car is necessary to fully explore the region properly. (A good selection of car rental agencies is found in Avignon and Marseille.)

The Vaucluse plateau is 40km (25mi) east of Avignon and 15km (9.3mi) east of Carpentras. By car, take the N100 (signposted "Apt") past L'Isle-sur-la-Sorgue and enter the area from the south (turn left onto the D2 north for Gordes; turn left onto the D4 north for Roussillon). Alternatively, from Avignon take the D942 to Carpentras and either continue on this road for the Gorges de la Nesque; or take the D4 south for Venasque and a scenic, though circuitous, route leading to Gordes and Roussillon from the north.

The westernmost part of the Luberon is 40km (25mi) east of Avignon. Three direct routes are possible, depending on your final destination. For villages in the north Luberon, including Oppède-le-Vieux, Ménerbes, Lacoste, Bonnieux and Apt, take the D100 east from Avignon (signposted "Apt") and turn where indicated. Alternatively, for the same villages, you can take the N7 east from Avignon. After 11km (6.8mi), continue on the same highway (the N7 turns sharply for Salon-de-Provence, which you don't want) which is now the D973 (signposted "Cavaillon"). After 4km (2.5mi), avoid the turn for Cavaillon and continue on the same highway which is now the D22 (signposted "Apt"). The D22 connects with the D100 after 18km (11mi).

A third option, useful for destinations in the southern parts of the Luberon, is to continue on the D973 circling Cavaillon. The D973 follows the banks of the Durance River towards Lourmarin, Cucuron and Ansouis.

Practical Information

Tourist Offices

Many village tourist offices offer informative guided tours lasting 1 to 2hrs and some provide local guides upon request. This is an excellent area for cycling and walking—if these activities interest

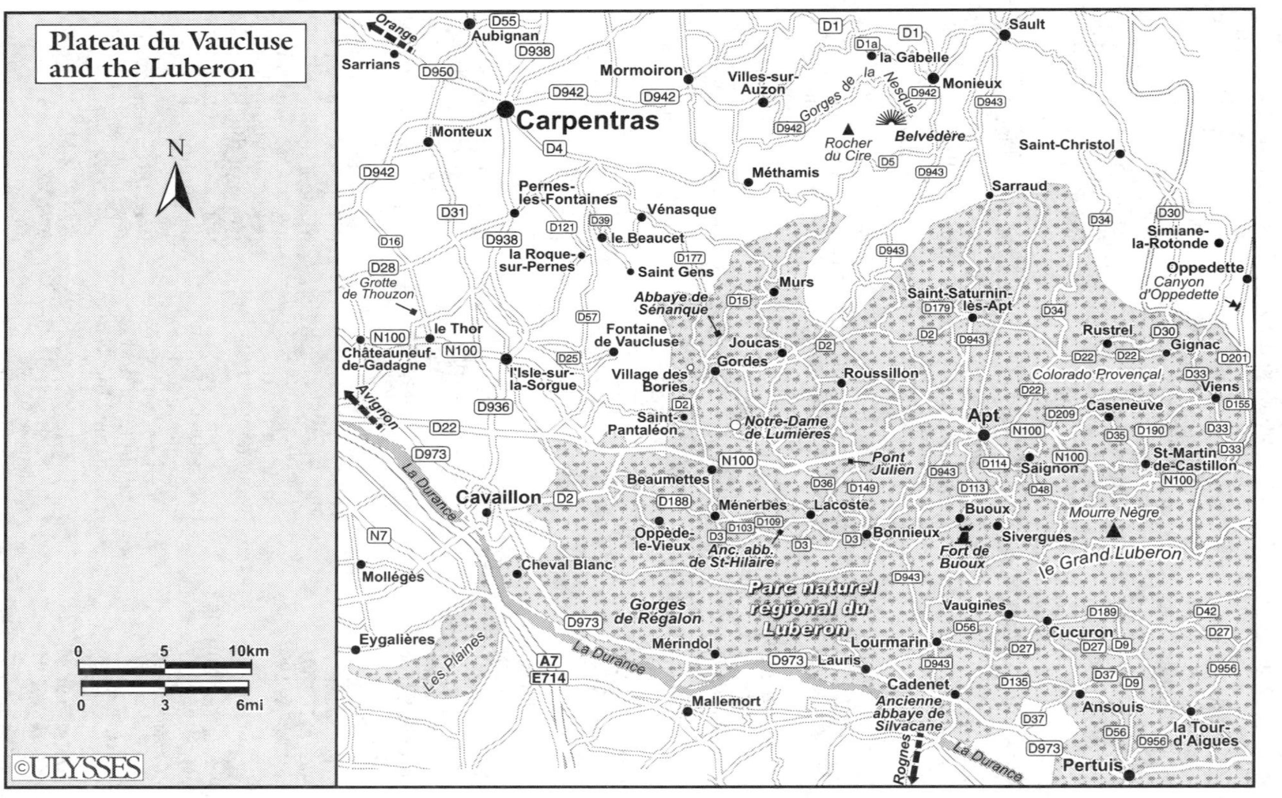
Plateau du Vaucluse
and the Luberon
N
0
5
10km
0
3
6mi
©ULYSSES
Orange
Sarrians
Aubignan
Carpentras
Monteux
Mormoiron
Villes-sur-Auzon
la Gabelle
Monieux
Sault
Gorges de la Nesque
Rocher du Cire
Belvédère
Méthamis
Saint-Christol
Sarraud
Simiane-la-Rotonde
Oppedette
Canyon d'Oppedette
Pernes-les-Fontaines
Vénasque
le Beaucet
la Roque-sur-Pernes
Saint Gens
Murs
Abbaye de Sénanque
Grotte de Thouzon
le Thor
Châteauneuf-de-Gadagne
l'Isle-sur-la-Sorgue
Fontaine de Vaucluse
Joucas
Gordes
Village des Bories
Roussillon
Saint-Saturnin-lès-Apt
Rustrel
Gignac
Colorado Provençal
Viens
Caseneuve
Apt
Avignon
Saint-Pantaléon
Notre-Dame de Lumières
Pont Julien
Saignon
St-Martin-de-Castillon
Beaumettes
Cavaillon
Ménerbes
Lacoste
Buoux
Bonnieux
Fort de Buoux
Sivergues
Mourre Nègre
Oppède-le-Vieux
Anc. abb. de St-Hilaire
le Grand Luberon
Cheval Blanc
Mollégès
Parc naturel régional du Luberon
Gorges de Régalon
Vaugines
Cucuron
Eygalières
Les Plaines
Mérindol
Lourmarin
Lauris
La Durance
Cadenet
Ancienne abbaye de Silvacane
Ansouis
Mallemort
Rognes
la Tour-d'Aigues
Pertuis
D55
D938
D950
D942
D1
D1a
D943
D4
D5
D31
D16
D28
D121
D39
D177
D15
D34
D30
D57
D25
D2
D179
D22
D201
D33
N100
D936
D209
D155
D190
D35
D973
D114
D36
D149
D113
D48
D188
D103
D109
D3
N7
D56
D189
D42
D27
D9
A7
E714
D135
D37
D956

you, contact the closest tourist office to obtain special maps and information about equipment rental.

Plateau du Vaucluse and Northern Luberon

Fontaine-de-Vaucluse
Chemin de la Fontaine
☎***04.90.20.32.22***
⇄***04.90.20.21.37***

Gordes
Place du Château
☎***04.90.72.02.75***
⇄***04.90.72.04.39***

L'Isle-sur-la-Sorgue
Place de l'Église
☎***04.90.38.04.78***

Pernes-les-Fontaines
Place de la Nesque
☎***04.90.61.31.04***
⇄***04.90.61.33.23***

Le Thor
Place du 11 Novembre
☎***04.90.33.92.31***

Venasque
Place de la Mairie
☎***04.90.66.11.66***

Cavaillon
79 Rue Saunerie
☎***04.90.71.32.01***
⇄***04.90.71.42.99***

Apt
Place Bouquerie, B.P. 15
☎***04.90.74.03.18***
⇄***04.90.04.64.30***

Bonnieux
7 Place Carnot B.P. 11
☎***04.90.75.91.90***
⇄***04.90.75.92.94***

Roussillon
Place de la Poste
☎***04.90.05.60.25***

South Luberon

Lourmarin
Avenue Philippe de Girard
☎***04.90.68.10.77***

Curcuron
Mairie Rue Léonce Brieugne
☎***04.90.77.28.37***

Ansouis
Hôtel de Ville
☎***04.90.09.96.12***
⇄***04.90.09.93.48***

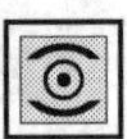

Exploring

The Plateau du Vaucluse

★★
L'Isle-sur-la-Sorgue

Two enchanting villages lie at the base of the Vaucluse plateau in the Comtat plain: L'Isle-sur-la Sorgue and Pernes-les-Fontaines. Canals run peacefully through both sites, making them pleasant stopping points before entering the nearby mountainous region.

L'Isle-sur-la-Sorgue is graced by a shallow canal system fed by the Sorgue River and is nicknamed the *Venise du Comtat* (the Venice of the Comtat). The first settlers here were fishers and they have since played a role in the town's history ever since. In the early 13th century, Raimond Bérenger VII granted the L'Isle-sur-la-Sorgue fishers the exclusive right to fish in the Sorgue, from its source to the Rhône. Nowadays, a *Roi de la Sorgue* (King of the Sorgue) is elected once a year. The town's street names reflect its fishy past—Rue de l'Anguille (eel), Rue de l'Écrevisse (crayfish) and Rue de la Truite (trout) for example.

You'll notice many waterwheels still in operation, reminders that L'Isle-sur-la-Sorgue was an important silk producer in the 17th century and paper manufacturer in the 19th century. The old city with its canals, streets shaded by plane trees and elegant buildings is best explored on foot.

Église Notre-Dame des Anges ★ *(Mon to Fri 10am to noon and 3pm to 6pm; Place de l'Église)* is a *collégiale* or collegiate church with a rich, 17th-century baroque interior, including a large ornate representation in gilded wood of the assumption and coronation of the Virgin Mary.

Hôtel Dieu *(free admission, must see concierge first, 10am to noon and 2pm to 6pm; ☎04.90.38.01.31)* Like the hospital in Carpentras, this 18th-century building has an interesting pharmacy with decorations painted by Duplessis and a fine collection of earthenware pots from Moustiers.

L'Isle-sur-la-Sorgue is an antique lover's paradise every Saturday and Sunday, year-round, when the entire town becomes an **antique and flea market** ★. This is the place to buy original glazed pottery jars in mustard yellow and green—for the same price as the mass-produced reproductions sold elsewhere. Many locals come here for Provençal furniture and objects for the home and garden. Whether you spend a little or a lot, the festive atmosphere in the streets is unbeatable (see p 158).

Pernes-les-Fontaines

Pernes-les-Fontaines is so named because of the 36 old fountains that dot this town. Once the capital of the papal territory Comtat Venaissin (968-1320), Pernes became an important community following the installation in the château in 1125 of the representatives of the counts of Toulouse (called *Sénéchaux*). Ramparts were built during the 15th and 16th centuries to protect the townspeople from plunderers, the Vaudois and carriers of the plague.

Only the rampart gates remain today (the walls were destroyed in the 19th century)—the most striking is the 16th-century **Porte Notre Dame** ★ *(Quai de Verdun, next to the Nesque river)*. At this spot, note the **Fontaine Cormorant** (built in 1761 and named after the bird on top) and the **Pont Notre** with the 16th-century chapel apparently stuck on one side. Across the river is the old **château** of the counts of Toulouse, where just the castle keep and wrought-iron cage bell tower remain. The sober **Église Notre-Dame-de-Nazareth** stands next to the square of the same name and dates from the 11th century.

Guided visits to the interesting **Tour Ferrande** *(15F, 20F for a combined tour of this sight and Tour de l'Horloge; Rue des Barbes; advance registration at the tourist office is required)*, a crenellated 18th-century structure that was originally attached to a large home, are also available. Frescoes from the same period can be seen inside it, as may the lovely **Musée du Costume Comtadin** *(free; Jul to Sep; corner of Rue de la République and Rue Victor-Hugo)*, which opened in 1991 in the abandoned shop of 19th-century clothing merchant Augustin Benoît Marbaud. Dresses, slips, lace bonnets and locally made cotton eiderdowns are exhibited here, all in an old-fashioned shop atmosphere. Even when closed, its display window is worth a look.

The Pernes tourist office provides a free map giving the names and dates of the fountains. Beware that you don't drink the water from the Fontaine de la Lune (of the moon) opposite the 14th-century Porte St-Giles. Legend has that it makes people *lunatique*, or crazy!

Le Thor

Le Thor *(5km or 3.1mi west of L'Isle-sur-la-Sorgue on the N100)* is a little burg that was founded in the 7th century. Its main attraction resides in the austere Église Notre-Dame-du-Lac; built in the 13th century. The church possesses only one nave, but nonetheless constitutes a remarkable example of Romanesque ecclesiastical architecture. Also take note of Porte Notre-Dame, which was transformed into a clock and bell tower in 1847.

Not far from Le Thor *(3km or 1.9mi on the D16)* is a subterranean cave, **Grotte de Thouzon** *(32F; Mar and Nov, Sun 2pm to 6pm; Apr 1 to Oct 31, every day 10am to noon and 2pm to 6pm; Jul and Aug 9:30am to 7pm; ☎04.90.33.93.65, ⇄04.90.33.74.90)*, which was formed naturally in the side of a chalky hill in the Cretaceous geological period. It was discovered in 1902. A guided tour leads visitors along a narrow path, explains the cave's strange rock formations and occasions the opportunity to see stalactites and stalagmites up close. Be aware that this is a privately run attraction; the commentary, although interesting, sometimes runs to the banal, and the 5min *son et lumière* "show" adds little to the experience.

★★ Venasque

Venasque is positioned on top of a steep-sided rocky crag overlooking the Nesque valley and Carpentras plain. This strategic location made Venasque the ideal second residence for the bishops of Carpentras, who came here (from the 6th to the 11th century) to escape Barbarian invasions in Carpentras. Nowadays, this charming village is worth a visit for its pretty streets, marvellous views and historical interest.

Most interesting is the **Baptistère** ★★ *(guided tour 10F; Thu to Tue 10am to noon and 3pm to 7pm; next to Église Notre-Dame)*, considered to be the oldest religious building in the region, and some say in all of France. Its origins are not clear. Legend indicates that a pagan building occupied the site during Roman times and that a sanctuary was built here in the 6th century (Merovingian period) by Saint-Siffrein de Lérins, who was consecrated Bishop of Venasque before 542 AD. The stone building was rebuilt in the 12th century and used as an episcopal funeral church. Its structure follows the Greek cruciform design: four semi-circular vaulted apses face a central square, with a hollow basin most likely used as a baptismal font. The north apse is the oldest, and its slender columns came from Roman temples.

Église Notre-Dame *(year-round, 9am to 7pm; Place de l'Église)* was built in the 12th century (only a semicircular apse remains from this era) and was expanded in the 13th, 17th and 18th centuries. The second chapel on the left displays an Avignon School painting of the Crucifixion, commissioned in 1498 by Seigneur Jean de Thézan on the occasion of his marriage with Siffreine de Venasque.

Vestiges of the ramparts that once surrounded the village are visible on the town perimeter, and a very beautiful 18th-century fountain is worth a look *(Place de la Fontaine)*. Just next to the latter stand three towers, the tallest of them reaching 18m (59ft); these were erected to defend the village, but they have gradually deteriorated over the years. Some of their stones were even used to build nearby houses and a neighbouring school.

Chapelle Notre-Dame-de-Vie lies at the foot of Venasque on Route D4. This little 17th-century temple encloses the tombstone of Boethius, Bishop of Carpentras, who died in the year 604. The structure's name was inspired by the ritual practice of baptizing stillborn children—it is said that they momentarily came back to life to receive the blessing—permitting their souls to ascend to heaven. This ceremony took place in a chapel that stood on this same site in the 6th century. A Carmelite convent now occupies the premises.

★ Le Beaucet

Near Venasque lies the picturesque village of Le Beaucet (one-way road D39 south), which is perched on a cliff-side and dominated by the ruins of a 12th-century château (built for the Carpentras bishops). Unfortunately, the 80 steps linking the village to the château are usually closed due to falling rocks or landslides, though you can see the ruined castle-keep, four walls of a chapel, cisterns and the drawbridge. A popular pilgrimage in memory of the 12th-century hermit Gens Bournareau has taken place in the area at midnight every May 16 since the 15th century. Gens was sainted for his miraculous ability to bring rain to the dry valley. During the pilgrimage, the hermit's statue is carried from the church in his birthplace of Monteux (near Carpentras) to the Saint-Gens Hermitage 15km (9.3mi) from Le Beaucet. Relics of Saint-Gens are found in the Hermitage, and the natural spring (*fontaine*) supposedly discovered by the hermit is marked along a pathway. An important artisans workshop is found at Le Beaucet, which holds internships promoting conservation and craft techniques *(information from Monsieur H. Morel, Les Ateliers du Beaucet, Centre Internationale de Formation en Métiers d'Art, 84210 Le Beaucet, ☎04.90.66.10.61).*

★★
Fontaine-de-Vaucluse

South of the village of Roque-sur-Pernes on the D57, and just 7km (4.3mi) from L'Isle-sur-la-Sorgue along the D25, lies Fontaine-de-Vaucluse. By following on foot the Chemin de la Fontaine pathway next to a pretty canal, past the tourist office and T-shirt vendors, you arrive at the famous natural spring from where the Rivière Sorgue originates. Set amongst a lush gorge, the spring is the most powerful in France and fifth most powerful in the world (it pumps out 630 million m^3 (22,248,119,250 cubic ft) of water a year on average). Winter and particularly the spring are the most spectacular times to see it in action—$90m^3$ (3,178 cubic ft) of water gushs out every second and pours down the river bed. During the summer, when the spout is low, you can see a calm, deep blue basin and appreciate the surrounding sheer cliff, eroded and sculpted by the powerful water. Divers have plunged as far as 205m (673ft) below the surface (the German Hasenmeyer in 1983), and exploratory measuring instruments have been dropped, but the spring's origin remains a mystery. Speleologists have discovered a complex underwater network in the limestone rock, aided by rain and melting snow from Mont Ventoux and the Vaucluse plateau in the springtime.

However, the spring is not the only thing to see here. In the 14th century, the Italian poet Petrarch stayed in Fontaine-de-Vaucluse many times and commissioned the construction of a cliff-side house on the other bank of the river, across the old bridge. It has been converted into a museum, **Musée Pétrarque** *(10F; Apr 15 to Oct 15, Wed to Mon, Sat and Sun for rest of year; left bank of the Sorgue; ☎04.90.20.37.20)*, dedicated to his work (collections of his writings explain the Petrarchan movement) and to his repeated sojourns in the Vaucluse. It also displays a small collection of modern art emphasizing humanist themes, including prints by Braque, Miro and Picasso. Petrarch's writings include the wonderful collection of sonnets *Canzonière*, which were inspired by a sighting of his beloved, Laure Chiabau, wife of Hugues de Sade, on April 6th, 1327 at Église Sainte-Claire d'Avignon.

Set on the site of an ancient pagan temple, right in the village, **Église Sainte-Marie et Saint-Véran**, which dates back to the 11th century, constitutes a beautiful illustration of Provençal Romanesque architecture with its groined vault and its three semicircular apses. In the chapel, it is possible to see the 2m-long (6.6ft) coffin of Saint Véran, a sixth-century hermit who introduced Christianity to the region and later became bishop of Carpentras.

Between the village and the fountain, three

museums of some interest succeed one another. Next to a large wooden paddle wheel, **Moulin Vallis Clausa** *(free; Chemin de la Fontaine, ☎04.90.20.31.72)* is a living museum dedicated to paper. A paper mill operated on this site from 1686 to 1887, and the Vallis Clausa today highlights traditional paper-making methods from the Middle Ages to the industrial age. A shop sells all sorts of paper goods made on the premises.

Musée du Santon *(20F; year-round, every day 10am to 12:30pm and 2pm to 6:30pm; Nov 15 to Feb afternoons only; in Galerie du Vallis Clausa, next to the mill, ☎04.90.20.20.83)* displays an incredible collection of over 1,000 old and new terracotta figurines, as well as Christmas crèches.

Musée de la Résistance *(10F; Apr 15 to Jun 30 and Sep 1 to Oct 15, Wed to Mon 10am to noon and 2pm to 6pm; Jul 1 to Aug 31, Wed to Mon 10am to 8pm; Oct 16 to Dec 31, Sat and Sun 10am to noon and 1pm to 5pm; Mar 1 to Apr 14, Sat and Sun 10am to noon and 2pm to 6pm; closed Jan and Feb; Chemin du Gouffre, ☎04.90.20.24.00)* deals with daily life under the German occupation during the Second World War and explains the role of the Resistance in the Vaucluse in a surprisingly interesting and modern fashion. The exhibition was designed by Willy Hot, who was the set designer for the film *Camille Claudel*.

Musée Norbert Casteret *(guided tour 27F; Feb to Apr and Sep to Nov, Wed to Sun 10am to noon and 2pm to 5pm; May to Aug, every day 10am to noon and 2pm to 6pm; closed Jan and Feb; Chemin de la Fontaine, ☎04.90.20.34.13)*, dedicated to the famous speleologist, re-creates an entire subterranean world with stalactites and stalagmites, waterfalls and prehistoric paintings.

A strong word of caution: Fontaine-de-Vaucluse is extremely crowded in the summer months and the souvenir stands along the Chemin de la Fontaine give the village an unfortunate touristy spirit.

★★★ Gorges de la Nesque

The Gorges de la Nesque is a spectacular canyon 400m-deep (1,312ft), carved into the Vaucluse plateau. Once inhabited by Paleolithic man, Celts and Ligurians, then by the Romans, the gorges offer marvellous panoramic views, unobstructed by evidence of modern humankind. A short half-day drive around an irregular circular route may start at either the village of Villes-sur-Auzon in the west or the town of Sault in the east.

Villes-sur-Auzon *(5km or 3,1mi east of Mormoiron on the D942)* is a charming village punctuated by the vestiges of ramparts, many fountains and adorable houses. Take the D1 in the direction of Sault and turn onto the more scenic, secondary Route D1A, which crosses the hamlet of La Gabelle before rejoining the D1. In **Sault**, pause in the little park that borders Avenue de la Promenade, from which there is a splendid view of the hills of Sault and of the Vallée de la Nesque. Here visitors will find the ruins of a castle; the Église de la Transfiguration (formerly called Église Saint-Sauveur), which dates back to the 12th century and prides itself on its rare groin-vaulted nave; and interesting houses constructed as early as the Middle Ages, interspersed with some beautiful 18th-century mansions. A large lavender fair is held here *(Aug; for information contact the Office de Tourisme, Avenue de la Promenade, 84390 Sault, ☎04.90.64.01.21)*, as is an attractive market that has run continuously every Wednesday since 1515. Finally, Sault is famous for its honey (often lavender honey) and its delicious nougat (see "Shopping," p 159).

Turn back along the D1 and after 2.5km (1.6mi), catch the D942 towards **Monnieux**. The village's Saint-Pierre church is Romanesque with later additions, and the ruins of a 12th-century watchtower can be seen as well. Carry on the D942 for 20km (12.4mi) back to Villes-sur-Auzon. This is the most impressive section of the Gorges de la Nesque. Along the twisty, steep road, you will pass a viewpoint (marked "Belvédère") overlooking the rock known as the Rocher de Cire (872m or 2,861ft) and drive through three short tunnels.

Gordes and the Petit Luberon

The Petit Luberon is indeed smaller—though no less spectacular—than the Grand Luberon mountain range due east. A number of typical Provençal towns perched on the cliffsides are found north of the Petit Luberon.

★ Gordes

One of the best known of these towns is Gordes. Its blond, drystone houses are arranged precariously around the edge of the Vaucluse plateau facing the Luberon hills. Panoramic views of both Gordes and the Luberon hills in the distance are best from the viewpoint on the D15 before entering the village. Gordes was once a centre for the pre-Roman indigenous peoples called the Vordeuses—hence the village's name (it has nothing to do with gourds!). Worth discovering are the pretty drystone houses dating from the 16th to the 18th century and cobble-stone pathways that encircle the Place du Château and the 18th-century Église Saint-Firmin. The community has been spoiled by the influx of wealthy people owning second homes in the area, as well as by tourism. For the most part, Gordes' restaurants and accommodations are over-priced and overrated.

The massive Renaissance **Château de Gordes** (1525-1541) with prominent circular towers was once a 12th-century fortress. The long dining room on the first floor has an immense stone fireplace more than 7m-long (23ft) with an ornate chimney.

Classified as a historical monument, the **Village des Bories** ★ *(35F; every day 9am to sunset; follow the signposted road at the junction of D15 and D2, south of Gordes, ☎04.90.72.03.48)* is a hamlet of curious shaped, drystone shelters with peaked roofs. Though the building technique was derived from neolithic period structures, most of the *bories* date from the 16th to the 19th century. They were usually used as shelters by shepherds and hunters and are found throughout the region. Yet as is visible here, self-sufficient communities lived in *bories*. On display are five groups of habitations, which include sheep pens, ovens for baking bread, and two-tiered living quarters with everyday objects such as wine vats and eating utensils.

Set in a verdant vale next to a field of lavender, the **Abbaye de Sénanque** ★★★ *(30F; Mar to Oct, Mon to Sat 10am to noon and 2pm to 6pm, Sun and Catholic holidays afternoons only; Nov to Feb, Mon to Fri 2pm to 5pm, Sat and Sun and school holidays 2pm to 6pm; Mass Sun 9am, Mon to Fri noon; 4km or 2.5mi north of Gordes on the D177, ☎04.90.72.05.72)* is one of the most remarkable monuments in Provence. Founded in 1148, the abbey is an exceptional example of austere Cistercian architecture. Its plan is based on a combination of squares and circles within each other. Though still an active Cistercian abbey, the public may visit the fully-restored, 12th-century buildings. There is a bookstore and a gift shop selling honey and lavender essence made at the abbey, plus the Sénancole liqueur invented by the monk

Marie Maurice. Because of Abbaye Sénanque's importance, it gets crowded during peak times.

Saint-Pantaléon

Saint-Pantaléon is a pleasant village south of Gordes that is enhanced by a graceful 12th-century Romanesque chapel. Olive-oil lovers will not want to miss the fascinating **Moulin des Bouillons** museum. Established in an old mas, it shelters one of the earliest surviving olive presses (16th century) made from the trunk of an oak tree. Through a series of display cases, the museum illustrates the process of making oil and the history of the valiant olive tree. Just next door is **Musée du Vitrail**, which mainly exhibits contemporary stained-glass works by Frédérique Duran and briefly recounts the history of the workshop. *(One ticket covers admission to both museums: 15F; Wed to Mon 10am to noon and 2pm to 6pm, closed Dec 15 to Feb 15; Route D 148, 5km or 3.1mi south of Gordes near Saint-Pantaléon, ☎04.90.72.22.11).*

Kit fox

★★ Roussillon

Rousillon is a splendid village perched high amongst the striking ochre quarries and rich green pine forests in the surrounding Fées valley. The ochre industry thrived in the late 19th century, reached its peak in the 1920s when 40,000 tons a year was quarried and is now no longer in operation. The ochre pigment is produced by separating then grinding the iron-oxide deposits in the earth into a dry powder. It is used in paint, cosmetics, food colouring (it's non-toxic) and plaster. As you'll see, Roussillon's houses are tinted with the rich ochre earth in hues ranging from pale yellow to rich red, while their doorways and windows are colourfully painted.

A couple of cafés face the shaded village square (Place de la Mairie), next to the town hall. A pretty pathway from this square winds up under an attractive bell tower (once a fortified gateway) with a typical wrought-iron bell cage, and leads to the simple Romanesque Église Saint-Michel. Follow a pathway behind the church to discover wonderful panoramic views facing north toward Mont Ventoux and the Alps. Other good viewpoints greet visitors at every turn.

The little villages of Joucas *(D102 to D102A)* and Murs *(D102A to D4)* lie a few kilometres north of Roussillon. **Joucas** possesses lovely winding roads lined by attractive houses, an 18th-century church and an interesting view of the ochre hills that rise to the south. As for **Murs**, it was the birthplace Crillon le Brave, a famous soldier under Henri IV, whose house *(now converted into a small museum of prehistory; information at the restaurant Crillon, ☎04.90.72.02.03)* flanks the Romanesque church. This village his a restored 15th-century castle, as well as what remains of the Mur de Peste, a wall erected in 1721 to protect the region from the plague.

Cavaillon

This town, famous for the delicious melons grown nearby in the Rivière Durance valley, lies at the edge of the Comtat plain at the approach to the Petit Luberon. As Cavaillon stands at the crossroads of such major roads as the D973 from Avignon and Aix-en-Provence, the D938 from L'Isle-sur-la-Sorgue, Pernes-les-Fontaines and

Carpentras and the A7 from Marseille, you're liable to circle around the town at some point in your trip. With so many interesting areas to visit in the region, there is no need to go right into Cavaillon if your visit to Provence is limited.

Melon

Incidently, the true Cavaillon melon is not a cantaloupe, which it closely resembles, but the smaller, rounder and sweeter *charentais*, with a smooth, pale-green outer skin.

Cavaillon proves to have been a very important market town, and some of its monuments attest to the role it likely played in the ancient history of Provence. First populated in the Neolithic Age, the town became a Roman colony in 42 BC, when it was named Cabellio. On Place François Tourel, opposite Place du Clos, lie the remains of a **Roman triumphal arch** that dates from the first century, which was moved and reconstructed at this site over 100 years ago. Behind it, a path leads to the little 12th-century Chapelle Saint-Jacques *(visits possible in the afternoon, ask the guard)* and then to the summit of **Colline Saint-Jacques**, offering a sumptuous view of the surrounding mountains *(the hilltop can also be reached by car via Cours Carnot and Route d'Avignon, namely the D938)*.

Cathédrale Saint-Véran *(every day; Place Joseph D'Arbaud, entrance at the south door)* dates originally from the 12th century, but certain additions were made in the 14th century and it was renovated from the 17th to the 19th century. Its ornately vaulted cloister and the golden wood panelling in its side chapels are worth seeing.

The elegant, Louis-XV-style **Synagogue** *(20F; Apr 1 to Sep 30, Wed to Mon 10am to noon and 2pm to 6pm; Oct 1 to Mar 31, 10am to noon and 2pm to 5pm; Rue Hébralque, next to Rue Chabran, ☎04.90.76.00.34; the same ticket is good for admission to the Musée Archéologique, Cours Gambetta; same schedule)* was built in the 18th century and is a reminder that Cavaillon was once home to a small Jewish community—one of only four in all of Provence under the reign of the Catholic popes, the others being those of Avignon, Carpentras and L'Isle-sur-la-Sorgue.

In the synagogue's old bakery there is an interesting little museum, the **Musée Judéo-Comtadin**, which relates the life of Jews in the Comtat Venaissin during this difficult period of intolerance and persecution. Ritual objects and historical documents are exhibited next to the marble block and the oven that were used to prepare unleavened bread.

The Petit Luberon South

A cluster of pretty villages in the Petit Luberon, south of the N100, manage to retain a natural charm and are less frequented than popular places farther north, such as Gordes, Roussilon and L'Isle-sur-la-Sorgue.

★★ Oppède-le-Vieux

A tiny community built on the peak of a rocky crag 12m (39.4ft) east of Cavaillon on the D176, Oppède-le-Vieux appears hidden amongst overgrown vegetation and pine trees. Access to the old village is by a well-marked pathway, leading up to the church and farther on the ruins of a Middle Age château, from which there are good panoramic views. Once abandoned, the hamlet has been gradually restored since the 1950s. Work has focused primarily on a few mansions dating from the 15th and 16th century and, more recently, the pretty 12th century church. There is little activity in Oppède, so enjoy the peaceful village square and cobblestone roads. The village once suffered a bad reputation because the château belonged to Baron Maynier, who authorized the massacre of the Vaudois people in 1545 (see p 132).

★★

Ménerbes

Passing along the D188 at the junction of the D103 lies Ménerbes. Built on a hilltop, it was the capital for the Protestant movement during the Wars of Religion in Provence in the 16th century. After the fall of other Protestant communities in the Luberon, the movement resisted French forces for over five years in the late 1580s before surrendering. Nowadays, visitors can see the 14th-century church, the imposing 12th- to 15th-century citadel and discover the magnificent old houses and charming cobblestone streets. Ménerbes is the birthplace of the Republican poet Clovis Huges, and the artist Nicholas de Staël lived in one of the village's two châteaux.

The attractive **Musée du Tire-Bouchon** *(30F; Jul and Aug, every day 10am to noon and 2pm to 7pm; off-season, 10am to noon and 2pm to 6pm except Sat afternoon and Sun; ☎04.90.72.41.58)*, a private museum exclusively devoted to corkscrews, appears on Route D103 Nord (in the direction of Beaumettes), on the wine-producing property of the Domaine de la Citadelle. Over 1,000 specimens in wood, bronze, gold and silver, from France, England, Germany, the Netherlands and the United States are displayed. Visitors are informed that this handy tool was invented in the 17th century in France (naturally!).

On the left side of the D103, 2km (1.2mi) south of Ménerbes, in the direction of Bonnieux and before the intersection with the D3 stands one of the Vaucluse's rare dolmens, which is actually one of the region's smallest as well. This prehistoric monument, composed of a stone lain horizontally across two other vertical ones bears the name **Dolmen de Pitchoun**, or **Pitchouno**.

The ancient **Abbaye de Saint-Hilaire** *(private property, afternoon visits by appointment; ☎04.90.75.88.83)*, which contains one small 12th-century chapel and another, vaulted chapel that dates back to the 13th century, appears on the D109, on the outskirts of Lacoste. On August 15 every year, a high mass is celebrated here in honour of Saint Louis.

Lacoste

Lacoste, 6km (3.7mi) east of Ménerbes on the D109, is famous as the home of the erotic writer Donatien-Alphonse-François, the Marquis de Sade, who penned *120 Days of Sodom* and *Justine*,. He fled a scandal in Paris caused by his libertine ways to his grandfather's château at Lacoste in 1771. He was imprisoned and condemned to death following later escapades and died in the Charenton asylum near Paris. The extraordinary château (dating from the 11th century) is now owned by a professor who has been restoring it for more than three decades *(visits on weekends can be arranged by contacting the owner, Monsieur André Bouër, ☎04.90.75.80.39)*.

Lacoste has many sloping cobbled streets and pretty blond-limestone houses (though a few are in a state of sad disrepair), spanning out from the main street Rue Basse. It is happily less frequented than other towns in the area. A striking view of Bonnieux across a valley can be had from the east side of the village.

★
Bonnieux

Bonnieux is a charming village with tiers of terracotta-roofed houses tumbling down a cliff side over the Calavon valley. It occupied a strategic position on the principal route between Italy and Spain during the Roman occupation of Provence. During the Middle Ages, the town moved up the hill to its actual site. Ramparts and towers were built during the 13th and 14th centuries to keep out marauding tribes (some ruins remain). The Catholic *Bonnieulais*, as the village's residents are called, held a certain animosity towards their Protestant neighbours in Lacoste. Some beautiful 16th-, 17th- and 18th-century mansions remind us that Bonnieux was once prosperous, when the Comtat Venaissin belonged to the Popes. Many bishops chose Bonnieux as their place of residence from the 14th century until the Revolution, and it therefore received special privileges. The town hall (Rue de la Mairie) occupies the former 18th-century residence Hôtel de Rouville.

Visit the **Musée de la Boulangerie** *(20F; Jun to Sep, Wed to Mon 10am to noon and 3pm to 6:30pm; Oct to May, Sat, Sun and holidays only; 12 Rue de la République, ☎04.90.75.88.34)* to discover the machines, techniques, posters and history of bread baking, as well as a surprising collection of different types of loaves in a former bakery.

A 12th-century Romanesque church simply called the **Vieille Église**, surrounded by beautiful cedar trees, dominates the upper ground *(follow 86 stone steps, contact the Tourist Office to visit inside)*. There are **good panoramic views** ★ from the small park, once the church's cemetery, looking north towards Gordes and Rousillon. The so-called new church (1870s) is located at the lower end of Bonnieux. It houses four 16th-century paintings in the primitive style representing the Passion and originating from the old church.

Don't miss the small Roman bridge *(9.6km or 6mi north of Bonnieux on the D149, next to the N100)* that crosses the Calavon river. Built in the year 3 BC, in cut stone without the use of mortar, the **Pont Julien** ★ is still in good condition. Its three arches span 70m (230ft).

Had enough of old churches and ratatouille? Head for **Galerie de la Gare** *(Easter to Oct 15, Wed to Mon 2:30pm to 6:30pm; between Bonnieux and Goult on a secondary road that branches off the D36 just south of the N100)*, a bright and airy art gallery that showcases temporary exhibitions of stimulating works by contemporary painters and sculptors. Just next door, Restaurant de la Gare serves drinks and light meals.

The Grand Luberon

Apt

Apt is an important commercial centre, serving the entire Grand Luberon area. It is famous for its lively Saturday morning Provençal market (Place des Martyrs-de-la-Résistance) where you can buy a mesmerizing array of local products, including hand made pottery. The town and its neighbouring communities are renowned for their colourful hand made ceramic tiles (called *carreaux d'Apt*) and pottery (see "Shopping," p 159), fruit jams and *confits* (delicious preserved fruits). Apart from these pleasures, Apt is not of great interest to tourists, as recent buildings have blotted the landscape.

The **old town**, surrounded by its old stone walls, has a few fountains, chapels and houses from the 16th, 17th and 18th centuries, and a beautiful **clock tower** *(Rue des Mar-*

chands) built in the 16th century that stands next to the cathedral. A chapel in the 12th and 14th century, **Cathédrale Sainte-Anne** *(Tue to Sat 9am to 11am and 4:30pm to 6:30pm, Sun 9am to 11am; Place de la Cathédrale)*, was added in 1660 after a visit by Anne of Austria during a pilgrimage; note as well the first- and 11th-century crypts and the treasury. The comprehensive **Musée d'Archéologie** *(10F; Oct to May, Mon and Wed 2pm to 5pm, Sat 10am to noon; Jun to Sep, Mon to Sat 10am to noon and 2pm to 5pm, Sun 10am to noon; 4 Rue de l'Amphithéâtre, ☎04.90.04.74.65)* contains a nice collection of items dating from prehistory and Gallo-Roman times, the remains of a Roman theatre, as well as a fine selection of Apt and Moustiers ceramics.

The **headquarters of the Parc Naturel Régional du Luberon ★** is based here *(Sep to Jun, Mon to Sat 8:30am to noon and 2pm to 6pm; Jul and Aug, until 7pm; Oct to Easter, closed Sat; 60 Place Jean Jaurès, ☎04.90.04.42.00)*. This is the place to pick up information about the many fascinating hiking trails or to book guided walking tours throughout the Luberon hills. Interesting exhibitions take place every year, based on regional themes. In addition, plus a permanent display in a cave-like setting describes the evolution of fossil life. For nature lovers, the gift shop offers an excellent selection of books on the Luberon and its walking trails, wildlife and history.

★★ Rustrel and the Colorado

Ten kilometres (6.1mi) northeast of Apt is the tiny village of **Rustrel** (along the D22) which was the centre for ochre production 100 years ago, and just prior to that, an important iron ore industry. A 17th-century château houses Rustrel's town hall. The main interest today is the nearby **Colorado Provençal ★★**. Lying south of the D22 road, between Rustrel and the hamlet of Gignac by the Dôa river, are a number of pathways leading to this incredible series of rust-coloured rocks jutting towards the sky in strange configurations, as well as to ochre quarries and numerous viewing points. Here, more than ever, one understands why the multi-coloured ground is called *terres d'ocres, de sang et d'or* (earth of ochre, blood and gold). The Colorado is only reached on foot, but the paths are clearly marked. The highlight is the cleverly named Cheminées de Fées (Fairies' Chimney). The Roussillon Tourist Office sells an informative booklet called *Circuits de Découverte du Colorado Provençal* by local expert, François Morénas *(30F)*.

Viens

A string of isolated, peaceful villages, each numbering no more than a few hundred residents, begins east of Apt. **Caseneuve** and **Saint-Martin-de-Castillon** are found between the D209 and the N100 on the D35, a narrow secondary road. Further along, at the junction of the D209 and the D33, the medieval town of **Viens** stands on the site it has occupied for over a millennium. This is a good place to stop, since Viens possesses a post office, bakery, small grocery store and restaurant-café with a lush patio, not to mention especially welcoming townspeople.

The **town hall** *(Place de l'Ormeau, ☎04.90.75.20.02, ≠04.90.75.31.10)* sells a photocopied brochure outlining an interesting walking tour of the village *(10F)*. Sights of note here include the village gate and its clock tower, the panoramic view that can be had from next to the renovated 16th-century castle and, on Chemin du Cimetière, Église Saint-Hilaire (16th and 17th centuries, flamboyant baroque altar) with its Romanesque Chapelle Saint-Ferréol *(open for services only, the first, third and fifth Sat of the month)*. Also take a look at the communal oven on Rue Notre-Dame, which was donated to the town in 1357 by Seigneur de Viens, Augier de Forcalquier. Villagers came here to bake dough they had prepared at home up until the 19th century.

Oppedette

North of Viens, along a winding narrow road (D201) past the pretty **Oppedette Canyon ★★**, is a village seemingly perched at the end of the world. Called Oppedette, it was once a Ligurian community before the Roman occupation of Provence. Not much is here—stone houses, a tiny café and a small 12th-century church (closed to the public). The perilous gorges along the Calavon river surrounding the village once sheltered Protestants fleeing persecution during the Wars of Religion.

Buoux

In the hills of the Grand Luberon, south of Apt and the N100, rests the charming village of Buoux. It possesses a château now owned by the Parc Naturel Régional du Luberon, as well as an 18th-century church.

The rugged surrounding area abounds with grottos and steep cliffs rising above the jagged Aigue Brun river. It is popular with professional rock climbers. Amongst the gorges nearby is **Fort de Buoux ★★** *(10F, every day sunrise to sunset; follow the signs along the D113 south of the village, cross over a bridge after a holiday camp—there is a car park next to the path leading to the fort which is only accessible by foot so wear siutable shoes, ☎04.90.74.25.75).* On top of the plateau are the ruins of a 14th- and 15th-century fort. The ruins of ramparts, an old village, fortress walls and a Romanesque chapel can be seen. Note the curious stone silos dug into the ground, a hidden stone staircase and, along the pathway, numerous tombs built into the rock face. The site has been a natural defence since prehistory; it was a Protestant stronghold in the 16th century but was destroyed in part soon after.

★★
Saignon

Saignon is a peaceful spot overlooking the Calavon valley with a very pretty Romanesque church called Notre-Dame (opposite the town hall), château ruins, a pottery workshop, and a tinkling fountain next to a charming small hotel-restaurant on the village square. In other words, this is a fine place to stop for a couple of nights and discover the Luberon's sites and walking trails. (Just don't tell too many people—Saignon is not over-run with visitors.) Hikers will enjoy climbing up to the **Mourre Nègre ★★** (1,125m or 3,691ft), the highest peak in the Grand Luberon. Stunning panoramas of the entire Vaucluse area greet you at the top (small car park 4km or 2.5mi south of Saignon, access by foot along the marked GR92 path).

Sivergues

Sivergues is an isolated hamlet 9km (5.6mi) south of Saignon that can only be reached by a small, winding road that branches off from the D232. The splendid sawtooth mountains that circle the village are alternately covered by forests and heather, and sheep farming is the region's main economic activity. Although the area has been inhabited since the fifth century, the town proper has only existed since the 16th century, in the era when the seven Vaudois families established themselves here. Their cemetery (Enclos de Cimetière) is found below the village. Sivergues is dominated by a small castle, the Castellas, and it is possible to explore the town's church (late 16th century) and its houses, as well as the ruins of Église Saint-Tropime (12th century).

★

Lourmarin

The picturesque **road D943** ★★ between Bonnieux and Cadenet winds through the Aiguebrun Valley, between the Petit and Grand Luberon. Surrounded by vineyards, olive and almond trees lies the village of Lourmarin. Livelier than its neighbours, you'll find a few cafés, bars, shops selling regional specialties and a couple of good restaurants. Locals like to point out that Nobel Prize winner Albert Camus lived and wrote here (he is buried in Lourmarin's cemetery). Needless to say, with all this activity amid such a pleasant setting, Lourmarin is popular with tourists during peak periods.

Apart from a Romanesque church, a temple and the pretty streets with their fountains, Lourmarin's principal site is the 15th-16th-century **château** ★ *(30F; Oct to Jun, every day guided tours at 11am, 2:30pm, 3:30pm and 4:30pm; Jul to Sep at 11am, 11:30am and every 30min 3pm to 6pm; Nov to Jun, closed Tue; ☎04.90.68.15.23)*. One wing is occupied by the École des Beaux Arts d'Aix-en-Provence, but visitors are offered an informative guided tour through the interesting Renaissance part with curious staircases, beautifully furnished apartments, a music room and two large stone fireplaces.

Curcuron

Seven kilometres (4.3mi) east of Lourmarin along the D56 is Curcuron. This is a peaceful village with an interesting clock tower and stone gate (remains of a 16th-century defensive wall) and some attractive houses. A magnificent 17th-century retable above the altar and a lifesize painted wooden statue of Christ, bound and pierced with thorns, rest in the 12th-14th- century **Église Notre-Dame de Beaulieu** ★. Lower down, next to a café, is a large rectangular water basin (called l'*Etang* or pond, and rather cloudy!) nicely bordered by tall plane trees.

★★

Ansouis

Further east is the village of Ansouis, which has a splendid 12th-century private residence well worth visiting for its collection of 17th- and 18th-century furniture, Flanders tapestries and its pretty facade. The **Château d'Ansouis** ★ *(guided tour 30F; Apr to Oct, every day 2:30pm to 6pm; Nov to Mar, closed Tue, Jul 14 and Aug 30, additional tour at 11am; ☎04.90.09.82.70)* has been occupied by the De Sabran family since it was built eight centuries ago. Otherwise, this charming village has pretty streets, a wrought-iron bell tower built into a 16th-century building and the 13th-century Église Saint-Martin attached to the château's ramparts.

An impressive skeleton is all that remains of the **Château de La Tour-d'Aigues** *(25F; Jul and Aug, every day 10am to 1pm and 3:30pm to 6:30pm; Oct to Mar, 9:30am to 11:30am and 2pm to 5pm, closed Tue pm and Sat and Sun mornings; Apr to Jun and Sep, 9:30am to 11:30am and 3pm to 6pm, closed Tue afternoon and Sat and Sun mornings; ☎04.90.07.50.33)*, which in no way prevents a visit of the ruins. It belongs to the Conseil Régional du Vaucluse and is the object of restoration work. The elegant proportions of its 16th-century facade are in sharp contrast to those of the more sober châteaux in the area. The Festival du Sud du Luberon, a summer festival of theatre, music and dance, , takes place every year in the castle's court *(contact the castle for more information)*.

The Rivière Durance Valley

Running west to east, parallel to the Petit and Grand Luberon is the Durance River and a number of villages along its banks. The durance often floods in the spring and a canal network is now in place, producing electricity and irrigating the plain. Many parts of this area lack the natural beauty of the nearby Luberon hills, as power stations and industry have taken over. However, there are a number of sites of interest. Starting from the west, near Cavaillon, lovers of steep, treacherous drives will be satisfied by a 10km (6.2mi) twisty one-way road across barren hills *(difficult access—head for the hamlet of Vidauque just east of the D31 side road and turn right up a steep incline of the narrow D30; this leads past two peaks, called the Tête des Buisses and Trou-du-Rat, and eventually looks over the Durance river and winds down to the major D973 road).*

For hikers, the **Gorges de Régalon ★** *(marked on the D973 road between Cheval-Blanc and Mérindol, park on the right and follow the indicated path past an informative panel describing the site's history and geological importance)* provides a fascinating short walk, though it is dangerous in wet weather.

A plaque commemorating the slaughter of the Vaudois is found on top of a hill overlooking **Mérindol**, a village which was destroyed along with many others in 1545 and rebuilt in the 17th century. South of Lourmarin and Cadenet, across the Durance River, lies one of the region's three Cistercian abbeys. The design of the **Abbaye Silvacane ★** *(27F; Oct to Mar, Wed to Mon 9am to noon and 2pm to 5pm; Apr to Sep, every day 9am to 7pm; occasional closure in Aug at 5pm when classical music concerts are held, call for details; ☎04.42.50.41.69)* resembles the sombre beauty of the slightly older Abbaye Sénanque near Gordes. Built between 1175 and 1230, it is not as well preserved and is no longer a working abbey, but is owned by the state department of historical monuments. Still, a visit through the cloister, the extremely high barrel-vaulted church and the monks quarters is worthwhile.

Outdoor Activities

Outdoor enthusiasts are advised to stop at the headquarters of the Parc Naturel Régional du Luberon for a gamut of helpful information from its welcome service and shop. This includes guidebooks on hiking trails in the area and the Luberon by car, thematic brochures about plant and animal life, and details about guided walks. Otherwise, tourist offices provide information about activities and services organized by local groups.

Parc Naturel Régional du Luberon
60 Place Jean Jaurès, B.P. 122
84400 Apt
☎04.90.04.42.00
⇌04.90.04.81.15

Hiking

This region has something to please everyone—from idyllic paths to challenging hills. Because much of the region is protected by legislation forbidding development, nature lovers may admire unique species of flora and fauna here, in addition to wonderful panoramic views. The tourist office in Lourmarin publishes a brochure regarding four marked trails in the South Luberon *Les Sentiers Promenades du Sub Luberon*. Similarly, the Venasque tourist office publishes a brochure outlining a number of walks (between 2.5hrs and 7hrs) in this lovely area. Guided visits of the Gorges de la Nesque with commentary are organized in July and August by the Sault tourist office.

Serious hikers will enjoy the following trails (Topo-Guides on sale in bookstores provide exact details):

GR4 (Mont Ventoux to Vaucluse Plateau), **GR9** (Mont Ventoux to

Vaucluse Plateau and the Grand Luberon), **GR91** (Mont Ventoux to Fontaine-de-Vaucluse), **GR6-97** (Vaucluse Plateau to Petit Luberon and the Gorges de Régalon), **GR91** (Mont Ventoux), **GR92** (Grand Luberon), **GR97** (Luberon).

Horseback Riding

Apt

L'École du Cheval
Quartier de Roquefure
☎*04.90.74.37.47*
L'École du Cheval equestrian centre and pony club organizes tours in the area on horseback.

Malaucène

Les Écuries du Ventoux
Quartier des Grottes
☎*04.90.65.29.20*
This *gîte* (farmhouse) arranges tours on horseback (plus hiking tours ans a private swimming pool).

Saignon

Centre Équestre de Tourville
Quartier des Gondonnets
☎*04.90.74.00.33*
Centre Équestre de Tourville give lessons as well as guided tours on horseback.

Mountain Biking

Mormoiron

G. Aubert
☎*04.90.61.83.90*
Monsieur Aubert organizes an exciting two-day mountain-bike circuit in the Gorges de la Nesque, as well as a descent of Mont Ventoux.

Downhill Skiing

Mont Ventoux

Mont Serein
north face of Mont Ventoux, 1400m to 1900m
☎*04.90.63.42.02*
Mont Serein has equipment rental, seven runs in winter, grass skiing in summer and a ski school. Chalet restaurant for the complete après-ski sensation.

Chalet Reynard
south face of Mont Ventoux, 1420m to 1640m
☎*04.90.61.84.55*
Chalet Reynard is a smaller version of the above, with four short runs.

Cross-Country Skiing

Comité Départemental de Ski
☎*04.90.63.16.54*
Cross-country skiing is limited to the forests around Mont Ventoux. For more information, contact the Comité Départemental de Ski.

Golf

Saumane (Fontaine de Vaucluse)

International Golf & Country Club
☎*04.90.20.20.65*
Practice greens and an 18-hole course.

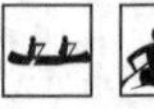 

Canoeing and Kayaking

The scenic Sorgue river in the Vaucluse is a favourite spot for canoeing and kayaking enthusiasts.

Fontaine-de-Vaucluse

Michel Melani, Kayak Ver
☎*04.90.20.35.44*
Michel Melani, Kayak Ver offers exciting guided trips down the Sorgue from Fontaine-de-Vaucluse to Isle-Sur-

la-Sorgue. Includes commentary.

Isle-sur-la-Sorgue

Club de Canoë-Kayak Islois La Cigalette
☎04.90.38.33.22
☎04.90.20.64.70
Club de Canoë-Kayak Islois La Cigalette give lessons for individuals and groups.

Accommodations

L'Isle-sur-la-Sorgue

La Méridienne
350F-400F
no credit cards
pb, ≈
Aux Fontanelles, Chemin de la Lône
☎04.90.38.40.26
⇄04.90.38.58.46
Each room in this pleasant bed and breakfast run by Muriel Fox (a photographer from Avignon) and Jérôme Tarayre (a former doctor in Paris) has a small terrace overlooking a pretty garden and a swimming pool. Quiet, peaceful location (off the N100 south of Isle-sur-la-Sorgue).

Mas de Cure Bourse
450F-650F
ℜ, ≈, tv
Route de Caumont-sur-Durance
☎04.90.38.16.58
⇄04.90.38.52.31
Chef Françoise Donzé's well-acknowledged talents in the kitchen are the first reason to come to this hotel, formerly an 18th-century inn. Along with her husband Jean-François, a banker, the colourful Donzé gave up her job as a chemist and started the hotel in 1980. Thirteen pleasant, Provençal-style bedrooms ideal for families. Patio and garden, seminar and reception facilities.

Lagnes

La Pastorale
330F
no credit cards
pb, locked garage
Route de Fontaine de Vaucluse
Les Gardioles
☎04.90.20.25.18
⇄04.90.20.21.86
A friendly couple, Elisabeth and Robert Negrel, recently moved from Paris and converted this pretty stone farmhouse into a bed and breakfast, next to fields and a small road. The bedrooms are spacious and comfortable, but simply furnished. Breakfast, served in a charming clay-tiled room, includes homemade jams and great coffee. Monsieur Negrel has a small antique/knick-knack shop next door. Well-situated (at the D24 and D99 crossroads, between the N100 and Lagnes village) for trips to L'Isle-sur-la-Sorgue and Fontaine-de-la-Vaucluse.

Pernes-les-Fontaines

Saint-Barthélémy
280F
no credit cards
pb or ps
☎04.90.66.47.79
The Saint-Barthélémy bed and breakfast is a restored, 18th-century stone house, once the residence of Baron Quiquerant, a royalist who fled to Russia during the French Revolution. The five rooms— four with showers and one with bath—are rather plain. The real pleasure here is the enclosed garden with flowering laurel trees. Breakfast can be served on the terrace, shaded by a large weeping willow tree. Swimming is possible in a small waterfall with private spring nearby. From Pernes, take the D1 direction Mazan for 2km, then turn right on the Chemin de la Roque.

Mas La Bonoty
300F-350F
pb, ≈, ℜ
Chemin de la Bonoty
☎04.90.61.61.09
⇄04.90.61.35.14
The peace and quiet of a restored farmhouse set in a low plain with a good restaurant *(menus at 145F and 195F)* and eight comfortable rooms lend this hotel a real country-inn atmosphere. Guests are warmly received like one of the family. Large pool and terrace. Good value.

(From Pernes, take the D28 to the village of Saint Didier, turn left on the Chemin de Barraud, leading to Chemin de la Bonioty.)

Hôtel Hermitage
410F-430F
pb, ≈, tv
Route de Carpentras
☎04.90.66.51.41
⇌04.90.61.36.41
Don't be put off by the busy road out front—this 20-room hotel faces its own large, leafy park and is a haven of tranquillity. This former residence of Captain Dreyfus is decorated with Provençal furniture. Rooms are attractively renovated; breakfast or drinks can be taken on a stone terrace. Unbeatable value.

Venasque

La Maison aux Volets Bleus
420F-780F
closed Nov 15 to Mar 15
pb, mini-bar
☎04.90.66.03.04
⇌04.90.66.16.14
violetbleu@aol.com
If you have ever dreamed of the ideal bed and breakfast, this might be it. Five tasteful rooms (one suite with two bedrooms) are freshly decorated with Provençal prints and have bathrooms with attractive tiling. Breakfasts are served on a long, narrow terrace with gorgeous clear views of the Vaucluse hills. The large front room offers the same view, a stone fireplace, local bric-a-brac, dried yellow wildflowers hanging from the ceiling and tons of books on Provence. The owner, Martine Maret, is a former chef and a warm, generous host—she'll suggest the best places to buy local chèvre, Provençal fabrics and olive oil. Evening meals for 135F without wine (recently roast rabbit, melon with Muscat and cheese feuilleté) if arranged in advance. They are served on a second terrace next to a fountain and flowering plants. Cats on the premises. No credit cards.

Auberge La Fontaine
800F
pb, K, ctv, ℜ, ☎
Place de la Fontaine
☎04.90.66.02.96
⇌04.90.66.13.14
fontvenasq@aol.com
Former businessman Christian Soehlke has been the host/chef of this comfortable inn for 20 years. Each large, fully-equipped apartment is two- or three-storeyed, has a small balcony, is decorated differently (modern, Provençal, country-style) and can accommodate families of four. Meals are served in the dining room or in the informal bistro. Good meals served in the first-floor rustic dining room include nice touches like thick homemade bread and delicious *tapenade* served while you ponder the menu. Monthly music recitals during dinner. The informal bistro on the ground floor is ideal for lunch *(both restaurants closed mid-Nov to mid-Dec).*

Fontaine-de-Vaucluse

Auberge de Jeunesse
45F
Chemin de la Vignasse
☎04.90.20.31.65
Located just outside Fontaine-de-Vaucluse, towards Gordes. Closed November 15 to Febuary 15. FUAJ (YHA) membership card necessary.

Gordes

Ferme de la Huppe
400F-750F
pb, ℜ, ≈
RD 156–Les Pourquiers
☎04.90.72.12.25
⇌04.90.72.01.83
This is a pretty stone farmhouse in the Luberon valley, just south of Gordes, with a landscaped garden and shaded terrace next to the pool. Eight attractive rooms (some in the 18th-century building, others in a new wing) and rustic-style restaurant. The owners, the Konnings, have created a friendly, relaxed atmosphere.

Le Domaine de l'Enclos
550F-1,900F
½b 490F-1,100F
pb, tv, ≈, ℜ
Route de Sénanque
This old stone farmhouse, surrounded by other buildings, is hidden in a wood overlooking the Luberon valley. Serge

Lafitte offers many rooms and suites here, each with a personalized decorative touch. During the summer, rooms are reserved in week-long blocks. This establishment proves calm and peace, for those who have the means to stay here. A tennis court figures among the amenities.

Mas de la Beaume
600F-700F and suite for 900F bkfst incl.
≈
Gordes Village
☎04.90.72.02.96
⇄04.90.72.06.89
la.beaume@wanadoo.fr
The Mas de la Baume has five charming, wonderfully renovated guestrooms and one suite, and is managed by the equally charming Camus couple. The decor exudes good taste, the colours are admirably selected and the bathrooms are impeccable. The owners opened this place in March 2000 and have managed to create a friendly, idyllic, rustic and comfortable ambiance. Located a few minutes from the centre of the village, the *Mas* has a peaceful garden graced with a very popular salt-water pool. We recommend this place for the gracious welcome and the elegance of the rooms.

La Gacholle
600F-750F
closed Nov 15 to Mar 15
pb, tv, ≈, ℜ
Route de Murs
☎04.90.72.01.36
⇄04.90.72.01.81
A friendly spot to stay while visiting the Luberon thanks to comfortable rooms (some are a bit dated), an unparalleled view of the hills and valley, excellent Provençal cuisine and, above all, the smiling, considerate welcome by Gerard Roux and his team, who are equally professional and personable. Reasonably priced for an area with inflated prices. Tennis court and pleasant swimming pool. Credit cards accepted, except Diners Club and American Express.

Les Bories
960F-2,280F
pb, ℜ, ≈, tv
Route de l'Abbaye de Sénanque
☎04.90.72.00.51
⇄04.90.72.01.22
For those tired of cute Provençal prints and country furnishings, try one of the 18 luxuriously appointed rooms in this hillside hotel that has more in common with the Côte d'Azur than the Luberon. Since 1994, a charming new manager is making great strides with the young staff (mainly student interns) and restaurant which, indeed, is a restored stone *borie*. Each bedroom has terrific views over pine-tree studded hills towards Gordes. Tennis court, incredible indoor marble swimming pool.

Lacoste

L'Herbier
300F
credit cards not accepted
ps, ≈
La Valmasque
☎04.90.75.88.98
Nestled at the foot of the Petit Luberon, set back from the D3 between Bonnieux and Ménerbes, this rudimentary bed and breakfast numbers but five poorly furnished rooms with showers and sinks; the toilet is in the hallway. The mild-mannered owner, Minouche Cance, great-granddaughter of Fauvist Henri Manguin, serves breakfast on a shady stone patio next to the pool. Also available are two comfortable apartments equipped with terraces, kitchenettes and private bathrooms *(2,600F-3,900F/week).*

Relais du Procurer
500F-700F
≈, pb, tv
Rue Basse
☎04.90.75.82.28
⇄04.90.75.86.94
Luxury bed and breakfast in a 17th-century stone house right in the middle of this pretty village. Well-equipped and furnished rooms, though a few are a bit dated for some people's tastes. A narrow outdoor swimming pool, surrounded by four walls, is found off an upper floor.

Bonnieux

L'Hostellerie du Prieuré
560F-700F
closed Nov 5 to Feb 15
ℜ, *pb*
Rue J-B Aurard
⇄04.90.75.96.00
A lovely hotel with character in a former 18th-century abbey. Ten comfortable rooms, a charming dining room in the old kitchen with an open hearth and a charming garden/terrace for breakfast. Note the delightful models of Paris theatre interiors illuminated in a display case under the bar in the sitting room. Restaurant menus at 98F (lunch) and 220F. Too bad the welcome is rather aloof.

Saignon

Auberge du Presbytère
290F-570F
closed Nov 15-30
ℜ, *pb*
Place de la Fontaine
☎04.90.74.11.50
⇄04.90.04.68.51
A number of the ten tasteful bedrooms have terraces and views of the Luberon, others overlook the fountain. (You'll find a stack of books instead of a television next to your bed!) Well recommended for the pleasant welcome and peaceful atmosphere. Drinks can be enjoyed in the bar or on the terrace next to the fountain *(11am to 1pm and 4:30pm to 8pm)*. A four-course fixed-price menu is offered and includes cheese and dessert.

Lourmarin

L'Hostellerie du Paradou
350F-390F
closed mid-Jan to mid-Feb
restaurant closed Thu, Sep to Jun
pb, ℜ
Route d'Apt, Trouée de la Combe
☎04.90.68.04.05
⇄04.90.68.33.93
Eight simple rooms in a peaceful garden setting with trees, next to the scenic D943. Restaurant meals are served in a pretty glassed-in veranda and on a shaded terrace *(menus at 100F and 145F)*. Discreet, friendly welcome. Good value.

Villa Saint-Louis
350F-450F
tv, pb
35 Rue Henri de Savournin
☎04.90.68.39.18
⇄04.90.68.10.07
Old *gendarmerie* (police station) and once a *relais de poste* (roadside inn), this charming 18th-century house is one of the best bed and breakfasts in Provence. Run by the exuberant Bernadette Lassallette and decorated with extraordinary taste by her husband Michel (a professional decorator). Bedrooms are filled with antiques and objects collected over the years from flea markets, plus a bohemian mix of fabrics, paintings and furniture. Each has a fireplace and bathroom; there is a pretty terrace and garden. The breakfast room has a kitchenette for client's use. Bicycles are lent out to guests to explore the region.

Le Moulin de Lourmarin
800F-2,800F
≈, ℜ, *pb, tv*
☎04.90.68.06.69
⇄04.90.68.31.76
moulin@provence-luberon.net
A stylish hotel in a renovated 18th-century mill. In the rooms, bright Provençal blue and yellow fabrics mix with wrought-iron and painted furniture, and cool stone floors. An inviting swimming pool faces soothing green fields.

Restaurants

L'Isle-sur-la-Sorgue

Le Jardin du Quai
$-$$
Thu to Tue, closed Tue pm
4 Avenue Julien-Guigue
☎04.90.38.56.17
This delightful restaurant is a favourite with antique dealers from nearby markets on weekends and it's easy to see why. A pretty shaded garden and fresh interior decorated with amusing bric-a-brac is the setting for some of this town's best food. Recent wonders included delicious fried red fish fillets, lamb chops with rosemary and superb des-

serts (cheesecake, rhubarb and plum pie). Everything is homemade and the service is friendly and efficient. Located next to the SNCF train station.

Le Caveau de la Tour de l'Isle
$$
Tue to Sun 9am to 1pm and 3pm to 8pm, closed Sun pm
12 Rue de la République
☎04.90.20.70.25
At the back of this charming, old-fashioned vintner (excellent selection of local bottles and knowledgeable, friendly staff) is a tiny *bar à vins*, where customers may try a glass of wine over a plate of *tapenade* (olive paste), chèvre or *cavier d'aubergine* (eggplant purée) and toasted bread.

Pernes-les-Fontaines

Dame L'oie
$-$$
closed Mon and Tue at lunch
56 Rue du Troubadour
☎04.90.61.62.43
Excellent authentic Provençal specialties including bouillabaisse and game, served in a rustic atmosphere. Three menus: lunch (70F), *menu gourmet* (105F) and *menu gourmand* (150F). Friendly, professional service.

Le Beaucet

Auberge du Beaucet
$$$
near the post office
☎04.90.66.10.82
The Auberge du Beaucet needs no introduction to locals who appreciate fine dining. This restaurant is a little gem the type of which very few remain. The refined Provençal food is served in an old home built against a cliff, in the lovely hamlet of Beaucet. The menu will please refined palates, as it is packed with mouthwatering specialties of southern France. Ravioli *de Baume*, duck terrine with foie gras, rabbit with morel mushrooms as well as mutton stew are among the owner-chef's accomplishments. To complement this divine cuisine, the cellar is stocked with the region's best wines, including Côtes-du-Rhône, Côtes-du-Ventoux, Côtes-du-Luberon and other excellent vintages. The menu certainly offers one of the best values for the price in the area. An absolute must for people who appreciate fine food. The service is courteous and attentive.

Fontaine-de-Vaucluse

Pétarque et Laure
$$
near the Romanesque church
☎04.90.20.31.98
You won't regret heading to Pétarque et Laure to enjoy the incredible terrace beneath the trees, in the shadow of the striking Fontaine-de-Vaucluse Romanesque church. Here, guests can admire the lush garden, adjoining a small stream and a windmill, as well as the majestic rock formations of the surrounding area. And the food? Very honest, with exceptional fish that deserves special mention.

Cavaillon (Cheval Blanc)

Alain Nicolet
$$-$$$
closed Sun pm and Mon in off-season
Route de Pertruis, B.P. 28
☎04.90.78.01.56
⇌04.90.71.91.28
A fine gourmet restaurant in a stone country house, emphasizing beautifully prepared, fresh seasonal products. During warmer months, diners can eat on the shaded terrace with striking unobstructed views of the countryside. Professional service and a pleasant welcome from Mireille Nicolet.

Cabrières-D'Avignon

Le Bistrot à Michel
$$
Jan Wed to Sun
Jul and Aug Wed to Mon
Grand Rue
☎04.90.76.82.08
Once a quiet village bistro run by the welcoming Bosc family, the Bistrot à Michel has become a trendy spot popular with Parisians and North Americans, thanks to recent media attention. Fortunately, it still serves great food using fresh ingredients, such as a warm tomato and tuna tart, fillet of cod or *pieds et paquets.* Amusing cartoons and old movie posters cover the walls.

Gordes

Le Mas Tourteron
$$
closed Mon and Tue and from Nov to Mar
Chemin de Saint-Blaise, Les Imberts
☎04.90.72.00.16
A stylish haven serving very good Provençal dishes, like rabbit terrine or aubergine mousse to start, followed by carpaccio of tuna and sword fish or pork fillet with mustard and honey. The shaded terrace, full of plants and flowers, has green metal tables, blue tablecloths and white chair cushions. The chef, Elizabeth Bourgeois, is well-known throughout France—her cookbook is available just about everywhere.

Tante Yvonne
$$
closed Wed and Sun evenings in low season
Place Genty-Pantaly (Place du Château)
☎04.90.72.02.54
A small tea room that becomes a restaurant in the evenings, Tante Yvonne is an unassuming establishment with a relaxed, familial ambiance. Everything is kept simple here, from the ordinary Provençal food to the sparse decor with bright lighting. The menu for 143F is nothing more than honest. This is a place to go if you're stuck for somewhere to eat because you don't feel like searching for a better restaurant further afield.

Le Clos de Gustave
$$$
closed Tue evening and Wed in low season
Route de Murs, several hundred metres from the Château traffic circle
☎04.90.72.04.25
Le Clos de Gustave is certainly a place to keep in mind among the restaurants in this charming village. Removed from the town centre, this fine dining establishment serves refined regional food beneath a bower, in one of the most enchanting rural settings. A good wine list offers some of the best regional vintages, which admirably complement specialties like the *Bohémienne au gratin*, made of eggplant, tomatoes and egg au gratin, as well as the *paquetoun de biou*, the poetic Provençal name for beef paupiette.

Le Temps des Saveurs
$$$
Route de Murs
☎04.90.72.17.47
The new restaurant at the Hôtel La Gacholle, Le Temps des Saveurs is worth the 3km (2mi) journey from the centre of Gordes. Guests can enjoy the marvellous landscapes of the Luberon from the lovely terrace. The fine food is typical of southern France, featuring lamb, fish and, of course, foie gras. A very affordable lunch menu includes an appetizer, main dish and a glass of wine.

Bonnieux

Henri Tomas
$
7 and 9 Rue de la République
☎04.90.75.85.52
The jovial Tomas offers his specialty, *galette Provençale* (tart) and other sweet things from his pastry shop in the front, and a tearoom in a couple of rooms behind which date from the 12th century and were once used as a press-house for olive oil. Perfect for a cup of steaming hot chocolate in cooler months. Situated opposite the Musée de la Boulangerie.

Le Fournil
$$
Tue to Sun
5 Place Carnot
☎ ***04.90.75.83.62***

Situated on a pleasant square with a fountain in the village centre, Guy Malbec and Jean-Christophe Lèche offer delicious and inventive twists to Provençal clas sics, such as a cold pistou with mussels and cockles, a lamb flan with eggplant, braised hake with violet artichokes and warm chocolate cake with pistachio sauce. A choice of menus (98F, 130F and 190F). Sum mer terrace.

Viens

Le Petit Jardin
$-$$
Thu to Tue, dinner only
Village centre
☎ ***04.90.75.20.05***

A typical village café (open all day) with a cozy restaurant behind serving no-nonsense classics like *salade chèvre chaud* and *confit de canard*. The menu includes mushroom terrine, roast lamb, cheese, dessert and a carafe of Côtes de Luberon wine. Service next to a stone hearth in winter, or in the beautiful garden in summer. Worth dropping by to meet Muguette, the colourful hostess.

Saignon

Auberge du Presbytère
$-$$
closed Nov 15 to 30
dinner only
Place de la Fontaine
☎ ***04.90.74.11.50***
⇄ ***04.90.04.68.51***

The restaurant in this delightful village proposes a fixed-price menu for only 145F including two courses, cheese and dessert. Drinks can be taken in the bar or on the terrace next to the fountain *(11am to 1pm and 4:30pm to 8pm)*.

Lourmarin

L'Oustalet de Georges
$-$$
Tue to Sun, closed Sun pm
Avenue Philippe-de-Girard
☎ ***04.90.68.07.33***

A definite emphasis on fresh, Provençal items (pistou soup, cod fillets with olives) in an old roadside house. The good three-course lunch menu (100F, weekdays only) includes a salad selection dressed with local olive oil or a fish terrine to start, and a fine *tarte du jour* to finish.

Michel Ange
$$
mid-Jun to mid-Sep every day
mid-Sep to mid-Jun, Thu to Tue, closed Tue pm
Place de la Fontaine
☎ ***04.90.68.02.03***

A cheery Mediterannean theme runs through this restaurant (formerly Maison Ollier) in the village centre. Clay-tile floors, Tuscany colours and lots of fish and pasta dishes. Menus at 108F, 158F plus a *Menu Dégustation* for 280F.

Rognes

Le Braséro
$
closed Mon, Tue lunchtime and Oct
9 Rue de l'Église
☎ ***04.42.50.17.63***

No awards for its interior, but Le Braséro serves the best pizza in the entire region—the chèvre and basil get top prize. Also pastas, salads and full menus. Rognes is 14km (8.7mi) south of Lourmarin (10min from the Silvercane Abbey) along the D543.

Entertainment

As in the Comtat Venaissin, the Vaucluse and the Luberon are rural areas with spectacular natural beauty but little nightlife. Visitors are here to soak up the region's rich history, to explore the countryside and its charming villages by foot and car and enjoy the delicious local food and wine. Evenings are not spent in a dance or smokey jazz club because there aren't any. But there are beautiful sunsets and great food to savour.

However, there is one huge exception: summertime is festival time in France and all of Provence is alive with festivals celebrating the region's culture, history and traditions. Major festivals in the Upper Comtat include:

Festival de Gordes
mid-Jul to mid Aug
Jazz, classical music and theatre.

Festival de Quatuors A Cordes
Jun to Sep
Fontaine-de-Vaucluse
Roussillon
Goult string quartet concerts.

Fête de la Lavande
Aug
Sault
Lavender festival.

Fête des Vendanges
Sep
Entrechaux
Wine harvest festival.

Festival du Sud-Luberon
Jul
La Tour-d'Aigues
Dance, theatre, music.

Rencontres d'Été
Aug
Apt
Events for historians and writers.

Festival International de Folklore
Fri, Jul and Aug
Cavaillon

Chansons Françaises
Sun, Jul and Aug
Cavaillon
Musical concerts.

Les Kiosques à Musique d'Été
Sun afternoons, Jul and Aug
Cavaillon

Musique d'Été and **Rencontres Méditerranéennes Albert Camus**
Aug
Lourmarin
Musical and writers' event.

Shopping

L'Isle-sur-la-Sorgue

Les Délices du Lubéron
270 Avenue Voltaire-Garcin
☎**04.90.38.45.96**
A good selection of the best Provençal food products, including olive oils, *tapenade*, herbs, nougat and candy.

Antique Markets

The entire village becomes an antique and flea market on weekends (arrive by 10am to find parking space during the summer). Try to bargain—start at 15% off the asking price and hope to get a 10% reduction. The choice is happily varied in taste, quality and price—here are some of the best spots to check out:

Espace Béchard
One Avenue Charmasson, Route d'Apt
☎**04.90.38.25.40**
Eleven professional dealers with quality furniture and objects.

L'Isle Aux Brocantes
Passage du Pont, 7 Avenue des 4 Otages
☎**04.90.20.69.93**
Over 35 dealers in a sheltered, antique village atmosphere, with a great mix of big and small items, including antique pottery and linens. Chez Nane, a busy restaurant/tearoom is found at the back *(weekends only, ☎04.90.20.69.93).*

Xavier Nicod
9 Avenue des Quatre-Otages
☎**04.90.38.07.20**
An eclectic selection of antiques and amusing objects chosen with a good sense of humour by Nicod and his wife.

Le Quai de la Gare
opposite the SNCF train station
☎**04.90.20.73.42**
An interesting array of antiques and brocante dealers in a pleasant gallery, offering furniture, mirrors and *objets d'art*, among other items.

Venasque

Atelier de Faïence
mid-Mar to mid-Oct, Thu to Tue 10am to 7pm
Place de la Fontaine
☎**04.90.66.07.92**
Pretty and original blue and white pottery in primarily geometric patterns, created by the friendly and sweet Anne Viard-Oberlin.

Apt

Dumas
Tue to Sat 8:30am to noon, 2pm to 7pm
16 Place Gabriel Péri
☎04.90.74.23.81
⇌04.90.74.63.59
Though you can find newspaper and magazine kiosks in the larger villages, it's hard to find a bookshop with a good selection of fiction and non-fiction works in the entire Luberon area. Here's the place for bibliophiles!

Jean Faucon
Mon to Fri 8am to noon and 2pm to 6pm, Sat 9am to noon and 3pm to 6pm, closed Sun
12 Avenue de Libération
☎04.90.74.15.31
Six generations of Jean Faucon's family have been making traditional Aptware. Each ceramic piece (from plates to pots and tobacco jars) uses local earth and a special technique to achieve the fine waves of yellow, red, green, brown and white. This attractive shop displays these refined and beautiful items at their best.

Sault

André Boyer
Mar to Jan, Tue to Sun 9am to noon and 2pm to 6pm
☎04.90.64.00.23
⇌04.90.64.08.99
For over 100 years, the Boyer family has been making the region's finest nougat and delicious macaroon-almond biscuits from this charming shop (you can't miss it in the village centre). André, great-grandson of the founder Ernest, continues to follow the traditional methods of preparation—his nougat is made from local almonds and lavender honey.

Goult

Pitot
Mon to Sat 9am to noon and 2pm to 6pm
signposted directly off the N100 at Ponty, near Goult
☎04.90.72.22.79
Inspired by 18th-century Aptware, Antony Pitot creates a fine white earthenware covered in typical solid mustard yellow or rich green glazes. These are not the reproductions you see all over the region, but original pieces, since Pitot makes his own moulds sold only at his studio.

Notre-Dame-des-Lumières

Edith Mézard
every day, 3pm to 6:30pm
Château de l'Ange
☎04.90.72.36.41
⇌04.90.72.36.69
Exquisite embroidered clothes for men and women, as well as a wonderful selection houses linens (sheets, pillow cases bed covers, serviettes, tablecloths and bath towels). Flowers, poems and initials are stitched by hand onto the finest quality linens and cottons. The cool, contemporary boutique was designed by Jacqueline Morabito and fits in surprisingly well with Mézard's tiny château-residence in Lumières, next to the village of Goult. Orders are taken.

Lourmarin

L'Ange Bleu
Tue to Sun 3pm to 7pm
25 Rue Henri de Savonin
☎04.90.68.01.58
A charming Flemish gentleman, Ignace Morreel, sells a good selection of antiques—regional and otherwise.

Cote Bastide
3 Rue du Grand Pre
☎04.42.97.31.00
Everything of impeccable quality for the bath—from deliciously perfumed soaps and scented candles to superb linen towels. Great for gifts for yourself and friends.

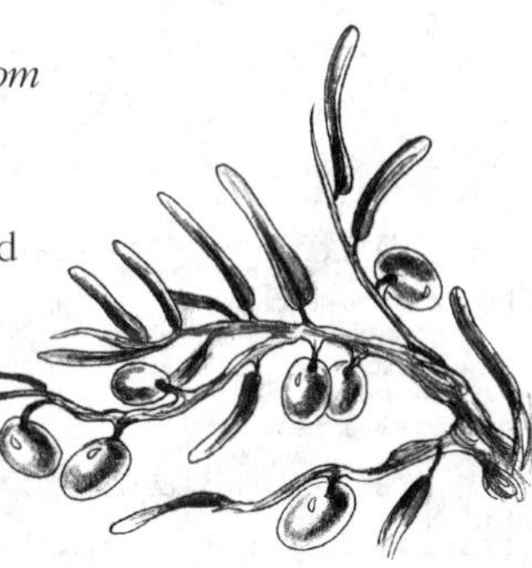

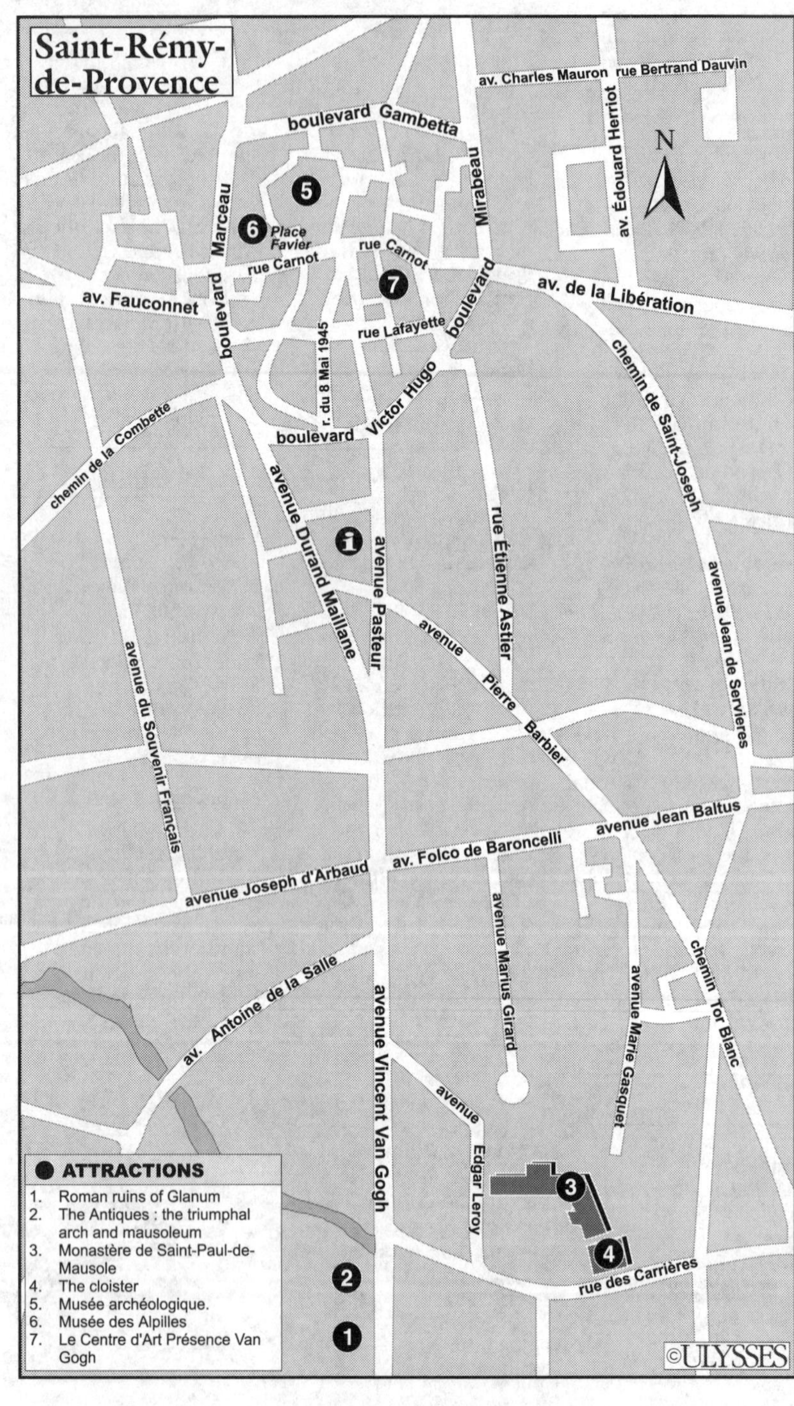
Saint-Rémy-de-Provence
av. Charles Mauron
rue Bertrand Dauvin
boulevard Gambetta
N
Mirabeau
av. Édouard Herriot
5
6 Place Favier
boulevard Marceau
rue Carnot
rue Carnot
7
av. Fauconnet
boulevard
av. de la Libération
rue Lafayette
r. du 8 Mai 1945
boulevard Victor Hugo
chemin de Saint-Joseph
chemin de la Combette
avenue Durand Maillane
avenue Pasteur
rue Étienne Astier
avenue Pierre Barbier
avenue Jean de Servieres
avenue du Souvenir Français
avenue Jean Baltus
av. Folco de Baroncelli
avenue Joseph d'Arbaud
avenue Marius Girard
chemin Tor Blanc
av. Antoine de la Salle
avenue Vincent Van Gogh
avenue Marie Gasquet
avenue Edgar Leroy
rue des Carrières
ATTRACTIONS
1. Roman ruins of Glanum
2. The Antiques : the triumphal arch and mausoleum
3. Monastère de Saint-Paul-de-Mausole
4. The cloister
5. Musée archéologique.
6. Musée des Alpilles
7. Le Centre d'Art Présence Van Gogh
©ULYSSES

The Alpilles, Arles and the Camargue

The surprising area of the Alpilles, Arles and the Camargue provides a bit of everything—world famous Roman ruins, beautiful scenery untouched by humans, quiet Provençal villages and stylish towns.

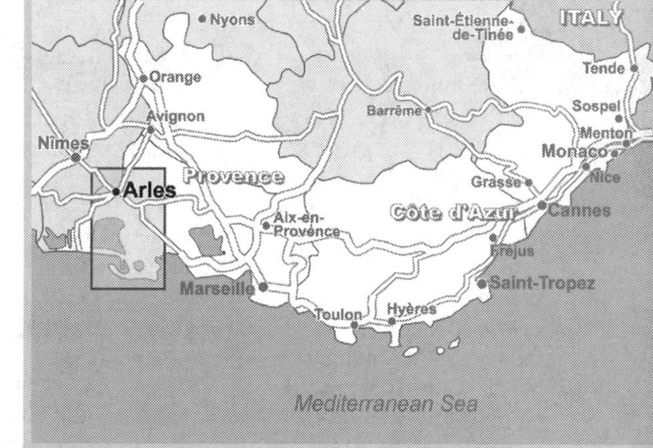

Welcome to an important part of the French department known as the Bouches-du-Rhône. The Alpilles is an impressive chain of white jagged limestone hills situated 25km (15.5mi) south of Avignon, encircled by three interesting towns: Saint-Rémy-de-Provence, Tarascon and Arles, plus a number of quiet villages. West of the Alpilles lie fields of golden wheat, to the north are orchards and due south is the Crau, a dry pebbly plain. Bordering the Crau and extending all the way to the Mediterranean Sea is the Camargue. This is the delta of the Rhône and much of the wet marshland is a regional park. Here rice and salt production and fishing are the main activities. Indigenous white horses roam and, somewhat remarkably, colonies of pink flamingoes live peacefully.

Before the stone age, the waters of the Rhône and the Durance rivers flowed into a huge gulf leading to the sea. Over thousands of years, the sea level lowered and earth deposits carried by the rivers' currents accumulated and formed small islands. Eventually, a landscape resembling that of today was created, allowing habitation in the area. Land was still being reclaimed as late as the 4th century—a considerable portion of the Camargue didn't exist until then and is naturally-formed reclaimed land.

Paleolithic man lived in the region, followed by the Celto-Ligurian tribes, then the Greek Phoecaeans. (The natural history museums in Arles, Saint-Rémy-de-Provence and Baux contain interesting artifacts from these times.) Great progress and growth occurred during Roman occupation, when Augustus Caesar stationed members of his 6th battalion in Provence.

After Marseille, Arles was perhaps the most important Roman settlement in the entire region. It was a great trading centre linking the sea to inland communities following the construction of a canal connecting Arles to the Golfe de Fos west of Marseille. Remains of the Roman arena, amphitheatre, baths and rampart walls with round towers can be visited today.

The region remained relatively calm from the 15th century onwards, as political and economic life continued to focus on Aix and Marseille. Its inhabitants carried on doing what they knew best—namely looking after the orchards, vineyards and olive groves, which existed here since Greek times, tending sheep north of the Alpilles, and raising cattle and horses in the Camargue. Though Arles was no longer in the limelight, it was still a commercial centre with a growing merchant-class. As a result, elegant buildings and *hôtels particuliers* were constructed there and in Saint-Rémy-de-Provence.

Among the many writers and artists who have lived here and immortalized the landscape and its people, three stand out. Fréderic Mistral, the poet and founder of the Félibrige movement to promote the Provençal language was born and lived in Maillane, north of Saint-Rémy. Alphonse Daudet, another native author to the region, wrote the famous satire *Les Aventures de Tartarin* in which he ridiculed the residents of Tarascon and *Les Lettres de mon moulin*. Finally, Dutch painter Vincent Van Gogh spent two years (1888-1890) of his life in Arles and at the Saint-Rémy asylum, the St-Paul-de-Mausole Monastery, before committing suicide in Auvers-sur-Oise near Paris three months later.

The world's social press carefully scrutinizes the comings and goings of famous personalities who have second residences here, among them model turned boutique-owner Inès de la Fressange, singer Charles Aznavour and designer/restaurateur Sir Terence Conran. Saint-Rémy's most famous part-time resident is Princess Caroline of Monaco, who in 1991 was offered a 99-year lease on a 17th-century stone farmhouse by Count Jacques Sénard.

Finding Your Way Around

The area is bordered by the Rhône and Durance rivers, due south of Avignon and serviced by good roads and the regional French SNCF train network.

By Train

Trains from SNCF's regional service TER run throughout the day from Avignon and Marseille to stations in **Arles**, **Saint-Rémy** and **Tarascon**.

By Car

From Avignon take the D571 south for **Saint-Rémy** and **Baux** (25km or 15.5mi); take the D570 south for **Arles** (34km or 21.7mi); take the D970 south for **Tarascon** (23km or 14.3mi). Saintes-Maries-de-la-Mer at the southern tip of the Camargue is 72km (44.7mi) south on the D570.

The major towns lie about 60km (37.3mi) from the Marseille Marignane airport. For **Saint-Rémy-de-Provence** and **Tarascon** (a further 16km or 10mi), take the A7– Autoroute du Soleil north to Cavaillon, then head west on the D99. For **Arles**, take the A7– Autoroute du Soleil north to Salon-de-Provence then head west on the N113–E80. For **Saintes-Maries-de-la-Mer**, follow directions for Arles, then take the D570 south (a further 38km or 23.6mi).

Practical Information

Tourist Offices

Saint-Rémy-de-Provence
Place Jean-Jaurès
☎***04.90.92.05.22***
⇄***04.90.92.38.52***

Fontvieille
5 Rue Marcel-Honorat
☎***04.90.54.67.49***
⇄***04.90.54.64.87***

Arles
Esplanade Charles de Gaulle
☎***04.90.18.41.20***
⇄***04.90.18.41.29***
ot-arles@visitprovence.com
www.arles.org

Tarascon
59 Rue des Halles
☎***04.90.91.03.52***
⇄***04.90.91.22.96***

Baux
Ilot "Post Tenebras Lux"
13520 Les Baux-de-Provence
☎***04.90.54.34.39***
⇄***04.90.54.51.15***

Saintes-Maries-de-la-Mer
5 Avenue Van Gogh
☎***04.90.97.82.55***
⇄***04.90.97.97.82***
saintes-maries@enprovence.com
www.saintesmariesdelamer.com

Exploring

Saint-Rémy-de-Provence

Extensive archaelogical work began on the Roman ruins of **Glanum** *(32F; Apr to Sep, everyday 9am to 7pm; Oct to Mar, everyday 9am to noon and 2pm to 5pm; guided tours possible if arranged in advance; 2km or 1.2mi south of Saint-Rémy-de-Provence on the D5,* ☎*04.90.92.23.79)* after the First World War and still continues today. Historians believe the Phocaeans first settled on this site as far back as the 6th century BC. Visitors now can distinguish a real Gallo-Roman city dating from 30 BC to 10 BC amongst the ruins—a large thermal bath with a number of rooms, a long avenue with residences, a temple and a natural spring. Barbians destroyed the city in the 3rd century AD, and a new community developed around present-day Saint-Rémy.

Two important monuments can be seen today next to the Glanum site: a **triumphal arch** and a **mausoleum** collectively called the **Antiques** ★★ *(free admission).*

Vincent's Provence

Scorned during his lifetime, the brilliant 19th-century painter Vincent Van Gogh (1853-1890) settled in Arles in February 1888, in search of a different quality of light. During his sojourn in Provence, the painter created vividly coloured canvasses with a hallucinatory rhythm and intensified forms that expressed the artist's passion and internal suffering. The light and colours of Provence led him to embark on his unique impressionistic style.

Everything here inspired him: nature, workers in the fields, the town, the people. Van Gogh was confined to an asylum in Arles after his argument with Gauguin that led him to mutilate his ear. Later, upon his request, he moved to the Saint-Paul-de-Mausole asylum in Saint-Rémy, where he continued to paint one canvas per day, before leaving Provence in 1890. Shortly thereafter, this tragic figure finished his days in Auvers-sur-Oise, north of Paris.

The arch dates from 6 BC, is decorated with reliefs commemorating Caesar's defeat of Gaul and is missing a top level. The scultpure work is particularly well-executed. The well-preserved 19m-(62ft) high mausoleum was built around 30 BC.

Not far from the Glanum ruins is the **Monastère Saint-Paul de Mausole** ★. The painter Vincent Van Gogh checked himself into the clinic here during the last year of his life (1890). In a peaceful, wooded setting, you may visit the pretty, 12th-century colonaded ***cloître***, or cloister next to the Romanesque chapel *(15F; 9am to noon and 2pm to 6pm; Avenue Edgar Leroy)*. A bust of the painter by the sculptor Zadkine, once stood along the path leading to the cloister, but was stolen in 1990.

The **Musée d'Archéologie** *(15F; guided 1hr visits every hour; Apr to Jun and Sep and Oct, 10am, 11am and 2pm to 5pm; Nov, 10am, 11am and 2pm to 4pm; Dec, 10am, 11am, 3pm and 4pm; Jul and Aug, 10am, 11am and 2:30pm to 6:30pm; Place Favier, ☎04.90.92.64.04)* situated in the pretty, 15th-century Hôtel de Sade contains columns, architectural pieces and everyday objects from the ruins of Glanum.

The **Musée des Alpilles** *(15F; Apr to Jun, Sep and Oct, open everyday 10am to noon and 2pm to 6pm; Jul and Aug, open everyday 10am to noon and 3pm to 8pm; Nov and Dec, open everyday 10am to noon and 2pm to 5pm, closed Jan to Mar; Place Favier, ☎04.90.92.08.10)* of ethnology, archaeology and daily life (costumes, furniture, objects) of the region is housed in the 16th-century Hotel Mistral de Montdragon, which has been restored (note the superb interior courtyard). There are interesting temporary exhibitions on the ground floor.

Another attractive 18th-century residence in the centre of Saint-Rémy is the Hôtel Estrine, now home to the **Centre d'Art Presence Van Gogh** *(20F; Sep to Jun, Tue to Sun 10am to noon and 2pm to 6pm; Jul and Aug, 10am to noon and 3pm to 7pm; 8 Rue Estrine, ☎04.90.92.34.72)*. It houses temporary exhibitions in beautifully restored rooms linked thematically or historically to Vincent Van

Gogh, as well as a permanent audio-visual exhibition about his work. However, this is not a Van Gogh gallery exposing the master's paintings. There is a well-stocked giftshop, selling books, postcards, posters, etc.

The **centre of Saint-Rémy ★**, with its winding narrow streets, is easily visited in a half day. Unfortunately, it is crowded with tourists during the summer, particularly during the day. Apart from fine 17th- and 18th-century mansions already mentioned, it is worth noting the Hôtel de Ville, or town hall in Place Pélissier, which is a former 17th-century convent, and the more recent Collégiale Saint-Martin church opposite Place de la République, with a world-famous organ entirely restored in 1985. Recitals are given as part of the "Oragana Festival" in summertime; inquire at the tourist office for details. At the corner of Rue Nostradamus and Rue Carnot is the mid-19th-century Nostradamus Fountain, commemorating the writer Michel de Nostredame, known as Nostradamus. He was born nearby in a house on Rue Hoche in 1503, but lived in Salon-de-Provence (see page 169).

The **Office du Tourisme** organizes 90min walking tours, one of which features the main sites and country landscapes painted by Vincent Van Gogh, and another that casts a historical eye on the architecture of the town centre *(30F per tour;* ***"Promenade sur les lieux peints par Van Gogh et Saint-Rémy"****, Apr 1 to Oct 15, Tue and Thu 10am, Sat 10am and 5pm;* ***"Au temps de Nostradamus"****, Apr 1 to Oct 15, Fri 10am; tours in English, German and Provençal are possible by prior arrangement).*

Maillane

A few kilometres north-east of Saint-Rémy on the D5 is the native town of Provençal hero Frédéric Mistral (1830-1914). This writer was the founder of the Félibrige movement of writers who worked in *langue d'oc*, a group of southern French dialects including Provençal, and an ardent protector of these languages, as well as being a Nobel-Prize recipient (1904). He spent his childhood in a nearby farmhouse, studied law in Aix-en-Provence and then returned to Maillane, where he lived first with his parents and then with his own family in the centre of town. In 1896, he created the Musée Arlatan in Arles with his personal collection of Provençal objects (see p 173). Mistral is mainly remembered for his poems *Mireille* and *Le poème du Rhône*, as well as for his *Mémoires*. His house, which has been converted into the **Musée Frédéric Mistral** *(admission fees still undetermined at press time; Apr to Sep 9:30am to 11:30am and 2:30pm to 6:30pm, Oct to Mar 10am to 11:30am and 2pm to 4:30pm; Rue de Lamartine, ☎04.90.995.74.06)*, provides a glimpse at how the writer lived; across the way is the Maison du Lézard, where he lived with his mother in an earlier period. The museum reopened its doors in 1995 following a three-year renovation project. Mistral's tomb can be seen in the Maillane cemetery.

Baux

Baux is remarkably situated on top of a craggy plateau with amazing panoramic views. The entire village has been classified a historical monument, and has therefore received subsidies to restore its charming stone buildings. It is one of the most popular tourist sites in all of France, and therefore is terribly crowded. This, coupled with the incredible number of souvenir shops, may diminish the pleasure of the visit for some.

Baux was an important military centre in the Middle Ages until the early 15th century when the Baux seigneurs controlled much of present-day southern France. They considered themselves descendants of Balthazar, the Magi King. The village's fortunes faded when the Baux line died out, at the same time as Provence became part of France. Following this, the village was abandoned for a time. The aluminum-rich mineral bauxite was discovered in the quarries of Baux in 1822, hence the mineral's name.

The village can only be visited on foot and the entrance is by the Porte Mage at the north end. The road on the right (Place Louis Jou and Rue de la Calade) leads past the old ramparts, the Porte Eyguières and ends at the Place de l'Église, which encompasses the 12th-century Église Saint Vincent and Chapelle Pénitents Blancs. There is a terrific view of the valley from here towards Arles. Straight ahead from the Porte Mage, the Grand'Rue leads past the 16th-century Hôtel de Manville (now the town hall and a contemporary art gallery) and the tourist office, and winds up to the old city.

The medieval city known as the **Citadelle** ★ *(39F; Mar to Nov, 8am to 7:30pm; Jul and Aug, closes at 9pm; Nov to Feb, 9am to 5:30pm; ☎04.90.54.55.56)* is at the top of the Rue de Traencat. Beyond the ticket office is the well-presented village museum, exhibiting objects found during archaeological digs. The citadelle itself occupies three-quarters of the Baux plateau. You'll need an hour to explore the sights marked out. These include the restored Chapelle Saint-Blaise, now housing a minor museum devoted to the olive tree, the ruins of a feudal château destroyed by Louis XIII's forces in 1631, the château's dungeon and a cemetery. The panoramic views are superb—especially overlooking the Val d'Enfer (Hell Valley).

The Alpilles

A pleasant day or two may be spent discovering the many small villages encircling the Alpilles chain. This is an area of contrasts—cherry orchards and fields of olive trees lead to pretty roads bordered by row upon row of tall plane trees, next to arid hills and white, jagged limestone hills. The Alpilles are famous for olive oil. Two types of olives are cultivated here: the Picholine and the Salonenque. They are cultivated by hand during the harvest months, September to February. Nowadays, three main co-operatives are the principal producers: Fontvieille, Maussane and Mouriès. For more details or information contact either **Comité de Promotion des Produits Agricoles** *(22 Avenue Henri Pontier, 13001 Aix-en-Provence, ☎04.42.23.06.11)* or **Comité Pour l'Expansion de l'Huile d'Olive** *(68 Boulevard Lazer, 13010 Marseille, ☎04.91.25.40.71).*

Our tour starts and ends at Saint-Rémy (adapt this circular tour to your own needs). Follow the scenic D99 road with its canopy of plane trees for 8km (5mi), then turn right on to the D74. Pass the handsome 16th-century Mas de la Brune mansion (private) and stop at **Eygalières** ★. The most interesting part is the old part of town, the **Vieux Village** ★, which is reached by leaving the Grand'Rue and ascending the Rue de l'Église, past pretty stone houses. At the top, near the old village gate, turn onto a pathway leading to the ruins of a château, circular watch-tower and Église Saint-Laurent. The 17th-century seigneurial Pénitents chapel contains the **Musée des Amis du Vieil Eygalières** *(free admission; Apr to Oct, Sun 3pm to 6pm; ☎04.90.95.91.52)*, a small museum with a collection of archaeological artifacts discovered in the Éygalières area—a reminder that

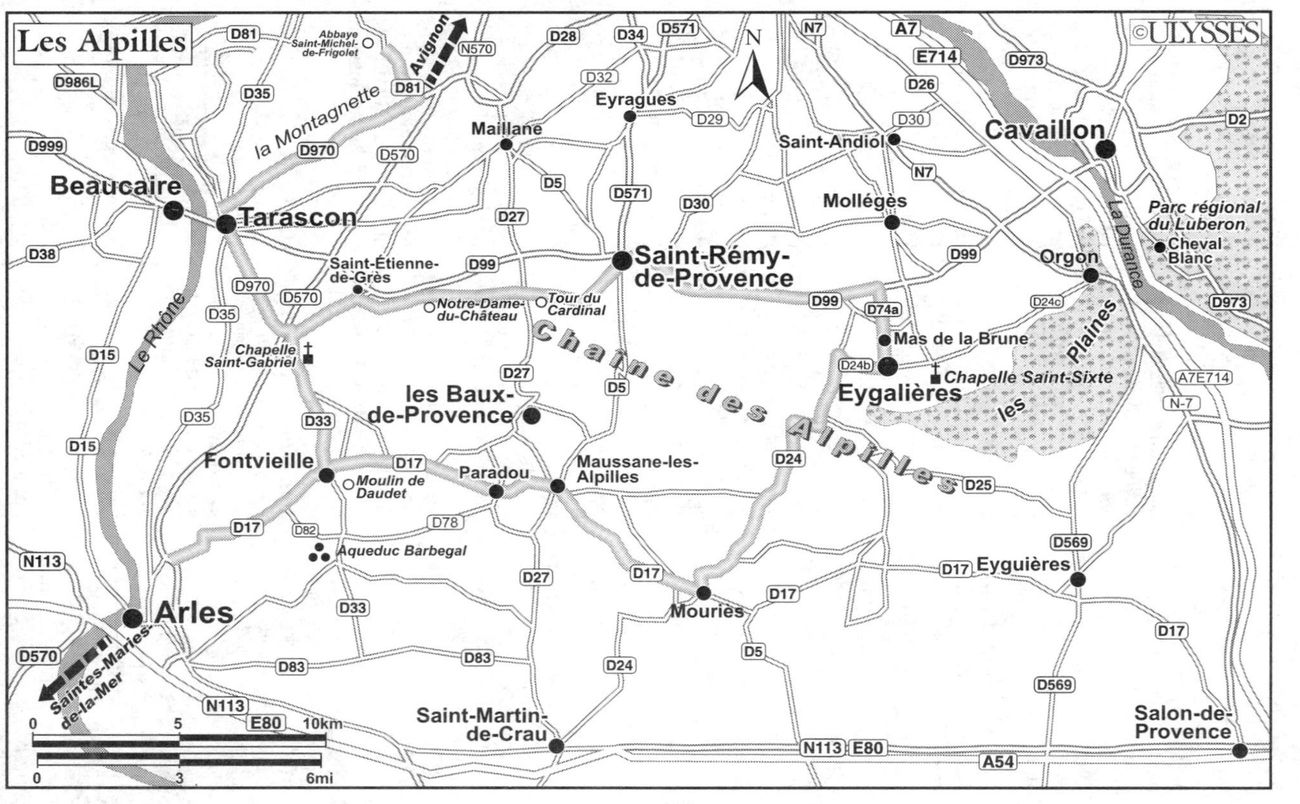
Les Alpilles
©ULYSSES
N
Avignon
Abbaye Saint-Michel-de-Frigolet
la Montagnette
Beaucaire
Tarascon
Le Rhône
Arles
Saintes-Maries-de-la-Mer
Eyragues
Maillane
Saint-Étienne-de-Grès
Notre-Dame-du-Château
Tour du Cardinal
Chapelle Saint-Gabriel
Saint-Rémy-de-Provence
Chaîne des Alpilles
les Baux-de-Provence
Fontvieille
Moulin de Daudet
Paradou
Maussane-les-Alpilles
Aqueduc Barbegal
Mouriès
Saint-Martin-de-Crau
Saint-Andiol
Mollégès
Cavaillon
La Durance
Parc régional du Luberon
Cheval Blanc
Orgon
Mas de la Brune
Eygalières
Chapelle Saint-Sixte
les Plaines
Eyguières
Salon-de-Provence
D81
D986L
D35
D999
D38
D15
D970
D570
N570
D28
D34
D571
D32
D29
D5
D27
D99
D30
N7
A7
E714
D26
D973
D2
D74a
D24b
D24c
A7E714
N-7
D33
D17
D78
D82
D83
D24
D25
D569
N113
E80
A54
D570
0
5
10km
0
3
6mi

the site has been inhabited since Neolithic times. The views are wonderful from here and along the pathway next to the buildings (marked "La Calade").

One kilometre (0.6mi) east of Eygalières, along the D24B (direction Orgon) is the 12th-century **Chapelle Saint-Sixte ★** *(interior often closed)*. It rests solemnly on a low hill, in the middle of a heat-scorched plain and is a simple but moving example of Romanesque architecture.

Return to Éygalières and turn south on the D24 for 12km (7.5mi) to **Mouriès**. It is the region's most important olive-oil producer, and visits of the co-operative mill are interesting. **Moulin à Huile Coopératif** *(Wed 2pm tp 6pm, Sat 8:30am to noon and 2pm to 6pm; Route D17 just outside Mouriès village centre, in the direction of Éyguières, ☎04.90.47.50.01)*.

Next, take the D17 west (past pretty fields of sunflowers in the summer) to **Maussane-les-Alpilles**. Activity in this lively village centres around the Place de l'Église, a typical Provençal square. There are a number of good restaurants and antique shops (see p 186 and p 192), and the place manages to be both animated and peaceful. Maussane's olive oil is famous throughout France for its high quality—you can buy it directly from the mill which dates from the 16th century, **Coopérative Oléicole de la Vallée des Baux** *(Mon to Sat 8am to noon and 2pm to 6pm, closed holidays; Rue Charloun-Rieu, ☎04.90.54.32.37)*.

Follow the D17 past Paradou to **Fontvieille** where the Provençal writer Alphonse Daudet spent much of his time. Daudet devotees will enjoy paying a visit to the superb, 19th-century **Château de Montauban** *(joint ticket allowing entry to the Moulin de Daudet: 20F; Apr to Sep, open everyday; Rue de Montauban, ☎04.90.54.62.57)*. The writer visited his friends here many times, and the chateau is now a small museum recreating these sojourns. A short way along the picturesque D33 sideroad is the mill that inspired Daudet's story *Les lettres de mon moulin*. A small museum in the **Moulin de Daudet** exposes manuscripts and items related to the author *(10F; Oct to May, open every day 9am to noon and 2pm to 5pm; Jun to Sep, every day 9am to noon and 2pm to 7pm; closed Jan except Sun 10am to noon and 2pm to 5pm; ☎04.90.54.60.78)*. Fontvieille is the third in the triumvirate of great Alpilles olive-oil towns—its mill the **Moulin de Bédaride** *(Mon to Sat 8am to noon and 2pm to 6pm, Sun 2pm to 6pm)* can be visited, but attracts loads of people during peak periods.

Farther along the D33, at the D82 crossroads, are the ruins of the two **Barbegal aqueducts**, which date from the 1st to 3rd centuries. Though eroding, they have still provided historians with important insight into the Roman mechanical mind. One channelled water into an ingenous mill-like apparatus which was used to grind wheat (access to the aqueducts is by a short pathway).

From Fontvieille, follow the D33 north 10m (6.2mi) to the Romanesque **Chapelle Saint-Gabriel**, built around a Gallo-Roman site. Make your way back to Saint-Rémy, along the small sideroad west of **Saint-Étienne-du-Grès**, the hometown of the Provençal fabric manufacturer Olivades. Pass the **Notre-Dame du Château** chapel and later the **Tour du Cardinal** (cardinal's tower, a 16th-century private residence). There are fine scenic views along the way.

Salon-de-Provence

Salon is centrally located east of the Alpilles and the Crau, north of the wetlands known as the Étang de Berre and west of the Trévaresse hill chain. The major highways

A7–*Autoroute du Soleil*, N113 and D578 pass through Salon. Although there is a pretty centre with a few shaded streets and fountains, Salon is a bustling commercial town lacking the formidable history and charm of comparable places such as Arles and Aix-en-Provence. Salon's reputation is centred around the olive-oil industry and the manufacture (along with Marseille) of the famous blocks of soap. An earthquake hit the region in 1909, damaging parts of Salon. A French Air Force training academy was created here in 1936. In the town centre, note the 17th-century **Mairie** *(town hall, Cours Victor Hugo)* and the **Porte de l'Horloge** (clock gate, transformed into a bell tower) along the rampart wall. In front of the Porte de l'Horloge on the Place Crousillat is the 18th-century **Fontaine Mousse**, a curious bulbous water fountain made from moss.

The old town is perched on a hillside, atop the imposing **Château de l'Empéri** fortress, where a crenellated watch-tower is found. This former residence for the archbishops of Arles has been heavily restored (12th, 13th and 16th centuries) and now houses a French military history museum. Afficionados will appreciate the rich and comprehensive collection of costumed mannequins, weapons and cavalry standards, dating back to the time of Louis XIV at the **Château Musée de l'Empéri** *(25F; Apr to Sep, open everyday 10am to noon and 2:30pm to 6:30pm; Oct to Mar, Wed to Mon closes 6pm; Rue du Château, ☎04.90.56.22.36)*. Chamber music concerts are held in the château's Renaissance courtyard in early August *(details from the Théâtre Municipal Armand, 67 Boulevard Nostradamus, 13330 Salon-de-Provence, ☎04.90.56.00.82, ⇄04.90.56.69.30; tickets 100F and 50F)*.

The **Musée de Salon et de la Crau** *(15F; Mon, Wed to Fri, 10am to noon and 2pm to 6pm, Sat and Sun, 2pm to 6pm; Avenue Roger Donnadieu, ☎04.90.56.28.37)* is a small museum housed in an elegant 19th-century mansion, Le Pavillion. It examines the history, ethnology and popular traditions of the Crau plain and Salon-de-Provence region. A display on the first floor explains the history of the famous "Extra Pure 72% Oil" soap industry which blossomed during the late 19th century, and Provençal furniture, objects and paintings are shown.

The 16th-century writer Michel de Nostradame, known as Nostradamus, lived and worked in Salon-de-Provence. Scenes from his life and writings about astrology, meteorology and medicine are on display in the home where he lived with his wife and children, the **Maison de Nostradamus** *(25F; mid-Jun to mid-Sep, 10am to noon and 3pm to 8pm; mid-Sep to mid-Jun, 10am to noon and 2pm to 6pm; 11 Rue Nostradamus, ☎04.90.56.64.31)*. Nostradamus was acclaimed for his predictions published in *Centuries*, such as the death of King Henry II on a battle-field. His acclaim spread nation-wide and even Catherine de Médicis, Henry's widow, stopped in Salon in 1564 to speak with him. Nostradamus is buried in the 14th-century **Église Collégiale Saint-Laurent** (outside the old town on the Carré Jean XXIII), a sober example of the Provençal Gothic style.

Arles

Arles is often called the Rome of Gaul. It offers a number of world-famous monuments within a very compact area bordered by old rampart walls. Evidence of human presence in the Arles area dates to 2,500 BC. Greek traders moved here after their founding of Marseille, and a Ligurian tribe lived in the region from the 6th century BC.

The Roman leader Marius linked Arles to the sea by digging a canal to the Mediterranean near the end of the 2nd century BC. Julius Caesar's lieutenant, Tiberius Claudius Nero, along with veterans of the Sixth Legion, founded the Roman colony of Arles on September 21, 46 BC. It quickly became a major trading centre. Arles was not only connected to the sea but was strategically placed at the junction of the Rhône and was the principal land route linking Italy and Spain. The Roman's developed a sophisticated urban centre during the next 200 years, which included a road network based on a grid pattern, an arena, amphitheatre, baths, hygiene systems, gardens and promenades.

Following a quiet period, Arles experienced a period of great prosperity during the late 3rd century AD and early 4th century AD when Constantine temporarily made Arles his operations base. The town was an intellectual, military, political and religious centre of world-wide importance. It was a major shipbuilder, weapons manufacturer and mint. Following the spread of Christianity in the 3rd century, Arles became a religious centre in 417 when it was designated primateship of Gaul by the Pope.

Problems began to arise during the course of the fifth century, after the fall of the Roman Empire. Tribes of marauders swept down on Arles, which ultimately fell to Euric, the Visigoth king. The town's population was further scattered by subsequent invasions.

Relative prosperity returned following the death of Charlemagne in 843, when his empire passed into the hands of Germanic leaders. The city became the capital of the kingdom of Arles founded by Boson, which encompassed almost the entire area of present-day Provence. One hundred years later, this domain was part of the realm of the kingdom of Burgundy. Arles remained moderately independent of the rest of the region and was administered by an elected council, as well as by religious leaders. From 1150 to 1250, numerous Romanesque chapels and churches were built in the area. Emperor Fréderic Barberousse was crowned in magnificent Cathédrale Saint-Trophime (see p 173) in 1178. An economic downturn in the 13th century delayed completion of the cathedral's half-built cloister for a full century.

In 1481, Arles was integrated with Provence, which was later made part of France (1535). Marseille and Aix-en-Provence would then become important political and economic centres, and Arles suffered greatly from this shift. Nonetheless, the town was sufficiently prosperous to support the construction of many residences, each more charming than the last, during the 16th and 17th centuries (the Grand Prieuré de Malte, the Hôtel de Laval-Castellane, the Hôtel de Ville). Arles did experience a serious economic crisis after the French Revolution of 1789; it no longer enjoyed the status of an important port town, industry was developing in other towns, and the region from this point on had to rely on its agricultural potential.

Nowadays, Arles is the business and supply centre for the vast agricultural territories of the Crau and the Camargue. Tourism is now an important source of economic activity. Take the time to discover the old, narrow streets and elegant mansions dating from the 17th and 18th centuries.

A museum pass costing 70F includes one visit to each of the following monuments and museums: Amphithéâtre, Théâtre Antique, Musée Réattu, Cloître Saint-Trophime, Alyscamps, Thermes de Constatine, Cryptoportiques du Forum, Musée Arlatan,

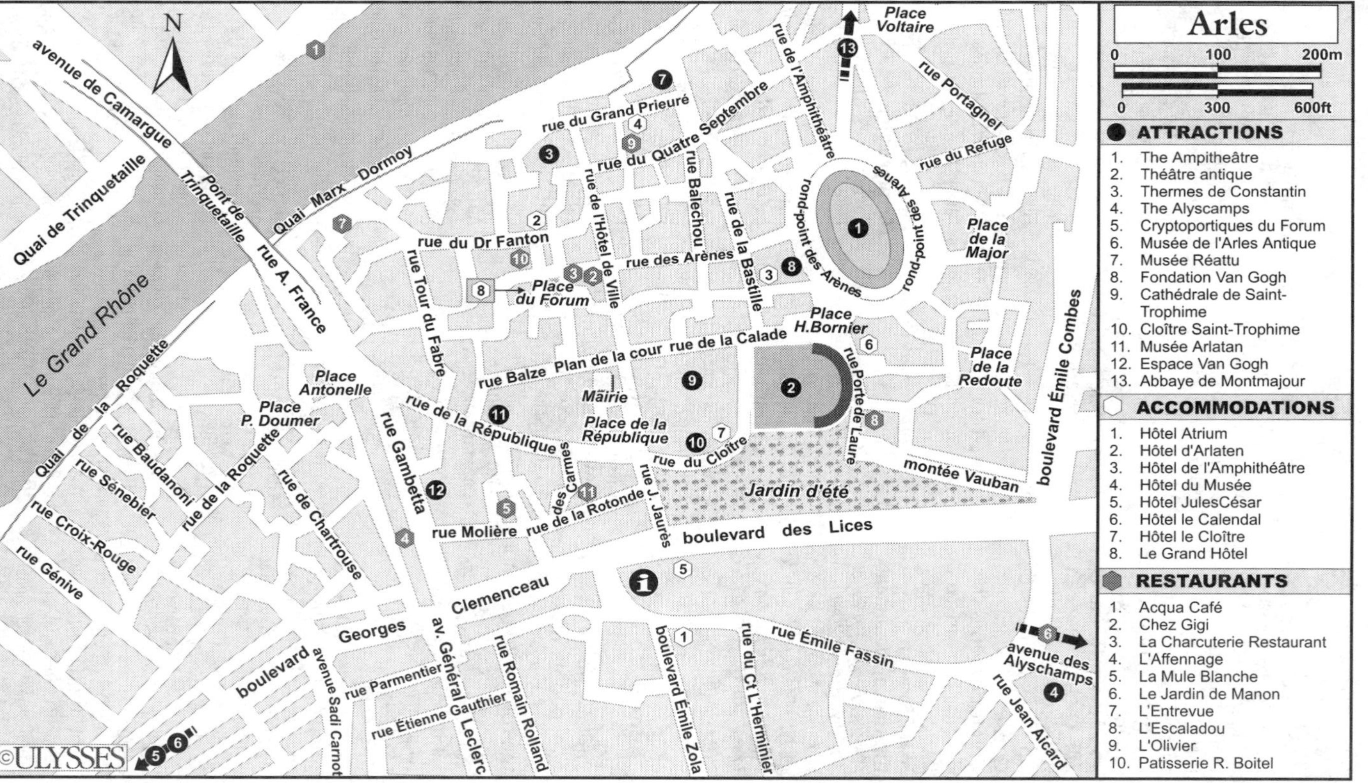
Arles
0
100
200m
0
300
600ft
ATTRACTIONS
1. The Ampitheâtre
2. Théâtre antique
3. Thermes de Constantin
4. The Alyscamps
5. Cryptoportiques du Forum
6. Musée de l'Arles Antique
7. Musée Réattu
8. Fondation Van Gogh
9. Cathédrale de Saint-Trophime
10. Cloître Saint-Trophime
11. Musée Arlatan
12. Espace Van Gogh
13. Abbaye de Montmajour
ACCOMMODATIONS
1. Hôtel Atrium
2. Hôtel d'Arlaten
3. Hôtel de l'Amphithéâtre
4. Hôtel du Musée
5. Hôtel JulesCésar
6. Hôtel le Calendal
7. Hôtel le Cloître
8. Le Grand Hôtel
RESTAURANTS
1. Acqua Café
2. Chez Gigi
3. La Charcuterie Restaurant
4. L'Affennage
5. La Mule Blanche
6. Le Jardin de Manon
7. L'Entrevue
8. L'Escaladou
9. L'Olivier
10. Patisserie R. Boitel
N
avenue de Camargue
Pont de Trinquetaille
Quai de Trinquetaille
Le Grand Rhône
Quai Marx Dormoy
rue A. France
Quai de la Roquette
rue Baudanoni
rue Sénebier
rue Croix-Rouge
rue Génive
rue de la Roquette
rue de Chartrouse
Place Antonelle
Place P. Doumer
rue Gambetta
rue Tour du Fabre
rue du Dr Fanton
Place du Forum
rue de l'Hôtel de Ville
rue du Grand Prieuré
rue du Quatre Septembre
rue Balechou
rue des Arènes
rue de la Bastille
rue de l'Amphithéâtre
Place Voltaire
rue Portagnel
rue du Refuge
rond-point des Arènes
Place de la Major
Place H.Bornier
rue Porte de Laure
Place de la Redoute
boulevard Émile Combes
montée Vauban
Jardin d'été
rue Balze
Plan de la cour
rue de la Calade
Mairie
Place de la République
rue de la République
rue du Cloître
rue des Carmes
rue de la Rotonde
rue J. Jaurès
rue Molière
boulevard des Lices
boulevard Georges Clemenceau
av. Général Leclerc
avenue Sadi Carnot
rue Parmentier
rue Étienne Gauthier
rue Romain Rolland
boulevard Émile Zola
rue du Ct L'Herminier
rue Émile Fassin
avenue des Alyschamps
rue Jean Aicard
©ULYSSES

Musée Réattu and the new Musée d'Arles Antique. It may be purchased at any one of the sites or at the tourism office; otherwise the major Roman monuments, Musée Arlatan and Musée Réattu cost 20F each, as does the Alyscamps, Théatre Antique, Thermes de Constantine and Cryptoportiques du Forum. The Musée de l'Arles Antique costs 35F. You can also visit the **Roman monuments** *(Nov to Feb, 9am to 11:30am and 2pm to 4:15pm; Mar to Oct, 9am to 12:15pm and 2pm to 6pm, though it is wise to check ahead for individual variations).*

★★★

Roman Monuments

Perhaps the first reason why people make their way to Arles is to see the town's Roman monuments. A convenient 70F ticket is available which allows admission to all the sites.

The **Amphithéâtre ★★★** *(20F; Rond Point des Arènes)* or arena, is the best-preserved of the lot. This Roman amphitheatre was built at the end of the first century AD for gladiator events and spectacles. It measures 136m by 107m (446ft by 351ft) and is 21m- (69ft) high, with two levels of 60 arcades. The large oval shape originally had 34 rows of seats and today holds 1200 people. The monument was saved in the Middle Ages when it was transformed into a fortress, which included 200 houses, two chapels, and a church. Four watchtowers where added which still remain. The arena was later restored in the 19th century by Charles X. Nowadays, it is used for Spanish (*corrida*) and local bull fighting (the non-violent *course à la cocarde*).

The **Théâtre Antique ★** *(20F; Place Henri Bornier)* or Roman theatre dates from the same period but little remains—two marble columns (out of 100 at the time), a part of the seating and the orchestra. Archaeologists surmise that it had 33 rows of seating and could accommodate 10,000 spectators.

The **Thermes de Constantine** *(20F; Rue du Grand Prieuré)*, the baths date from the 4th century AD, and despite heavy damage over the years, a large section of the hot baths, parts of the underground heating system and remains of the warm baths can be still seen.

The **Alyschamps ★** *(20F; Avenue des Alyscamps)* is a pretty, tomb-lined promenade that once was a Roman cemetery in the 3rd century AD. A tree-lined alley leads to the ruins of the necropolis, the Église Saint-Honoratus. It was used for this purpose up until the 12th century. In November 1888, Van Gogh painted the pleasant allies, and later, Gaughin did likewise. The more interesting decorated sarcophagi from the Alyscamps are on display in the newly-opened (April 1995) archeological museum.

Access to the **Cryptoportiques du Forum ★** is through the former museum of Christian art, the Musée Lapidaire d'Art Chrétien *(20F; Rue Balze)*. These are U-shaped underground galleries measuring 89m- (292ft) long and 59m- (194ft) wide, acted as the foundations of the former Place du Forum, while serving as a granary and warehouse.

The **Musée de l'Arles Antique** *(35F; call ahead for opening times; Avenue de la Première Division Française Libre, ☎04.90.96.92.00)* This recently opened museum, created in 1995, in a new building designed by Peruvian architect Henri Ciriani, is situated where the Roman Circus once stood. It houses the collections from the former Museum of Pagan Art and the Musée Lapidaire d'Art Chrétien (mosaics, statues, sarcophagi), plus a reference library, gift shop, seminar rooms and a cafeteria.

The **Muséon Arlatan ★★** *(20F; Nov to Mar, 9am to noon and 2pm to 5pm; Apr, May, Sep and Oct, closes at 6pm; Jun and Jul, closes at 7:30pm; Oct to Jun, closed Mon; Rue de la République, ☎04.90.96.08.23)*. Dusty and old-fashioned for some people, this museum is an absolute must for visitors who are interested in the rich local folklore of the Arles region. Housed in a 16th-century mansion, the Palais de Laval-Castellane, and founded in 1896 by the Provençal writer and Nobel Prize winner Frédéric Mistral, the Muséon Arlatan is a veritable treasure chest of discoveries. It is a major source of information on traditional life in Provence, with displays of furniture, costumes, ceramics and crafts—some of the descriptive tags are hand-written by Mistral himself. The recreated scenes of a large bedroom, women's sewing room, kitchen with hearth and generously laden table are well-prepared. The female attendants wear the Arlésienne dress—dark and sober in the winter time and colourful in the summer.

The **Musée Réattu ★** *(20F; Nov to Feb, 10am to 12:15pm and 2pm to 5:15pm; Mar, closes at 5:45pm; Apr to Sep, 9am to 12:15pm and 2pm to 6:45pm; Oct, 10am to 12:15pm and 2pm to 6:15pm; Rue du Grand Prieurié, ☎04.90.18.41.20)* houses a small selection of paintings and prints from the Provençal and European schools of the 18th and 19th centuries, plus tapestries, contemporary art and a small photography collection. Picasso donated 57 sketches to the museum—some of which are displayed. The beautiful 17th-century building is the former priory of Saint Gilles, once resided in by Arles painter Jaques Réattu. His work is well-represented here.

The **Foundation Van Gogh** *(30F; every day 10am to 12:30pm and 2pm to 7pm; 26 Rond-Point des Arènes, ☎04.90.49.94.04)* is an art centre that exposes the work of artists and writers who have paid homage to Van Gogh, including some set apart in a gallery dedicated to the creations of well-known contemporary figures such as Francis Bacon, César and Jasper Johns. The foundation occupies the rooms of the Palais de Luppé, across from the Roman amphitheatre.

The **Cathédrale Saint-Trophime ★★** *(Place de la République)* dates from the 12th century. After seven years of restoration, the outstanding beauty of the west door can now be fully appreciated. This celebrated door is a good reference point to better understand the Provençal Romanesque style. Its inspiration has been drawn from Roman architecture (notably triumphal arches): pediments supported by pilasters, Corinthian columns, and the perfectly proportioned figures whose costumes are accurately depicted. Statuary reflect scenes from the Last Judgement, the Adoration of the Magis, the Massacre of the Innnocents and Jesus' life. The interior is also a fine representation of the Provençal Romanesque style—simple lay-out, single nave, exceptionally-high broken vaulted ceiling and rounded narrow windows.

Cloître Saint-Trophime ★★ *(20F; every day 9am to 6:30pm)* or cloister, is reached by passing through the courtyard of the Palais de Archeveché (Archbishop's palace, now the municipal library) located right beside the cathedral. Two of the cloister's galleries are Romanesque, dating from the 12th century. Building stopped, however, when the monks ran out of money halfway through the construction process. Almost two hundred years later, when sufficient funds were gathered, the style of the day had changed. Gothic was in vogue and so the two remaining galleries are in this style. Miraculously, there is a harmony of vision—no wonder some consider the Saint-Trophime Cloître one of the most refined in the Western world. It should really be seen at different times during the day, when the sunlight gently falls on the sculptures adorning the columns and arches. The Roman gallery recounts scenes from the Old and New Testament, while the Gothic gallery represents events in the life of Saint Trophime, as well as the legend of Sainte Marthe of Tarascon and some mean-looking monsters.

L'Espace Van Gogh *(admission fees and opening hours vary according to the exhibitions; Rue du Président Wilson, ☎04.90.49.39.39)*, an ancient hospital where Van Gogh was once a patient, now serves as a media library, and a cultural and academic centre. Each year interesting temporary exhibitions are featured. (For more information concerning upcoming exhibits, contact the Arles tourist office.)

Abbaye Montmajour ★★ *(35F; Oct to Mar, open everyday 9am to noon and 2pm to 5pm; Apr to Sep, open everyday 9am to 7pm; 7km or 4.3mi from Arles, north along the N570, then the D17 towards Fontvieille, ☎04.90.54.64.17)*. A beautiful Benedictine abbey, originally built in the 10th century, although it primarily displays the Romanesque style which dates from the 12th century. It was closed down by Louis XVI following the French Revolution. The town of Arles and the state's historical monuments department have restored the 12th-century cloister, the severe-looking abbey with its formidable tower, plus the Notre-Dame church and crypt. If you have the strength to climb more than 120 steps, the panoramic view from the abbey tower is wonderful. Photographic exhibitions take place in the cloister every summer, as part of the Rencontres Internationales de la Photographie.

Tarascon

Tarascon lies on the banks of the Rhône River, facing the town of Beaucaire. Originally a trading port, Tarascon is now dependent on agriculture and industry for its livelihood. It is not crowded with visitors, and so a visit to the château, chuch and old town makes a pleasant half-day outing.

The town is famous for the story of Sainte Marthe, Tarascon's patron saint. According to legend, a diabolical land and sea monster known as the Tarasque, who lived in the Rhône under the present-day château, gobbled up women and children and caused havoc for river boats. He had a lion's head, dragon's body, spikey back and long serpent's tail. Sainte-Marthe came to Tarascon from Sainte-Maries-de-la-Mer in 48 AD to introduce Christianity to the pagan population. She converted the people by performing a miracle—with holy water and a cross, she tamed the horrible Tarasque. She threw her belt around the monster and brought it to the people of Tarascon who promptly pummelled it to death. Ever since the days of King René in the 15th century, the defeat of the beast is marked every June by a celebration, the *Fête de la Tarasque* (on the last Sunday in June), where a 6m (20ft) effigy of the monster is paraded through the streets.

The **Château du Roi René** *(32F; Apr to Sep, open everyday 9am to 7pm; Oct to Mar, 9am to noon and 2pm to 5pm; Boulevard du Roi René, ☎04.90.91.01.93)* is one of the best-preserved fortresses in France. Apart from a fine tapestry collection, the château is completely empty—its beauty is found in studying the magnificent stone structure itself. Built on the riverbank, it dates from the 13th century, but the present building was constructed by Louis II of Anjou and completed by his son, King René, Count of Provence, who lived here from 1471 until his death in 1480. It was a prison from the 1700s up until 1926, when it was restored by the historical monuments department.

be had from the open roof terrace.

Château du Roi René

The château is surrounded by a moat and tall defensive walls with imposing crenellated watch towers. Past the entrance gate, is a building once used as the castle's kitchen. Beyond the present-day gift boutique is a room housing the old apothecary of Tarascon's Saint Nicholas hospital. A remarkable collection of 205 earthenware pharmaceutical jars and pots dating from 1742 line the wooden shelves. Turning into the château's courtyard, the Cour d'Honneur, you'll find the vaulted Chapelle Basse and the Chapelle des Chantres. Upper floors include large reception rooms with huge stone fireplaces, the Queen's apartments and a council chamber. British marines, prisoners in the château, carved their names in the blond stone walls—their "graffiti" dating between 1757 and 1778 can be seen by the windows in the Salle des Fêtes. Exceptional **panoramic views ★★** can be had from the open roof terrace.

La Collégiale Sainte-Marthe ★ *(Boulevard du Roi René and Place de la Concorde)* was built following the supposed discovery of the relics of Sainte-Marthe in 1187. Part Romanesque, part Gothic, this church holds a rich collection of 17th- and 18th-century religious paintings, primarily by Provençal artists including Mignard and Vien. Note the 3rd-century crypt in the basement, with two sarcophagi— that of Sainte Marthe's dates from the late 4th century.

The **Cloître des Cordeliers** *(5F; Jun to Sep, 10am to noon and 3pm to 7pm, Oct to May, 2pm to 6pm; Place Frédéric Mistral, ☎04.90.91.00.07)* is a beautiful Franciscan nunnery built in the 14th century that today welcomes interesting exhibitions in the summertime.

Théâtre de Tarascon *(Rue Eugène Pelletan, ☎04.90.91.24.30)* recaptured its baroque splendour in 1987, with its charming pediment depicting two angels holding a lyre and, in its interior, 1,000 seats spread over three levels. The apse of an old Dominican church that had occupied the site since 1489 forms the stage wall. The theatre was destroyed in 1884 when an angry actor set fire to it following a performance of *Oedipe*, but it was rebuilt and opened its doors again four years later. It was further neglected after the Second World War, and closed down completely in 1963. Today, dance and opera troupes, as well as musical groups, appear here from September to May.

The **Hôtel de Ville** *(corner of Rue des Halles and Rue du Château)* dates from 1648, and its sculpted façade, with its stone balcony, figures on the register of historic monuments. Take note of the old, narrow streets that radiate from the street arcade, Rue des Halles, especially Rue Arc de Boqui, which was first used in the Middle Ages.

Another figure contributed to the notoriety of Tarascon in the French-speaking world: Tartarin, the main character in a series of satirical stories collected under the title *Les Aventures de Tartarin*, written in 1872 by local hero Alphonse Daudet (see Fontvieille, p 168). At the time, the people of the region were not particularly pleased to see their city and their customs ridiculed in this way on paper, but the feeling is quite different today. Fans of Daudet's work can even visit **La Maison de Tartarin** *(10F; Mar 15 to Apr 14 and Sep 15 to Dec 14, 10am to noon and 2pm to 5pm; Apr 15 to Sep 14, 10am to noon and 2:30pm to 7pm, closed Sun and from Dec 15 to Mar 14; 55bis Boulevard Itam,* ☎*04.90.91.03.52)*, where every room re-creates a scene from the life of Daudet's famous character.

Abbaye Saint Michel de Frigolet *(regular free guided visits, usually Mon to Fri 2:30pm, Sun and holidays 4pm, enquire at the shop first; the churches are open to the public during the day; along the D81, off the D970, 12km or 7.5mi from Tarascon and 17km or 10.6mi south of Avignon,* ☎*04.90.95.70.07)*. Resting on the pretty hill range known as the **Montagnette ★**, Saint Michel de Frigolet is a working abbey of the Prémontré order of monks. Visitors may see the 12th-century Notre-Dame du Bon-Remède chapel, which was altered in the 17th century with baroque decorations and gilded wood-panelling. The abbey includes a shop, an inn and a restaurant.

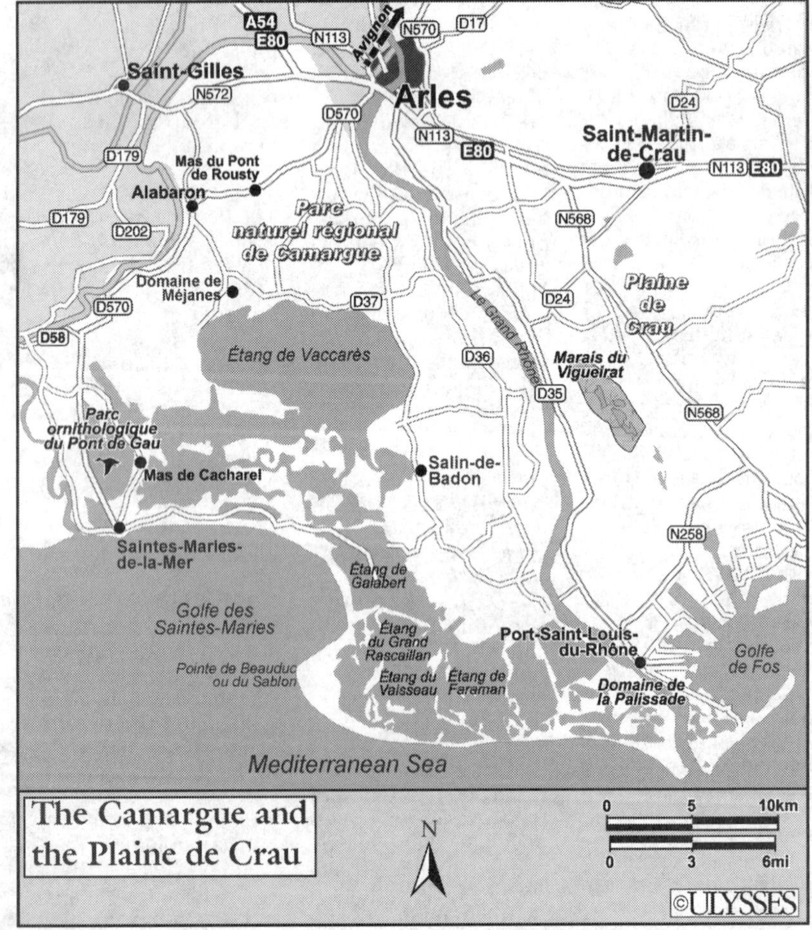

The Camargue and the Plaine de Crau

Crau

This vast plain area measuring 60,000ha (148,258 acres) south-east of Arles is the last natural steppe in Europe. The irrigated northern half is used for growing an excellent variety of hay, known as *foin de Crau*. The semi-arid terrain of the southern half, once the river bed of the Durance, is covered by millions of pebbles, and measures 11,500ha (28,416 acres). The plain is principally used for raising sheep, who graze here during the cooler months, generally mid-October to mid-February.

Crau's irrigation system, the air-force base in nearby Istres and the industrial complex in Fos-sur-Mer all threaten the plain's ecosystem, where a unique fauna and flora abound. For example, the pin-tailed sandgrouse (*ganga cata*), an endangered species that inhabits the region, numbers only 150 pairs throughout France, and this figure is decreasing. Recently, however, French and European environmental-protection groups have been drawing public attention to Crau's problems.

Saint-Martin-de-Crau

Saint-Martin de Crau *(N453 then N213 east of Arles)* is the most important town in the area. Here you'll find the modest **Écomusée de la Crau** *(free admission, open everyday 9am to noon and 2pm to 6pm; Route N113, ☎04.90.47.02.01)* which explains the flora, fauna and history of the area. Next to the museum is a 14th-century late-Romanesque church.

Seven kilometres (4.3mi) further south-west on the D24, the hamlet of **Dynamite** appears. This was once an autonomous community with dormitories, a store, a church and a post office. These were all of these set around a factory that produced explosives (hence the town's name) that were used in agriculture, road construction and military armament. For health and safety reasons, the workers were moved to Saint-Martin-de-Crau in 1988, and the village was intentionally razed.

The Camargue

The Camargue wetlands delta are bound to surprise and fascinate first-time visitors to southern France. Leave behind the post-card image of charming Provençal villages perched on the sides of cliffs, with rolling fields of lavender and fruit orchards nearby. Here, 72,000ha (177,910 acres) of flat terrain, marshes, ponds and beaches, lie south of Arles wedged for the most part between the Petit Rhône and the Grand Rhône rivers and the Mediterranean Sea.

Much of the Camargue is a natural park and protected from excessif development. As a result, large colonies of pink flamingoes (unique in Europe) and a variety of rare birds make this area an ornithologists paradise. The principal economic activities are agriculture and tourism.

Flamingo

The area is renowned for its black bull ranches, known as *manades*, and for the semi-wild Camargue horse. Traditionally used to help herders (*gardiens*) control their bulls and to grind wheat, the Camargue horses are now primarily bred for the tourists, who hire them to explore the region with a guide. Though pale-grey or white as an adult, ponies are born with dark, sometimes black, coats. They are relatively small, with large feet and hard hooves, particularly adapted for the soft earth.

Apart from horseback-riding, bird-watching, visiting a *manade* to see a local rodeo (usually open to groups only) and visiting the seaside, there is not a lot to do in the Camargue. Some people spend days or a week enjoying the natural habitat. Others drive down from Arles or Avignon for just half a day, to get a taste of the region and say hello to the flamingoes (don't forget to bring along a pair of binoculars). Services like gas stations are difficult to find (there are none between Arles and Saintes-Maries-de-la-Mer), so fill your tank before setting out, and bring drinking water and insect repellent (mosquitoes and marshlands are the best of friends!).

To find out more about the area's unique history and flora and fauna, visit the **Musée Camarguais** *(30F; Oct to Mar, Wed to Mon 10:15am to 4:45pm; Apr to Sep, everyday 9:15am to 5:45pm; Jul and Aug, closes at 6:45pm; Mas du Pont de Rousty, 12 km or 7.5mi southwest of Arles on the D570, ☎04.90.97.10.82).*

Explore the exceptional 1,000ha (2,471 acres) of the **Marais du Vigueirat** *(55F; reservations for visits can be made at the Mas-Thibert, tours Apr to Jun and Sep, Tue, Thu, Sat and Sun 4pm to 8pm, Jul and Aug every day 4pm to 8pm, Oct to Dec and Jan to Mar, Sat and Sun 10am to 4pm; take the D35 from Arles, ☎04.90.98.70.71, marais-du-vigueirat@wanadoo.fr)* by going on a pleasant nature-discovery walk. The trail has six observation posts and allows you to explore on foot the vast marshes where the horses and bulls of the Camargue graze. Small groups accompanied by a naturalist guide give you the opportunity to experience this wildlife up close. You will also see flora that has adapted wonderfully to this area and come to understand the powerful bond between humans and nature in the Camargue. As of mid-2000, a 450m (2,126ft) trail is open during summer, allowing for recreational and instructive exploration of the Camargue.

Formerly a private hunting estate, the **Domaine de la Palissade** *(15F; every day 9am to 5pm; Route de la Mer, D36d, take the D570 from Arles then the D36, ☎04.42.86.81.28)* has now been designated one of the nature preserves of Europe (Natura 2000) that is open to the public. This estate is the last of these preserves to be located outside of the dykes that separate the Camargue from the river and the sea. Exhibits and trails allow visitors to discover on foot or on horseback the flora and fauna that live around the mouth of the Rhône.

Saintes-Maries-de-la-Mer

A seaside tourist town that was once a tranquil fishing port, Saintes-Maries-d-la-Mer is now host to sun-loving vacationing families and teenagers. Legend has it that in 40 AD, Mary Salome (mother of the apostles Jack the Major and John) and Mary Jacob (sister of the Virgin Mary), as well as Mary Magdelene, Martha, Lazarus and Maximus, were forced from Jerusalem by the Jews and landed by boat at this port, accompanied by their Ethiopian servent Sarah (patron saint of the Tsiganes or gypsies). Mary Salome and Mary Jacob remained in the Camargue (thus becoming the town's patron saints) with Sarah, while the others parted to spread Christianity to Provence. Pilgrimages every year celebrate the arrival of this trio of women: there is the very colourful gypsy festivals the Fête des Gitans on the 24th and 25th of May, and another in October (see p 191).

In the late 1980s, the Camargue's own Gypsy Kings popularized the latin guitar songs native to this region, some of which topped music charts around the world. The group is no longer together, but one of its members, Chico, occasionally performs in the area. Some restaurants provide live gypsy music during the summer season (for example, La Manade in Sainte-Maries-de-la-Mer, see p 190).

Saintes-Maries de la Mer is touristy in the summer months. Visitors will be overwhelmed by street after street of seafood restaurants (with identical menus, some serving frozen fish) and the number of souvenir stands selling suntan lotion and ice-cream cones.

However, it is worthwhile noting the **Église Notre-Dame ★★** *(Place de l'Église)*, which dates from the 12th century, and was fortified in the 15th century against invasions by pirates and invaders. The upper chapel includes a shrine holding the relics of the two Sainte Maries found in 1448, while the **crypt** *(May to mid-Sep, 8am to noon and 2pm to 7pm; mid-Sep to Oct, Mar and Apr, 8am to 7pm; Nov to Feb, 8am to 6pm)* holds an eerie statue of Sarah next to her altar. Near the vending machine inside the church door, are the stairs leading to the rooftop terrace *(10F; closed between noon and 2:30pm)* which has superb **panoramic views ★★** of the Camargue and seacoast.

Spring and autumn are the best times to see the greatest variety of birdlife in the Camargue, which includes all nine species of herons living in Europe. The **Parc Ornithologique du Pont de Gau** *(35F; everyday 9am to sunset; Route D570 just north of Saintes-Maries-de-la-Mer, ☎04.90.97.82.62)* is a 12ha (30 acres) outdoor bird sanctuary with explanatory panels that let you see the real thing up close with a museum describing the area's rich ornithological life.

Outdoor Activities

Hiking

One of the nicest trails is the GR6, which crosses the Alpilles from west to east, passing by Les Baux-de-Provence. The path follows the ridge of the craggy hills and offers panoramic views as far as the Camargue, Mont Ventoux and the Luberon. Shorter, well-marked trails are found along the hilly area known as La Montagnette (starts at the Abbeye Saint-Michel-de-Frigolet north of Tarascon) and in the Alpilles starting from Saint-Etienne-du-Grès, Saint-Rémy-de-Provence, Les Baux-de-Provence and Éyguires. The Saint-Rémy tourist office publishes a free leaflet suggesting a number of walking trails of varying degrees of difficulty in the region. Note: outdoor activities are prohibited in wooded areas of the Alpilles during July and August due to the risk of forest fires. However, many fine walking trails are accessible around the villages and in the plains year-round.

Mountain Biking

Although the hilly Alpilles attract hardy mountain bikers, the scenic plains and pretty villages of this area are ideal for those seeking less taxing rides.

Bike Rentals

Saint-Rémy-de-Provence

Ferri
35 Avenue de la Libération
☎04.90.92.10.88

Arles

Peugeot
15 Rue du Pont
☎*04.90.96.03.77*

Dall'Oppio
Mar to Oct
Rue Portagnel
☎*04.90.96.46.83*

Tarascon

Cycles Christophe
70 Boulevard Itam
☎*04.90.91.25.85*

MBK
1 Rue E. Pelletan
☎*04.90.91.42.32*

Saintes-Maries-de-la-Mer

Camargue Vélos
27 Rue Frédéric Mistral
☎*04.90.97.94.55*

Le Vélociste
1 Place des Rempaarts
☎*04.90.97.83.26*

Le Vélo Saintois
8 Route de Cacharel
☎*04.90.97.74.56*

Horseback Riding

The following associations, farms and *manades* (ranches) propose guided tours of the region on horseback.

Saint-Rémy-de-Provence

Club Hippique des Antiques
Rue Etienne Astier
☎*04.90.92.30.55*

Tarascon

Ferme Equestre de Bernercac
Grand Domaine de Frigolet
☎*04.90.90.53.66*

Centre Equestre de Lansac
Mas Lansac
☎*04.90.91.42.87*

Manades

There is a plethora of *manades* in the Camargue and not all can be mentioned here, so inquire at your hotel or local tourist office for exact details. These four have good reputations:

Manade Jalabert
La Chassagne en Camargue
☎*04.90.97.00.54*

Domaine de Méjanes
Albaron
☎*04.90.97.10.62*
Large complex with a restaurant next to the Étang de Vaccares pond; rodeo shows, tourist train and tours on horseback.

Manade Jacques Bon
Le Sambuc
☎*04.90.97.20.62*
Professional ranch with rodeos and tours on horseback; managed by Jacques Bon, the charismatic host of the new luxury bed and breakfast Mas de Peint (see p 184).

Golf

Baux

Golf des Baux de Provence
Domaine de Manville, 13520 Les Baux-de-Provence
☎*04.90.54.40.20*
Proshop, restaurant, equipment rental, nine-hole course.

Mouriès

Golf Club de Servannes
Château de Servannes, B.P. 6
☎*04.90.47.59.95*
Proshop, restaurant, equipment rental, 18 hole course.

Swimming

Beaches for sun-bathing and swimming are found in the Camargue along the seacoast. Long sandy beaches are best at Saintes-Maries-de-la-Mer (east and west of the village) and are popular during the summer months.

For followers of naturism, there is an authorized nudist beach 1km (0.6mi) east of the access road to the Plage d'Arles (Arles beach), located in the Camargue in the Salin de Giraud area. A second nudist beach created by the local municipality is located about 6km (3.7mi) east of Saintes-Maries-de-la-

Mer, just before the Phare de la Gacholle lighthouse. It is reached only by walking along the Saintes-Maries-de-la-Mer beach.

Accommodations

Saint-Rémy-de-Provence

Hôtel Ville Verte
200F-280F
pb
Place de la République
☎04.90.92.06.14
⇄04.90.92.56.54
A simple hotel with a homely style and owners full of local wit and colour. Fully equipped studios with kitchenettes are available for two people or four people.

Mexican Café
240F
open Easter to late Aug
ps
4 Rue du 8 Mai 1945
☎04.90.92.17.66
Overlooking Monsieur Cecchi's Mexican restaurant are a few bedrooms—rustic, colourful and among the least expensive in Saint-Rémy.

Hôtel du Cheval Blanc
280F-310F
pb/ps, tv
6 Avenue Fauconnet
☎04.90.92.09.28
⇄04.90.92.69.05
A comfortable, though basic, hotel for a moderate price in a town with rather elevated prices.

Auberge de la Reine Jeanne
350F
closed Jan and Feb
pb, tv, ℜ
12 Boulevard Mirabeau
☎04.90.92.15.33
⇄04.90.92.49.65
Set back from Saint-Rémy's main street, this hotel offers 11 freshly decorated rooms in a country-inn atmosphere. Shaded courtyard for summer meals (lunch and dinner) and rustic restaurant with large hearth in cooler months.

Le Castellet des Alpilles
520F
closed Nov 1 to late Mar
pb, ℜ
6 Place Mireille
☎04.90.92.07.21
⇄04.90.92.52.03
Many of this hotel's simply decorated rooms dispose of small patios or balconies facing south, and Madame Canac-Roux greets all of her guests with a warm and friendly welcome. The furniture is outdated, however, and the restaurant is to be avoided if at all possible.

Le Mas des Carassins
600F
closed mid-Nov to mid-Mar
pb
One Chemin Gaulois
☎04.90.92.15.48
⇄04.90.92.63.47
Just south of the town centre off Avenue Van Gogh lies this quiet hotel nestled by a pretty garden with a variety of trees, shrubs and flowers. The rustic-style rooms are a bit outdated, but very clean and comfortable, and the hosts are very hospitable.

Vallon de Valrugues
780-1,165F
ℜ, bar, ≈, ⌂, ⊙, ≡, pb, mini-bar, tv
Chemin Canto Cigalo
☎04.90.92.04.40
⇄04.90.92.44.01
vallon.valrugues@wanadoo.fr
A four-star luxury resort, decorated with style, though lacking in local charm. Every need is taken care of, and the renowned gastronomic restaurant is excellent. A variety of fixed-price menus make good use of fresh Provençal ingredients. All around professional, friendly service.

Baux

La Burlande
380F
≡, pb, tv
13520 Le Paradou
☎04.90.54.32.32
Tranquil bed and breakfast, each of the three rooms and the one suite has its own terrace. A cold lunch platter by the pool and evening meal are available. Signposted from the D78, south of Baux, near Le Paradou. Warm and considerate welcome. No credit cards.

Auberge de la Benvengudo
650F-980F
closed end of Oct to Mar 1
ℜ, ≈, pb, tv
☎04.90.54.32.54
⇄04.90.54.42.58
benvengudo@aol.com
Tasteful rooms, pretty garden and inviting pool. True comfort in an exceptional site, though the Route d'Arles road rumbles quietly nearby.

Eygalières

Mas dou Pastré
380F-690F
≈, pb, tv, some rooms with mini-bar
Route d'Orgon
☎04.90.95.92.61
⇄04.90.90.61.75
In a stone farmhouse, 10 spacious, recently decorated rooms in charming Provençal style. Well-equipped bathrooms, and each room has a wicker basket with an extra towel for the swimming pool. Friendly hostess.

Maussane

L'Oustaloun
320F-400F
closed Jan 2 to Feb 10
ℜ, pb, tv
Place de l'Église, 13520 Muassane
☎04.90.54.32.19
A friendly, attentive welcome greets you in this attractively decorated nine-room hotel, next to the shaded town square and church. The restaurant (closed Wednesdays) is recommended for its simple, Provençal cuisine—served in front of the town's fountain in good weather.

Salon-de-Provence

Hôtel Vendôme
255F-300F
pb
34 Rue Mal Joffre, 13300 Salon-de-Provence
☎04.90.56.01.96
There's not much choice in this town where most hotels face noisy roads or lack charm. You can't go wrong with the Vendôme: 23 simple rooms (many face a quiet central courtyard with small basin) in an oldish building. Very clean, very friendly.

Arles

Auberge de Jeunesse
closed Dec 16 to Feb 5
Avenue Maréchal Foch
☎04.90.96.18.25
Restaurant, garden, tv room, 108 beds (dormitories and rooms).

Hôtel du Musée
230F-490F
closed early Jan to early Feb
ps/pb, tv
11 Rue du Grand Prieuré
☎04.90.93 88 88
⇄04.90.49 98 15
A very pleasant two-star hotel. Rooms are bright and decorated with Provençal-style furniture. In warm weather, breakfast is taken on a sunny interior courtyard.

Hôtel Le Cloître
250F-410F
closed Jan and Feb
pb
16 Rue du Cloitre
☎04.90.96.29.50
⇄04.90.96.02.88
hotel_cloitre@hotmail.com
Arles lacks adequate, inexpensive accommodation, but this one does the trick. Thirty clean rooms, with small bathrooms. Large breakfast room with a 13th-century stone arch. Rooms 20 and 18, though tiny, have glorious views overlooking the Saint-Trophime cloister and church.

Hôtel Saint Trophime
290F-345F
closed late Nov to Mar
ps/pb, tv
16 Rue de la Calade
☎04.90.96.88.38
⇄04.90.96.92.19
A centrally located hotel in a 17th-century building. Rooms are simple and somewhat outdated.

Hôtel Le Calendal
290F-450F bkfst incl.
pb/ps, tv
22 Place Pomme
☎04.90.96.11.89
⇄04.90.96 05 84
contact@lecalendal.com
www.lecalendal.com
A sunny, bright hotel near the Arenes with Proveçal decor. Breakfast buffet and light meals are served on a pretty, shaded garden terrace. A new terrace has also been installed on the side facing the Rue Port de Laure.

Hôtel de l'Amphithéâtre
310F-360F
pb/ps, tv
5 Rue Diderot
☎04.90.96.10.30
⇌04.90.93.98.69
www.hotelamphitheatre.fr
Open since 1997, this charming hotel is in a renovated *hôtel particulier* and is decorated simply yet with great style (bathroom floors of terracotta tiles, warm yellow walls and attractive furnishings). It is opposite the pretty Place Jacques Henri Lartigue and steps away from the Roman amphitheatre.

Hôtel d'Arlatan
350F, 500F and 950F
bar, pb, ≡, mini-bar, tv
26 Rue Sauvage, 13631 Arles
☎04.90.93.56.66
⇌04.90.49.68.45
www.hotel-arlatan.fr
An utterly charming hotel in the elegant former residence of Roi René's intendant, the Count Jean d'Arlatan de Beaumont. Thirty individually decorated rooms (plus 11 apartments: 1,050-1,550F) with lovely Provençal furniture and antiques. Delicious breakfast with fresh croissants and pastries, jams and terrific coffee (served in the inner-courtyard next to a fountain during the summer). Friendly service and sincere smiles from the Desjardins family. Near the Place du Forum.

Hôtel Atrium
540F-630F
pb, ≡, tv, minibar, ≈, ℜ
1 Rue Émile Fassin
☎04.90.49.92.92
⇌04.90.93.38.59
atrium.arles@nanadoo.fr
www.hotelatrium.com
Hôtel Atrium offers comfortable lodgings right in the centre of town. Its decor is comparable to that of many establishments affiliated with large international hotel chains, and there is a swimming pool on the roof. Most popular with organized tours and business people.

Hôtel Jules-César
680F-1,250F
ℜ, pb, ≡, mini-bar, tv
Boulevard des Lices, 13631 Arles
☎04.90.93.43.20
⇌04.90.93.33.47
www.hotel-julescesar.fr
Centrally located, luxury hotel (part of the Relais & Châteaux chain), in a former 16th-century convent. Well-equipped rooms, newly decorated in bland Provençal style. Excellent dining room with good wine list; the superb breakfast *(and lunch menu at 105F)* is served in the pretty, landscaped cloister. Professional welcome.

Le Grand Hôtel Nord-Pinus
840F-990F
closed Feb
ℜ and bar, pb, ≡, mini-bar, tv
Place du Forum
☎04.90.93.44.44
⇌04.90.93.34.00
info@nordpinus.com
www.nord-pinus.com
Ideally-situated on the Place du Forum, this hotel has welcomed numerous toreadors and celebrities in its past. Anne Igou reopened the hotel in 1989, and has kept the Nord-Pinus' charm, blending good taste with a touch of kitsch. Wrought-iron beds and a fun mix of antiques and bric-a-brac items are found in each room; spacious, well-equipped bathrooms. Old photos and bullfighting memorabilia fill the salon and bar (frequented by the fashion-designer and Arles native Christian Lacroix, among others).

Tarascon

Auberge de Jeunesse
closed annually Dec 15 to Mar 1
48F
31 Boulevard Gambetta
☎04.90.91.04.08
⇌04.90.91.54.17
tarascon@fuaj.org
Reception room, six dormitories (eight or 12 beds each), 65 places in total. Member of FUAJ (YHA).

Mas de Gratte Semelle
500F
≈, pb, K, tv
Route d'Avignon
☎04.90.95.72.48
⇌04.90.90.54.87
In her old stone Provençal farmhouse, Thécla Fargepallet offers a large, split-level apartment with sitting room, two bedrooms, fully-equipped kitchen (including clothes and dish washer) and a large terrace with views of the rolling

Montagnette hills. Another smaller room is also available. An evening meal is available, even for non-residents. Can be rented for weekends or by the week. Close to all the Alpilles sites. No credit cards.

The Crau

Château de Vergières
850F
pb
13310 Saint-Martin-de-Crau
☎04.90.47.17.16
⇌04.90.47.38.30
www.ila-chateau.com/manade
A bed and breakfast in a late-18th-century château? Why not! Jean and Marie-Andrée Pincedé welcome you warmly, without ostentation, to their tasteful home that is set in a surprisingly verdant spot amidst the pebbly Crau plain. Six spacious bedrooms.

Camargue

Le Mas de Pioch
265F-285F or 295F-305F
≈, ps or pb, tv in some rooms
Route d'Arles, 13460 Saintes-Maries-de-la-Mer, D570 just south of the D38
☎04.90.97.50.06
⇌04.90.97.55.51
The Camargue has a surplus of expensive, often mediocre, motel accommodations. This bungalow-style hotel with 12 basic, though clean rooms in a shaded park setting won't break your budget. Unfortunately located too close to the highway.

Le Mas de Peint
1,195F-2180F
ℜ, ≈, ≡, pb, tv, mini-bar
Le Sambuc, 13200 Arles, on the D36 road between Arles and Salin de Giraud
☎04.90.97.20.62
⇌04.90.97.22.20
peint@avignon.pacwan.net
Brand-new luxury accommodations in the middle of the Camargue: 11 rooms, with mezzanine bathrooms, are superbly decorated with fine furnishings and materials. The tasty breakfast (not just good croissant and coffee but fresh fruit, cereal and yogurt) is served on a large wooden table in the lovely kitchen (lunch and dinner are available too, prepared by the resident cook). The charismatic Bon, a successful rice-farmer and *manade*-owner, and his architect wife Lucille, succeed in creating a warm and relaxed place with a low-key, refined atmosphere. Private tours of Bon's farm can be arranged.

Lou Mas Dou Juge
½b 1,300F
no credit cards
pb, tv
Quartier Pin Fourcat, Route du Bac du Sauvage, 13460, Saintes-Maries de la Mer, Route D85, next to the Petite Rhône, below the D58 road towards Saintes-Maries-de-la-Mer
☎04.66.73.51.45
⇌04.66.73.51.42
This renovated farm house-inn is renowned for jovial dinners, where Renée Granier whips up a fine meal (usually fresh grilled fish) and husband Roger Granier entertains his guests with naughty tales, music and dancing—made all the merrier with a running supply of his famous peach and pear *eau de vie* liqueurs. Though popular with corporate groups, individual guests are welcome to join in on the fun (though this is not a place for introverts!). Basic rooms, with tired furnishings. Horseback riding is arranged to discover the Camargue region.

Saintes-Maries-de-la-Mer

Auberge de Jeunesse
Piocht-Badet, Route de Cacharel
☎04.90.97.51.72
⇌04.90.97.54.88
Member of FUAJ (YHA); 76 beds, 10km (6.2mi) from Saintes-Maries-de-la-Mer.

Hôtel Mediterranée
280F
pb in some rooms
4 Boulevard Frédéric Mistral
☎04.90.97.82.09
⇌04.90.97.76.31
Fourteen simply decorated rooms in a hotel near the beach and port; pleasant garden courtyard. Jovial host.

Hôtel Mas de Rieges
300F-500F
closed Oct to Mar
≈, pb, tv
Route de Cacharel
☎04.90.97.85.07
⇄04.90.97.72.26
Low-key, calm ranch resort with small but nicely-decorated rooms and an inviting pool. Possibility of light meals at lunchtime, or drinks from the bar (dinner not available).

Hôtel le Boumian
440F-490F
ℜ, ≈, pb, tv
Le Pont des Bannes
☎04.90.97.81.15
⇄04.90.97.89.94
Twenty-eight comfort able rooms, many bor dering the swimming-pool. Good value din ner menu in the attrac tive dining room in cludes cheese, dessert and wine for 150F. Friendly greeting. Horse-riding arranged. Along the D570, just north of Saintes-Maries-de-la-Mer.

Restaurants

Saint-Rémy-de-Provence

Lou Planet
$
7 Place Favier
☎04.90.92.19.81
Simple and attractive creperie, in a pretty tranquil square opposite the restored façade of the Musée des Alpilles, where salads, crepes and galettes are tasty and won't hurt your pocketbook in a town with inflated prices. For lunch or dinner, but also open all afternoon for cool drinks, ice cream and coffee.

L'Assiette de Marie
$$
open everyday, dinner only
One Rue Jaume-Roux
☎04.90.92.32.14
The young chef, Marie shows a confident hand in the kitchen, offering a three-course set menu, which might include grilled red peppers, chèvre and spinach cannelloni, osso bucco and delicious *crème brulée*. Meals are served in a charming room with blond stone walls, fresh flowers and wooden tables and chairs. Meals arrive on an eclectic selection of dinner plates—no two are alike! Friendly service.

Le Bistrot des Alpilles
$$
closed Sundays and Nov 15 to Dec 15
15 Boulevard Mirabeau
☎04.90.92.09.17
Large and jolly brasserie-restaurant in dark green and red, with Provençal touches, serving pricey meals to the Saint-Rémy jet set.

Le Bistro Decouverte
$$
closed Mon
19 Boulevard Victor-Hugo
☎04.90.92 34 49
A small, simple and smart restaurant with a great selection of wines by the glass. The menu at 115F offers dishes such as king prawns, duck or filet mignon.

La Gousse d'Ail
$$
closed Thu at lunch
25 Rue Carnot
☎04.90.92.16.87
A cosy bistrot with wooden beams, bric-a-brac, old prints on the walls and white tablecloths. The food is equally comforting—fresh pasta with pistou, Roquefort salad, fish soup. Jazz evenings on Thursdays, with a set-price menu.

La Maison Jaune
$$
closed Mon and Tue
15 Rue Carnot
☎04.90.92.56.14
A pleasant restaurant serving Provençale specialties (lamb filet with tapenade, fresh fish) on a terrace with a number of teak tables and chairs overlooking old Saint-Rémy. Menus at 120F *(lunch Tue-Fri)*, 180F, 265F and 305F.

Le Monocle
$$
closed Sun and from Dec 20 to Feb 10
no credit cards
48 Rue Carnot
Le Monocle, run by very friendly young women, has a certain originality to it. The small restaurant has a dozen tables and walls covered in fanciful frescoes, and exudes simplicity and conviviality. Guests are seated around tables where vinyl records serve as tablemats, menus come

in old record sleeves and the dessert menu is printed on a CD case. The southern-French food is inexpensive and comes in hearty portions. There is a fixed-price lunch menu for 48F (three courses), and fixed-price dinner menus are 68F to 88F. No reservations accepted, and there is no telephone.

Olivade
$$
closed late Oct to mid-Mar
closed Tue lunch
12 Rue Chateau
☎04.90.92.52.74
Best enjoyed during the warmer months, when dinner on the stone terrace is most pleasant. Provençale dishes include meat, fish and salads.

L'Orangerie Chabert
$$
closed Mon
16 Boulevard Victor Hugo
☎04.90.92.05.95
A charming restaurant set back from the street at the far end of a courtyard adjoining a house where you can sample olive oil, L'Orangerie Chabert has a lovely terrace beneath the trees, with tables shaded by large parasols. The subtle and sophisticated cuisine includes, among others, dishes like a unique hake *gougonnette* with the juice of green apples, tender pork filet with cardamom and moist chicken liver loaf.

XA
$$
closed Wed and Dec to Mar
24 Boulevard Mirabeau
☎04.90.92.41.23
Comfortable restaurant with an emphasis on fresh products.

Vallon de Vallrugues
$$$
Chemin Canto Cigalo, Saint-Rémy-de-Provence
☎04.90.92.04.40
⇌04.90.92.44.01
The entirely renovated gourmet restaurant of the Vallon de Vallrugues proves excellent. Its menus, at 195F *(lunch only)*, 290F, 390F and 480F *(menu dégustation)*, make ample use of fresh Provençale ingredients. The service is professional and courteous in every regard.

Eygalières

Sous Les Micocouliers
$$
closed Tue and Wed
Traverse Monfort
☎04.90.95.94.53
Mediterranean emphasis in a trendy casual restaurant behind the village centre, with, indeed, a wonderful terrace shaded by many *micocouliers* (nettle trees). Cooler months are pleasant inside where a large open hearth greets you, and you might see lamb roasting over a wood fire. The menu changes daily (*terrine de poisson, médallion de lotte, filet de boeuf sauces aux cèpes*, etc).

Maussane-les-Alpilles

Ou Ravi Provençau
$$$
closed Tue, Nov 20 to Dec 20 and Jun 20 to 30
34 Avenue de la Vallée-des-Baux
☎04.90.54.31.11
A friendly restaurant, very popular with locals, serving Provençal specialties (beef *daube*, *pieds et paquets* (sheep tripe), fresh cod with tomato *coulis*). Cheery, rustic decor with lampshades covered with Provençal fabrics and copper pans and bric-a-brac on the walls.

Salon-de-Provence

La Salle à Manger
$$
closed Sun pm and Mon
6 Rue du Maréchal Joffre
☎04.90.56.28.01
The Miège family moved south after owning a restaurant in Normandy, and opened this fabulous spot in 1993. Housed in an 18th-century mansion and renovated by designer Gilles Dez, the Salle à Manger proposes a refined Provençal menu offering remarkably good value. Delicious grilled red mullet, mouth-watering roast lamb stuffed with *tapenade* (black olive paste). The menu includes two courses plus a selection from the extensive *Grand Mère* dessert menu. Pretty courtyard

patio for summer dining.

Arles

Pâtisserie P. Boitel
$
7:30am to 8pm, tearoom closes at 7pm, closed Feb
4 Rue de la Liberté
☎**04.90.96.03.72**
Pâtisserie du Forum is a traditional pastry shop coupled with a small tearoom where they serve croissants and coffee in the morning, light meals (quiches, salads) at noon and delectable cakes throughout the day.

Tart'in
$
7 Rue des Carmes
☎**04.90.93.36.77**
An amazing number of tarts, from leek and gruyère or onion and ham to red fruits or apple, cinnamon and raisins, plus numerous types of mixed salads, all at reasonable prices. Extremely friendly hosts.

Vitamine
$
closed Sun
16 Rue du Docteur-Danton
☎**04.90.93.77.36**
More than 30 types of salads and pasta dishes are available, freshly prepared and delicious, in this light and pleasant eight-table café in the old part of town.

L'Affenage
$$
closed Tue and Wed PM in off-season and Sun year-round
4 Rue Molière
☎**04.90.96.07.67**
Good restaurant serving traditional dishes in the charming wood-beamed stable of a former 18th-century inn. Reasonably priced menu includes a "flavours of Provence" buffet offering a selection of *saucisson d'Arles* (sausage), fresh salads and terrines, followed by leg of lamb with thyme, duck confit or grilled fish, topped off with home-made desserts (excellent lemon meringue pie, hazelnut tarte). Efficient service, though locals appear to get preferential treatment.

La Charcuterie Restaurant
$-$$
Tue to Sat, noon to 3pm, 7pm to 1am
51 Rue des Arènes
☎**04.90.96 56 96**
A rustic bistrot with old-tile floor, long wooden tables, and even a bath tub hanging from the ceiling. The cooking is part Provençale (saucisson d'Arles, lamb with thyme), part Lyonnaise (tripes, charcuterie). Open late in a town where it's difficult to find a restaurant serving past 10pm.

La Mule Blanche
$-$$
Mon to Sat
9 Rue du Président Wilson
☎**04.90.93.98.54**
Casual and friendly restaurant enjoyed by locals and serving a reasonably priced Formule du Bistro. Otherwise, a selection of hearty salads, pasta and meat dishes.

L'Olivier
$$
Tue to Sat
1 bis, Rue Réattu
☎**04.90.49.64.88**
One of the better, refined tables in Arles where chef Jean-Louis Vidal's imagination turns fresh Provençale ingredients into inspired creations such as grilled mushrooms with a garlic and parsley cream sauce, poached haddock cakes with *chèvre purée*, roast lamb with rosemary and a steaming *pot au feu* with seafood rather than beef. Menus at 168F, 238F, 288F and 348F (six courses, each served with a different glass of wine). Professional service.

L'Entrevue
$$
closed Sun
Place Nina Berbevova
☎**04.90.93.37.28**
Set on a small square adjoining the docks on the Rhône is a restaurant that will whisk you away to Morocco in the blink of an eye. Delicious couscous, *tajines* and *pastillas* are prepared with great skill and in summer are served on a splendid

terrace from which you can admire the sunset over the Rhône. In addition to these mouthwatering meals, the chef prepares some classic French dishes of grilled meat and fish. If the terrace is inviting, the dining room is just as pleasant with its warm North African decor and walls covered with retro posters.

L'Escaladou
$$
noon to 2:30pm, 6:30pm to 11:30pm
15 Rue Porte de Laure
☎04.90.96 70 43
Provençale cuisine including fresh fish, roast beef with Carmague rice, fish soup, served in a cheery room with yellow tablecloths and white-tiled floors. Menus at 85F, 105F and 140F.

Acqua Café
$$
closed Sun
Riverside dock
☎06.08.45.91.66
Acqua Café is more than your average restaurant, to say the least. In 1996, the friendly owners had the brilliant idea of setting up the restaurant in a barge moored on the Rhône. Guests can admire historic Arles bathed in the low-angled rays of the setting sun as they enjoy excellent Provençal dishes that are light, subtle and flavourful. Delicacies include eggplan with tomato purée, rabbit in tapenade and filet of bull in an anchovy sauce. The delicious, fresh desserts are also worth lingering over. A superb dining experience at a reasonable price, in a magnificent setting. No credit cards.

Chez Gigi
$$
closed Mon
49 Rue des Arènes
☎04.90.96.68.59
Michel, an Arles native chef and Gigi, an energetic woman from Québec, invite you on a culinary odyssey in their very charming restaurant. These feisty globetrotters have collected a thousand and one souvenirs and, more important, a thousand and one recipes from around the world, from Corsican *gnocchis* to guacamole, New Orleans-style fried calamari and cod fritters and authentically Québécois smoked meats. The atmosphere could not be warmer, friendlier and more relaxed and the owners' optimism and *joie de vivre* are infectious. The menu changes often, and Michel and Gigi always have some surprises in store for their guests.

Le Jardin de Manon
$$-$$$
closed Wed
14 Avenue Alyscamps
☎04.90.93.38.68
This little gem is only a few minutes from the town centre. Carefully and tastefully decorated, Le Jardin de Manon has a seasonal menu with delicious, subtle and sophisticated choices. For example, the sublime sweet onions melted in a tomato and basil coulis, the *gigotin de volaille* with tapenade made with seasonal vegetables and the excellent deboned rabbit stuffed with goat cheese, savory and olive juice. The recently redecorated terrace, with large yellow parasols and wrought-iron furniture, could not be more peaceful and inviting.

Tarascon

Bistrot des Anges
$$
closed Sun
Place du Marché
☎04.90.91.05.11
The Bistrot des Anges offers a cordial reception and friendly service, a charming terrace just a few steps from the town hall and good food.

The dining room has a minimalist feeling, with its bare yellow walls. The friendly owners have a fixed-price lunch menu for 86F (one main course and an appetizer or dessert), daily specials for 65F and a full menu for 100F.

Saint-Martin-de-Crau

De Moro Pâtissier
$
6am to 1pm and 2:30pm to 7:30pm, closed Mon
Avenue de la République
☎04.90.47.11.02
De Moro Pâtissier is the place to go for mouth-watering pastries, cakes and croissants; all of these sweets may be savoured on the premises in a comfortable tearoom.

L'Oustau de Mamette
$$
closed Sun pm and Aug 15-30
13 Avenue de la République
☎04.90.47.04.03
Lovely restaurant on the ground floor of an old house on this quiet town's main street. Fresh Provençale ingredients are cooked the way they should be—simply, without fuss so that the natural flavours shine through. Recent items included eggplant in filo pastry with a tomato *coulis*; a light salad of chicken livers with raspberry vinaigrette; frogs' legs with garlic and basil grilled sole. Delicious homemade, fresh fruit pies. Courteous service, shaded terrace.

Camargue

Marc et Mireille
$
Plage de Beauduc
☎04.42.48.80.08
There is nothing like a trip to the isolated beach of Beauduc, for adventurers whose cars have good shocks, to savour tasty grilled fish caught fresh the same day at Marc and Mireille's rustic restaurant. Incomparable *tinades* (tiny molluscs) in garlic; extraordinarily succulent white fish, such as *corb* and *marbré*; and *poutargue*, a spread of eggs and fish purée, are some of the delicacies to be found here. Even though it is barely larger than a canteen, this restaurant is very popular in the summertime; reservations are recommended. From Arles, take the D36 5km (3mi), then turn right onto the D36B South, which passes the pond at Vaccarès and provides a chance to see beautiful pink flamingos. This road becomes the D36C past the villages of Salin-de-Badon and Paradis, but be careful not to take the sharp left turn toward Salin-de-Girard; instead, continue south and then make a sharp right at the small hand-painted sign that reads, "Marc et Mireille—Beauduc." Also, be sure to fill up on gasoline before heading out on this excursion, as there are no service stations in the area.

Saintes-Maries-de-la-Mer

Les Vagues
$-$$
12 Avenue Théodore Aubanel
☎04.90.97.84.40
Les Vagues presents itself as a beach-side café, ideal for a snack or a simple refreshment, although it also offers a varied menu of perfectly respectable fish dishes.

Hôtel Le Boumian
on the D570, just north of Saintes-Maries-de-la-Mer; Le Pont des Bannes, 13460 Saintes-Maries-de-la-Mer
☎04.90.97.81.15
≠04.90.97.89.94
The restaurant of the Hôtel Le Boumian offers a dinner menu that is a good deal no matter how you look at it, served in an attractive dining room *(180F including cheese, dessert and wine)*.

Lou Cardelino
$$
closed Wed, Feb and late Nov and Dec
25 Rue Frédéric Mistral
☎04.90.97.96.23
Pretty seafood restaurant with a blue interior and friendly management. Fresh grilled fish such as sole or catfish for 40F/100g. Menus from 75F to 120F.

Entertainment

Saint-Rémy-de-Provence

Bars and Nightclubs

La Forge
Avenue de la Libération
☎***04.90.92.31.52***
Discotheque.

La Haute Galine
Quartier de la Galine
☎***04.90.92.00.03***
Dance club.

Café Latin
Rue Roger Salengro
Café with live music some evenings.

Organa Festival
Association Organa
☎***04.90.92.08.10***
Concerts given with the newly-restored organ (one of the most important in France) at the Collégiale Saint-Martin church *(Boulevard Marceau, opposite place de la République)*, plus classical concerts from July to September (call for a programme). Organ rehearsals in Saint-Martin every Saturday at 5.30pm, July to September.

Concerts de Jazz. Inquire at the Saint-Rémy Office de la Culture *(☎04.90.92.08.10, extension 394)* or at the tourist office for more detailed information on the jazz evenings organized at various locales during the summer.

Festivals and Cultural Events

One of the most unusual festivals in the area must be the **Fête de la Transhumance** ★ held annually every Pentecost Monday (late May). Shepherds in traditional costume parade their 3,000 lambs through the town's streets, supposedly before taking them from the torrid Crau plain to the cool hill ground where they spend the summer. As well, a display of *chèvres* from local farms (with prizes for the best one), an all-day brocante fair with exhibitions.

Arles

Bars and Nightclubs

Le Tropicana
7 Rue Molière
☎***04.90.93.34.70***
Piano bar, crêperie.

Le Café La Nuit
11 Place du Forum
☎***04.90.96.44.56***
Also known as the Café Van Gogh, as this is the subject of a famous 1890 painting by the artist. For drinks and animated conversation in the heart of Arles—a popular meeting place.

Cargo de Nuit
Thu to Sat, 8pm to 4am
7 Avenue Sadi Carnot
☎***04.90.49.55.99***
Popular night spot with very good live music—African, salsa, jazz. 300-seat concert hall, bar and restaurant (serving until 2am).

Le Grenier à Sel
49 Quai de la Roquette
☎/⇌***04.90.93 05 23***
Performance venue with cabaret, theatre, jazz. Well-worth checking out for its adventurous—and fun—programming.

Cinéma Le Mejean
Quai Marc Dormoy
☎***04.90.93.33.56***
Cinéma Le Mejean presents a good selection of recent independent films from around the world, as well as commercial successes, retrospectives and meetings with directors, in three cinemas. A restaurant that serves salads and light meals, and a very good bookstore, Actes Sud, are also located on the premises.

Manades

Arles and the Camargue area are rich with tradition—many revolve around bulls and bull-fighting. Numerous *manades* (Black bull farms) dot the region, many with public rodeos once a week in the summer (times, prices, and quality vary, so check with the local tourist office for details). Bullfighting in the Arles region is done both in the Spanish style as well as a local non-violent variation where the animal is not injured; rather the goal is to deftly pluck a tight string from between the bull's horns.

Festivals and Cultural Events

The most colourful and interesting festival in Arles is the **Fête des Gardiens ★**, which occurs on May 1 every year. Costumed men on horses and pretty *Arlésiennes* (local women dressed in traditional long skirts, white blouses and carefully draped shawls) parade through the streets, and special bullfighting and equestrian games take place.

Other annual events in Arles include:

La Feria Pascale, during the three-day Easter weekend, when toreadors and herdsman run their bulls to the Roman arena;

La Pégoulado, in the first week of July, a torchlight procession, folkloric singing and dancing in the streets;

Les Rencontres Internationales de la Photographie, for one week in July, top-class photography festival attracting professionals and amateurs from around the world;

Les Prémices du Riz, in mid-September, a rice harvest festival featuring a parade with floats and entertainment.

Tarascon

Theatres

Théâtre de Tarascon
Rue Eugénie Pelletan
information
☎*04.90.91.51.45*
reservations
☎*04.90.91.24.30*
Théâtre de Tarascon presents a range of dramas, operas and musical entertainment from September to May, produced by touring troupes that come here specifically to perform in this adorable, entirely restored baroque theatre. Phone ahead of time for the program.

Festivals and Cultural Events

Eight costumed young men parade a huge model of the fabled monster, the Tarasque, through Tarascon's streets during the **Fête de la Tarasque** *(last Sunday in June every year)*. Befitting the monster's grisly demeanor, the Tarasque menaces any on-lookers attempting to block its path!

Saintes-Maries-de-la-Mer

Bars and Nightclubs

Flamenco - Bar Le Commerce
13 Rue Victor Hugo
☎*04.90.97.84.11*
Café with live entertainment, and yes, often flamenco shows.

Toward the end of the 1980s, the Gypsy Kings, natives of Camargue, earned a new popularity for the guitar-accompanied Latin melodies that are characteristic of this region; a few of these traditional songs even hit the top of the charts in countries around the world. While the band has since broken up, one of its members, Chico, occasionally appears in the region. As well, some restaurants present gypsy musicians in the summertime, like La Manade de Sainte-Marie-de-la-Mer (see p 190), for example.

Festivals and Cultural Events

There are dozens of traditional festivals in this region celebrating local customs, religious events and significant historic moments. The following are the most important *(complete lists of festivals are prepared by local tourist offices)*.

The popular **Fêtes des Gitans** in Saintes-Maries de la Mer *(May 24-25 every year)* sees a bejewelled statue of Sarah carried through the town's streets by *gitans*, followed by a procession of *Arlésiennes* (women in traditional Arles costume) and *gardiens* (horse and bull herders). Various entertainments takes place by the sea and through the streets, including games with the Camargue bulls. A similar event occurs on a Sunday around October 22.

Mouriès

A green-olive festival is held in September (usually on the next-to-last Sunday of the month), just after the harvest of this precious fruit, in the streets of this village.

Shopping

Saint-Rémy-de-Provence

Confiserie des Alpilles
Sun to Fri 8am to noon and 2pm to 6pm
5 Avenue Albert-Schweitzer
☎04.90.92.11.08
For three generations the Lilamand family has been making their famous *fruits confits* (candied fruits) using the finest local produce (apricots, melons, mirabelles, etc.).

Galerie Noir et Blanc
30 Rue Carnot
☎04.90.92.55.21
Galerie Noir et Blanc is a small photography gallery run by a talented young man named Éric Pexxali, who sells framed prints and postcards made from black and white and colour photographs of the region that he takes himself. He also offers professional printing services. Next to the Fontaine Nostradamus.

Forum Santé Pharmacie
closed Sun
4 Boulevard Mirabeau
☎04.90.92.08.05
Conveniently located drug store with extended opening hours.

Saint-Rémy Presse
12 Boulevard Mirabeau
☎04.90.92.05.36
Newsagent with a large selection of international newspapers and magazines.

Atelier de Photographie
closed Sun and Mon in winter
9 Rue Carnot
☎04.90.92.36.76
One-hour photo developing.

La Maison d'Araxie
1 Place Joseph Hilaire
☎04.90.92.58.87
An enchanting fine food shop with a great selection of local products, including nougat, herbal teas, honey bonbons and fruit jams.

Poivre d'Ane
closed Sun in winter
25 Boulevard Victor Hugo
☎04.90.92.17.08
Provençal gifts and objects for the home of superior quality to those found elsewhere.

Maussane-les-Alpilles

Bastide Saint-Bastien
Tue to Sun 10am to 12:30pm and 3pm to 7pm
99 Avenue de la Vallée des Baux
☎04.90.54.37.64
Superb antique shop in a 19th-century residence with pretty front garden. A large choice of Provençal furniture and objects, selected by François Calvia (press attaché for the French Ministry of the Interior until 1981) and Daniel Pourchez (descendent of a family of renowned jewellers).

Arles

Antiquités Maurin
9am to noon and 2pm to 7pm, closed Sun and Sat morning
4 Rue de Grille
☎04.90.96.51.57
Antiquités Maurin presents an amusing mix of antiques and miscellaneous items including glassware, porcelain, paintings and furniture.

Provençal Market
Sat am
along the Boulevard des Lices
Arles' Provençal market is particularly colourful and varied. In addition to the usual stands selling fresh regional vegetables, fruits,

Like other towns along the coast, Villefranche-sur-Mer has a lovely seaside promenade bordered by charming, colourful houses.
- *Tibor Bognár*

Perched on the mountainside, Moustiers-Sainte-Marie enjoys a serene setting in a magnificent landscape.
- *Mehlig*

The Place de l'Hôtel de Ville in Aix-en-Provence is flanked by a splendid 15th-century clock tower with a wrought-iron campanile. - *Tibor Bognár*

spices, herbs, flowers, soap and fabrics, you may find bric-a-brac dealers, plus harness-makers crafting bridles, saddles and stirrups for the horsemen of Camargue. It's also an opportunity to the see the *Arlésienne* women in traditional dress.

Pierre Milhau
Tue to Sun 6:30am to 1pm and 3pm to 7:30pm closed Sun pm
11 Rue Réattu
☎***04.90.96.16.05***
This *traiteur* (gourmet food shop) is famous for its own tasty Arles dried sausage (*saucisson d'Arles*) made from pork, beef and mild spices.

L'Arlésienne
Mon to Sat 10am to noon and 2pm to 7pm
12 Rue du Président Wilson
☎***04.90.93.28.05***
Traditional Provençal and Camarguais clothes, including the dresses and wide hair ribbons worn by woman for local festivals.

Librairie Actes Sud
Wed to Sun 10am to 9pm, Mon 2pm to 9pm, Thu 10am to 8pm
Passage Méjan, 47 Rue du Docteur-Fanton
☎***04.90.49.56.77***
Belgian publisher Hubert Nyssen created the Actes Sud publishing house in 1978. A year later, his daughter Françoise took control of the Arles-based firm that now publishes about 10 titles a month, with an impressive roster of French and international authors (the American Paul Auster, the Russian Nina Berberova, plus Asian, Arab and Scandinavian writers). The Actes Sud bookjackets have won awards for their distinctive graphics; the entire collection is sold in this bookshop, along with a good selection of other publisher's work. Regular seminars and readings; art-house cinema and restaurant.

InterSport
closed Mon am and Sun
20 Place de la République
☎***04.90.96 17 70***
The place to come for sports equipment and clothes.

Labo Photo Valtier
58 Rue du 4 Septembre
☎***04.90.96.43.61***
Photographs developed in one hour, plus film supplies.

Pharmacie Poix-Wattrelos
closed Sun
1 Rue de la Place
☎***04.90.96.13.69***
This drug store has friendly, professional service and extended opening hours.

De Moro Patissier
Sun and Mon closed between 1pm and 2:30pm
Rue Wilson
☎***04.90.93.14.43***
One of the finest pastry shops in the region with a hallucinating selection, including the house specialty Alexandrian (light chocolate mousse on hazelnut biscuit).

Forum
closed Sun
Rue Wilson
☎***04.90.93.65.39***
This smart-looking bookstore has a good selection of travel guides, road maps, literature and culture.

Saint-Martin-de-Crau

Chèvre Fermier Malbosc-Espique
sign-posted 400m east of the D27, between Maussane and Saint-Martin de Crau
☎***04.90.47.05.95***
A wonderful variety of farm-house chèvre on sale direct from the manufacturer. The Malbosc's goats produce a rich milk due to careful breeding and their diet of select Crau hay.

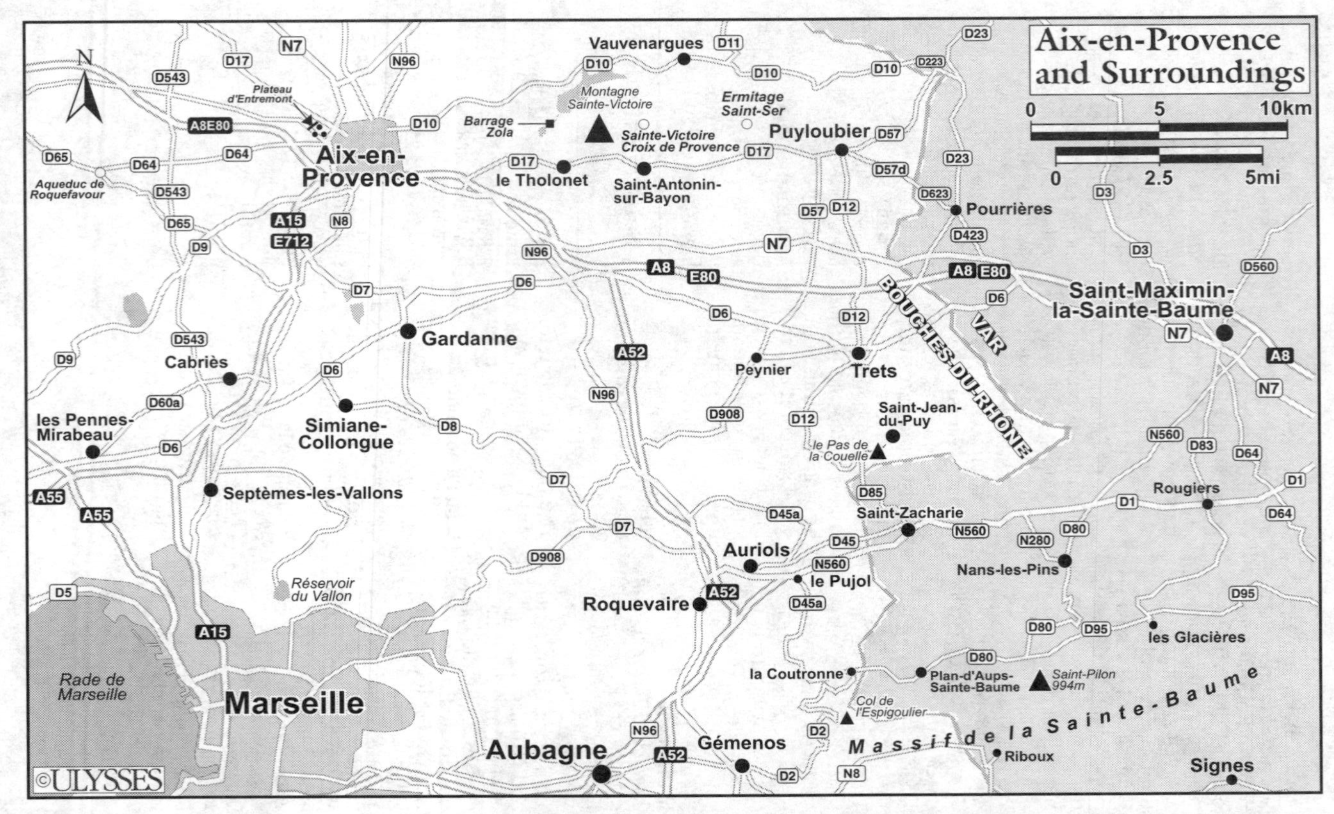
Aix-en-Provence and Surroundings
0
5
10km
0
2.5
5mi
N
Aix-en-Provence
Plateau d'Entremont
Aqueduc de Roquefavour
Barrage Zola
Montagne Sainte-Victoire
Sainte-Victoire Croix de Provence
Ermitage Saint-Ser
Vauvenargues
le Tholonet
Saint-Antonin-sur-Bayon
Puyloubier
Pourrières
Saint-Maximin-la-Sainte-Baume
VAR
BOUCHES-DU-RHÔNE
Gardanne
Cabriès
Simiane-Collongue
les Pennes-Mirabeau
Septèmes-les-Vallons
Peynier
Trets
Saint-Jean-du-Puy
le Pas de la Couelle
Rougiers
Saint-Zacharie
Nans-les-Pins
Auriols
le Pujol
Roquevaire
Réservoir du Vallon
Rade de Marseille
Marseille
Aubagne
Gémenos
la Coutronne
Col de l'Espigoulier
Plan-d'Aups-Sainte-Baume
Saint-Pilon 994m
les Glacières
Massif de la Sainte-Baume
Riboux
Signes
©ULYSSES

Aix-en-Provence

Aix-en-Provence is a beautiful Provençal city with tree-lined streets, elegant historic residences and numerous squares with almost 100 pretty fountains.

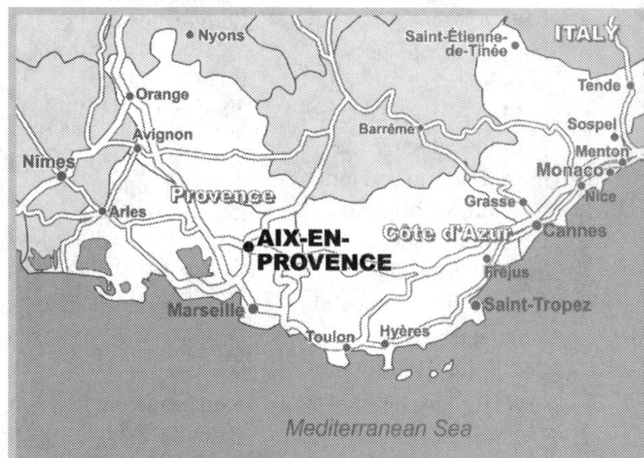

The many interesting buildings and monuments along the pedestrian streets in the centre town must obviously be visited on foot. It is worth spending a few days in the Aix region. The Mont Sainte-Victoire hill range (painted so often by Cezanne) and the wooded Sainte-Baume Massif offer dramatic panoramic views and wonderful fragrant pathways. An added plus—this region is less frequented, yet just as pretty as the Luberon hills to the north.

Aix became a Roman colony under Caesar and Augustus, and archaeological evidence suggests that an amphitheatre, as well as temples and ramparts existed in the area. But just as the ancient Entremont settlement was destroyed by the Romans, successive marauding over hundreds of years ruined these structures. Two invasions stand out—that by the Visigoths in 477 and by the Saracens in 731.

Aix became the capital of the Provence county in the 12th century. Rapid expansion started in the 13th century when the counts of Provence resided permanently here. They gathered cultural figures, poets, musicians and, most notably, the famous troubadours around them. Building architecture advanced, principally of a religious nature, and a huge Palace was constructed. A university was founded in 1409 by Louis II. Aix was hit by the Black Plague of 1348 when it struck the whole region.

The height of Aix's splendour occurred during the reign of King René, Count of Provence (1471-1480). He was a great patron of the arts, and possessed intelligence, enthusiasm and a common touch despite his aristocratic bearing. Civic building projects were undertaken, canvases by important Italian and Flemish painters were commissioned, and cultural events flourished. The *bon roi* René (good king René), as he was known by a beloved public, is even credited with introducing the muscat grape to France. In contrast, popular legend also indicates that the King didn't speak the Provençal language and only drank the Anjou wine from his ancestors' territory, thus shunning locally produced varieties!

Along with the rest of Provence, Aix joined France in 1486. Following the installation of the Provence Parliament in 1501, the city experienced a second golden age. Parliament members brought new prosperity to the town and supported the cultural community. Just the same, the working class accused them of voting for more privileges for themselves and increasing taxes for the poor.

Delicacies of Aix

It has to weigh between 10 and 14g (0.35 to 0.49 oz), and only contain almonds grown around the Mediterranean. It consists of one-third almonds, one-third sugar and one-third candied fruit, 99% of which is melon. What is it? Connoisseurs and those with a sweet tooth will quickly answer "calisson!" Still, the origins of this sweet from Aix remain a mystery. Some claim it has been made since antiquity, while others, including the 19th-century author Alphonse Karr, maintain it was first created for the marriage of René of Anjou and Jeanne de Laval in 1474. History, or rather legend, has it that the future queen never smiled. Sad to see the sovereign so dejected on such a festive occasion, the royal cook concocted her a little sweetmeat made with sugar, almonds and candied fruit. From the very first bite, the titbit put a radiant smile on Jeanne's face. Stupefied, the courtiers asked themselves what had transpired and one is said to have responded it was the caress, or *di calin soun* in Provençal. If you pause to reflect on the origins of this local delicacy, the second version of which is certainly more poetic, its shape also may puzzle you. Why a diamond shape? Only its creator knows the answer.

Aix was at the height of its splendour during the 17th and 18th centuries. Louis XIV visited the city and encouraged urban reconstruction. The aristocratic class built fabulous private residences called *hôtels particuliers* (notably along the Cours Mirabeau and neighbouring streets), made from blond limestone and featuring narrow terraces with pretty wrought-iron railings on the upper levels. There are more than 160 *hôtels particuliers* in Aix. One of the most important building projects was undertaken in 1646 by Michel Mazarin (archbishop of Aix and brother to Cardinal Mazarin). An entire neighbourhood south of the Cours Mirabeau was constructed with elegant homes, squares and fountains—still known today as the Quartier Mazarin.

In the 1780s, Aix sent the prominent anti-monarchist Mirabeau to represent them as its elected member of the new Tiers État governing body in Paris, which replaced the absolute monarchy. His memory lives on today, as Aix's principal avenue, the Cours Mirabeau with its four lovely rows of tall plane trees, is named after him.

Following the Revolution, Aix lost much of its prestige and power. No longer the Provençal capital, it became a sub-prefecture of the newly created French department Bouches-du-Rhône.

Aix today is made up of executives and workers employed by surrounding industry, magistrates from the important Court of Appeal, a large student population and an important influx of tourists. Summer months are lively—not the least due to the renowned summer music festival in August (unfortunately affected by budget difficulties and therefore presenting a reduced season since the early 1990s).

Finding Your Way Around

By Plane

Aix is a convenient 25km (15.5mi) from the **Marseille-Marignane Airport** (☎*04.42.89.09.74*). The D9 road links the airport and Aix-en-Provence. Avignon Airport is 85km away—the N7 highway or the A7 Autoroute du Soleil and bear left on the A8 La Provençal highway, after Salon-de-Provence and 17km (10.6mi) before Aix.

By Train

Aix-en-Provence SNCF Train Station
Rue G. Desplaces (at the base of Avenue Victor Hugo)
Information
☎***04.91.08.50.50***
Reservations
☎***04.91.08.84.12***

Aix is served by regional services (TER) of the SNCF French national train service. Overseas visitors arriving in Paris should take the TGV from either Charles-de-Gaulle Airport or Gare de Lyon and stop at Avignon or Marseille, then take one of numerous regional trains to Aix, which run many times throughout the day. Overseas visitors flying to Lyon Satolas Airport may pick up the TGV to Avignon or Marseille from the SNCF train station connected to the terminal.

SNCF information desks in all French train stations can organize the fastest, most efficient itinerary for you. The TGV ticket and the ticket to Aix by regional train may be purchased at the same time and from any station. Special "Joker" fares offer substantial discounts (50% or more) on train journeys for many destinations, if purchased two weeks or one month in advance.

By Bus

Bus Station
Avenue Camille Pelletan
☎***04.42.27.17.91***
Aix can be reached by bus from numerous destinations in Provence, notably Marseille, and Avignon.

Practical Information

Tourist Offices

Aix-en-Provence
Place du Général-de-Gaulle
☎***04.42.16.11.61***
≠***04.42.16.11.62***

Aix's large tourist office is professional, efficient and loaded with useful brochures about the city and its events, and provides details about what to do in the surrounding countryside. The concise and extremely informative *Circuit Cézanne/In the Footsteps of Cézanne* leaflet (in French, English and Italian) offers a self-guided walking tour through the streets of Aix, past the buildings and sites which influenced the painter's life, plus a 40km (24.9mi) round-trip circuit in the Mont Sainte-Victoire region. The tourist office also offers walking tours of the city *(mid-Jun to mid-Sep, everyday at 10am and 3pm; mid-Sep to mid-Jun, Wed and Sat at 3 pm)* and excursions in the region. A small boutique sells books, T-shirts, local Coteaux d'Aix wine and souvenirs.

Saint-Maximin-la-Sainte-Baume
Place de l'Hôtel de Ville
83470 Saint-Maxim-la-Sainte-Baume
☎***04.94.59.84.59***

Parking

Many of the streets in the centre of Aix are narrow or for pedestrians only, which makes sight-seeing enjoyable but also causes traffic problems. Avoid taking your car into the city-centre. Many well-lit, video-controlled underground parking lots are provided near-by (charged by the hour), just a few minutes walk from the centre. They are indicated by signs upon entering Aix-en-Provence, and the tourist office at Place du Général de Gaulle publishes a map with these parking lots indicated.

Car Rental

Avis
11 Boulevard Gambetta
☎***04.42.21.64.16***

Budget
16 Avenue des Belges
☎***04.42.38.37.36***

Europcar
55 Boulevard de la République
☎***04.42.27.83.00***

Hertz
43 Avenue Victor Hugo
☎***04.42.27.91.32***

Bicycle Rental

Troc-Velo
62 Rue Boulegon
☎***04.42.21.37.40***

Cycles Naddeo
Avenue de Lattre-de-Tassigny
☎***04.42.21.06.93***

Exploring

Aix-en-Provence

Aix-en-Provence's principal street, the elegant **Cours Mirabeau** ★★ divides the city in two. It was created in the mid-17th century and was lined with rows of tall plane trees and numerous mansions (built between 1650 and 1760 for the most part, and now with banks and businesses). Cézanne's father founded a millinery business in 1825 at number 55. Three fountains stand along the road, the most unusual being the **Fontaine Moussue** that is fed from a hot spring underneath and looks like a giant-green mushroom. Farther east, the **Fontaine Roi René** shows him holding a bunch of muscat grapes, which he introduced to Provence.

Paul Cézanne

Surely the best-known painter from Provence, at least after his death, Paul Cézanne (1839-1906) painted beautiful canvasses of Aix-en-Provence, the city where he was born and raised, and its surroundings. A childhood friend of writer Émile Zola when the latter lived in Aix, Cézanne moved to Paris in 1863, where he had contact with the Impressionists, without achieving much success in their circles. Returning to the Midi, he began, like the Impressionists, to translate the vibration of light and its variations into the subtleties of colour and reflections. Nevertheless, he soon put his own stamp on the technique that had been developed by his friends, working on his treatment of colour and density. After a revelatory stay in the Estaque beginning in 1870, the importance of his work was finally acknowledged in Paris in 1904, two years after his death. Fascinated by the light, colours and landscapes of the region around his native Aix, Cézanne produced truly marvellous work, notably some 60 canvasses of his favourite subject, the Montagne Saint-Victoire. He painted the Provençal landscape in a way that won him recognition as the grand master of the art. The founder of a new type of painting and the forerunner of cubism, Cézanne dcreated a new conception of pictoral space that had an impact on his successors.

Cafés, restaurants and shops line the right side of the Cours Mirabeau. Street musicians and performers entertain crowds here at night.

Musée Arbaud *(15F; 2pm to 5pm, closed Sun and holidays; 2A Rue de Quatre Septembre, ☎04.42.38.38.95)* occupies a drab 18th-century home and contains a library, paintings and—its most interesting feature—a marvellous collection of earthenware from Moustiers and Marseille, all of which was generously bequeathed by collector Paul Arbaud.

From the Fontaine de La Rotonde *(Place du Général de Gaulle)* heading towards Place Forbin, the calm **Quartier Mazarin ★★** neighbourhood is on the left of the Cours Mirabeau. The streets (designed in 1646 by the archbishop Michel Mazarin) follow a grid-pattern and reveal numerous *hôtels particuliers* from the period, antiques shops and museums.

Musée Granet ★★ *(15F; Sep to May, everyday except Tue and holidays 10am to noon and 2pm to 6pm; Jun to Oct, everyday, same hours; closed Christmas to late Jan; Place Saint-Jean-de-Malte, ☎04.42.38.14.70)*. Aix's fine arts museum contains a very good selection of oil paintings from the 16th to 19th centuries (Dutch, Flemish and Italian schools) and a number of rooms devoted to French masters which shouldn't be missed, notably works by Quentin de Latour, Nicolas de Largillière and Ingres. The elegant building, a former 19th-century priory, also possesses important works by Provençal painters and sculptors (Mignard, Puget, the Le Nain brothers), a contemporary art department, Impressionist paintings and a small gallery devoted to the city's celebrated painter **Paul Cézanne ★★**. The basement and ground floor of the Musée Granet are full of archaeological treasures, including the ruins found at the Entremont site (the Celto-Ligurian settlement just north of Aix and dating from the 3rd century BC).

At the intersection of Rue des Quatre Dauphins and Rue Cardinale is the pretty **Fontaine des Quatre Dauphins** (four dolphins fountain) in the centre of the square of the same name.

The most lively areas of Aix are found to the left of the Cours Mirabeau. They are riddled with an astonishing number of clothes shops, cafés and restaurants (see our selection of Restaurants and Shopping). The **Quartier des Prêcheurs** or preachers neighbourhood, includes **Place de Verdun**, the **Palais de Justice**, **Place des Prêcheurs**, the **Église de la Madeleine** (Cézanne was Christened here on February 22, 1839) and **Chapelle du Collège des Jésuites**. The **Quartier Saint-Sauveur** is the oldest in Aix, and includes the cathedral and archbishop's residence.

Musée d'Histoire Naturelle/Hôtel Boyer d'Eguilles ★ *(15F; everyday 10am to noon and 1pm to 5pm, closed Sun am; 6 Rue Espariat, ☎04.42.26.23.67)*. A striking late 17th-century mansion houses Aix's museum of palaeontology, mineralogy, botany and prehistory. To be seen, if only for the elegant U-shaped building and its interior, including a wrought-iron staircase and painted panelling.

Of all the many fountains and squares in Aix, the 18th-century **Place d'Albertas ★★** must be one of the most elegant and simple. Three-sided symmetrical façades with wrought-iron upper balconies face a central fountain of the same name. Occasionally,

● ATTRACTIONS

1. Cours Mirabeau
2. Fontaine Moussue
3. Fontaine du Roi René
4. Musée Arbaud
5. Quartier Mazarin
6. Musée Granet
7. Fontaine des Quatre Dauphins
8. Quartier des Prêcheurs
9. Place de Verdun
10. Palais de justice
11. Place des Prêcheurs
12. Église de la Madeleine
13. Collège des Jésuites
14. Musée d'Histoire naturelle/Hôtel Boyer d'Eguilles
15. Place d'Albertas
16. Hôtel de ville
17. Musée du Vieil Aix
18. Musée des Tapisseries
19. Cathédrale Saint-Sauveur
20. Atelier Cézanne
21. Pavillon de Vendôme

⬡ ACCOMMODATIONS

1. Grand Hôtel Nègre-Coste
2. Hôtel Cardinal
3. Hôtel de France
4. Hôtel des Augustins
5. Hôtel des Quatre Dauphins
6. Hôtel Le Manoir
7. Hôtel Le Prieuré
8. Hôtel Paul
9. Hôtel Saint-Christophe
10. La Villa Gallici
11. Les Infirmeries du Roy René
12. Les Résidences Pierre et Vacances
13. Résidence Les Floridianes

⬢ RESTAURANTS

1. À la Cour de Rohan
2. Café de l'Horloge
3. Chez Antoine Côté
4. Chez Feraud
5. Chez Maxime
6. Haagen-Dazs
7. Hub Lot Cybercafé
8. Jacquou le Croquant
9. La Maison des Fondues
10. Le Basilic Gourmand
11. Le Bistro Latin
12. Le Cintra
13. Le Comté d'Aix
14. Le Petit Verdot
15. Le Poivre d'Ane
16. Les Agapes

evening classical music concerts take place here in the summer.

In the Quartier Saint-Sauveur lies the animated Place de l'Hotel de Ville, with the 15th-century **Tour de l'Horloge ★** or clock tower, and wrought-iron bell cage, the handsome **Place de l'Hôtel de Ville ★** with its the baroque facade and **post office ★** containing the 17th-century *halle aux grains* or seed exchange.

Musée du Vieil Aix ★★ *(15F; Oct to Mar, Tue to Sun 10am to noon and 2pm to 5pm; Apr to Sep, 10 am to noon and 2:30pm to 6:30pm, closed Oct; 17 Rue Gaston-de-Saporta,* ☎*04.42.21.43.55)* is a marvellous 17th-century baroque mansion containing a wonderful collection of decorative objects (mirrors, ceramics, dolls), and furniture. Plus, special rooms devoted to *santons* (clay figures for Christmas nativity

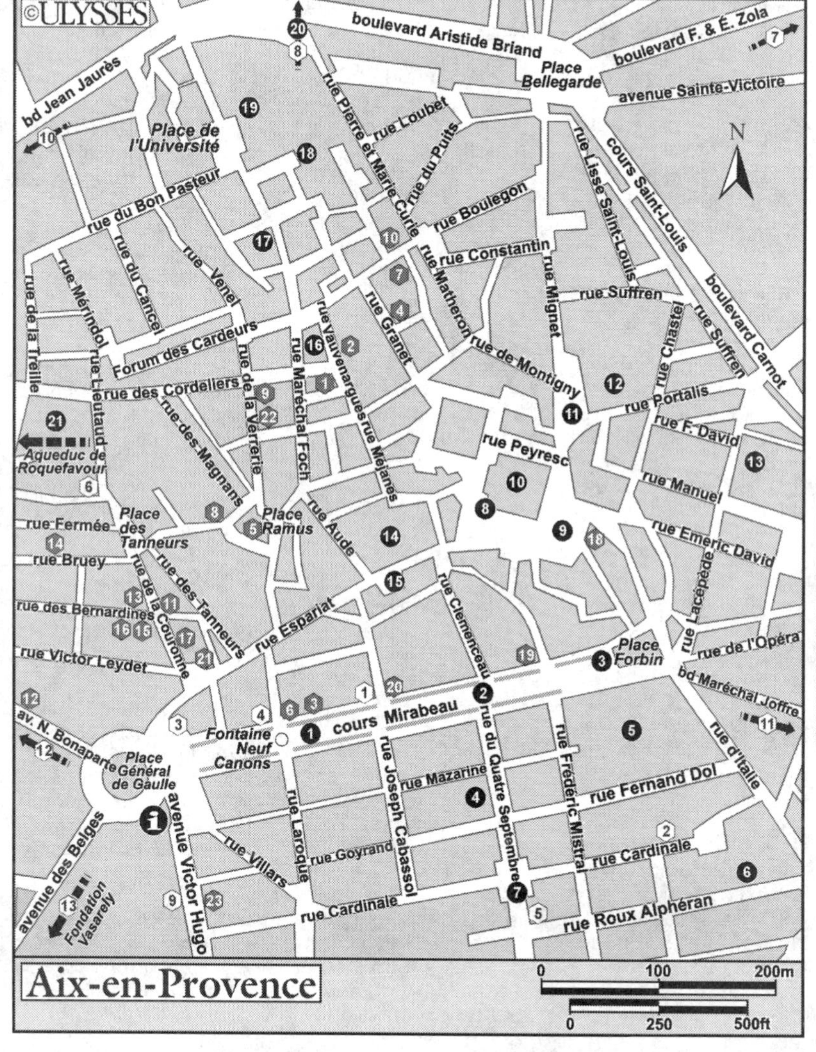

scenes) and marionettes from the 19th century.

Musée des Tapisseries *(13F; Wed to Mon 10am to noon and 2pm to 5:45pm; Place de l'Ancien Archevêché/Place des Martyrs de la Résistance, ☎04.42.23.09.91)* presents a celebrated collection of very beautiful tapestries from Beauvais, which will please connoisseurs of this art form and simple admirers of pretty objects alike. The museum is on the ground floor of the **Archevêché**. Temporary exhibitions are also put on here, as is the famous Festival de Musique d'Été.

Cathédrale Saint-Sauveur *(8am to noon and 2pm to 6pm; Rue Gaston de Saporta)*. The cathedral offers a mix of styles, as seen in the austere Roman section (12th century), octagonal baptistry (5th century), Provençal Gothic nave (16th century) and baroque nave (17th century). The pleasant arcaded **cloître ★★**, or cloister dates from the 12th century and was renovated in the 17th. Saint-Sauveur holds a beautiful triptych, the ***Buisson Ardent*** **★★** (the burning bush) painted for King René by Nicolas Froment in the late 1400s. The centre panel represents the parable of the Virginity of Mary, positioned beside Moses and the flaming green bush; amongst the religious figures, King René appears on a side panel; his wife Jeanne on the other. The triptych is often closed, so ask the attendant on duty to open the panels.

Atelier Cézanne ★ *(14F; Oct to May, Wed to Mon 10am to noon and 2pm to 5pm closed holidays; Jun to Sep 10am to noon and 2:30pm to 6pm; 9 Avenue Paul Cézanne, ☎04.42.21.06.53)*. Paul Cézanne (1839-1906) was born in Aix and studied law, then art, here. He spent most of his life painting this region, particularly the rugged limestone hills of the Mont Sainte-Victoire range with its ever-changing light and colours. He lived at this address for the last seven years of his life. The studio and garden where he worked is now a museum. Cézanne's furniture and personal objects haven't been moved since his death, making a visit here a solemn, moving experience for fans of the artist.

Pavillon de Vendôme ★ *(13F; Mon to Sun 10 am to noon and 2pm to 5pm; Jun to Sep, 10am to noon and 2pm to 6pm; 32 Rue Célony, ☎04.42.21.05.78)*. Very pretty *hôtel particulier* set in its own landscaped park and French garden, dating from 1665. An entire upper level was added in the 18th century. The interior was meticulously renovated in 1992, and includes a number of fine paintings and period furniture. The facade includes an ensemble of Doric, Ionic and Corinthian columns, with two heroic Atlantes sculptures propping up an elegant balcony.

Outside Aix

The **Oppidum d'Entremont** *(free; Wed to Mon 9am to noon and 2pm to 6pm; Plateau d'Entremont, 3km or 1.9mi north of the centre of Aix on Route de Puyricard, no ☎)* displays the vestiges of the first colony of Aix, which date back to the end of the 3rd century B.C. when the Salyens, a Celto-Ligurian tribe, occupied this plateau. There is not much to see here, although archeologists have identified the remains of a rampart wall and established the layout of the village, which consisted of dwellings, roads and an irrigation system. The findings of archeological digs at Entremont can be seen at Musée Granet.

Roquefavour Aqueduct ★ *(17km or 10.6mi west of Aix along the D64)*. Part of the Marseille Canal, this impressive arched aqueduct was built between 1842 and 1847 to carry water from the Durance River across the Arc River to the south.

La Fondation Vasarely *(Avenue Marcel Pagnol - Jus de Bouffan, 4km (2.5mi) west of Aix city centre via Avenue de* *l'Europe,* *☎04.42.20.01.09).* Hungarian-born, Paris-based artist Victor Vasarely was known as the Master of op Art—his graphic, geometric paintings and tapestries are present in large art galleries and private collections around the world. For years, the Vasarely Foundation near Aix has exposed a large selection of his work in this contemporary edifice. It was forced into liquidation in early 1997 because of mismanagement of funds and was dissolved in March 1997. Vasarely died of prostate cancer the same month. It is worth enquiring at the Aix tourist office to find out if this extraordinary exhibition site has reopened as so many supporters hope.

Montagne Sainte-Victoire

The Montagne Sainte-Victoire hill range extends for 20km (12.4mi) west of Aix-en-Provence. The site contains a number of quiet villages, excellent hiking trails and, hidden amongst the aromatic pine trees, vacation homes for wealthy *Aixois.* The north face is generally verdant and undulating, the south face is dramatic and craggy.

Forest fires devastated parts of Mont Sainte-Victoire in 1989. Since then, a number of precautions have been put in place—notably the installation of "anti-fire" mist-making machines and a surveillance team of 22 men and women on horseback (with uniforms inspired by the famous Royal Canadian Mounted Police). They control a territory of more than 700ha (1,730 acres), give assistance to hikers and mountain bikers and evaluate the growth of vegetation in the area destroyed by fire.

Sainte-Victoire is known as the favourite subject matter of the artist Paul Cézanne. He is thought to have painted the mountain more than 60 times, capturing its varying geometric shapes and changing hues throughout the day and across the different seasons. In a letter to his son in 1906, Cézanne said, "I spend every day in this landscape, with its beautiful shapes. Indeed, I cannot imagine a more pleasant way or place to pass my time."

A full day is necessary to explore this area, if a lunch or walking tour are planned. An easy circular circuit is suggested, starting and finishing at Aix-en-Provence. Take the D17 eastward (past Le Tholonet and Puylobier) to Pourrières. Turn north on the D23, then left, westward onto the D223, which soon becomes the D10, for the return journey to Aix (past Vauvenargues). Sites along the way include:

Le Tholonet is a pretty village nestled in park and woodlands, and a suitable spot to explore the countryside without venturing far from Aix. Obviously due to its proximity to Aix, it is crowded on weekends and in the summer. A pathway is indicated which leads to an arched dam (the barrage Zola), built by François Zola, father of the writer and Aix native Émile Zola. At the exit of Le Tholonet, in front of a mill, is an effigy of Cézanne. After passing the D46 (leading to the peaceful hamlet of Beaurecueil) is the Roque-Hautes Park, and a walking path leading to the Refuge Cézanne resting point. From here, eastwards to **Saint Antonin-sur-Bayon**, the road becomes quite twisty and provides spectacular views of the bald hill range up close.

L'**ermitage de Saint-Ser** can be reached on foot by a path leaving the D17, before it reaches Puyloubier *(about a 1hr walk).* Nestled in the country you will see a charming little 11th-century chapel (which is often close).

From **Puyloubier**, take the D57D (the D623

when crossing into the Var department) past sloping vineyards to **Pourrières**. Pass through the town, and head north through the Bois de Pourrières woodlands, climbing the D223 for 7km (4.3mi). Make a sharp left, westwards onto the D223, just before the hamlet of **Puits-de-Rians**. The D223 becomes the D10 upon re-entering the Bouches-du-Rhône department and passes through wooded spaces with a variety of wildflowers in season. The *conseil général* (regional government) has placed information panels in this area (known as the Puits-d'Auzon) describing possible walking paths. Sheltered picnic tables are provided off the roadside.

Vauvenargues is a charming small village at the foot of the north side of Mont Sainte Victoire. The wonderful view from the village is dominated by the Château de Vauvenargues (not open to the public), a 17th-century castle with two low, round towers and clay-tile roof. It was bought by the Spanish artist Pablo Picasso (1881-1973) in 1958, who painted the region in the years to follow.

Just west of Vauvenargues, a pathway is marked indicating the walking trail leading to the **Prieuré de Sainte-Victoire** and the **Croix de Provence** ★★★. (The walk takes a good hour, and requires proper footwear.) From the hilltop site of the 28-metre (92-foot) cross and base, are spectacular panoramic views as far as the Luberon hills, Sainte-Baume Massif and Alpilles range. From the D10, Aix-en-Provence is 13km (8mi) westward.

Saint-Maximin-la-Sainte-Baume

Saint-Maximin-la-Sainte-Baume *(42km or 26.1mi east of Aix-en-Provence along the N7 highway)* is famous throughout France for one thing—its splendid **Basilique** ★★. Experts consider it the most important Gothic structure in all of Provence. Construction started in 1295 under orders by Charles II (future Count of Provence) on the site of a 6th-century Merovingian church, but stopped in 1316 when only partially completed. Lack of funds meant work was delayed until the early 15th century, and then again in the early 16th century. Such stop-and-go construction methods remarkably did nothing to harm the harmony nor beauty of the finished structure.

Inside, the pure, luminous space is decorated with a magnificent wood pulpit by Louis Gudet and many paintings (unfortunately many need restoring), including a retable of the Crucifixion by Françoise Ronzen. The organ dating from 1773 (one of the oldest still in use in France) was created by Jean-Esprit Isnard. Recitals are presented on Sunday afternoons and a series of organ concerts takes place in summer; both are well worth attending *(for the exact program contact the tourist office or consult the basilica's bulletin board).*

Legend has it that after landing at Saintes-Maries-de-la-Mer, having been chased out of Jerusalem, Mary Magdalene went to the region of Saint-Maximin to perform her penance, which explains why the basilica's crypt encloses the sarcophagi of Mary Magdalene and Saint-Maximin, among others. Her skull rests in a golden reliquary.

The **Couvent Royal** ★ and verdant cloître *(15F; Apr to Oct, Mon to Fri 10am to 11:45am and 2pm to 5:45pm, Sat, Sun and holidays 2pm to 6:45pm; Nov to Mar, Mon to Fri 10am to 11:45am and 2pm to 4:45pm, closed weekends; Place de l'Hôtel de Ville, ☎04.94.78.01.93).* The former 17th-century Dominican convent is administered by the Collège d'Échanges Contemporains, who organize temporary art exhibitions and classical music concerts of high standard. The **Hôtel de Ville** ★ *(Place de* *l'Hotel de Ville)* is housed in the former hostel belonging to the convent.

The Sainte-Baume Massif

This hilly forest area offers dramatic views and excellent walking opportunities. The untouched beauty and remarkable variety of coniferous and deciduous trees make the Sainte-Baume Massif similar to that of the Vosges Mountains in northeastern France. An easy circular tour, with stops at sites with access by foot only, will take at least half a day.

From Saint-Maximin-la-Sainte-Baume, take the N560 to Saint-Zacharie (16km 9.9mi). Turn right onto the D85, where a very twisty road affords a number of remarkable south-westerly views, over the Régagnas Mountain. Continue past the mountain pass called Pas de la Couelle, until you reach **Saint Jean-du-Puy**. On foot, past the private chapel, there are fine panoramic views of the entire region.

Return to Saint Zacharie and take the D45 for 5km (3.1mi), turning south onto the D45A at the hamlet of le Pujol. At la Coutronne, turn south onto the D2, another twisty road, and head towards the village of Gémenos.

This scenic stretch of road passes by the **Col de l'Espigoulier**, with the Pic de Bertagne and Roque Forcade mountain peaks on the east side. Following a series of hairpin turns, the tree-lined Saint-Pons valley appears upon descending the road. About 3km (1.9mi) before Gémonos is the **Parc de Saint-Pons**. Here, the ruins of the **Abbaye de Saint-Pons** are discovered by following a marked pathway on foot for a short distance. It was once a Cistercian convent for women, and visitors may discern the nuns' cloister, chapel and living quarters.

Gémenos ★ is a pretty village with a Hôtel de Ville dominating its central square. The building of the former town château was started in the Middle Ages but its main features date primarily from the 17th and 18th centuries. Next to it are the large Granges du Marquis d'Albertas, agricultural buildings dating from around 1750.

Return to la Coutronne by the same road (D2) and turn right onto the D80 (direction Saint-Maximin-la-Sainte-Baume). Past the hamlet of Plan-d'Aups, is the Hôtellerie de la Sainte-Baume. This former Dominican convent is now a religious retreat.

Stop at the junction of the D80 and D95 (known as the Trois Chênes). According to legend, Mary Magdelene served penitence for 30 years in a cave here, the Grotte de la Baume *(30min on foot; follow the indicated pathway and steps, wear proper footwear, everyday 8am to 6pm)*. Pilgrimages occur twice a year (Jul 22, Dec 24) to the cave, in which a natural spring and marble statue of Virgin Mary are found.

Spectacular panoramic views can be had from the peak, **Saint Pilon** ★★ (994m or 3,261ft) south to the Mediterranean Sea, west to Marseille, and north to the Sainte-Victoire Mountain. The steep pathway is marked from the Grotte (cave) and takes another half hour on foot. This circuit finishes back at Saint-Maximin-la-Sainte-Baume, after passing the village of Nans-les-Pins on the D80, and picking up the N560 northeast.

Outdoor Activities

Hiking

The Aix region is ideal hiking territory, as it offers a variety of easy to challenging trails, many with spectacular views. One of the most scenic paths is the GR9, which starts from the D10 road just west of Vauvenargues, leads to the Croix de Provence, continues along the Montagne Sainte-Victoire to the Pic des Mouches (1,011m or 3,317ft) and descends to Puyloubier. A shorter path leads north from Vauvenargues (also marked GR9) through gently sloping wooded landscape to the hamlet of Lambruise.

A third arm of the GR9 heads south from Sainte-Victoire towards the Sainte-Baume Massif. Between Puyloubier and Trets (a village off the D6 road), this path trails through vineyard territory and is relatively easy. The GR9 continues on the south side of Trets—it becomes more rugged but the effort is worth it because it includes some amazing scenery. Here the GR9 heads south of Trets, past the breath-taking Saint-Juan-du-Puy viewing point to Saint-Zacharie, trails the Huveaune River and reaches the Saint-Pilon peak (after crossing the D80 and D95 junction known at the Trois Chênes).

The Sainte-Baume Massif may be crossed using the steep GR98 trail. This extensive route heads southwest in the direction of Gémenos, past the Parc de Saint Pons, and includes views over high cliffs. Many kilometres later, it eventually ends at Mont de la Saoupe, the scenic fishing port of Cassis. This latter section of the GR98 offers lovely views of the Mediterranean coastline.

Local tourist offices will put you on the right path, or you can buy one of the many fine maps and guidebooks in local bookshops. Please note that the major paths (Mont Sainte-Victoire and the Saint-Baume Massif) are closed during the summer (generally Jul 1 to Sep 15). This is to prevent forest fires that have recently destroyed many of these *grandes zones boisées* (large woodland areas).

Fishing

Trout, salmon and eels may be caught in the rivers of this region. For more information on the best spots and local fishing regulations, contact the tourist office or, better yet, the Fédération de Pêche *(Chemin Beauville, 13100 Aix-en-Provence, ☎04.42.26.59.15)*

Golf

The following 18-hole golf courses offer equipment rental and the services of a resident pro. Green fees and admission prices vary, between 200F and 300F a day, so call ahead.

Golf Club Aix-Marseille
Domaine de Riquetti, 13290 Les Milles
☎04.42.24.20.41

Golf International Pont Royal Country Club
Route N 7, 13370 Mallemort
☎04.90.57.40.79

Horseback Riding

Club Hippique Aix-Marseille
Avenue du Club Hippique, Chemin des Cavaliers, 13100 Aix-en-Provence
☎04.42.20.18.26

La Provence à Cheval
Quartier Saint Joseph, 13950 Cadolive
☎04.42.04.66.76

La Galinière Provence Équitation
Route N 7, Châteauneuf-le-Rouge, 13790 Rousset
☎*04.42.53.32.55*

Tennis

Tennis Club de l'Arbois
Route de Calas, 13480 Cabries
☎*04.42.22.20.84*

Tennis Part
Chemin d'Eguilles, 13090 Aix-en-Provence
☎*04.42.92.34.19*

Tennis de l'Oliveraie
126 Cours Gambetta 13100 Aix-en-Provence
☎*04.42.27.87.87*

Bicycling

The following Aix-en-Provence companies rent bicycles for touring the city, as well as sturdy mountain bikes for exploring the surrounding countryside.

Troc-Vélo
62 Rue Boulegon
☎*04.42.21.37.40*

Lubrano Location
37 Boulevard de la République
☎*04.42.21.44.85*
Lubrano also rents mopeds and motorbikes.

Sports Centres

The municipal sports centre of Aix-en-Provence offers a multitude of facilities including an outdoor pool *(May to Sep)*, tennis courts and even a training wall for novice mountain climbers. It is no surprise that it is invariably overrun on hot summer days.

Complexe Sportif du Val de l'Arc
Chemin des Infirmeries, 13100 Aix-en-Provence
☎*04.42.16.02.50*

Country Club Aixois
Bastide des Solliers, Chemin de Cruyès, 13090 Aix-en-Provence
☎*04.42.92.10.41*
If the above options are not appealing, travellers can try the Country Club Aixois, which offers a pool and tennis and squash courts, not to mention a warm, friendly staff.

Accommodations

Aix-en-Provence

Auberge de Jeunesse
82F first day
69F each following day
3 Avenue Marcel-Pagnol
Quartier Jas-de- Bouffan
☎*04.42.20.15.99*
Well-equipped with tennis and volleyball courts, bar, library, laundromat, restaurant, tv room; 100 places in dormitories; 10min from city centre. Meal for 50F.

Hôtel Paul
193F-253F
ps, pb
10 Avenue Pasteur
☎*04.42.23.23.89*
An inexpensive and upbeat budget hotel. Ask for a room over the garden as those overlooking the road tend to be noisy. Television room. Extremely clean. Pretty breakfast room with ratan furniture next to the garden.

Hôtel Cardinal
260F, 350F and 400F
pb, tv
24 Rue Cardinale
☎*04.42.38.32.30*
04.42.26.39.05
A good-value hotel in a restored 18th-century building, across from the Musée Granet and St.Jean de Malte church in the calm Mazarin neighbourhood. Rooms are bright and decorated with taste—most

have Provençal wood furniture.

Hotel de France
300F-370F
ps, pb, tv
63 Rue Espariat
☎04.42.27 90 15
⇌04 42 26 11 47
Just off the Place de la Rotonde and the Cours Mirabeau, this is a simple two-star hotel that offers good value in what is otherwise a pricey city. Bedrooms are dated, but can you complain at these prices?

Hôtel Le Manoir
325F, 400F and 490F
ps or pb, tv
8 Rue d'Entrecasteaux
☎04.42.26.27.20
⇌04.42.27.17.97
A 14th-century arched cloister is the stunning feature of this city-centre hotel which once was a monastery. Some of the 42 rooms have interesting features such as wood-beamed ceilings and antiques, but the furnishings and wall-paper are from another era and need refreshing.

Hôtel le Prieuré
330F-400F
pb
Route de Sisteron
☎04.42.21.05.23
Comfortable, quiet hotel, just 5min from the city-centre. Most rooms look out over the lovely 17th-century Pavillon de L'Enfant park (no access however). Romantically decorated in lush reds, royal blues and pinks. Friendly. Off-street parking.

Les Infirmeries du Roy René
350F-550F
1,900-3,300F per week
pb, tv, K, ≈
Chemin des Infirmeries
☎04.42.37.83.00
⇌04.42.27.54.40
Les Infirmeries du Roy René occupies the site of an old 16th-century hospital, 10min from the centre of Aix. This is a modern hotel with 66 fully equipped apartments that are perfectly suited to couples or families who want to spend several days in this town. Each apartment, while simple, presents a harmonious decor and possesses a dining area (the hotel does not serve breakfast). A coin laundry, an outdoor parking lot and access to the neighbouring municipal pool complete the list of amenities on offer.

Hôtel des Quatre Dauphins
380F-400F
ps or pb, mini-bar, tv
54 Rue Roux Alphéran
☎04.42.38.16.39
⇌04.42.38.60.19
Located in the quiet, elegant Quartier Mazarin just a few steps from the Fontaine des Quatre Dauphins and the Cours Mirabeau, this charming hotel offers prettily decorated bedrooms with Provençal fabrics and clay-tile floors. Modern bathrooms are small, but for location, comfort and price, who's complaining?

Résidences Les Floridianes
390F
≡, tv, ℜ, K, ≈
24 Boulevard Charrier
☎04.42.37.23.23
⇌04.42.64.00.18
The centrally located Résidences Les Floridianes is a good, economical option for short visits as well as longer stays. The small $20m^2$ (215 sq ft) studios have terraces and come fully equipped, allowing guests to prepare their own meals. With nondescript surroundings and no charm to speak of, the studios are still worth considering for their location. Guests sleep on sofa beds that are comfortable, but still not as firm as a box spring mattress.

Hôtel Saint Christophe
420F-460F
ps, pb, tv, ℜ
2 Avenue Victor-Hugo
☎04.42.26.01.24
⇌04.42.38.53.17
Hôtel Saint Christophe is an inviting hotel with Art Deco touches throughout. Service is very professional and friendly. Renovated in 1994. The restaurant Brasserie Leopold serves Parisian brasserie dishes including fresh seafood, steak tartare and sauerkraut, and is popular with guests and non-guests alike.

Grand Hôtel Nègre-Coste
420F, 600F and 750F
ps, pb, tv
33 Cours Mirabeau
☎*04.42.27.74.22*
⇄*04.42.26.80.93*
Rather grand hotel with 19th-century furniture and faded atmosphere. Staff are helpful, and the place has an unparalleled location right on the Cours Mirabeau—thankfully the rooms are sound-proofed.

Les Résidences Pierre & Vacances
470F
pb, tv
3-5 Rue des Chartreux
☎*04.42.37.98.98*
⇄*04.42.37.98.99*
This national chain offers not just double rooms by the night, but also fully equipped apartments with kitchenettes available by the week (studios and three-room units suitable for up to eight people for 3,290F). The decor is cheery yet banal.

Hôtel des Augustins
700F-1,500F
≡, pb, tv
3 Rue de la Masse
☎*04.42.27.28.59*
⇄*04.42.26.74.87*
Sombre, elegant hotel in a former 15th-century convent, fully-restored in 1984 with good-sized, fully-equipped rooms.

Villa Gallici
1,350F-3,050F
≈, ℜ, pb, mini-bar, tv
Avenue de la Violette / Impasse des Grands Pins
☎*04.42.23.29.23*
⇄*04.42.96.30.45*
This exquisite grand villa set amongst fragrant pine trees is Aix's most charming and sophisticated hotel. The salons, dining room and 17 bedrooms have benefited from the hand of interior decorator Gilles Dez, who mixes fabrics, textures and colours in perfect harmony. The pretty pool is surrounded by tall cypresses. Located in a tranquil haven a few minutes north of the city centre.

Beaurecueil

Relais Sainte-Victoire
400F-800F
≈, ℜ, pb, tv
Route D58
☎*04.42.66.94.98*
This auberge is nestled in the wilderness, next to Mont Sainte-Victoire, and is perfect for a peaceful break. It has nine spacious rooms (recently decorated yet in an outdated style), with terraces facing the wooded grounds. It is run with great care and attention by Gabrielle Jugy and René Bergès. Of course, the excellent restaurant is just a few tempting steps away (see p 213). Delicious breakfast with home-baked croissants, fresh fruit and very good coffee.

Pourrières

Mas des Graviers
500F bkfst incl.
pb, ≈
Route de Rians
☎*04.94.78.40.38*
⇄*04.94.78.44.88*
Mas des Graviers is a small winery, whose owners, Norwegian painter Ian Olaf and Andrea McGarvie-Munn, put on art exhibitions in the summertime. Surrounded by flowers and trees typical to the Mediterranean coast, this farmhouse was recently renovated and converted into a bed and breakfast offering seven tastefully decorated rooms. A majestic pool overlooks the vineyard and neighbouring lavender fields. The establishment is closed to the public in winter and spring when it is transformed into an artists' retreat. Credit cards not accepted,

Gémenos

Le Provence
180F, 220F and 250F
Route d'Aix
☎*04.42.32.20.55*
A rustic country inn, simple and reasonably priced. Although the luxuries of grander places are missing, Le Provence does have a delightful terrace and gardens as well as a restaurant serving home-cooked meals. Popular with guests hiking in the Massif de Sainte Baume.

Le Relais de la Magdeleine
630F, 730F and 890F
pb, tv
☎***04.42.32.20.16***
⇄***04.42.32.02.26***
A magnificent 18th-century bastide with lovely parklands originally designed by royal landscape architect Le Nôtre. It feautures a total of 23 tastefully decorated rooms, a dining room serving excellent Provençal classics and a serene swimming pool set amidst the trees. Friendly, warm greeting from the Marignane family. A good base from which to discover Aix and the Sainte-Baume Massif, or Marseille, Cassis and the Mediterranean coast.

Restaurants

Aix-en-Provence

Café de l'Horloge
$
6am to 2am
38 Rue Vauvenargues
☎***04.42.23.35.10***
Whether for a coffee and croissant in the morning, a salad or croque monsieur at noon or a hot meal later, this typical café has it all. Baguette sandwiches and a small pitcher of wine are 20F. Relax a while on the terrace under two rows of towering plane trees on Place Richelme.

Haagen-Dazs
$
every day 12:30pm to 10:30pm
15 Cours Mirabeau
☎***04.42.27.63.30***
This branch of the American ice-cream king offers the perfect, indulgent antidote to healthy Provençal cooking. Café/take-out counter with a small terrace on Cours Mirabeau.

Hub Lot Cybercafé
$
17 Rue Paul Bert
☎***04.42.21.96.96***
Aix's very own Cybercafé, decorated with flags of the world and football pendants, is better for a coffee or drink than a meal. Football matches transmitted on a giant tv screen, billiards, happy hours *(7pm to 9pm; draught beer 10F)*. Breakfast menu. Internet usage: 30F half-hour, 50F hour; e-mail facility: 15F.

Pizza Capri
$
One Rue Fabrot
☎***04.42.38.55.43***
Pizza Capri appeases the appetites of Aixois on their way out to the movies or to meet friends. At just 13 or 17F for a slice, or 42 to 50F a pie, who could blame them for frequenting this friendly pizza stand? Take out only.

Pizzéria La Grange
$
2 bis Rue Nazareth
☎***04.42.26.19.85***
Dependable and popular pizzeria, with typical red-checkered tablecloths and *al fresco* dining along this pedestrian-only street near the Cours Mirabeau. Menu at 99F.

À La Cour de Rohan
$-$$
everyday 11am to 7pm, Fri and Sat until 11:30pm May to Sep, everyday until 11:30pm
10 Rue Vauvenargues-Place Hôtel de Ville
☎***04.42.96.18.15***
Large café with light lunches (eggplant purée on toast, poached egg on a bed of spinach), and numerous cakes and varieties of tea. The excellent location with a sunny terrace in front of the town hall makes this a popular afternoon spot, though 25F for a cup of tea might put some people off.

Le Cintra
$-$$
24 hours/day, every day
14 Place Jeanne d'Arc
☎***04.42.27.57.01***
A restaurant and café ready to satisfy whatever your heart and stomach desires, such as fish soup, chicken salad, steak tartar and sauerkraut. A colourful mix of tourists and locals make themselves at home on Le Cintra's red banquettes.

Le Petit Verdot
$-$$
closed Sun and Mon pm
7 Rue d'Entrecasteaux
☎**04.42.27.30.12**
Charming wine bar serving terrines and meat dishes to accompany the good selection of bottles. An Aix-en-Provence institution and worth stopping into for a glass or two.

Tapas Café
$-$$
closed Sun
6 Place des Augustins
☎**04.42.26.77.72**
A spot favoured by young Aixois, tempted by the piped-in pop music, bold yellow interior and selection of 30 tapas (mackerel croquettes, chicken or lamb brochette, marinated anchovy filet). Margaritas and sangrias are served by the glass and in pitchers. Terrace.

Le Basilic Gourmand
$$
closed Sun, Mon and Wed
6 Rue du Griffon
☎**04.42.96.08.58**
A very pleasant place for lunch or dinner (especially on the front terrace), serving unfussy but delicious meals with a Provençal slant. Excellent value three-course menus and two-course lunch menu. Located off Rue Paul Bert, away from the crowds.

Le Bistro Latin
$$
18 Rue de la Couronne
☎**04.42.38.22.88**
Chef Bruno Ungaro offers superb contemporary Provençal cuisine made with the freshest local ingredients, such as profiteroles of sautéed snails and olive cream or baked chèvre tart followed by braised lamb with pistou or fried-red mullet with spices. Professional service and excellent wine list. Casual, sophisticated grey and pink decor; a good place for a refined dinner.

Le Verdun
$$
every day 6am to 2am
20 Place de Verdun
☎**04.42.27.03.24**
A comfortable and friendly local café serving breakfast, lunch and dinner. Items include roast pork with garden vegetables, a Saint-Marcellin and walnut salad and rich chocolate cake. Those watching their waistline will fall for the *plats diététiques*, which might be a fish, chicken- or vegetable-based dish. Handy location opposite the Palais de Justice for the thrice-weekly outdoor flea market.

Chez Antoine Côté Cour
$$
closed Sun and Mon lunch
19 Cours Mirabeau
☎**04.42.93.12.51**
Fresh, luminous restaurant situated in the verdant inner courtyard of an elegant Cours Mirabeau *hôtel particulier*. New owners, Monique and Roger, serve dishes with an Italian slant: rabbit polenta, fresh fish, sweetbreads with capers.

Chez Féraud
$$
closed Sun
8 Rue du Puits Juif
☎**04.42.63.07.27**
A charming restaurant hidden away from the busy streets nearby, serving Provençal cuisine prepared with great care. Starters include eggplant gratin and pistou soup; main dishes might be medallion of tarragon chicken and cannelloni with thyme. Blue and yellow fabrics and wicker chairs contribute to the relaxed atmosphere.

Le Comté d'Aix
$$
closed Sat lunch and Sun
17 Rue de la Couronne
☎**04.42.26.79.26**
Provençal specialties and shellfish dishes are Le Comté's strong points. The rustic room has Provençal-print tablecloths and posters on the walls. A choice of six menus ranging from 95F to 200F.

Jacquou le Croquant
$$
closed Sun lunch, Mon and mid-Aug to mid-Sep
2 Rue de l'Aumône Vieille
☎**04.42.27.37.19**
A variety of tasty *tourtons* (whole-wheat crepes with different fillings) and salads are served by the bubbly, friendly female staff. Everything is fresh and appealingly presented—we enjoyed the *Salade Mistral* (chèvre, tapenade, herbs and olive oil).

The midday menu includes either salad or *tourton* followed by home-made dessert (caramelized apple pie, pear flan).

La Maison des Fondues
$$
13 Rue Verrerie
☎***04.42.63.07.78***
Over 60 types of fondues are available—from chicken, beef and lamb to the more unusual duck, fish and even ostrich. Most cost around 100F; children's menu 55F. Country-inn decor with table cloths and wooden chairs.

Le Poivre d'Ane
$$
closed Sun
7 Rue de la Couronne
☎***04.42.93.45.56***
A cosy restaurant, long and narrow, with blue painted wood chairs, Provençal tablecloths and low lights on the tables. Menus range from one and two dishes to three courses. Recent dishes included delicious basil-laden pistou soup, beef tournedos and fillet of cod. To finish: baked pear with lavender honey.

Tây-Lai
$$
closed Sun
16bis Rue des Marseillais
☎***04.42.23.53.79***
A colourful restaurant specialising in Chinese and Vietnamese cuisine. A variety of dishes is offered—fish, chicken, pork, duck, beef, and Chinese noodles. The house specialty is Asian brochettes— delicious pieces of beef, chicken, shrimp or tiger prawns barbecued at the table. Lunch, dinner and children's menus are available.

Les Agapes
$$
11 Rue des Bernardines
☎***04.42.38.47.66***
Les Agapes has a Provençal ambiance thanks to its dining room with exposed ceiling beams and warm, yellow colours, embellished with small pictures and dried flowers. Expect honest and hearty food like peppers grilled with local cheese, sardines *à l'escabèche*, *brandade* (a dish made with cod), rennet stomach, casserole and coquerel. The restaurant certainly offers good value for the price given the tastiness and size of the portions. Les Agapes is popular with the Aixois, who enjoy a pleasant location that makes the most of the architectural qualities of this old building in the heart of the old city of Aix.

Les Bacchanales
$$
0 Rue de la Couronne
☎***04.42.27.21.06***
Reputed to be one of the best dining establishments in Aix, Les Bacchanales offers generous portions of excellent, genuine rural Provençal cuisine. The wide price range on the lengthy menu guarantees appeal to a variety of diners. Guests enjoy a peaceful, traditional setting and refined service. If you ask anyone from Aix about the best places to eat in the city, they're sure to recommend Les Bacchanales.

Yoji
$$-$$$
closed Mon
7 Avenue Victor Hugo
☎***04.42.38.48.76***
An exciting Japanese and Korean restaurant serving a tasty Bento box (salad, Yakitori, rice, vegetables and coffee) at mid-day, with a large selection of à la carte dishes such as sushi, sashimi, bulgoki (Korean barbecue) and sukiyaki (Japanese fondue) at lunch and dinner. The restful spot has a shaded terrace, teak chairs and crisp white tablecloths.

Chez Maxime
$$$
closed Sun and Mon at noon
12 Place Ramus
☎***04.42.26.28.51***
Without a doubt one of the best-known dining establishments in Aix-en-Provence, Chez Maxime opens onto a pretty little square under the benevolent watch of a three-hundred-year-old plane tree. Set in the old Saint-Antoine chapel, this restaurant, which has been a fixture in Aix for 15 years, specializes in delicious, simple, authentic Provençal cuisine, and is especially known for its meat. The cuts are chosen by owner Maxime who, in fact, carves them as you

watch on the old butcher's block. Maxime was a butcher and grocer/caterer for nearly 30 years before entering the restaurant business, so he knows his meat. Guests enjoy a warm, relaxed atmosphere both in the dining room and on the terrace, reflecting the personality of the friendly owner who takes the time to welcome his regulars personally with a firm handshake. We can't help but urge you to try one of the many beef or lamb dishes. The crisp mullet (*croustillant de rouget*) is a simple and tasty appetizer, while the *foie gras* with figs is positively divine! Ordering à la carte can get pricey, but Maxime offers some affordable set-price menus, or a real culinary feast for 270F. The restaurant also has an exceptionally well-stocked wine cellar with approximately 500 vintages carefully and lovingly chosen and highly praised by the owner.

Beaurecueil

Relais Sainte-Victoire
$$-$$$
closed Sun evening and Mon, first week of Jan, Feb and Easter school holidays
Route D58 Beaurecueil
☎***04.42.66.94.98***
René Bergès has established a reputation reaching far beyond this tiny hamlet near Aix for his refined Provençal cooking. Local suppliers provide the best ingredients, from vegetables and olive oil, to fish, lamb, rabbit and pigeon. Recent starters included mushroom-stuffed zucchini, flower or lobster terrine with pistou and a white-bean vinaigrette, followed by fresh red mullet with lavender butter or a lamb confit with ratatouille. The cheese trolley offers a particularly good selection of chèvre varieties. Desserts are sublime. Pleasant oak-panelled dining room or conservatory. Professional service. Worth the detour and best to book ahead as it is popular with local dignitaries and well-off Aixois.

Vauvenargues

Le Couscoussier
$
Tue to Sun 9am to midnight
☎***04.42.66.00.57***
Although eating here is not particularly recommended, this roadside café makes a good rest stop. Travellers can sip cool drinks on its quiet terrace, which has an excellent view of Château de Vauvenargues where Picasso lived, and of the undulating hills that served him as a backdrop. Credit cards not accepted.

Le Garde
$-$$
Mon to Wed pm only, Thu to Sat mid-day and pm, Sun mid-day and pm during the summer only
Route D10 2km (1.2mi) west of Vauvenargues
☎***04.42.24.97.99***
Within viewing distance of the hill-top cross of the Prieuré de Sainte-Victoire, this friendly roadside restaurant serves up good grilled meats and fish, salads and home-made desserts. There's even a *boules* track next to the brightly-tiled patio bar. No credit cards.

Au Moulin de Provence
$-$$
open mid-Mar to Oct. 31
Avenue des Maquisards
☎***04.42.66.02.22***
⇌***04.42.66.01.21***
Though the decor is nothing to write home about, the cuisine is: superb Provençal dishes cooked with care by Monsieur and Madame Yemenidjian which highlight the ingredients' natural flavours (eggplant terrine with a tomato-basil *coulis*; *daube à la Provençale*; *nougat glacé*).

Entertainment

Aix-en-Provence

Les Thermes Sextius
One day 380F to 440F
Six days 1,980F to 2,370F
55 Cours Sextius
☎***0.800.639.699***
≠***04.42.95.11.33***
thermes.sextius@wanadoo.fr
Hot springs have made the city of Aix-en-Provence a lively place for more than 2000 years. Located on the site of ancient thermal baths that had been abandoned for several years, Les Thermes Sextius have brought new life to this place loaded with history. Wishing to combine the richness of the past with modern amenities, the designers of this new establishment have left some of the marvellous Roman ruins exposed, skilfully blended with an ultramodern glass and metal structures. As well as providing an impressive array of treatments, Les Thermes Sextius captures the spirit of past and present through its unusual architecture that combines the lines and arches of the 18th century with ultramodern infrastructure. Although we recommend the series of treatments that come with the six-day hydrotherapy cure (four treatments per day), those fortunate enough to come here can opt to take their favourite treatments individually or by the day. The friendly, welcoming staff will guide you throughout your stay. We encourage you to indulge in a little sensuous pleasure at this exceptional spa in the heart of Aix.

Les 2 Garçons
53 Cours Mirabeau
☎***04.42.26.00.51***
An elegant café with a large sidewalk terrace which is perfect for watching the parade of people passing along the Cours Mirabeau, while sipping a coffee or a drink, night and day. Known as the "2 G," it was founded in 1792 and is an Aix institution. Service can be rushed and aloof; eat somewhere else.

Bar Brigand
17 Place Richelme at Rue Fauchier
☎***04.42.26.11.57***
Better than the average bar serving over 40 types of Belgian and European beers.

Café le Verdun
every day 6am to 2am
20 Place Verdun
☎***04.42.27.03.24***
This pleasant café (see p 211) is open late and offers a large selection of beers and wines by the glass. With its late-opening hours and tables spread out on the Place Verdun, there could be no finer place to pass a warm evening, watching the world go by.

Dixie Clipper
closed Sun, 10pm to 2pm
34 Rue Verrarie
no ☎
This small club overflows with a young crowd dancing to techno music and some hip-hop.

Hot Brass
Route d'Eguilles, Celony
☎***04.42.21.05.57***
Laid-back club with jazz music and frequent visiting musicians. Worth the trip from the city centre *(take Route N7, direction Eguilles/Avignon)*. During concerts, the entrance charge is 100F per person, including one drink.

Keaton Club
Tue to Sat, from 8:30pm on
live music from 10pm
9 Rue des Bretons
☎***04.42.26.86.11***
Great live jazz at this small club *(30-50F cover charge)*.

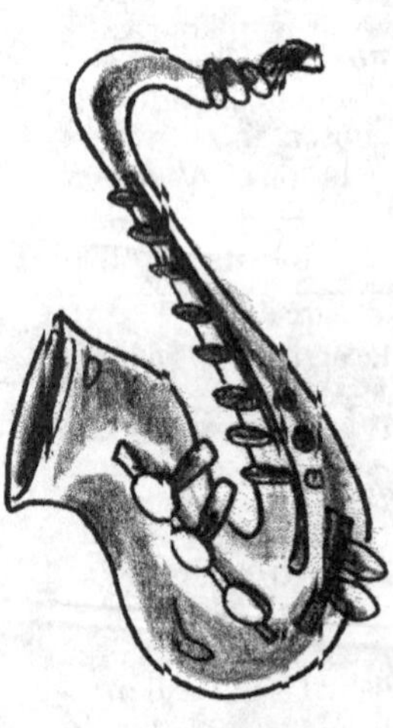

Le Scat
Tue to Sat from 11pm
on 11 Rue Verrerie
☎*04.42.23.00.23*
A cool club in a vaulted cellar with live soul, blues and funk. Drinks are pricey—beer 40F, spirits 60F.

Pub Honky Tonk
closed Sun, 10pm to 2pm
38 Rue Verrarie
☎*04.42.27.21.82*
An industrial decor with records on the wall and a biker theme set the tone for this club with a live DJ playing everything from rock and disco to techno and funk music.

Theatres

Cézanne
21 Rue Goyrand Prolongée
☎*04.42.26.04.06*
The Cézanne is a cinema that presents a mix of popular films and recently produced art films.

Ciné Mazarin
6 Rue Laroque
☎*04.42.26.99.85*
The latest award-winning art films from around the world in three cinemas. Reduced prices Mon and Wed.

Théâtre de l'Archevêché *(Palais de l'Ancien Archevêché, ☎04.42.17.34.00)* and **Théâtre Municipal** *(Rue de l'Opéra, ☎04.42.38.07.39)*, the two main recital halls in Aix, present a whole range of theatre pieces, operas and concerts throughout the year. Current programs are available at their ticket offices and at the tourist office. Aix also possesses many other smaller-scale theatres, dinner-theatres and concert halls, and the local press publishes information on performances presented at these halls.

Festivals and Cultural Events

The **Festival International d'Art Lyrique et de Musique d'Aix-en-Provence**, commonly known as the **Fesitval d'Aix**, is an acclaimed annual music festival running since 1948. Internationally renowned musicians and singers perfom in recitals, concerts and excellent opera productions (in the Théâtre de l'Archevêqué), plus many impromptu events take place throughout the city. The festival generally runs between July 10 and 30. For a programme and guide contact the Festival d'Aix office *(Palais de l'Ancien Archevêché, 13100 Aix-en-Provence, ☎04.42.17.34.20, ≠04.42.96.12.61)* or the city's tourist office.

Shopping

Aix-en-Provence

Confiserie d'Entrecasteaux
closed Sun
2 Rue d'Entrecasteaux
☎*04.42.27.15.02*
Confiserie d'Entrecasteaux prepares chocolates and excellent Aix *calissons* (ground-almond sweets).

Decathalon
closed Sun
13 Rue Chabrier
☎*04.42.21.62.93*
For all your sports clothing and equipment needs—from swimwear and hiking gear to sunglasses, sports shoes and sun hats.

Gérard Paul
closed Sun
45 Boulevard Georges Clemenceau
☎*04.42.23.16.84*
A vast choice of cheeses from Monsieur Paul of the *Guilde des Fromageurs*.

IC Aix en Provence
closed Sun
33 Boulevard de la République
☎*04.42.38.28.08*
Vast choice of computer equipment. Professional service.

Kennedy's General Store
2 Boueno Carriero, at the corner of Rue Monclar
no ☎
Kennedy's General Store is the joy of homesick American

and British tourists, who can procure, among other things, Pop Tarts, English beer, cherry pop and nacho-style corn chips!

Léonard Parli
closed Sun and Mon
33 Avenue Victor Hugo
☎***04.91.26.05.71***
Manufacturers of the famous *Calissons d'Aix* since 1874. Delicious oblong candies made from almond paste, syrup and preserved melon, the *calissons* reportedly were first served for the wedding banquet of good king René and his second wife, Queen Jeanne.

Librairie de Provence
closed Sun
31 Cours Mirabeau
☎***04.42.26.07.23***
Large bookshop with a good choice of regional titles (travel, literature, cuisine, etc.), including Ulysses travel guides!

Makaire
closed Sun and Mon
Rue Thiers/Place du Palais
☎***04.42.38.19.63***
Quality bookshop with the latest fiction and non-fiction releases (strong on Provençal titles), rare books, plus a large section devoted to paper supplies and writing instruments. Professional service.

Micro Informatique Conseil
closed Sun
8 Avenue Paul Cezanne
☎***04.42.96.46.00***
⇄***04.42.96.14.65***
Computer and multi-media equipment sales and repair.

Paradox Librairie Internationale
closed Sun
15 Rue du 4 Septembre
☎***04.42.26.47.99***
A large bookshop, favoured by Aix's large student population with titles in Spanish, German, Italian and English.

Pharmacie Landi
closed Sun
15 Avenue Marachel Foch
☎***04.42.26.13.78***
Convenient pharmacy with extended opening hours.

Pharmacie des Prêcheurs
closed Sun
2 Rue Peyresc
☎***04.42.23.54.32***
Convenient pharmacy with extended opening hours.

Photo Clic Clac
2 bis Avenue Belges
☎***04.42.26.80.00***
⇄***04.42.38.17.95***
The place to come for 1hr photo developing and film purchases.

Photo Service
1 Rue des Cordeliers
☎***04.42.96.50.01***
Photographs developed in 1hr (copies in the same amount of time, too) plus passport photos. Professional service includes cold water dispenser and on-screen weather bulletins.

Richart
closed Sun
8 Rue de Thiers
☎***04.42.38.16.19***
Superb chocolates from this contemporary shop, plus delicious chocolate cones filled with a variety of refreshing fruit-flavoured sorbets. Dark chocolate is Richart's speciality.

Riederer
6 Rue Thiers
Long-established (five generations) pastry shop for morning croissants and a large selection of cakes, including the house specialty, *tarte aux pommes* (apple pie). Continental breakfast, light lunches and afternoon cake are served in a pleasant tearoom.

Rue d'Italie. A visit to the shops along this street *(south of Place Forbin at the east end of Cours Mirabeau)* to prepare a picnic is recommended before heading out for a day-trip to the Sainte-Victoire Mountain or Sainte-Baume Massif areas. There are a couple of fruit and vegetable sellers, a cheese shop, **La Baratte** *(21 Rue d'Italie)*, a wine shop, **Bacchus** *(25 Rue d'Italie)* and two bakeries for fresh bread. **La Paneria** *(45 Rue d'Italie)* sells a mesmerizing selection of whole wheat varieties. (These shops are generally open 8am to 12:30pm and 4pm to 7:30pm.)

Sienne
closed Sun and Mon
9 Rue Rifle Rafle
☎***04.42.21.42.20***
A fine selection of tasteful gifts (decorative objects, household linens and furniture) and no Provençal fabrics in sight! Promise.

Vents du Sud
closed Sun
7 Rue Maréchal Foch
☎*04.42.23.03.38*
A well-stocked bookshop with everything from best-sellers to travel. Superior service. Situated facing Place Richelme.

Markets

Flea Market
Tuesday, Thursday and Saturday mornings
Place Palais de Justice

Fruit and Vegetable Market
Tuesday, Thursday and Saturday mornings
Place de la Madeleine
Every morning
Place Richelme.

Flower Market
Tuesday, Thursday and Saturday mornings
Place de la Mairie
Sunday morning
Place de la Madeleine

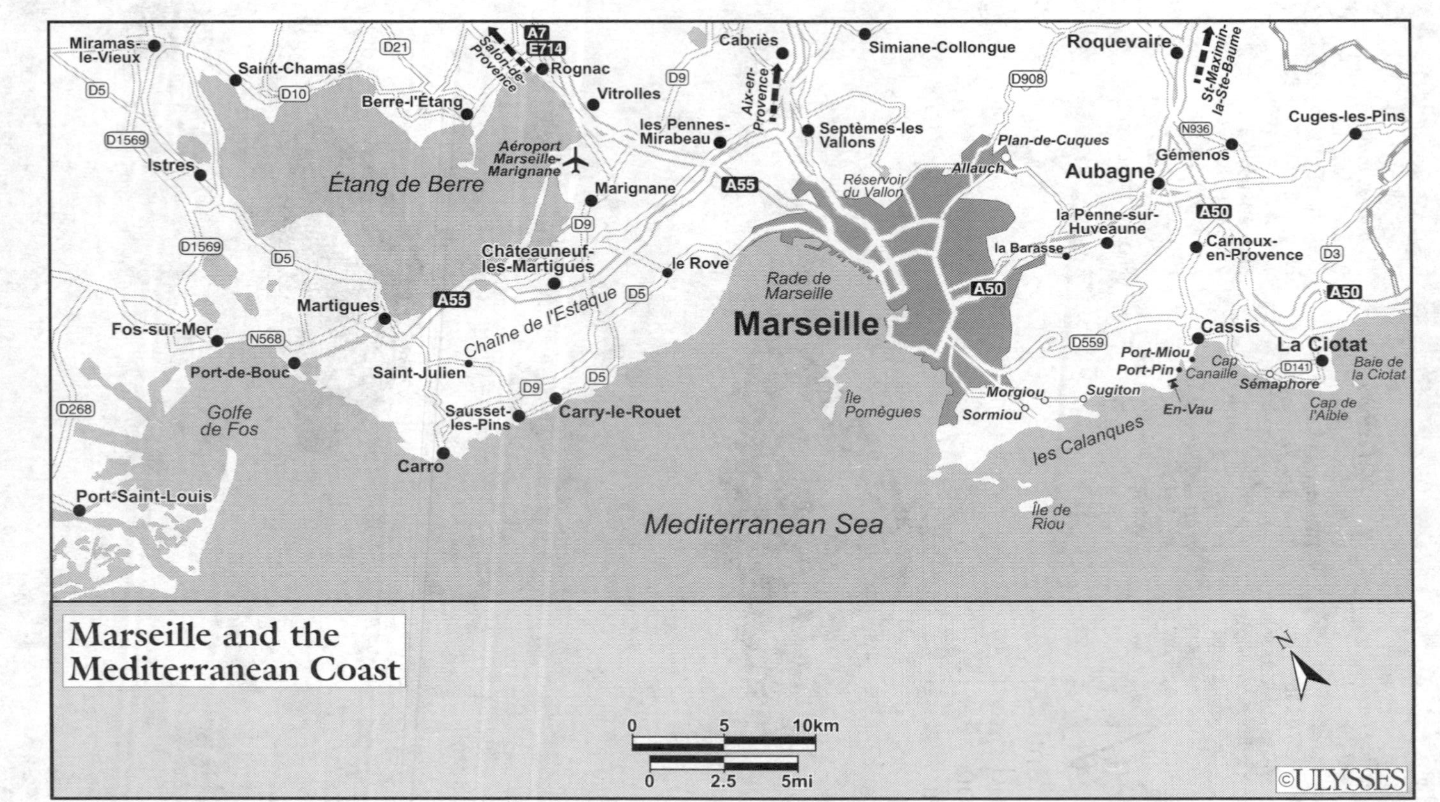

Marseille and the
Mediterranean Coast
Miramas-le-Vieux
Saint-Chamas
Salon-de-Provence
A7
E714
Rognac
Berre-l'Étang
Vitrolles
Istres
Étang de Berre
Aéroport Marseille-Marignane
Marignane
Châteauneuf-les-Martigues
Martigues
Fos-sur-Mer
Port-de-Bouc
Saint-Julien
Chaîne de l'Estaque
Golfe de Fos
Sausset-les-Pins
Carry-le-Rouet
Carro
Port-Saint-Louis
le Rove
les Pennes-Mirabeau
Cabriès
Aix-en-Provence
Septèmes-les Vallons
Simiane-Collongue
A55
Rade de Marseille
Marseille
Réservoir du Vallon
Allauch
Plan-de-Cuques
Île Pomègues
Morgiou
Sormiou
Sugiton
Île de Riou
les Calanques
Mediterranean Sea
Roquevaire
St-Maximin-la-Ste-Baume
Aubagne
Gémenos
Cuges-les-Pins
la Penne-sur-Huveaune
la Barasse
A50
Carnoux-en-Provence
Cassis
Port-Miou
Port-Pin
En-Vau
Cap Canaille
Sémaphore
La Ciotat
Baie de la Ciotat
Cap de l'Aigle
D5
D10
D21
D1569
D9
D908
N936
D3
D559
D141
N568
D268
N
0
5
10km
0
2.5
5mi
©ULYSSES

Marseille and the Mediterranean Coast

Marseille has an image problem. France's oldest city is frequently misunderstood, due to negative press reports and public misconceptions formulated from afar. Let's clear things up.

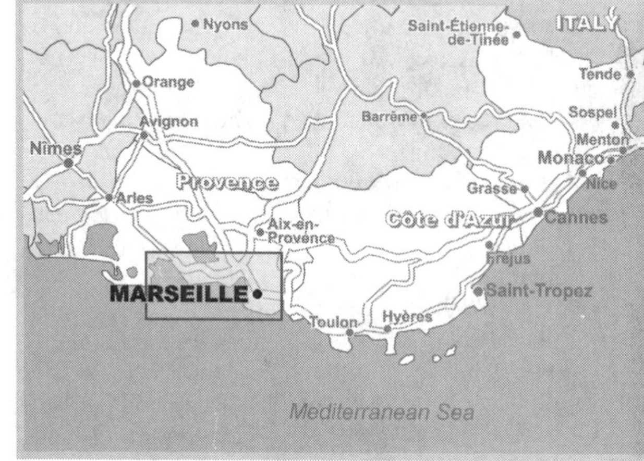

Marseille and the Mediterranean coast are great places to visit. The spectacular white cliffs (Les Calanques) that rise above the turquoise sea are unique in southern Europe. The small fishing port of Vallon des Auffes remains untouched by modern property developers yet is part of the city-centre. Age-old neighbourhoods, whose shops and market-stalls are reminiscent of the streets of a Greek village or Arab souk, entice passersby. Not far away, boutiques sell the finest fashion and luxury goods. Cathedrals charged with history, prized art collections and a dizzying variety of museums provide an endless fix for even the most demanding culture junkie. Countless eating possibilities exist, ranging from an incredible number of pizza spots to restaurants offering the best bouillabaisse and fresh seafood that France has to offer.

So Marseille provides a variety of sightseeing possibilities whether your interest is the great outdoors, cultural, culinary or more blatantly, materialistic. What doesn't it offer? It is not for those seeking out a quaint little corner of Provence, like something out of an old French film. These spots exist in the Vaucluse and Bouches-du-Rhône departments and are described in the preceding chapters.

Neither is it an upscale place with beautiful, harmonious

architecture in the city-centre like Bordeaux or Paris. Years of neglect and the lack of a cohesive urban development policy (until recently that is) have denied it that. Marseille has grown in fits and starts, building projects seem to have been erected willy-nilly and events such as World War II (the occupying German forces destroyed much of the Vieux Port) have left their mark. Instead, Marseille has isolated sites and individual buildings of architectural importance, at times plunked down in undistinguished areas. The 19th-century Hôtel de Ville on the Quai du Port is squeezed between low-rise apartment blocks designed by the architect Pouillon, the elegant opera house rests in an area frequented by *femmes de charme* (call girls) and the brilliantly-restored Vieille Charité museum is in the heart of the colourful working class neighbourhood known as Le Panier.

Indeed, Marseille is more accurately termed picturesque than beautiful. Apart from the extraordinary Calanques, which extend eastwards from Marseille all the way to the port of Cassis, the city offers a couple of vantage points from which to enjoy amazing panoramic views. From the Notre Dame de la Garde Cathedral, visitors get a 360° view of Marseille—it is best at sunset when the multicoloured sky reflects on the sea and places Château d'If (the island fortress immortalized in Alexandre Dumas's *The Count of Monte Cristo*) in silhouette. Otherwise, the lovely views looking back over the entire Vieux Port from the gardens of Napoléon III's Palais du Pharo are picture-postcard beautiful.

The city has been a trading centre since day one, which in Marseille's case, was around 600 BC when Greek merchants from Phoenecia landed on the coast. Protis, the Greek leader, was chosen by Gyptis, daughter of the local Celto-Ligurian chief, to marry her. Thus started a tradition of mixed-marriages in the city. Marseille has been proudly multicultural ever since.

The Greeks called the spot Massalia, and they competed with the Etruscans and the Carthaginians for trade routes throughout the Mediterranean region. The Marseillais even pushed north by sea towards the British Isles and Scandinavia, and south towards Senegal in search of new markets. Outposts along the coastline, notably at present-day Antibes, Nice and Hyères, were established. The community had its ups and downs as a trading centre— 6 BC and 4 BC were prosperous periods, but 5 BC was particularly difficult.

Skirmishes were frequent between the Greek settlers and the Celto-Ligurian tribes. The Marseillais twice called upon the Romans to help them defend their trading colony, in 181 BC and 154 BC. Thus started a Roman presence in the region, which grew following 125 BC. The Roman consul Sextius Calvinus took hold of the Celto-Ligurian settlement at Entremont in 124 BC and created a base nearby, called Aquae Sextiae (present-day Aix-en-Provence).

Roughly 6,000 people lived in the Marseille area at this time.

Between 118 BC and 472 AD, a permanent Roman colony known as Provincia Romana, dominated the area today called Provence (soon after called Narbonne). Strategically, Provence gave the Romans control of the all-important land route between Italy and Spain. Arles became its principal city—both on land and by sea (a canal was dug linking it to the Mediterranean). Because of Arles importance, Marseille fortunes floundered somewhat during the Roman occupation, although the city continued to develop trade. Christianity grew, especially after a bishop was installed in the city in the early 5th century AD, and with the creation of the Saint-Victor monastery at the same time.

Relative stability came to the region in the 10th and 11th centuries following the establishment of political and geographic boundaries, administered by the Counts of Provence. Marseille profited economically by the increased trade passing through its port. Spices, silk, precious wood and foodstuffs came from newly-established trading posts in north Africa and the Orient. Though ruled by the Counts of Provence, Marseille was an independent force with its own city council made up of trade leaders and craftsmen.

A series of political crises elsewhere, along with the plague of 1348 and competition from Italian trading ports, brought economic difficulties in the 14th century, which took over one hundred years to resolve. Following the arrival of King René in 1470, and then the union with France in 1481, Marseille developed its trade routes over the next century and a half. Cotton, carpets, leather, wheat, fish and coral were added to the list of imported goods. These were exchanged notably for cloth, refined sugar and soap—three growing Marseillais industries.

Lather up!

A traditional product of Marseille, said to be endowed with many life-enhancing qualities, the soap made in this region has left its mark on the economy and on the city itself. Just before the start of the WWII, Marseille produced 120,000 tonnes (118,000 tons) of soap annually, accounting for half of the soap produced in France. The same recipes had been followed since the 16th century, based on soda and vegetable oils imported from the Orient. But beware of immitations! To claim the designation "*savon de Marseille*" the soap must contain 72% olive oil. Le Sérail is the only traditional soap factory left in Marseille.

The city controlled its own affairs for most of the 16th and 17th centuries, though the situation was anything but calm. A consulate, based at the Aix Parliament and made up of the aristocracy was often criticized for looking out for its own interests, leading to popular uprisings in Marseille. The plague struck again in 1649. Throughout France, Louis XIV replaced the consulats in 1669 with local municipal councils headed by a *viguier*, a hand-picked royal representative.

Perhaps the greatest economic period lasted from the late-17th century to the late-18th century. Local industries flourished, abetted by successful foreign trade. Raw goods were made into manufactured goods and exported; new contracts with the French state ensured steady work. Overseen by a newly formed Chamber of Commerce, Marseille controlled trade to the East and exported cloth, soap and sugar. The plague of 1721 struck Marseille particularly hard, and half of its population of 80,000 died.

Marseille was anti-monarchist and supported the revolutionary activities with vigour following the storming of the Bastille prison in Paris in 1789. France was declared a Republic by the country's ruling Assembly, known as the Convention, and controlled by the Girondist party. In 1793, Louis XVI was guillotined, yet France was far from being the ideal democratic nation wished for by the children of the Revolution. She lacked consolidation and order. The country lead a war against Austria and Prussia and was invaded by a coalition of European powers including England, Holland and Spain. At home, the Paris-based political group known as Jacobins struggled for political control against the Girondins. Girondin deputies were sent to the scaffold as traitors in the 1790s. Later, in Marseille and other southern communities, the Girondins rebelled and imprisoned Jacobin supporters during a period known as the *terreur blanche*, (the white terror). At one point, in June 1795, Jacobin prisoners in Marseille's Fort Saint Jean were massacred.

The arrival from Corsica of the brilliant General Bonaparte in the 1790s (later crowned head of state and known as Emperor Napoléon), settled many of France's domestic and foreign affairs. England, with her mighty sea power, resisted Napoléon's forces, and in retaliation, the Emperor forbade trade with the British Isles. The traders in Marseille suffered greatly as a result of these politically motivated economic sanctions. It was only following the downfall of Napoléon in 1815 and the return of the monarchy during the period known as the Restoration, that Marseille could recover its financial losses.

Indeed, the city returned to the world market-place with renewed vigour. Old markets were revitalised and new territories exploited. Marseille was at the height of its economic power during the entire 19th century. It was a major world business centre during the so-called Second Empire in the 1850s (under Napoléon III), followed by the Troisiéme République (third republic). Trading activity was centred around the Joliette docks due north of the old port. The agglomeration included a series of docks running perpendicular to the quay, huge warehouses and a maritime train station linking a new coastal railroad. French colonization in the East and in Africa introduced new trade routes. The population hit the 300,000 mark in 1869, nearly doubling in 30 years.

The local economy has suffered greatly during the 20th century, although rapid industrialization has brought some respite. Marseille was hit hard by the world-wide depression of the 1930s. The city was isolated from Paris and northern France during the World War II, and was itself occupied by German forces (November 11, 1942 to August 29, 1944). They destroyed parts of the city and most of the Vieux Port. Post-war political events, namely the Indochina war in the 1950s and French decolonization in Africa (particularly the loss of Algeria in 1962), have meant a reduction of markets.

Marseille has been an attractive refuge for immigrants fleeing political troubles. Greeks arrived in the 1820s and Italians in the 1870s and 1880s. During this century, immigrants have included Armenians (1915), Greeks and Armenians fleeing Turkey (1920s), Italian anti-Fascists (1930s), north-African Arabs from Morocco, Algeria and Tunisia (since the end of World War II, including an influx of Algerians following their country's independence in 1962). They settled in the city-centre, principally in two neighbourhoods—Besunce (east of the Vieux Port) and Le Panier (north of the Vieux Port). Both merit a visit today.

Until recently, the former ship-building docks known as Les Arcenaux (just south of the Vieux Port below the Quai de Rive Neuve) housed a hideous 1960s above-ground concrete parking lot. It was torn down and replaced by a harbour-side site with restaurants and a few shops. Centred around Place Thiers and Cours d'Esteinne d'Orves, it is now particularly lively at night.

One of the most important projects is the cleaning up of the grand Boulevard Le Canebière, which leads right to the Quai des Belges and the Vieux Port. Built by Haussman under orders by Napoléon III in the 1850s, it once housed elegant residences and smart shops, but over the years has been banalized by offices, fast food outlets and down-scale shops. The city is currently revitalising the Canebière. Already it has restored the Bourse, created a fashion museum in an attractive building—the Musée de la Mode, renovated Place du Général de Gaulle and pedestrianized near-by streets, Rue Saint Ferréol for example.

This intoxicating cocktail of commerce, industry, politics and a multi-cultural population is nothing new to Marseille. Such a dynamic concoction spills over at times—hence the stories of violence, racial tension, drug hauls, football hooliganism and political corruption. Marseille is France's second most populous city (after Paris) and third largest in terms of area (after Paris and Lyon). The city is shrinking however; in 1982 there were 878,689 people, and in 1990 just 807,726.

Visitors are safer here than in most international capitals. Simply follow the usual precautions: keep a close eye on your wallet, stick to well-lit areas at night, don't keep valuables in your car. The Marseillais are friendly and helpful to tourists. Visitors who take the time to discover this city agree, in everything it does, Marseille is different. So much so that you might feel you're in a completely different country.

Finding Your Way Around

By Plane

The Vieux Port of Marseille is a convenient 25km (15.5mi) from the **Marseille-Marignane Airport** *(information ☎04.42.14.14.14, reservations ☎04.91.91.90.90).*

The A55 highway links the airport and Marseille. Numerous daily flights link Paris' Orly Airport and the Marseille-Marignane Airport *(the major carrier is Air Inter, 14 La Canebière, 1300 Marseille, ☎04.91.39.36.36).* Special shuttle buses (navettes) connect the airport to the central Saint Charles SNCF train station. They leave every twenty minutes from the airport, from 6:30am to 8:50pm, then at 9:15pm, 9:40pm, 10pm, 10:30pm, 10:50pm, 11:15pm, and from the train station, from 6:10am to 9:50pm, and at 5:30am and 5:55am. For information: ☎04.42.14.31.27 or 04.91.50.59.34.

By Train

Gare SNCF Marseille Saint Charles (train station)
Avenue Pierre Semard (Place des Marseillais)
information and reservations:
☎08.36.35.35.35

Recorded message: late arrivals and departures: ***☎04.91.50.00.00***

Overseas visitors arriving in Paris may pick up the TGV from either Airport Charles-de-Gaulle or Gare d'Austerlitz travelling to Marseille Saint-Charles train station. Eleven Paris-Marseille TGV trains make this journey daily (not all are direct); it takes 4hrs and 15min; the distance is 813km (505mi). Overseas visitors flying to Lyon Satolas Airport from abroad may pick up the TGV to Marseille from the SNCF train station connected to the terminal. Take a taxi or the efficient Marseille subway system, the métro, from the train station to your accommodation or city centre. There is a tourist office (opening times below) in the train station.

Marseille is conveniently close to a number of important destinations in Provence. The TER regional train service links Marseille to coastal ports including Cassis and La Ciotat, to larger centres including Cannes and Nice, and to inland towns including Aubagne and Aix-en-Provence. For example, 19 TER trains travel to Aix every day; the journey is 30min. The information desk on the ground floor of Saint Charles station provides local train schedules and will answer travel questions. Special "Joker" fares offer substantial discounts (50% or more) on train journeys for many destinations (including Paris-Marseille), if purchased two weeks or one month in advance.

By Bus

Gare Routière
(bus station)
Place Victor Hugo
☎***04.91.08.16.40***
The Gare Routier bus station is next to the main Marseille-Saint-Charles SNCF train station, making connections from the Paris-Marseille TGV to a local bus easy. Local buses (*autocars régionaux*) run regularly to destinations throughout Provence and the Côte d'Azur. Visitors making day-trips to nearby places like Aubagne and Cassis might prefer the convenience of the local bus (for example, Cassis' Gare Routier/bus station is centrally-located, yet its SNCF train station is 3km (1.9mi) from the port).

Public Tranport

By Métro

An efficient, inexpensive and safe way to quickly get around Marseille is to take its subway, a rapid-transit underground system called the métro. A single ticket for the two-line system costs 8F. All métro stations and the tourist office can provide you with a map; otherwise contact Info RTM *(6 Rue des Fabres, 13001, Marseille, ☎04.91.91.92.10)*. Métro service runs from 5am to 9pm, although métro ticket offices are open from 6:30am to 7.30pm.

By Bus

A good bus network serves the city and its outskirts. The fare is the same as for the Métro, and one ticket suffices for a trip that involves both the bus and the Métro. Regular bus service ends at about 9pm, after which special night buses (fluobus) go on duty. Less frequent but still regular service is offered until 1am (one bus every 15 to 30min) on a limited number of routes.

By Taxi

Some Marseille taxi drivers have a bad reputation. For example, many don't like to make the journey from the Saint-Charles train station to the city-centre (presumably they feel it's not worth the effort because of horrible traffic and the short distance). Note the denomination of the bank note you give the driver, so that you are sure you receive the correct change in return.

Local taxi companies:

Marseille Taxis
☎***04.91.02.20.20***

Taxis France
☎***04.91.34.51.06***

Taxis Tupp
☎***04.91.85.80.00***

Taxis Plus
☎***04.91.09.28.79***

Eurotaxi
☎***04.91.05.31.98***
Multi-lingual drivers

Taxi Tourisme Marseille (Tourist Taxis) is a new scheme organised by the tourist office in which visitors are given a guided tour of Marseille in a designated taxi (drivers are rigourously selected) equipped with professionally-made taped commentary of the sites. Four circuits are offered in French, English or German. Tickets are sold at the tourist office 5min in advance *(duration 1h30 to 4hrs; 140F to 500F)*.

By Car

Car Rental

Ada
24 Avenue de Toulon
☎***04.91.79.37.17***
34 Rue d'Alger
☎***04.91.48.20.56***
23 Rue de la loge
☎***04.91.90.24.66***
19 Rue du Marché
☎***04.91.84.72.00***
Economical, with the best prices available for week-end rentals.

Astuce
219 Avenue Roger Salengro
☎***04.91.08.02.08***
One of the most economical agencies in Marseille (approximately 240F/day for a compact, insurance and 100km or 62mi included.

Avis
SNCF Gare Saint Charles, 13101 Marseille
☎***04.91.08.41.80***
267 Boulevard National, 13103 Marseille
☎***04.91.50.70.11***
92 Boulevard Rabatau, 13108 Marseille
☎***04.91.80.12.00***

Hertz
27 Boulevard Rabatau, 13108 Marseille
☎***04.91.79.22.06***
16 Boulevard Nédelec, 13101 Marseille
☎***04.91.14.04.22***

Service Stations

Shell
44 Boulevard des Dames

Total
35 Boulevard Rabatau

Emergency Travel Help / (SOS Voyageurs)
☎***04.91.62.12.80***

All are open late at night.

Parking

The downtown area is especially congested in the morning and afternoon during rush hour. Avoid driving during these periods; it will save you quite a bit of time.

Since most attractions are right downtown, they are accessible by foot to most visitors, and the Métro provides efficient service to other neighbourhoods, so why bother with the car?

If you do have a car, know that it sometimes takes patience to find a parking spot on the streets of Marseille (circle the block a few times and you will end up nabbing a spot).

There are a few municipal parking lots spread through the city, but these can prove expensive if you leave your car for a prolonged period. They are well identified, but here is a list of the best situated: Cours d'Estienne d'Orves, Cours Julien, Allées Léon Gambetta, Centre Bourse (all in the 1er Arrondissement); Rue des Phocéens, Place du Mazeau, Place Villeneuve-Bargemont, Place Victor Gélu (2e Arrondissement); Gare Saint-Charles (3e Arrondissement); Cours Pierre-Puget, Place Monthyon/Palais de Justice (6e Arrondissement). As you would in any other large city, leave nothing of value in your car.

Practical Information

Tourist Offices

Marseille
Jul to Sep: Mon to Sat 9am to 8pm, Sun and holidays 10am to 6pm; Oct to Jun, Mon to Sat 9am to 7pm, Sun and holidays 10am to 5pm
4 La Canebière, 13001 Marseille
☎***04.91.13.89.00***
⇌***04.91.13.89.20***
www.destination-marseille.com

SNCF Gare Saint Charles
(in the train station)
Mon to Fri 10am to 6pm
13003 Marseille
☎***04.91.50.59.18***

Ville d'Art et d'Histoire
reservations are necessary for some tours
start at 2pm
40F, 50F, 90F or 130F depending on the tour chosen
36 different guided walking tours are organized by the tourist office and conducted by professional guides in a choice of seven languages. Several tours examine parts of Marseille unknown to most tourists, in addition to more classic circuits: the 18th-century mansions of Marseillais notables; the Estaque hills favoured by Braque, Cézanne, Dufy and where Cubism was born; the old docks and warehouses in the Joliette area.

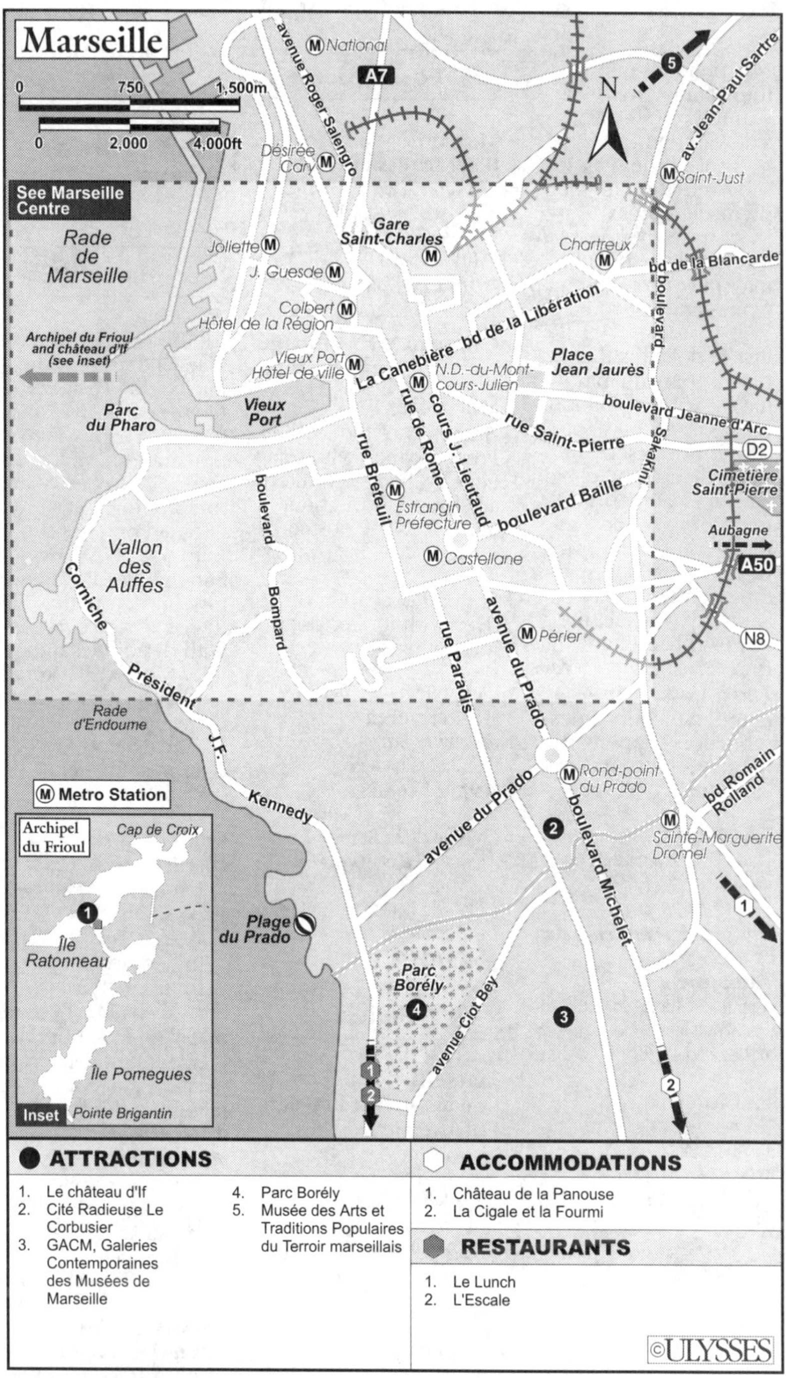
Marseille
0 750 1,500m
0 2,000 4,000ft
N
See Marseille Centre
Rade de Marseille
Archipel du Frioul and château d'If (see inset)
Parc du Pharo
Vieux Port
Vallon des Auffes
Corniche Président J.F. Kennedy
Rade d'Endoume
Plage du Prado
Parc Borély
avenue Roger Salengro
National
A7
Désirée Cary
Joliette
J. Guesde
Colbert
Hôtel de la Région
Vieux Port Hôtel de ville
Gare Saint-Charles
La Canebière
bd de la Libération
Chartreux
Saint-Just
av. Jean-Paul Sartre
bd de la Blancarde
boulevard Sakakini
Place Jean Jaurès
N.D.-du-Mont-cours-Julien
boulevard Jeanne d'Arc
rue Saint-Pierre
rue de Rome
cours J. Lieutaud
rue Breteuil
boulevard Baille
Estrangin Préfecture
Castellane
boulevard Bompard
Périer
rue Paradis
avenue du Prado
Rond-point du Prado
boulevard Michelet
bd Romain Rolland
Sainte-Marguerite Dromel
avenue Ciot Bey
D2
Cimetière Saint-Pierre
Aubagne
A50
N8
Metro Station
Archipel du Frioul
Cap de Croix
Île Ratonneau
Île Pomegues
Inset
Pointe Brigantin
ATTRACTIONS
1. Le château d'If
2. Cité Radieuse Le Corbusier
3. GACM, Galeries Contemporaines des Musées de Marseille
4. Parc Borély
5. Musée des Arts et Traditions Populaires du Terroir marseillais
ACCOMMODATIONS
1. Château de la Panouse
2. La Cigale et la Fourmi
RESTAURANTS
1. Le Lunch
2. L'Escale
©ULYSSES

Independent-minded tourists may follow a painted red line on the sidewalk, which passes in front of the major sites and conduct their own self-led city tour (it starts at the tourist office, where people may pick up a free map explaining the route).

Bon Week-End is the name of a valuable nation-wide operation, which is strongly followed in Marseille. More than 40 hotels in all price categories offer two nights accommodation for the price of one, provided you arrive either Friday or Saturday. Contact the tourist office in advance to receive its *Bon Week-End à Marseille* brochure, which includes reduction coupons for the city's museums and car rental.

Cassis
Place Baragnon, 13260 Cassis
☎***04.42.01.71.17***
⇄***04.42.01.28.31***
www.cassis.enprovence.com

Aubagne
Esplanade Charles de Gaulle
13400 Aubagne
☎***04.42.03.49.98***

La Ciotat
Boulevard Anatole France
13600 La Ciotat
☎***04.42.08.61.32***
⇄***04.42.08.17.88***

Post Office

Marseille
Hôtel des Postes
Mon to Fri 8am to 7pm, Sat 8am to noon
Place de l'Hôtel des Postes
13101 Marseille
☎***04.91.15.47.00***

Currency Exchange

Marseille
Branches of the leading French banks with foreign exchange counters are found throughout Marseille. They close at 4pm.

Foreign exchange offices with longer opening hours include:

Comptoir de Change Méditerranéen
everyday 8am to 6pm
Gare Saint Charles
☎***04.91.84.68.88***

Change de la Bourse
Mon to Sat 8:30am to 6:30pm
3 Place du Général de Gaulle
13101 Marseille
☎***04.91.13.09.11***

Police

Marseille
Commissariat Central de Police (central police station)
24hrs/day
2 Rue Antoine Becker
13102 Marseille
☎***04.91.39.80.00***

Exploring

Marseille

All the museums in Marseille, except the Musée de l'Histoire, the Musée de la Mode and the Galerie des Transports, are open Oct to May, Tue to Sun 10am to 5pm; Jun to Sep, Tue to Sun 11am to 6pm. Entrance is free on Sunday mornings and for children under 10, the over-65s, persons with disabilities and the unemployed. Tickets are half price for students, children between 10 and 16 and teachers. The museums are closed Monday.

Centre de la Vieille Charité ★★★ *(2 Rue de la Charité, métro Joliette,* ☎*04.91.14.58.80,* ⇄*04.91.90.63.07)*. The 17th-century hospice with its pretty pink arcades facing a **central chapel** ★★★ built by Pierre Puget is now an exciting arts complex, including the **Musée d'Archéologie Méditerranéenne** ★ *(12F)*, with an Egyptology collection, plus artifacts from Mediterranean civilisations, tracing customs and daily life; the **Musée des Arts Afrcains, Océaniens, Amérindiens** *(12F)*, a fresh insight into the art and culture

Little Saints

Figurines typical of Marseille and Provence, *santons* are firmly rooted in the country's popular traditions. The word "santon" comes from the Provençal word *santoun*, which means "little saint."

The origin of *santons* remains vague, but most historians agree they came from somewhere in Italy. Although they certainly originated outside the country, the little saints are still quintessentially *Marseillais*. They came to be created due to the locals' resistance to French republican prohibitions at the end of the 18th century, namely the suppression of the midnight mass in 1789 and the suspension of religious worship and the closure of churches in 1794. So as not to debase the celebration of Christmas, the people of Marseille fashioned improvised crèches in their homes, marking the beginnings of the first *santons*.

The oldest model, dating back to 1797, is attributed to Jean-Louis Lagnel, considered the father of Marseille's *santons*. He was in fact the first to make these little grey or red baked clay figurines—the clay comes from around Aubagne—and to establish them as a distinct artistic genre. His observations of daily life in the streets of Marseille and subsequent fashioning of secular figures added a new element to the traditional crèche. It became a minutely detailed account of the population of Marseille and, more broadly, of Provence. The scene usually includes a shepherd, a fisher, a fishmonger, a *tambourinaïre* (tambourine player), a "*ravi*" (astounded figure), an *amouraïre* (grinder), a *boufareou* angel (with a trumpet) and many other figures. Soon, each family had its own crèche, the preparation of which started on the Sunday before Christmas.

Throughout the century that followed, this type of craft continued to develop at an impressive rate, and many families still pass on this rich tradition that is both sacred and secular, but above all reflects the milieu of Marseille and Provence.

of different ethnic groups, particularly West African; opened in 1992; a very good book shop and small café. Good temporary exhibitions *(12F)*.

Musée des Docks Romains *(10F; Place de Vivaux, métro Vieux-Port, ☎04.91.91.24.62)*. A unique museum in that it sits on the actual site of the subject examined. It deals with commercial life in the Marseille port during Roman times. Housed in the former Roman warehouse on the south quay, its ruins and artifacts bears witness to an important moment in Marseille history when it controlled Mediterranean trade routes.

Musée du Vieux Marseille ★★ *(12F; Maison Diamantée, Rue de la Prison, métro Vieux Port, ☎04.91.55.10.19)*. This 16th-century residence has a facade

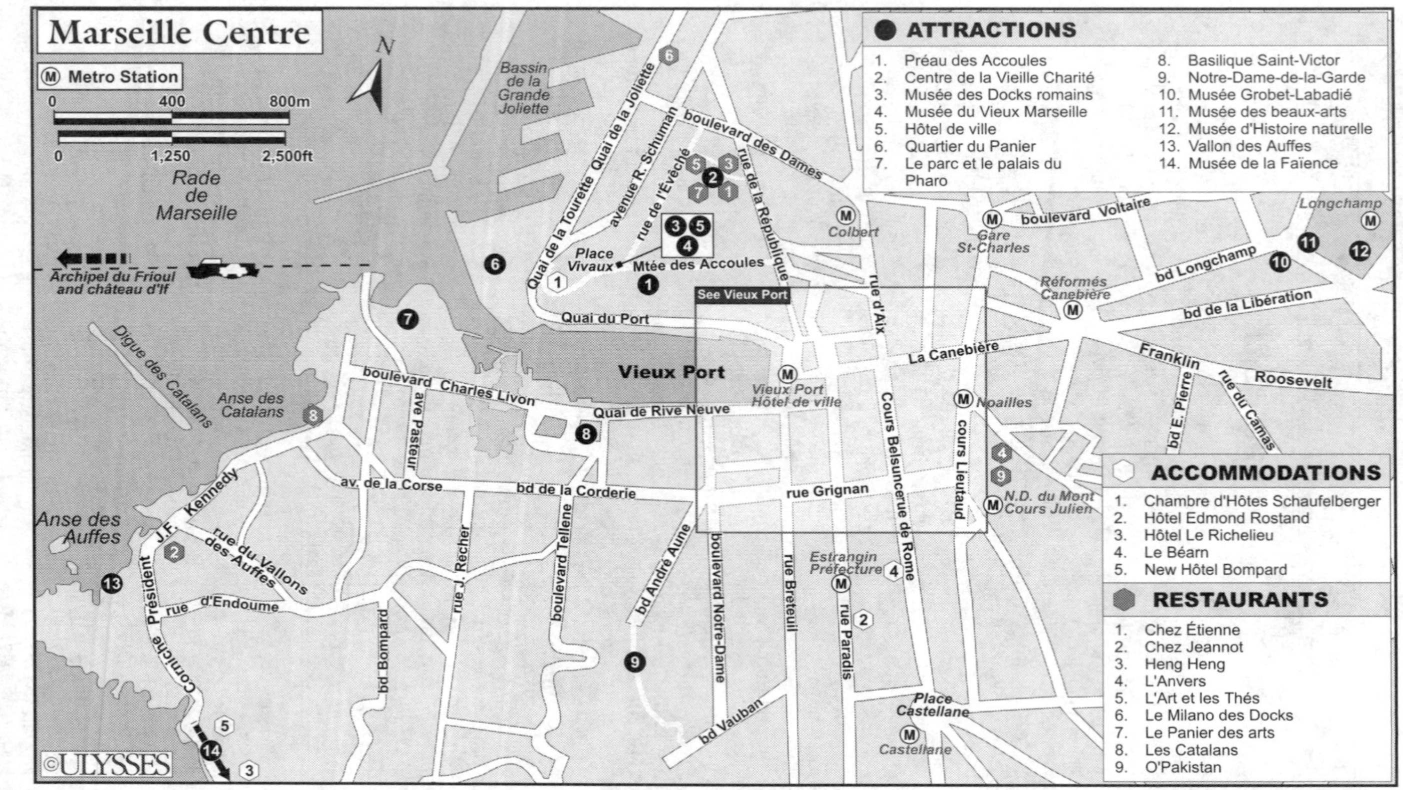

Marseille Centre
Metro Station
0
400
800m
0
1,250
2,500ft
N
Rade de Marseille
Archipel du Frioul and château d'If
Bassin de la Grande Joliette
Digue des Catalans
Anse des Catalans
Anse des Auffes
Vieux Port
See Vieux Port
Quai de la Tourette
Quai de la Joliette
avenue R. Schuman
rue de l'Évêché
boulevard des Dames
rue de la République
Place Vivaux
Mtée des Accoules
Quai du Port
Quai de Rive Neuve
boulevard Charles Livon
ave Pasteur
av. de la Corse
bd de la Corderie
rue Grignan
J.F. Kennedy
rue du Vallons des Auffes
rue d'Endoume
Président
Corniche
bd Bompard
rue J. Recher
boulevard Tellene
bd André Aune
boulevard Notre-Dame
bd Vauban
rue Breteuil
rue Paradis
Cours Belsunce
rue de Rome
cours Lieutaud
rue d'Aix
La Canebière
Franklin
Roosevelt
bd E. Pierre
rue du Camas
bd de la Libération
bd Longchamp
boulevard Voltaire
Colbert
Gare St-Charles
Réformés Canebière
Vieux Port Hôtel de ville
Noailles
N.D. du Mont Cours Julien
Estrangin Préfecture
Place Castellane
Castellane
Longchamp
ATTRACTIONS
1. Préau des Accoules
2. Centre de la Vieille Charité
3. Musée des Docks romains
4. Musée du Vieux Marseille
5. Hôtel de ville
6. Quartier du Panier
7. Le parc et le palais du Pharo
8. Basilique Saint-Victor
9. Notre-Dame-de-la-Garde
10. Musée Grobet-Labadié
11. Musée des beaux-arts
12. Musée d'Histoire naturelle
13. Vallon des Auffes
14. Musée de la Faïence
ACCOMMODATIONS
1. Chambre d'Hôtes Schaufelberger
2. Hôtel Edmond Rostand
3. Hôtel Le Richelieu
4. Le Béarn
5. New Hôtel Bompard
RESTAURANTS
1. Chez Étienne
2. Chez Jeannot
3. Heng Heng
4. L'Anvers
5. L'Art et les Thés
6. Le Milano des Docks
7. Le Panier des arts
8. Les Catalans
9. O'Pakistan
©ULYSSES

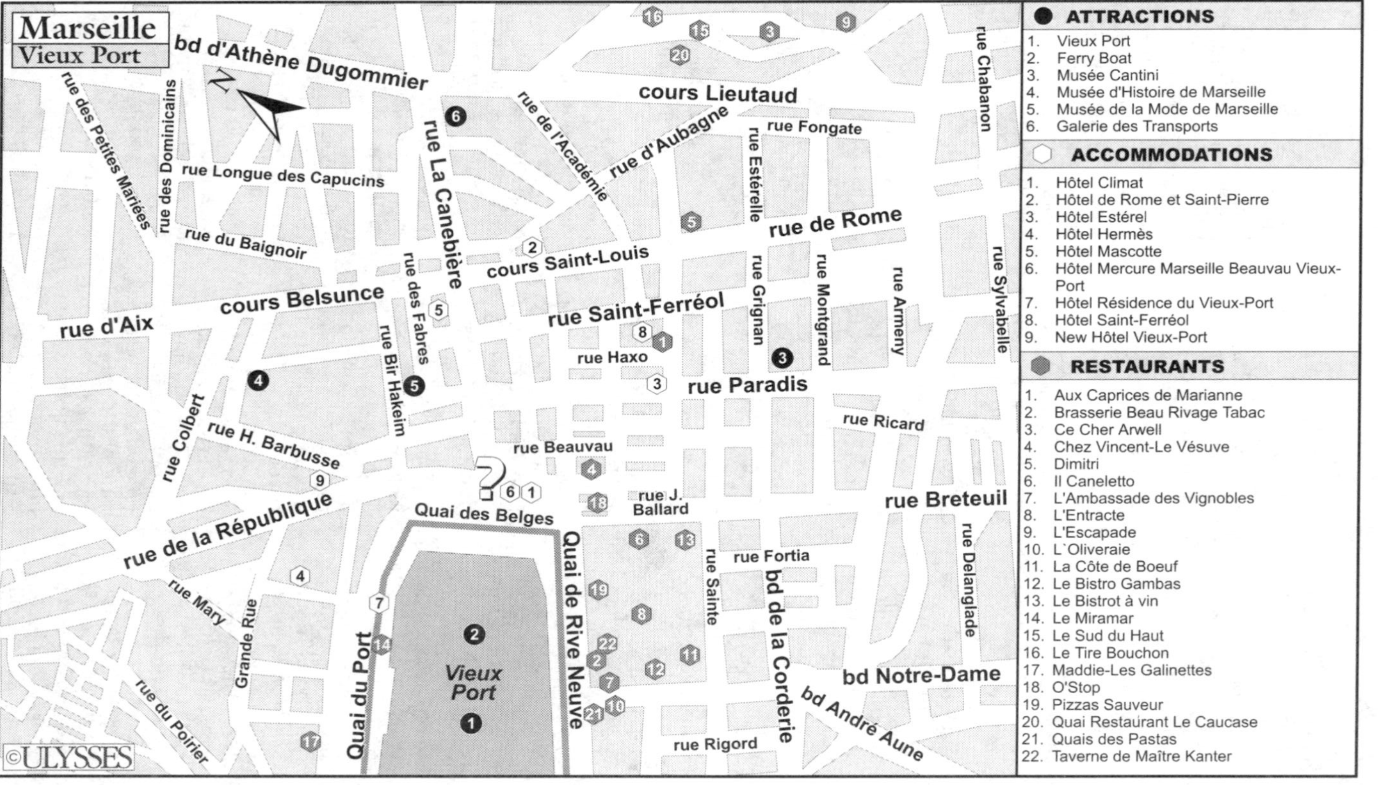

Marseille
Vieux Port
bd d'Athène Dugommier
N
rue des Petites Mariées
rue des Dominicains
rue Longue des Capucins
rue du Baignoir
rue d'Aix
cours Belsunce
rue Colbert
rue H. Barbusse
rue Bir Hakeim
rue des Fabres
rue La Canebière
rue de l'Académie
rue d'Aubagne
cours Lieutaud
rue Fongate
rue Estérelle
rue de Rome
cours Saint-Louis
rue Saint-Ferréol
rue Haxo
rue Grignan
rue Montgrand
rue Armeny
rue Sylvabelle
rue Chabanon
rue Paradis
rue Ricard
rue Beauvau
rue J. Ballard
rue Breteuil
Quai des Belges
rue de la République
Quai de Rive Neuve
Quai du Port
Vieux Port
rue Fortia
rue Sainte
bd de la Corderie
rue Delanglade
bd Notre-Dame
bd André Aune
rue Rigord
rue Mary
Grande Rue
rue du Poirier
©ULYSSES
ATTRACTIONS
1. Vieux Port
2. Ferry Boat
3. Musée Cantini
4. Musée d'Histoire de Marseille
5. Musée de la Mode de Marseille
6. Galerie des Transports
ACCOMMODATIONS
1. Hôtel Climat
2. Hôtel de Rome et Saint-Pierre
3. Hôtel Estérel
4. Hôtel Hermès
5. Hôtel Mascotte
6. Hôtel Mercure Marseille Beauvau Vieux-Port
7. Hôtel Résidence du Vieux-Port
8. Hôtel Saint-Ferréol
9. New Hôtel Vieux-Port
RESTAURANTS
1. Aux Caprices de Marianne
2. Brasserie Beau Rivage Tabac
3. Ce Cher Arwell
4. Chez Vincent-Le Vésuve
5. Dimitri
6. Il Caneletto
7. L'Ambassade des Vignobles
8. L'Entracte
9. L'Escapade
10. L`Oliveraie
11. La Côte de Boeuf
12. Le Bistro Gambas
13. Le Bistrot à vin
14. Le Miramar
15. Le Sud du Haut
16. Le Tire Bouchon
17. Maddie-Les Galinettes
18. O'Stop
19. Pizzas Sauveur
20. Quai Restaurant Le Caucase
21. Quais des Pastas
22. Taverne de Maître Kanter

made of stone cut in diamond shapes (hence its name, Maison Diamantée) and now houses a charming museum devoted to furniture, Provençal costumes and folklore from the time when Marseille was at the height of its power and influence during the 18th and 19th centuries.

The **Hôtel de Ville** proudly faces the old port on the Quai du Port. The three-story 17th-century building was not damaged during the bombing by German forces during World War II (though much of the surrounding quayside was).

The **Vieux Port**. Surrounded on three-sides by the Quai du Port, the Quai des Belges and the Quai du Rive Neuve, the old port is the symbolic centre of Marseille. Fishermen still display their morning catch along the Quai des Belges (at the base of La Canebière). Avoid eating in any of the fish and seafood restaurants situated directly on the quais and supposedly serving the *vrai bouillabaisse* (authentic bouillabaisse). They are touristy and not all reliable (see Restaurants for our choice).

Le Ferry Boat *(5F; between the Hôtel de Ville on the Quai du Port and the Place Aux Huiles on the Quai du Rive Neuve).* A quick way to cross from one side of the old port to the other is to hop on this water bus just like the Marseillais, who call it Le Ferry *Bo-At.* It's been operating since 1880.

Quartier du Panier *(south of the Quai du Port).* This is Marseille's oldest area and source of many colourful tales of rough living and prostitution from days gone by. Today it is a colourful working-class neighbourhood whose buildings and narrow streets are slowly being restored. It is still home to fishermen, small businesses and artisans and has kept its authentic character.

The **Préau des Accoules** *(free admission; Wed and Sat 1:30pm to 5:30pm; 29 Montée des Accoules, Métro Joliette/Vieux Port, ☎04.91.91.52.06)* is located at the centre of the historic district of Paier. Behind the austere walls of what is now the École des Accoules, you'll be surprised to discover a well-proportioned room fitted with stone in warm yellow-and-rose hues. Surrounded by Doric columns and covered by a flat-vaulted ceiling, this is an original example of neoclassical architecture. This building's history is varied. Erected at the beginning of the 18th century, it has served several functions: a scientific observatory, the seat of the Académie de Marseille and the school of hydrography. More recently, since 1991, it has served as a children's space at the heart of the Direction des Musées (Museum Headquarters) and has playful exhibits related to art. The programming covers a diverse set of themes including archaeology, fine art, American and African culture, regional heritage, history, photography and contemporary art. The Préau des Accoules hosts three exhibits each year, accompanied by different events, concerts, performances and festivals.

The **Parc et Palais du Pharo** *(entrance on the Boulevard Charles Livon, at the end of the Quai de Rive-Neuve)* is well located, right at the entrance to the Vieux Port. The palace has been turned into a convention centre and includes a performance room for classical music among its facilities. The gardens surrounding the centre are pleasant and are an excellent **vantage point ★★** from which to view the sailboats and buildings of the old port and the 17th-century Saint-Nicholas fort that lies right across from it. You can enjoy a delightful breakfast beneath the trees while admiring this exceptional panorama.

Basilique Saint Victor ★★ *(every day 8am to 6pm; Place Saint Victor ☎04.91.54.23.37).* Founded in the 5th century by the monk

Saint John Cassian, this basilica is one of the oldest in France. Much was destroyed during raids by the Saracens in the 8th century, leading to its reconstruction in the 11th century. Be sure to descend the stone stairs to visit the crypts *(10F)*, one of which dates from the original 5th century structure.

Notre-Dame de la Garde *(basilica and crypt: Oct to May, 7am to 7pm; Jun to Sep, 7am to 8pm; a steep walk or take bus 30 from the Vieux Port)* The Romanesque-Byzantine Basilique Notre-Dame de la Garde dominates Marseille and has become the city's symbol much like the Eiffel Tower in Paris or Statue of Liberty in New York. Like those two monuments, there are spectacular panoramic views from the terraces surrounding the basilica. (It's best to come at sunset for splendid views of the old port and of the Mediterranean.) Though swamped with tourists, the 19th-century structure is a place of worship. It's patron saint is Mary Magdelene, and the rows of model fishing boats hanging by chains above the nave remind us that this is the fisherman's basilica.

Musée Cantini ★ *(12F; 19 Rue Grignan, métro Estrangin-Préfecture, ☎04.91.54.77.75, ≠04.91.55.03.61)*. The contemporary canvases have been transferred to the new MAC gallery, and so the Musée Cantini now specializes in the modern period dating from 1900 to 1960. This intimate museum is worth a visit just for its good Fauve and Cubist selection. Housed in the impressive, 18th-century Hôtel de Mongrand mansion. Excellent temporary exhibitions (see tourist office or the local press for details).

Musée d'Histoire de Marseille ★★ *(12F; same hours as other museums except closed Sun and Mon; Centre Bourse-Square Belsunce, métro Vieux-Port, ☎04.91.90.42.22)*. Starting with the Phoceaen occupation of the city in 600 BC, Marseille's history museum displays a number the city's archaeological treasures including items found in the underwater sea cave known as the Grotte Cosque and a 3rd-century Roman trading ship (found on this spot while building around the new stock exchange in 1974). Greek and Roman artifacts dating from the 1st to 4th centuries are also on view in the **Jardin des Vestiges** garden.

Musée de la Mode de Marseille *(12F; noon to 7pm, closed Mon; Espace mode Méditerranée, 11 La Canebière, métro Vieux-Port, ☎04.91.56.59.57)* opened in 1993. The small permanent collection has little to show for this highly creative industry; the temporary exhibits are more worthwhile. The boutique *(☎04.91.14.92.13)* offers an original selection of books and fashion accessories. The restaurant, Café de la Mode *(☎04.91.14.92.12)*, serves light meals.

Musée Grobet-Labadié ★★ *(12F; 140 Boulevard Longchamp, métro Longchamp Cinq-Avenues, ☎04.91.62.21.82)*. The elegant *hôtel particulier* built in 1873 for the industrialist and art collector, Alexandre Labadié, holds a marvellous collection of furniture, paintings (16th-18th-century French), Medieval and Renaissance sculptures, Moustiers ceramics and Flemish tapestries. An absolute must for amateurs of painting and decorative arts.

Musée des Beaux-Arts ★ *(12F; Palais Longchamp, métro Longchamp-Cinq-Avenues, ☎04.91.62.21.17, ≠04.91.84.73.72)*. Fine-arts museum situated in the grand rooms of the left-wing of the marvellous Palais Longchamp. The ground floor includes the works of 16th- and 17th- century masters, and sculptures including that of local hero Pierre Puget, while the first floor displays 18th- and 19th-century French artists, as well as works by Provençal painters. Behind the museum is a very pretty garden with tree-lined paths and a waterfall, which is popular with locals and little-known by tourists.

The **Musée d'Histoire Naturelle** *(10F; Palais Longchamp, métro Longchamp-Cinq-Avenues, ☎04.91.14.59.50)* is an aged museum that occupies the right wing of Palais de Longchamp and recounts the natural history of Provence and the Côte d'Azur. The Salle de Provence presents an exhibition on the region's flora and fauna.

Vallon des Auffes ★★ *(Corniche Président John Kennedy, immediately south of the Monument au Morts d'Orients, under the bridge)* is an authentic fishing port, untouched by modern development and imperceptible from the Corniche and cliff-side above. Colourful fishing boats, rows of *cabanons* (fishers' huts) and three popular restaurants.

Chateau d'If ★★ (*25F; open everyday except Monday during school periods, 9am to 5pm, ☎04.91.59.02.30).* Visitors may take a short boat-ride to this small island and visit its château, immortalized by the writer Alexandre Dumas in his book, *The Count of Monte-Cristo.* The 3ha (7.4 acres) area of white rocks was untouched by man up until the 16th century. On a visit to Marseille in 1516, François I realised the island's strategic position and gave orders to build a fortress there. The heavy triple-towered structure was completed in 1531. However, it quickly became a prison and following 1689, had a particularly grisly history when many Protestants perished there under horrible conditions. It has been open to the public since 1890. Visitors can see the famous dungeons and the escape hole dug by Dumas' famous Count, Edmond Dantès, plus the courtyards and prisoners' cells. The panoramic view is spectacular. *(Boats for the island leave regularly from the Quai des Belges, ☎04.91.55.50.09).*

Cité Radieuse Le Corbusier *(280 Boulevard Michelet, south of the Rond Point du Prado)* is an all-in-one high-rise building, created by avant-garde architect Le Corbusier in 1954 and controversial in its day; includes apartments, shops, a school, sports facilities and a hotel.

GACM, Galeries Contemporains des Musées de Marseille ★ *(15F, 69 Avenue d'Haïfa, bus 23 and 45, ☎04.91.55.50.09 ≠04.91.72.17.27).* Opened in 1994, this museum of contemporary art holds a particularly rich collection (one of the best in France outside of Paris) of works created post-1960. Also on the premises: a cinema, contemporary art bookshop and restaurant "Au Macaroni."

Parc Borély ★★ *(free, Avenue du Parc Borély, south of Avenue du Prado, ☎04.91.73.21.60).* This beautiful botanic garden includes roses, pretty pathways and a lake. The elegant Château Borély dates from the 18th century (closed for renovations).

Musée de la Faïence ★★ *(12F; closed Mon; 157 Avenue de Montredon, bus 19, ☎04.91.72.43.47).* This new museum is an absolute must-see for lovers of ceramics. It is housed in a beautifully restored 19th-century mansion, the Château Pastré, and set between the inland hills and the sea in peaceful Parc Montredon. Some 1,500 ceramic pieces covering a period of 7000 years are exhibited; Provençal items from Apt, Marseilles and Moustiers are well-represented. Work by contemporary designers is displayed on the top floor.

Founded in 1928 in Château-Gombert by the *félibre* (a poet who writes in occitan, or *langue d'oc*, a regional dialect of southern France) Jean-Baptiste Julien Pignol, the **Musée des Arts et Traditions Populaires du Terroir Marseillais** *(20F; Wed to Mon 2:30pm to 6:30pm; 5 Place des Héros, Métro Malpassé then local bus*

No. 5, ☎*04.91.68.14.38)* uses lively and vivid displays to recount how people lived in the Marseille region during the 12th and 13th centuries. Furniture, clothing and artefacts reconstruct the setting of traditional life in Provence, while the collection of religious objects and crèches with their ornamental figures evoke the festive season. One of the highlights is the museum's exhibit of a table featuring 13 desserts, bringing to mind the Christmas season and its regional traditions that are still practiced today.

The Calanques

The Calanques are a series of fjords or rocky inlets along the coastline between Marseille and Cassis. The wonderful white cliffs are loved by rock-climbers, while the clear turquoise waters favoured by swimmers and small pleasure craft. **Sorgiou ★**, **Morgiou ★** and **Sugiton ★** are closest to Marseille and may be visited by car *(Oct to May only)* or by boat *(trips start from Quai des Belges, details about prices and times from the tourist office).*

The most beautiful calanques lie just west of Cassis: **Port-Miou ★**, **Port-Pin ★★** and the most glorious **En-Vau ★★**. Small, sandy beaches lie hidden at the end of Port-Pin and En-Vau. Boat trips lasting about 1hr *(45F, numerous boats depart between 9am and 6pm)* leave the port of Cassis and visit all three. Unfortunately, because of their natural beauty, the calanques are crowded on summer weekends and one wonders if those petrol emissions from pleasure boats are helping the already polluted Mediterranean coast. Port-Min and En-Vau are not accessible by road, but there are well-marked trails leading to each of them. A hiking visit to En-Vau will take a complete day; wear sturdy footwear and carry appropriate supplies (notably drinking water). Fires devastated trees and vegetation in this area in the early 1990s, so some walking trails are prohibited to hikers during summer months, such as in the Sainte-Victoire hill range near Aix-en-Provence. Inquire before setting out.

Aubagne

This town is worthy of a stop for a few hours. It is laid-out in two levels: the *ville haute,* dating from the medieval period, and the *ville basse,* dating from the 17th century. Of special note is the 14th-century **Porte Gachiou** and the **Tour de l'Horloge**, or clock tower, built in 1900.

Aubagne's most famous citizen is Marcel Pagnol, who was born here on February 28, 1895. The region was a great inspiration for his numerous books and films. The house where he grew up is found at 16 Cours Barthélémy. Visitors may see a rather sentimental reconstruction in miniature (over 200 *santons*—clay figurines) of the sites and figures described by Pagnol in his works at the **Musée du Petit Monde de Marcel Pagnol** *(free admission; Tue to Sun 9am to noon and 2pm to 6pm; Esplanade de Gaulle,* ☎*04.42.84.10.22).* A permanent retrospective of the famous Aubagne *santons,* as well as a look at the much-heralded local pottery and ceramic tradition is to be found at **Les Ateliers Thérèse Neveu**, an exhibition space opened in 1995 *(free admission; Tue to Sun 9am to noon and 2pm to 6pm; Cour de Clastre,* ☎*04.42.03.43.10).*

Cassis

Situated at the foot of Cap Canaille, the highest maritime cliff in Europe (416m or 1,364ft), Cassis is a charming fishing port loved by artists such as Matisse and Dufy at the turn of the century. It is famous for the nearby calanques *(one-hour*

The Son of Aubagne

Born in Aubagne, Marcel Pagnol (1895-1974) depicted Provence and its people more than any other artist of his time. Raised in the La Pleine district of Marseille, this writer, man of the theatre and talented director, who was appointed to the Académie Française in 1946, was an attentive observer of the people of Marseille and the region of Provence. His love for Provence, its untamed nature and the people who lived there, gave rise to his unique style that was both profoundly southern French and resoundingly humanist. Naïve, touching, delightful, excessive, funny and profound, the dialogue in his comedy touched on every level of human experience. With his tireless pen and gift for colourful repartee, Pagnol knew how to enthral his readers and theatre audiences both with locally-flavoured comedy and drama (*Topaza*, 1928), melodrama with an easy-going folk tone (*Marius*, 1929; *Fanny*, 1931; *César*, 1946) and nostalgic tenderness (*La Gloire de mon père*, 1957; *Le Château de ma mère*, 1958; *Le Temps des secrets*, 1960).

Pagnol also made his mark on southern-French cinema. With his representations of daily life in the region so dear to him, Pagnol began his film career in 1931 when he adapted his successful stage piece *Marius* to the screen. The following year, the director founded his own production studio in the heart of Marseille, near the Prado. The success of the film versions of his first trilogy encouraged Pagnol to make other films, including *Angèle* (1934), *Regain* (1937), *Le Schpountz* (1938), *La Filledu puisatier* (1940) and, of course, *La Femme du boulanger* (1939), based on a work by Jean Giono, another highly talented writer from Provence, born in Manosque. With his distinctly Provençal films, Marcel Pagnol managed, among his other successes, to bring the exceptional actor Jules Muraire, known as Raimu, to the Midi. Countless directors and actors followed and continue to follow in Pagnol's footsteps.

visits by boat with commentary, 45F; departures from the Cassis port from 9am to 6pm by a number of different boats), the fresh, fruity white wine produced nearby, a couple of beaches, but most of all, for its fishing community. Coral and sea-urchins are its specialty. Cassis is crowded in the summer-time so try to visit the port in the morning or off-season. Be sure to see the **port ★★** with its tall, narrow houses and cafés, as well as the 17th-century Hôtel de Ville near the pretty Place de l'Église. Above the tourist office is the **Musée des Arts et Traditions Populaires** (*free admission; Wed to Sat 4pm to 7pm; Rue Xavier d'Authier/Place Baragnon, ☎04.42.01.88.66)* devoted to archaeological ruins found in the near-

Fernandel and Raimu

Marcel Pagnol, who loved Provence and its people, was able to find two exceptional vehicles to bring all the vivid colour, humour and emotion of his writing to the screen. These two personalities were larger than life, and the dramatic and touching performances of Fernandel and Raimu could not have better represented the world of Pagnol. Born near Marseille in Carry-le-Rouet, Fernand Contandin, known as Fernandel (1903-1971), began his career on the small stage as part of a comedy troupe, performing as well in operettas and comedy performances. This actor, with horsey facial features that won him a number of nicknames, brought his humour, naiveté, emotions and modesty to Pagnol's characters, which won him some of his best on-screen roles (*Angèle*, 1934; *Regain*, 1937; *Le Schpountz*, 1938; *La Filledu puisatier*, 1940).

Also starting his career in the *café-concerts*, Toulon native Jules Muraire, known as Raimu (1883-1946), gained recognition rather late in life, at the age of 42, thanks to his legendary interpretation of the role of César in Pagnol's *Marius* (1929). His natural instincts as an actor allowed him to move seamlessly between comedy and tragedy, and made this giant of the stage and the screen one of the first stars of French cinema. His plump physique and facial expression of habitual complaint appear in Pagnol's finest works, notably the trilogy *Marius*, *Fanny* and *César*, *La Femme du boulanger* and *La Fille du puisateur*.

by Baie de l'Arène, local history and a small number of Provençal paintings.

La Ciotat

The spectacular **coastal road linking Cassis to La Ciotat ★★★**, known as Route des Crêtes (D141) passes along the sheer cliff-sides of **Cap Canaille** and **Sémaphore**. This coastal city lacks the charm of the smaller ports along the Mediterranean, perhaps due to its shipyards and post-World War II urbanization. However, it does shelter the **Chapelle des Pénitents**, a pretty chapel dating from 1626, and a local history and folklore museum in the old town hall, the **Musée Ciotaden** *(free admission; Mon, Wed, Fri and Sat 4pm to 7pm, Sun 10am to noon, closed Tue and Thu)*. La Ciotat was home to the first movie theatre (Cinéma Eden, still open) in the world, created by the Lumière brothers.

Outdoor Activities

Marseille's location on the rugged Mediterranean coast means water sports and hiking are favourite activities for locals and visitors alike. The tourist office publishes a free comprehensive guide called *Marseille By The Sea* (in French, English, and German) with full details about what to do in the great outdoors. Here are some ideas:

Swimming

Plage du Prophète
Corniche John F. Kennedy, take bus 83 from the Vieux Port
Large sandy beach with lots of activities including sailing, windsurfing, canoeing and volleyball. Services include showers, toilets, a first-aid post and refreshment stand.

Sometimes called the Plages Gaston Defferre, the **Prado Beach** south of the city-centre is actually a series of beaches: **Plage du Roucas Blanc** sand and pebble, includes volleyball court, a playground, raft and diving boards; **Plage du David** pebble; **Plage Borely** pebble, good for windsurfing; **Plage Bonneveine** pebble, includes restaurants, swimming pool, scooter and waterski hire; **Plage de la Vieille Chapelle** pebble, children's games and skate-board track and finally, one which is not accessible by bus 83, **Plage de la Pointe Rouge** sand, restaurant, good for windsurfing.

Frioul Islands
50F
20min shuttle boat service throughout the day from the Quai des Belges, Vieux Port, contact Groupement des Armateurs Cotiers de Marseille
☎***04.91.55.50.09***
A series of rocky islands next to Château d'If (see p 234), with a number of beaches (pebble except for the sand beach Plage de la Maison des Pilotes) and a few restaurants in the village Port Frioul. An idyllic spot to relax.

Scuba Diving

The Mediterranean coastline offers unparalleled opportunities for scuba divers to discover plant and marine life and even shipwrecks. An important archaeological find was made in July 1991 by the professional diver Henri Cosquer, who discovered an underwater prehistoric cave with rock paintings at the Morgiou Calanque near Marseille. A number of scuba clubs provide supervised half-day initiation courses, weekend packages or longer excursions, plus equipment rental. Among the many interesting possibilities are:

ASPTT
Port de la Pointe Rouge
☎***04.91.16.35.90***
Special Friday afternoon to Sunday training sessions, plus five-day courses.

Label Bleu Vidéo
19 Rue Michel Gachet
☎***04.91.33.27.28***
From its base of operation in the old port on Frioul Island, this group offers beginners' courses on weekends (including a video taping of your first dive to keep as a souvenir of the occasion).

Club du Vieux Plongeur
116 Cours Lieutaud
☎***04.91.48.79.48***
Another club based on Frioul Island, this one offers short- and long-term courses, plus dives looking at wrecks, archaeological discoveries and trips for underwater photographers. All-inclusive packages including accommodation (boats, hotels, studio apartments) are arranged.

Other agencies also offer a wide range of services and activities. They include, to name but a few:

Abyss Adventures
26 Rue de la République Claude Wagner
☎***04.91.91.98.07***

Centre de Loisirs des Goudes Plongée
2 Boulevard Alexandre Delarbre Les Goudes, Marie-Carmen and Bertrand Ricard
☎***04.91.25.13.16***

Océan 4
83 Avenue Pointe Rouge, Patrick Bogaerts
☎***04.91.73.89.00***

Palm Beach Plongée
2 Promenade de la Plage, Patrick Brissac
☎***04.91.22.10.38***

Pleasure Boating

An alternative to landlubber vacations consists of renting a yacht to explore the region on the water. Daily, weekly and monthly rentals are available, with or without crews. Interested travellers can contact **Midi Nautisme** *(13 Place aux Huiles, ☎04.91.54.86.09)*, **Soleil Rouge** *(74 Quai du Port, ☎04.91.54.86.09)*, **Boramar** *(77 Rue Peyssonal, ☎04.91.64.75.23)* or **Compagnie Méditerranéenne des Armateurs Gérants** *(1 Square Protis, ☎04.91.56.15.59)*. Motorboats can also be rented for the day or for longer periods from **Groupement des Armateurs Côtiers Marseillais** *(Quai des Belges, ☎04.91.55.50.09)*, from Soleil Rouge, from Boramar and from the Compagnie Méditerranéenne des Armateurs Gérants.

Natrium *(22 Place aux Huiles, ☎04.91.33.95.33)* also rents out boats, as does the **Don du Vent** *(☎04.91.90.85.67)* society.

Windsurfing

The Prado Beach area offers excellent facilities for windsurfers. Equipment is hired out by **Sideral's Time Club** *(☎04.91.25.00.90)* at the Port de la Pointe Rouge Beach.

Waterskiing

At the port of Pointe Rouge, the **Roquette Club Marseille** *(139 Rue François Mauriac, ☎04.91.75.19.33)* organizes waterskiing outings at sea and rents the necessary equipment. The **Jet Sea Club Marseillais** *(61 Boulevard des Neiges, ☎04.91.72.62.23)* dedicates itself equally to waterskiing and jetskiing.

Sailing

A couple of groups at the Port de la Pointe Rouge Beach rent small sail boats and catamarans by the hour:

Pacific Palissades *(☎04.91.73.54.37)* or by the day: **Sideral's Time Club** *(☎04.91.25.00.90)*.

Calanques by the Sea and by Foot

A visit to Marseille is not complete without seeing the spectacular white limestone cliffs rising from the clear turquoise Mediterranean. The series of inlets or fjords known as the Calanques stretch for 20km (65.6mi) between Marseille and Cassis. Though a few may be reached by road from October to May, the Calanques are primarily accessible by sea or by foot, see p 235.

The Calanques are favourite spots for scuba divers and rock-climbers. Most satisfying, if you have the time and are physically-fit, are the numerous walking trails in the area. Only one main trail, the GR98, is open during the summer months (others are closed from mid-June to mid-September due to forest fire threat). The Marseille tourist office publishes a free brochure on the Calanques, with a detailed map of walking trails.

The following hiking clubs offer walks through the Calanque trails, with experienced guides: **Le Club Alpin Français** *(12 Rue Fort Note Dame, ☎04.91.54.36.94)*, **La Société des Excursions Marseillais** *(16 Rue de la Rotonde, ☎04.91.84.75.52)*, **Touring Provence Méditerranée** *(11 Place Général de Gaulle, ☎04.91.33.40.99)*.

Directed by Christian Tamisier, **SERAC** also organises hikes in the Calanques *(25 Rue Kruger, ☎04.91.08.96.08)*.

The sheer cliffs of the Calanques are perfect for dedicated rock-climbers (non-professionals should not attempt to climb them). Contact the local chapter of the **Fédération Française de la Montagne et de l'Escalade** *(Comité Départemental 13 de la FME, Daniel Gorgeon, 5 Impasse du Figuier, 13114 Puylobier, ☎04.42.66.35.05)* for guide books and names of local groups.

You don't need to start from Cassis to discover the Calanques by boat. For 120F per person, you can take 4hr organized excursions to Cassis, which depart from the Quai des Belges in the Old Port every day at 2pm and 6pm in July and August. The rest of the year these tours are available only on Wednesdays, Saturdays and Sundays and in good weather. Departure time is 2pm.

Kayaking

Raskas Kayak Rando
Tue to Sat 9am to noon
☎04.91.73.18.33
Discover the coast around Marseille and its islands and rocky inlets with Raskas Kayak Rando, a state-certified canoe and kayak agency that specializes in sea kayaks.

A guided half-day excursion costs 150F while a daylong excursion costs 250F.

Hiking

Apart from hiking through the Calanques area, there is a wonderful inland walking trail starting north of Cassis. The GR98 trail starts south of Cassis, turns inland past the Mont de la Saoupe and rises sharply in the direction of the Sainte-Baume Massif (see p 205). Looking back, there are superb views of the Provençal coastline.

Aubagne

Sur les traces de Pagnol is a rather special series of marked trails on the Garlaban Massif (710m or 2,329ft) that groups together the numerous sites popularised in Marcel Pagnol's books (*The Glory of My Father, The Chateau of My Mother, Manon des Sources*). Trails are marked by level of difficulty (red, green and blue). The sites are closed in July and August. Information from Les Amis du Garlaban *(winter, Sun 9am to 5pm; summer, 9am to 8pm; Chemin du Ruissatel, Aubagne, ☎04.42.03.23.59)*.

Mountain Biking

Mountain bike rental, plus excursion packages, are offered by:

SERAC
25 Rue Kruger
☎04.91.08.96.08

In-line Skating

Explore Marseille on skates? It's possible every evening after 9:30pm. Several hundred roller blade fans convene at the Vélodrome stadium, then set out on the city's main arteries including the Avenue du Prado, La Canebière, Les Corniches, the quays, the Quai de Joliette and the docks, under the increasingly vigilant surveillance of the police, who ensure that the event is safer by temporarily closing these streets to traffic. Those who wish to participate in this 3 to 4hr ritual event but don't have the necessary equipment can rent it at the Escale Borély.

Accommodations

Marseille

Auberge de Jeunesse Bonneveine
66F-130F
47 Avenue Joseph Vidal
☎04.91.73.21.81
Near the Prado beaches, open from mid-January to mid-December. Shaded terrace, 150 places in dormitories and single rooms; cafeteria; travellers with handicaps welcome.

Auberge de Jeunesse Bois Luzy
74F
Allée des Primevères
☎04.91.49.06.18
Situated in the east of Marseille in a quiet suburb surrounded by greenery and with a view over the harbour. Rooms with four and six beds, plus individual rooms; 90 places in total. Open all year.

La Cigale et la Fourmi
from 100F
early Jun to late Sep
19 Rue Théophile Boudier
☎/⇄04.91.40.05.12
A smashing guest house painted in bright blue and yellow and run by larger-than-life Marseillais Jean Chesnaud. Popular with a young crowd (the narrow, steep stairs are for the spritely) who are drawn to La Cigale et la Fourmi (the locust and ant) by the comfortable dormitory-style rooms, each of which has a bathroom (shower only) and kitchenette. A laundry room with a washer and an iron is available. Located 15min from the centre of Marseilles (there is convenient local bus service) in the Mazargues neighbourhood. The Calanques are a short drive away.

Le Béarn
180F-200F
pb, ps, tv
63 Rue Sylvabelle
☎04.91.37.75.83
⇄04.91.81.54.98
A one-star wonder! Friendly, family-run and good value, though of course at this price there isn't much luxury about the place. Located off the popular Rue du Rome, near the local *préfecture.*

Hôtel Le Richelieu
190F-370F
pb, tv
52 Corniche Kennedy
☎04.91.59.38.09
⇄04.91.59.38.09
Worth staying here only if you can get a room overlooking the Mediterranean and the Château d'If, as the view is the establishment's key feature. The 21 rooms are nothing special—guests spend their time on the sunny terrace (a breakfast-room facing the sea is slated to be built).

Hôtel Esterel
200F-350F bkfst incl.
pb, tv
124-125 Rue Paradis
☎04.91.37.13.90
⇄04.91.81.47.01
Another budget-conscious choice, many consider the Esterel to be the best two-star hotel in Marseille. Rather small rooms, though recently renovated, and a central location behind the Vieux Port. The gracious hosts serve a copious breakfast.

Hôtel Edmond Rostand
250F-295F
bp, tv
31 Rue Dragon
☎04.91.37.74.95
⇄04.91.57.19.04
For those on a budget, this is a fine option—simple, modern rooms at a price that won't break the bank.

Chambre d'Hôtes Schaufelberger
280F-300F, bkfst incl.
pb, tv
2 Rue Saint-Laurent
☎04.91.90.29.02
Chambre d'Hôtes Schaufelberger, the inviting bed and breakfast of Monsieur and Madame Schaufelberger, is on the 14th floor of an apartment building near the Vieux Port, and it enjoys superb views of the comings and goings of sailboats, the docks, Notre-Dame de la Garde and the Mediterranean. Breakfast is served on the balcony. One unglamorous but comfortable room with a private bathroom is rented; a second room

is available, but only if a group is too large to stay in the first. The hosts reach their own room through a private entrance.

Hôtel Climat
280F-355F
pb, tv
6 Rue Beauveau
☎***04.91.33.02.33***
⇄***04.91.33.21.34***
Another good budget hotel, with 45 basic, modern rooms. Centrally-located off the Canebière, near the tourist office and Quai des Belges.

Château de la Panouse
300F-350F, suite 450F, bkfst incl.
198 Avenue de la Panouse
☎/⇄***04.91.41.01.74***
Jean-Yves and Martine Dussart, the happy owners of the Château de la Panouse, have a unique and magical place that they've arranged beautifully, taking full advantage of its setting. Nestled peacefully between the sea and the mountains, this two-room establishment overlooks the city of Marseille. In 1881, a ship-owner from Marseille built the Château as his summer residence in the architectural style of the day, with a few colonial details. Now, after numerous renovations, part of the building serves as an exceptionally charming guesthouse. Guests can enjoy the 100-m^2 (1,076 sq ft) swimming pool surrounded by hills. The 14,000-m^2 (150,696 sq ft) property is a protected site and home to a rich variety of Mediterranean flora and fauna. It is also the starting point for superb hikes into the wild massif of the Saint-Cyr Mountains.

Hôtel de Rome & Saint-Pierre
330F-420F
bp, tv
7 Cours Saint-Louis
☎***04.91.54.19.52***
⇄***04.91.54.34.56***
The central position near the business district is this hotel's greatest asset. Common rooms have a family atmosphere; the bedrooms are large and well equipped. Though the owners have renovated extensively, the taste in decor (flock wallpaper, old-fashioned materials) is quite ghastly!

Hôtel Saint Férréol
300F-500F
pb, tv
19 Rue Pisançon
☎***04.91.33.12.21***
⇄***04.91.54.29.97***
Marseille's best hotel for comfort, value and location. Rooms are named after famous painters and each is decorated with appropriate prints and furnishings; smallish marble bathrooms. Breakfast includes better--than-average croissant and coffee, plus freshly squeezed orange juice. The owners, Bernard Brulas and his wife, are friendly and helpful. Located on the corner of Rue St Férréol, a bustling pedestrian shopping street during the day.

Hotel Mascotte
350F-420F
bp, tv
5 La Canebière
☎***04.91.90.61.61***
⇄***04.91.90.95.61***
Well-placed hotel on the city's main street. Thankfully, the rooms are not only attractive but sound-proofed; some are designated as non-smoking. The top-floor bedroom has a bathroom in a small tower overlooking the street!

Hôtel Hermès
350F-470F
≡, ≈
2 Rue de la Bonnetterie
☎***04.96.11.63.63***
⇄***04.96.11.63.64***
hotel.hermes@wanadoo.fr
Located on a small street that runs perpendicular to the Quai du Port, the Hôtel Hermès has 28 air-conditioned rooms that have been perfectly soundproofed and recently renovated. The four rooms on the upper floor have a pleasant terrace where guests can enjoy splendid views along the old port and Notre-Dame-de-la-Garde. Although they're small, the rooms are comfortable and well maintained. In addition, the excellent location of the Hôtel Hermès and its reasonable rates make it the perfect choice if you want to stay right in the heart of Marseille. The cordial and very professional staff proffers a warm welcome.

New Hôtel Vieux-Port
395F-440F
≡, pb, tv
3 bis Rue Reine Elisabeth
☎04.91.90.51.42
⇌04.91.90.76.24
Charmingly renovated hotel in an 19th- century building centrally located two steps from the old port. Guest rooms are decorated in tasteful blue and cream tones; staff are a helpful, friendly bunch. Bright breakfast room; four meeting rooms.

Nouvel Hôtel Bompard
420F-460F
bp, tv, ≈
2 Rue des Flots Bleus
☎04.91.52.10.93
⇌04.91.31.02.14
info@new-hotel.com
www.new-hotel.com
Situated in one of Marseille's peaceful residential neighbourhoods, the New Hôtel Bompard is located in a delightful park above the Corniche Kennedy. The big plus here isn't just the clean, pretty rooms nor the refined villa setting, but the relaxing swimming pool which is hard to resist on hot days.

Hôtel Résidence du Vieux Port
490F-765F
≡, pb, tv
18 Quai du Port
☎04.91.91.91.22
⇌04.91.56.60.88
hotel.residence@ wanadoo.fr
Hôtel Résidence du Vieux Port is situated next to the old port and every room has a balcony and a view overlooking the glorious bay, across to the Notre Dame de la Garde basilica. The 40 air-conditioned rooms, renovated in 1997, are nicely decorated with soft colours and wooden armoires and desks. The manager is helpful and genuinely pleased to welcome his guests.

Hôtel Mercure Marseille Beauveau Vieux-Port
550F-1,575F
pb, tv
4 Rue Beauveau
☎04.91.54.91.00
⇌04.91.54.15.76
H1293@accor-hotels.com
A European-style hotel in operation since 1816 (recently renovated) and facing the old port on the Quai des Belges, its 72 rooms offer sober Provençal furnishings and a number of 19th-century antiques. Several rooms overlook the old port and are thankfully sound-proofed against traffic noise. The copious buffet breakfast includes whole-grain bread, yogurt and fresh fruit for the health conscious. Some guests might want to stay in the Chopin Suite where the composer and author George Sand sojourned in 1839.

Cassis

Hôtel Cassitel
290F-390F
tv
Place Clémenceau
☎04.42.01.83.44
⇌04.42.01.96.31
www.hotel-cassis.com
cassitel@hotel-cassis.com
Guests stay at the Hôtel Cassitel because of its central location, just a few steps from the beach and the port, and for the comfortable rooms. The Cassitel is impeccably maintained, but only a few of its 32 rooms have a view of the marina and port.

Le Jardin d'Émile
350F-650F
closed two weeks in Nov and in Jan
pb, tv
La Plage du Bestouan
☎04.42.01.80.55
⇌04.42.01.80.70
Charming hotel set amongst pine trees overlooking the sea. Good taste abounds: soothing terracotta colours and clay tile floors are found throughout. The six bedrooms are simply, yet elegantly furnished—ask for one with a sea view. The delightful terrace restaurant means guests need not go far to seek out a good meal. Private parking.

Le Clos des Arômes
390F-550F
ℜ, pb
10 Rue Paul Mouton
☎04.42.01.71.84
⇌04.42.01.31.76
In the centre of Cassis, not far from the port

lies this charming homey inn with eight nicely decorated rooms (the most pleasant face the garden). Breakfast is served on the garden terrace in good weather, and the very good dinner menu includes freshly prepared Provençal classics.

Hôtel de la Plage du Bestouan
430F-650F bkfst incl.
pb, tv, ≈, ℜ, tennis
Avenue Amiral Ganteaume
☎04.42.01.05.70
≠04.42.01.34.82
Hôtel de la Plage du Bestouan proves modern and clean, but lacks character. Its location is nonetheless ideal, since it directly overlooks the Bestouan Beach. The hotel possesses a long terrace on which meals and drinks are served.

Les Roches Blanches
950F-1,300F
closed Nov to late Jan
≈, ℜ, pb, tv
Route des Calanques
☎04.42.01.09.30
≠04.42.01.94.23
For those in need of pampering by the seaside, this restored 19th-century residence is the place. There's a swimming pool facing the sea and a small private beach, while the hotel itself is nestled in sweet-scented pine groves. Though some rooms are compact, all are comfortable and tastefully decorated. Unsurprisingly, considering its location, the restaurant specialises in seafood.

Restaurants

Marseille

Marseille has hundreds of restaurants suiting everyone's taste and pocketbook. For convenience's sake, our selection is divided by area:

Vieux Port/ Le Panier/Les Docks

L'Art et Les Thés
$
10am to 6pm
Centre de la Vieille Charité, 2 Rue de la Charité
☎04.91.14.58.71
Light meals are served at lunch-time, while cakes and drinks are available throughout the day in this small café within the Vieille Charité museum complex. Inventive offerings include spinach and mussel gratin, chicken curry pie and tagliatelle with salmon. Cakes are home-made.

Chez Etienne
$-$$
closed Sun
43 Rue de Lorette
Etienne Cassaro's restaurant and his pizza and home-made pasta dishes are famous throughout Marseille. The place is bustling, the food terrific, and you're likely to strike up a conversation with your neighbour while waiting for a table (don't try reserving—there's no telephone!). Situated in the colourful Quartier Le Panier, north of the old port.

Le Milano des Docks
$-$$
Mon to Fri for lunch
10 Place de la Joliette, Atrium 10.4
☎04.91.91.27.10
The restoration of the old 19th-century docks in the 1980s has certainly resulted in a resounding success for the urban and architectural environment. The buildings were converted from obsolete, neglected warehouses into stunning architectural sensations that highlight Marseille's rich maritime history. Each day, thousands of employees come to work in the many offices and studios located here. Le Milano des Docks is a magnificent café that is popular with those now working at the docks, and is a distinctive place to enjoy an eclectic lunch of good bistro food. We can only dream of having an office down here!

Dimitri
$$
closed Sun and Mon
6 Rue Méolan
☎04.91.54.09.68
Dimitri, a restaurant established long ago now, offers nourishing Russian and Hungarian specialties. Try the *blinis*, the smoked and marinated fish, the beef Stroganoff and the thick cheesecake.

Le Panier des Arts
$$
closed Sun
3 Rue du Petit Puits
☎**04.91.56.02.32**
A new bistrot near the Vieille Charité (see p 228) run by an adorable couple from Sierra Leone. They have renovated an old house in the quaint Panier neighbourhood and created a dining room in warm yellow tones where simple, delicious meals are served. Great value lunch menu for three courses.

Le Miramar
$$-$$$
closed Sun and first three weeks of Aug
12 Quai du Port
☎**04.91.91.10.40**
Marseillais love to debate over which seafood restaurant serves the best bouillabaisse. The name Le Miramar comes up time and time again. The decor is 1960s kitsch, but what's important is that the fish here is delivered fresh every day. Patrons don't leave disappointed. However, such goodness has a price; count on 500F for two people with wine (there are no set-price menus).

Vieux Port/Quai de Rive Neuve/Les Arsenaux

Aux Caprices de Marianne
$
25 Rue Francis Davso
☎**04.91.55.67.71**
Located above the Chocolatier Puyricard, Aux Caprices de Marianne is a teahouse that will please those who love pastries and tea. Homemade, calorie-rich sweets and about 20 kinds of tea are served in unremarkable surroundings. A buffet with *crudités* (raw vegetables), cold cuts and a hot dish is also available. We recommend this establishment to those who enjoy this kind of dining.

O'Stop
$
16 Rue Saint-Saens
☎**04.91.33.85.34**
Known as a "snack-cafeteria" this is a handy and friendly place to grab a meal at any time, as it is open 24 hours a day, seven days a week.

Brasserie Beau Rivage Tabac
$
13 Quai de Rive Neuve
☎**04.91.33.32.37**
Tourists tend to pass this brasserie by but shouldn't, as it is as good a place as any for a reasonable hot lunch in the winter and for cool drinks and ice cream in the summer.

Chez Vincent-Le Vésuve
$-$$
closed Mon
25 Rue Glandevès
☎**04.91.33.96.78**
Unpretentious, simple and congenial, Chez Vincent-Le Vésuve has for years been a meeting place for regulars. The reception and service are friendly at this little restaurant-pizzeria with a decor that seems frozen in time, creating a pleasant atmosphere that will please those who appreciate modest establishments. Pizzas baked in a wood-burning oven complete a menu that features pasta, brochettes, fish and daily specials.

Le Bistrot à Vin
$-$$
closed Sun and Sat lunch
17 Rue Sainte
☎**04.91.52.02.20**
A small though bustling wine bar attracting a youngish clientele, which offers a large selection of wines by the glass *(18-39F)* and tasty bistro dishes such as a charcuterie plate, the famous tripe dish *pieds et paquets Marseillais (76F)*, plus salads, meat dishes and cheeses.

Quai des Pastas
$-$$
15 Quai de Rive Neuve
☎**04.91.33.46.39**
Now this is fun! This restaurant facing the old port specialises in all things pasta, from risotto with eggplant or olives and basil to delicious tagliatelli with crayfish. Turquoise walls, bare wood tables and chairs and wacky light fixtures (metal colanders as wall sconces and cheese graters as hanging lamps) create a relaxed atmosphere. Rolling pins fixed to the wall act as coat hooks.

L'Ambassade des Vignobles
$$
closed Sun
42 Place Aux Huiles
☎04.91.33.00.25
With the same ownership as the Côte de Boeuf next-door (see below), this popular spot proposes four menus where each dish is accompanied by a different glass of wine.

Le Bistro Gambas
$$
closed Sat lunch and Sun
29 Place Aux Huiles
☎04.91.33.26.44
This simple yet refined restaurant serves a variety of *gambas* (crustaceans) in a number of inventive ways: grilled, on salads, with fragrant Asian flavours. Several affordable local white wines are offered.

Il Caneletto
$$
closed Sunday
8 cours Jean Ballard
☎04.91.33.90.12
Many locals agree, the best Italian food in Marseille is found here in this charming tratorria next to the Arsenaux complex and old port. The fresh home-made pasta and carpaccio of tuna are excellent; be sure to leave room for the heavenly tiramisu. No set-price menu.

La Côte de Boeuf
$$
closed Sun
35 Cours d'Estienne d'Orves
☎04.91.54.89.08
This long-established restaurant serves up succulent roasted meats in a refined rustic atmosphere, with dark wooden beams and a hearth at the back. Reputed for the quality of its meat, as well as for the impressive (and heavy!) wine list.

Les Menus Plaisirs
$$
no credit cards
closed Sat and Sun and every evening
1 Rue Haxo
☎04.91.54.94.38
A tiny café serving simple but good lunchtime meals (roast pork with rosemary, braised lamb) to an appreciative local clientele. The rich home-made chocolate cake is out of this world. Reservations advised.

Maddie-Les Galinettes
$$
138 Quai du Port
☎04.91.90.40.87
There is a real mix of establishments around the Quai du Port and while there are some acceptable finds, most are mediocre restaurants that serve rather banal fare. Maddie-Les Galinettes definitely does *not* belong to the latter category, and sets itself apart with its quality food and carefully chosen, artistic decor. The fish dishes are excellent, and the quality of the meat selections has won this restaurant its reputation. The *pieds et paquets* (tripe), casserole, lamb and calves' liver are divinely prepared. In summer, of course, you can enjoy the terrace on the port, but even if you dine outside, take a look at the dining room, which is beautifully decorated with paintings by contemporary artists from Marseilles. Excellent value for the price.

Taverne de Maitre Kanter
$$
9 Quai de Rive Neuve
☎04.91.33.84.85
When you think you can't face another bouillabaise or ratatouille but still want something hearty and comforting to eat, this is the place to come. Maitre Kanter's speciality is Alsatian cooking, so expect platters of steaming sauerkraut and sausages. Oysters and fresh seafood also appear on the menu. Pine banquette seating and rich red and green colours predominate.

L'Oliveraie
$$$
closed Sat at noon and Sun
10 Place aux Huiles
☎04.91.33.34.41
A charming little restaurant that distinguishes itself among the many establishments on the Place aux Huiles, L'Oliveraie has a typical Provençal ambiance. The pretty dining room with a vaulted ceiling and warm, sun-drenched colours admirably complements the terrace, which is very popular in summer. The food is honest, generous and authentic, never failing to delight diners. The chef skilfully prepares appetizers featuring zucchini,

eggplant and goat cheese while the main courses highlight rabbit, cod and pork filet. The desserts are a brilliant finale to the restaurant's meals, served by a discreet, attentive and cordial staff.

Direction Escale Borely/Calanques

Les Catalans
$
May to Sep, for lunch and dinner
Oct to Apr, lunch only
closed Dec 22 to Jan 31
Bains de Mer, 3 Rue des Catalans
☎04.91.52.37.82
Les Catalans, is a pizzeria ideally set on the beach between the Palais du Pharo and the Plage des Catalans. Patrick Martin and his friendly team serve delicious thin-crust pizzas *(around 45F for a small to 75F for a large)* cooked in a wood-burning oven. Pasta, fish and grilled meat dishes are also available; Provence wines are featured on the wine list. The spot is simple (concrete floor, white plastic chairs on the covered terrace)—the pleasure here comes from dining next to the glorious sea away from traffic.

Chez Jeannot
$-$$
closed Mon, Sun evening Oct to May and mid-Dec to mid-Jan
129 Vallon des Auffes
☎04.91.52.11.28
Chez Jeannot is a real Marseille institution, a place to eat good pizzas and salads right in front of the tiny Vallon des Auffes fishing port in the city's 7e Arrondissement. Popular during hot weather when the large terrace is open.

L'Escale
$$
2 Boulevard Alexandre Delabre, Les Goudes
☎04.91.73.16.78
A new owner has arrived at this restaurant which is ideally situated on the roadside overlooking the spectacular port of Goudes. The non-descript interior is not a problem as customers come from all around for the superb sea view and the fine seafood dishes. It is necessary to drive here as it is south of Marseilles near the Calanques (see p 235).

Le Lunch
$$
open Apr to mid-Oct, no lunch no Jul and Aug Mon to Fri because the Calanque is closed to cars until 7pm
Calanque de Sormiou
☎04.91.25.05.37
Not easy to find (at the end of the Calanque de Sormiou, right of the parking lot) but worth the effort as customers find themselves perched on a terrace between turquoise waters and the impressive cliffside. The house specialty is fresh fish, which arrives daily—recently sea bass, sea bream and red mullet were featured. Finish the meal with a delicious raspberry clafoutis. It is essential to make reservations for Saturday and Sunday lunch during July and August in order to obtain a pass to use the Route de Sormiou.

Cours Julien/ La Plaine

Restaurant Le Caucase
$
closed Sun
62 Cours Julien
☎04.91.48.36.30
Billed as an "Armenian Auberge", this spot does a great job in transporting customers to the Caucasus. The food is simple and reasonably priced—grilled meats for 55F, mixed kebab 75F and, for the adventurous, the Grand Mezze plate of 15 starters for two people *(250F)*. The interior is very 1950s, beige and very Formica.

L'Anvers
$-$$
closed Sunday
2 Rue des Trois Rois
☎04.91.42.05.46
As the name suggests, this restaurant serves up Belgian cuisine to an appreciative crowd. Of course, it serves mussels in an amazing selection of sauces (safran, pistou, basil, garlic) with French fries and there's also salmon waterzooi (stew) and a good choice of beer.

Heng Heng
$-$$
closed Tue
65 Rue de la République
☎04.91.91.29.94
Heng Heng is a tiny restaurant serving the best Chinese food in Marseilles to a loyal local clientele. The Vietnamese soups are meals in themselves; the glazed duck is divine. Best of all is the charming welcome from the Chaung family, who make everyone feel right at home.

O'Pakistan
$-$$
closed Sat lunch
11 Rue des Trois Rois
☎04.91.48.87.10
Try the *Plateau des Rois* for a tour of Pakistani cuisine: nine different dishes on one plate (including chicken curry, samosa, grilled fish and saffron rice). The decor is kitsch—pink-and-white walls with 1960s-style wooden panelling; the management is extremely friendly.

Le Sud du Haut
$$
closed Sun to Wed at noon
80 Cours Julien
☎04.91.92.66.64
Le Sud du Haut is a small, charming and fresh restaurant that opened on the Cours Julien four years ago and is now located at the top of the steps, which is how it got its new name. Both the food and the service are flawless. This hip and friendly establishment serves superb dishes that combine local ingredients with exotic spices. The result is exquisite: delicious, melt-in-your-mouth chicken liver with spiced onion jam, excellent spiced lamb baked in *papillotte* pastry and tender curried beef fricassee. Guests who are so inclined can use the pens thoughtfully provided by the establishment to graffiti the bathroom walls.

Le Tire-Bouchon
$$
Tue to Sat for dinner
11 Cours Julien
☎04.91.42.49.03
Le Tire-Bouchon has a warm, retro atmosphere with lots of wood trim and old furniture, in the purest French bistro tradition. This place opened several years ago and serves food typical of this sort of establishment, such as grilled meats, meat with sauce and other French dishes.

Ce Cher Arwell
$$$
no credit cards
96 Cours Julien
☎04.91.48.30.41
Ce Cher Arwell treats its guests like royalty. This tiny restaurant has a comfy, intimate setting with low ceilings and exposed beams, and serves delicious, delicate southern-French cuisine. There is no fixed-price menu. This place is an absolute must on the Cours Julien.

Cassis

La Marine
$
closed Nov 15 to Jan 2
5 Quai des Baux
☎04.42.01.76.09
A typical bar/café with lots of rustic character facing the Cassis port, it started in the 1930s and has been a meeting place for locals ever since. Marcel Pagnol filmed scenes for a number of his movies here.

Bonaparte
$-$$
closed Sun to Mon and Oct to Mar
14 Rue du Général Bonaparte
☎04.42.01.80.84
The atmosphere at the Bonaparte is so friendly and relaxed that you'll feel right at home. The owner welcomes and waits on his loyal clientele with an incredible energy and obvious good humour, creating an amicable ambiance that couldn't be more inviting. Regulars come to the Bonaparte to enjoy the simple Provençal cuisine that is largely based on fish: sea-perch, salmon, scorpion fish and sea bream are served in minimalist surroundings. At lunch, the terrace on the pedestrian street as well as the small, open dining room overflow with customers. The speedy, efficient but still attentive service is beyond reproach. The menu has items to suit all budgets.

Le Grand Large
$-$$
Plage de la Grande Mer
☎04.42.01.81.00
What could be finer than facing the Mediterranean, sitting on a terrace next to the beach eating fresh fish and seafood? Customers at this busy, simple restaurant can sip a pastis or grab a dish of ice-cream between meals, or enjoy oysters, clams, fish soup or a tasty salad of warm red mullet and scallops at lunch and dinner.

Le Dauphin
$$
closed Wed and Thu at noon
3 Rue du Docteur Séverin Icard
☎04.42.01.10.00
Le Dauphin will please those who enjoy traditional Provençal cuisine and have a penchant for seafood. In addition to the fixed-price menus, you can order delectable seafood chowders, which have become the house specialty. A small, unassuming establishment decorated in warm orange-and-yellow hues, Le Dauphin has a lively atmosphere that is reflected in its friendly service. Guests can choose between the indoor dining room and the small terrace, which consists of a few tables set out on the pedestrian street.

Restaurant Romano
$$
closed Sun evening
15 Quai Barthélémy
☎04.42.01.08.16
Restaurant Romano has a splendid location on the port and specializes in seafood with a Provençal flavour. Appetizers include tomato and basil mousse and mussels stuffed with garlic and parsley, as well as the classic fish soup with its *rouille.* The main dishes feature sea bream, sardines *à l'escabèche*, the traditional bouillabaisse, not to forget the Provençal larks and the *pieds et paquets*. Restaurant Romano extends over two floors, with a terrace on port level and a dining room with large bay windows on the upper level. Meticulous, attentive service.

La Fleur de Thym
$$-$$$
open for dinner only
18 Rue M. Arnaud
☎04.42.01.23.03
Located on a small street set back from the port, La Fleur de Thym is a good place in Cassis for those in search of fine cuisine with a Mediterranean accent, served in a charming setting that is both typical and upbeat. The dining area is dominated by an imposing fireplace right in the middle of the room, that adds to the character of this excellent spot to enjoy the flavours of Provence. As well as the pleasant dining room, there is a terrace with several tables on the small pedestrian street in the centre of the village. Different types of meat, most notably lamb, duck and beef, are featured here, but there are also some fish and seafood selections.

Aubagne

Le Florentin
$
Cours Foch
☎04.42.03.00.86
A relaxed town-centre café with a good choice of French standards—crêpes, omelettes, large salad plates. In the summer, tables are set out on the Cours Foch in front of a World War II memorial.

Le Parc
$$
closed Sun pm
Avenue du 21 Août 1944, Parc Jean Moulin
☎04.42.84.15.14
A good restaurant with reasonably priced set menus from 50F to 120F. Its pretty setting in the Parc Moulin means the restaurant is popular on weekends.

La Ferme
$$
open Tue to Fri and Sun for lunch only, and Fri and Sat evenings
Quartier Font de Mai, Chemin du Ruissatel
☎04.42.03.29.67
A truly wonderful spot, where, for a price, guests are treated to a cuisine based on fresh, local produce including *daube provençale* and *pieds et paquets*. The

luminous interior leads to a series of outdoor terraces; the whole restaurant is set next to trees at the foot of the Garlaban hillside.

Entertainment

Pick up the free weekly newspaper *TakTik* (available in the tourist office, bookshops, cafes and bars) and the brochure *In situ* (Marseille's cultural calendar) for an up-to-date guide to what's on in Marseille and the region. The following list, though far from complete, indicates a wealth of things to do in Marseille.

Marseille

Bars and Nightclubs

The area known as La Plaine (Place Jean Jaurès leading to the nearby Cours Julien) and the Arsenaux area (Cours d'Estienne d'Orves, Place Aux Huiles) are two lively places at night-time, with loads of restaurants, bars and nightclubs. Take your pick, according to your taste.

Bar de l'Avenir
55 Place Jean Jaurès
☎***04.91.78.11.22***
This Bohemian bar doesn't look like it has changed much since the 1950s—lots of bric-à-brac and a collection of old bank notes displayed behind the bar counter. Popular with a scruffy, arty local crowd.

Chocolat-Théâtre
closed Sun
59 Cours Julien
☎***04.91.42.19.29***
During the day this is an arty hangout where Bohemian types grab a coffee or lunch. Each evening it turns into a terrific live-performance venue: improv comedy on Monday nights *(40F)* and theatre and musical-comedy from up-and-coming stars the rest of the week *(70F to 110F)*. Special dinner-theatre prices from 178F.

Cyber Café Hors Limites
35 Rue de la Paix
☎***04.91.55.06.34***
Cyber Café Hors Limites claims to have been the first cyber café in France. Created by art historian Sophiane Vautier-le-Bourhis, who has decorated and furnished the large room with great care.

Le Degust Rock
12 Place Jean-Jaurès
no ☎
Le Degust Rock is a small bar that organizes concerts year-round (mainly rock, reggae and blues). Good selection of beers.

Espace Julien
39 Cours Julien
☎***04.91.24.34.14***
Very happening, established space with live music from 9pm (entry is sometimes free though most nights tickets cost 40F to 50F and are available at the door or in advance at Virgin and FNAC). Bands vary from world music to pop and rock.

L'Espace Snooker
Nov to Mar, closed Mon
148 Avenue Pierre Mendés France
☎***04.91.71.24.12***
Over 700m^2 (7,535 sq ft) devoted to billiards and snooker as well as a brasserie, creperie, bar and 1950s-style restaurant called Les 3 Coups. Open terrace over-looking the sea during the summer.

L'Intermédiaire
63 Place Jean Jaurès
☎***04.91.47.01.25***
Funky spot with live music ranging from blues to reggae every Wednesday through Saturday. Check local press for details on shows.

La Maronnaise
winter, Fri and Sat; summer, Thu to Sat
Anse Croisette, Les Goudes
☎***04.91.73.98.58***
In the Goudes area next to the sea, this disco is a true Marseillais institution. Fun and loud, with an all-ages group.

Méditerranée Café
51 Quai des Belges
☎***04.91.55.58.32***
A casual café and bar where customers sit on the terrace facing the old port and linger over coffee or a cold beer. Ideal for people-watching.

O'Brady's Irish Pub
378 Avenue de Mazargues
☎*04.91.71.53.71*
Irish theme-pubs have become enormously popular in France. O'Brady's, in the eighth arrondisement, is one of Marseille's first and still the busiest. Expect a young, jovial atmosphere.

Le Pelle-Mêle
5pm to 2am
45 Place Aux Huiles
☎*04.91.54.85.26*
Piano bar with established jazz groups.

Quai 9
closed Sun and Mon
9 Quai de Rive Neuve
☎*04.91.33.34.20*
Nightclub/discotheque for Marseillais youth, particularly students, with the latest music (top 40 to house).

Transbordeur
every day 9pm to dawn
12 Quai de Rive Neuve
☎*04.91.54.29.43*
Popular bar with music videos, billiards and a pub atmosphere; live music from local rock and pop groups.

Trolleybus
24 Quai de Rive Neuve
☎*04.91.54.30.45*
A smart young crowd shows up at this discotheque every Saturday night for the latest music and dancing into the wee hours.

Gay and Lesbian Life

Provence's gay scene seems extremely limited to travellers who are used to the variety of cafés, bars and services available in a large metropolis, such as Paris, New York and London. The local gay community in the region is not nearly as open as it is in more cosmopolitan cities. However, Marseilles is happening compared to Aix, Arles and Avignon. The Côte d'Azur offers more vibrancy and choice. For information about the latest events, contact **Collectif Gai et Lesbian Marseille Provence** *(93 La Canebière, 13001 Marseille, ☎04.91.55.39.50)*. There is a local chapter of action group **ACT UP** *(40 Rue Senac, 13001 Marseille, ☎04.91.94.08.43)*. The group **AGIS-Ibiza** *(Association Gay d'Infos sur le Sida, 22 Rue L. Bourgeois, 13001 Marseille, ☎04.91.50.50.12, ⇄04.91.84.64.93)* publishes a free magazine, *Ibiza News*, with details about the local gay scene.

Gay Bars

Enigme Bar
daily from 5pm to 2am
22 Rue Beauvau
☎*04.91.33.79.20*
Centrally-located male gay bar, near Métro Vieux-Port.

MP
every day from 5pm
10 Rue Beauvau
☎*04.91.33.64.79*
MP is another gay bar, also for men, situated near the Énigme (Métro Vieux-Port).

The New Cancan
Wed to Sun, 11pm onwards
3-5 Rue Sénac
☎*04.91.48.59.76*
Near Métro Noallies, the largest gay male disco in the area. Live entertainment Thursdays and Sundays.

Theatres

Cinéma César
4 Place Castellane
☎*04.91.53.27.82*
Cinéma César is the best repertory theatre in Marseille. The most recent releases from such diverse film-makers as Atom Egoyan and Jean-Luc Godard are presented, as are various retrospectives. New commercial films are presented in many other cinemas in town; consult the local papers for schedules.

Les Variétés
138 La Canebière, near the street and the Métro Noailles
Les Variétés cinema is another good movie theatre in Marseille's city centre. Films are screened in their original language.

La Cité de la Musique
4 Rue Bernard du Bois
☎*04.91.39.28.28*
Classical and contemporary music concerts are performed regularly in the **Auditorium** of this arts complex, while some excellent jazz masters groove in the **Cave à Jazz**, playing standards and contemporary selections.

La Criée/Théâtre National de Marseille
30 Quai de Rive Neuve
☎04.91.54.70.54
Excellent home-grown productions plus pieces created elsewhere (often major works from Paris) are performed here.

Other theatres to look out for are: **Théatre du Gymnase** *(4 Rue du Théâtre Francais, ☎04.91.24.35.24)* and the **Théâtre Gyptis** *(136 Rue Loubon, ☎04.91.11.00.91)* plus countless smaller venues, including cabarets and café-theatres.

Espace Odéon
162 La Canebière
☎04.91.92.79.44
Espace Odéon is a cultural centre that puts on cinematographic retrospectives and theatre pieces with a contemporary slant (in the Théâtre de l'Odéon).

Maison de l'Étranger
12 Rue Antoine Zattara
☎04.91.28.24.01
Maison de l'Étranger puts on theatre pieces and lively concerts presented by guest performers, most of whom come from European Mediterranean countries and North Africa.

Opéra Municipal
1 Place Reyer
☎04.91.55.00.70
Call ahead or pick up a programme in order to catch one of the in-house or travelling opera and dance productions, performed in this grand Art-Deco masterpiece.

La Passerelle
noon to midnight
26 Rue des Trois Mages
☎04.91.48.46.40
A dynamic arts centre attracting lots of local young people, incorporates **La Planete Livres** *(for "BDs" comic books for all ages)*, **Gégé le Chinois** *(used books, open 3pm to 8pm)*, **Marseille Café** *(lunch menu 45 F, dinner menu 60 F)* and a small cinema showing experimental films.

Zénith Le Dôme
☎04.91.12.21.21
Zénith Le Dôme welcomes all of the big shows that pass through Marseille, including international stars as diverse as Roch Voisine, Charles Aznavour and Janet Jackson.

Festivals and Cultural Events

Le Chandeleur *(Feb 2)* Procession of the Vierge Noir (the Black Virgin) to the Saint Victor basilica;

Festival de Musique *(Oct to Apr)* recitals in the Saint Victor basilica;

Festival de Création de Musique du XXe Siecle *(early May)* Contemporary music festival;

Festival Marseille *(Jul)* Dance, theatre, music;

La Fiesta des Suds *(Oct)* Music, dance, concerts, bodegas;

Pastorales *(Jan)* Live enactment of the Nativity with spoken text and sometimes Provençal songs at Théâtre du Lacydon *(1 Montée du Saint Esprit, 13002, ☎04.91.90.96.70)*, Théâtre Mazenod *(88 Rue d'Aubagne, 13001 Marseille, ☎04.91.54.04.69)*, Espace Odéon *(162 La Canebière, 13002 Marseille, ☎04.91.92.79.44)*, and at Théâtre Nau *(9 Rue Nau, 13006, ☎04.91.92.36.97)*.

Crêches *(Dec and Jan)* Christmas nativity scenes with coloured Provençal clay figurines, some a large as $60m^2$ (645 sq ft), in local churches. *Santons* are sold throughout the region in *foires aux santons* (santon fairs). Check local papers or tourist offices for details.

Foire aux Santons *(late Nov to late Dec)*: exhibits showcasing the best figurines of saints typical of the region's crèches since 1803. On the Allées de Meilhan (above La Canebière).

Aubagne

Festival International de l'Humour et des Rires *(Jun and Jul)* Comedy festival;

Crêche *(Dec)* Christmas Nativity scene with santons, held in the tourist office; at the same time the clay figurines are sold at the **Foire Aux Santons** held along the Cours du Maréchal-Foch;

Biennale de l'Art Santonnier *(mid-Jul to late Aug, Dec)* Aubagne is the centre for the manufacturing of *santons*, therefore it is only natural that its artisans proudly display their stuff (exhibition/display on the Cours du Maréchal-Foch);

Pastorale *(Dec)* Live enactment of the Christmas Nativity *(Théâtre la Comoédia, ☎04.42.71.19.88)*.

Cassis

Fête des Pêcheurs (Fishermen's Festival) last Sunday in June;

Fêtes des Vins *(early Sep)* Wine tastings from the reputable Cassis vineyards, plus Provençal dancing;

Pastorale *(Jan)* Live enactment of the Christmas Nativity story *(Centre Cultural, ☎04.42.01.77.73)*.

La Ciotat

Lumières du Jazz *(last two weeks of July)* Jazz music festival.

Shopping

Marseille

For smart, upscale shops head to Rue Grignan between Rue Paradis and Rue St Ferréol (Louis Vuitton, Alain Figaret, Façonable) and Rue Paradis (Max Mara, John Lobb, Ikks Compagnie, Marine).

Arterra
1a Rue du Petit-Puits
☎04.91.91.03.31
Originating in Marseille at the end of the 18th century, *santons* (ornamental crèche figures) are now a flourishing industry. The Arterra shop and studio is especially worth mentioning, with its magnificent collection of baked clay figurines and *santons.*

Faïencerie Figuères
10-12 Avenue Lauzier, Pointe Rouge district, near the Musée de la Faïence
☎04.91.73.06.79
The last establishment of its kind in Marseille, the Faïencerie Figuères specializes in making surprising *trompe l'oeil* fruits, vegetables, meats and fish. Strikingly lifelike, you almost want to bite into these little gems, which are displayed alongside lovely reproductions of traditional 18th-century Provençal earthenware.

Au Cygne D'Or
29 Quai des Belges
☎04.91.33.47.46
A handy *librairie-presse* selling local, national and international newspapers and magazines. Closed May 1st.

La Chocolatière du Panier
4 Place des Treize Cantons
☎04.91.91.67.66
Michèle Le Ray has recreated her father's artisanal chocolate-making business with great success. Her specialties are bars with nuts or perfumed with orange or passion fruit. The white-chocolate galette, perfumed with real lavender, is sublime. Le Ray doesn't keep fixed hours, so just knock on her door if there doesn't appear to be anyone around.

Compagnie de Marseille
One Rue Caisserie, in the Panier district
☎04.91.56.20.97
Soaps have certainly had an impact on Marseille's economy and image. If you're looking for a gift or souvenir to bring back with you, the Compagnie de Marseille is a good place to visit. Here you will find authentic items made in Marseille, which is rare, and your purchases will be beautifully gift-wrapped.

Dromel Ainé
Mon 2:30pm to 7pm, Tue to Sat 9pm to 7pm, closed Sun
6 Rue de Rome
☎04.91.54.01.91
Specialty candy manufacturer since 1760, with excellent *marrons*

glacés (preserved candied chestnuts), plus teas and coffees. Dromel Ainé sells three types of navettes which are tastier and softer than its rival Le Four des Navettes (see below).

Eupalinos
Mon to Sat 9:30am to 12:30pm and 2pm to 7pm
72 Cours Julien
☎***04.91.48.74.44***
Comprehensive selection of books on architecture, photography, music, cinema and art.

FNAC *(Centre Commercial Bourse, ☎04.91.39.94.00)* and **Virgin Megastore** *(75 Rue St Ferréol, ☎04.91.55.55.00)* both satisfy every music and book-lover's needs—travel, business, computers, sports books, etc. Each has a concert ticket desk for advance sales to local concerts and clubs.

Four des Navettes
everyday 7am to 7:30pm
136 Rue Sainte
☎***04.91.33.32.12***
The oldest bakery in town (founded in 1782) is famous for its *navettes*, small boat-shaped sweet biscuits which supposedly symbolise the Saintes-Maries' arrival to Provence by sea. The recipe is kept secret. Every February 2 during the Fête de la Chandeleur (Candlemas celebration), the wooden statue of the Vierge Noir (Black Virgin) is taken from the crypt of the nearby Saint-Victor abbey. According to tradition, the *four des navettes*, the oven and its production, is blessed, whereupon the participants buy green-coloured candles and freshly-blessed biscuits following the service. The two items will protect the owner's household for the rest of the year.

Le Fournil des Rois
Tue to Sun 6:30am to 8pm
8 Rue Breteuil
☎***04.91.33.26.40***
Le Fournil des Rois is a bakery and pastry shop renowned for its traditional Gâteau des Rois Provençal (cake of the kings of Provence), prepared in the month of January.

Galeries Lafayette
40 Rue St Ferréol
☎***04.91.54.92.20***
Department store selling everything from clothes to luggage to housewear. The place to go for an umbrella when you're caught without one in a downpour, and a swimsuit and beach towel when you forget yours at home.

Georges Bataille
Mon to Sat 8am to 12:30pm and 3:30pm to 8pm
16-18 Rue Fontange
☎***04.91.47.06.23***
A marvellous gourmet food shop selling bread, a vast selection of cheese (including a delicious house camembert), wine, prepared meats, fresh meat, prepared foods, *oreillettes* (sugar coated, deep-fried, dough shaped lard in the form of ears), smoked salmon and house foie gras. A veritable feast for the eyes and stomach.

Invitation au Voyage
132 Rue Paradis
☎***04.91.81.60.33***
Bookstore selling general literature, books in foreign languages, plus books on travel and cinema.

Librairie de la Bourse Frezet
8 Rue Paradis
☎***04.91.33.63.06***
Specialty bookstore selling maps and guides, plus lots more.

Les Arsenaux
10am to midnight, closed Sun
25 Cours d'Estienne d'Orves
☎***04.91.59.80.37***
Housed in a unique cultural centre that conveys an incredibly rich history, the Les Arcenaulx bookstore wonderfully complements its collection of books, which features fine dining and restaurants. The knowledgeable sales staff guides you through the shelves of books, which include a section on Provence. An absolute must to visit, if only to appreciate the spectacular historic building, which has been renovated over the past few years.

Librairie Maurel
95 Rue de Lodi
☎***04.91.42.63.44***
English-language bookshop.

Librairie Regards
every day 10am to 6:30pm
Centre de la Vieille Charité, 2 Rue de la Charité
☎**04.91.90.55.34**
Librairie Regards is a magnificent art bookstore that also sells elegant postcards.

Madame Zaza de Marseille
Mon to Sat 10am to 1pm and 2pm to 7pm, open the second Sun of every month
Madame Zaza de Marseille is a fashion designer whose creations are especially coveted by young (and young-at-heart) women. Parisians can now purchase her original clothing pieces at a new shop in the Marais district *(18 Rue Sainte Croix de la Bretonnerie).*

Phamacie du Vieux Port
4 Quai du Port
☎**04.91.90.00.57**
Drug store with extended hours and staff who speak English, Italian and Spanish.

Photo Station
126 Rue Rome
☎**04.91.81.61.97**
3 Rue Paradis
☎**04.91.33.35.63**
For all your film and developing needs.

Torréfaction Noailles
56 La Canebière
☎**04.91.55.60.68**
Renovated in 1996, Torréfaction Noailles is a coffeehouse in the purest Italian tradition and serves about 40 kinds of tea and a dozen varieties of coffee, roasted on the premises.

Le Père Blaize
4 Rue Méolan
☎**04.91.54.04.01**
A healer who came from the Alps, Le Père Blaize set up shop selling herbs and medicinal products in 1815. Today, the same heady aromas as must have prevailed two centuries ago fill the air in the faithfully preserved interior. Plants from around the world, as well as essential oils and *tisanes* prepared on the premises are sold to customers hoping to prolong their lives through herbal remedies.

Markets

Monthly Second-Hand and Rare Book Market
second Sat of the month, all year
Cours Julien

Fish Market
every morning
Quai des Belges (Vieux Port)

Flea Market (Marché Aux Puces)
Fri, Sat and Sun
Cours Julien

Brocante Market
second Sun of the month
Cours Julien

Fruit and Vegetables
everyday except Sun
Cours Pierre-Puget, Cours Julien, Boulevard Michelet
everyday
Place des Capucins

Flower Market
Mon morning
Place Félix-Baret and Cours Pierre-Puget
Tue and Sat morning
Allées de Meilhan
Thu morning
Boulevard Michelet
Fri morning
Avenue du Prado

Marché Paysan: This country market is open on Tue, Sat and Sun. Inquire at the tourist office for further details.

Marché de la Poterie: in summer, this event brings together artisans and makers of the crèche figurines from across the region. The Espace Thérèse Neveu also has a lovely pottery collection. Inquire at the tourist office for further details.

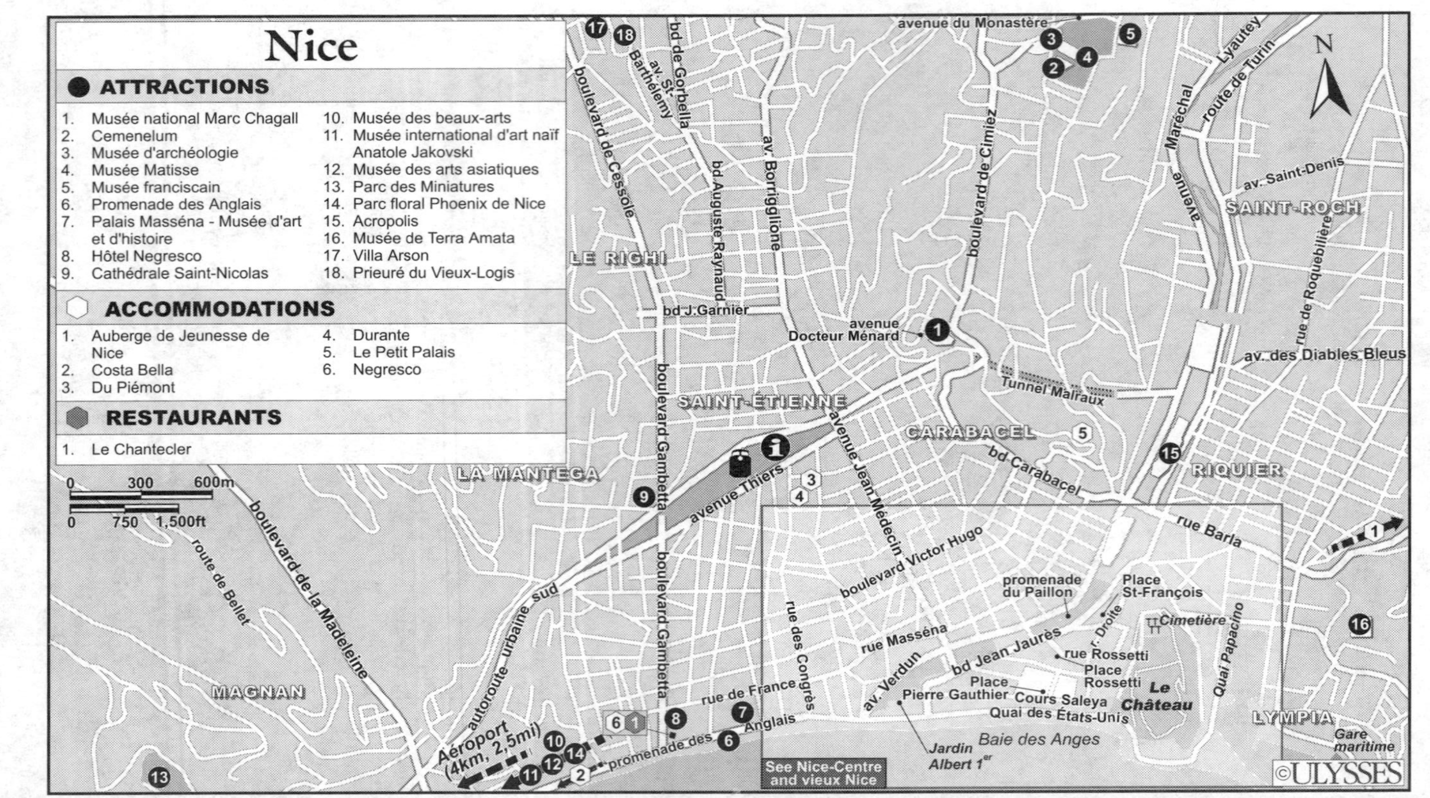
Nice
ATTRACTIONS
1. Musée national Marc Chagall
2. Cemenelum
3. Musée d'archéologie
4. Musée Matisse
5. Musée franciscain
6. Promenade des Anglais
7. Palais Masséna - Musée d'art et d'histoire
8. Hôtel Negresco
9. Cathédrale Saint-Nicolas
10. Musée des beaux-arts
11. Musée international d'art naïf Anatole Jakovski
12. Musée des arts asiatiques
13. Parc des Miniatures
14. Parc floral Phoenix de Nice
15. Acropolis
16. Musée de Terra Amata
17. Villa Arson
18. Prieuré du Vieux-Logis
ACCOMMODATIONS
1. Auberge de Jeunesse de Nice
2. Costa Bella
3. Du Piémont
4. Durante
5. Le Petit Palais
6. Negresco
RESTAURANTS
1. Le Chantecler
0 300 600m
0 750 1,500ft
N
avenue du Monastère
boulevard de Cessole
av. St-Barthélemy
bd de Gorbella
bd Auguste Raynaud
av. Borriggliore
boulevard de Cimiez
avenue Maréchal Lyautey
route de Turin
av. Saint-Denis
SAINT-ROCH
rue de Roquebillière
av. des Diables Bleus
LE RIGHI
bd J.Garnier
avenue Docteur Ménard
Tunnel Malraux
SAINT-ÉTIENNE
CARABACEL
bd Carabacel
RIQUIER
LA MANTEGA
avenue Thiers
avenue Jean Médecin
boulevard Gambetta
rue Barla
boulevard Victor Hugo
promenade du Paillon
Place St-François
Cimetière
r. Droite
rue Rossetti
Place Rossetti
Le Château
Quai Papacino
rue des Congrès
rue Masséna
bd Jean Jaurès
av. Verdun
Place Pierre Gauthier
Cours Saleya
Quai des États-Unis
Baie des Anges
Jardin Albert 1er
LYMPIA
Gare maritime
rue de France
promenade des Anglais
autoroute urbaine sud
Aéroport (4km, 2,5mi)
boulevard de la Madeleine
route de Bellet
MAGNAN
See Nice-Centre and vieux Nice
©ULYSSES

Nice

The capital of the Côte d'Azur, Nice ★★★, is blessed with the kind of climate that sun-lovers dream of.

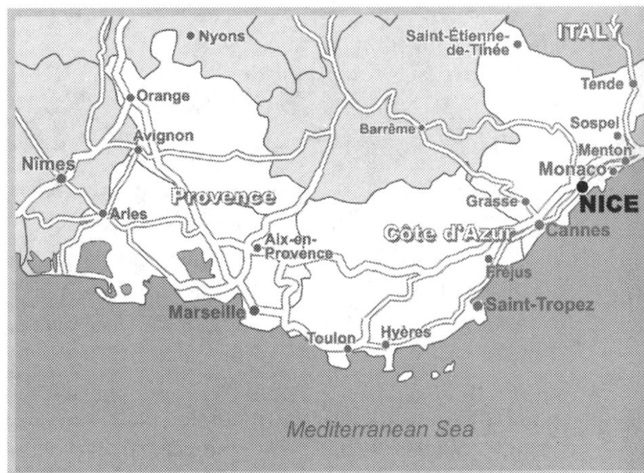

It also has the advantage of being exceptionally well located, on one of Europe's most beautiful bays. The Baie des Anges is surrounded by hills that offer a sort of natural protection, and essentially explain why Nice was so popular even in prehistoric times. The Terra Amata encampment and Lazaret cave, which date back 400,000 years, are a living testimony to this ancient heritage.

Nice itself has a very favourable microclimate, with pleasant temperatures in the winter (around 11°C), and temperate warmth from mid-June to September (around 24°C). The weather in September is especially pleasant. As early as 1850, the English and Russian upper-classes were already spending winters here to escape their own colder climates. Thanks to the development of a major tourist infrastructure, Nice has since become a leading international tourist centre, drawing visitors year-round.

Despite its status, Nice remains a friendly city and a pleasant place to explore on foot. It offers all the advantages of a much larger city, in an urban environment that has retained a human dimension. In the summer, Nice is overrun with tourists, as is the entire Côte d'Azur. But what saves Nice is its abundance of delightful neighbourhoods, that have benefited from careful urban planning.

True to their reputation, the locals are as friendly as one would expect of the so-called "Southerners" of any country in the northern hemisphere. Furthermore, these French "Southerners" have been greatly influenced by their Mediterranean neighbours.

Nice has a turbulent history, especially because its geographical location places it unavoidably on the route between Italy and France. Around 600 BC, the Greeks established a trading post here. Nikaïa, a town of modest size, served mainly as a military base and was easily defended from a castle atop a hill. The castle was later razed during the reign of Louis XIV.

In the first century BC, the Romans built the Via Julia, a high road which follows the coastline. Cemenelum, on the Cimiez Hill, became the administrative capital of the Roman province of Alpes-Maritimes. The reign of Cemenelum ended with the fall of the Roman Empire in the fifth century, and the Roman town disappeared after it was pillaged by barbarians. Fortunately today, the Cimiez hill has regained some of its former glory, thanks to its museums and attractive parks. Cimiez is also a lovely residential area, very popular with the Niçois.

Comté de Nice, or the county of Nice, belonged to Provence until 1388, when it was annexed to the house of Savoy. In those days, Europe was made up of various duchies, counties and kingdoms. France was a kingdom whose borders changed according to the outcomes of the constant wars that were fought between these entities.

It was not until 1860 that France was able to reclaim the county of Nice once and for all by virtue of the treaty signed on March 24, 1860, by Napoleon III and the King of Piémont-Sardinia. Following this treaty a plebiscite was held in April of the same year, the results of which indicated that 84 per cent of the Niçois were in favour of the county of Nice joining France. Of course, between 1388 and 1860, there were times when Nice did belong to France, for example under Louis XIV, or during the post-Revolution years.

Nice's population of 50,000 in 1860 grew within a century to approximately 400,000 (475,000 including the suburbs), making Nice the fifth-largest city in France after Paris, Marseille, Lyon and Lille. The Niçois and inhabitants of the surrounding area take a certain pride in their region; they consider themselves Niçois first and French second.

Nice enjoys an enviable world-class status. Indeed, the city hosts many national and international conferences. At the end of the year 2000, Nice will be the centre of Europe for several days when it hosts the special summit of the leaders of the European Union, meeting here to discuss the community's eastward expansion, decision-making processes and the future of its institutions.

Nice has also benefited from the location of many important industries in the region. The city is a major cultural hub. There are numerous performance halls (opera, concerts, ballet, theatre, variety shows) and a multitude of museums, most of which do not charge admission.

L'École de Nice and Nouveau Réalisme

At the end of the World War II, international artist Yves Klein started a major artistic wave in Nice which would come to be known as the École de Nice, or the Nice School. He became famous worldwide for creating a colour: a deep blue, which he often juxtaposed with gold in his paintings and sculptures. In the 1950s, he organised "art-happenings", featuring young, beautiful, naked women coated with fresh paint, who danced and slithered on canvasses. Later Klein, together with now well-known Arman and Raysse, created Nouveau Réalisme.

École de Nice (Arman)

Today, artists Ben and César are key figures in the French neo-realism style. Ben, himself an enthusiast of "art happenings,' has mostly become famous for his work with graffiti art. César was known for his work in bronze, and his sculptures made from compressed objects.

L'École de Nice is strongly represented at both the **Museé d'Art Moderne** and the **Musée d'Art Contemporain**, as well as at Château Notre-Dame-des-Fleurs (see "Outskirts of Vence," p 291). This is quite exceptional in itself, since compared to other countries such as the United States, Germany or Italy, contemporary art is for the most part under represented in the museums in France.

Finding Your Way Around

To help you discover Nice, we suggest five walking tours: **Vieux-Nice** ★★★ (see p 264), **Nice-Cimiez** ★★★ (see p 266), **Promenade des Anglais** ★★ (see p 266), **Quartier du Paillon** ★★ (see p 269) and **Quartier du Port** ★ (see p 270).

By Car

You can reach Nice via the **A8** highway, which follows an east-west axis. This autoroute allows you to cross the region, and connects Aix-en-Provence in the west, to Menton, on the Italian border to the east. This is the fastest way to get to Nice. Nice is only 200km(124.3mi) from Aix-en-Provence, and Menton is only 40km (24.9mi) away. The autoroutes charge tolls, which are on the expensive side, as is fuel, for that matter. But you can also get there by the *routes nationales* **N7**, **N98**, and **N202** (from the north) and Route Napoléon (coming from Grasse, in the north-west). The N7 and N98 are very busy in July and August. Traffic is often at a standstill and it can take hours to travel just a few kilometres.

Car Rentals

There are several car rental agencies at the airport and at the SNCF station. Rental rates at the station are usually better because of the packages they offer. This also goes for independent agencies located in the cities and the villages.

By Plane

Nice Côte d'Azur International Airport
☎*04.93.21.30.30*

Air France
☎*08.02.80.28.02*

Air Littoral
☎*08.03.83.48.34*

Helicopters
Héli Air Monaco
☎*04.93.21.34.95*
☎*04.93.21.34.62*

By Ferry

SNCM *Ferryterranée* car ferry (regular service to/from Corsica)
Gare Maritime, Quai du Commerce
☎*04.93.13.66.66*
⇄*04.93.13.66.81*

By Train

The TGV links Paris to Nice in 7hrs, with two departures every day (three, from June to September). There are many daily connections from large cities within France, and regular connections from outside of France.

Train Stations

Gare SNCF
avenue Thiers
Information, sales (direct line)
☎*08.08.36.35.35.35*
Schedules, train info., automated message.
☎*08.36.67.68.69*

Circuit Digne-Nice, Chemins de Fer de Provence
4 bis, Rue Alfred Binet
☎*04.97.03.80.80*

By Bus

National and international connections:

Gare routière de Nice (train station)
5 Boulevard Jean Jaurès
☎*04.93.85.61.81*

Public Transportation

Bus transit maps and schedules are available at the tourist office. You can purchase a tourist pass which entitles you to unlimited access to bus transportation for one, five or seven days.

Bus Masséna
Mon to Fri 7:15am to 7pm, Sat 7:15am to 6pm
Parc Autos Place Masséna
☎*04.93.16.52.10*

Taxis

Central Taxi Riviéra
Main stations
Esplanade Masséna, Promenade des Anglais, Place Garibaldi Gare SNCF and Acropolis, airport
☎*04.93.13.78.78*

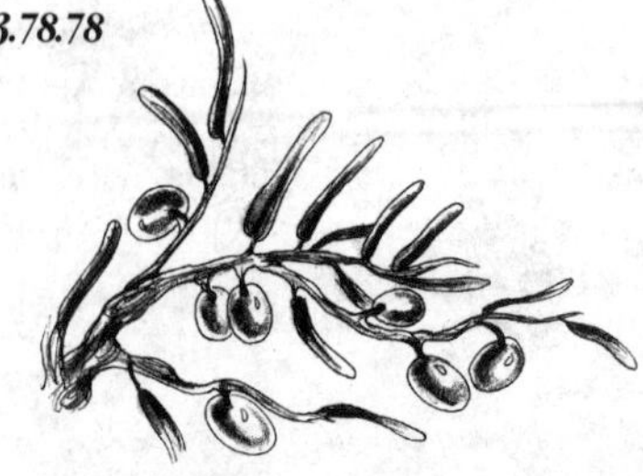

Independent Taxi Companies
Avenue Thiers
☎*04.93.88.25.82*

Transportation for Travellers with Disabilities
2 bis Avenue du Petit Fabron
Mon to Thu 8:30am to 5pm, Fri 8:30am to 3:45pm
☎*04.93.86.39.87*

Hitchhiking

Ridesharing
Ridesharing from Paris
☎*01.42.46.00.66*
Other points of departure
☎*01.47.70.02.01*

Practical Information

Tourist Offices

To obtain information before you leave, write to the **Office de Tourisme et des congrès de Nice** *(mail: B.P. 79, 06302 NICE CEDEX 4, ⇄04.93.92.82.98, www.nice-coteazur.org, otc@nice-coteazur.org).* Include return postage in stamps or international reply coupons.

On Site

Gare SNCF (train station)
mid-Jun to mid-Sep, every day 7:30am to 8pm; Oct to Jun, every day 7:30am to 8pm
Avenue Thiers
☎***04.93.87.07.07***
mid-Jun to mid-Sep, every day 8am to 8pm; Mon to Sat 9am to 6pm in off season
5 Promenade des Anglais
☎***04.92.14.48.00***

Mon to Sat 8am to 8pm; Mon to Sat 9am to 6pm in off season
Nice Ferber (near the airport), Promenade des Anglais
☎***04.93.83.32.64***

Comité Régional du Tourisme
55 Promenade des Anglais
☎***04.93.37.78.78***
crt06@crt-riviera.fr
This organization can provide you with a multitude of useful brochures for travelling in this region, such as camping vacations, youth accommodation, golfing destinations, water sports, active nature adventures, art and nature and adventure experiences.

Centre Régional d'Information Jeunesse de la Côte-d'Azur (regional youth information centre)
Mon to Fri 10am to 7pm
19 Rue Gioffredo
☎***04.93.80.93.93***
⇄***04.93.80.30.33***

Informatique et Multi-Services
11 Avenue Malaussean
☎***04.93.16.12.36***

Emergencies

Police
☎***17***

Commissariat Central de Police
Ville de Nice
One Avenue Maréchal Foch
☎***04.92.17.22.22***
Service Accueil Touristes Etrangers (service for tourists and foreigners)
☎***04.92.17.20.31***

Hôpital St-Roch (24hr hospital)
5 Rue Pierre Devoluy (pedestrian entrance)
☎***04.92.03.33.75***

SOS Médecins
for medical emergencies 24hrs
☎***04.93.85.01.01***

SOS Dentaire
☎***04.93.76.53.53***

SAMU–Centre 15
☎***15***

Urgence Centre 15 S.A.M.U. St. Roch
☎***15***

Children's Emergencies
Hôpital Lenval, 57 Avenue de la Californie
☎***04.92.03.03.03***

24hr Pharmacy
every day 24hrs
7 Rue Masséna
☎***04.93.87.78.94***

Lost and Found
Municipal Police, Cours Saleya
☎***04.93.80.65.50***

Banks

Banks are usually open from 8:30am to 11:45am, and from 1:30pm to 4:30pm, from Monday to Friday. Most have automatic teller machines.

In case of credit card loss or theft:

American Express
☎***01.47.77.72.00***

Visa
☎***01.42.77.11.90***

Mastercard
☎***01.45.67.84.84***

Currency Exchange

American Express
9am to noon and 2pm to 6pm
11 Promenade des Anglais
☎***04.93.16.53.53***

B.P.C.A. Nice Côte d'Azur Airport
8am to 10pm
☎***04.93.21.39.50***

Change Sans Frontières
every day 8am to 8pm, 24hrs in the summer
36 Rue de France
☎***04.93.88.56.07***

Thomas Cook
every day 7:15am to 10:00pm; 8am to 8pm in winter
13 Avenue Thiers
☎***04.93.88.59.99***

Post Office

The postal code in Nice is **06000**.

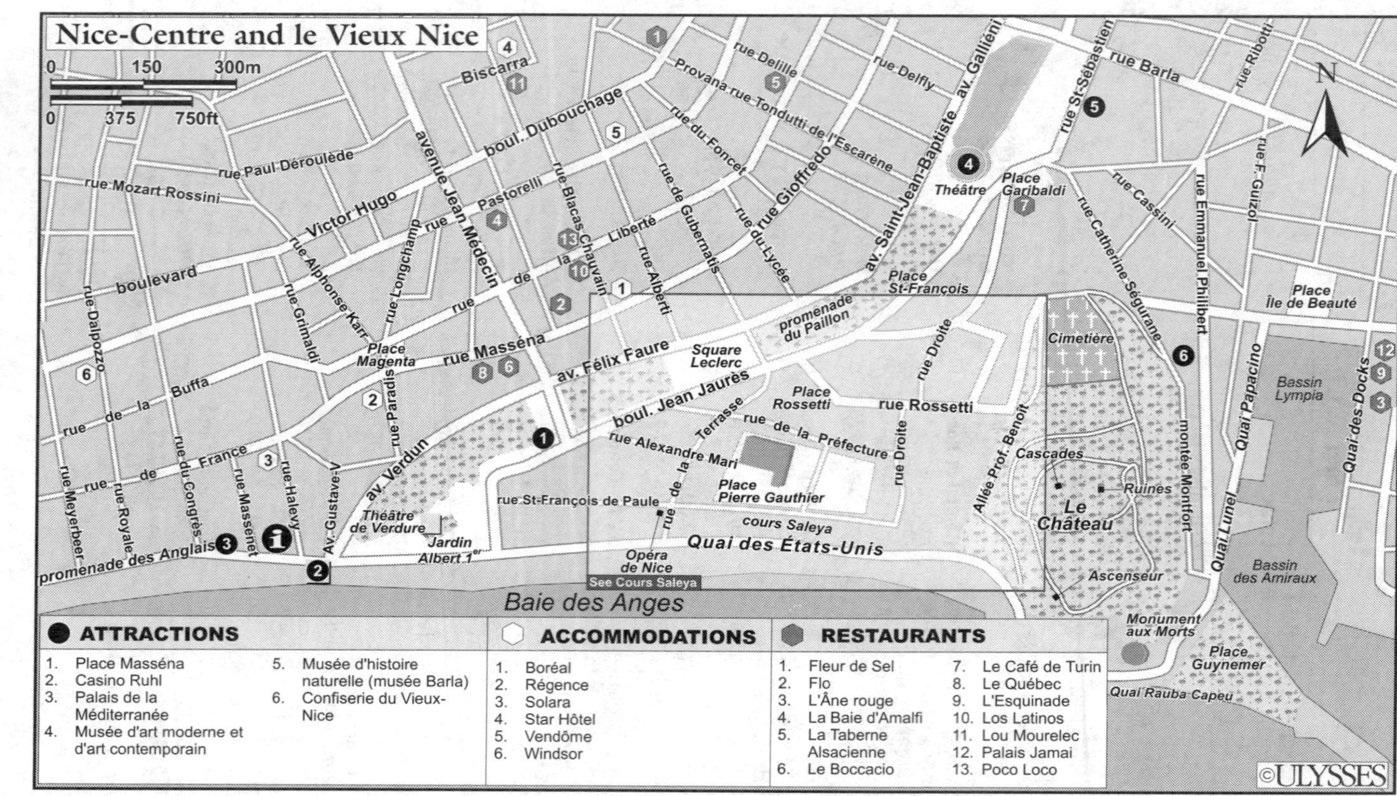

Nice-Centre and le Vieux Nice
0 150 300m
0 375 750ft
N
rue Barla
rue St-Sébastien
rue Riboti
rue F. Guizol
rue Emmanuel Philibert
rue Cassini
rue Catherine Ségurane
montée Montfort
Quai Lunel
Quai Papacino
Quai des Docks
Bassin Lympia
Bassin des Amiraux
Place Île de Beauté
Place Guynemer
Quai Rauba Capeu
Monument aux Morts
Ascenseur
Le Château
Ruines
Cascades
Cimetière
Allée Prof. Benoît
Place Garibaldi
Théâtre
av. Galliéni
av. Saint-Jean-Baptiste
rue Delfly
rue Delille
Provana rue Tondutti de l'Escarène
rue du Foncet
rue Gioffredo
rue du Lycée
rue de Gubernatis
rue Alberti
rue Blacas Chauvain
rue de la Liberté
rue Pastorelli
boul. Dubouchage
Biscarra
boulevard Victor Hugo
avenue Jean Médecin
rue Longchamp
rue Alphonse Karr
rue Grimaldi
rue Paul Déroulède
rue Mozart Rossini
rue Dalpozzo
rue de la Buffa
rue de France
rue Meyerbeer
rue Royale
rue du Congrès
rue Massenet
rue Halevy
Av. Gustave-V
rue Paradis
Place Magenta
rue Masséna
av. Félix Faure
Square Leclerc
promenade du Paillon
Place St-François
boul. Jean Jaurès
rue Droite
Place Rossetti
rue Rossetti
rue de la Préfecture
rue de la Terrasse
rue Alexandre Mari
Place Pierre Gauthier
rue St-François de Paule
cours Saleya
Quai des États-Unis
Opéra de Nice
See Cours Saleya
av. Verdun
Théâtre de Verdure
Jardin Albert 1er
promenade des Anglais
Baie des Anges
ATTRACTIONS
1. Place Masséna
2. Casino Ruhl
3. Palais de la Méditerranée
4. Musée d'art moderne et d'art contemporain
5. Musée d'histoire naturelle (musée Barla)
6. Confiserie du Vieux-Nice
ACCOMMODATIONS
1. Boréal
2. Régence
3. Solara
4. Star Hôtel
5. Vendôme
6. Windsor
RESTAURANTS
1. Fleur de Sel
2. Flo
3. L'Âne rouge
4. La Baie d'Amalfi
5. La Taberne Alsacienne
6. Le Boccacio
7. Le Café de Turin
8. Le Québec
9. L'Esquinade
10. Los Latinos
11. Lou Mourelec
12. Palais Jamai
13. Poco Loco
©ULYSSES

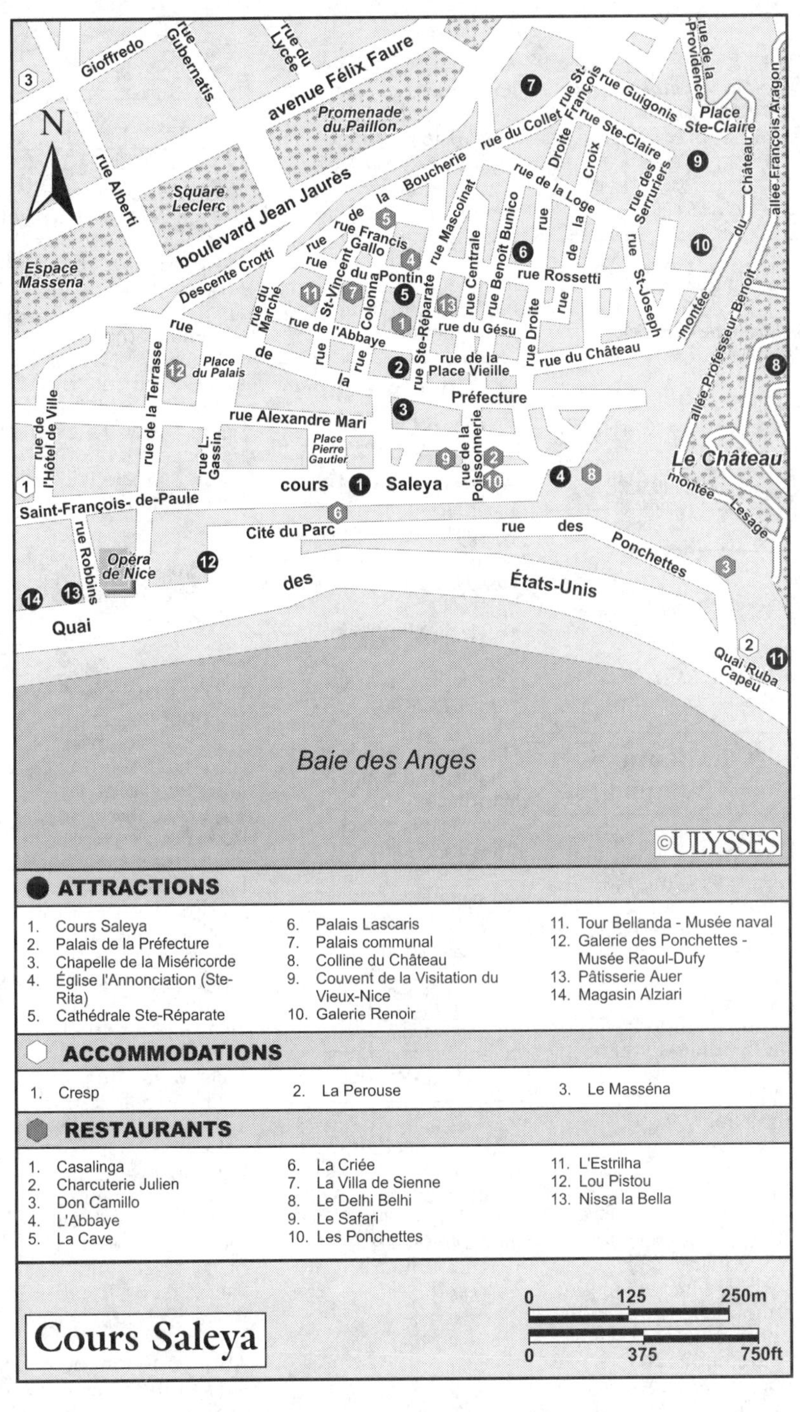
Cours Saleya
Baie des Anges
Le Château
Quai des États-Unis
cours Saleya
boulevard Jean Jaurès
avenue Félix Faure
Promenade du Paillon
Square Leclerc
Espace Massena
Opéra de Nice
Place du Palais
Place Pierre Gautier
Place Ste-Claire
rue de la Préfecture
rue Alexandre Mari
rue des Ponchettes
Cité du Parc
Saint-François-de-Paule
Quai Ruba Capeu
©ULYSSES
ATTRACTIONS
1. Cours Saleya
2. Palais de la Préfecture
3. Chapelle de la Miséricorde
4. Église l'Annonciation (Ste-Rita)
5. Cathédrale Ste-Réparate
6. Palais Lascaris
7. Palais communal
8. Colline du Château
9. Couvent de la Visitation du Vieux-Nice
10. Galerie Renoir
11. Tour Bellanda - Musée naval
12. Galerie des Ponchettes - Musée Raoul-Dufy
13. Pâtisserie Auer
14. Magasin Alziari
ACCOMMODATIONS
1. Cresp
2. La Perouse
3. Le Masséna
RESTAURANTS
1. Casalinga
2. Charcuterie Julien
3. Don Camillo
4. L'Abbaye
5. La Cave
6. La Criée
7. La Villa de Sienne
8. Le Delhi Belhi
9. Le Safari
10. Les Ponchettes
11. L'Estrilha
12. Lou Pistou
13. Nissa la Bella
0 125 250m
0 375 750ft

P. T. T.
Mon to Fri 8am to 7pm, Sat 8am to noon
Main Office – Information:
23 Avenue Thiers
☎04.93.82.65.00

International Press

Maison de la Presse
One Place Masséna;
Gare SNCF;
at airport;
Kiosque du Ruhl (Casino)

Internet

Cybercafé

La Douche
every day from 2pm
34 Cours Saleya
☎04.93.62.81.31
ladouche@wanadoo.fr

Telecommunications

If you want to communicate with the French, a mobile phon28e is indispensable. First, they all have one—many homes have one for each family member. Secondly, unless you're using one yourself, calling a mobile is shockingly expensive. Otherwise, expect to go through many phone cards.

So, if you expect to make many calls, you're better off renting a mobile since even the phone booths seem to be getting scarce. If you arrive near or at the airport, you can rent one at **Ellinas Communications** (*☎04.93.18.88.18, ≠04.93.18.96.18, www.ellinas.com*). The company doesn't have a permanent counter at the airport but will quickly send someone to meet you if you haven't made previous arrangements.

Government Services

Préfecture des Alpes-Maritimes
147, Route de Grenoble, 06286 Nice Cedex 3
☎04.93.72.20.00

Mairie de Nice (town hall)
5 Rue de l'Hôtel de Ville
☎04.97.13.20.00

Chambre de commerce et d'industrie des Alpes-Maritimes
20 Boulevard Carabacel
☎04.93.13.73.00

Car pound
31 Rue Fontaine de la Ville
☎04.93.89.18.08

Exploring

You will need at least two to three days to really see Nice. There are a lot of museums and interesting neighbourhoods to be explored.

Vieux-Nice

Vieux-Nice, the old town, is best visited by foot. If you have a car, leave it in one of the four parking lots in the area, where you pay at the end of the day. Street parking is extremely difficult to find in Nice, in addition to being costly. There are parking meters everywhere, so you will have to fill the meter all day.

The tour begins at the western limit of the Cours Saleya, which is near the seashore.

Le Cours Saleya ★★ is a long public square where, every morning, merchants sell flowers and vegetables. On Mondays, the area becomes an enormous flea market for second-hand goods. On Wednesday and Saturday evenings, the square is taken over by artists and artisans selling their work. You can also stop at one of many bars and restaurants in the area to really get a feel for the action, and there is plenty of it. Of course high prices, but not necessarily quality, are part of the deal, with the possible exception of "La Criée" and "Le Safari" (see "Restaurants" section).

Also located in the square, the **Palais de la Préfecture** is the former residence of the Savoy dynasty rulers and of the kings of Sardinia in the 17th century. The palace's current appearance dates back to 1907, when the main façade was redone. The interior decoration is a tribute to the *belle époque*. The building was completely restored and now serves as a residence for the president of the Conseil Général and the prefect of the Alpes-Maritimes. Also, there is a lovely 16th-century house at 18 Rue de la Préfecture.

At the corner of Place Pierre Gautier you will find the **Chapelle de la Miséricordia** ★★, the work of an 18th-century Piedmontese architect. The arrangement of curves and use of space in the lavishly decorated interior produce a rather spectacular effect.

L'Église de l'Annonciation or Sainte-Rita, one of the oldest churches in Nice, is located at the far east end of the Cours Saleya. Originally, around AD 900, it was the site of a Benedictine priory; in the 17th century, under the authority of L'Ordre des Carmes (the White Friars), it became a baroque-style church.

Leave the Cours Saleya.

Here Vieux-Nice's picturesque alleys abound with artisans' booths, fragrant produce stalls, little restaurants, sweetshops, churches, and art galleries.

Sooner or later you will end up at the **Place Rossetti** where you will find the **Cathédrale Sainte-Réparate**, a baroque-style building, originally built in 1650. Its current appearance is the result of several centuries of construction (the bell-tower was completed only in 1757 and the façade was finished in the 19th century). The cathedral was also restored in 1980.

After visiting the square, an ice cream at Fenocchio's is a must! Their old-fashioned ice cream and sherbets are home-made and are among the best in Nice, if not the best in the world.

Leave the square by Rue Rossetti.

Turn left on Rue Droite, and the **Palais Lascaris** ★★ *(free admission; 10am to noon and 2pm to 6pm, closed Mon and certain holidays)* is only a few metres away. This aristocratic house dates from 1648 but has undergone several transformations over the years. The City of Nice purchased it in 1942 and recreated a noble's household, exhibiting rooms with painted ceilings. There is even a recreation of an 18th-century apothecary shop on the main floor. A grand staircase leads up to apartments that have been furnished and decorated in the manner of the 17th and 18th centuries.

A few metres further, you will find the **Palais Communal** in the Place Saint-François. Today, this square is famous for its fish market.

The **colline du château** ★★, the chateau's hill, is at the far east end of Vieux-Nice. As you go up the hill, you will pass the **Couvent de la Visitation du Vieux Nice** and the **Galerie Renoir**. Go along the edge of the cemetery and take one of the little lanes to the waterfall, the castle ruins (11th century) and finally to the Frédéric-Nietzche terrace at the top. There is a **magnificent view** ★★★ of the city and surrounding area from here.

To go back down, there is an elevator on the waterfront side. At the bottom, you will see the **Tour Bellanda**, a historical monument which houses the **Musée de la Marine** *(15F; summer, Wed to Sun 10am to midnight and 2pm to 7pm; winter until 5pm; ☎04.93.80.47.61)*. Here, you can see a collection of weapons, maritime paintings, and models of sailboats and fishing boats. A little further, on the Quai des États-Unis (the boulevard along the sea), you will find two art galleries. The **Galerie des**

Ponchettes *(Tue to Sun 10am to noon and 2pm to 6pm)* showcases contemporary art exhibitions.

Further along this street you will find the **Opéra de Nice**. The main entrance is in the rear, on Rue St-François-de-Paule. Originally, the Opera was but a small wooden theatre in the Italian style. After falling victim to fire, it was rebuilt in 1885 and was completely renovated in 2000. The theatre is characteristic of the Second-Empire style. Drop in at the **Pâtisserie Auer**, just beside the opera. This family bakery, decorated in the rococo style (an extremely ornamental baroque style), has been around since 1820. A bit further along the street, be sure not to miss the **Magasin Alziari**, a store specializing in olive products. It offers a wide array of different olives and olive oils, including the small Nice olive.

Nice-Cimiez

To get to Cimiez, take Boulevard Caracel, which becomes Boulevard de Cimiez further along. In any case, up is the only way to go since Cimiez is on a hill. Once you reach the top, you will soon see signs for the **Musée National Marc Chagall** ★★ *(30F; summer, Wed to Mon 10am to 6pm; off-season 10am to 5pm; ☎04.93.53.87.20)*, located on Avenue du Docteur Ménard. This museum was built at the heart of a small park filled with flowers, where a charming cafe is open during tourist season. The permanent collection includes the 17 large paintings of the *Message Biblique* by Chagall. There are also many sketches, gouaches, etchings, and lithographs that were donated to the museum after the artist's death in 1985.

Continuing further along Boulevard de Cimiez, you will come to the former Roman site of **Cemenelum**, where the ruins of the public baths and arenas stand. *(Buses number 15, 17, 20 and 22, "Arènes" stop)*. Beside the Arènes, on Avenue Monte Croce, is the **Musée d'Archéologie** *(25F; summer, Tue to Sun 10am to noon and 2pm to 6pm; off-season until 5pm; closed holidays; ☎04.93.81.59.57)*. This museum, inaugurated in 1989, recalls the life and history of the people who lived at Cemenelum and in the Roman province of Alpes-Maritimes. A collection of objects of all kinds is displayed, including ceramics, glass, and money, in a recreation of the situations in which they were used. These articles date as far back as 1100 BC.

The **Musée Matisse** ★★ *(25F; Apr to Sep, Wed to Mon 10am to 6pm; ☎04.93.81.08.08)* stands a few steps from the Roman site. During the 1992 renovation of the original pink, 17th-century Genoese villa, a new, modern-style concrete wing was added—a highly criticised architectural accomplishment. The museum contains Matisse's personal collection of works. The painter lived in Nice from 1917 until his death in 1954. You will see works from every period of the painter's life, from his first works painted in the 1890s to his last, painted in the '50s. Finally, there are several drawings and etchings as well as an entire collection of books illustrated by Matisse.

Musée Franciscain *(free admission; Mon to Sat 10am to noon and 3pm to 6pm; ☎04.93.81.00.04)* is housed in the Cimiez monastery, which dates from the 17th century. This museum recalls the way in which Franciscans in Nice lived from the 13th to 18th centuries. The Gothic church boasts, among other things, three Renaissance reredos created by Bréa.

Promenade des Anglais

The Promenade des Anglais is the place *par excellence* to take long walks while admiring the magnificent sea, with its sweeping colours ranging from deep blue to emerald green. This is where Nice's beaches are located. The public beaches have no admission charge and no sand, only small flat pebbles called *galets* (shingles). Privately-owned beaches, often belonging to hotels, offer lounge chairs or beach mats for rent for about 50F per day. In all, there are 6km (3.7mi) of beaches, of which 4km (2.5mi) are public. The water is surprisingly clean, considering the crowds of bathers.

The area bordering the Promenade des Anglais has an abundance of stores and restaurants. Many of the streets allow only pedestrian access.

The tour begins at Place Masséna and heads west.

Place Masséna is the true heart of Nice. The fountain has a bronze representation of the planets in the solar system and attracts crowds of tourists who come to cool off. The public square is bordered on the north by handsome buildings painted in warm Niçois colours. The major French department store, **Les Galeries Lafayette**, is located here.

Leave the square and take Rue Masséna.

Rue Masséna is Nice's largest pedestrian street, with many shops and restaurants. The restaurants have large patios and offer pleasant meals at reasonable prices, although the quality of the meals is not always outstanding. Once you get to Place Magenta, there are several places that offer delicious ice cream.

Leave Place Magenta and return to Avenue de Verdun towards the seashore.

You will come across the Jardins Albert Ier gardens and their spectacular foliage. A few steps away is the Promenade des Anglais and the departure point of a little tourist train. If you continue west along the promenade, you will pass by the **Casino Ruhl**. It is located in a building featuring very ordinary modern architecture that hasn't aged well. A sad sight made even sadder when one sees the **Palais de la Méditerranée**, a bit further along the promenade, at the corner of Rue des Congrès. Built in 1929, only the exterior walls remain of this Art-Deco building, which used to hold an extravagant casino with a monumental staircase. The Palais has been closed since 1977, and has since been designated as a historical monument; it was supposed to be restored as a conference and recreation centre. However, nothing has been done as of yet.

A few museums can also be found in this part of the city. Farther along the Promenade at number 35, the **Palais Masséna** *(summer, Tue to Sun 10am to noon and 2pm to 6pm; verify by phone; ☎04.93.88.11.34)* is a magnificent villa built around 1900 in the first-empire Italian style. Since it reopened in 2001, it houses a permanent collection focussing on the Napoleonic army. This museum is devoted to regional history and houses a library containing over 10,000 rare books and manuscripts on the ground floor.

Next door is the famous **Hôtel Negresco ★**, which was constructed in 1913 and was designated a historical monument in 1974. The majestically adorned salons and high-class boutiques inside the palace are sights to behold. The Salon Royal is in the shape of an ellipse with a large cupola, and features a Baccarat crystal chandelier. The Negresco is private property and the most luxurious hotel in Nice, receiving celebrities from all over the world, particularly those in show business. Those who have stayed here: Anthony Quinn, The Beatles, Liz Taylor and Richard Burton, Michael Jackson, Phil

Collins and many, many more...

Continue west until Boulevard Gambetta, then head north.

The onion-dome-shaped towers of the **Cathédrale Saint-Nicholas** Russian Orthodox church are unusual sights considering their location. However, the church's construction, at the beginning of this century, was deemed necessary by Nice's large Russian community. The cathedral is a bit out of the tourist area but it is worth visiting. Built in a splendid Russian architectural style, it is definitely a change of scenery.

Return to Promenade des Anglais and head west.

The **Musée des Beaux-Arts** *(25F; summer, Tue to Sun 10am to noon and 2pm to 6pm; ☎04.92.15.28.28)* is on a street just north of the Centre Universitaire Meditérranéen at 33 Avenue des Baumettes. This museum, also known as Musée Chéret, is located in an unusual house that was built in 1876. Its vast European collection includes works from the 17th to the 20th century. The museum offers an overview of the École Française of the 19th-century, from neoclassicism to impressionism and everything in between, with academicism being particularly well-represented. Some artists of note featured here are Van Loo Fragonasd, Boudin, Monet and Sysley. Sculptures by Rodin and Carpeaux are also part of the collection.

Cathédrale Saint-Nicholas

Still farther west is the **Musée International d'Art Naïf Anatole Jakovski** *(25F; Wed to Mon 10am to noon and 2pm to 6pm; ☎04.93.71.78.33)*. This naïve art museum is located in the Château Sainte-Hélène, a turn-of-the-century villa, on Avenue Val-Marie. Visitors can get here by car or by bus (nos. 9, 10 or 12), getting off at the Fabron stop. The museum boasts no less than 600 works representing naïve art from around the world.

If you continue east along Rue Fabron and turn left on Chemin de l'Élysée des Grottes, you will reach a small hill on which lies the **Parc des Miniatures ★** *(47F)*. This amusement park contains hundreds of models built on a scale of 1/25 the actual size and recounts the history of the Côte d'Azur, from prehistory to modern times. The park is set in woodlands, which afford panoramic views of Nice and the Baie des Anges.

Finally, head for the Nice airport, at the city's west entrance, where you can visit the **Parc Floral Phoenix de Nice** *(40F; spring and summer, 9am to 7pm; off season, 9am to 5pm; 405 Promedade des Anglais, ☎04.93.18.03.33; use the underground parking lot)*. This greenhouse, the largest in the world, is home to fish, birds, exotic butterflies and, of course, flowers by the thousands. Various activities and exhibitions are also organized here.

At the entrance to this park, stop to admire the simple and superb architecture of the building which houses the **Musée des Arts Asiatiques ★** *(35F; May to mid-Oct, Wed to Mon 10am to 6pm, low season 5pm; 405 Promenade des Anglais-Arénas, T*04.92.29.37.00)*, designed by Japanese architect Kenzo Tange. The building consists of circles, cubes and pyramids, symbolizing the cosmogony of the Far East, and seems to float on Parc Phoenix's small artificial lake. Inside, magnificent works of Asian art (mainly sculptures) are found on the main floor, most of them from India, Cambodia, China and Japan. The works, borrowed from public and private collections, are gorgeous and show off the different materials they are made of, mainly ceramics and painted, sculpted wood.

You can take an audio-guided tour that brings you to the upper floor, where you can follow an itinerary representing the path to Buddhist enlightenment. The exhibit on the lower level shows a more contemporary side of Asia, but is just as aesthetic and artistic in its presentation of everyday objects. An area devoted to multimedia lends the museum a dynamic and entertaining aspect. A small footbridge leads to a section dedicated to the tea ceremony, where a multitude of different teas are displayed, which are also for sale in the boutique. Be sure to climb up to the roof to appreciate the exterior design, the sky and the adjoining park.

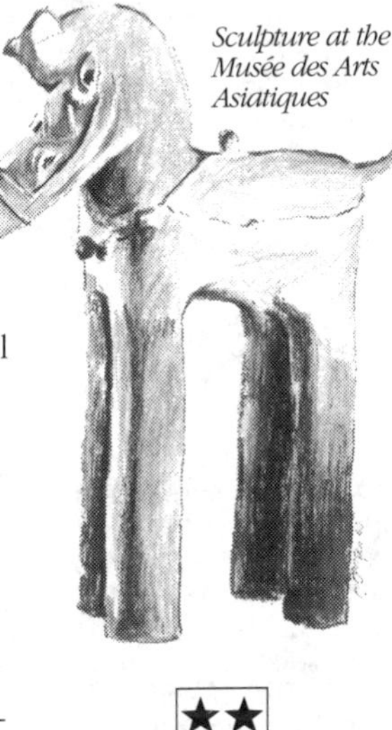

Sculpture at the Musée des Arts Asiatiques

★★

Quartier du Paillon

The Paillon River used to flow into the sea exactly where the Jardins Albert Ier now stand. The banks at the mouth of the river, where the water level was low, were filled in and developed. The parts close to the sea were set up as green spaces, ideal for walks. To get to the Masséna area from the Jardins Albert Ier, cross Place Masséna. The fountains here are very refreshing in the summer.

You will reach the end of Promenade du Paillon, where a row of cultural complexes begins. The first, built of grey Carrare marble, houses the new theatre and the **Musée d'Art Moderne et d'Art Contemporain ★** *(25F; Tue to Mon 10am to 6pm, Fri until 10pm; closed on holidays; ☎04.93.62.61.62)*. The artistic movements of the '60s and '70s, such as neo-realism, pop art, American abstraction, minimalism and, of course, the École de Nice are especially well-represented in this museum's collection. There is even one very beautiful room entirely devoted to Yves Klein. Before leaving the museum, go up to the terraces at the very top, where you can catch a breathtaking view of Nice. The theatre holds 1,100, and the very red interior is the work of designer Jacqueline Morabito. To finish off, you might enjoy a cocktail at the bar between the theatre and the museum.

Across from this complex, on the Boulevard Jean-Jaurès side, you will come to Place Garibaldi.

Continuing your stroll along the Paillon will lead you to the **Musée d'Histoire Naturelle**, also known as **Musée Barla** *(reopening in 2001 with an exhibition on octopi,* *squid, etc.; ☎04.93.55.15.24).* This natural history museum has four galleries, dealing primarily with mineralogy. It also boasts a major natural-sciences library that can be used upon request.

A bit further along the same boulevard stands the **Acropolis**, a monster of a building that was constructed in 1983. It contains a bowling alley, shops, the Cinémathèque, a large exhibition room and an auditorium with 2,500 seats and a stage measuring 1,200m^2.

Finally, the **Palais des Congrès** and its various expostions, with a capacity of 20,000 people, is located on the Paillon. The river flows behind it.

If you want to continue your walk, return toward the Musée Barla and cross the Paillon to reach Boulevard Caracel. Lavish 19th-century buildings of the Nice bourgeoisie line the boulevard. Turn left at Boulevard Dubouchage and continue to Avenue Jean Médecin. Cinemas and the Étoile de Nice shopping centre border this busy shopping street. Farther up the avenue are the train station and the tourist information centre. The train station was built in 1863, in the Louis-XIII style.

Quartier du Port

There are two ways to get to the port. You can take the road along the seashore that follows the castle hill where you will find the **Monument aux Morts** (dedicated to the 4,000 Niçons who did in the war from 1914 to 1918). The other way is via Place Garibaldi to the north, on the other side of the hill. The port hardly has any tourist attractions, with the possible exception of the flea market at Place Guynemer, that is much nicer now after the restoration of the *palais*.

As you leave place Guynemer, heading towards the central area of the port, you will pass by the **Confiserie du Vieux-Nice**, at 14 Quai Papacino. This sweet-shop sells handmade candies flavoured with local fruits and flowers (violets, mimosa and vervain), chocolates and jam, at factory prices. Further along, in the main port area, Place Île-de-Beauté awaits, surrounded by a few beautiful buildings and a church.

In general, be wary of restaurants at the port. The quality leaves a lot to be desired. But there are some wonderful exceptions (see "Restaurants")!

At the eastern end of the port, a piece of land juts out into the sea. Ferry boats destined for Corsica, a French island in the Mediterranean, dock at the end of this point (see p 260).

For lovers of things Prehistoric, the **Musée de Terra Amata** *(25F; Tue to Sun 10am to noon and 2pm to 6pm; ☎04.93.55.59.93)*, is located at 25 Boulevard Carnot, about 500m (5,382ft) from the port. There you can see, among other things, a recreation of an elephant-hunters' camp in Nice as it may have looked 400,000 years ago.

Other Points of Interest

Visiting the **Villa Arson** *(admission fee; summer, Wed to Sun 1pm to 7pm; Oct to May, 1pm to 6pm; ☎04.92.07.73.73)* and its École Nationale d'Arts Décoratifs, is a must for lovers of conceptual contemporary art. Perched on a hill in the northern part of the city, the villa is hard to reach. The Villa Arson, a superb 18th-century residence, now includes a stunning modern building set amidst vast green spaces. Its location affords magnificent views, all the way to the sea. It is a privileged place of creation, research and education in the field of contemporary art.

Right nearby, after making your way east down the hill, is the **Prieuré du Vieux-Logis** *(Wed, Thu, Sat and the first Sun of the month 3pm to 5pm and by appointment for groups; ☎04.93.84.44.74)*. This 16th-century residence boasts the reconstructed interior of a priory from the late Middle Ages.

Outdoor Activities

Nice is a popular spot for water sports, although perhaps a bit too popular. Along the Promenade des Anglais private beaches offer food and refreshment, and equipment rentals such as catamarans, pedal boats, sailboards, waterskis and parasails.

The Promenade des Anglais is also a popular place for taking a stroll or going for a run. However, the public park on the Colline du Château is still the nicest place to take a walk. The view is magnificent and the shade it offers is appreciated on hot summer days.

Accommodations

Nice is a major tourist city, and consequently also has a multitude of hotels to choose from, in a wide range of categories. Unfortunately, the heavy traffic and very limited number of pedestrian streets make it quite difficult to find a truly peaceful hotel. Of course, this is not a problem in exclusive hotels, since they usually have double- or triple-glazed windows as well as air conditioning. We have nevertheless managed to find a few hotels that are sheltered from the noise of the traffic.

Suggestion: Reserving well in advance is strongly recommended, especially during high season, since Nice hosts several international conferences and receives many tourist groups. By booking in advance, you're one step ahead.

Relais International de la Jeunesse Clairvallon
75F/pers. bkfst incl.
½b 140F
26 Avenue Scudéri
☎04.93.81.27.63
The prices are reasonable here. This hotel is located at Cimiez in a park with a swimming pool. To get there, take bus number 15 from the station or Place Masséna and get off at the "Scudéri" stop.

Auberge de Jeunesse de Nice
85F/pers. bkfst incl.
Route forestière du Mont Alban
☎04.93.89.23.64
⇄04.92.04.03.10
It's better to get here early in the morning to secure a space; these go fast thanks to the youth hostel's very reasonable rates and its magnificent hilltop location. To get there, take bus number 17 from the train station, then transfer to the 14 at the "sun bus" station. Take note that reservations are *not* possible.

Vieux Nice

Hôtel Cresp
280F
pb, ≡ in some rooms, K, tv
8 Rue Saint-François-de-Paule
☎04.93.85.91.76
Beside the old opera and a few steps from the sea: the Hôtel Cresp. This hotel is our favourite in the "one-star" category. It offers a family *pension* atmosphere. A large hallway leads to a terrace overlooking the sea. Very good value. Note: credit cards are not accepted.

Hôtel la Pérouse
750F-2,000F, 3,500F for a suite
pb, ≡, ℝ, tv, ≈, ℜ, ⌂, ⊙, tv
11 Quai Rauba-Capeu
☎04.93.62.34.63
⇄04.93.62.59.41
ep@hroy.com
If luxury is what you're looking for, the Hôtel la Pérouse is for you. Although it's just steps from Vieux-Nice, you might not even notice it. The front of the building facing the street is quite small, but the back of the building extends to the hill that overlooks the Baie des Anges. A sublime spot, this is a modern hotel with rustic decor

and a truly charming appeal. There's a large rooftop terrace nestled against the hill, which provides a spectacular panoramic view. There is also a small meeting room that can accommodate 20 people.

Nice-Cimiez

Le Petit Palais
480F-810F
pb or ps, tv, ≡
10 avenue Bieckert
☎04.93.62.19.11
≠04.92.62.53.60
petitpalais@provence-riviera.com
Former residence of Sacha Guitry, Le Petit Palais has the advantage of a superb location with a garden and magnificent views of the sea. As part of the Relais du Silence chain, tranquillity has a special place here. You'll hardly realize you are in a big city. With a welcoming atmosphere, this hotel is very comfortable and even offers parking, which is a rarity in Nice.

La Promenade des Anglais

Hôtel Solara
280F-500F
ps, , ≡, tv, elevator, ⇑
7 Rue de France
☎04.93.88.09.96
≠04.93.88.36.86
The Hôtel Solara, also in the pedestrian zone, is a family business that has been around for a few years, so guests can expect friendly, personalized service. Its 14 rooms are undeniably comfortable and also well soundproofed. The ones on the sixth floor have a pretty terrace looking out over the rooftops of Nice. Good value.

Régence
350F-390F
pb or ps, ≡, tv, elevator
21 Rue Masséna
☎04.93.87.75.08
≠04.93.82.41.31
regence@aol.com
Right in the heart of the pedestrian zone, away from the traffic, you'll find the charming Régence, which is also just 200m (656ft) from the beach. The hotel has an arrangement with the Plage du Galion, so guests get a discount. The Leaõs, wife and husband, will greet you with a smile. Since they took the helm, the hotel's 40 rooms have been undergoing constant renovations. With its tasteful, sober decor, the Régence offers a tranquil atmosphere right in the middle of all the action. If you really want peace and quiet, ask for a room on the fourth floor or on courtyard side.

Hôtel de Florel
370F, suites 890F
pb, ≡, ℝ, ℜ, tv
2 Rue Maccarani
☎04.93.87.26.20
≠04.93.87.71.11
The Hôtel de Florel is a three-star hotel, and therefore somewhat more luxurious. It is close to many of the city's tourist attractions and to the sea.

Hôtel Costa Bella
485F-550F
pb, ≡, tv, ℜ, ≈, P
50 Avenue de la Lanterne, 06200 Nice
☎04.93.18.29.00
≠04.93.83.31.16
www.costa-bella.com
The Hôtel Costa Bella is located in a quiet residential quarter but is just a few minutes from the airport and the sea. Buried in vegetation, the hotel resembles a private villa and promises a pleasant stay. The rooms are comfortable and ideal for catching your breath; from the moment you cross the threshold, time seems to slow down. And there is no reason to leave: you can sprawl out by the pool and, when hungry, dine at their Italian restaurant, the **Nisa Bella** *(\$\$; closed Mon)*. The hotel offers two specialized stays to help you better discover the region: a cultural one, "In the Footsteps of the Painters of Light" (*Sur les pas des peintres de la lumière*), and an invigorating one, "The Footpaths of the Riviera" (*La Côte d'Azur au fil des sentiers*).

Windsor
550F-750F
pb, ≡, ℝ, ≈, ℜ, ⊙, tv
11 Rue Dalpozzo
☎04.93.88.59.35
≠04.93.88.94.57
windsor@webstore.fr
For traditional style, we strongly recommend the Windsor. The hotel is less than 10min from the sea, and close to

pedestrian streets filled with antiques shops and art galleries. There's lots of ambience, beautiful Chinese furniture and several *objets d'art*. Some of the rooms were decorated by local artists, and the results are often spectacular. What gives this hotel its charm is the garden. With a pool, terrace and the sounds of singing birds, it is a small paradise. Very good value. Try to get a room on the garden side. There is pay parking close by.

Negresco
1,750F-2,750F, 3,500F-8,600F for a suite
pb, ≡, ℝ, tv, ℜ
37 Promenade des Anglais, B.P. 379
☎04.93.88.39.51
⇌04.93.88.35.68
And of course we can't forget the famous and illustrious Negresco, the favourite hotel of international celebrities. Sometimes you can see people lining up at the entrance to the hotel, hoping to get an autograph from their favourite star. The hotel, with its pink turret and roof, and little yellow lights, is the most beautiful address on the Promenade des Anglais. Even if you don't spend the night, it is at least worth seeing the interior of this unique building (see detailed description on p 267).

Hotel Negresco

Centre/Gare SNCF

Hôtel du Piémont
140F-270F
s or ps
19 Rue Alsace Lorraine
☎04.93.88.25.15
⇌04.93.16.15.18
Hidden away on a small street a few minutes from the train station is the Hôtel du Piémont. Though anything but fancy, this 30-room hotel has a certain charm, thanks to small details like the tiny window in one of the rooms, which looks out onto a picturesque little yard. In addition, budget travellers will receive a warm welcome from the owner and can even do their own cooking here, since several of the rooms are equipped with kitchenettes.

Hôtel Durante
430F-550F
pb, K 50 F/day, tv
16 Rue Durante
☎04.93.88.84.40
⇌04.93.87.77.76
durante.3soleils@informa.fr
There are many hotels around the station, but they are often noisy. However, we've found a very pleasant one, the Hôtel Durante, on a private street, removed from the noise. Completely renovated and impeccably clean, the rooms look out over the small garden where breakfast is served during tourist season. This hotel is close to the main commercial streets of modern Nice and is only 10min from the sea and Vieux Nice. The new owner extends a warm welcome.

Downtown

Star Hôtel
320F-350F, bkfst 30F
pb, ps, ≡, tv, elevator
14 Rue Biscarra
☎04.93.85.19.03
⇌04.93.13.04.23
Located in an attractive 19th-century building that has been completely restored, the simple Star Hôtel is very clean and friendly. The rooms are pretty, often decorated in rose and brown tones, and also quiet thanks to the double-glazed windows. Guests can enjoy its location in the commercial section in the centre of town, just 400m (1,890 ft) from the beaches of the Baie des Anges, with several

movie theatres nearby and charming little restaurants in the vicinity (see especially the Lou Mourelec restaurant, p 278).

Hôtel Boréal
570F
pb, tv, ≡, ℜ
9 Rue Paul Déroulède
☎04.93.82.36.36
⇌04.93.82.34.94
The Hôtel Boréal, located by the Nice-Étoile shopping centre, has 46 completely renovated, very comfortable rooms. The stores on the pedestrian streets in the "*quartier des musiciens*" (musicians' sector) are right near by and the ocean is about a 10min walk away. Furthermore, guests can use the private Plage Lido for 55F per day, parasol and chaise longue included. Finally, the hotel also has a restaurant with outdoor seating by the street.

Hôtel Vendôme
590F, 770F for a studio with mezzanine
pb, ≡, ℝ, *tv*
26 Rue Pastorelli
☎04.93.62.00.77
⇌04.93.13.40.78
contact@vendome-hotel-nice.com
In a completely different architectural style, is the very well-maintained Hôtel Vendôme. It is 5min from Nice's modern city centre and 15min from the sea. This hotel, an old private villa dating back to the end of the 19th century, has been completely renovated. There is a beautiful central staircase and a lounge with period furnishings. The pastel decor and the owner's warm reception combine to create a friendly and welcoming atmosphere. This old-fashioned hotel has rooms with large terraces on the fifth floor, and a small parking lot. The owner can also recommend some little restaurants nearby. How's that for service!

Hôtel Masséna
790F-990F
pb, tv, ≡, *elevator*
58 Rue Gioffredo
☎04.93.85.49.25
⇌04.93.62.43.27
info@hotel-massena-nice.com
The Hôtel Masséna is a charming, well-established hotel next to the Place Masséna. It has a superb *belle époque* facade. The atmosphere inside is hushed, and the lobby's harmonious coloured frescoes echo the Provençal tones of the 105 guestrooms. The hotel has private parking, which is a huge advantage in a city with as much traffic as Nice. Reserve early and ask for a top-floor room with a large balcony. The rooms are rather small given the price, but they're lovely and tastefully decorated.

Restaurants

Vieux Nice

L'Abbaye
$
Place Rossetti
L'Abbaye is a small *crêperie.* It also serves pasta and Niçois specialties. What makes this place really appealing, though, are its low prices: 59 F for a salad, daily special and dessert. Hard to beat!

Lou Pistou
$
closed Sat and Sun
4 Rue de la Terrasse
☎04.93.62.21.82
Lou Pistou offers Niçois specialities such as *beignets de fleurs de courgettes* (no oil), *pâtes au pistou,* small *farcis* and tripe stew. This small family restaurant has only 24 seats, and the tables are practically on top of each other, creating a very convivial atmosphere. The attentive service is provided by Isabelle, whose husband Michel prepares the food. We discovered a succulent local appetizer here, the *troucha,* an omelet made with garlic, *blette* (a kind of spinach grown in these parts) and parmesan cheese. Furthermore, If you like profiteroles, you'll be in heaven here. Two delicious kinds are available: traditional chocolate or strawberry

Nissarde Cuisine—Upholding the Tradition

The *Union départementale des offices de tourismes et syndicats d'initiative des Alpes-Maritimes Riviera Côte d'Azur* has compiled a list of 24 restaurants in Nice and its surroundings that serve authentic, high quality "*à la nissarde*" cuisine, prepared according to traditional recipes. Six of these establishments are included in the Ulysses guide:

Casalinga
4 Rue de l'Abbaye, Old Nice
☎04.93.80.12.40

Don Camillo
5 Rue des Ponchettes
Old Nice
☎04.93.85.67.95

L'Âne Rouge
7 Quai des Deux Emmanuel
☎04.93.89.49.63

Le Petit Provençal
25 Boulevard de la Madeleine
☎04.92.15.07.92

Le Safari
1 Cours Saleya, Old Nice
☎04.93.80.18.44

Lou Mourelec
15 Rue Biscarra
☎04.93.80.80.11

with red fruit coulis. What sets them apart is that the pastry isn't soft but rather slightly crunchy.

La Villa de Sienne
$-$$
closed Sun at lunch
10 Rue Saint Vincent
☎04.93.80.12.45
One of the finest Italian restaurants in Nice, La Villa de Sienne is located on a little side-street, behind the Cours Saleya, close to the Palais de Justice. You can sit outside on the little terrace, or inside in a simple, rustic atmosphere. The servings are generous. Try the excellent *soupe au pistou*, the *ratatouille*, the *raviolis à la niçoise*, the osso bucco, the rabbit cooked in a wood-burning oven, or one of their many pasta dishes. The service is extremely friendly and very efficient under the watchful eye of the owner.

Nissa La Bella
$-$$
6 Rue Ste-Réparate
At the heart of the old city, on a small street that leads to the Place Rossetti, you can enjoy good Niçoise cuisine at Nissa La Bella. Try the *beignets* (fritters), *farcis* (vegetables stuffed with ground meat) or *pissaladière*. A charming young family runs the restaurant. No matter what the season, this place always has a cozy feel.

Le Casalinga
$$
closed Sun
4 Rue de l'Abbaye
☎/≠04.93.80.12.40
Nestled in the heart of old Nice, this little restaurant is thoroughly enjoyable. With an enthusiastic welcome, Marie-Luce will attend to your every desire with infectous friendliness and an irreplaceable smile. Then there is Gerard who, at his stove, will send your taste buds to seventh heaven with a whole range of typical Nice and Pièmont cuisine. Excess is not their style; they serve simple yet savoury dishes. The *pistou* pasta (vegetables with basil and garlic) is superb. Everything is fresh and homemade, whether it is the zucchini-flower fritters, the ravioli, the Nice *farcis* specialties or the gnocchi. Basically, expect deliciously fresh cuisine in an ambiance you would otherwise only find in your parent's kitchen when they feel like spoiling you!

Le Delhi Belhi
$$
closed last three weeks of July and Sun
22 Rue de la Barillerie
☎04.93.92.51.87
Also in old Nice, this restaurant serves Indian food in a cozy setting reminiscent of an old stable (it has exposed beams). Its candle-lit dining room with chairs strewn about is charming. And just like the owner, you can't escape this charm. So, if you're in the mood for a change of decor or taste...

La Cave
$$-$$$
Rue Francis Gallo
closed Mon
☎04.93.62.48.46
Also in Vieux-Nice, La Cave distinguishes itself with a slightly more sophisticated menu (*scampis à la provençale, fois gras maison, magret de canard...*). It stands at the corner of two narrow, picturesque streets with tables set up along them, making for a very pleasant atmosphere. The interior is equally charming, with its warm, vibrant colours. Unfortunately, the welcome is not up to par with the rest of the establishment. Try experimenting with the different menus offered.

L'Estrilha
$$-$$$
6 Rue St-Vincent
If the terrace of the above restaurant is full and you'd still like to eat outside in this little alleyway, try L'Estrilha just opposite. This establishment is owned and run by former students of the École Hôtelière. Niçoise specialties are served, as well as "*L'amphore de la mer*," a unique dish based on monkfish and mullet.

Cours Saleya

For years, most of the many restaurants on the Cours Saleya had a bad reputation. Today, the situation has improved and the competition has increased between restaurant owners, thus benefiting customers. Nevertheless, you can still end up paying a lot of money for food that is not particularly special, just to enjoy the prime location of these restaurants. Here, we suggest a few good or very good establishments.

Charcuterie Julien
$
8 Place de la Poissonnerie
If you simply want to buy a tasty sandwich to eat on the spot or in the narrow streets of the old town, let yourself be tempted by the Charcuterie Julien, located at the far northeast corner of the Cours Saleya. Just a few blocks further is the Fenocchio ice cream shop. A good, inexpensive lunchtime option.

Les Ponchettes
$-$$
3 Place Charles Félix
If you prefer to sit down to a meal for lunch, head to Les Ponchettes with its immense, sunny terrace located at the eastern corner of the Cours Saleya. Here you can enjoy the spectacle unfolding on the square for the price of an aperitif or a beer. The meals are very generous and we especially recommend the different salad combinations, as well as the fries. Good value for the price.

La Criée
$$-$$$
22 Cours Saleya
☎04.93.85.49.99
La Criée is a good choice in the Cours Saleya, especially because it offers good value. For 125F, you can enjoy the *menu navigateur*, complete with appetizer, entrée and dessert. If you're not in the mood for this, the seafood, oyster and shellfish platters are always tempting. Finally, the service is skilfully orchestrated by the friendly and efficient manager.

Le Safari
$$-$$$
One Cours Saleya
Lastly, Le Safari is a must because of its lovely blue-and-white terrace, its cozy interior, its stylish service and its food. The latter is rather pricey, but the quality makes it worthwhile. Most of the dishes are prepared over a wood fire (inside). The restaurant is one of the "institutions" of the old town. Guests

dine on seafood as well as pasta, pizza and the excellent pork.

If you leave the Cours Saleya heading (east) toward the large rock outcropping, you'll find yourself in the Rue des Ponchettes.

Don Camillo
$$$
closed Sun and Mon
5 Rue des Ponchettes
☎04.93.85.67.95
The Don Camillo falls into a higher category in every respect, including price. Their excellent meals are served in an enlightened upper-class ritzy decor. House specialities include rabbit *porchetta, pithiviers de pigeons,* and ravioli *farcis.* In general, everything here is special. Located in the east end of Vieux-Nice, this restaurant is a favourite with many Niçois. The new chef-owner, Stéphane Viano, guarantees quality, refined cuisine that offers good value for the price.

La Promenade des Anglais

I Gelati di Pinocchio
30 Rue Masséna
If you're in the mood for a snack, you'll have a hard time resisting the homemade Italian ice cream displayed at I Gelati di Pinocchio. If you're thirsty, try a *granita,* a sort of Italian slush made with fruit juice.

Le Québec
$
43 Rue Masséna
☎04.93.87.84.21
⇄04.93.87.30.48
Located on a pedestrian street, Le Québec is a pizzeria that belongs to a chain with two other locations on the same street. They all offer a simple menu made up mainly of pizza, salads and pasta. Because it has lots of tables right on the pedestrian street, this place gets very lively in warm weather.

Le Boccacio
$$-$$$
7 Rue Masséna
☎04.93.87.71.76
⇄04.93.82.09.06
Also on Rue Masséna, Le Boccacio is a more upscale restaurant in a superb *belle-époque* style. It specializes in fish and seafood and serves up four different paellas. Of course, it also has outdoor seating on the street.

Le Chantecler
$$-$$$
37 Promenade des Anglais
☎04.93.88.39.51
If you can't afford to stay at the "modest" hotel Negresco, at least go and eat there. Le Chantecler offers good cuisine at a relatively reasonable price in a very unique setting. In the *"menu plaisir"* the chef combines colours and fresh produce from the Provençal market to create a work of art: soft-boiled eggs on bread with the crusts removed and truffles, crisp Mediterranean prawns with basil, pesto and tartar sauce and fish and meat like bouquets of exquisite flavours. The desserts are also absolutely delicious. It's a change from regular tourist fare. Formal dress.

Quartier du Paillon

There are two noteworthy restaurants on Place Garibaldi, where you'll also find a repertory cinema:

Fleur de Sel
$-$$
closed Sun pm and Mon
10 Boulevard Dubouchage
☎04.93.13.45.45
Not far from Nice-Étoile, Fleur de Sel is a recently-opened restaurant with a lovely, shady, outdoor seating area—right in the heart of Nice. The atmosphere is particularly lively in the evening. The light and innovative regional cuisine is a refined blend of colours, fragrances and flavours that occasionally tend toward the exotic. Not to be missed!

Le Café de Turin
$$
☎04.93.62.29.52
If you're more in the mood for seafood, Le Café de Turin is just the place. For starters, it boasts a prime location in one corner of the square and has recently been expanded. This restaurant is very popular with local residents and is almost always full. You can also stop

by for drinks on the terrace. The perfect place to take in the nonstop action!

Centre

Le Latinos
$
closed Tue
6 Rue Chauvin
Le Latino is a must in this area if you want to grab a small lunch. It features Spanish specialties, as its name suggests. The tapas are especially recommended.

Poco Loco
$-$$
closed Sun at noon
10 Rue Chauvin
To stick with the Latin American theme, head to the Mexican restaurant Poco Loco. Here you can enjoy reasonably-priced fajitas, burritos, tacos, nachos, and *chili con carne.*

Flo
$$
4 Rue Sacha Guitry
☎04.93.13.38.38
Located behind the Galeries Lafayette, Flo is part of the Parisian brasserie chain of the same name. The decor and the value for the money are both very good. Beside steak and grill dishes, seafood platters are the house specialty. After 10pm, there is a more affordable, "*faim de nuit*" (midnight snack) menu for 119F.

Lou Mourelec
$$-$$$
15 Rue Biscarra
☎04.93.80.80.11
To discover Niçoise cuisine, we strongly recommend the Lou Mourelec, a family-run restaurant located right in the middle of town. The parents wait on tables while the son does the cooking, and everything about the familial atmosphere is pleasant, from the warm welcome to the excellent food and the good value for the price. You can come here for lunch (daily specials and à la carte selections) or dinner (a more elaborate menu and à la carte selections) and enjoy dishes like homemade ravioli and gnocchi, tripe and octopus *Niçoise, farcis a la brousse de brebis*, stuffed veal, real stockfish and more.

La Taberne Alsacienne
$$-$$$
49 Rue de l'Hotel-des-Postes
☎04.93.62.24.04
If you like sauerkraut, you'll find a little bit of Alsace at La Taberne Alsacienne. This establishment has a typically Alsatian decor, but also serves Niçoise cuisine in a warm, *heimelig* (cozy) atmosphere.

La Baie d'Amalfi
$$-$$$
closed Mon
9 Rue Gustave Deloye
☎04.93.80.01.21
La Baie d'Amalfi is a large, family style Italian restaurant with a southern environment, located near the Étoile de Nice shopping centre (Avenue Jean Médecin). Both the food and service proved to be quite good. The place is very popular with the locals—always a good sign!

Quartier du Port

Don't waste much time hunting down too many good restaurants in the port district. The quality leaves something to be desired. Nonetheless, we managed to find four restaurants that stand out.

La Zucca Magica
$-$$
4bis Quai Papacino
☎04.93.56.25.27
If you prefer vegetarian cuisine, head to La Zucca Magica by the port (west side). This restaurant is strongly recommended by locals who enjoy vegetarian food.

L'Esquinade
$$-$$$
closed Sat for lunch and Sun
5 Quai des Deux Emmanuels
☎04.93.89.59.36
L'Esquinade serves delicious bouillabaisse, grilled fish and spit-roasted meats, in an old-style stone and wood decor. Marcel and Liliane Béraud, the proprietors, have been offering their patrons a warm welcome, fine cuisine and good value for the money for 40 years. Culinary highlights include lobster ravioli, seafood salad,

bass grilled in its skin on a bed of fennel (a real treat!) and, for dessert, red-fruit soup.

Palais Jamai
$$-$$$
3 Quai des Deux Emmanuels
☎***04.93.89.53.92***
If you crave Moroccan cuisine, let yourself be spoiled at the Palais Jamai, managed by Madame Ben Moulay Ali Alaoui Lalla Charna. Crossing the threshold of this restaurant will make you feel like you're entering Alibaba's cave, with an elegant decor where you can sample the thousand and one flavours of traditional Moroccan cuisine (including *tajines*, lemon chicken, couscous and *méchouis* (roast sheep). We also recommend the Couscous Prince Albert de Monaco.

Âne Rouge
$$$-$$$$
closed Wed
7 Quai des Deux Emmanuels
☎***04.93.89.49.63***
The Âne Rouge takes you into a whole new class of food and prices. You can enjoy local flavours and elaborate menus as well as à la carte selections in the genteel, all-white decor.

Entertainment

For an overview of cultural activities, sporting events and nightlife, buy *l'Officiel des Loisirs* or *La semaine des spectacles*, available at all newsstands.

Bars and Nightclubs

La Civette du Cours
every day 7:30am to 2am
1 Cours Saleya
☎***04.93.80.80.59***
An inviting bar with a young, mixed clientele. The terrace gets sun most of the time and is the perfect spot for a drink at any time of day.

L'ambassade
Wed to Sat 11pm to 5am
18 Rue du Congrès
☎***04.93.88.88.87***
L'ambassade is a hip and very exclusive nightclub (on the basis of both age and dress of the clients). The special events are very popular.

Le Forum
Fri to Sat
45-47 Promenade des Anglais
☎***04.93.96.68.00***
Le Forum is one of the largest and most popular nightspots in Nice. The atmosphere is electric!

Le Ghost
every day 9:30pm to 2:30am
3 Rue Barillerie
☎***04.93.92.93.37***
Le Ghost has been updated, without losing its cosy atmosphere. The DJ guarantees good music every night. There is also a computer that allows guests Internet access.

L'Escalier
every day 9pm to 4am
10 Rue de la terrasse, beside the Opera
☎***04.93.92.64.39***
DJs or rock and jazz groups play in the lively atmosphere of the main room at L'Escalier. The second room, below, has pool tables and a giant T.V. screen. An added bonus: a small pitcher (half litre or one pint) of beer starts at 18F.

Au Pizzaïolo
170F
4 Bis Rue du Pont-Vieux
☎***04.93.62.34.70***
Dinner theatre, Provençale cuisine. Ambience, shows, dancing.

Le Trap's
from 2pm, closed Sun
26 Boulevard Risso
☎***04.93.56.88.77***
A swinging pub with a very casual atmosphere.

Gay and Lesbian Bars

Le Blue Boy
11pm to 5am
closed Mon and Tue from Oct to May
9 Rue Spinetta
☎***04.93.44.68.24***
Two bars on two floors. A truly pleasant ambiance.

L'Ascenseur
6pm to 3am
18 bis, Rue Emmanuel Philibert
☎***04.93.26.35.30***
Gay night club with space to play pool. Warm welcome.

Flowers and Fragrances

People living in Provence and on the Côte d'Azur know how to celebrate. As a result, flowers, fruits and scents have given rise to annual festivals. Here are the best-known.

Menton:
Lemon Festival *(February)*

Mandelieu:
Mimosa Festival *(February)*

Tourrettes-sur-Loup:
Violet Festival *(March)*

Villefranche-sur-Mer:
International Floral Show *(April)*

Cagnes-sur-Mer:
International Floral Exposition *(April)*

Grasse:
Expo-Rose *(May)*

Mougins:
Mougins Flora *(May)*

Monaco:
International Bouquet Competition *(May)*

Grasse:
Jasmine Festival *(August)*

Coursegoules:
Lavender Festival *(August)*

Saint-Paul:
Saint-Paul Floral Festival *(November)*

Antibes:
Exhibition of Flowers and Birds *(November)*

Casinos

Casino Ruhl
1 Promenade des Anglais
☎***04.93.87.95.87***
Gaming room: blackjack, *punto banco*, French and English roulette *(8pm to 4am, Fri and Sat 5pm to 5am, Sun 5pm to 4am)*. Slot-machine room *(10am until dawn)*.

Festivals and Cultural Events

Festival de l'École au Théâtre *(first half of April)*. Théâtre Lino Ventura; information: ☎***04.93.27.37.37***.

Festival de Musique Sacrée *(June)*. Cathédrale Sainte-Réparate and other venues; information ☎04.93.13.20.52.

Carnaval de Nice

Each year, during the second half of February, Nice is transformed. Stands are erected in Place Masséna and along the sea, so people can watch the parades of allegorical floats, cheerful masquerades and cavalcades. Of all of France's carnivals, Nice's stands out for its extravagant costumes and parades. This tradition dates back to the 13th century. Of course, the Church tried many times, most often in vain, to control this flood of excitement. Beginning in 1539, in the middle of the Renaissance, city officials charged designated *abbés des fous* with organising and managing the event. In the 18th century, the Carnaval was celebrated in accordance with very specific rules. There were four celebration locations, for four classes: the nobles (the Dukes of Savoy sometimes joined in with this crowd), the merchants, the artisans, and the fishermen. Later, beginning in 1873, a Festival Committee was set up to give this traditional celebration a new orientation. There was a break between the two world wars, but festivities resumed in 1946 with even greater splendour. Soon Nice will be celebrating the 50th anniversary of this revival.

Shopping

Caves Cambillau
277 Chemin de Saquier, St-Roman de Bellet
☎04.93.29.85.87
Located in the hills behind Nice, the Caves Cambillau offers wine tasting from the Bellet area, some of the best wines in Provence. Try the Clot dou Baile vintage, Provençal for "The Shepherd's Vineyard."

Aux Parfums de Grasse
10 Rue Saint-Gaëtan
☎04.93.85.60.77
A dream shop in the land of fragrances: Aux Parfums de Grasse. A tiny little shop where the air is filled with the scent of 84 perfumes. The miniature bottles at 14F make ideal gifts. For 15F, you can buy large soaps, and as for lavender, well, it comes by the litre.

Bijoux et Sculptures Rémy
32 Rue Droite, in Vieux-Nice
☎04.93.80.62.60
If you have a passion for old bronze jewellery, take a peek at Bijoux et Sculptures Rémy. The jewellery is made using age-old techniques, with only a few produced of each. A bracelet costs about 280F, a necklace, 380F.

Every Monday *(8am to 5pm, except the day before holidays)*, you will marvel at the variety of things for sale in the kiosks of the Cours Saleya in Vieux-Nice. There is a bit of everything, and at a range of prices. Unfortunately, quality is becoming more expensive and harder to find. You have to bargain.

Promenade des Antiquaires
7 Promenade des Anglais
The Promenade des Antiquaires houses no less than 22 shops. You can spend hours rummaging through the Provençal objects that are sold here.

Le Village Ségurane
Rue Antoine Gauthier
Le Village Ségurane, at the port, is another area for second-hand shops. You will find no less than 80 shops of various sizes and quality.

Hôtel des Ventes
50 Rue Gioffredo
☎04.93.85.85.50
If you feel like attending an auction, inquire at the Hôtel des Ventes, as getting "good deals" at public sales in France requires some knowledge of prices. You stand to lose a great deal otherwise...

Loft Galerie
2 Rue Saint-Suaire, at the end of Cours Saleya
☎04.93.85.51.20
To find practically anything you want, visit the Loft Galerie. In an unexpected way, this shop combines everything ranging from retro second-hand goods to contemporary art.

Alziari
14 Rue St-François-de-Paule
☎04.93.85.76.92
You can't leave Nice without buying a bottle of extra-virgin olive oil at Alziari. Not only can you choose from a variety of the best olives in the world, but you can also buy honey in this store, where a welcoming atmosphere is the order of the day. What's more, they recently opened a little restaurant, **La Table Alziari** *(4 Rue François Zanin, ☎04.93.80.34.03)*.

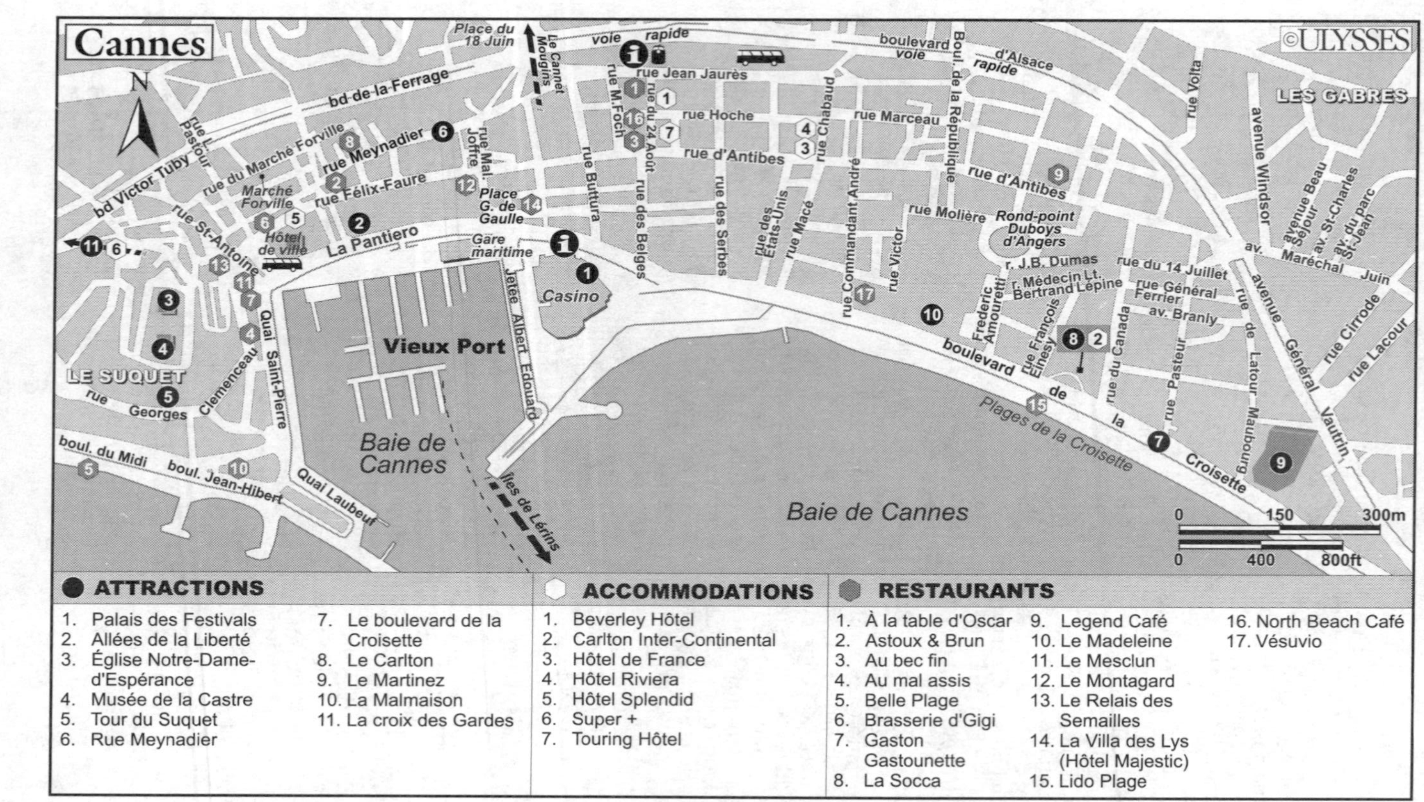
Cannes
©ULYSSES
N
Place du 18 Juin
Le Cannet Mougins
voie rapide
boulevard voie d'Alsace rapide
rue Jean Jaurès
bd de-la-Ferrage
LES GABRES
rue L. Pastour
bd Victor Tuby
rue du Marché Forville
Marché Forville
rue Meynadier
rue Félix-Faure
rue Mal. Joffre
Place G. de Gaulle
rue M.Foch
rue du 24 Août
rue Hoche
rue Buttura
rue des Belges
rue d'Antibes
rue des Serbes
rue des États-Unis
rue Macé
rue Chabaud
rue Marceau
rue Commandant André
rue Victor
Boul. de la République
rue Molière
Rond-point Duboys d'Angers
rue Volta
avenue Windsor
avenue Beau Séjour
av. St-Charles
av. du parc St-Jean
av. Maréchal Juin
r. J.B. Dumas
r. Médecin Lt. Bertrand Lépine
Frederic Amouretti
rue François Einesy
rue du 14 Juillet
rue Général Ferrier
av. Branly
rue du Canada
rue Pasteur
rue de Latour Maubourg
avenue Général Vautrin
rue Cirrode
rue Lacour
rue St-Antoine
Hôtel de ville
La Pantiero
Gare maritime
Casino
Jetée Albert Edouard
Vieux Port
Quai Saint-Pierre
Clemenceau
LE SUQUET
rue Georges
boul. du Midi
boul. Jean-Hibert
Quai Laubeuf
Baie de Cannes
Îles de Lérins
boulevard de la Croisette
Plages de la Croisette
Baie de Cannes
0 150 300m
0 400 800ft
ATTRACTIONS
1. Palais des Festivals
2. Allées de la Liberté
3. Église Notre-Dame-d'Espérance
4. Musée de la Castre
5. Tour du Suquet
6. Rue Meynadier
7. Le boulevard de la Croisette
8. Le Carlton
9. Le Martinez
10. La Malmaison
11. La croix des Gardes
ACCOMMODATIONS
1. Beverley Hôtel
2. Carlton Inter-Continental
3. Hôtel de France
4. Hôtel Riviera
5. Hôtel Splendid
6. Super +
7. Touring Hôtel
RESTAURANTS
1. À la table d'Oscar
2. Astoux & Brun
3. Au bec fin
4. Au mal assis
5. Belle Plage
6. Brasserie d'Gigi
7. Gaston Gastounette
8. La Socca
9. Legend Café
10. Le Madeleine
11. Le Mesclun
12. Le Montagard
13. Le Relais des Semailles
14. La Villa des Lys (Hôtel Majestic)
15. Lido Plage
16. North Beach Café
17. Vésuvio

Between Nice and Cannes

This part of the Côte d'Azur (between Nice and Cannes) evokes not only splendour and opulence but also landscapes whose natural beauty inspires great spirituality as you get farther away from the coast.

However, this region is famous mostly for its great artistic and cultural strength. Above and beyond the fashionable myth, fed by grandiose events—namely the Cannes Film Festival—this area remains an exceptional site where the soul may wander freely between waves of nostalgia and heavenly visions. This is why many artists settled here, leaving behind a rich artistic and cultural heritage.

Unfortunately, there are two sides to every coin. This region, still undeveloped at the turn of the century, experienced rapid urban growth and an enormous wave of construction, and the resulting heavy flow of traffic has become difficult to manage. To meet the need for more roads, the region, department and urban communities had to sacrifice much of their wilderness areas.

New roads have been built, but some of them are congested to the point of being unusable at certain hours in July and August. A prime example is the N98, which is the main link between Nice and Cannes. It is so crowded that bumper-to-bumper traffic inches along for hours under the hot sun.

So don't make a mistake you'll regret. Avoid travelling on the main roads to the beaches during rush hours, which are usually between 10am and 1pm, and between 5pm and 8pm.

This magnificent region abounds in beautiful natural and cultural attractions. The food is excellent. The Côte d'Azur remains a place of great charm and grace with many interesting places to see. Although superficially quite accessible, the "real" Côte d'Azur, only reveals itself to life's true pleasure-seekers, according to the *Comité Régional du Tourisme* in Nice (*55 Promenade des Anglais, ☎04.93.37.78.78, ⇌04.93.86.01.06*).

You may wish to see architectural treasures, take the time to examine the ancient stones, tour through all the museums and discover the many artists on whom this region has left its indelible mark. But the simpler pleasures are also within reach, such as a stopping in a quaint inland village where contact with people is easier and more real, and where nature holds a place of honour.

Finding Your Way Around

By Plane

The closest international airport is in Nice (see p 336). From the airport, a vast transportation network provides access to the city or town of your choice.

By Car

Highway A8 is the fastest route linking Nice to Cannes and is accessible from Nice's airport. If you have time, the N98 follows the river, if not, the N7, part of which has four lanes, is faster. These two roads lead to Cannes via Cagnes-sur-Mer, Antibes and Junales-Pins. There are also exits to the near interior (Cagnes, Vence, Mougins, Grasse, etc.) from these roads.

To get to the backcountry (Digne, ski resorts, the western part of the Mercantour, etc.), follow the national route N202 to Digne and Grenoble, which is accessible from Nice's airport.

Car Rental

Cannes

Avis
(SNCF Station)
☎04.93.39.26.38
⇌04.93.21.44.53

Europcar
Downtown: Palais de Festival
☎04.93.06.26.30
Airport: Aéroport Mandelieu
☎04.93.90.40.60

Bicycle Rental

Cagnes

Motorcycle and Bicycle Rental
3 Rue du Logis
☎04.93.22.55.85

Cannes

Bicycle Rental
5 Rue Allieis, (near the SNCF Station)
☎04.93.39.46.15

By Train

There are many daily connections to the seashore between Nice and Cannes, via St-Laurent-du-Var, Cagnes-sur-Mer and Antibes. During the summer, trains run frequently, ensuring a link between the many seaside resorts. Train stations are also departure points for the network of buses that provide transportation to the interior. For information on train schedules and bus services available from the stations, inquire at the information service at the SNCF stations:

Cagnes
information (sales)
☎***08.36.35.35.35***

Antibes
Avenue Robert-Soleau, Antibes exit, toward Nice, behind the Port Vauban, hotel and train information
☎***08.36.35.35.35***

Cannes
Information and sales (direct line)
☎***08.36.35.35.35***
Schedules (direct line)
☎***08.36.67.68.69***
Traffic
☎***04.93.87.30.00***

To get to **Digne-Les-Bains** *(150km or 93.2mi from Nice)*, there are several daily connections from Nice. This train also serves Colomars-La Manda, Castangniers, Saint-Martin-du-Var, Villars-sur-Var, Puget-Théniers, **Entrevaux** (a very attractive town), Annot, Saint-André-les-Alpes and Barrème. Three daily connections equally guarantee your return trip. *For information, ☎04.93.82.10.17.*

Nostalgic for old trains? Contact the Groupe d'Études pour les Chemins de Fer de la Provence *(GECP, ☎04.93.05.04.82)*. This association operates a steam train from May to September on weekends.

By Bus

A vast network of bus and coach services provides many connections. Inquire at the bus station or tourist office in each city or town. Phone numbers are listed below.

Antibes

Rue de la République, near Place du Général-de-Gaulle
Note that buses for Nice (with a stop at the airport), Cannes, Juan-les-Pins and Cagnes leave from Place du Général-de-Gaulle.

Cannes

Next to the SNCF Station
☎***04.93.39.31.37***
for buses to Grasse, Mougins, Golfe-Juan and Vallauris.

Place de l'Hôtel de Ville
☎***04.93.39.11.39***
to get to Juan-les-Pins, Antibes, Nice, Saint-Raphaël and Vallauris.

City bus: Société des Transports Urbains (city bus service)
Place de l'Hôtel de Ville
☎***04.93.39.11.39***
There are 11 city bus lines.

By Ferry

Ferry from Cannes to the Îles de Lérins

Compagnie Esterel Chanteclair
At the port, next to the Palais des Festivals
☎***04.93.39.11.82***

Practical Information

Tourist Offices

Cagnes-sur-Mer
6 Boulevard du Maréchal-Juin
☎***04.93.20.61.64***
20 Avenue des Oliviers, Cros-de-Cagnes
☎***04.93.07.67.08***

Vence
8 Place du Grand-Jardin
☎***04.93.58.06.38***

Saint-Jeannet
open in summer, Thu to Mon 9:30am to 12:30pm and 3pm to 7pm
in the village centre
☎***04.93.24.73.83***

Saint-Paul-de-Vence
Thu to Tue 10am to noon and 2pm to 6pm
2 Rue Grande
☎***04.93.32.86.95***

Villeneuve-Loubet
Rue de l'Hôtel de Ville
☎***04.93.20.20.09***

Biot
6 Place de la Chapelle
☎***04.93.65.05.85***

Antibes
Mon to Fri 9am to noon and 2pm to 6pm and Sat morning; in summer, every day from 9am to 8pm except Sat morning
11 Place du Général-de-Gaulle
☎***04.92.90.53.00***
⇄***92.90.53.01***

Juan-les-Pins
Avenue Amiral Courbet
☎***04.92.90.52.05***

Suggested Itineraries

Itinerary I: for nature and landscape lovers

From Nice: one day, about 130km (80mi)

Saint-Jeannet *(take the N98, exit at Saint-Laurent-du-Var, then take the D118)*, Vence *(D2210)*, Coursegoules *(D2)*, Gréolières *(D2)*, Gourdon *(D3)*, Bar-sur-Loup *(D2210)*, Tourrettes-sur-Loup, Vence, Saint-Paul-de-Vence *(D2)*, La Colle-sur-Loup, Cagnes-sur-Mer, Nice.

From Cannes: one day, about 130 km (80mi)

Mougins *(via the N285)*, Grasse *(N85)*, Châteauneuf-de-Grasse *(D2085)*, Gourdon *(D3)*, Coursegoules *(D2)*, Vence *(D2)*, Saint-Paul-de-Vence *(D2)*, La Colle-sur-Loup, Haut-de-Cagnes, then take highway A8 to Cannes.

Itinerary II: for art and history lovers

From Nice: one day, about 60km (37mi)

Haut-de-Cagnes *(take the N98, then highway A8; take the exit for Vence, drive about 7km or 4.3mi towards Vence, then take the D36)*, Vence *(D36)*, Saint-Paul-de-Vence *(D2)*, La Colle-sur-Loup *(D2)*, Biot *(via highway A8)*, Antibes *(N98)*, Vallauris *(N7)* and returning to Nice via highway A8.

From Cannes: one day, about 100km (62mi)

Grasse *(N285)*, Gourdon *(via Châteauneuf-de-Grasse D2085 and D3)*, Bar-sur-Loup, Tourrettes-sur-Loup *(D6)*, Vence, Saint-Paul-de-Vence *(D2)*, La Colle-sur-Loup *(D2)*, Haut-de-Cagnes may also be added, before returning to highway A8, in the direction of Cannes.

Itinerary III: for lovers of modern art

From Nice: one day, about 120km (75mi)

Haut-de-Cagnes *(see itinerary II)*, Vence *(take the D2210 towards the Château Notre-Dame-des-Fleurs)*, Saint-Paul-de-Vence *(return to Vence and take the D2)*, La Colle-sur-Loup *(D2)*, Biot *(via highway A8)*, Antibes *(N98)*, Cannes *(N7)*, Mougins *(N285)*, Mouans-Sartoux, then return to Nice via the D32 and the A8.

From Cannes: one day, about 100km (62mi)

Mougins *(N285)*, Mouans-Sartoux, Antibes *(D35)*, Biot *(N98 toward Cagnes-sur-Mer, then the D4)*, La Colle-sur-Loup *(A8, then the D6 toward Saint-Paul)*, Saint-Paul-de-Vence, Vence *(D2 and D2210 toward the Château Notre-Dame-des-Fleurs)*, Haut-de-Cagnes *(return to Vence and take the D36 to the sign)*, return to Cannes via the A8.

Itinerary IV: for families

From Nice: one day, about 50km (31mi)

Haut-de-Cagnes *(see itinerary II)*, Marineland-La Brague *(N98 toward Antibes, near Biot)*, Biot *(D4)*, Antibes *(N98)*, swim at Antibes or Juan-les-Pins, return to Nice *(A8)*.

From Cannes: one day, about 40km (25mi)

Vallauris *(D803)*, Golfe-Juan, Juan-les-Pins, Antibes *(stop at the beach)*, Marineland-La Brague *(about 5km or 3.1mi from Antibes, in the direction of Cagnes-sur-Mer on the N98)*, return via highway A8.

Itinerary V: tour deep into the backcountry

Take in the **Gorges de la Vésubie**, Utelle, Madone d'Utelle, Lantosque, Saint-Martin-Vésubie, Saint-Dalmas, Saint-Sauveur-de-Tinée, Beuil, then descend through the **Gorges du Cians ★★** or via Valberg and the **Gorges de Daluis ★**, ending up in **Entrevaux**.

Vallauris
Avene Georges Clémenceau
☎04.93.63.82.58

Cannes
Bureau de la Place de la Gare
☎04.93.99.79.77
www.cannes-on-line.com
Palais des Festivals, Boulevard de la Croisette
☎04.93.39.24.53
semloimb@palais-festivals-cannes.fr

Mougins
15 Avenue Jean-Charles-Mallet
☎04.93.75.87.67

Grasse
in summer Mon to Sat 9am to 7pm, Sun 9am to noon and 1:30pm to 6pm
Palais de Congrès
☎04.93.36.66.66

Cabris
☎04.93.60.55.63

Entrevaux
at the entrance to the old city, by the drawbridge
☎04.93.05.46.73

Valberg
☎04.93.23.24.25

Isola 2000
☎04.93.23.15.15

Auron
Immeuble la Ruade
☎04.93.23.02.66

Digne-Les-Bains
Le Rond-Point, Place Tampinet
☎04.92.36.62.62

Telecommunications

If you want to communicate with the French, a mobile phone is indispensable. First, they all have one—many homes have one for each family member. Secondly, unless you're using one yourself, calling a mobile is shockingly expensive. Otherwise, expect to go through many phone cards.

So, if you expect to make many calls, you're better off renting a mobile since even the phone booths seem to be getting scarce. If you arrive near or at the airport, you can rent one at ***Ellinas Communications*** *(☎04.93.18.88.18, ≠04.93.18.96.18, www.ellinas.com)*. The company doesn't have a permanent counter at the airport but will quickly send someone to meet you if you haven't made previous arrangements.

Emergencies

Cannes
Central Police Station
15 Avenue de Grasse
☎04.93.39.10.78

Post Office

Cannes
Main Post Office
22 Rue du Bivouac-Napoléon
☎04.93.39.13.16

Exploring

It takes at least a week to properly explore the beautiful natural areas of this region as well as its many cultural points of interest, especially if you wish to take full advantage of the many magnificent hiking opportunities in the interior in summer. In winter and early spring, there is skiing at Isola 2000, Valberg or Auron. All of this is only 90min from Nice.

Organizing a schedule is no easy task, since there are so many towns and magnificent places to see, each with their own cultural and historical richness. It all depends on where you decide to stay. Because distances are so short, you could opt to stay in just one place. Accommodations on the Côte d'Azur are very different from those available inland, and are more expensive. It all depends on your tastes and personal interests.

To help you organize your trip in this region, and to more adequately address your preferences, we propose some itineraries (see box "Suggested Itineraries"). These tours can start from either Nice or Cannes, and concentrate essentially on places offering a particular interest. The best way to do these tours is by car.

Cagnes-sur-Mer

The urban area of Cagnes is divided into three parts: **Le Cros-de-Cagnes**, an old fishing village that has become a tourist town and seaside resort with a water sport centre and an internationally-famous racetrack; **Cagnes-centre**, a new town with no points of interest for tourists and **Haut-de-Cagnes ★★**, the old town on the hill, dominated by its castle. Cagnes was densely populated in the early Middle Ages. In the 6th century, monks from Lérins founded a monastery here. Haut-de-Cagnes was built as protection against the Saracens, and later became a castle-fortress under the protection of one of the Grimaldis. It was later destroyed during Charles Quint's rule.

In 1625, Jean-Henri Grimaldi built a beautiful residence out of the

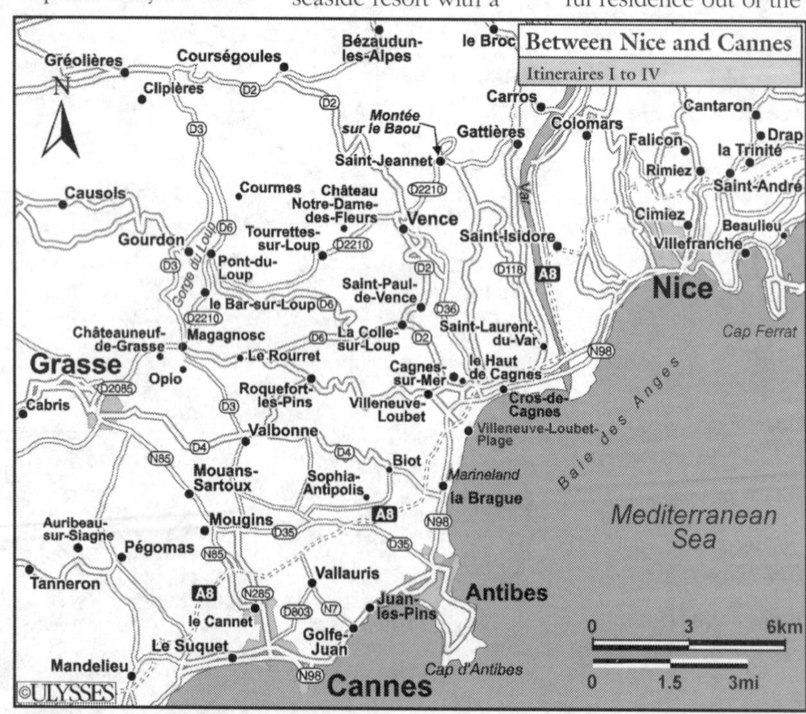

The Camargue is famous for its horses. Traditionally used by herdsmen to watch the bulls, the horses are relatively small, with broad feet and tough hooves that have adapted to the region's spongy ground.
- *Hinous*

the Luberon, ails run along Provence's Colorado, leading to a plendid series oddly-shaped rust-coloured cks and ochre quarries.
- *E. Luider*

The pleasures of strolling amidst the colourful stalls are evident at this fruit and vegetab market, set up in one of Nice's narrow streets. - *Tibor Bognár*

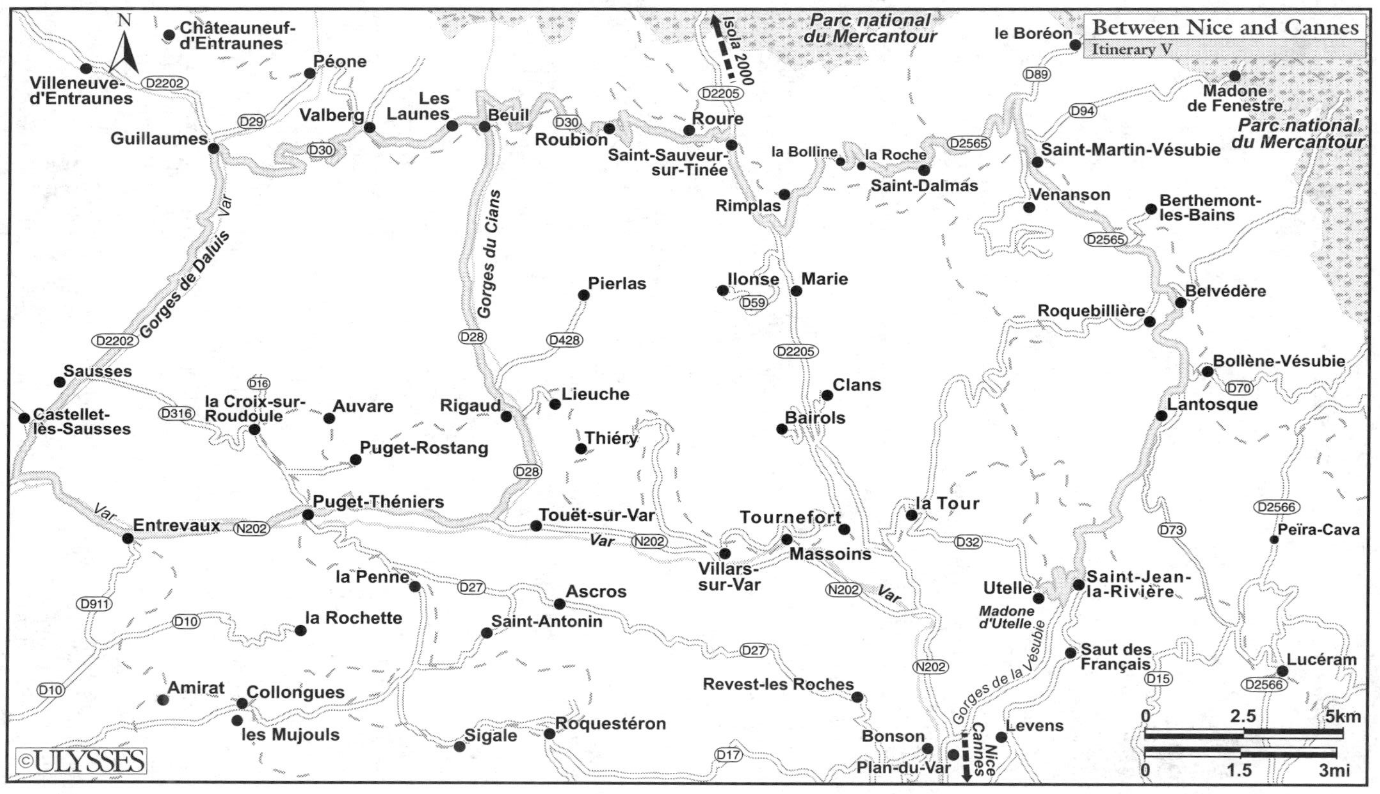
Between Nice and Cannes
Itinerary V
N
Châteauneuf-d'Entraunes
Villeneuve-d'Entraunes
Péone
D2202
D29
Guillaumes
Valberg
D30
Les Launes
Beuil
Roubion
Roure
D2205
Isola 2000
Parc national du Mercantour
le Boréon
D89
D94
Madone de Fenestre
Parc national du Mercantour
Saint-Martin-Vésubie
D2565
la Bolline
la Roche
Saint-Dalmas
Saint-Sauveur-sur-Tinée
Rimplas
Venanson
Berthemont-les-Bains
Var
Gorges de Daluis
Gorges du Cians
Pierlas
Ilonse
D59
Marie
Belvédère
Roquebillière
D2202
D28
D428
D2205
Sausses
D16
Bollène-Vésubie
D70
Clans
Lieuche
Castellet-lès-Sausses
D316
la Croix-sur-Roudoule
Auvare
Rigaud
Lantosque
Bairols
Thiéry
Puget-Rostang
D28
Puget-Théniers
la Tour
Var
Entrevaux
N202
Touët-sur-Var
Tournefort
D2566
Var
N202
D73
Peïra-Cava
D32
Massoins
Villars-sur-Var
la Penne
D27
Ascros
N202
Var
Utelle
Saint-Jean-la-Rivière
D911
Madone d'Utelle
D10
la Rochette
Saint-Antonin
D27
Saut des Français
Lucéram
N202
Gorges de la Vésubie
D15
D2566
Revest-les Roches
Amirat
Collongues
D10
0
2.5
5km
Roquestéron
Levens
Bonson
les Mujouls
Sigale
Nice
Cannes
D17
Plan-du-Var
0
1.5
3mi
©ULYSSES

castle, blending Renaissance and baroque styles.

Today, the castle houses the **Musée de l'Olivier** and the **Musée d'Art Moderne Méditerranéen** ★★ *(admission charge; summer, Wed to Mon 10am to noon and 2:30pm to 6pm; winter, 10am to noon and 2pm to 5pm; ☎04.93.20.87.29)*. The most spectacular area within the castle is without a doubt the indoor courtyard, overlooked by three floors connected by a monumental staircase. A beautiful ceiling with frescos painted in 16th-century post-Raphaelesque style graces the audience hall. The old boudoir is devoted to portraits of the famous singer Suzy Solidor. There are also works from the 1930s to the 1960s by many of Jean-Henri Grimaldi's artist friends, among them Dufy, Cocteau, Kisling and Picabia. This stunning collection features many different styles of contemporary painting. As well, an international art festival is held here every year in the winter, with prizes awarded under the sponsorship of UNESCO.

The Musée de l'Olivier occupies the ground floor and basement. It contains a collection of ancient tools used in the production of olive oil.

Place du Château has several restaurants and is a pleasant spot for cocktails or a light meal. It also houses the **Maison des Artistes**, which holds painting exhibitions featuring various artisitc styles and tastes.

In a small square, below the Forteresse Grimaldi, is the **Chapelle Notre-Dame-de-Protection** ★ *(Wed to Mon 2:30pm to 5pm, until 6pm in summer; closed Fri afternoons)*. The chapel boasts iridescent-coloured frescoes, dating from 1530. They were discovered, somewhat by accident in 1936, by a priest who noticed a fragment of lime on the apse's vault.

Cagnes-sur-Mer is also home to the **Domaine Renoir (Maison de Renoir)** ★★ *(Wed to Mon 10am to noon and 2pm to 5pm; summer until 6pm; closed mid-Oct to mid-Nov; ☎04.93.20.61.07)*, bought in 1907 by the famous impressionist painter. Access is easier from Cagnes-sur-Mer (follow the signs). This is where Renoir spent the last years of his life, after having spent time in Magagnosc, Le Cannet, Villefranche, Cap-d'Ail, Vence, La Turbie, Biot, Antibes and Nice. The spirit of the artist still haunts this enchanting garden where ancient olive and orange trees grow. Inside hang about ten of his paintings, and his studio, which has remained just as it was when inhabited by the artist and his ever-present rocking chair, is open to visitors. *Les Grandes baigneuses*, which the master considered the highest point of his art, was painted here.

Finally, there are many lovely places to walk near Cagnes, for example to Hautes Colettes.

Vence

Vence is a medieval city where art and tradition are sovereign. It is the essence of Provence.

Vence's origins go back to the Roman Empire; "Vintium" was then the heart of a region where pastoral cultures prospered. In the Middle Ages, however, Grasse surpassed Vence because of its superior location. Nevertheless, Vence remained a bishopric until the French Revolution. Alexandre Farnèse, who was later to become the future Pope Paul III, was its bishop for many years.

This city has retained a special charm. Situated on a plateau at an elevation of 325m (1,066ft), the ancient city's narrow streets with its countless shops and bistros, the portals of its medieval fortifications and its fountains make Vence a most attractive place indeed. Gide, Valéry, Soutine, Dufy, Céline, Cocteau, Matisse, Chagall, Carzou, Dubuffet and many more have stayed here. Today, the city enjoys a rich artistic life with its many art galleries, exhibitions and concerts.

A bird's eye view of the city reveals an oval shape inside its medieval walls. Its charming rooftops give the city a special character.

If you are travelling by car, it may be difficult to find parking, especially during peak season. The city can be accessed by one of three doors at the east, south and west. Any of the narrow streets will inevitably lead to Place Clémenceau, where the city hall and the **Cathédrale ★** stand. The nave and aisles of this 11th-century building betray its Romanesque origins. The façade is late-19th century. The cathedral contains a superb mosaic by Chagall entitled *Moïse sauvé des eaux* (Moses saved from the waters).

At the west entrance to the old city, at Place du Frêne, the **Château de Villeneuve–Centre d'Art Moderne et Contemporain ★** *(admission charge; summer, Tue to Sun 10am to noon and 3pm to 7pm; winter 10am to noon and 2pm to 6pm; ☎04.93.58.15.78)* is open to visitors. This entirely renovated museum was formerly the home of the Seigneurs of Villeneuve. Its bright spaces are used for temporary exhibitions. Part of the museum is dedicated to works by artists such as Matisse, Dufy, Chagall, Dubuffet and many others, created during their visits to Vence.

Outskirts of Vence

On the road to St-Jeannet, the **Chapelle du Rosaire,** also called the **Matisse Chapel ★** *(admission charge; Tue to Thu 10:30am to 11:30pm and 2:30 pm. to 5:30pm; closed beginning of Nov to mid-Dec; ☎04.93.58.03.26)* includes an artistic collection which Matisse considered his "masterpiece despite all its imperfections." Completed in 1951, this chapel was a gift from Matisse to the Dominican Sisters who had nursed him back to health during a period of exhaustion. The chapel is designed in a profoundly simple style: "The inner soul is moved all the more by simple colours" (Matisse). The play of light is most fascinating. The cactus motif, symbolizing the tree of life, is repeated throughout the stained-glass windows. Ceramic tiles are brush-painted with ink and then enamelled. The stations of the Cross, which the artist rendered in all their drama and torment, is represented on the white ceramic walls.

On the road to Grasse, follow the signs to **Château-Notre-Dame-des-Fleurs ★★** *(entry fee; Mon to Sat 11am to 7pm; closed Nov; ☎04.93.24.52.00)*. This magnificent castle recently became a foundation under the patronage of the owners of the **Galerie Beaubourg** *(Apr to Sep 11am to 5:30pm)* in Paris. On the way to the castle, visitors walk through a garden of sculptures created, for the most part, by artists from the École de Nice (Klein, Arman, César, Ben, etc.), and by other illustrious sculptors, such as Niki de Saint-Phalle, Stellas, Spoerri and many more. Inside, the huge spaces contain exhibits of a multitude of works by artist friends and protegés of the owners over the past 25 years. In addition to works by the artists represented in the garden, there are works by Vol, Boisrond, Combas, Villeglé, Dado and more. The old Romanesque chapel contains mechanical sculptures by Jean Tinguely, who died in 1992. The stained-glass windows are by Jean-Pierre Raynaud. The entire collection honours French and international Nouveau Realists. It is also possible to buy artworks or souvenirs in the boutique.

Saint-Jeannet

Saint-Jeannet, only 7km (4.3mi) from Vence (or 20km or 12.4mi from Nice), makes for a nice change of scenery. Here you can stroll through a superb ancient town perched upon a famous rock peak, the Baou de Saint-Jeannet. Driving is difficult in this village, so visitors leave their vehicles in the parking lot (with security guards on duty at night) and continue on foot. We recommend you check out the **Place sur le Four**. It can be reached via a narrow passageway behind the church. This square is truly charming and offers a panoramic view encompassing Nice and the sea.

Before leaving the village, make sure you stop at the Roatta bakery, surely one of the best in the region. You can even buy the ingredients for a picnic lunch at the peak of the Baou. The bakery is actually affiliated with Rond-Pont (before heading to the village).

The **peak of the Baou ★★** *(elevation 400m or 1,312ft; duration about 3hrs, return)* can be reached by a path from the village. The Provençal word *Baou*, often used in the region to designate rocky peaks, comes from a word meaning "precipice". The summit is a desert-like area at an elevation of 800m (2,625ft). It offers a magnificent view of the town, the Baou de la Gaude and the sea. It's a bit of a shame that the surrounding hills have undergone so much development over the past few years. The view is nonetheless spectacular, and extends to the hills behind Nice, and even as far as Cap d'Antibes.

There is also a second path leading to the summit, one that will appeal to more athletic types. The steep path goes right up the Baou's sheer side. It remains fairly accessible nevertheless, for it requires no special equipment.

It is hardly surprising that St-Jeannet and its Baou have been a source of inspiration for painters such as Poussin, Carzou and Chagall; nor that it has attracted the likes of Ribemont-Desaignes (one of the founders of the Dada and Surrealist movements), great art collector Tzara and musician Kosma, who left us the unforgettable *Les Feuilles mortes*, interpreted by some of the world's greatest singers.

Today, St-Jeanet has become a lively village with numerous popular cultural events.

Saint-Paul-de-Vence

It's hard to believe that a town like Saint-Paul was once as quiet and "normal" as Saint-Jeannet. Its remarkable beauty makes it a popular stopover for tourists visiting the region. Of course, fame does come at a cost. The best way to appreciate the natural charm of this village at its best is to go in the early morning before the tour coaches arrive, or at the end of the day to admire the sunset.

Despite its "tourist attraction" side, this village has indeed earned its fame. Located on a slightly rocky plateau, its harmonious beauty conquers the heart, especially when seen from the road coming from La Colle-sur-Loup. This is undoubtedly one of the most beautiful villages in the world.

The oldest mention of the town's name dates back to 1016, when the "community" became free of serfdom and feudal taxes. In 1536, François I ordered the construction of ramparts to surround the town. This made it an imposing fortress capable of rivaling Nice, which was becoming more and more powerful. Later, when the town no longer had a strategic role to play,

Saint-Paul shifted to a more pastoral lifestyle, like other medieval cities. *Art de vivre* reigned above all else. Local customs, celebrations, and the Provençal language were guarded like treasures.

From 1925 onwards, some of the most illustrious painters, poets and writers visited or settled here, no doubt entranced by the area's natural beauty.

After the war came the stars of the silver screen, who would stop at the Colombe d'Or, at the entrance to the town. They included Simone Signoret and Yves Montand (Montand would play pétanque in the main square at the entrance), Marcel Carné and Prévert, to name only a few. Tobiasse and Blais also came here to paint.

However, the town wasn't completely taken over by artists and tourists. Today, farmers still represent almost a third of the actual population, which no doubt contributes to Saint-Paul's charm.

The tour begins at the main square.

Rue Grande crosses from one end of town to the other. This strictly pedestrian street is lined with stone buildings dating back to the 16th and 17th centuries, magnificent reminders of the town's former prosperity. Souvenir shops, artisans' workshops and art galleries can be found on the street level.

The street runs through several small squares. One of these contains the magnificent **Grande Fontaine ★★**, which has been photographed thousands of times. The noble **Collégiale ★** (description below), the **Campanelle**, the ancient **Donjon Seigneurial**, which now houses the city hall, the **Chapelle des Pénitents** and the **Tour des Remparts** are also along this street. The cemetery where Chagall is laid to rest is at the other end of town. The tour ends with a stroll along the ramparts, featuring breathtaking views over the hills and sea.

La Collégiale de la Conversion-de-Saint-Paul ★ was built in the 12th century, but has since undergone many transformations. The Romanesque choir is the oldest part of the building. The bell tower was built in 1740. Chapelle Saint-Clément, with its rich blue and white decor, is worth seeing as well. The portrait *Sainte-Catherine d'Alexandrie*, attributed to Tintoret, hangs to the left as you enter.

The **Trésor de l'Église ★**, among the richest and the most beautiful of the Alpes-Maritimes, has a remarkable ciborium.

Several trails begin at the entrance to the town, providing an opportunity for a pleasant stroll over the hills north of the Poste. One of these trails heads west to the wooded estate of the Fondation Maeght.

The **Fondation Maeght ★★★** *(40F, 10F for cameras otherwise they must be checked; summer 10am to 7pm; winter 10am to 12:30pm and 2:30pm to 6pm, ☎04.93.32.81.63)* is a wonderful place; a perfect union of nature, architecture and art. Created in 1964 by art dealers Marguerite and Aimé Maeght, it was inaugurated by André Malraux, the illustrious Minister of Cultural Affaires during the De Gaulle administration. The Maeghts worked closely with Catalonian architect Joseph Luis Sert and their artist friends, who included Miro, Braque, Calder and Chagall.

To reach the museum, visitors must first go through a small park where pine trees and sculptures stand side by side. The large windows allow the exhibition rooms to come together in harmony with the gardens and terraces outside. Domed skylights let in a profusion of natural light.

The gardens contain a collection of statues by Giacometti (not always on exhibit), a labyrinth of sculptures and ceramics designed by Miro, "moving" sculptures by Calder, a Chagall mosaic and stained-glass by Braque, who was the subject of a retrospective in 1994. Finally, a small, modest chapel and several ornamental ponds add a freshness and spiritual dimension to this heavenly place.

Major exhibitions are held here every year. Catalogues, posters and etchings are sold in the pretty little bookstore, recalling the tributes paid in past years to artists such as Dubuffet, Max Ernst, Fernand Léger, Nicolas de Staël and many more. The permanent collection contains works by Bonnard, Kandinsky, Matisse, Hartung, and Klee. Among the more recent works are those by Tapiès, Paul Bury, Tal-Coat and Québec artist Jean-Paul Riopelle.

Various artistic and musical events are held here. Contemporary art enthusiasts and experts can also consult the films, books, magazines and catalogues at the documentation centre. Finally, a small bar-restaurant serves refreshments during the summer.

La Colle-sur-Loup

Only 3km (1.9mi) from Vence, on the road for Villeneuve-Loubet, this village boasts a few wonderful antique shops. Modern-art lovers will also want to check out the Evelyne Canus art gallery. The very dynamic and jolly proprietress is well up on everything going on in the area with regard to modern art. She herself has a small but beautiful and special collection of very modern paintings, sculptures and artist's videos.

Agriculture was once of great importance in La Colle, with its orange trees, olive trees and fragrant roses, the considerable production of which once earned it the title of "Capital of the Fragrant Rose".

Villeneuve-Loubet

Much like Cagnes, Villeneuve-Loubet boasts a superb old village dominated by a medieval château, which Dante referred to in *The Divine Comedy*. Its alleys and stairways wind their way amidst flowered balconies and lovely porches.

Unfortunately, the seaside scenery is marred by a string of camp sites, motels, hotels and restaurants of all kinds. On the other hand, fans of thalassotherapy can take advantage of two such centres at the Marina Baie des Anges.

Those interested in the culinary art and who enjoy eating and cooking should visit the **Musée de l'Art Culinaire** ★ *(10F; Tue to Sun 2pm to 6pm, summer until 7pm; closed public holidays and Nov; Fondation Auguste Escoffier, ☎04.93.20.80.51)*, which attracts gourmets from all over the world, Japan in particular. For a complete change of pace, you can then drop by the **Musée Militaire** *(Tue to Sun 10am to noon and 2pm to 5pm; closed holidays; Place de Verdun, ☎04.92.60.39)*, only a stone's throw away.

Finally, a visit to the **Parc de Vaugrenier**, stretching over 100ha (247 acres) to the ocean, is in order for those who enjoy wooded spaces. The place is also much prized by picnickers.

Biot

Biot has always been famous for its pottery. Already in Roman times, Biot pottery was of particular importance. Bizoto, as Biot was called in the 11th century, had many dark periods in its history, with a succession of wars and dominations, as well as a plague that ravaged the town in the

14th century. At the end of the 15th century, when the town was almost deserted, King René encouraged its repopulation by welcoming Italian families from Impéria, in Italy. Agriculture and the potter's art were revived. But Biot's trials continued and the town was again ravaged by two wars in the 18th century. Since then, Biot has flourished and the population is still growing.

The **church** ★★, rebuilt toward the end of the 15th century, was more or less spared by the two wars that ravaged Biot in the 18th century. The church's patron saint occupies a place of honour over the portal, which dates from 1638. The nave's large columns are those of the former church, which was built by the Templars in 1367. The church boasts two beautiful 15th-century retables, one of which, attributed to Ludovico Brea's studio, represents "kneeling Christendom". The baroque interior dates from the 17th century.

Pottery is an age-old tradition in Biot that has carried on because the area is rich in clay, sand and stones. Up until the early 20th century, Biot's reputation spread far and wide with the exportation of its beautiful earthenware jars. Biot dishes are characterized by their pale-yellow enamel marbled with green and brown. But it seems that the most beautiful pieces ever made in Biot remain the apartment fountains. They stand in testimony to the skill of the artisans of the 18th and 19th centuries. It was during this time that pottery art in Biot was at its height. The fountains speak of a tradition that is not completely lost, even today.

Great blown-glass artists, painters, potters, basket makers, ceramists, and silver and goldsmiths settled in this town. Their works can be admired in the **Musée d'Histoire de Biot** ★★ *(10F; Thu to Sat and Sun 2:30pm to 6:30pm; 9 Rue Saint-Sébastien, enter through the tourism office ☎04.93.65.54.54).*

If you are interested in glassware, the **Ecomusée du Verre** ★ *(8am to 7pm; Chemin des Combes, ☎04.93.65.03.00)*, at the bottom of the village, is open to visitors. This factory employs about 80 people.

Absolutely worth visiting is the **Musée Fernand-Léger** ★★★ *(30F; 10am to 12:30pm and 2pm to 5:30pm, summer until 6pm; ☎04.92.91.50.30).* It is well-indicated before the town, and is 3km (1.9mi) from the seashore. This lovely museum is dedicated to the great French painter Fernand Léger (1881-1955). It was built by his widow in a beautiful park and was expanded in 1989. The museum was architecturally designed to harmonize with the incredible multicoloured ceramics that dominate the facade. Fifty-thousand enamelled tiles, covering an area of 500m² (5,382 sq ft) are mounted at different angles to better reflect the sunlight.

Two floors of the gallery house the painter's works showing the evolution of his art, from his purely impressionist *Portrait de l'oncle,* to his powerful, characteristic cubist style, and finally the painting he was working on shortly before his death. The collection includes *Les Constructeurs* (1950), his greatest work. This painting is an excellent example of the "social realist" style that characterizes his work. Moved by the drama of the two world wars, Léger wanted to express the causes of the people, whom he felt were his equals in a universe of technological advancement.

Antibes

Even though Antibes has traces of civilization that are 3,000 years old, its true history begins with the Greeks. Around the 4th century BC, the Greeks founded Antipolis—

meaning "city in front of"—on this site which served as a supply port between Corsica and Massalia (Marseille). In 43 BC, it became a Roman city and was chosen as the site of great Roman constructions including an arch of triumph, theatre, amphitheatre, forum, aqueducts and thermal baths. Christianity arrived later, with the first bishop settling here in AD 442. Eight centuries of religious administration followed. The city's name was changed to Antiboul and it became an episcopal centre. But the repeated invasions by barbaric peoples and the murderous pillages by the Saracens during this period forced the population to abandon the city in the 9th century. They fled into the interior, only to return one hundred years later.

With the departure of the bishop to Grasse in 1236, Antibes lost much of its status and shifted to a new, more democratic administration. Under the rule of Henri III near the end of the 16th century, Antibes regained some status when the impressive **Fort Carré ★★** , fortification wall and bastions were built. The fort, which can be seen on the way from Nice, was restored in 1967. Henry IV later bought the city from the Grimaldis in 1608 and made of it a royal city and powerful stronghold, taking advantage of its strategic location. Unfortunately, the fortifications were destroyed in 1894.

After 1920, the city began to grow, and many artists, writers and actors came to stay in this spectacular area of the Côte d'Azur. They included Guy de Maupassant, Georges Sand, Mistinguett, Rudolf Valentino, Max Ernst, Picasso, Prévert, Sydney Bechet, Nicolas de Staël, Hans Hartung, Scott Fitzgerald and Julien Greene.

Antibes and Juan-les-Pins have grown together, encompassing Golfe Juan, to form a single urban community called **Antibes-les-Pins** with a population of 80,000. While Antibes is "alive" all year round, Juan-les-Pins is rather deserted during the winter.

Many cultural events are held here in the spring. Antibes hosts a large antique show. During the first two weeks of July, the **Chantier naval Opéra ★★** invites opera enthusiasts for the Musique au coeur festival, where Wilhamina Fernandez, among others, often performs. And of course the Festival International de Jazz, is held here in mid-July.

A tour of Antibes usually begins with a stroll in the old yachting port, where wealthy boat owners show off their luxurious crafts. Follow the ramparts (Quai Rambaud) to the small bay and pretty sandy beach. Nearby is the Marine door leading to the old city, which is divided in two. The high part is the site of the ancient Ligurians, Greek and Roman cities. The lower city is where the market is held. The streets leading towards the sea take you back to the ramparts. A magnificent view of Cap d'Antibes and the seashore extends to Nice, with the Mercantour appearing behind it on the horizon. Only a few steps away sits the Château Grimaldi, an old episcopal residence which now houses the **Musée Picasso ★★★** *(20F; Tue to Sun 10am to 6pm; winter, 10am to noon and 2pm to 6pm; closed on public holidays; ☎04.92.90.54.20)*. This museum owes its existence to a fortunate coincidence by which Picasso met the castle's curator in 1946. He suggested that Picasso set up his studio in the building. The painter spent several months here creating a multitude of works. These, along with others that were either bought or donated, are now on exhibit.

The works here can be grouped into three main themes: mythology, nudes in cubic style, and the every day life of fishers, fish, etc.

Other rooms in the museum display works of Fernand Léger, Modigliani, Picabia, Magnelli, Ernst and Hartung. The most spectacular room is the one dedicated to Nicolas de Staël. It contains, among others, his enormous painting entitled *Le Grand Concert*, de Staël's final work prior to taking his own life in Antibes in the mid-1950s.

The terrace facing the sea features sculptures by Calder, Miro, Arman, and Patrick and Anne Poirier, who created a sculpture incorporating tons of white marble and Roman remnants.

Finally, ceramic lovers can admire 150 ceramic works created by Vallauris potters between 1947 and 1949.

Next to the museum stands the **Cathédrale ★**, which contains pieces representing very different periods and styles. The choir and the transept date back to 1125, but the recently restored façade was built in 1751.

A market is held every morning near the Cours Masséna. Vegetables, fruit and fish rival each other in flavour and freshness. The nearby streets constitute the lower city.

The picturesque Rue du Bas and Rue du Haut-Castelet both lead to Placette du Safranier. This small square is a special place. It is the heart of a tiny, almost independent community whose city hall is located in a little restaurant.

Near Square Albert I, Bastion Saint-André houses the **Musée d'Histoire et d'Archéologie ★** *(6F; Tue to Sun 9am to noon and 2pm and 6pm; winter until 6pm, closed Nov; ☎04.92.90.54.35)*. It contains artifacts from ancient Antipolis, compiled during various underwater searches and land digs.

Walk along the beaches to the cape's entrance.

Around Antibes

Marineland *(150F; summer 10am to midnight, winter until 8pm, two or three shows from 2:30pm, Jul and Aug evening shows at 9:30pm; ☎04.93.33.49.49)* is around 4km (2.5mi) from Antibes, towards Cagnes-sur-Mer on the N7 (near Biot). The aquarium and shows featuring dolphins, sea lions and seals will delight children young and old.

The area around Marineland is like a huge theme park because, next to it, there are several activities for children. **Adventure Golf** *(45F; summer Wed to Sat and Sun 2pm to midnight)* is an enchanting spot for miniature golf enthusiasts because of its exotic setting. **Aquasplash** *(85F; mid-Jun to mid-Sep 10am to 7pm; ☎04.93.33.49.49)*, is a refreshing (though expensive) spot with its water slides and a wave pool. **La Jungle des Papillons** *(45F; 10am to sunset; ☎04.93.33.49.49)* is a unique place where hundreds of butterflies fly freely. **La Petite Ferme** *(10am to 6pm)*, with its farm animals, is always fun for children.

Cap d'Antibes

Although Cap d'Antibes is really only the southern tip of the peninsula, the name is often used to refer to the entire area, whose highest elevation is 73m (240ft). You can go all the way around it by following the beach, or walk through narrow streets to reach the tip. Famous for its sumptuous estates, the cape is also the site of the Hôtel du Cap Eden Roc, considered one of the most luxurious establishments in the world. All along the cape, there are numerous inlets with little ports and velvet beaches. The beaches of the Garoupe are very popular. Beyond these beaches the landscape becomes more wild. The rocks provide excellent opportunities for fishing and scuba-diving. A walk along the **Sentier Tire-poil ★★**, a pretty trail, is a wonderful way to enjoy all this wild beauty.

The top of **Phare de la Garoupe** *(summer 2:30pm to 6pm; winter 3pm to 5pm; 30min guided tour; ☎04.93.61.57.63)*, a lighthouse, offers a wonderful vantage point from which to admire the view of the seashore spanning from l'Estérel to the Italian Alps. On a clear day, you can even see Corsica in the distance. Next to the lighthouse stands a small chapel from which Notre-Dame de Bon-Port watches over sailors.

Those interested in Napoleon will want to visit the **Musée Naval et Napoléonien** *(20F, Mon to Sat 9:30am to noon and 2:15pm to 6pm; closed Sat pm and Oct; avenue J.F. Kennedy, ☎04.93.61.45.32)*. This museum recounts, among other things, the Emperor's epic, after his escape from Elba.

Cap d'Antibes owes its fame mostly to the many celebrities from all spheres who have lived or visited the area. They include wealthy shipping tycoons, royalty, politicians and writers, not to mention those who have stayed at the Hôtel du Cap Eden-Roc. This hotel is very popular with film stars during the Cannes Film Festival.

The cape also has a botanical garden, the **Jardin Thuret** *(free admission; Mon to Fri 8am to 6:00pm; 1 Boulevard du Cap, ☎04.93.67.88.66)*. It covers an area of 7ha (17.3 acres) and contains a vast number of plant species, including 10 very rare ones.

Finally, if you're curious to see what's hidden inside some of the Cap d'Antibes sumptuous estates, stop in at the **Villa Eilen-Roc** *(Wed 1:30pm to 5:30pm; Bd du Cap, ☎04.92.90.50.00)*. This villa, with its palatial facade, was built by Charles Garnier, architect of the Opéra de Paris. Among other things, it contains a bathroom featuring a green marble bath.

Juan-les-Pins

Although it's hard to imagine, Juan-les-Pins was covered by a huge pine forest before 1880.

Unfortunately, those days are gone. The history of Juan-les-Pins is best summed up as a series of miscalculated real estate speculations, but you can be the judge.

It was only from 1927, however, that Juan became a real success, thanks to the construction of a huge luxury hotel, the Provençal. Juan thus became a summer seaside resort, not only a winter resort, luring the upper crust of international celebrities, royalty, etc.—in a word, "money"!

Jazz then appeared, attracting luminaries such as Armstrong, Count Basie, etc. After the war, Edith Piaf and Juliette Greco became regular visitors. It was a non-stop party!

Today, the **Festival International de Jazz à Antibes-Juan-les-Pins** *(Pinède Gould, ☎04.92.90.53.00)* remains Juan's main point of interest. Each year since 1960, the stars of the jazz world have been coming here to perform during the second half of July. For several years now, the Festival's most famous performer has been Keith Jarrett.

Unfortunately, Juan has little to offer tourists besides the festival. There is a spirited nightlife during the summer months, but in the winter the scene is quite dead.

Vallauris

Situated between the sea and mountains, Vallauris-Golfe-Juan is actually made up of two communities, with a total population of 25,000. Vallauris is a pottery town, Golfe-Juan, a seaside resort.

Vallauris' past is similar to that of Biot. Devastated by the plague and one war after another, the village was repopulated by Italian families from Genoa, who brought with them their pottery skills. Even today, pottery is the primary craft and commercial activity in Vallauris. The town's streets are lined with pottery shops which, unfortunately, are not always in the best taste.

Between 1946 and 1955, Picasso took up residence in Vallauris. In 1952, upon the community's request, he created an enormous fresco entitled *Guerre et paix*, which can be admired in the **Musée National Picasso** ★ *(17F; Wed to Mon 10am to 6:30pm, off-season 10am to noon and 2pm to 5pm; closed on public holidays; Place de la Libération, ☎04.93.64.16.05)*. This museum has found a home in a Renaissance-style castle, whose 12th-century **Chapelle Sainte-Anne** houses the Picasso fresco. Otherwise, the museum is dedicated mostly to pottery, including some produced by the great master himself. Every two years, the museum hosts the *Biennale Internationale de Céramique d'Art*.

At the same place, you can visit the **Musée de la Céramique** *(25F; Wed to Mon 10am to 6:30pm, off-season 10am to noon and 2pm to 5pm; Place de la Libération; ☎04.93.64.16.05)*. Contemporary ceramics that placed in the International Biennial Exhibition are on the main floor, while canvasses by renowned abstract artist Alberto Magnelli hang on the second floor. There is also a collection of Art Nouveau works and Art Deco ceramics.

Another small **museum** here devotes itself to **pottery** ★ *(15F; Mon to Sat 9am to 6pm, Sun 2pm to 6pm, summer until 7pm; Rue Sicard, ☎04.93.64.66.51)*, featuring pottery-making techniques in a reconstructed turn-of-the-century potter's studio.

Cannes

Cannes, world famous for its Festival International du Film, devotes all of its energy to being the second largest tourist, commercial, conference and tradeshow city in France. Over 400 events are held here each year. Top television, cinema, recording, real estate and computer professionals from all over the world come here to meet.

Cannes' real history began when the Roman colony *canoïs* was established in AD 154. A succession of invasions and wars followed, testimony to the attractiveness of this splendid site. The territory was coveted in turn by the Saracens, the German Empire under Charles Quint, the Spanish, the Duke of Savoy Victor-Amédée II and once again by the German imperial troops in the 18th century.

The tides turned for Cannes in 1834 with the arrival of an English aristocrat, Lord Brougham. He commissioned the construction of a sumptuous winter residence, a move which was later imitated by the international aristocracy. There was a proliferation of homes and luxury villas in Cannes around this time. But it wasn't until after 1853 that Cannes really took off, with the arrival of the railroad, followed by the construction of a yachting harbour, hotels and creation of the illustrious Croisette. Cannes had already established itself as *the* place to go in winter. And so, rich Northern-Europeans, especially the English, French and Russians, came each winter to take advantage of the healthy, mild climate.

Cannes' economy has been based mainly on tourism since the 1930's, when the city also became a summer tourist spot. Since the end of World War II, Cannes has been transformed by real estate developers who have built thousands of apartment buildings, all for the benefit of those who come seeking a calm and pleasant place to stay. Fortunately, many luxurious residences, often of rather extraordinary design, have resisted the assault of time, thus keeping alive a certain nostalgia in this part of the Côte d'Azur. Every year since 1939, this nostalgia is perpetuated with the Festival de Cannes, where the stars and starlets create a commotion by their appearance or absence thereof on the famous Croisette.

It is extremely difficult to find a place to park on the street. The underground parking lot of the **Palais des Festivals**, located at one end of the Croisette, offers a convenient alternative. This building, whose architecture in no way resembles the palaces of old, has sparked many comments (usually negative) since its inauguration in 1982. In any case, it is very practical and well-equipped to accommodate the conferences and many events that are held there.

West of the Palais, the old port harbours many pleasure yachts. The boat service to the Îles de Lérins leaves from here. Across the street, among the ancient plane trees, lie the **Allées de la Liberté**, the site of the Hôtel de Ville. The old part of the city can be reached from here by going up Rue de Montchevalier.

The old city, the cradle of Cannes, with its medieval buildings overshadowing the old port, is also known as **Suquet**. The square at the top of the hill is surrounded by the ruins of the old 14th-century castle and its ramparts. **Église Notre-Dame-d'Espérance**, a church built in 1627, is an example of late Gothic Provençal architecture.

The square offers a captivating panoramic view of the city, the port, l'Estérel and the Îles de Lérins. The **Nuits Musicales de Suquet** *(program information and reservations: ☎04.92.98.62.77)* is held here every year in July, featuring many concerts and classical music recitals.

Inside the castle, the **Musée de la Castre** *(10F; Wed to Mon 10am to noon and 2pm to 5pm, summer 3pm to 7pm; closed Jan; ☎04.93.38.55.26)* offers ethnological and archaeological collections from five continents. Paintings from Cannes and Provence are also represented, with 19th-century works on exhibit. The **Tour du Suquet**, towers 22m (72.2ft) above the yard, and the entire area. Construction of the tower began in 1070 and was completed in 1385. There is a terrace at the top of the tower and viewpoint indicator that points to some of the region's interesting sites.

To go back downtown, take Rue Saint-Antoine. This picturesque street is lined with flowery old houses and little restaurants. The old city streets often carry the names of families who lived in the area, or recall the trades that were practised there long ago.

At the foot of Suquet, behind the old port, is the Forville market, where vegetables, fruits and fresh fish are sold. The commercial area begins a little further along, where the street is lined with a multitude of shops of all kinds. Some of these are pedestrian streets, such as the **Rue Meynadier ★★**. This narrow street has a special ambience and an intimate atmosphere despite the bustling crowds. There are many narrow streets and vaulted passages to discover. Well-renowned specialty shops offer all the delicacies needed to put together an exquisite picnic lunch. For shopping of any kind, Rue d'Antibes is a must because it has the most shops.

Boulevard de la Croisette ★ professes to be the quintessence of luxury with its exorbitantly priced hotels and boutiques. People parade along the Promenade on the beach, often in a great show of prestige. The name Croisette comes from a small monument with a cross on the site where the Casino Palm Beach has stood since 1929, at the end of the bay.

With the construction of the boulevard in the second half of the 19th century, Cannes officially entered in competition with Nice, which already had its beautiful Promenade des Anglais.

La Croisette houses several palaces that date back to the end of the last century or the beginning of the 20th century. They include the **Carlton**, with its *belle époque* architecture, and the **Martinez**, with its Art Deco interior. At Number 47, **La Malmaison** was formerly a pavilion of the Grand Hôtel, a colossus built in 1864. Repurchased by the city, it hosts large exhibitions each year, dedicated to modern and contemporary painters and sculptors.

Visitors can end their tour of the city with a stroll of its oldest residential district, the **Croix-des-Gardes** hill, located in the northwest part of Cannes. This is where Lord Brougham, an Englishman, decided to settle in 1835, having a magnificent villa built here. Emulated by many of his compatriots, this led to the birth of this district, which was nicknamed the Quartier des Anglais (English quarter). The view of the bay of Cannes and the Esterel from its summit is magnificent.

In the same vein, the Quartier de la Californie (California quarter), east of the city, boasts numerous luxury villas. The Russian colony chose this area in which to settle in the 19th century.

Les Îles de Lérins

Buy tickets at the Gare Maritime (on the west side of the Palais des Festivals) for the two magnificent islands that you see when you stroll along the Baie de Cannes. In summer, there are departures almost every hour and sometimes even more often depending on the

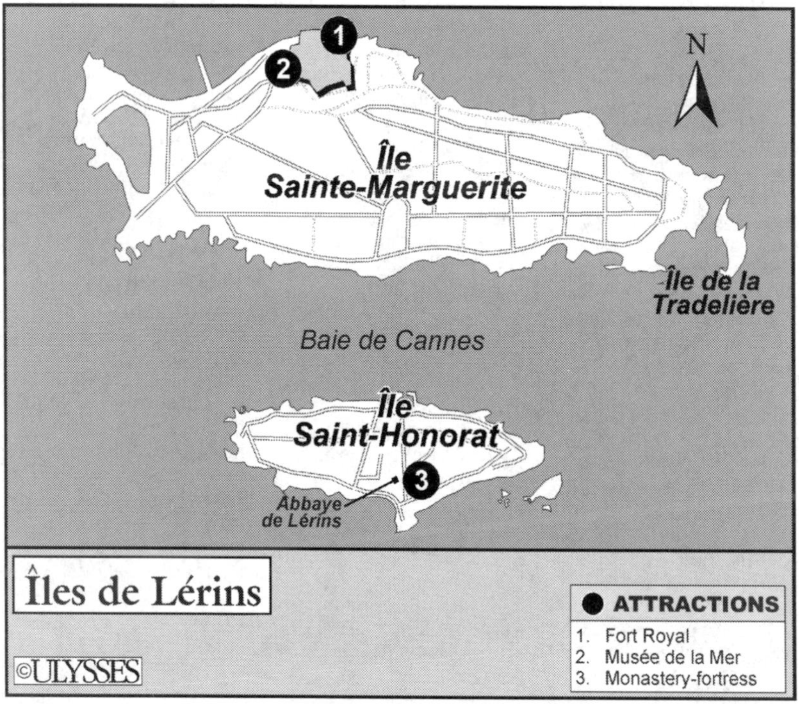

Île Sainte-Marguerite
Île de la Tradelière
Baie de Cannes
Île Saint-Honorat
Abbaye de Lérins
N

Îles de Lérins

ATTRACTIONS

1. Fort Royal
2. Musée de la Mer
3. Monastery-fortress

flow of tourists *(return fare 40F for Sainte-Marguerite or Saint-Honorat and 60F for both islands, keep your tickets! ☎04.93.39.11.82, ≠04.92.98.80.32; for a tour of the ocean floor, ☎04.93.38.66.33)*. On the islands you can visit historic sites, stroll through the Alep pine and eucalyptus forest, and swim and dive from the top of rocks.

The Îles de Lérins were already well known to navigators in Antiquity, as confirmed by archaeological evidence. Today these islands continue to attract pleasure craft, many of which drop anchor here.

Sainte-Marguerite

The island was originally called Lero. The Ligurians, the Greeks and the Romans each occupied it in turn, as the artifacts on exhibit in **Fort Royal** *(10F; Wed to Mon 10:30am to 12:15pm and 2:15pm to 5:30pm, until 4:30pm in winter; ☎04.93.38.55.26)* show. The fort, built under Richelieu, was used as a prison from 1685 until the early 20th century. Its most illustrious occupant was without a doubt the "Masque de Fer", who was imprisoned here in 1687. The search for his identity has given rise to all sorts of theories, including one claiming that he was Louis XIV's eldest brother. The mystery has yet to be resolved. Visitors can see the cell where he was held. Other cells are decorated with mural frescoes painted by French artist Jean Le Gac in the early 1990s. The painter created the collection after being inspired by the site.

Now restored and reorganized, the fort houses a diving centre, a centre for dance and artistic expression for children and the **Musée de la Mer** *(10F; Wed to Mon 10:30am to 12:15pm and 2:15pm to 4:30pm, until 6:30pm in summer; ☎04.93.43.18.17)*, which occupies the oldest part of the building. This museum contains artifacts collected on archaeological digs on the island, and objects recuperated from ships sunken off the island's shores. An interesting note: some of these collections are presented in the ancient Roman cisterns that used to hold the island's drinking water. Temporary photography exhibits are also showcased here.

A tour of the island could not be complete without a long stroll on its walking paths. The area is protected and there is a wide variety of plant species to discover.

Saint-Honorat

This island is smaller than Sainte-Marguerite, and belongs to the Congrégation Cistercienne de Sénaque, a community of monks who have maintained a very active monastery here since 1869. They strictly observe the 72 monastic rules established by Saint-Benoît, which dictate that spiritual and physical life must be balanced. Accordingly, the monks devote a certain amount of time to meditation, but they also cultivate lavender and grapes, harvest honey and produce a liqueur made from aromatic Provençal plants. The liqueur is known as *Lérina*, which comes from the name of the island in Antiquity.

An important Christian landmark, Saint-Honorat's monastery, has a history that reaches far into the past. The monastery, where many theologians, bishops and even several saints were trained, had an unparalleled reputation as early as the 6th century.

Despite all the piety on the island, the monastery wasn't spared from the pillages by the Saracens and the wars waged during the Middle Ages. Shortly after the French Revolution, the monastery was closed with the secularization of the area by the pope. Monastic life resumed only after the second half of the 19th century.

Monastère-Fortresse Saint-Honorat

The **monastère-fortresse**, which was built in 1073, is open to visitors during tourist season. On the first floor, the cloister opens up to two levels of galleries with Gothic vaults. The cistern in the centre dates back to Roman times. The upper gallery provides access to Chapelle Sainte-Croix. Its original vault contains relics of Saint-Honorat.

Finally, there is a shaded trail that leads all the way around the island. It is a beautiful place for a walk, and along the way you can discover the seven chapels scattered across the island. The most interesting is Chapelle de la Trinité. It has three vaults forming a trefoil, reminiscent of Byzantine art.

Le Cannet

Visitors can enjoy a charming stroll through the old streets of this village, only 3km (1.9mi) from the centre of Cannes and accessible by bus from the town hall. The village, whose beginnings date back to the late 13th century, was significantly marked by the immigration of Italian families in the 15th century. Finally, this is the place where painter Pierre Bonnard lived out his last days.

While here, make a point of dropping by the **Chapelle Saint-Sauveur/Musée Tobiasse** *(every day 2pm to 6pm; ☎04.93.46.74.00)*. The chapel was decorated by contemporary artist Tobiasse. Using a movingly poetic form of expression, the painter chose to treat subjects both religious and profane within the context of a central theme: "Life is a celebration".

Mandelieu-la-Napoule

If you love old chateaux that have been restored, we recommend a stop at Mandelieu-la-Napoule's **Château-musée** *(25F; Wed to Mon, guided tours at 3pm and 4pm, in summer also at 5pm, closed Nov to Feb; ☎04.93.49.95.05)*, which is surrounded by magnificent gardens. Two towers (14th century) are all that remain of the old chateau. The chateau was restored by the architect wife of American sculptor Henry Clews (1876-1937), some of whose works are on display here. The place has an astounding mix of styles (Romanesque, Gothic and a touch of Orientalism).

Mougins

This lovely town is located 7km (4.3mi) from Cannes, at an elevation of 260m (853ft). It is a wonderful place to take a walk. And since walking works up an appetite, Mougins is the right place to be, with its many gourmet restaurants of long-standing reputation. It's difficult to go through Mougins without stopping to eat here. The hardest part is choosing a restaurant, since there are so many good ones. See p 327.

Mougins is almost a thousand years old (not to be mistaken with Haut-de Mougins!). It is built around the old church at the top of the hill, according to the typical layout of Provençal villages in the Middle Ages. The Romanesque church dates back to the 11th century, and has since undergone several modifications.

Take the time to stroll about in the lanes of the old town. The soft light and welcoming ambience of the Place de la Mairie are positively charming on summer evenings.

For those interested in photography, the **Musée de la Photographie** *(5F; Jul to Aug, 2pm to 11pm; Sep and Oct, Wed to Sun 2pm to 6pm; Porte Sarrazine, ☎04.93.75.85.67)* is located at the Place de l'Église. The first floor features temporary exhibitions. The second floor displays the permanent collection, which formerly belonged to Picasso. It includes photographs by Doisneau, Lartigue, Clergue, Colomb, Quinn, Duncan and others. You can also admire a beautiful collection of antique cameras.

Somewhat different in style, the **Musée de l'Automobiliste** *(40 F; Oct to Mar, 10am to 6pm; Apr to Sep, until 7pm; Aire des Bréguières, on the Nice-Cannes highway, ☎04.93.69.27.80)* features around 200 antique and modern cars.

Finally, a little to the east of Mougins, Notre-Dame-de-Vie is where Picasso spent the last 12 years of his life, until his death in 1973.

Mouans-Sartoux

This commune arose, in the 19th century, from the merging of two villages: Mouans, on the plain, and Sartoux, on the hill. There is a delightful château here, which now houses **Espace de l'Art Concret** *(15F; winter, Wed to Mon, 11am to 6pm, summer until 7pm; ☎04.93.75.71.50)*. Three exhibitions are organized here every year, over and above a seminar in early September, where themes related to artistic and scientific research are explored.

Valbonne

This village differs from the others on account of its checkerboard layout, characteristic of North American cities. The old abbey was founded in the 12th century by Chalaisien monks, a mountain order that followed the strict rules of Saint-Benoît. The abbey's beautiful, sober church was built according to the "Latin cross" plan and has two side chapels.

Finally, visitors should not miss out on the Place des Arcades, a lovely square lined with arcades.

Sophia-Antipolis

This "technopolis," or high-tech industrial park, brings together about 1000 companies from 50 different countries that provide over 20,000 jobs. Its early history is reminiscent of the Silicon Valley's in California. After IBM set up its headquarters in Europe, in the village of La Gaude (15km or 9.3mi from the Nice airport), senator Pierre Laffitte had the idea of creating a centre for high-tech industries on the Côte d'Azur.

Today, Sophia-Antipolis covers an area of 2,300ha (5,683 acres).

The industrial park currently stretches over a territory adjoining the communes of Antibes, Biot, Mougins, Valbonne, Vallauris, Villeneuve-Loubet, Roquefort-les-Pins, La Colle-sur-Loup and Opio.

Quality of life has always been respected here where planning was concerned: 650ha (1,606 acres) have been set aside for economic activity, 150ha (371 acres) for housing and 1,500ha (3,706 acres) have remained or become natural areas for pleasant walks or for mushroom growing. In the summer, thousands of people flock here to go for a walk or have a picnic.

A veritable laboratory of the future, the park encompasses, among other things, a European telecommunications centre and research laboratories in the fields of biotechnology and health sciences. The economic contribution provided by Sophia-Antipolis currently exceeds 12 billion francs per year.

Finally, a host of sports and cultural activities are organized to make this an appealing place in which to live. Every July, master classes are held for young, international, aspiring musicians.

Grasse

Located 16km (9.9mi) from Cannes and 35km (21.7mi) from Nice, Grasse is known internationally for its perfumes. Signs along the roads to Grasse point out how closely the history of the town and the perfume industry are intertwined.

Parking spots are hard to find, so we suggest leaving your car in a public parking lot.

Place aux Aires is the site of a flower market every morning. From this square, the winding streets lead into the old medieval town surrounding Puy, the peak that used to protect the city against attacks. Many beautiful homes line these streets. Three major 13th-century buildings dominate the medieval town: The **Donjon** ★; the **Palais de l'Évêque** ★, which is now the Hôtel de Ville; and the **Cathédrale** ★, a modest church built of limestone, which houses works by Rubens and Fragonard as well as a Ludovico Brea reredo.

Right behind the cathedral, on the Place du 24-Août, stands the **Tour de l'Horloge**. This clock tower recalls the loss of Grasse's free Republic status, which it had acquired for a few years in the beginning of the 12th century, for the city had to be ceded to the Count of Provence upon his return to power.

This market city abounds in superb residences, tokens of its commercial success: the Pontévès mansion, which houses the **Musée de la Marine** *(Mon to Sat 10am to noon and 2pm to 6pm; closed Nov; Boulevard du Jeu-de-Ballon, ☎04.93.40.11.11)*, the Court de Fontmichel and the De Clapier-Cabris mansions, among others.

The lower part of town has three museums. The **Musée International de la Parfumerie** ★ *(summer 10am to 7pm; Place du Cours, ☎04.93.36.80.20)* is the most interesting. It is dedicated to the history and evolution of perfume-production techniques. The entire process of creating a perfume is revealed, from combining raw plant, animal or synthetic materials to actually producing the perfume (*enfleurage*, distilling and extraction). This journey into the land of fragrances leads into a room where a remarkable collection of flasks, some dating back to Antiquity, are displayed in glass cabinets. The tour ends on the roof, in the museum's greenhouse where fragrant plants such as jasmin, vetiver, *rose de mai* and vanilla are cultivated.

The **Musée d'Art et d'Histoire de la Provence** *(summer, 10am to 1pm and 2pm to 7pm; off-season, 10am to noon and 2pm to 5pm; Rue Mirabeau, ☎04.93.36.01.61)*, located in Grasse's most elegant residence, evokes scenes of daily life. Complete with furniture, paintings and accessories, the museum illustrates a true Provençal *art de vivre*.

At the entrance to the town, coming from Cannes, there are many signs indicating the **Villa-Musée Fragonard** *(summer, 10am to 1pm and 2pm to 7pm; off-season, 10am to noon and 2pm to 6pm; 23 Boulevard Fragonard, ☎04.93.36.01.61)*. A native of Grasse, famous 18th-century painter Jean-Honoré Fragonard made a gift of four paintings representing the stages of a suitor's conquest—*Le Rendez-Vous, La Poursuite, Les Lettres,* and *L'Amant Couronné*—to the Comtesse du Barry, mistress of Louis XV. Magnificent replicas of these paintings adorn the rooms of the Villa.

Gorges du Loup

In the countryside around Vence, visitors can take a **wonderful tour** by car (or bicycle, if you are the athletic type) to the Gorges du Loup. This 70km (43.5mi) round-trip excursion from Vence begins on the D2210, toward Tourettes-sur-Loup, Bar-sur-Loup, to Châteauneuf-de-Grasse, and continues along the D3 toward Gourdon, Gréolières and Coursegoules. The excursion ends with the crossing of the Col de Vence (970m or 3,182ft in altitude), through magnificent bare hills.

★★

Tourrettes-sur-Loup

After having survived invasions by the Franks, the Huns, the Visigoths and the Lombards, ramparts were finally built around this ancient town during the Middle Ages. All that remains of them now are two doors that open onto the church square, and the 13th-century dungeon that now houses the city hall.

It is said that, over the last century, the shade of the Tourrettes olive trees has provided a perfect climate for the violets to grow. These flowers are used in decoration, distillation in the perfume factories in Grasse and in the manufacture of sweets (candied violets). Tourrettes boasts of being the "city of violets" because of their abundance here.

This town is a wonderful place for a leisurely stroll. Go in one door, to the square, and out the other—the Grand'Rue forms a loop between the two. Discover the beautiful romantic houses, pleasant restaurants and many artisan shops, many of which belong to the artisans themselves. Built outside of the ramparts, the **early 15th century church ★** contains, among other things, paintings from the School of Bréa. If you like naïve frescoes, stop for a moment at the **Chapelle Saint-Jean**, just outside of the village.

In Pont-du-Loup, between Touretes and Bar, you can visit a confectionery (see p 332).

★

Le Bar-sur-Loup

In ancient times, the Ligurians, Celts, Gauls and Romans all went through here. The latter erected two tombs on the current site of the **château**. An engraved tombstone from one of these monuments is embedded in the base of the bell tower.

The château was destroyed on more than one occasion between the 9th and 15th centuries: first by the Saracens, then by the Moors. The two towers flanking the château date from the 13th and 15th centuries.

Admiral de Grasse, one of whose naval victories helped the United

States achieve independence, was born in this village in 1722.

Le Bar affords a panoramic view of Gourdon, the Gorges and the Vallée du Loup. This old village has successfully retained its authentic character, making it worth a visit. The very old, closely huddled houses form a still perceptible rampart. Among the village's treasures is the **Eglise St-Jacques le Majeur** ★, a Gothic-style parish church built between the 13th and 15th centuries. The main door of this asymmetrical structure (it comprises two naves rather than three) is surmounted by a diagonal rib and bordered by columns. The flamboyant, Gothic-style carved panels are the work of Jacotin Bellot, who also created the stalls in the Vence cathedral. Inside, behind the high altar, is a retable of the Brea school. At the far end of the church, below the gallery, you can admire a peculiar 15th-century painting, entitled *La danse macabre.*

★★

Gourdon

Gourdon and its hamlet, **Pont-du-Loup**, form a picturesque village with only 242 inhabitants. The imposing 13th-century **château** *(admission charge; guided tours, Wed to Mon, closed Tue)*, rebuilt in the 17th century, is sure to capture your attention. Constructed in pure Provençal style, it surrounds a square courtyard flanked by two towers and a dungeon which was destroyed during the French Revolution. It contains a collection of antique weapons, a torture table and isolation chamber in the old prison, old paintings (French, Flemish, Dutch and Rhenish) and, in the chapel, a statue of Saint-Sebastien attributed to El Greco. The first floor houses a museum of naïve painting. This castle has had a succession of owners during the 20th century. It was last restored in 1972-73.

Place Victoria ★★★ offers breathtaking panoramic views of astonishing depth and scope over the entire Côte d'Azur, with colours that change according to the time of day and the season. From left to right, the view encompasses Cap-Ferret, Nice, the mouth of the Var, Cagnes, Antibes and its cape, Juan-les-Pins, the Îles de Lérins, Cannes, and even Mont-Chevalier, Napoule, l'Estérel and the Maures. In the foreground you will see the huge green valley, the Loup River, fields, olive, orange and cypress trees. In the distance you can just make out Mougins.

Gourdon has lots to offer shoppers, including several establishments that sell regional products, such as pâté, Provençal herbs, tapenade, goat's cheese, jams and honey.

★

Gréolières

Gréolière is perched on a spur of the Cheiron, at an altitude of 820m (2,690ft). The **church**, built in the 12th century but extended in the 16th century, houses a retable painted by an artist of the Brea school in the late 15th century.

Gréolières-les-Neiges, a ski resort at an altitude of 1,450m or 4,757ft (see p 310), is 18km (11.2mi) away. To reach the resort, follow the D2, then the D802. A chairlift takes visitors to the summit of the Cheiron in summer.

★

Coursegoules

An old royal city in the 17th century, the village has since lost some of its importance due, in part, to its inaccessibility. Paradoxically, the old village is now experiencing renewed interest for the very same reason. Indeed, the village, miles from nowhere in the back country, offers an oasis of peace away from the hectic life of the Côte d'Azur. Several houses have consequently been renovated to be converted into holiday homes.

The village boasts a lovely, Provençal defensive-type architectural unity and has managed to retain the distinctive charm and character of old villages. Make the most of it and explore its alleys and stairways, and take the time to stop and examine the doors' lintels, all sober yet different.

The 12th-century Romanesque **Église Sainte-Marie-Madeleine** was restored in 1658, and contains a reredos attributed to Brea. The **Chapelle Saint-Michel**, situated on the path that skirts the small valley of Cagne, is even older, dating from the 11th century.

The area makes for some pleasant strolls to observe the magnificent flora during spring and summer.

Outdoor Activities

This area is perfect for all kinds of sports, including winter sports from December to April. Tennis courts are in great abundance, and the tourism office can direct you to the closest one.

Beaches and Water Sports

Every kind of beach can be found along this coast. There are sandy beaches, rocky beaches and near Nice, pebble beaches. They tend to get sandier as you approach Cannes. Cap d'Antibes has a few pleasant little beaches; some of them charge admission but do offer certain facilities. Beaches on the Cape are mostly rocky but become sandy again towards Juan-les-Pins. At Cannes, the beaches offer many facilities. There is an admission charge to most of these beaches since they belong to the hotels on the Croisette. Lounge chairs and parasols can be rented by the day or half-day, with prices ranging from 35 to 70F. These beaches usually offer water sports equipment rentals at reasonable prices.

For **windsurfing**, Antibes (at the entrance to the Cape) or Cannes (near the Palm Beach Hôtel, at the far end of the Croisette) are the best places to go. Rental costs about 60F per hour.

Boats and sailboats can also be rented. Enquire at the tourism offices at the beach resorts for more information.

Golf

In this region of about 20 golf courses, the biggest and most beautiful one is between **Opio** and **Valbonne**, 16km (9.9mi) from Cannes and 35km (21.7mi) from Nice *(Château de la Bégude; Route de Roquefort-les-Pins, ☎04.93.12.00.08, ⇄04.93.12.26.00)*. This golf course was established in a beautiful nature park by Club Med, whose vacation "village" is in Opio.

Dolphins

The **Golf de la Grande Bastide**, an 18-hole golf course with a par of 72, is laid out near **Châteauneuf-de-Grasse**, 6km (3.7mi) east of Grasse, via Route D2085 *(Chemin des Picholines, ☎04.93.77.70.08, ≠04.93.77.72.36)*.

For information on other golf courses, call ***☎04.93.63.73.43 ≠04.93.63.74.36 o2c.omega@wanadoo.fr***

Horseback Riding

Nice

Tango
everything for horses and jockeys
☎04.93.80.01.09

Cagnes-sur-Mer

Les Écuries d'Azur
☎04.93.73.19.49

Cannes

Centre Équestre Poney Club de Tanneron
☎04.93.60.66.16

Vence

Ranch El Branco
for riding and boarding horses
☎04.93.58.09.83

Rock Climbing

The Alps of Nice are a canyon enthusiast's paradise. If such an adventure appeals to you, contact **Séquence Action** *(Parc Montmeuille, La Colle-sur-Loup, ☎04.93.32.06.93)*. A team of certified experts will lead you through an unforgettable experience. All equipment is supplied, but participants must be over 10 years of age.

For more information, contact:
Comité Régional de Canoë-Kayak
☎04.92.00.44.50
≠04.93.89.05.33

Hiking

From Antibes

The Cours de la Brague *(elevations between 100 and 120m or 328 and 393ft; duration: 3.5hrs)*. Go to Biot (by N98 and D4) and park in the village. Take Chemin de l'Ibac. An Office National des Forêts sign indicates the way to the river. Go to the sign indicating the Pont des Tamarins and continue to Point de la Verrière. Double back along the same route.

Gorges de la Cagne *(starting elevation: 425m or 1,394ft, highest point: 730m 2,395ft; duration: 6hrs)*. Begin at **Vence**. Take D2 towards Coursegoules for 1km (0.6mi), then turn right on Chemin du Riou. Follow this road for 3km (1.9mi) and leave the car at the little parking lot. Cross over the footbridge and follow the red markers. The trail climbs up along the Cagne River. Take a dip along the way in one of the little ponds. At the fallen bridge of the abandoned mine, go back along the same trail. You could also continue on one of the trails indicated on the sign, either the GR51 or the Cap S.S.E, which is the marked trail connecting Baou des Blancs in the west to Baou des Noirs in the east. Go back to the sign and go down the hill. Head towards the Chemin du Riou and walk 2km (1.2mi) to the parking lot.

Baou de St-Jeannet ou de la Gaude *(starting elevation: 400m or 1,312ft, highest point: 800m or 2,625ft and 750m or 2,461ft respectively; duration: 3 or 4hrs there and back)*. Go to St-Jeannet (see p 292). Leave your car at the parking lot. Climb up to the village and turn right after the Auberge St-Jeannet. Climb up and follow the signs. The huge peak on the left is the Baou de St-Jeannet; the smaller peak on the right is the Baou de La Gaude. A pretty little oak forest stands at its peak. The Summit of Baou de St-Jeannet offers a fabulous panoramic view over St-Jeannet, the neighbouring hills and the Côte d'Azur.

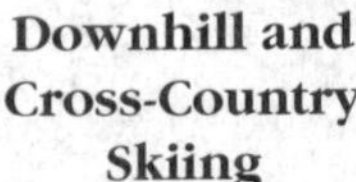

Downhill and Cross-Country Skiing

The climate and skiing conditions in the Alpes-Maritimes vary considerably from year to year. Call for information before heading out (see p 71 for the telephone numbers). The best months for skiing are January, February and March. Trails and runs usually have enough, even a lot of snow at this time. Equipment rental is available on-site at reasonable prices.

Gréolières-les-Neiges

Just under an hour from the Côte d'Azur, this winter sports resort is also very pleasant in summer.

The place is primarily recommended for cross-country skiing. Downhill skiing is more difficult due to a lack of snow. In summer, the pleasant woods are ideal for walking, horseback riding or cycling. Visitors can also take the chairlift up to the top of the Cheiron.

Valberg

This pretty winter resort has a multitude of mountain chalets.

A bus service connects Valberg to Nice *(from the bus terminal, Promenade du Paillon,* *☎04.93.85.61.81)* and the airport. Information: Tourist Office *(☎04.93.23.02.66, ot@valberg.com)*. Note: Reservations required.

By car, take N202 from the Nice airport towards Digne-Les-Bains for about 50km (31.1mi), then take D28 towards Beuil. The road crosses the Gorges du Cians. Valberg is just 6km (3.7mi) from Beuil.

Isola 2000

This modern resort was built in the 1970s in a completely remote area. Concrete must have been a bargain when this town was built, with its succession of chairlifts, restaurants, hotels, shops, cinemas etc. All is very functional, but you won't find romantic ambience here!

To get to Isola from Nice by car, take N202 towards Digne for about 30km (18.6mi), then take D2205 towards St-Sauver-de-Tinée. The D97 rises 17km (10.6mi) up to Isola.

Auron

This is the third biggest ski resort in the Alpes-Maritimes. Situated on a beautiful plateau at an altitude of 2,000m (6,562ft), Auron offers every opportunity for winter sports.

Ski School
☎04.93.23.02.53

Auron can be reached by car by following directions for Isola 2000, then continuing for 15km (9.3mi) more along the D2205 to the fork toward Auron.

Accommodations

Cagnes-sur-Mer

Val Duchesse
250F-360F
apartment 340F-490F
ps or pb
11 Rue de Paris
☎04.92.13.40.00
⇄04.92.13.40.29
Although we don't really recommend that you stay in Cagnes-sur-Mer, the Val Duchesse provides good accommodation. Among the advantages of this congenial place are its quiet location, just a few steps from the sea, the private parking and the garden with palm trees that offers a swimming pool and facilities for various outdoor games.

Vence

L'Hôtel Le Provence
200F-380F
400F for three people
closed mid-Jan to mid-Feb
ps or pb
9 avenue Marcellin Maurel
☎***04.93.58.04.21***
⇄***04.93.58.35.62***
L'Hôtel Le Provence is a pretty, fully renovated little hotel in a quiet courtyard, located near the south entrance to the old town. Ask for room six *(380F)*, which has a large rooftop terrace, or rooms one and two *(380F)* each with smaller terraces.

La Roseraie
395F-750F
pb or ps, tv, ℝ, ≈
Avenue Henri Giraud
☎***04.93.58.02.20***
⇄***04.93.58.99.31***
On the other side of Vence, at the beginning of Route du Col de Vence, La Roseraie offers good value. Surrounded by a most beautiful garden, this hotel has a pool and a lovely view over the old medieval town. La Roseraie is not pretentious; its canopy beds make you feel at home. The staff is very friendly, and the copious breakfasts are not to be missed!

Auberge des Seigneurs
400F
closed in winter
ps, ℜ
Place du Frêne
☎***04.93.58.04.24***
⇄***04.93.24.08.01***
Treat yourself to a royal getaway and stay at the Auberge des Seigneurs. Under the command of Madame Rodi and her small, welcoming staff and dog, guests will be immersed in grand medieval surroundings. This establishment lies right next to the chateau of Villeneuve, which houses a museum, on the western ramparts of Vence. Don't expect great luxury, but you are guaranteed to be comfortable in the six rooms named after the different painters who inspired their decor. The beds are large, and the rooms are tastefully furnished with antiques. Flowers and a small fruit platter are placed in each room, for guests nostalgic for a different era of travel. Try to stay in the Bonnard room if possible. The place offers excellent quality for the price.

Saint-Jeannet

Hôtel l'Indicible
300F-330F, bkfst 30F
ps, pb, tv, ℜ
Rue du Saumalier
☎***04.92.11.01.08***
⇄***04.92.11.02.06***
Discover the authentic village life of the back country (and near the sea) while comfortably accommodated at the Hôtel l'Indicible. Peter and Els, a young Belgian couple, have magically transformed this aging hotel into a pleasant, clean and modern establishment. The rooms are rather small, but very bright. In short, the place offers superb value for the price. To get there, head up to the kiosk at the entrance to the old town. Leave your luggage at the hotel and drive the car back to the parking lot a little further down.

Haut-de-Cagnes

Le Cagnard
950F-1,500F, apt. 1,700F-2,600F
pb, ≡, ℝ, ℜ
Rue Pontis-Long
☎***04.93.20.73.21***
⇄***04.93.22.06.39***
Hôtel Le Cagnard is at the heart of the old town and is a member of the Relais et Château. All the rooms have modern bathrooms. Most of the apartments have large terraces with panoramic views of the sea and the hills. The area both exudes and encourages romance. Unfortunately, the prices have skyrocketed in recent years, though the location is remarkable. Getting there is a bit complicated, but a valet service is available to take care of your car. The hotel is 8km (5mi) from the Nice Airport. Horseback riding, tennis, golf and a pool aren't far away.

Saint-Paul-de-Vence

Hostellerie Les Remparts
300F-520F
ps, pb, ℜ
72 Rue Grande
☎04.93.32.09.88
⇌04.93.32.06.91
HR@saintpaulweb.com
Not everything is expensive in Saint-Paul: you can enjoy a pleasant stay at the Hostellerie Les Remparts. It is a little difficult to reach, but you'll delight in a panoramic view (from the most expensive rooms) once you've settled in. The entire place is charming with its antique furnishings, and guests are made very welcome. Warm reception.

Hostellerie de la Fontaine
360F
ps, ℜ
centre of town
☎04.93.32.80.29
☎04.93.32.74.12
The Hostellerie de la Fontaine offers the charm of days gone by. For those who like an old-fashioned, modest style, this hotel offers rooms with a rustic appeal. The floors are tiled with *tomettes*, traditional Provençal ceramic. A strong family atmosphere prevails here. Only a door separates this romantic hotel from the heart of the city. The food ***($)*** is also simple, but hearty and delicious. Enjoy a piece of home-made pie on the terrace overlooking the town's beautiful fountain.

Le Hameau
580F-790F
closed mid-Nov to mid-Feb except Christmas and New Year's
pb or ps, ≡, tv in some rooms, ℝ, ≈
Route de La Colle
☎04.93.32.80.24
⇌04.93.32.55.75
www.le-hameau.com
Le Hameau is one of the best places to stay in terms of value. It is just 1km (0.6mi) from town, close to the Fondation Maeght. The large garden offers splendid views of Saint-Paul. The hotel was built in modern Provençal style with special attention paid to detail. The garden is a bit wild, just enough to give it a charming and romantic, natural appeal. This is a paradise of beautiful flowers and green foliage. Families or groups of friends can take advantage of a special arrangement: two rooms (for four people), which share a living room that opens directly onto the garden and the pool, are available for 900F.

Le Mas d'Artigny
1,000F-2,300F
apt. 3,400F
pb, ≡, ℝ, ≈
Route de la Colle
☎04.93.32.84.54
⇌04.93.32.95.36
In a huge 9ha (22.2 acres) park perched high in the Niçois interior, this place offers a splendid view of the sea and the neighbouring hills. The hotel has a large pool measuring 11 by 25m (36.1 by 82ft) right in the park, and guests in the apartments enjoy exclusive use of their own smaller pool in absolute privacy. The hotel has a large boutique and organizes painting exhibits throughout the year. Finally, the hotel is very well run. The reception is friendly, and the efficient staff are always available to help you. Guests are guaranteed a pleasant stay. This is also a perfect place for a conference or celebration.

Hôtel Saint-Paul
1,300F-1,700F, suite 1,900F-2,800F
closed Nov to Dec 22
pb, ps, tv, ≡, ℝ, ℜ, elevator
86 Rue Grande
☎04.93.32.65.25
⇌04.93.32.52.94
stpaul@relaischateaux.fr
If you're looking for luxury, the Hôtel Saint-Paul is the place to stay. Located at the heart of this celebrated village, it has a spectacular panoramic view (from the most expensive rooms and suites). The reception is gracious and professional, and the staff will see to your luggage (since there is no direct access to the hotel). The owners have created a very stylish establishment that has been tastefully decorated. You'll be plunged into the Middle Ages, but with all the conveniences of the 21st century.

La Colombe d'Or
1,500F-1,750F
½ b 1,980F
pb, ℝ, ≈
☎04.93.32.80.02
⇌04.93.32.77.78
www.la-colombe-dor.com
La Colombe d'Or is among the most prestigious hotels in the area. Formerly a post house, and later a modest inn run under the name of Robinson, this hotel was transformed into a hotel-restaurant by the son of the innkeeper. Over the years, a number of famous or soon-to-be-famous artists have stayed here. The owner, an art-lover, has created a living museum here. Sleep in a sumptuous setting among paintings by the great masters, including Picasso, Matisse, Léger and many more. The rooms are as rustic as they are elegant. Here, art and space are one. The pool in the indoor courtyard is highlighted by a large moving sculpture by Calder. Yves Montand and Simone Signoret adored staying here so much that at one time they actually became co-owners. Today, there are celebrities who rent out the rooms for the whole year.

La Colle-sur-Loup

La Vallon Rouge
bungalow and trailer rental
stores, ps, ℝ, ≈
Route de Grólières
☎04.93.32.86.12
To get here from La Colle, take D6 towards Gréolières. Alongside the river, on a flat, shaded area, you will enjoy the charming Niçois countryside, just 10min from the sea. Lawn bowling, entertainment, sports, videos and evening activities are offered.

Le Castellas
trailer and bungalow rental
ps, ℝ
Route de Roquefort
☎04.93.32.97.05
To get here from La Colle, follow D7 towards Roquefort for 5km (3.1mi). This campground is 6km (3.7mi) from the sea, in a shaded area beside a river. Facilities are clean. Leisure activities, fishing, swimming.

Hôtel Marc Hély
390F-520F
apartment 530F-770F
pb, ps, tv, ≡, ≈
on the road from Cagnes to La Colle
☎04.93.22.64.10
⇌04.93.22.93.84
On the road to Cagnes, there is a sign indicating the Hôtel Marc Hély at La Colle. This establishment is part of the Relais du Silence hotel chain and offers a magnificent view of Saint-Paul-de-Vence. It has its own parking area and a very well-tended garden. Don't hesitate to take one of the less expensive rooms, since they offer excellent quality for the price.

L'Abbaye
450F-1,300F
pb or ps, tv, ≈, ℜ, ≡
541 Boulevard Honoré Teisseire
☎04.93.32.68.34
⇌04.93.32.85.06
l-abbaye@wanadoo.fr
If you feel like idling away the day in magnificent surroundings, L'Abbaye is the perfect place. This hotel and restaurant occupies a 12th-century building that has been listed as a historic site. The owner, Sylviane Hugues, has given the place a major overhaul, equipping it with all the modern comforts but preserving all its character and charm. You'll be amazed by how many places there are to lounge about here. Be it the chapel, the sitting room with its fireplace, the gardens, or simply the poolside, there is a spot for everyone here. Furthermore, you don't have to spend a fortune, though the larger rooms are superb. Finally, if you don't want to venture too far to eat, you can have a meal in the magnificent courtyard.

Villeneuve-Loubet

Le Sourire
trailer and mobile home rentals
shops, ℝ, ≈
Route de Grasse, D2085
☎04.93.20.96.11
This camp site is located in the heart of a secluded, wooded area near the village itself and boasts a large swimming pool. More-

over, sports and leisure activities are also organized here.

La Vieille Ferme
cottages with tv for rent
shops
ℝ, ≈
Boulevard des Groules
☎*04.93.33.41.44*
Near the beach, this camp site is reached from Nice by the RN7 and by turning right a little before the Marineland amusement park as indicated by the signs. The site and its swimming pool are open year round. The pool is covered during the colder months.

Biot

Hôtel des Arcades
300F-500F
pb or ps, tv
16 Place des Arcades
☎*04.93.65.01.04*
⇄*04.93.65.01.05*
Hidden away at the very top of this charming old village is the magnificent Hôtel des Arcades. This place is incredible! It has 12 rooms, the most expensive of which are huge and furnished with antiques. The building dates from the 15th century and is as charming as can be, with a maze of corridors decorated with contemporary paintings, old fireplaces and mosaics adorning some of the bathrooms. A number of the rooms have private terraces.

Originally, the place was only a restaurant, and it is worth coming here just for the food (see p 324). Please note that they only accept cash.

Antibes

Le Rossignol
tent and trailer rental
stores
s, ℝ, ≈
2074 Avenue Jules Grec
☎*04.93.33.56.98*
From Nice take N7 towards Antibes. About 2km (1.2mi) before Fort Carré turn right on Chemin des 4 Chemins, and then turn right on the fourth street. The lush green setting is perfect for relaxation. The beaches are 1km (0.6mi) away. Reserve by mail.

Hotels are abundant in this very beautiful coastal city. Here are a few establishments that are well-known for the charming and quiet atmosphere they offer their guests:

La Jabotte
270F-370F with shower on the landing or ps
½b 540F-670F
closed Nov
13 Avenue Max Maurey, Cap d'Antibes
☎*04.93.61.45.89*
⇄*04.93.61.07.04*
If you're on a budget and are looking for good value in a town where hotels are rather expensive, go to La Jabotte.

To find this quaint little hotel, head towards the Cap along Boulevard Maréchal Leclerc and then Boulevard James Wyllie. At La Salis Beach, turn right and go up the very narrow Rue Max Maurey. The hotel is only 50m (164ft) from the sea, yet is a quiet spot. It is run by a very nice young couple and offers comfort above its class. The owner serves typical French cuisine and can also suggest some good places to enjoy "Antiboise" cuisine. The sunny garden is peaceful. It's the perfect place for the young at heart!

Petit Castel
540F
closed mid-Feb to beginning of Mar
ps or pb, ≡, *tv*
22 Avenue des Sables
☎*04.93.61.59.37*
⇄*04.93.67.51.28*
info-pcastel-djoliba.com
For a more comfortable place to stay, we suggest the Petit Castel. This charming 1930s-style villa, whose rooms have been completely renovated, sits at the edge of Cap d'Antibes, in a residential area close to the beach, casino and convention centre. The hotel has a rooftop solarium with views of the sea and the mountains. It offers all the modern comforts but lacks a restaurant. However, breakfast is served on a beautiful veranda decorated with flowers.

Le Ponteil
½b 600F-800F
½b mandatory during high season
closed late Nov to late Dec
ps, ℜ
11 Impasse Jean Mensier
☎04.93.34.67.92
⇌93.34.49.47
Le Ponteil is located at the gates of Cap D'Antibes (at the corner of Avenue Général Maizière) and is a member of the Logis de France (association of small hotels in France). We loved this place! The hotel is in the heart of an oasis of flowers and greenery, sheltered from the noise, yet still close to the sea. A warm family ambience makes you feel welcome right away. All the rooms have been redone in 2000/2001 to make them more comfortable. The owners themselves do the cooking, and during the summer you can eat on the tree-shaded terrace. In short, a carefully-tended country inn right in the heart of the city.

Opio

Caravan Inn
studios, duplexes and rooms for rent
shops, ℝ, ≈, tennis
18 Route de Cannes
☎04.93.77.32.00
There is some wonderful camping situated in the backcountry of Cannes, not very far from the sea (15km or 9.3mi).

Saint-Martin-Vésubie

La Mério
trailer and studio rentals
ℝ
Route de la Colmiane
☎04.93.03.30.38
The camp site lies at the gateway to the Parc du Mercantour and 1hr from the sea. It is 1.5km (0.9mi) past Saint-Martin-Vésubie on the Route de la Colmiane, on wooded grounds, by a river filled with trout. To get here from Nice: take the road skirting the ocean, then the N202, toward Digne, and the D2565, for 10km (6.2mi) more. Only open from mid-June to mid-September.

Collonges

FonFrède
bed and breakfast
☎04.93.05.80.76
Sheep rearing, mountain gardening, hunting, pond fishing.

Guillaumes

La Ferme du Troc
three rooms accommodating two to six people
☎04.93.05.54.64
Thirteen kilometres (8.1mi) from Guillaumes. Cattle breeding, agro-biology, mountain gardening, set menu, vegetarian and meat-based meals.

Juan-les-Pins

Juan Beach
250F-400F
closed Nov to Apr
ps or pb, tv room
5 Rue de l'Oratoire
☎04.93.61.02.89
⇌04.93.61.16.63
juan.beach@atsat.com
Bed and breakfast hotel Juan Beach is near the Pinède Gould, 100m (328ft) from the beaches, close to the convention centre and the casino. The owners guarantee you a relaxing and enjoyable holiday. Although the rooms are rather small, they are clean and well-kept. A few rooms have terraces. Meals are alfresco, and breakfast is served in the garden shaded by lime and orange trees. The owner prepares regional specialities.

Le Pré Catelan
550F-950F
ps or pb, ℜ, ≈
22 Avenue des Lauriers
☎04.93.61.05.11
⇌04.93.67.83.11
trevoux@club-internet.fr
Close to Antibes and away from the main thoroughfares, we strongly recommend Le Pré Catelan. This 1930s-style hotel is surrounded by trees and has been entirely renovated. The only sound to be heard is that of birds singing. Surprisingly, it is only 200m (656ft) from the beach and the casino.

The hotel has a warm, country-inn atmosphere. The interior is tastefully decorated with beautiful antiques. The bathrooms are original and very well maintained. A separate pavilion overlooking the large garden could accommodate four to six people.

Hôtel Sainte-Valérie
670F-930F
½b 345-410F
closed Oct to mid-Apr
pb, tv, ≡, ≈
Rue de l'Oratoire
☎04.93.61.07.15
⇄04.93.61.47.52
saintevalerie@juanlespins.net

The nearby Hôtel Sainte-Valérie is two hotels rolled into one. The cheaper rooms, in the Villa Christie, offer direct access to the same amenities as the more expensive ones, namely a lovely pool and a flower-filled garden. The difference lies in the level of comfort: the former have neither air conditioning nor private terraces. The choice is yours. In any case, the most important thing is that the sea is right nearby. The hotel also has a restaurant that serves Provençal specialties inside or outdoors in the garden.

Vallauris/Golfe-Juan

Beverly Hôtel
300F-400F
ps, elevator, tv
14 Rue Hoche
☎04.93.39.10.66
⇄04.92.98.65.63
beverly-hotel_cannes@csi.com

Situated on a pedestrian street this family-run hotel guarantees a pleasant stay. The rooms are slightly outdated, but clean and comfortable nevertheless. The lobby is modest and a bit "American."

Touring Hôtel
350F-450F
ps, tv, elevator
11 Rue Hoche
☎04.93.38.34.40
⇄04.93.38.73.34
infos@cannes.hotels.com

The Touring Hôtel appealed to us because of its old 19th-century façade. It is located in the centre of the city on a semi-pedestrian street. The huge French doors open onto balconies, which makes the old-fashioned rooms very bright. The interior decoration is quaint in aesthetics and modern in comfort.

Beau Soleil
400F-600F
pb, ≡, *tv, K,* ≈
Impasse Beau Soleil
☎04.93.63.63.63
⇄93.63.02.89
contact@hotel-beau-soleil.com

The Beau Soleil is part of the Relais du Silence chain. Situated between Cannes and Nice and only 500m (1,640ft) from the fine sand beaches, this hotel offers all the modern comforts, including a pool.

Cannes

Hôtel Riviera
350F-470F
440-490F for studios
closed Nov and Dec
ps, ≡, *tv, K in studios*
35 Rue Hoche
☎04.93.38.33.67
⇄04.93.38.65.22

If the two previously mentioned hotels have no vacancies, try the Hôtel Riviera, also in the downtown area, 200m (656ft) from the train station and 300m (984ft) from the beaches. Guests of the hotel will benefit from the peaceful pedestrianized street and rooms with triple windows. The decor is modern and the studios are equipped with well-equipped kitchenettes. This hotel will do nicely for both families and those travelling alone. The proprietors are very gracious and put all their time and effort into offering guests the most for their money.

Hôtel Splendid
580F-960F
pb, ≡, *K, tv*
4 Rue Félix-Faure
☎04.97.06.22.22
⇄04.93.99.55.02
infos@cannes.hotels.com

We strongly suggest the Hôtel Splendid. This huge hotel (with two top-floor suites with sloping ceilings and 62 rooms, 42 with K) is marvellously situated in the centre of a huge public garden. The hotel is in the heart of Cannes and faces the sea and the Vieux Port. It is also close to the casino and the Palais des Festivals, and only a few steps from the sandy beaches. You will be delighted with the comfort and excellent service of this late-19th-century-style hotel. Beautiful antique furniture graces the lounges as well as the rooms. Most of the rooms have balconies or terraces overlooking the sea. The comfort is irreproachable, and the bathrooms are very modern. Bathrobes are provided. This hotel offers very good value.

Hôtel de France
650F-690F bkfst 50F
closed Dec
pb, ≡, tv
85 Rue d'Antibes
☎04.93.06.54.54
⇌04.93.68.53.43
Renovated in 1997, this little hotel located on Cannes's commercial street surprisingly offers tranquility and an opportunity for relaxation. Its proximity to the beaches and activity as well as its comforts are guaranteed to make your stay a most agreeable one. What makes this hotel stand out, however, is its rooftop terrace. You can lounge there while gazing onto the Cannes panorama.

Guests from the hotel also benefit from a special rate at the Le Goéland Beach.

The Carlton Inter-Continental
2,995F-4,090F
7,950F-17,950F for suites
ps or pb, tv, ≡, ℝ, ℜ
58 La Croisette, B.P. 155
☎04.93.06.40.06
⇌04.93.06.40.25
cannes@interconti.com
The Carlton Inter-Continental is at the height of luxury. Resembling a majestic, turn-of-the-century palace with a magnificent, white façade, this hotel is the most spectacular building in Cannes. Its large terrace and superb lobby are located in the centre of the Croisette and 5min from the Palais des Festivals. The Carlton has its own private, sandy beach with restaurant service. Many different outdoor activities are offered such as windsurfing. On the top floor, you can dine in a splendid decor with magnificent views of the sea. This floor, located under an impressive rooftop terrace, is also equipped with a casino, conference rooms, a solarium and a sauna. For an amusing time, spend a night or two in one of the deluxe suites on the top floor; the spectacular bathrooms are nestled in the turrets of this grand hotel. Take note that from November through March (after conference season), you can stay at one of the magnificent palaces of La Croisette (*☎08.10.06.12.12 or 04.97.06.53.07, ⇌04.93.99.06.60, centrale@cannesreservation.com*), such as **Le Carleton**, **Le Majestic** or **Le Martinez**, relatively cheaply ("relatively" being the key word here!). During this period, some attractive packages (two or five nights) are offered. On top of accommodations, the packages include a multitude of freebies like an excursion to the Îles de Lérins and access to their private beach with beach mats and umbrellas.

Cannes–La Bocca

Hôtel Super +
249F
pb, tv
242 Avenue F. Tonner
☎04.92.19.64.64
⇌04.92.19.64.65
www.super-plus.claranet.fr
This eccentric hotel, though lacking in character, is in the lead when it comes to offering decent rooms at pretty unbeatable prices (for Cannes that is).

Mougins (old town)

Les Muscadins
950F-1,400F
1,800F for the suite
½b 200F extra
closed Feb and for two weeks before Christmas
pb, ≡, tv, ℝ, ℜ
18 Boulevard Courteline
☎*04.92.28.28.28*
⇄*04.92.92.88.23*
muscadins@alcyonis.fr
If you're looking for a hotel with unbelievable charm and style, go to Les Muscadins. There are eleven rooms, the two most expensive of which look out over the sea. Every room is comfortable, and each is different, decorated with *objets d'art,* old paintings and specially selected pieces of furniture. The bathrooms are spacious and very modern. The main floor has a British pub and a restaurant that opens onto the large terrace. The house, tucked away at the bottom of the old town exudes a modest sort of beauty. The value becomes better when you opt for half-board, since the food is amazing (see p 328).

Mougins

Le Moulin de Mougins
Chemin du Moulin
☎*04.93.75.78.24*
⇄*04.93.90.18.55*
Le Moulin de Mougins is not only a very fine restaurant, (see p 328) but also a wonderful place to stay. It offers three rooms *(850-950F; pb, ≡, tv)* and four suites *(1,800F; pb, ≡, lounge, tv),* two of which are in a separate building. You will enjoy the magnificent fairy-tale surroundings, which abound with trees and flowers.

Cabris

This little village, much loved by Gide, Saint-Exupéry and many others, lies 5km (3.1mi) from Grasse, in the hills. It is truly worth the trip, if only for an brief stay while you're in the area. A number of good lodgings are available here.

Chambres d'Hôte Mme Faraut
260F-320F
closed Nov to Mar
ps
14 Rue de l'Agachon
☎*04.93.60.53.36*
For a simple yet pleasant and clean establishment, we recommend the Chambres d'Hôte Mme Faraut. The four rooms, two of which offer panoramic views, are located in an old house with a yellow facade in the old town.

Hôtel Horizon
340F-640F
pb or ps, elevator, tv, ≈
☎*04.93.60.51.69*
⇄*04.93.60.56.29*
A member of the Relais du Silence chain, the Hôtel Horizon offers peace and quiet in a warm atmosphere. What's more, most of the rooms are not only comfortable but also have panoramic views of the area. The big pool, which gets lots of sunshine throughout the day, is as inviting as can be. Visitors might be interested to know that it was here that Saint-Exupéry proofread his novel *Terre des hommes.*

Le Vieux Château
400F-600F
ps, tv
Place Mirabeau
☎*04.93.60.50.12*
⇄*04.93.60.50.12*
Le Vieux Château, an inn and restaurant, stands at the very top of the village, near the ruins of—that's right—an old chateau. First and foremost a restaurant (see p 323), it only has four rooms. Country specialties.

If you're on a tight budget, stop by the tourist office, whose staff can direct you to the local guesthouses. Don't waste any time, though, since these rooms are almost always taken.

Grasse

Hôtel des Parfums
675F-780F, apartment for 4 ppl. 915F-1,020F, on a weekly basis, bkfst 60F
pb, ps, tv, ≈, ℝ, ℜ, *elevator*
Boulevard Eugène Charabot
☎/⇄*04.92.42.35.35*
www.hoteldesparfums.com
These days, it's worth spending a night in Grasse! If you're a fan of Best Western hotels, head for the Hôtel des Parfums.

This large hotel (71 rooms) is located high up, near the very centre of town, and has a lovely panoramic view. The restaurant opens out onto a large terrace and an attractive swimming pool. Another advantage is the private parking just a few minutes from the town centre. The only negative feature is the large advertisement on the hotel's facade, quoting a misleading price.

Grasse Country Club
800F-1,000F
rooms with mezzanine 1,050-1,300F
pb, ≡, *elevator,* ≈
Route des 3 Ponts (D11)
☎04.93.60.55.44
⇄04.93.60.55.19
info@grasse-country-club.com
If you like golf, you can stop over at the Grasse Country Club, a big resort with all the amenities. Guests enjoy the use of a sauna and even a pool table. The rooms, of course, are spacious and impeccable, and each has a large private terrace. The club also offers golf packages with half-board. The airy restaurant ***($$$)*** serves traditional cuisine and offers both indoor and outdoor seating. A bit on the expensive side, but if you've got the golf bug...

Tourrettes-sur-Loup

La Camassade
trailer and studio rental
stores, s, ℝ, ≈
523 Route de Pie Lombard
☎04.93.59.31.54
To get here, follow the signs around Tourrettes. This campground lies between the sea and the mountain, at an elevation of 400m (1,312ft). It is most peaceful here in the shade of century-old oaks and olive trees.

L'Auberge Belles Terrasses
250F-290F bkfst incl.
½b 400F
ps, pb, tv, ℜ
☎04.93.59.30.03
L'Auberge Belles Terrasses makes quite an impression. This Provençal establishment, in a lush, natural setting, is on Route de Vence, 1km (0.6mi) from Tourrettes-sur-Loup, and only 15min from the sea. The rooms have terraces overlooking either the Côte d'Azur or the garden. The hotel is kept by a family whose first priority is quality and comfort. Simplicity and a good atmosphere prevail. The hotel offers good value, but the place could use a face lift. See p 330 for a description of the restaurant.

Le Mas des Cigales
450F, bfst incl.
pb, ps, tv, =
1673 Route des Quenières
☎04.93.59.25.73
⇄04.93.59.25.78
macigale@aol.com
If you're looking for a high-end bed and breakfast that offers excellent quality for the price, book your stay at the Mas Des Cigales. This villa is surrounded by a magnificent garden and has private parking and a tennis court located 5km (3mi) from Tourrettes, heading in the direction of Grasse (CD2210). The rooms (Capucine, Pivoine, Papillon, Violette and Olive) are charming, well maintained and comfortable with furniture that has been lovingly hand-painted and decorated.

Résidence des Chevaliers
580F-850F
closed Oct to Mar
pb, tv, ≈
Route du Caire
☎04.93.59.31.97
⇄04.93.59.27.97
A more comfortable, more exclusive and very quiet place to stay is the Résidence des Chevaliers. This Provencale-style *bastide* resembles an enormous villa. Perched on a hillside above the village, the hotel offers lovely panoramic views of the sea. It is run by a very discrete couple. The rooms have terraces and beautiful bathrooms. The two rooms in the southeast and southwest corners are especially charming. The beautiful garden

and the lovely pool make this hotel a fair value.

Bar-sur-Loup

Les Gorges du Loup
tent rentals
shops, ℝ, ≈
965 Chemin des Vergers
☎04.93.42.45.06
To get here from Vence: follow the D2210, pass the D6, cross the small bridge and turn left a short distance after, onto Chemin des Vergers. Beneath the olive trees at the foot of the village, this camp site lies in the triangle formed by Cannes, Nice and Grasse. Campers will enjoy these peaceful surroundings with magnificent views of the Vallée du Loup.

La Thébaïde
145F-275F
pb or ps
54 Chemin de la Santoline
☎04.93.42.41.19
If you're looking for peace and quiet in a simple, sequestered spot with lots of charm, head to La Thébaïde. An old Provençal *mas* or farmhouse located in the midst of an olive grove out in the countryside, this place has a homey atmosphere. It has eight rooms, ranging from no frills (nothing but a bed) to fully equipped. Guests enjoy access to a number of common rooms as well as to a living room, a library with a fireplace and a TV room. Outside, you can stroll about or simply sit back and relax in the huge garden. The service is always friendly, and the unbeatable rates make this secluded place well worth the detour.

Restaurants

Vence

Le Pêcheur de Soleil
$-$$
every day in summer, Tue to Sat in winter
Place Godeau
☎04.93.58.32.56
If you love pizza, stop at the Pêcheur de Soleil where 500 different kinds of pizza are made to order. The decor of this small establishment evokes a *tcharafi* (bazar), with dozens of antique kitchen utensils hanging from the ceiling. Christian and Marie-Françoise serve up light meals that are great quality for the price. In summer you can eat outdoors on the pretty, peaceful little square.

Le Pigeonnier
$-$$
closed Fri and Sat at noon
Place du Peyra
☎04.93.58.03.00
The Pigeonnier is a pleasant place (both inside and on the terrace) to enjoy Provencal dishes (such as homemade ravioli and pasta, salmon *tagliatelles*, a dozen escargots in puff pastry) and the house specialty, homemade tiramisu. What's more, this establishment is protected from the traffic even though it's right in the tourist area, surrounded by attractive Provençal shops.

P'tit Provencal
$-$$$
closed Sun evening and Mon
4 Place Clémenceau
☎04.93.58.50.64
If you want to go more upscale but eat at comparable prices, have a meal at the P'tit Provençal. The fixed-price lunch menu is only 69F, but very enticing since the food is great and well presented. This charming little restaurant (with a small terrace on the street) offers "country" specialties (meat and fish).

La Cassolette
$-$$$
10bis Place Clémenceau
☎04.93.58.84.15
A few steps away, La Cassolette serves traditional food from the southeast region of France, including *cassoulet* and *magret de canard*. Claude Berlin guarantees a warm reception and good food at reasonable prices.

La Farigoule
$$-$$$
closed Tue and Wed at noon
15 Avenue Henri Isnard
☎04.93.58.01.27
Situated west of the historic town centre, La Farigoule features a

charming and unique setting. You can enjoy tasty meals highlighting the flavours of Provence (pasta, meat, fish) in a rustic interior decor or on the delightful large patio.

Auberge des Seigneurs
$$$
closed Mon to Wed at noon
Place du Frêne
☎04.93.58.04.24
⇌04.93.24.08.01
The Auberge des Seigneurs is the best place for a classy evening in a medieval atmosphere. Located beside the "Château-Musée de Villeneuve," this restaurant serves fine regional cuisine in an interior that is carefully maintained and full of character. The menu offers selections like *tian vençois* and *tourton des pâtres* (a local type of shepherd's pie), followed by a rack of lamb or half chicken, both cooked on skewers over a wood fire. To top it off, the gracious welcome extended by Madame Rodi and her staff adds to the restaurant's appeal. It is quite possible that a mischievous ghost will swipe your table-napkin or your bill, adding to the light-hearted charm and family ambiance of the place.

Saint-Jeannet

Au Vieux Four
$
closed for lunch and Tue evening (except in Jul and Aug)
23 Rue du Château
☎04.93.24.97.41
Au Vieux Four offers pizza cooked in a wood-burning oven. But pizza is not all you will find here, since Martin, the young chef, also prepares quality fish and meat dishes. The atmosphere is warm and convivial.

Chante Grill
$-$$
42 Rue Nationale
☎04.93.24.97.41
We recommend the Chante Grill for lunch (and for other meals as well). Maguy and Philippe serve food prepared according to family tradition, their specialty being rabbit bouillabaisse. A small terrace overlooks the lane that runs directly to the wash-house.

L'Indicible
$$
closed Thu
at the entrance to the old town
☎04.92.11.01.08
At the Hôtel L'Indicible, the food is also guaranteed to be good. The young Belgian couple who owns the place are well acquainted with Provencal herbs as well as traditional Belgian recipes, which use beer as a basic ingredient. The atmosphere is pleasant, and the service and reception are excellent.

Haut-de-Cagnes

This charming village has several good and very good restaurants:

Le Vertigo
$-$$
closed Jan
Place du Château
On the square of the château we recommend Le Vertigo, primarily because of its wonderful location under the acacia trees, its delectable salad combinations and its exceptional desserts (with home-made ice cream). The owner is not stingy with the vodka, which he adds liberally to the lemon ice cream, making sure that the "colonel" special lives up to its name!

Entre Cour et Jardin
$-$$
pm only except on Sun, closed Tue
102 Montée de la Bourgade
☎04.93.20.72.27
Entre Cour et Jardin, located on one of the little streets leading to the chateau, is a small restaurant with a relaxed, friendly atmosphere. It serves decent, unpretentious regional cuisine, and the service is extremely cordial. The apéritif included with the table d'hôte and the snacks are good starters.

Les Peintres
$$-$$$
closed Wed and Mon for lunch
71 Montée de la Bourgade
☎04.93.20.83.08
The more upscale Les Peintres is sure to win you over—first, with its decor, which highlights the work of local artists, and then with its cuisine. Young chef Frank Ria hails from Toulouse and concocts dishes that blend the flavours of southwest of France with those of Provence, all for very good value. One distinctive touch is that instead of the usual selection of cheeses, guests are offered a delicious *aumônière de reblochon* (Savoie cheese pockets).

Le Cagnard
$$-$$$
Rue Pontis-Long
☎04.93.20.73.21
The restaurant in the Hotel Le Cagnard lives up to the good reputation of the Relais et Châteaux chain. The dining room is quite spectacular, with a view of the surrounding landscape. The roof opens, enabling guests to admire the sky as well as the horizon. The cuisine is delicious, but the stiff service—which seems to be the norm in establishments like this—detracts a bit from the pleasure of eating here. If you're looking for an exclusive atmosphere, however, this is the place to go. See hotel description, p 311.

La table d'Yves
$$-$$$$
closed Tue and Thu at noon and Wed
85 Montée de la Bourgade
☎04.93.20.33.33
Several restaurant guides recommend La table d'Yves, and for good reason. You can choose among the different menus (*saveur*, *gourmand* or *plaisir*) according to your taste, budget and appetite, or order à la carte. The house specialties are fillet of *pagre*, a velvety pea soup with white truffle oil and duck *lardon*, as well as strawberries marinated in sweet wine and mint for dessert. Irresistible!

Saint-Paul-de-Vence

Café de la Place
$
☎04.93.32.80.03
The Café de la Place is located in the most strategic spot in Saint-Paul: you have go past it to enter the village. It's an extremely inviting place, with a big outdoor seating area, where the "ringside seats" for the pétanque games played on the square are located. The simple fare is perfect for lunch. Of course, this is also a great place to have drinks before dinner. Don't get too irritated by the high stress level of the servers at lunchtime.

La Voûte
$-$$
☎04.93.32.09.47
There are several quaint little restaurants along the ramparts at the west end of the town. We especially recommend La Voûte. Provençale and Italian cuisine are served here. Make a reservation or arrive early to get a table on the little terrace from which you can enjoy the magnificent views.

La Colombe d'Or
$$$
☎04.93.32.80.02
≠04.93.32.77.78
La Colombe d'Or is among the most prestigious establishments in the area. Formerly a post house, and later a modest inn run under the name of Robinson, this hotel was transformed into a hotel-restaurant by the son of the innkeeper. The owner, an art-lover, has created a living museum here. Dine in a sumptuous setting among paintings by the great masters, including Picasso, Matisse, Léger and many more. The dining areas is as rustic as it is elegant. Here, art and space are one. In the summer, guests can enjoy breakfast or lunch in a very beautiful, shaded garden. But this sought-after little place is fairly expensive. They do not offer a table d'hôte, and a basic but fine gourmet meal costs about 300F per person. Yves Montand and Simone Signoret adored staying

here so much that at one time they actually became co-owners.

Le Saint-Paul
$$$-$$$$
closed late Nov to late Jan, except Christmas, New Year and Tue noon
86 Rue Grande
☎04.93.32.65.25
The hotel-restaurant Le Saint-Paul is worth a detour for food enthusiasts. At lunch, you can choose among three excellent daily specials or order à la carte. Meals are served on a small, shady terrace. In the evening, the lovely interior awaits you to sample house specialties like Mediterranean sea-perch with lemon, baked in clay. For dessert there is *crème brulée* with Provençal flavours such as basil, rosemary and thyme. Those who prefer to finish their meal with a cheese course can feast on *reblochon* farm cheese with truffles.

La Colle-sur-Loup

L'Abbaye
$$$
541 Boulevard Honoré Teisseire
☎04.93.32.68.34
Set in a building that dates back to the 10th century, L'Abbaye has a truly enchanting location. If you come during high season, you can enjoy lunch or dinner in a garden that lets in the perfect amount of light; if not, Madame Hugues or one of her staff will direct you to the inviting dining room. In this interior decorated with venerable antique furnishings, guests can sample the aperitif (a house specialty) and then savour the cooking of Chef Hervé Rozec who strains his ingenuity to marry different flavours that will seduce your palate. The asparagus-and-shrimp salad as well as the roasted young chicken (*coquelet*) with lemongrass is very tasty. Dining at L'Abbaye is an experience that won't disappoint. After your meal, be sure to visit the chapel where religious ceremonies are still held.

Villeneuve-Loubet

Le Festival de la Moule
$-$$
on the coastal road, near the Géant Casino
☎04.92.02.73.25
Do you like mussels and fries? Come to Le Fetsival de la Moule. Whether you sit inside or on the huge terrace (open-air or covered depending on the weather), you can enjoy all-you-can-eat mussels prepared in a variety of ways. The French fries are good, and the pizzas and pasta (also all you can eat) come highly recommended as well. The atmosphere is youthful and lively, and the service is efficient.

La Vieille Auberge
$-$$
closed Wed
11 Rue des Mesures
☎04.93.73.90.92
Right in the heart of the old village, La Vieille Auberge is a restaurant with a Provençal decor and a charming little outdoor seating area. Chef Fabienne Pradier, a disciple of Escoffier (the museum of culinary art is right near by), cooks up regional cuisine using local produce, which you can wash down with a local wine.

Cabris

L'Auberge le Vieux Château
$-$$
closed Tue evening and Wed in off season
Place Maribeau
☎04.93.60.50.12
L'Auberge le Vieux Château stands near the ruins of the chateau, at the top of the village. They serve local specialties like *pigeon farci aux noisettes et aux choux.*

La Chèvre-d'or
$$-$$$
at the entrance to the village
☎04.93.60.54.22
In a different category, namely that of finer and more expensive dining, you can try La Chèvre-d'or. The chef prepares dishes including veal sweetbread, Tournedos Rossini, fillet of beef with morel mushrooms, as well as fish, *coquilles Saint-*

Jacques and prawns *à la provençale.*

Biot

Boulangerie H. Dessoit
15 Rue St-Sébastien
Whether you arrive in this ancient village at lunchtime or during the course of the afternoon, stop at the Boulangerie H. Dessoit for a bite if you're hungry. You'll be met with a warm welcome, and there is a little area where you can eat sandwiches, quiches and other little treats made at the bakery.

Hôtel des Arcades
$$
16 Place des Arcades
☎04.93.65.01.04
⇌04.93.65.01.05
Hidden away at the very top of this charming old village is the magnificent Hôtel des Arcades. The building dates from the 15th century and is as charming as can be. It is worth coming here just for the food. The menu includes Provençale specialties like sautéed rabbit with herbs, as well as osso bucco (the owners are of Italian and Norman descent). You should also try the house ravioli. This restaurant, where celebrities dine, is a definite must!

Valbonne

Moulin des Moines
$-$$
closed Sun evening and Sat at lunch
Place de l'Église
☎04.93.12.03.41
The Moulin des Moines has a charming 12th-century interior. Outside, a lovely shaded terrace awaits. House specialties include home-made foie gras *au torchon*, various fish dishes, and a gourmet plate with six different mouth-watering deserts. The restaurant prides itself on having a large cellar of good vintage wines. Meal prices are fairly reasonable since they include wine and coffee, giving you decent value for your money.

Antibes

Restaurant de la Gravette
$
closed Tue
48 Boulevard d'Aguillon
☎04.93.34.18.60
The Restaurant de la Gravette, offers seafood specialities including bouillabaisse, grilled fish, scampi and fried seafood. This restaurant has a huge terrace looking out onto a pedestrian street. It is just behind the big wall on the right side just past the entrance to Vieux-Antibes. They offer a lunch menu which includes appetiser, main course and dessert for 58F.

Le Pistou
$
pm only, closed Sun
18 Rue James Close
☎04.93.34.73.51
Located on one of the prettiest little commercial streets in the Antibes, Le Pistou is a bargain. The chef and owner is first and foremost an artist—not just when it comes to food—he is actually a sculptor. This place, adorned with his father's works, is convivial, in the best sense of the word. What an ambiance! No one, no matter how gargantuan an appetite they might have, will leave hungry. The 110F menu starts with a tureen of thick, flavourful *soupe au pistou*. It's so delicious that you can't help but have seconds, even though you know there's more food coming. This place is a real gem, and the prices are unbeatable.

La Taverne du Safranier
$
closed Mon and Tue at noon
Place du Safranier
☎04.93.34.80.50
La Taverne du Safranier looks out over a pleasant, calm square where the many lanes and streets of Vieux-Antibes begin. The restaurant is removed from the crowds since it is off the beaten tourist path of the town. This square is most charming, and in the summer is so very Provence. You can enjoy your meal outdoors beneath the awning or under

the stars. Provençal specialities and mussels are served. For dessert, we suggest their excellent home-made pie.

La Toscana
$
20 Avenue du 24 Août
☎04.93.64.18.02
For a quick meal, try La Toscana, a pizzeria near the bus station. Pasta, *fondue bourguignonne* and grill appear on the menu as well.

Le Brûlot
$-$$
closed Sun, and Mon to Wed at noon
3 Rue Frédéric Isnard
☎04.93.34.17.76
We highly recommend Le Brûlot, located a few steps from the restaurant above, also on the little street between the Place du Marché and the Place Nationale. Here you can eat *socca*, couscous, pizzas and grilled dishes in a pleasant room or in the large vaulted room below. This restaurant is very popular with the Antibois and Antiboises.

Le Caméo
$$
closed Nov and Dec
Place Nationale
☎04.93.34.24.17
Le Caméo is a combination of hotel, bed and breakfast and bar. Their specialities are paella and *marmite des pêcheurs* (fish stew). Other dishes are more ordinary like the *fondue bouguinon* (as much as you want). The value is very good, and you can eat outdoors under the plane trees of the Place National, in the heart of Vieux-Antibes.

Jardin de Justine
$$
5 Rue Sade
☎04.93.34.64.74
Don't hesitate to sample the offerings at the Jardin de Justine. Provençal specialties are served in a lovely walled garden. The ambiance is very welcoming.

Le Sucrier
$$
closed Tue, closed Jan and Feb
6 Rue des Bains
☎04.93.34.85.40
Le Sucrier serves innovative regional cuisine by adding a touch of the exotic. The resulting combinations will make your mouth water. As an added bonus, you can eat outside in the little garden. This establishment sometimes presents dinner shows.

L'Auberge Provençale
$$-$$$
closed Mon and Tue noon
Place Nationale
☎04.93.34.13.24
L'Auberge Provençale is also in the square, in the heart of the city. Inside, there is a very attractive summer garden. The setting is rustic and spacious. The menu consists of fish, seafood and shellfish, and the house speciality is bouillabaisse.

La table ronde
$$-$$$
5 Rue Frédéric Isnard
☎04.93.34.31.61
La table ronde is right next door to the restaurant above. This establishment has a Breton atmosphere, and the house specialties are bouillabaisse, *jambettes d'agneau* (lamb shanks) and frogs' legs. More exotic specialties such as ostrich, kangaroo, swordfish and shark round out the menu.

Juan-les-Pins

L'Oasis
$-$$
closed in the evenings during winter
Boulevard du Littoral
☎04.93.61.45.15
For a meal that is truly a seafood feast, go to L'Oasis. This popular restaurant is right on the beach. Guests may park in the large lot across the boulevard, just behind the railroad tracks.

During the summer you can eat outside, on the beach. Otherwise, the dining room has large bay windows, which are all that separate you from the sea. The view extends from Cap d'Antibes to the Îles Lérins. The restaurant is well maintained by the very friendly Bruno Charles. Try the *marmite du pêcheur*, (fish stew). For dessert, the creamy, delicious chocolate mousse is a must. You can enjoy a walk on the beach after dinner. The value and service are both excellent. Finally, the restaurant offers service on the beach with unbeatable lunch specials.

Cannes

Brasserie d'Gigi
$
5 Rue Meynadier
☎***04.92.98.81.88***
If you'd like to take a break for coffee and dessert, stop at Brasserie d'Gigi. Enjoy a piece of *tarte tatin* along this lively pedestrian street. At noon, you can enjoy a daily special, wine and dessert for 70F.

North Beach Cafe
$
closed Sun
8 Rue du 24 Août
☎***04.93.38.40.51***
On a pedestrian street between the sea and the station, the North Beach Cafe offers a table d'hôte at 67F. House specialities are pasta, crepes and salads. It's an "in" spot, decorated all in white and very bright. Highly recommended.

La Socca
$-$$
62 Rue Meynadier
☎***04.93.39.91.39***
La Socca is located in the middle of town on a lively little street. The Boughambouz family, of Algerian origin, spares no effort to ensure that guests receive a warm reception and good food at a reasonable price. Dishes include succulent pasta with pesto, burbot *bourride*, paella and grilled fish. The owner, who is a pastry-chef, bakes the bread. Try his excellent lemon tart.

Vesuvio
$-$$
68 La Croisette
☎***04.93.94.08.28***
If you prefer Italian cuisine, go to Vesuvio. Excellent pizza and fresh pasta can be enjoyed at the bar or on the terrace. The ambiance and decor are truly agreeable.

Au Bec Fin
$$
closed Sun and Mon
12 Rue du 24 août
☎***04.93.38.35.86***
This little restaurant, opened in 1955 by the Hugues family, offers simple, traditional fare at affordable prices *(69-112F)*. Excellent value for the money is assured by Phillippe and his brother Antoine. And the service is great.

Au Mal Assis
$$
closed mid-Nov to Christmas
15 Quai Saint-Pierre
☎***04.93.99.19.09***
Don't worry, you'll be comfortable at Au Mal Assis. This pleasant restaurant at the Vieux-Port offers a fixed menu for 120F. You can sit outside on the terrace and enjoy the house specialities including local fish, bouillabaisse, *bourride maison* and *lotte proivrée* in soup.

Le Madeleine
$$-$$$
closed Nov and Tue
13 Boulevard Jean Hibert
☎***04.93.39.72.22***
This brasserie is a little removed from the bustle of the port because it is located on the coast on the way to Mandelieu. But this doesn't mean it's wanting in atmosphere: it's often packed and the elevated, rooftop terrace is very lively. As in all seaside restaurants, fish and seafood are served.

Le Montagnard
$$-$$$
closed Sun and Mon
6 Rue Maréchal Joffre
☎***04.93.39.98.38***
This is the place to go if you're looking for tasty fish dishes or vegetarian cuisine made with fresh, organic products which is a rarity in Cannes. This restaurant is centrally located.

Astoux & Brun
$$-$$$
telephone reservations are not accepted
27 Rue Félix Faure
☎***04.93.39.21.87***
A restaurant for connoisseurs: Astoux & Brun has a very good reputation, and the prices are surprisingly reasonable. House specialities include fish and shellfish served on the air-conditioned terrace. Not to be confused with "Chez Astoux."

Le Mesclun
$$$
closed Dec and Wed
16 Rue St-Antoine, Le Suquet
☎***04.93.99.45.19***
This restaurant is nestled in a little street that leads to Le Suquet, the oldest, most picturesque and most becoming part of Cannes. Choose the slightly raised terrace if you want to dine with atmosphere. For a little more calm, choose the dining room inside. The restaurant serves regional specialties and the ambiance is truly enjoyable. We strongly recommend it!

La Palme d'Or
$$$
closed Mon and Tue and Nov 15 to Jan 15
Hôtel Martinez, 73 La Croisette
☎***04.92.98.77.14***
Haute cuisine is featured at La Palme d'Or, which offers a 340F (275F at lunch) menu. Guests here will enjoy dining to music on the air-conditioned terrace. This restaurant is the talk of the town when it comes to fine dining.

Le Relais des Semailles
$$$
closed Sun from Nov to Mar
9 Rue Saint-Antoine, Le Suquet
☎***04.93.39.22.32***
In the old city, we recommend Le Relais des Semailles. This restaurant prepares market fare served on an air-conditioned terrace. The 190F menu is expensive enough, but is high in quality.

Gaston Gastounette
$$$-$$$$
closed for two or three weeks in Jan
7 Quai Saint-Pierre
☎***04.93.39.47.92***
Also in the Vieux-Port is another highly recommended restaurant. The Gaston Gastounette specializes in fish dishes, bouillabaisse and lobster, which are served on the air-conditioned terrace.

La Villa des Lys
$$$$
closed December
Hôtel Majestic, 14 La Croisette
☎***04.92.98.77.41***
This restaurant, hailed by all, is a refuge of culinary art. The decor is polished, the service is attentive and the food delicious; but it's all included in the price. Definitely a place to check out if you're looking for something new.

Restaurants on the Beach

Among the many restaurants along the beach (obviously closed in winter), these two are especially worthwhile:

Lido Plage
$-$$$
on the Croisette (promenade), across from the Hôtel Carleton
☎***04.93.38.25.44***
The Lido Plage serves generous portions at reasonable prices. Patrons enjoy Italian and Provençal specialties right by the sea, shaded from the sun. Fred ensures a friendly reception and efficient service. We recommend the daily lunch special. The desserts, which include fruit tarts, are great.

Belle Plage
$-$$$
on the beach by Boulevard De Midi
The Belle Plage is located just west of the port, as you leave Cannes via the coastal road. This establishment is recommended by the Canois, and offers good food at decent prices.

Mougins (old town)

Mougins is a beautiful town to see, and also a good place for a gastronomic adventure or two. The restaurants listed below are all close to each other.

Resto des Arts
$-$$
14 Rue du Maréchal Foch
☎***04.93.75.60.03***
At the Resto des Arts, Denise and Gregory serve *petits farcis* (vegetables stuffed with ground meat), Provençal stew, rabbit with two kinds of mustard and many lighter, less elaborate dishes, all in an artistic decor with a friendly ambiance.

La Villa Romaine
$-$$
12 Rue du Maréchal Foch
☎***04.93.75.54.25***

You can also nibble on good food at La Villa Romaine. The theatrical decor is perfect for the pasta, pizza and salad served here.

À la Table d'Edmond
$-$$
closed Wed and Thu at noon
7 Avenue de l'Église
☎04.92.92.15.31
À la Table d'Edmond is an excellent establishment, right across from the two restaurants above. Edmond and Rosa-Marie welcome you on the shady terrace or in the unique interior. Good food.

Feu Follet
$$-$$$
closed Mon and Tue at noon and mid-Dec to mid-Feb
Place de la Mairie
☎04.92.92.15.31
The Feu Follet is well known and for years has consistently served good, classic menus as well as more original selections. We especially liked its location on the terraces and the views from the upstairs windows, which open onto the square.

Brasserie de la Méditerranée
$$-$$$
closed Jan
Place de la Mairie
☎04.93.90.03.47
We recommend the Brasserie de la Méditerranée because of its superb interior decor and large terraces offering both sun and shade. The "trio" that owns it strives to ensure that their guests receive the best, and each owner brings their own particular qualities to the enterprise. In spite of some weaknesses, such as inattentive service, the food is very good, as is the presentation. Try the mustard and saffron pike, but avoid the sorbet, which is nothing special.

Muscadins
$$$
18 Boulevard Courteline
☎04.92.28.28.28
Muscadins is an absolute must. The young cook, Noël Mantel, uses only quality ingredients. With his Provençale-Italian flavours, he convinced us of his talent. Indulge your taste buds with huge poached lobster *ravioles* in a clear shellfish broth. But then you'd have to do without the Italian *risotto* with *fleurs de courgettes* or the *rougets* fried in olive oil with purple artichokes and fresh herbs. Of course, there is the *magret de canard sur la peau* in pepper sauce sweetened with honey. In other words, meals are fit for a king. The atmosphere is equally pleasant in winter in the beautiful dining room, and in summer when the recently expanded blue-and-white terrace with sparkling silverware comes to life.

Mougins

Le Moulin de Mougins
$$ at noon
$$$-$$$$ in the evening
closed Mon, Thu noon and Feb and Mar
Chemin du Moulin
☎04.93.75.78.24
mougins@relaischateaux.fr
Another great master of French cuisine is Roger Vergé, who runs Le Moulin de Mougins with his wife Denise. This restaurant is set in a marvellous 16th-century mill, in the Notre-Dame de Vie district, on the old road that used to lead up to the old town. It is surrounded by a lush garden. Every dish prepared in this kitchen is a culinary masterpiece. The presentation is beautiful, and sophisticated ingredients are often used. The always-attentive service is discreet, impeccable and sprinkled with good humour. In the dining rooms, marvellous attention has been paid to the decor, where the modest setting is complemented with period furniture and works of art from the École de Nice. You can enjoy your meal in one of the mill's lounges, or in the beautiful room with windows overlooking the garden. There are two set menus, one at 550F (*"de chauds parfums"*) and the other at 740F (*"tradition"*). Expensive... yes... but worth every *sou*.

A business lunch is served at noon for 280F. Here is a wonderful opportunity to discover this prestigious Mougins restaurant and meet a master chef.

If you'd like an introduction to Vergé's techniques, his cooking school offers an enlightening and amusing course *(Moulin de Mougins; ☎04.93.75.35.70)*. A small boutique also sells home-made products. And finally, *La lettre de mon Moulin*, published on an irregular basis, provides all sorts of information about Monsieur Vergé's establishment.

La Ferme de Mougins
$$-$$$$
closed Sun evenings and Mon
10 Avenue St-Basile
☎04.93.90.03.74
La Ferme de Mougins is another good place attesting to Mougins' epicurean status. The farmhouse is near the old village, in the heart of a very well-tended, flowered property. The setting is rustic and airy. The place is magnificent in summer, beautifully rural. Diners will enjoy traditional, richly flavoured French cuisine in the glassed-in dining room, or outside, on the splendid terrace looking out on the garden. Attentive service and excellent value for your money, though good wine is rather expensive.

The lunchtime menu during the week is less expensive at 250F a head.

Mouans-Sartoux

Although it may be tempting to eat on the square, we recommend two establishments that are popular with the locals and serve more original fare:

La Fiancée du Désert
$-$$
21 Rue Durand de Sartoux
☎04.92.28.19.14
If you like Middle Eastern food, acquaint yourself with La Fiancée du Désert, located in the heart of town. The original decor transports you to another world as you savour Lebanese cuisine (hummus, *mottabal*, taboule, couscous) in the dining room or on the terrace. There is an interesting Moroccan craft shop across the street.

La Gabbia
$-$$
closed Mon
corner of Rue Docteur Geoffrey and Rue Durand de Sartou
☎04.93.75.69.68
Head to La Gabbia to enjoy some local cuisine. The menu offers characteristically southern specialties such as guinea-fowl with honey, leg of mutton *à la romaine* and small dishes like spinach with goat cheese or tomatoes with courgettes.

Grasse

Gazan
$-$$
3 Rue Gazan
☎04.93.36.22.88
Gazan offers an attractive interior as well as a charming terrace where you can enjoy simple but original dishes like Gazan *galettes*, roast leg of mutton *à la farigoulette* and other house specialties.

Hôtel des Parfums
$$-$$$
Boulevard Eugène Charabot
☎04.92.42.35.35
⇄04.93.36.35.48
You can also dine at the Hôtel des Parfums (see p 318). Inside, the large restaurant offers a panoramic view, while outside there is a large shaded terrace by the pool. The cusine is regional with numerous meat and fish dishes, all good quality for the price.

Tourrettes-sur-Loup

La Barbacane
$
Place de la Libération
☎04.93.59.34.81
You can be refreshed and restored with a light lunch at La Barbacane, situated on the large square. The young owners ensure a warm reception and serve salads and *paninis* at good prices.

Le Mediéval
$-$$
closed Thu
6 Grand'Rue
☎04.93.59.31.63
Le Mediéval is on the little street that goes around the old town close to the main square. On the ground floor there is a little terrace looking out onto the surroundings. In a medieval-Provençal setting, you will enjoy Provençal cuisine at very reasonable prices.

Auberge Belles Terrasses
$-$$
☎04.93.59.30.03
The restaurant at the Auberge Belles Terrasses offers two standard menus. Their specialities are *cuisses de grenouilles provençales* (frogs legs), *civet de porcalet* (jugged piglet) and *lapin à la moutarde* (rabbit). Game is also served in the fall. See p 319 for a description of the inn.

La Treille
$-$$
closed Mon and Tue
770 Route de Grasse
☎04.93.59.29.39
The irresistible little La Treille, run by a husband and wife team (he welcomes the guests, she does the cooking), is located just outside the village. The food is served on a pretty, shady terrace with a gorgeous view of Tourrettes. Even better than the view, however, are the excellent regional dishes prepared with fresh country produce. The *farcis niçois* were delicious and very light compared to those elsewhere. Still, the most succulent dish of all is the gnocchi, which are remarkably light and not at all sticky. It's rare to find gnocchi that don't feel like rocks in your stomach. For more traditional tastes, the menu also includes veal or beef served with Roquefort, cream or forestière sauce.

Chez Grand-Mère
$$
closed Wed and Sat at noon
Place Maximin Escalier
☎04.93.59.33.34
If you go to the oldest section of the village, by way of the gate on the east side, you'll find the friendly little restaurant Chez Grand-Mère not far from the town hall. The owners (three generations) specialize in the art of Moroccan cooking (couscous, lemon chicken and grill dishes), and they do it well. The mother takes the orders, the father efficiently serves the food, and the son is busy in the kitchen while the grandmother rests up... The atmosphere is extremely pleasant and very welcoming, which explains why it is often full.

Bar-sur-Loup

L'École des Filles
$$
☎04.93.09.40.20
This new restaurant was built in an old girls' school (*École des Filles* means Girls' School) and serves family-style regional cuisine in an intimate setting. The owner is from an old local family; her mother is Simone Gauthier, the enchanting Provençal woman who runs the Galerie de Provence in Gourdon (see p 332).

Entertainment

To find out about all the events in the area, consult the ***L'Officiel des Loisirs*** or ***La Semaine des Spectacles***, sold at newstands.

During July and August, there are little music and theatre festivals in almost all the towns along the Côte d'Azur. Check with the tourist office in each town for dates and programmes.

Cagnes-sur-Mer

Le Diamant
1 Chemin du Lautin, RN7 Pont de la Cagne
☎04.93.73.48.22
Le Diamant is a private nightclub.

Biot

Musical Recitals
End of May to end of Jun
Église de Biot
☎04.93.65.05.85

Antibes

Bar de la Porte du Port
every day 7am to 2:30am in summer, 12:30am in winter
32 Rue Aubernon, Old Antibes
☎04.93.34.68.94
The Bar de la Porte du Port is a bistro worth getting acquainted with: a lively, friendly ambiance seems guaranteed here. This is also a good place to meet the locals.

Casino La Siesta
May to Oct
Route du Bord de Mer
☎04.93.33.31.31
Slot machines, French and English roulette, blackjack.

Antibes Music Festival
early Jul
Chantier Naval Opéra, Port Vauban
☎04.92.90.54.60

Juan-les-Pins

Antibes Juan-les-Pins International Jazz Festival
late Jul
Pinède Gould
☎04.92.90.53.00

Le Village
every day in summer, Fri and Sat in winter
Carrefour de La Nouvelle Orléans
☎04.92.93.90.00
This bar has a hot, sexy ambiance (hip dress is a must). It is a well-known spot that anchors the town's nightlife.

EDEN Casino
8pm to 5am
Boulevard Baudoin, across from the Pinède
☎04.92.93.71.71
Roulette, black jack and slot machines.

Cannes

Le Palais Oriental
10 Boulevard Jean Hibert
☎04.93.39.00.16
Le Palais Oriental is a large restaurant offering traditional Moroccan cuisine. A dance show is featured every night.

Le Sérérin
3 Rue Félix Faure, in Place de l'Hôtel de Ville
☎04.93.39.74.00
This restaurant, with its elegant decor, is open 24hrs.

Le Loft
Rue du Docteur Monod
Le Loft is an absolute must. Find refreshment at the bar before following the lively music up to the second floor or engaging in conversation in one of the lounge areas.

Le Whisky à Gogo
every day in summer, Fri and Sat in winter
115 Avenue Lérins
☎04.93.43.20.63
This bar is considered an establishment not to be missed. The room is magnificent, spacious and airy. You also find festival-goers and "real" VIPs here.

Lobby Bar
Royal Hôtel Casino, 605 Avenue du Général-de-Gaulle
☎04.92.07.70.00
Relaxing, comfortable, convivial atmosphere. Dance floor.

Gay and Lesbian Bars

Le Zanzibar
men only
85 Rue F. Faure
☎04.93.39.30.75
Definitely the most renowned gay bar in Cannes, and the easiest to find. It is located at the heart of the action, a few feet from the Palais des Festivals, the Suquet and the Port. The pleasant terrace is perfect for being seen or for eyeing the Cannes *gratin*...

Vogue
20 Rue Suquet
Techno and house music.

Casinos

Carlton Casino Club
70F
7:30pm to 4am
58 La Croisette
☎04.93.68.00.33
English and French roulette, black-jack, punto banco.
From Thursday to Sunday, you can dance at Jimmy'Z de Régine. It has a terrace with an exceptional panoramic view of the old port and Suquet. Frequented by a 40-plus crowd.

Casino Croisette
11am to 3am, until 4am on weekends, until 5am Jul-Aug
Palais des Festivals
☎**04.93.38.12.11**
Two rooms with 290 slot machines; English and French roulette, black-jack, chemin-de-fer, punto banco.

Festivals and Cultural Events

Cannes Musique Passion
late Apr
Palais des Festivals
☎**04.92.99.31.08**

International Film Festival
mid-May
Palais des Festivals
☎**04.93.39.01.01**

Nuits Musicales du Suquet
late Jul
Parvis de l'Église Notre-Dame d'Espérance
☎**04.92.98.62.77**
Music Festival.

International Dance Festi val
Last week of Nov
Palais des Festivals
☎**04.92.99.31.08**
⇄**04.92.98.98.76**

Mougins

Dinner-theatre

Saint-Petersbourg
45 Ave. Saint-Basile
☎**04.92.92.98.43**
Romantic and quintessentially Russian environment.

Grasse

Festival International des Maîtrises is an international choir-singing festival held in July at the cathedral *(☎04.93.36.70.18).*

Shopping

Saint-Paul-de-Vence

Faune et Flore
67 Rue Grande
☎**04.93.32.56.32**
studio ☎**04.93.08.37.54**
Faune et Flore is a family business run by real artists, who happen to be very friendly as well. They make pretty animal sculptures (ducks, cats, etc.), as well as charming serving trays decorated with lavender, dried plants and other natural ornaments. The owner, Robert Jean, is also a painter. Fascinated by Africa, he creates unique canvasses and sculptures inspired by African themes. Though relatively figurative, the compositions of his paintings also tend toward the abstract, lending them a very original style. This shop sets itself apart by selling high quality products and steering clear of tourist-trap kitsch.

Galerie Jean Carré
1 la Placette
☎**04.93.32.56.32**
Here you will find particularly beautiful works of art and artisan items.

Pont-du-Loup

La Confiserie des Gorges du Loup
9am to noon and 2pm to 6pm
12km (7.5mi) from Grasse, on Route de Vence
☎**04.93.59.38.32**
La Confiserie des Gorges du Loup offers traditionally prepared jams and candied fruit. Entirely decorated with 18th and 19th-century Provençal furniture, the store features beautiful armoires, buffets, bread boxes, tables and benches. Free guided tours demonstrate how everything is made. At the end of the tour, you can buy the confections sampled or displayed. This may be a bit out of the way for tourists; however, this place is well worth the detour for the quality of its products. They also have a store in the port district of Nice.

Gourdon

Galerie de Provence
☎**04.93.09.68.64**
The Galerie de Provence is situated upstairs from the castle exit.

Although the village is brimming with boutiques, there is only one run by Simone Gauthier. Provençal to the core, she is overflowing with energy and merriment. And she never stops! A great lover of the land, Simone insists on the unmatched quality of her *calissons* and nougat. Flavoured with orange or lemon "straight from my garden," she'll tell you, her products are definitely unique.

Mougins (old town)

La Boutique du Moulin et la Cave du Moulin
at the entrance to the village, going up towards the main square
☎***04.93.90.19.18***
☎***04.92.92.06.88***

La Boutique du Moulin et la Cave du Moulin is one of Roger Vergé's sidelines. He is the head chef at the Moulin de Mougins. This store sells the Produits du Soleil line, which includes seasonings, jams and jellies, mixed spices as well as a selection of teas and books by Roger Vergé. There are also quality wines, including some selected by Vergé himself. Exquisitely gift-wrapped bottles of cognac, eau-de-vie or champagne can be sent abroad as gifts.

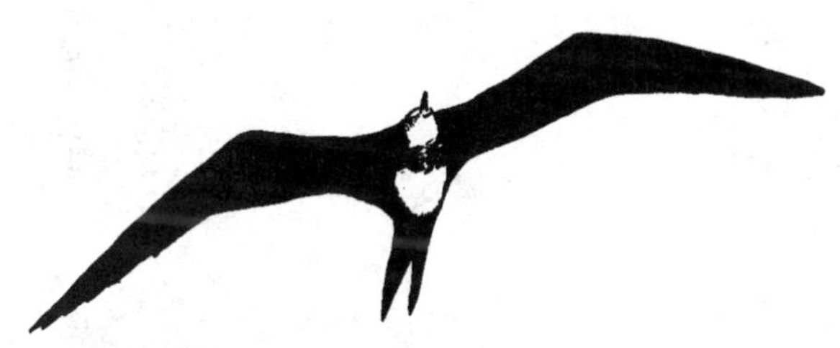

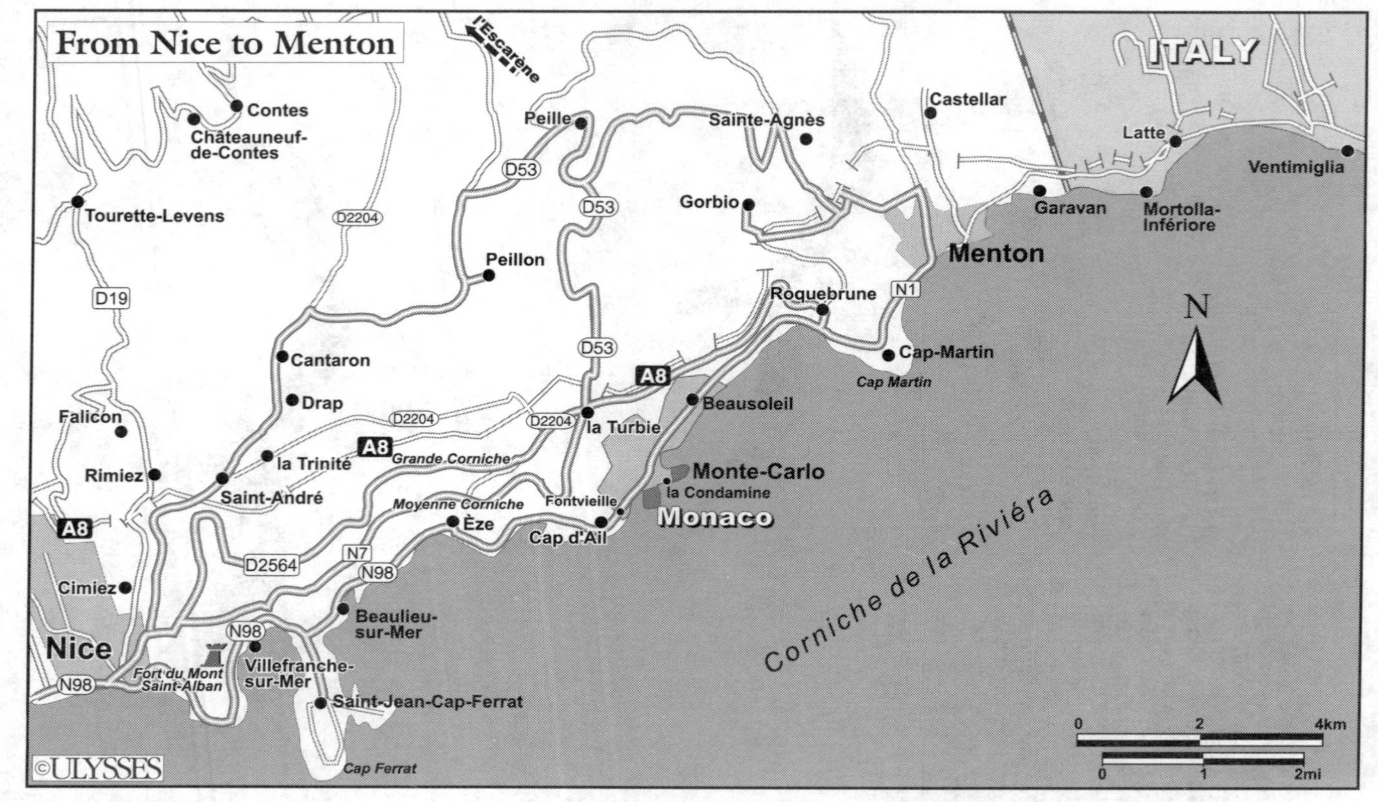
From Nice to Menton
l'Escarène
ITALY
Contes
Châteauneuf-de-Contes
Tourette-Levens
Peille
Sainte-Agnès
Castellar
Latte
Ventimiglia
Gorbio
Garavan
Mortolla-Inférieure
Menton
Peillon
D53
D2204
D19
Roquebrune
N1
N
Cantaron
Cap-Martin
Cap Martin
A8
Drap
Beausoleil
Falicon
la Turbie
la Trinité
Grande Corniche
Monte-Carlo
Rimiez
Saint-André
la Condamine
Moyenne Corniche
Fontvieille
Monaco
Èze
Cap d'Ail
D2564
N7
N98
Corniche de la Riviéra
Cimiez
Beaulieu-sur-Mer
Nice
Villefranche-sur-Mer
Fort du Mont Saint-Alban
Saint-Jean-Cap-Ferrat
Cap Ferrat
0
2
4km
1
2mi
©ULYSSES

From Nice to Menton

The splendid region from Nice to Menton stretches from the eastern part of the Côte d'Azur to the Italian border.

The Italian influence is clearly present here, in the inhabitants' names, their appearance and in the local dishes. This is not at all surprising since throughout its history, the region actually belonged more often to Italy than to France.

This part of the Côte d'Azur has to be seen, above all for its landscape. It is traversed by three mountain roads called *corniches*, which follow the coastline at different elevations. They are called La Basse, La Moyenne and La Grande.

Finding Your Way Around

Since each *corniche* offers a different panorama, having your own car is almost the only way to experience all of the beauty of the various landscapes. Other modes of transportation don't allow the flexibility of changing from one road to the next.

The villages and towns that border the sea are all accessible by train and bus. However, those located inland can only be reached by bus, which limits access considerably. For example, there are a few daily connections from Menton to Ste-Agnès, Gorbio and Castellar (inland villages in the Menton area).

We strongly recommend renting a car at one of the rental agencies in Nice for this part of your trip.

To get to the three *corniches* from Nice, leave the city from the east end near the port.

The Basse Corniche is to be avoided absolutely in July and August. The road follows the coastline and is jammed with traffic, especially in the late afternoon and early evening when everyone is coming back from the beach. This is an experience that you can afford to miss! In any case, there are many smaller roads that connect the *corniches*, which allow you to go from one to the other.

By Plane

Menton and all the towns east of Nice are less than 30km (18.6mi) from the airport in Nice.

Aéroport International de Nice
☎***04.93.21.30.30***
☎***04.93.21.30.12***
Flight information
☎***08.36.69.55.55***

Air France
☎***08.02.80.28.02***

By Train

There are a number of trains serving the region between Nice and Menton every day. They run to almost all the towns on the Côte d'Azur, and a few go as far as Vintimille in Italy.

Enquire at the SNCF stations:

Menton
☎***08.36.35.35.35***

Beaulieu
☎***04.93.01.15.31***

Nice
☎***08.36.35.35.35***

By Bus

Menton-Nice: every half-hour with Rapides Côte-d'Azu
☎***04.93.55.24.00 (Nice)***
☎***04.93.85.64.44 (Menton)***

Menton serves nearby inland villages (Gorbio, Ste-Agnès and Castellar) with a relatively regular schedule.

Microbus, Menton
☎***04.93.28.19.94***

Bus Station

Menton
Avenue de Sospel, (near the SNCF station)
☎***04.93.28.43.27***
Rapides Cote-d'Azur at Autocars Breuleux
☎***04.93.35.73.51***

By Car

Three *corniches* link Nice to Menton:

- The **Grande Corniche** or **D2565**
- The **Moyenne Corniche** or **N7**
- The **Basse Corniche** or **N559**, which is the coast road. It provides access to all the seaside resorts between Nice and Menton.

The quickest route from Nice to Menton is the **A8**.

Car Rentals

Menton
Avis
9 Rue Victor Hugo
☎***04.93.35.50.98***

Europcar
9 Avenue Thiers
☎***04.93.28.21.80***

Practical Information

Tourist Offices

Villefranche-sur-Mer
Jardin François Binon
☎***04.93.01.73.68***
⇄***04.93.76.63.65***

Saint-Jean-Cap-Ferrat
57 Ave. D. Séméria
☎***04.93.76.08.90***
⇄***04.93.76.76.67***

Beaulieu-sur-Mer
at the station
☎***04.93.01.02.21***
⇄***04.93.01.44.04***

Èze-Bord-de-Mer
Summer only
☎***04.93.01.52.00***

Èze-Village
Place du Général de Gaulle
☎***04.93.41.26.00***
⇄***04.93.41.04.80***

Cap d'Ail
104, Avenue du 3 Septembre, Centre Guillaume-Apollinaire
☎***04.93.78.02.33***
⇄***04.92.10.74.36***

La Turbie
Mon to Fri
at the Mairie (town hall)
☎***04.93.41.10.10***

Peille
Mon to Fri
at the Mairie
☎***04.93.91.71.71***

Peillon
open during the week only
at the Mairie
☎*04.93.79.91.04*
⇄*04.93.79.87.65*

Roquebrune Cap-Martin
Mon to Fri
☎*04.93.35.62.87*
⇄*04.93.28.57.00*

Menton
Palais de l'Europe; 8 Avenue Boyer, B.P. 239
☎*04.92.41.76.50*
☎*04.92.41.76.76*
Maison du patrimoine
5 Rue Ciapetta
Mon to Sat 8:30am to 12:30pm and 1:30pm to 6pm in winter, 8:30am to 6:30pm in summer, Sun 10am to noon
☎*04.92.10.33.66*
At the Mairie (town hall) 17 Rue de la République
☎*04.92.10.50.00*

Hospital

Menton
Hôpital La Palmosa
Rue A. Péglion
☎*04.93.28.77.77*
emergencies
☎*04.93.28.72.41*

SOS – Médecins
☎*04.93.41.41.41*

Banks and Currency Exchange

Menton
Currency Exchange
Office de Change St-Michel, 5 Rue St-Michel
☎*04.93.57.18.31*

Foreign exchange machine
43 Quai Bonaparte
☎*04.93.35.79.86*

Crédit Lyonnais
Avenue Boyer
☎*04.93.28.60.60*

Banque Nationale de Paris
14 Avenue Félix Faure
☎*04.93.35.80.87*

Exploring

Leaving Nice, take La Moyenne Corniche.

The road passes by the **Fort du Mont Alban**, one of the most beautiful examples of Renaissance military architecture. Transformed into a fortress in the 18th century, this fort was an important military installation until World War II. It offers magnificent views of the coast. Nearby Mont Boron, closer to the sea, is a nice place for a hike.

Whichever road you choose, make sure to stop in Villefranche-sur-Mer.

Villefranche-sur-Mer

Villefranche-sur-Mer is the first town east of Nice. This seaside village was founded in the 13th century on the site of Olivula, an old Roman port and commercial centre. The village has a network of charming pedestrian side-streets. One of these lanes, **Rue Obscure** ★, has remained unchanged since the 13th century, when it served as a refuge during periods of instability. It is completely covered, (a little like a tunnel) and is very dark, hence the name.

Though there are many small restaurants and bars pleasantly situated by the sea or on small squares in the village, the quality of the food they serve is rather wanting. Visitors would perhaps do better only dropping by for a drink. One exception is the La Grignotière restaurant (see p 353).

In the village stands **La Citadelle Saint-Elme**, a restored 16th-century building. The citadel was built by Emmanuel Philibert, Duke of Savoy, in reaction to the siege of Nice by François I in 1543. Later, the citadel became an important defence complex, after the occupation of the port by a Muslim fleet. Today, it is still a port-of-call for some of NATO's military units and for cruise ships. The citadel is also host to the **Fondation Musée Volti** *(free admission; summer, 10am to noon and 3pm to 6pm; Oct to May, 10am to noon and 2pm to 5pm; ☎04.93.76.33.27)*, where large sculptures depicting women in the Rodin style are on display.

At the port, make sure you visit the tiny

Chapelle Saint-Pierre ★★ (*12F; Tue-Sun, closed mid-Nov to mid-Dec; ☎04.93.76.90.70*), built in the 14th century. In 1957, Jean Cocteau decorated the inside of the chapel with paintings honouring "his friends the fishermen." The **Galerie Jean Cocteau** (*Sep to Jun, 10am to 7pm; Jul and Aug, 10am to 11pm; ☎04.93.01.73.92*) is on the first floor.

Across the street from the church, there are lovely terraces where visitors can stop for a drink. Tourists might not want to stay overnight in Villefranche. There is only a tiny beach and very few hotels.

Continue on the Bord-de-Mer road.

Saint-Jean-Cap-Ferrat

This cape extending out into the sea is famous for the great wealth of its residents. Yet, before the turn of the century, it was nothing more than a fishermen's hamlet, a still untamed place without any buildings to speak of. Everything changed when Béatrice de Rothschild had the **Villa Ephrussi-Rothschild** ★ (*entrance fee; Apr to Oct, everyday 10am to 6pm; Jul and Aug until 7pm; Nov to Mar. 15, Sat and Sun only; ☎04.93.01.45.90*) built here at the beginning of this century. If you like formal splendour, you will love this place. This home stands in testimony to the grandeur of the wealthy families of the *belle époque*. It contains a collection of paintings, furniture, rare objects, porcelain pieces, tapestries and sculptures. The grounds are also worth seeing as they include seven gardens in various themes (Spanish, Japanese, Provençal, Oriental, Exotic and, of course, French) complete with ornamental ponds, waterfalls, benches for visitors to rest on, and even a Temple of Love!

Villa Ephrussi-Rothschild

Finally, visitors can stop at the tea-room located in a lovely glassed-in rotunda that looks out onto the garden.

The cape can be toured on foot, by bicycle or by car. Hikers might want to set off on the 11km (6.8mi) trail that follows the coastline all the way around the cape. Along the path, visitors will catch an occasional glimpse of the grounds of the magnificent villas hidden behind the pine trees.

This excursion begins near Plage de Passable, not far from Villa Ephrussi-Rothschild and the **Zoo** (*58F; everyday 9:30am to 5:30pm, summer until 7pm; ☎04.93.76.07.60*), which has a wide variety of animals in the unique setting of tropical and Mediterranean vegetation. There is a lighthouse at the tip of the cape. Beyond it lies the Hôtel Bel-Air, a very luxurious palace built at the turn of the century.

This building is a member of the Relais et Châteaux chain and has its own private beach.

There are lots of places for sunbathing on the rocks surrounding the cape, which plunge into the sea. There are also several little inlets to be discovered. Nude suntanning is very commonly practised on the rocks, but almost exclusively by men.

On the other side of the cape, the path continues towards the peninsula which retains a rugged look. Near the eastern point, your walk will take you up towards the pretty little **Chapelle Sainte-Hospice**. This site offers a lovely view of the surrounding area. A little further, on the north side, is the charming La Paloma Beach where you can get a bite to eat and rent water-sports equipment. A little further is the port, with its many shops and a variety of restaurants.

Leave the cape and go back to the Bord-de-Mer road.

Beaulieu-sur-Mer

You can also go to Beaulieu-sur-Mer on foot via Promenade Maurice-Rouvier from the cape. It makes for a most pleasant walk. The path follows the coast and has several benches where you can rest in the shade of pine trees and admire the magnificent view.

A visit to the **Villa Kerylos** ★★ *(45F; summer, Mon to Sun 10:30am to 7pm; winter, 2:00pm to 6:00pm; mid-Feb to mid-Nov, 10:30 to 6pm; ☎04.93.01.01.44)* is a must. When it was built at the beginning of the century, the owner intended it as a tribute to life in ancient Greece, but with all the modern comforts of the 20th century. Designated a historical monument in 1967, this seaside residence features an exceptional wealth of materials and a highly luxurious decor: walls, floors and ceilings made of white, yellow or lavender Italian marble, frosted glass, alabaster, ivory and bronze.

Leave Beaulieu, still following the Bord-de-Mer road.

Èze

Éze is made up of three communities: **Èze-Bord-de Mer** on the Basse Corniche, **Èze-Village** ★★★, higher up on the Moyenne Corniche, and finally **Le Col d'Èze** ★★ even higher up on the Grande Corniche.

Èze-Bord-de-Mer has two public beaches that are still undeveloped, one private beach and a sailing club near the train station. Make a short stop at **Chapelle Saint-Laurent**, built in the 12th century.

From there you can reach Èze-Village by car. The more athletic will want to hike up via the Chemin Nietzsche. This trail offers magnificent vantage points over the sea and takes around 1hr to complete. The incline is, however, quite steep!

You should stop in at the **tourist office** *(Place Général de Gaulle, ☎04.93.41.26.00)* as soon as you arrive at Èze-village. They have an excellent brochure about Éze called *Èze Guide Pratique*, as well as a pamphlet for hikers about various trails in the area.

Èze-Village is located on a rocky peak at an altitude of 429m (1,407ft). Ligurians had already settled here by the Middle Ages for the protection the terrain offered. Today, it is a perfect place for relaxing, except maybe in July and August. You can enter the village by the **Paterne**—two guard-towers, now designated historical monuments, which were built in the 14th century to guard the only entrance to the village. Beyond them is the church, which was built around 1772. Its sober façade, pierced by a single bull's-eye window, contrasts sharply with the very rich baroque-style interior.

Next comes the trek up through charming, narrow streets. Near the top, two luxurious hotels offer excellent service in a virtual paradise. The **Jardin Exotique** *(12F; summer, 9am to 8pm; off-season, 9am to 6:30pm; ☎04.93.41.10.30)* is at the top of the village. This garden contains numerous species of cacti, most of which are native to South America. The garden is laid out on several levels, and the top level features a large terrace offering a spectacular panorama that spans from Cap Ferrat to l'Estérel. On a clear winter day you can even see Corsica.

From Èze-Village, head up towards the **Grande Corniche** ★★★, a road built under the orders of Napoleon I. It offers even more spectacular panoramas stretching as far as Hyères to the west, and Italy to the east. At the top, there is a wilderness park covering 60ha (148.3 acres) from Mont Vinaigre to the Mont Bataille promontory. You can learn about the park at the Maison de la Nature, where there is also a parking lot. At the Révère, an old military building, there is a viewing table indicating the location of the region's various capes, bays, seaside towns and alpine peaks.

Next to the Hôtel Hermitage (see p 349), a walking trail invites hikers of all ages on a short excursion (1.4km or .9mi). There is also a small playground for children, and picnic tables shaded by oak trees.

Also in the vicinity is the **Astrorama** *(40F, 60F with show; May to Sep, Tue, Fri and Sat 6:30pm to 11pm; Oct to Apr, 5:30pm to 10pm; ☎04.93.85.85.58)*, which is sure to delight children who will enjoy observing the stars.

Head east out of Éze, regardless of whether you are taking the Moyenne or Grande Corniche.

La Turbie

If you've planned a different itinerary than that proposed, La Turbie can also be reached via the A8. In fact, this is the fastest way to get there, as there is an exit specifically for the town.

La Turbie

Already populated during prehistoric times, La Turbie was at its height during the Gallo-Roman era. It was located on Via Julia Augusta, a strategic road at the time. In Emperor Augustus' days, the Roman senate decided to erect a monument, **Le Trophée** *(25F; 18 Avenue Albert 1er; closed Mon, 9:30am to 7pm in summer, 5pm in winter; ☎04.93.41.20.84)*, to commemorate Augustus' victories over the rebels he conquered.

In the early 1930s, this monument was partially restored to its original architecture thanks to generous donations of a wealthy American art patron. There is even a museum devoted to the evolution of the monument throughout the years.

The sovereigns of Genoa, Savoy and France had always fought over La Turbie, because of its location on the borders of these kingdoms. In 1713, Monaco gave the village back to France once and for all.

The town and surrounding area is truly spectacular. Don't miss visiting the **Église Saint-Michel**, built in 1777. This beautiful pink and grey Renaissance-inspired church contains two magnificent paintings: a Brea original and a work said to be by Veronese, in the Chapelle de la Piétà. The altar is decorated with 17 sculpted roses.

Hint: This spot on the *corniche* offers a very beautiful view of Monaco and is generally off the tourist track in summer. It is cooler than right by the seaside, and the restaurant and hotel prices are much more reasonable.

Leave La Turbie by D53 for a short excursion inland.

Here is a short tour which will allow you to discover Monaco's interior via Peille and Peillon. This side-trip can be done by car or even by bike. This road allows you to discover some splendid landscapes. It is best, however, not to undertake this adventure during the summer vacation period, when car traffic is heavier, as the road is rather narrow.

Peille

In the Middle Ages, Peille was a consular city. The town is worth visiting mostly for its unusual location, almost hidden below the road. Visitors can park their cars in a roadside parking lot and walk down to the town below. Peille has some very lovely squares, including one near a gorgeous Gothic fountain. This square is home to the tiny Musée des Arts et Traditions Populaires, which is worth visiting. The village also contains the Chapelle Saint-Martin de Peille, a uniquely designed chapel built in the 1950s.

The lovely little **Musée du Terroir** *(free admission; in summer Wed, Sat and Sun 2pm to 6pm)* displays crafts and everyday objects from the 19th century.

The Peille area offers many possibilities for excursions and walks in the nearby forests. Hikers can set out for 20min or 3hrs. Some of the walking trails even go all the way to Monaco.

The road winding out of Peille, D53, leads past the Vicat cement quarry, which is a bit of a blemish on the landscape. The white Turbie stone, which was used to build the cathedral and the ocean museum in Monaco, came from this quarry.

Fans of the baroque style should make their way to **Escarène**, about 7.5km (4.7mi) farther north, on Route du Sel *(for more information, see the "From Nice to Tende" chapter, p 369).*

If you head down south, you will soon arrive at Peillon.

Peillon

Perched way up high, Peillon is one of the most beautiful towns on the Côte d'Azur. Many artists have immortalized the view over this village. There are two reasons why you absolutely must stop here: first to stroll through the narrow streets, stairways and vaulted passages that climb to the church at the top; and second, to eat or even spend the night at the Auberge de la Madone (see p 350).

There's not much to see in the village, save the **Chapelle des Pénitents Blancs**, decorated with gorgeous frescoes. However, you will find tranquillity and a haven from the tourist frenzy. This village has fortunately not been invaded by the many businesses which often undermine the charm of some other very beautiful towns on the Côte d'Azur, Saint-Paul-de-Vence for example.

Continue on D53 to D2204, which leads to the highway to Roquebrune.

Roquebrune Cap-Martin

Superbly situated between Menton and Monaco, this community offers great diversity. Its climate (annual average 17°C) is said to be the best in Europe, and is characterised by dazzling skies and an absence of fog. The lush fauna comes as no surprise.

This town's past is marked by the history of its castle, which dominates the picturesque medieval village of **Roquebrune ★★★**. The castle was built in AD 970 and is one of France's only Carolingian castles, a precursor of those erected two centuries later, which mark the height of the feudal era. Over the centuries, it belonged to the Counts of Vintimille, then the Counts of Provence, and finally to the Grimaldis. The castle was designated a historical monument in 1927.

You can enter the **Château ★** *(20F; 10am to 12:30pm and 3pm to 7:30pm in summer, 10am to 12:30pm and 2pm to 5pm in winter; ☎04.93.35.07.22)* by a stone bridge which has replaced the ancient 16th-century drawbridge. The ground floor, carved out of rock for the most part, holds a guard's room that has also served as a prison, and a water cistern, fed by rain water. The first floor once contained the great hall used for banquets and ceremonies but it is now an open courtyard. The second floor housed the castle guards. The third floor housed the seigneurial apartments: two vaulted rooms and a kitchen. In the 10th century, one of the two bedrooms

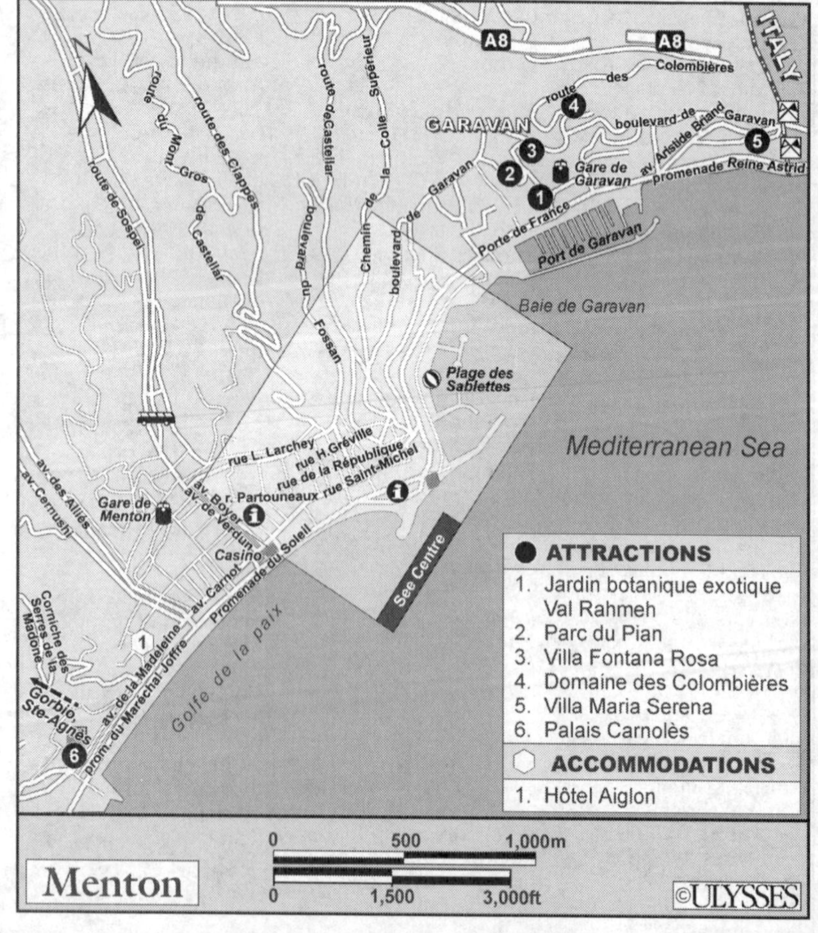

doubled as a dining room. The parapet walk on this floor allowed guards to survey the surrounding area. It offers a beautiful view of the landscape. Finally, on the top floor were the lodgings for the watchmen.

Take the time to explore the stairways and vaulted passages and charming little squares. Rue Pié has a large number of support arches very close together.

Cap-Martin ★ is a magnificent rocky overhang scattered with villas and gardens hidden among pine trees and secular olive trees. Nature lovers will be delighted by its walking trail, the **Promenade Le Corbusier ★★**, which follows the wild and steep contours of the coastline.

Cap-Martin shelters luxurious villas set in magnificent gardens, which can be explored on foot (no cars are allowed). This site has attracted many famous people: royalty, writers, artists, stage and screen stars, including Empress Sissi of Austria, the great architect Le Corbusier and Coco Chanel.

You can walk about these luxurious villas surrounded by magnificent gardens on foot along the wide avenues that make up the residential area that occupies the greater part of the island.

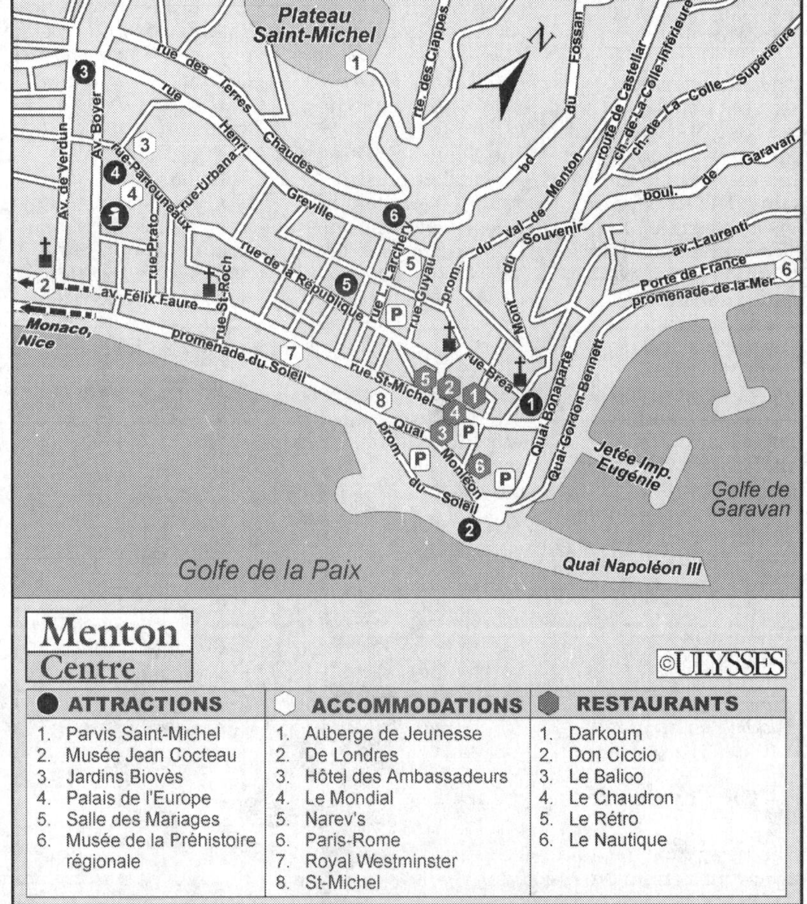

Finally, you can practise a host of water-sports activities or simply lounge on one of the beaches here.

Menton

Because of Menton's proximity to the Italian border, it has long been influenced by that country's culture. The colours of the houses attest to this. In fact, Menton only really became French in the 19th century, under Napoleon III.

The city enjoys an exceptional climate because of its advantageous location between the sea and the mountains. The result is an average temperature of 17°C in January. Furthermore, this microclimate has allowed Menton to cultivate citrus trees and tropical plants. It is known as the "lemon capital of the world", and for good reason. Its climate attracted many visitors near the end of the 19th century, including wealthy Northern-Europeans hoping to be cured of tuberculosis.

Menton has a lot of green spaces, which is why the city has adopted the slogan: *"Ma ville est un jardin"* (My city is a garden).

The City Centre

The best place to begin your tour is from the square in front of l'Église Saint-Michel, in the heart of the old city. Guided tours organised by the Service du Patrimoine start in front of this church *(30F; ask at the tourist office for schedule information).*

The **Parvis St-Michel** is an important place in Menton. This square, situated between two beautiful renaissance *(the Chapelle de l'Immaculée Conception or des Pénitants–Blancs)* and baroque *(the Basilique Saint-Michel-Archange; closed Sat morning, otherwise every day 10am to noon and 3pm to 5pm)* churches, is a mosaic of black and white cobblestone. A chamber music festival has been held here since 1949. An excursion up the Rue du Vieux-Château, reveals quaint houses painted in warm colours interspersed with splashes of green vegetation. At the top of the street lies the cemetery, which was founded on the site of the old castle.

Take one of the winding side streets to go back down to the square. Head towards Rue St-Michel, a commercial pedestrian street.

There are many stores and restaurants along Rue St-Michel. It's the perfect place to stop for a coffee or a light lunch.

Head towards the water, in the direction of the port and the bastion.

The bastion was built in the 17th century for the purpose of defending the city. Today it houses the **Musée Jean Cocteau** *(free admission; Wed to Mon 10am to noon and 2pm to 6pm; ☎04.93.57.72.30).* The only museum in the world dedicated to this artist, it holds a permanent exhibition of his works including drawings, tapestries, watercolours, pastels, ceramics and writings.

Walk west, towards the tourist office.

Église Saint-Michel

The market is directly across from the tourist office. Here, regional specialities such as *la pichade, la socca,* and *la fougasse,* to name but a few, await sampling. This is a must-see. Continuing west is the Promenade du Soleil and the casino; this is a popular place for a stroll.

Behind the Casino lie the **Jardins Biovès** where the 10-day long **Fête du Citron** (lemon festival) takes place every year in February. The **Palais de l'Europe** stands on the avenue bordering the gardens to the east. Site of the old casino, this building is now home to the tourist office and the municipal library. Various shows and cultural events are held here as well.

Go back east by Rue Parouneaux.

You will soon reach Rue de la République. At number 17 is the **Salle des Mariages de Jean Cocteau** *(5F; Mon to Fri 8:30am to 12:30pm and 1:30pm to 5pm; ☎04.93.57.87.87)*, decorated from 1957 to 1958 with frescoes by this celebrated French artist.

Continue to Rue Lorendan Larchey.

At the end of the long esplanade, is the **Musée de la Préhistoire Régionale** *(free admission; Wed to Mon 10am to noon and 2pm to 6pm, summer until 7pm; ☎04.93.35.84.64)*. It displays a collection of regional prehistoric specimens that were collected over the last one hundred years or so, including the "Menton man" skeleton that dates back to 25,000 BC. In the basement, there is a section devoted to the traditional arts and customs of Menton.

Garavan

This area is on the Italian border at the eastern edge of the town. A garden-lover's paradise, Garavan is overflowing with parks and gardens. Start with the **Jardin Botanique Exotique Val Rahmeh ★** *(20F; everyday 10am to 12:30pm and 2pm to 5pm, summer 3pm to 6pm; Avenue St-Jacques, ☎04.93.35.86.72)*. The gardens at this designated historical site are stunning, and the staff is friendly. You can stroll along the little footpaths that feature more than 650 plant species native to five continents. Just beside, is the **Parc du Pian**, a thousand-year-old olive grove. Three hectares (7.4 acres) of olive trees growing on the terraced hillside overlooking the sea can be visited.

A bit further to the east lie the gardens of **Villa Fontana Rosa** (*Avenue Blasco Ibanez)*, designed by the dramatist and writer Ibanez. The Valencia-style garden features benches, pergolas and ornamental ponds. The gardens are only open to the public on the third Saturday of the month at 10am *(Contact the tourist office, ☎04.92.10.33.66)*.

A bit further to the north is the **Domaine des Colombrières** *(20F; visit possible on demand at the Maison du Patamoine; Route des Colombrières, ☎04.93.35.71.90)*. A tour of the garden is like a trip around the Mediterranean.

Finally, just beside the border, is the **Villa Maria Serena** *(30F; Promenade Reine Astrid)*, built in 1880 by Charles Garnier (Opéra de Paris). The gardens include a large collection of exotic plants. They are open on Tuesdays at 10am. *(Contact the tourist office, ☎04.92.10.33.66)*.

Go back downtown to the Promenade du Soleil.

The **Palais Carnolès** *(free admission; Wed to Mon, 10am to noon and 2pm to 6pm, in summer until 7pm; ☎04.93.35.49.71)* is located at the very end of the Promenade du Soleil, at the far west end of the town. It houses the Musée des Beaux-Arts. The contemporary collections acquired at the biennial festivals of Menton are on display here. This old palace was built in 1717 as a summer residence for the Prince of Monaco. The park in which the building stands is the oldest garden in Menton. It contains over 400 trees of 50 different species.

Leave Menton by taking the D23 for Gorbio, in the backcountry of Menton. If you are short of time, head toward Ste-Agnès instead, on the D22, north of town.

Gorbio

The road to Gorbio is very tortuous. Though the journey is short, getting there will take some time. Be that as it may, the scenery is magnificent, particularly come nightfall.

A small village with a medieval character, Gorbio can be an interesting place in which to stop for a breather, far from the bustling Côte d'Azur. Moreover, the drive from here to Sainte-Agnès or Roquebrune-Village is beautiful.

Sainte-Agnès

This old Saracen town perched on the mountain is the highest town along the European coast. Here, the proud beauty of the rugged landscape embraces the coast. Sainte-Agnès is charming, and hikers will find it a great place to stop.

In fact, the surrounding area offers many possibilities for hiking, whether you prefer a short or long, easy or difficult trail. One possibility is a hike to Gorbio or Roquebrune-village from here.

Since 1999, friends of this medieval site have undertaken exceptional efforts to make accessible the ruins of this chateau overlooking the village. Visitors can cross the parapet, walk along the tops of the remains of the walls and explore the medieval garden. The amusing attendant posted at the entrance to the site quipped that if the Côte were a cake, this would be the cherry on top!

Outdoor Activities

Between Nice and Menton, the beaches are generally small and often privately owned (by a hotel or vacation-resort chain). The largest beaches (public and private) are at Menton and Èze.

This area offers many beautiful hiking trails along or close to the water.

Hiking

Saint-Jean-Cap-Ferrat

The walk around the cape makes a wonderful excursion for the young and not so young alike. Start at Pointe de Passable (at the northwest end of the peninsula, close to the zoo), where there is a small sandy public beach and a restaurant (on a private beach). The path follows the sea as far as the lighthouse (southern point) and then continues on the Chemin de la Carrière, which leads you to the new port. Duration of the tour: 90min. For more information, ask for a map at the tourist office.

Èze

Around Èze there are many beautiful walking trails that are easy, even where there are inclines. From here you can hike from Èze Bord de Mer to Èze-Village (Moyenne Corniche) to Saint-Laurent d'Èze and to Col d'Èze (Grande Corniche). Ask for the *Les Chemins d'Èze* map at the tourist office.

Roquebrune Cap-Martin

A beautiful and picturesque walking trail leads around the cape. The avenues on the privately-owned area in the interior of the peninsula are wide and peaceful, with magnificent villas along the way.

Menton

Menton, with its many botanical and exotic gardens, is perfect for those who enjoy a casual stroll. (See "Exploring" section). The city has a Service du Patrimoine, which tends the numerous gardens. Some of the gardens may only be seen with the permission of this administrative service.

Golf

La Turbie

Monte-Carlo Golf Club
18 holes
Route du Mont-Agel, La Turbie
☎04.93.41.09.11
The Monte-Carlo Golf Club is situated at an altitude of 900m (4,252ft), between mountains and sea, and is one of the most beautiful courses on the Côte d'Azur. The course is unique because it is so narrow.

Accommodations

There are two options—to be close to the sea, and all the action (including the nightlife), or to get away from the hustle and bustle and enjoy the tranquillity of the countryside. Of course, hotel prices are higher by the sea. However, as you head uphill, you will still enjoy panoramic views of the water.

Villefranche-sur-Mer

Hôtel Patricia
240F-300F
½ b 260-340F
closed Nov and Dec
ps
Avenue Ange Gardien, Pont Saint-Jean
☎04.93.01.06.70
⇄04.93.01.29.38
The well-located Hôtel Patricia is a family boarding house as well as a restaurant. The rooms are very basic, but the beaches are just 300m (984.3ft) away; you can take your pick between the ones in Villefranche or those in Cap-Ferrat, since the Patricia lies right at the border between the two. The restaurant ***($$)*** has lots of tables in the garden, part of which is shaded throughout the day. Balcony-lovers take note: only one room, #3, has one.

Hôtel Provençal
380F-590F
ps, ℜ, tv
in the centre of the village
☎04.93.76.53.53
⇄04.93.76.96.00
provencal@riviera.fr
There is really only one hotel in this town that is worth mentionning: the Hôtel Provençal. In July and August, the accommodation is half-board *(330-435F per person)*. The hotel, which was built in the 1930s, has been restored and offers spectacular views of the sea and the public garden behind. The rooms are pretty, bright and modern, and some also have terraces. The hotel's restaurant has a glassed-in terrace overlooking a garden where you can eat during the summer.

Hôtel Welcome
690F-950F
closed mid-Nov to mid-Dec
pb or ps, tv, elevator
on the seaside, Villefranche
☎04.93.76.27.62
⇄04.93.76.27.66
welcome@riviera.fr
The Hôtel Welcome really stands out in this town. To start with, it has lovely architecture, but more importantly, it is located in the middle of all the action, right near the port and the chapel decorated by Cocteau. The common terrace where breakfast is served, and the private terraces adjoining a number of the rooms, offer superb views of the port and the sea. The corner rooms are quite spectacular. Furthermore, since Cocteau's presence is strongly felt here, two of the rooms are decorated in his style.

Résidence Pierre & Vacances
3,360F-6,650F for a studio-cabin and 3,600F-7,200F per week for a two-room apartment
pb, K, ℜ, tv extra
☎04.93.76.40.00
If you're planning to stay for one week or longer, we recommend the Résidence Pierre & Vacances. Built on terraces facing the sea and overlooking the bay, the residence opens up to a lovely park, a beautiful pool and tennis courts. The beach is only 300m (984.3ft) away. Note: minimum stay is one week, beginning on a Saturday.

Saint-Jean-Cap-Ferrat

Here's a place we strongly recommend if you want to spend a few pleasant days on the coast. The cape has plenty of magnificent villas and lots of greenery.

Résidence Bagatelle
360F-500F
ps, tv
Avenue Honoré Sauvan
☎04.93.01.32.86
⇄04.93.01.41.00
hotelbagatelle@libertysurf.fr
Hidden in the middle of a lush garden, a stop at the Résidence Bagatelle is a must. The owner offers her guests a warm welcome and her *joie de vivre* is contagious. The hotel is near the Ephrussi-Rothschild villa (see p 338). The garden at this establishment is stunning and includes 2,000-year-old olive trees.

Hôtel Brise Marine
730F-790F
pb, ps, ≡ in some rooms
58 Avenue Jean Mermoz
☎04.93.76.04.36
⇄04.93.76.11.49
info@hotel-brisemarine.com
This hotel is particularly attractive, offering tranquillity in a pleasant setting with magnificent views. Close to Paloma Beach, with all the facilities and services that a beach should offer. However, this hotel is a bit on the expensive side—but then again, it all depends on your budget!

Beaulieu-sur-Mer

Beaulieu is a sailing harbour and therefore has many hotels.

Le Select
320F
ps/pb, tv
Place Générale de Gaulle
☎04.93.01.05.42
⇄04.93.01.34.30
If you're on a limited budget, here's a good address: Le Select. In the very heart of the village, this simple but fully-restored hotel is located in a quaint old building. There is a Crédit Lyonnais branch on the main floor. It is in a pleasant square but, because the road passes just beside the hotel, it can be a bit noisy especially in the summer.

If this hotel is full, you can try the **Hôtel Riviera** *(220-280F; 6 Rue Paul Doumer; ☎04.93.01.04.92)*, which is closer to the sea.

Réserve de Beaulieu
3,400F-4,900F
7,975F-9450F for a suite
≡, ℜ
☎04.93.01.00.01
⇄04.93.01.28.99
reservebeaulieu@relaischateaux.fr
Looking for luxury? Head to the family-run Réserve de Beaulieu. This turn-of-the-century-style hotel was completely renovated. There are enormous, tastefully decorated rooms that look out onto the sea. This little palace has a small beach with rocky cliffs and a pier from which you can dive into the sea. Pleasure boats can also dock here. If you're not in a hurry, relax beside the big beautiful pool. As for value, it's expensive, but it is the height of luxury, after all! Its gastronomic but pricey restaurant is located in a bright, open space offering splendid views of the sea.

Èze-Village

Camping Les Romains
98F
Grande Corniche, Èze
☎04.93.01.81.64
Camping Les Romains is in a totally different category. To get there: take D2564 (Grande Corniche). If you're coming from the water, go up by D45. This

campground, on Italy's doorstep, offers magnificent panoramic views of the Alps, the sea, and Cap-Ferrat. Sunshine, tranquillity and comfort, hot showers and a snack-bar can be found here as well as beaches, sports and recreation. The campground is 10min from Nice and 15min from Monaco.

The "queen" of the *corniches*, and with a view!

Hôtel Hermitage
170F-320F
pb, tv, ℜ, ≈
Èze Grande Corniche
☎04.93.41.00.68
The Hôtel Hermitage is another good address. A member of the Logis de France chain, this establishment is 5km (3.1mi) from Èze-Village, and still relatively close to Nice and Monaco. It is located at the entrance to a departmental park with several walking trails. Sure to satisfy anyone with a taste for the backcountry. Reserve the room with the extra-big bathroom. This hotel also has a pool.

Auberge des 2 Corniches
340F
ps, tv
15 Boulevard Maréchal Leclerc
☎04.93.41.00.68
Around 1km (.6mi) from the village, in the direction of Col d'Èze, the Auberge des 2 Corniches, will appeal to travellers seeking a comfortable and reasonably priced hotel. Monsieur and Madame Maume, the friendly owners, offer you a quiet spot away from the tourist scene. You'll feel like you're out in the country! Ask for the corner room in the front; it has two windows and a nice view. Very good value.

For an unforgettable night in a dream hotel, choose one of these two luxury hotels located in the very heart of the old medieval village: **Le Château de la Chève-d'Or** *(1,700F-3,700F; every comfort, luxurious, ℜ, ≈, Èze-Village; ☎04.93.41.12.12, ⇄04.93.41.12.24)*, and **Le Château Eza** *(2,000F-3,500F; every comfort, luxurious, ℜ; Èze-Village, ☎04.93.41.12.24, ⇄04.93.41.16.64)*. These two hotels offer essentially the same services and have the same advantages. The atmosphere is most refined and there are pretty gardens and terraces overlooking the sea. The food is very also good. The restaurant at Château Eza is more spectacular because the terrace literally looks down over the sea. Both of these places are out of this world, simply extraordinary.

Cap d'Ail

If you want to avoid the tinsel of Monaco/Monte Carlo, here is a good place to stay in this small adjacent village.

Résidence Pierre & Vacances
studio 2,450F-5,750F per week, 2 rooms 2,050F-6,100F per week
pb, K, ℝ, ≈, tv extra
☎04.93.41.73.00
capdail@cierre-vacances.fr
If you're planning to stay for a week or more, the Résidence Pierre & Vacances is a must! This impressive building made of glass and stone was designed by Jean Nouvel, a well-known French architect. Perched way up high over the sea, the hotel was built on terraces at various levels to offer a spectacular view. The swimming pool is absolutely fabulous. Note: although it's only 800m (2,625ft) from the village, it is still off the beaten path—and a most vertical path it is! Generally the best way to get there is by car or taxi. There is pay parking. **There is a minimum one-week stay, starting on a Saturday.** The two-room apartments are ideal for families, since there is a separate room for the children. Good value!

La Turbie

Hôtel Napoléon
300F-450F, ½b 560F
closed Sun evening
pb, tv, ℜ
7 Av. de la Victoire
☎04.93.41.00.54
⇄04.93.41.28.93
The Hôtel Napoléon is located in the centre of the village, facing the town hall. This establishment combines modern comfort with

traditional architecture. Ask for a room at the back where it is more peaceful.

Peille

Hôtel Belvédère
200F-240F; ½b 260F
ℜ
One Place Jean Miol
☎04.93.79.90.45
If you're on a budget, the Hôtel Belvédère will fit the bill. The rooms are plain but proper, with views looking over Nice and the hills of Monaco. Unfortunately, they also look out over a huge rock quarry. This hotel offers a rustic atmosphere and a large dining room with an open terrace. Ask for room #2 or #4! Member of Logis de France chain.

Peillon

Auberge du Portail
290F-410F
ps
For travellers on a smaller budget, the owner has added an annex below the hotel. The Auberge du Portail opened only recently.

Auberge de la Madone
470F-780F
pb, tv
☎04.93.79.91.17
⇌04.93.79.99.36
Let yourself dream a bit, and enjoy life at the Auberge de la Madone. Located at the entrance of a most beautiful medieval village, this hotel is furnished with lovely antiques. The modern, spacious rooms overlook the village. There is also an excellent restaurant on the premises (see p 354). This hotel exudes elegance, and benefits from the owner's very fine taste. All of this makes it worth seeing!

Roquebrune Cap-Martin

Hôtel Europe Village
390F, ½b 580F
ps, tv, ℜ
Avenue Virginie Hériot
☎04.93.35.62.45
⇌04.93.57.72.59
The Hôtel Europe Village is nestled in the heart of Cap-Martin, 3km (1.9mi) from both Monaco and Menton. You will be impressed, if not seduced, by the beauty and tranquillity of the garden surrounding the hotel. It is an oasis of nature between these two cities. The rooms are comfortable and some have a terrace overlooking the garden. It is located at the starting point of a superb walking trail that leads around the cape. The hotel also offers a reasonably-priced restaurant.

Hôtel Westminster
380F-500F
closed Dec and Jan
pb or ps, tv, ≡
14 Avenue Louis Laurens
☎04.93.35.00.68
⇌04.93.28.88.50
westminster@ifrance.com
The Hôtel Westminster is located just before Cap-Martin, on a small dead-end street heading down to the sea. A comfortable, family-style hotel, it stands 200m (656.2ft) from the beach. If you happen to be a hang-gliding enthusiast, this is the perfect place for you, since the Westminster takes a special interest in fans of this sport and can provide any information needed. The hotel also has a restaurant *(closed Wed)* overlooking the sea, which serves traditional French specialties prepared by the proprietress.

Les Deux Frères
545F-595F
pb or ps, tv
☎04.93.28.99.00
⇌04.93.28.99.10
Located in a strategic spot in the medieval village of Roquebrune, the hotel and restaurant Les Deux Frères is a pleasant place to stay. It stands on a pleasant square with a lovely view of the surroundings, just steps away from the village's charming little streets. All the rooms have been renovated and are named for their individual decors: "mer" (sea), "africaine" and so on.

Vista Palace Hôtel
1,200F-2,300F
suite 2,300F-4000F
apt. 3,000F-7,000F
elevator, ≡, ≈, ⊙, ℜ, *tv*
Grande Corniche
☎04.92.10.40.00
⇌04.93.35.18.94
vistapalace@webstore.fr
Set between the sea and the sky, the Vista

Palace Hôtel is positively spectacular. Its status as one of the "Leading Hotels of the World" is well-deserved. Perched on a rocky spur overlooking the sea from a dizzying height, it boasts a unique location. Equipped with all the modern comforts, the Vista Palace falls squarely into the "dream resort" category, with its pool, fitness centre, gardens, gourmet restaurant, and above all, stunning views everywhere you look. The hotel has three, corner junior suites whose series of wide picture windows afford breathtaking panoramas of Monaco, the Hong Kong of the Riviera, on one side, and the unspoiled beauty of Cap-Martin on the other. One final note: during summer, you can eat lunch and dinner outside, next to the pool.

Menton

Camping Fleurs de Mai
67 Val de Gorbio
☎*04.93.57.22.36*
To get there: from Autoroute A8 take the Menton exit and go towards D23. This campground offers a peaceful, green setting and is within 1.5km (.9mi) of the beaches. Pool, tennis, supermarket, stores, etc.

Auberge de Jeunesse
80F bkfst incl.
Plateau Saint-Michel
☎*04.93.35.93.14*
A minibus goes to the youth hostel from the bus station. Note: reservations made by telephone are not guaranteed.

Hôtel de Londres
230F-460F
½b 220F-360F
closed mid-Oct to mid-Dec
pb or ps, tv, elevator
15 Avenue Carnot
☎*04.93.35.74.62*
⇄04.93.41.77.78
Nestled away just 200m (656.2ft) from the casino, right near the beach, is the Hôtel de Londres. Thanks to its big front garden, where guests can enjoy drinks or a meal, the hotel is set back a bit from the street. The owner has renovated all the rooms and their double windows provide extra peace and quiet. This place is enchanting, not only for its garden but also for its wonderful "old France" charm. The welcome extended is exemplary and the quality for the price is excellent.

Le Mondial
230F-270F
ps, tv, ℜ cafeteria-style
12 Rue Partouneaux
☎*04.92.10.20.66*
⇄04.92.10.20.70
The Hôtel Le Mondial is 5min from the sea, across from the chic Hôtel des Ambassadeurs. Le Mondial offers everything and then some of what you would expect from a simple, inexpensive hotel. The decor is pleasantly old-fashioned, with a turn-of-the-century look. The hotel offers small, basic but very clean rooms. The cafeteria-style restaurant serves breakfast and a variety of simple meals that you can take into the hotel's garden, which seats up to 80 people. This hotel is a very good value and very popular! With only 14 rooms, it can be full even in January, so reserve in advance. Unfortunately, the owner's welcome is no more than mediocre.

Hôtel Paris-Rome
360F-470F
pb, ≡, tv, ℜ
79 Porte de France
☎*04.93.35.73.45*
⇄04.93.35.29.30
The Hôtel Paris-Rome faces the sea near the sailing harbour. It is a quaint little hotel, with a tiny garden where you can relax over breakfast. A few of the rooms look out over the sea, and also over the busy road in the summertime. This can be noisy, but second-floor rooms (which are the most expensive) have double-glaze windows. The decor is rustic and the restaurant features a fireplace. Member of Logis de France. Good service. If you spend a week here, you can take advantage of a package deal which includes free guided tours of the city's five exotic gardens.

St-Michel
360F-480F, ½b 350-380F
pb, tv, ℜ
1684 Promenade du Soleil
☎04.93.57.46.33
The St-Michel is another hotel facing the sea. Run by an Italian *bon vivant* and his wife, this hotel is just at the entrance to the old city. There are a few quiet rooms in the back, as well as rooms with views of the sea. Very good value.

Narev's Hôtel
375F-550F
pb, ≡, tv
12 bis, Rue Lorédan Larchey
☎04.93.35.21.31
⇄04.93.35.21.20
The Narev's Hôtel is another great place. In a higher category than Le Mondial, Narev's is a newly-built hotel surrounded by 19th-century buildings. It is a friendly family business run by Pascale Veran, who knows a lot about the city and its restaurants. The very pleasant rooms (some with terraces) are furnished with all the comforts of a modern hotel. Well-located, it is 5min from the sea and faces the Musée de Préhistoire Régionale. The hotel also has a conference room and is open year-round.

Hôtel Aiglon
550F-720F
1/2b 495F-580F
two suites 960F
pb, ≡, tv, ≈, ℜ
7 Avenue de la Madone
☎04.93.57.55.55
⇄04.93.35.92.39
aiglon.hotel@wanadoo.fr
It is primarily fans of Québéc literature who'll want to experience this superb hotel which claimed writer Anne Hébert (who died in 2000) as a regular visitor over the course of 50 years. The hotel is, of course, the Hôtel Aiglon. We found this to be the most charming establishment in Menton, with a lovely swimming pool surrounded by a spectacular garden. What's more, it's close to the sea and the town centre. Guests can dine outside or in a charming pavilion. Owner Madame Solange Stiffa, together with Nathalie, ensures that guests are received with warmth in this hotel "with soul."

Hôtel Royal Westminster
590F-770F
closed Nov
pb, ℜ, ⊙, ≡, elevator
1510 Promenade du Soleil
☎04.93.28.69.69
⇄04.92.10.12.30
If you're looking for luxurious accommodations near the beach, the Hôtel Royal Westminster is the place for you.

The front entrance is just steps from the sand, where guests of the hotel enjoy complimentary use of a sunmat and a parasol. The back entrance offers access to the pedestrian zone, with all its stores and restaurants. The lovely grounds that surround the elegant building are a protected area. A fitness centre, pool room, grand piano and a bar can all be found on the premises, along with a restaurant with outdoor seating.

Hôtel des Ambassadeurs
800F-1,150F
1,650F for a suite
pb, ≡, ℝ, tv, ℜ
3 Rue Partouneaux
☎04.93.28.75.75
⇄04.93.35.62.32
ambassadeurs-menton@wanadoo.fr
For luxury in the heart of the city centre, choose the Hôtel des Ambassadeurs. This late-19th-century-style hotel was completely restored and is quite an impressive sight with its pink exterior. The entrance is extravagant, and the hotel's lounges are decorated with Art-Deco furniture. The rooms are bright and offer the modern comforts of a world-class luxury hotel. Bathrobes are even provided. Finally, the hotel has a very chic bar and two conference rooms that can hold from 40 to 150 people. Overall good value.

Restaurants

Villefranche-sur-Mer

There are two restaurants on the premises of the Hôtel Welcome, the **Carpe Diem** *($-$$)*, which serves simple, traditional fare, and the **Saint-Pierre** *($$$)*, specializing in more sophisticated cuisine, with an emphasis on fish.

La Grignotière
$$-$$$
3 Rue du Poilu
☎04.93.76.79.83
La Grignotière is a small, wonderful restaurant. Located in one of the narrow streets in the old village, this restaurant has been serving fine cuisine for years. The fish soup with its *rouille* comes in generous portions and is a pure delight. House specialities are meat and salmon pastries. The menu, which includes two appetizers, a main dish, cheese and dessert, is recommended. Servings are very generous. Finishing your plate would be quite a feat. The manager is friendly, and the service is efficient.

La Mère Germaine
$$
At the port, there are several restaurants with terraces overlooking the sea. Beware, however, because you will pay for this luxury. Locals prefer La Mère Germaine. Although the setting is delightful, the 195F menu offers only one choice of appetizer.

Saint-Jean-Cap-Ferrat

Two restaurants captured our attention at the port on the peninsula. Both are simple restaurants that nonetheless serve quite good fare.

La Goélette
$-$$
Pizza, pasta, salads and fish make up the menu. Pretty terrace. Children's menu. Regarding specialties, the attentive owners recommend the *aïoli provençal*.

Le Capitaine Cook
$-$$
11 Avenue Jean-Mermoz
☎04.93.76.02.66
Le Capitaine Cook - features mainly fish specialities and Bouillabaisse. A very popular restaurant.

Make sure you grab a bite at **Bas du Port**, the meeting place for joyful and friendly locals.

Beaulieu-sur-Mer

African Queen
$-$$
☎04.93.01.10.85
The African Queen, on the sailing harbour, serves Mediterranean cuisine featuring fish and meat with the occasional touch of curry. Pizzas cooked in a wood-burning oven and other simple fare also appear on the menu. Still, the main attraction here is the magnificent outdoor seating area, where you'll feel like lingering for hours.

Èze-Village

If you prefer a terrace with a view, stop at the very top of the village, near the entrance to an exotic garden. Perfect place for a cocktail!

Le Troubadour
$-$$$
closed Sun and Mon morning
☎04.93.41.19.03
Le Troubadour is a highly recommended "classic" restaurant at the entrance to the village. You should definitely try the *foie de gras* grilled with grapes. The atmosphere is drenched in old-fashioned charm, and the value is good.

Château Eza
$$
If money is no object, try one of the two château (see p 349) restaurants. We did, however, prefer the Château Eza because its marvellously situated terrace affords a wide-open views over the sea. Both châteaux offer equally fine cuisine at similar prices.

Cap d'Ail

La Pinède
$-$$$
closed Wed
10 Boulevard de la Mer
☎04.93.78.37.10
If you enjoy grilled fish, don't miss La Pinède. The large terrace where you can eat literally hangs over the sea and is completely covered when the weather is poor.

You can also dine inside, in a rustic, warm setting. There is even a tree that is integrated into the architecture of the building! The friendly owner, Monsieur Guglielmi, makes sure that everything is perfect, from the reception to the service to the food. This is an address to remember!

La Turbie

Restaurant de l'Hôtel Napoléon
$-$$
7 Avenue de la Victoire
☎04.93.41.00.54
If you'd like to savour some delicious soup, try the restaurant at the Hôtel Napoléon. Jeanine and Dominique Kolinsky also guarantee the quality of their two fixed-price menus and the à la carte selections.

Peille

Relais Saint-Martin
$-$$
☎04.93.41.16.03
On the road joining La Turbie and Peille, is the Relais Saint-Martin. Take in the panoramic views of Monaco's inland hills while dining. The huge fireplace gives this restaurant a rustic atmosphere. There is also a terrace and a banquet hall. An ideal place to enjoy the local cuisine and savour the taste of food grilled over a fire.

Peillon

L'Auberge de la Madone
$$-$$$
L'Auberge de la Madone promises hearty, gourmet, traditional Provençal cuisine. You can eat outside on the pretty terrace or in the lovely dining room (see p 350).

Roquebrune

At the entrance of the old town, at the Place des Deux Frères, there are two restaurants with outdoor dining.

La Grotte
$-$$
Place des Deux Frères
Excellent pizza and excellent salads are served at La Grotte. As for the fries, they're good and crisp. The bar inside is tucked away in the actual "grotto." The service is efficient and the quality is superb for the price.

Casarella
$-$$
15 Rue Grimaldi
Run by a Corsican family that has lived here for quite some time, Casarella serves family cooking in a friendly atmosphere. This restaurant is also recommended by locals.

Au Grand Inquisiteur
$-$$
Rue du Château
☎04.93.35.05.37
Au Grand Inquisiteur is a restaurant with a special setting. It is located in a medieval cave, which, in years gone by, was a shelter for livestock. The restaurant is listed in several restaurant guides and is very popular for its superb wine cellar. Not to be missed!

L'Idée Fixe
$-$$
☎04.93.28.97.25
L'Idée Fixe is a small restaurant perched at the top of a staircase. It offers an intimate atmosphere, and small temporary art exhibitions are held here. Gnocchi lovers must stop here if only for the selection of sauces. Over the past few years, the owners have begun to add fish and meat specialties to the menu. Open in the evening.

Les Deux Frères
$$
closed Sun evening and Mon from mid-Nov to mid-Dec
Place des Deux-Frères
From among the several good restaurants in this medieval village, we also recommend Les Deux Frères. The restaurant serves food made with fresh local ingredients, such as grilled fish, as well as homemade *foie gras.*

Menton

Le Rétro
$
3 Rue Saint-Michel
☎04.93.35.46.16
For a snack or drinks before dinner, Le Rétro is highly recommended. People come to this bar and tea room to relax on the charming pedestrian street and watch the parade of passersby. Le Rétro is one of the oldest establishments in Menton, and the staff is very friendly. If you like cocktails, try the house apéritif, a mixture of freshly squeezed orange and lemon juice perked up with Napoléon mandarin liqueur. Delicious and refreshing! Also make sure to try the delectable crepes!

Darkoum
$-$$
closed Mon and Tue
23 Rue St-Michel
☎04.93.35.44.88
For a change from southern French cuisine, head to Darkoum where you can enjoy wonderful Moroccan specialties. We sampled the lemon chicken, *tachine* and couscous--all were excellent. You can eat inside or on a little terrace—both are pleasant. This restaurant is also very popular with the Mentonais.

Don Cicco
$-$$$
11 Rue St-Michel
☎04.93.57.92.92
For fish and Italian cuisine, try Don Cicco. You won't be disappointed, but prices have escalated.

Le Balico
$-$$$
closed Tue
Place aux Herbes
☎04.93.41.66.99
Located on one of the most picturesque squares in old Menton, Le Balico serves Mentonnais cuisine that scores high points with everyone, including local residents. The service is friendly and efficient. Guests eat on the terrace, squeezed up against one another—which is what gives the place its charm. A bargain for Mentonnais flavours and ambiance.

Le Nautique
$-$$$
27 Quai de Monléon
☎04.93.35.78.74
Le Nautique is also recommended for fish-lovers.

Le Chaudron
$$-$$$
closed Tue
26 Rue St-Michel
☎04.93.35.90.25
On the other side of the pedestrian street is Le Chaudron, where you can eat delicious meat and fish dishes in a lovely interior or on the small terrace. This restaurant is also highly recommended by many locals.

Gorbio

Beau Séjour
$-$$
closed Wed
☎04.93.41.46.15
The Beau Séjour, located on the town square, serves regional cuisine in a rustic setting with views of the bucolic surroundings. Naïl and Yvan serve up fish soup with garlic cream, ravioli stuffed with *blettes* and sauteed rabbit with marjoram. To top it off, the prices are reasonable.

Sainte-Agnès

La Vieille Auberge
$-$$
closed Tue
☎04.93.35.92.02
If you'd like a change from the city, take a breath of fresh air at La Vieille Auberge in Ste-Agnés. The village is magnificently situated. You can enjoy simple, typical country fare in a modest setting and even spend the night at the hotel, run by the Revel family for

the past four generations.

Entertainment

Inquire at the tourist office in each town and village for their *Info-Animations*. Here are a few suggestions:

Beaulieu-sur-Mer

Grand Casino de Jeux: *7pm to 4am Mon to Thu, 6pm on weekends and 5pm in summer*
Avenue Blundell Maple
☎ ***04.93.76.48.00***

La Réserve de Beaulieu
5 Boulevard Maréchal Leclerc
☎ ***04.93.01.00.01***
Piano Bar.

Menton

Festivals and Cultural Events

Menton holds a number a fairs and festivals each year, including:

La Grande Foire d'Antiquité Brocante-Troc
end of Jan
Antiques and collectibles.

La Fête du Citron
Feb
Lemon festival.

La Bourse Numismatique et philatélique
one Sun in May
Coin and stamp exchange.

La Festival de Musique de Chambre
Aug
Parvis de l'Église St-Michel •
Chamber Music festival.

La Festival des Oiseaux
mid-Nov
Bird festival.

Le Salon de l'Artisanat d'Art
mid-Dec
Arts and crafts fair.

Casino

Casino de Menton
slot machines 11am to 3am, gambling room (roulette, blackjack, punto banco) 8pm to 3am, 5pm to 4am on weekends
Avenue Félix Faure
☎ ***04.92.10.16.16***

Recreational Park

Parc de Loisirs de la Madona-Koaland
10am to noon and 2pm to 6pm, 10am to 1am in summer
5 Avenue de la Madone

Bars and Nightclubs

Brasserie de l'Europe
1 Rue Partouneaux
☎ ***04.93.35.82.93***
Brasserie de l'Europe is a pub open in the evenings.

Le Brummell
cover charge 90F one drink included
open till dawn on weekends
☎ ***04.92.10.16.16***
Le Brummell is the Menton casino's discotheque.

La Case du Chef
Avenue R. Schumann
☎ ***04.93.35.91.43***

Le Queenie Club
One Avenue Pasteur
☎ ***04.93.57.58.46***

Monaco

After the Vatican, the Principality of Monaco is the world's smallest sovereign state.

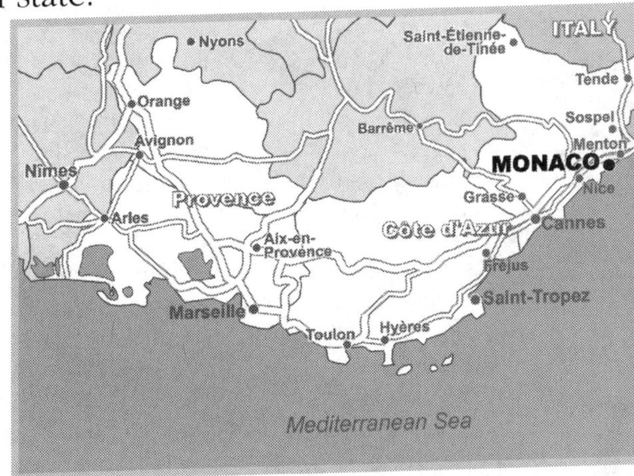

It is only 195ha (482 acres) in area, but with its population of approximately 30,000, it has the greatest population density per square metre in the world. Monaco's unique status in the world is attributed to its size, its great wealth and its somewhat incredible history. The marriage of Prince Rainier III to the stunning and famous American actress Grace Kelly in 1956 was a historical event that enchanted millions all over the world. It was a modern fairy tale that ended tragically in 1982 when Princess Grace was killed in a car accident on one of the area's winding roads. Since then, the royal family seems to have had its share of misfortunes, at least according to the tabloids, that track the family's every move.

Monaco's real history goes back much further. It begins at the end of the 13th century, at a time when the Genoese nobility fought over control of the territory. They were divided in two camps: the Guelfes, who were papal supporters; and the Gibelins, who were partisans of the German empire. In 1297, Rainier Grimaldi, of the Guelfes nobility, took control of the rocky land that is Monaco. In 1342, this dynasty, today more than 700 years old, expanded its territory by taking over Roquebrune and Menton.

In the 16th century, Monaco became a Spanish protectorate and remained so until 1641, when France took over. It only regained a semi-sovereign status in 1815, after the Vienna Conference. This agreement reinstated all the European monarchies in their territories as they had existed before the French Revolution. Monaco was therefore placed under the protectorate of the King of Sardinia.

The 50-year period that followed was somewhat difficult economically, especially because of the loss of Menton and Roquebrune, to France. Monaco only began to regain its former glory in 1863 with the creation of the Société des Bains de Mer and the construction of a casino. Monaco's rapid development continued when the principality was linked to Nice by rail in 1869. Shortly afterwards, Charles Garnier, architect of the Opéra de Paris, was commissioned to add a theatre to the luxurious casino. Finally, in 1910, Prince Albert I, who was an oceanographer, decided to add to the city's wealth by having an ocean museum and an exotic garden built.

Monaco launched into a new chapter of its history in 1949 with Prince Rainier III's ascension to the throne. An era of great economic growth had begun. From then on, the adoption of favourable laws attracted many investors and real-estate speculators. They have provided Monaco with luxurious buildings, and have built new museums and theatres as well as a huge sports stadium. Monaco has become the real-life dream world of an exclusive and privileged society.

Today, the principality hosts several sporting and cultural events that have brought it international acclaim. The Festival du Printemps des Arts, a spring arts festival, under the patronage of the Prince, welcomes many of the big names in music and dance each year. And don't forget the world-famous Monaco Grand Prix. Moreover, Monaco has its own orchestra, L'Orchestre Philarmonique de Monte-Carlo, as well as a dance troupe, Les Ballets de Monte-Carlo. Much emphasis is placed on the cultural life in Monaco. Indeed, patronage is widely practised and Monaco allocates 5% of its national budget to culture. Finally, Monaco's climate and exceptional site make it an ideal place for many international seminars and conventions (often of a scientific nature).

Monaco's special statutes are mainly what set it apart from other states. Indeed, the Prince retains absolute legislative, executive and judiciary power. The customs union between Monaco and France has been in place since 1865, and following a treaty signed between the two states in 1919, the Prince of Monaco must conjugate his sovereign rights with France's political, military, naval and economic interests. Nevertheless, Monaco's status as a fiscal paradise remains its most lucrative trademark.

Two things are striking about Monaco: the impressive body of security forces and the cleanliness. There are police officers everywhere, and numerous cameras watch over and protect all the billionaires, millionaires and even the everyday tourists that stroll through its streets.

Finding Your Way Around

During the summer, because the roads are

ATTRACTIONS

1. Musée océanographique et son aquarium
2. Cathédrale de Monaco
3. Le Palais Princier - Musée des Souvenirs napoléoniens et Collections des Archives historiques du Palais
4. Historial des Princes de Monaco
5. Chapelle de la Miséricorde
6. Musée du Vieux-Monaco
7. Place du Casino
8. Casino
9. Café de Paris
10. Jardin japonais
11. Musée national
12. Jardin exotique
13. Grotte préhistorique de l'Observatoire
14. Musée d'Anthropologie préhistorique
15. Port de Monaco
16. Église Sainte-Dévote
17. Vieux marché de La Condamine
18. Jardin animalier
19. Parc paysager
20. Roseraie Princesse Grace
21. Terrasse de Fontvieille
22. Musée naval
23. Musée des timbres et des monnaies
24. Collection des voitures anciennes

ACCOMMODATIONS

1. Ambassador-Monaco
2. Balmoral
3. Cosmopolite
4. Hermitage

RESTAURANTS

1. Au gâteau des rois
2. Le café de Paris
3. Le Florestan
4. Le Périgourdin
5. Quai des Artistes

so congested with traffic, the train is your best bet for a day trip to Monaco. The Métrazur, which links Saint-Raphaël to Vintimille, stops in Monaco about every half-hour.

By Plane

Monaco is about 22km (13.7mi) from the Nice Côte d'Azur International Airport. From there you have the choice of helicopter transport *(Héli Air Monaco, ☎92.05.00.50)*, coach or taxi. Many daily connections are available.

By Train

All the international trains stop at the Monaco/Monte-Carlo station on Avenue Prince Pierre.

Information ***☎36.35.35.35***

By Boat

Pleasure boats of all sizes may dock at the various ports with landing facilities: the Monaco-Condamine port in the Baie d'Hercule or either of the two ports in Fontvieille, one of which is located at the foot of the Monaco rock cliff, and the other in Cap d'Ail, in France. For more information, enquire at:

Services de la Marine - Direction des Ports
7 Avenue du Président J.-F. Kennedy, B.P. 468, MC 98012 Monaco Cedex
☎93.15.86.78

By Car

Monaco is accessible by the **A8** road from the east or the west. If you are coming from Nice, you may want to choose a more scenic route via one of the three departmental roads, the Basse, Moyenne and Grande Corniche. Of course, this way takes more time, especially in summer. Once in Monaco, you can park your car in one of the many covered parking lots. There are 6,000 pay parking spaces available in the city.

Car pound (Parking des Écoles)
Ave. des Guelfes
☎93.15.30.84

Automobile Club de Monaco
23 Blvd. Albert 1er
☎93.15.26.00

Car Rental

Budget
9 Avenue J.-F. Kennedy
☎92.16.00.70

Hertz
27 Boulevard Albert I
☎93.50.79.60

Avis
9 Avenue d'Ostende
☎93.30.17.53

By Bus

A coach service also offers connections between the Nice airport and Monaco every 90min from 9am to 7:30pm daily. The coach travels along the highway and makes the trip in 45min. Once in Monaco, it stops in several places.

The Compagnie des Autobus de Monaco has six urban bus lines that serve the main corridors of the territory. During the week, the buses generally run every 11min, between 7am and 9pm.

3 avenue du Prés. J.-F. Kennedy
☎93.50.62.41

By Taxi

The central telephone number for taxis is:
☎93.50.56.28

Practical Information

Area code: ***00377***

Since Monaco is built on ridges, public elevators are available to facilitate access to various locations.

There is also a tourist train, the *Azur Express (20F; Jul and Aug, 8:30pm to midnight; tour commentary in English and French, depar-*

ture/arrival: Stade Nautique Rainier III, Quai Albert I, ☎*92.05.64.38)* which offers two routes within the principality, by day or by night.

Monaco's beaches are all located east of Monte-Carlo and can be reached via Avenue Princesse Grace. Bus service to the beaches is also available.

Tourist Offices

Direction du Tourisme et des Congrès de la Principauté de Monaco
2a Boulevard des Moulins
Monte-Carlo, MC 98030 Monaco Cedex
administration:
☎**92.16.61.16**
⇄**92.16.60.00**
information:
☎**92.16.61.66**

Monaco Govenment Tourist and Convention Office
London (G.B.)
☎**(171) 352.99.62**
New York, N.Y., (U.S.A.)
☎**(212) 286-3330**

Police

Sûreté Publique
3 Rue Louis Notari
☎**93.15.30.15**

Emergencies
☎**17**

Hospital

Centre Hospitalier Princesse Grace
Avenue Pasteur
☎**93.25.99.00**

Emergencies
☎**93.25.98.69**

Exploring

To make exploring easier, the principality can be divided into four tours: **Monaco-Ville** ★★★ (Le Rocher, which encompasses the cathedral, the royal palace and several museums), **Monte-Carlo** ★★ (with the Casino and the Musée National), **Quartier du Jardin Exotique** ★★, and **Quartiers Portuaires** ★ (Condamine and Fontvieille, located on either side of the Rocher of Monaco-Ville).

Monaco-Ville

Since cars from other countries are not allowed in this part of the city, there are only two ways to explore the area known as the Rocher de Monaco: by foot or on board the tourist train ***Azur Express*** *(35F; 10:30am to 6pm, 5pm in winter; tour commentary in French, English, Italian and German, departure/arrival: Musée Océanographique, Avenue St-Martin,* ☎*92.05.64.38)*. This tour passes alongside the main monuments of the Rocher and can help you decide which sites are worth a closer look.

To get to the Rocher, take either the Rampe Major, a wide stairway that leads to Place du Palais, or the elevator located in the covered parking lot at the end of Avenue de la Quarantaine, which leads to the Musée Océanographique. On this street stands Fort Antoine, an early 18th-century fortress that was transformed into a summer theatre.

If you are taking the elevator, you can learn about the history of the Lords and Princes of Monaco through a multimedia presentation called the **Monte-Carlo Story: History of a Dynasty** *(38F; Mar to Oct, everyday 11am to 5pm; Jul to Aug, until 6pm; winter, 2pm to 5pm;* ☎*93.25.32.33)*. The elevator brings you to the **Musée Océanographique** ★★ and its **Aquarium** *(60F; Mar to Oct, 9:30am to 7pm; Jul to Aug 9am to 8pm, winter 10am to 6pm; avenue St-Martin,* ☎*93.15.36.00)*. It took 11 years to build this museum; its impressive façade overlooking the sea is made of white stone from La Turbie. Prince Albert I, an oceanographer and lover of the sea, inaugurated it in 1910. The museum contains remarkable collections of marine fauna presented on two floors with huge open rooms. The aquarium, at the basement level, exhibits several rare species in some 90 tanks fed directly from the sea. In addition, Jacques Cousteau's films are shown all day long in the conference room. Finally, the terrace offers a very beautiful panorama over the sea and the coast, from Italy to l'Estérel.

Leave the museum and head towards the gardens known as the Jardins de Saint-Martin, facing the open sea.

Here is a wonderful opportunity to take a pleasant stroll through gardens that stretch out along the coastline. Your walk will take you to Ruelle Sainte-Barbe, which opens up onto Place du Palais. A little before Ruelle Sainte-Barbe there is a wonderful view of the **Cathédrale de Monaco**, where Monaco's former princes are buried. The cathedral, built out of white stone from La Turbie in 1875, also contains a reredos by Brea that dates back to 1500.

Head towards Ruelle Sainte-Barbe.

Ruelle Ste-Barbe opens up onto Place du Palais. Visitors can watch the changing of the guard everyday at 11:55am, in front of the main gate of the royal palace. The Garde des Carabiniers are an impressive sight, in their black winter uniforms or their white summer ones.

The **Palais Princier** ★★★ *(30F; Jun to Oct, 9:30am to 6:30pm, 5pm in Oct; ☎93.25.18.31)* stands on the site of a fortress built by the Genoese in 1215. Visitors can see the Grand Appartements, which include: the Salon Louis XV decorated in blue and gold; the Salon Mazarin; the Throne Room, where Prince Rainier and Grace Kelly were married; the Chapelle Palatine, built in the 17th century and, finally, the Tour Ste-Marie, from the top of which the royal colours are flown when the Prince is in residence.

Cathédrale de Monaco

In the south wing of the Palace, you can visit the **Musée des Souvenirs Napoléoniens et Collections des Archives Historiques du Palais** *(20F; summer, everyday 9:30am to 6:30pm; Oct, 10am to 5pm; Dec to May, Tue to Sun 10:30am to 12:30pm and 2pm to 5pm; closed mid-Nov to Dec; ☎93.25.18.31)*. This museum contains a collection of objects and documents from the First Empire and its emperor, Napoléon I, as well as various items that recall the history of the principality.

Leave the square via Rue Basse.

You are now in the very heart of the Vieux-Monaco of medieval times, on one of the most picturesque streets of the Rocher. At 27 Rue Basse, the wax museum **Historial des Princes de Monaco** *(22F; Feb to Sep, everyday 9:30am to 6pm; Oct to Jan, 11am to 4pm; ☎93.30.39.05)* recalls the historical events of the Grimaldi dynasty, from the end of the 13th century to the present, with life-sized wax statues.

The street opens up onto Place de la Mairie, where the **Chapelle de la Miséricorde** stands. Built in 1639, it was the seat of the Confrérie des Pénitents Noirs. This little chapel has a small **museum** *(20F, children 10F; Tue to Sun 10am to 4pm)* that contains works from the

profess to sophistication.

Location, location, location... that is the name of the game in Monaco, and higher prices are the result.

Au Gâteau des Rois
$
Rue Princesse Caroline (pedestrian zone)
Right near the port, on the small terrace of the Au Gâteau des Rois bakery, you can enjoy excellent sandwiches, zuchinni tarts, *pissaladières* and delicious little chocolate or fruit tartlets. The place serves only homemade products and specializes in pastries.

Le Florestan
$$-$$$
corner of Rue Princesse Caroline and Princesse Florestan
You'll eat very well at Le Florestan. Selections include Italian pasta and fish baskets, as well as popular dishes such as *socca aux gambas*, *daraude royale* and sliced breast of duck cooked with *cèpes* (mushrooms).

Quai des artistes
$$-$$$
4 Quai Antoine Ier
☎*97.97.97.77*
This Parisian-style brewery is located right by the port, namely on the Quai des Artistes. The interior, with high ceilings, was decorated by painters, most of whom work in the vicinity of the port.

There is a set-price lunch menu including a drink, and a more expensive dinner menu in the evenings. The menu is seasonal (in winter, for example, it includes *pot-au-feu)*, but specialties like gnocchi and seafood are served year-round.

Monte-Carlo

Le Périgordin
$$-$$$
closed Sat noon and Sun
5 Rue des Oliviers
☎*93.30.06.02*
There is a cute little restaurant on Monte-Carlo's only old street: Le Périgordin. Gérard, the restaurant's very welcoming manager, offers specialties from the southwest of France, such as *magrets et confits de canard* (duck cutlets and preserves) and foie gras, cassoulet. The menu also lists other delicacies such as sea-perch fillet with champagne or fricassee of guinea fowl. Of course, this restaurant has meanwhile made its way into various fine-dining guides. You'll be welcomed into a decor that seems like it's a world away from the glitter of Monaco. Portions are generous and the service is friendly and personal. This restaurant is a pleasant spot to enjoy a lovely evening at a reasonable price.

Le Café de Paris
$$-$$$
Place du Casino
☎*92.16.20.20*
Le Café de Paris, located on Place du Casino in Monte-Carlo, offers the most beautiful and elegant *belle époque* decor. If you want to be where the action is, have a cocktail or dessert on its large terrace. However, we have our doubts as to the value this restaurant offers, and the service does leave something to be desired.

Louis XV
$$$-$$$$
Hotel de Paris, Place du Casino
☎*92.16.36.36*
If you hit the jackpot at the Casino and you want to blow it all in a very luxurious setting, treat yourself to an evening at the Louis XV, Hotel de Paris. The decor is princely and very ornate. The chef, Alain Ducasse, is internationally famous. This is one of the finest restaurants of the Côte d'Azur.

Entertainment

Casino

Casino de Monte-Carlo
Place du Casino
☎*92.16.21.21*
European and English roulette, chemin de fer, black jack, craps and European rooms from

noon, private rooms from 3pm.

The Casino also houses the **Opéra de Monte-Carlo** and a cabaret club where musicals are performed.

Bars and Nightclubs

JIMMY'Z
Monte-Carlo Sporting Club, Avenue Princess Grace
☎*92.23.16.22.77*

Piano-Bar The Living Room Club
7 Avenue des Spélugues
☎*93.50.72.24*
Refined decor with cozy atmosphere. To make your evening last into the night...

Stars 'N' Bars
6 Quai Antoine 1er
☎*93.50.95.95*
This large and stylish North-American-type bar has a young, classy ambiance.

Festivals and Cultural Events

The **Festival du Printemps des Arts** begins in April. It presents a multitude of musical events featuring famous as well as new artists.

Le **Grand Prix de Monaco** also takes place in May each year. It is one of the most prestigious car-racing events for the Formula I World Cup.

From Nice to Tende

Let us now take a brief excursion into the countryside.

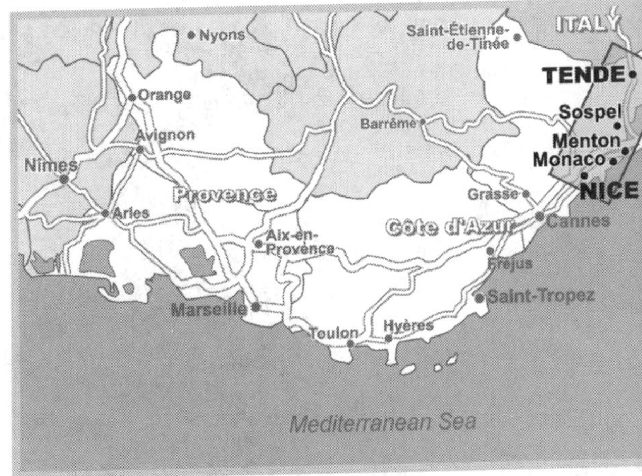

This region is the ideal place for hiking enthusiasts, who can go for short treks across the hills and valleys that grace this corner of the backcountry. More athletic types will also find something to satisfy them here: the magnificent Vallée des Merveilles. The area is even worth spending a few days in.

If hiking is not your cup of tea, the region nevertheless has lovely little villages that rival those of Provence.

Finding Your Way Around

Tourist information centres will provide you with useful information on the various ways of getting from one place to another.

By Car

Renting a car gives you the flexibility to travel where and when you want. Buy a good road map, as the route often involves many small roads.

From Nice, the "famous" Route des Cols, literally the "passes route," is the most picturesque and interesting route, passing through Col de Nice, Col de Braus, Sospel, Col de Brouis, Breil-sur-Roya and several charming small villages of the backcountry of Nice. The journey from Nice to Breil can be made in 1hr 45min, but this all depends on how many stops you make along the way.

If you are short of time, take the A8 from Nice to Menton, then the D2566 to reach Sospel. This is the shortest way, and the scenery remains interesting nonetheless. This will save you about 30min of travelling time.

Those who wish to visit the **Vallée des Merveilles** must go to St-Dalmas-de-Tende, just before Tende. From there, follow directions for Casterino.

By Train

The train runs through most villages in the

backcountry located in the Nice-Menton-Tende triangle. In fact, by setting off from Nice, travellers can stop at Drap, Le Moulin, Peillon, l'Escarène, Sospel, Breil-sur-Roya, Saorge, St-Dalmas-de-Tende and Tende. From Ventimiglia, right across the Italian border from Menton, passengers can travel directly to Breil-sur-Roya and Tende. Once in Tende, you can even continue to Cuneo and Turin, both situated in Italy. Travelling through this region by train will allow you to take full advantage of picturesque landscapes; the journey by car, on the other hand, is made along narrow, tortuous roads.

Contact the Nice, Menton and Monaco SNCF train stations (see below) for schedules and routes.

Nice and Menton
☎*08.36.35.35.35*

Monaco/Monte Carlo
☎*00377-36.35.35.35*

Breil-sur-Roya
☎*04.93.04.40.15*

Tende
☎*04.93.04.65.60*

By Bus

A network of buses serves the major cities on the Côte d'Azur (Nice, Monaco and Menton) as well as the small towns or villages located within a 30km or 18.6mi-radius. For instance, there are two buses per day, one early in the morning and another in the evening departing from the Nice bus station, and running through the backcountry.

A bus from Tende goes to the **Vallée des Merveilles**, passing through Saint-Dalmas and Casterino, in July and August.

Bus Stations

Nice
☎*04.93.85.61.81*
☎*04.93.80.08.70*

Menton
☎*04.93.28.43.27*

Tende
☎*04.93.04.65.60*

Practical Information

If you would like to stay with local people in their own homes in Breil, Fontan or Tende contact the **Gîtes de France** office in Nice:

Gîte de France
55 Promenade des Anglais, B. P. 602, 06011 Nice
☎*04.92.15.21.30*

The Gîtes de France label guarantees a standard of quality. Rentals are made for the week and stretch from Saturday at 4pm to the following Saturday at 10am. Prices range from 1,040F for one person to 1,800F for six people.

Tourist Offices

Sospel
Office de Tourisme et d'Animation de Sospel (OTAS)
Pont-Vieux, 06380 Sospel
☎*04.93.04.15.80*
⇄*04.93.04.19.96*

Breil-sur-Roya
open afternoons only in the off season
☎*04.93.78.01.55*
⇄*04.93.78.79.87*

Saorge
Mairie (town hall)
☎*04.93.04.51.23*

La Brigue
open in summer only
Place St. Martin
☎*04.93.04.36.07*
⇄*04.93.04.36.09*

Haute-Roya Tourist Office
off season
☎*04.93.04.73.71*

Tende
Haute-Roya Tourist Office
(Tende–La Brigue)
☎*04.93.04.73.71*

Emergencies

Sospel
Police Station
Gendarmerie
☎*04.93.04.02.67*

Medical Clinic
☎*04.93.04.18.88*

Hospital
☎*04.93.04.30.30*

Pharmacy
☎*04.93.04.01.48*

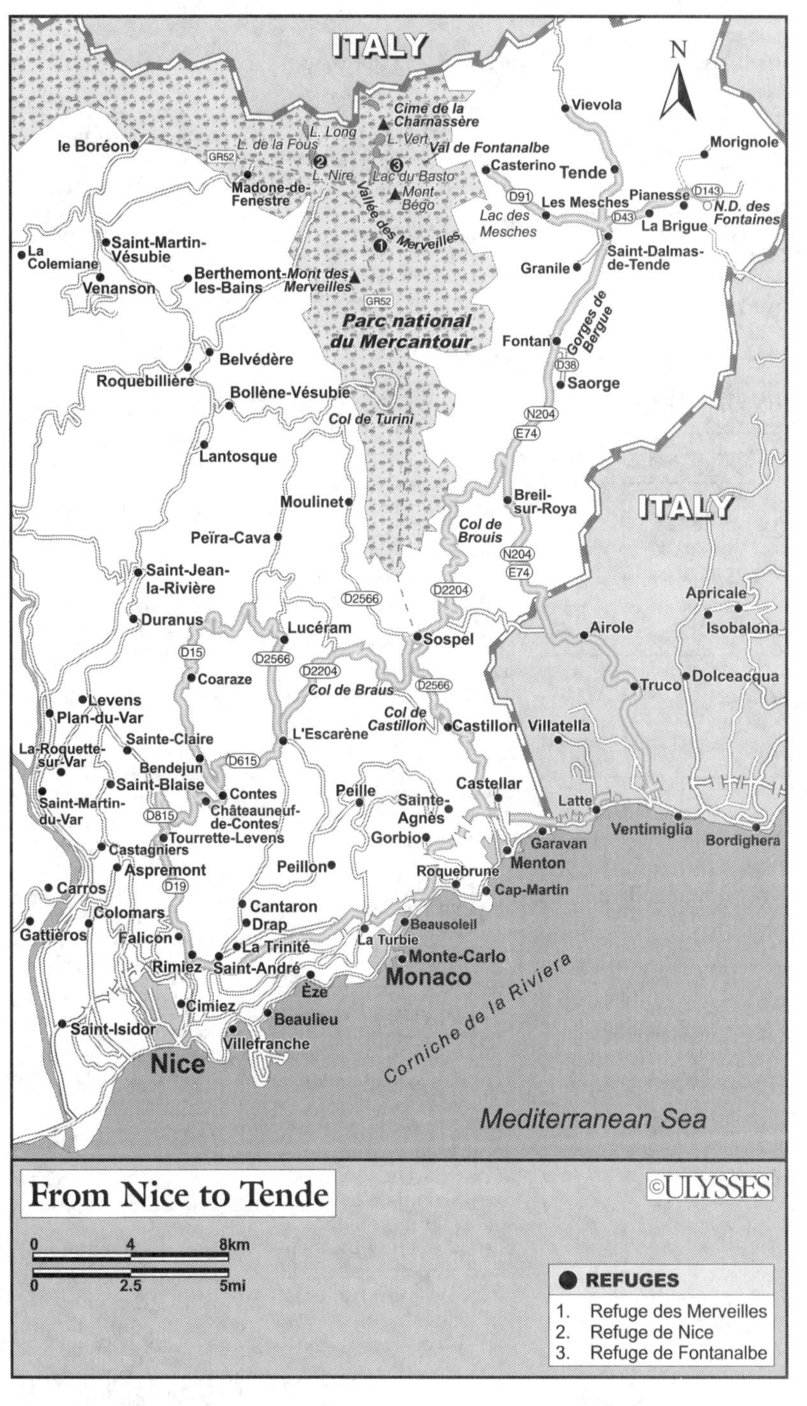

ITALY
N
Cime de la Charnassère
L. Long
L. Vert
Val de Fontanalbe
le Boréon
L. de la Fous
GR52
L. Nire
Lac du Basto
Mont Bégo
Madone-de-Fenestre
Vallée des Merveilles
Vievola
Morignole
Casterino
Tende
D91
Les Mesches
Pianesse
D143
N.D. des Fontaines
Lac des Mesches
D43
La Brigue
Saint-Dalmas-de-Tende
Granile
La Colemiane
Saint-Martin-Vésubie
Venanson
Berthemont-les-Bains
Mont des Merveilles
GR52
Parc national du Mercantour
Fontan
Gorges de Bergue
D38
Saorge
Belvédère
Roquebillière
Bollène-Vésubie
Col de Turini
N204
E74
Lantosque
Moulinet
Breil-sur-Roya
ITALY
Col de Brouis
Peïra-Cava
N204
E74
Saint-Jean-la-Rivière
D2566
D2204
Apricale
Isobalona
Duranus
Lucéram
Sospel
Airole
D15
D2566
D2204
Coaraze
Col de Braus
D2566
Truco
Dolceacqua
Levens
Plan-du-Var
Col de Castillon
Castillon
Villatella
Sainte-Claire
L'Escarène
La-Roquette-sur-Var
Bendejun
D615
Saint-Blaise
Contes
Peille
Castellar
Saint-Martin-du-Var
Châteauneuf-de-Contes
Sainte-Agnès
Latte
D815
Tourrette-Levens
Gorbio
Ventimiglia
Bordighera
Garavan
Castagniers
Menton
Aspremont
Peillon
Roquebrune
D19
Carros
Cap-Martin
Cantaron
Colomars
Drap
Beausoleil
Gattières
Falicon
La Trinité
La Turbie
Monte-Carlo
Rimiez
Saint-André
Monaco
Èze
Cimiez
Beaulieu
Saint-Isidor
Villefranche
Nice
Corniche de la Riviera
Mediterranean Sea
From Nice to Tende
©ULYSSES
0 4 8km
0 2.5 5mi
REFUGES
1. Refuge des Merveilles
2. Refuge de Nice
3. Refuge de Fontanalbe

Breil-sur-Roya
Hospital
☎04.93.04.37.00

La Brigue
Hospital
☎04.93.04.60.29

Tende
Hospital
☎04.93.04.60.50

Vallée des Merveilles
Ambulance
☎04.93.04.64.15

Taxis

Sospel
☎04.93.04.01.40
☎04.93.04.01.24

Banks

Sospel
Bank machine
Avenue Jean Médecin

Hostels

Shelters are open from June to September.

A 30% deposit is required for all reservations.

Refuge des Merveilles
86F, 185F ½b
60 places
summer
Gardien du Refuge des Merveilles, 06430 St-Dalmas-de-Tende
☎04.93.04.64.64
winter
Mr. Ferrier, 40 Rue Lascaris, Tende
☎04.93.04.69.22

Refuge de la Valmasque
86F, 185F ½b
62 places
Gardien du refuge de Valmasque, 06430 St-Dalmas-de-Tende

Refuge de Fontanalbe
50F, 146F ½b
30 places
Mr. Ferrier, 40 Rue Lascaris, 06430 Tende
☎04.93.04.69.22

Exploring

One or two days are sufficient to cover this region. Spending more time is necessary, however, if you wish to take full advantage of the many outdoor activities the Parc National du Mercantour has to offer. The following is a complete tour of the main attractions between Nice and Tende.

Leave Nice via the D19, toward Contes.

Tourette-Levens

This little village seems to have remained frozen in time. A street lined with beautiful houses, some decayed, rises from the small square at the village entrance. Only the bell tower remains of an old chapel. Up above, the old château dominates the village.

Tourette-Levens also features a wonderful small **museum** *(free admission; every day 2pm to 6pm)* devoted to the most beautiful butterflies and insects in the world, with around 3,500 species.

Continue along the D19 and take the D815 toward Contes.

Châteauneuf-De-Contes and Contes

Because of the insecurity that prevailed at the end of the Middle Ages, the inhabitants of Contes built Châteauneuf-De-Contes in the neighbouring hills to protect themselves against potential devastation. The ruins of Châteauneuf's old château and ramparts attest to this. It was not until the 18th century that a significant number of villagers returned to Contes. This village is worth the trip for the magnificent view of the Alps from the château (10 to 15min away). You can also visit the **Église Madone-De-Villevieille**, which attests to the breakthrough of Romanesque art in Provence, despite the fact that the vertical stripes on its façade are of Lombard influence.

Contes' **Église Sainte-Marie-Madeleine ★**, built in the 17th century, contains a portal dating from 1575, as well as a lovely polyptych of the Brea school, inside.

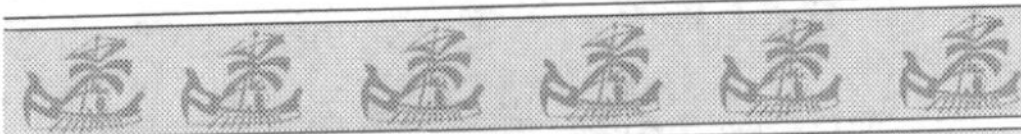

Maupassant's "Bonheur" on the Côte d'Azur

The famous Norman author Guy de Maupassant described with great accuracy the harshness of peasant life in Normandy and the sweetness of days on the Côte d'Azur. He spent several summers on the bay of Nice, seeking refuge here by the peaceful sea.

Better than anyone else, he found the words to describe the sensation that overcomes you when, by the sea, you watch the day's relentless sun give way to the shimmering evening light: *"La ville dominait la mer; le soleil disparu avait laissé le ciel tout rose de son passage, frotté de poudre d'or; et la Méditerranée, sans une ride, sans un frisson, lisse, luisante encore sous le jour mourant, semblait une plaque métal polie et démesurée."*

[The city overlooked the sea; the departed sun left in its wake a pink sky, dusted with gold powder; and the Mediterranean without ripple or shiver, calm, and still gleaming beneath the dying day like a polished sheet of metal.]
(our translation)

Le Bonheur, Guy de Maupassant

Upon leaving Contes, you can go straight to l'Escarène on the D615 or, if you have more time, make a big detour toward Coaraze and Lucéram on the D15.

Coaraze ★★ and Lucéram ★★

Visiting the **Chapelle Saint-Sébastien**, just 2km (1.2mi) before the village of Coaraze, is a real must. The chapel displays beautiful frescoes from the early 16th century, depicting the martyred Saint-Sebastien, Sainte-Ursule and Sainte-Lucie, who had her eyes torn out.

Several ceramic sundials created by different artists can be admired in the Place de l'Église in Coaraze. Worth noting, in particular, is the one signed by **Jean Cocteau**, which graces the town hall's facade. These sundials contributed to Coaraze's inclusion on the prestigious list of the most beautiful villages in France.

Lucéram is a fortified medieval village that has a few Gothic-style houses, as well as a tower at a rather impressive angle. Until the 19th century, its inhabitants lived from the trade and production of olives, cattle breeding and the distilling of wild lavender.

The **Église Sainte-Marguerite ★★**, which was designed in the Italian rococo style in the 18th century, boasts five wooden reredos of the Nice school dating from the 1500s. The church also has a lovely little collection of silverware, among which the silver reliquary statuette, *Sainte Marguerite Issant du Dragon*, is of unparalleled beauty.

The stunning view of the hills, the tall houses clinging to the rock and the Place de l'Église, with its fountain and washhouse, all contribute to make the village of Lucéram one of the most beautiful in Nice's backcountry.

L'Escarène

Starting in the late 16th century, this village occupied a strategic position on the "*route du sel*" ("salt route"), which linked Nice to

Tende. At the time, salt was an essential staple, as it was used for preserving food.

Fans of the baroque style will be delighted with the village of L'Escarène, and its **Église Saint-Pierre-aux-Liens ★** in particular. Construction of the church was completed in 1656; it is the work of Guibert, the engineer of the Cathédrale Sainte-Réparate in Nice, a masterpiece of baroque architecture. Though the main part of the Saint-Pierre church bears a rather simple architecture, the baroque style appears in all its splendour in the side chapels.

Leave l'Escarène via the D2204. Sospel is 22km (13.7mi) away.

Sospel

The road to Sospel runs over the Col de Braus (pass), at 1,002m (3,287ft) in altitude. Sospel is a small town nestled in a verdant basin that was long a stopping place on the road from Nice to Turin. The old city has a certain charm (though unfortunately it is in quite decrepit shape), and the surroundings are ideal for many walks and hikes.

Tour of the City

The walking tour begins at the town hall (Mairie). Those with cars can park here or behind the Place des Platanes.

Opposite the **town hall**, visitors can see a few columns graced with capitals, the last remnants of the old Saint-Pierre church, whose foundations are buried beneath the Place des Platanes.

*Head toward the **Rivière Bévéra**.*

Along the river's edge, you will notice rather striking houses painted in *trompe l'œil* before reaching **Pont-Vieux**, a symbol of the old village and headquarters of the tourist office. Up until the 16th century, this bridge was made of wood. The central tower served as a residence, and a toll had to be paid to cross it. The two arches were rebuilt in 1951, after having been demolished during the German retreat in 1944.

On the other side of the bridge is the **Place Saint-Nicholas**. When the town was granted autonomy under the protection of the Counts of Provence, the central building, known as the "Loggia", was used for Sospel's syndic and parliament sessions. The sculpted lamb adorning the façade represents divine protection. The fountain dates from the 18th century.

Take Rue de la République.

In the Middle Ages, this street was called "Rue Longue" (long street) and bustled with activity. Lined with workshops under the arcades (which were later filled in), it was sheltered from the elements of bad weather. Notice the lintels above the doors engraved with the coat of arms of certain families. Continue your stroll to the Ruelle des Tisserands, the narrowest street in the village, whose name recalls the cultivation of hemp and mulberry practised in the valley, for the purpose of breeding silkworms.

On **Place Sainte-Croix** stands the Chapelle des Pénitents Blancs, built in the 16th century and restored in Italian colours. The triangular bell tower dates from the 19th century.

Return to the Pont-Vieux and go back across. Head up Rue Saint-Pierre.

The former **Palais de la Gabelle**, where the salt tax was collected, is on this street graced with old façades. This freestone house boasts a Renaissance window and very beautiful sculpted mouldings.

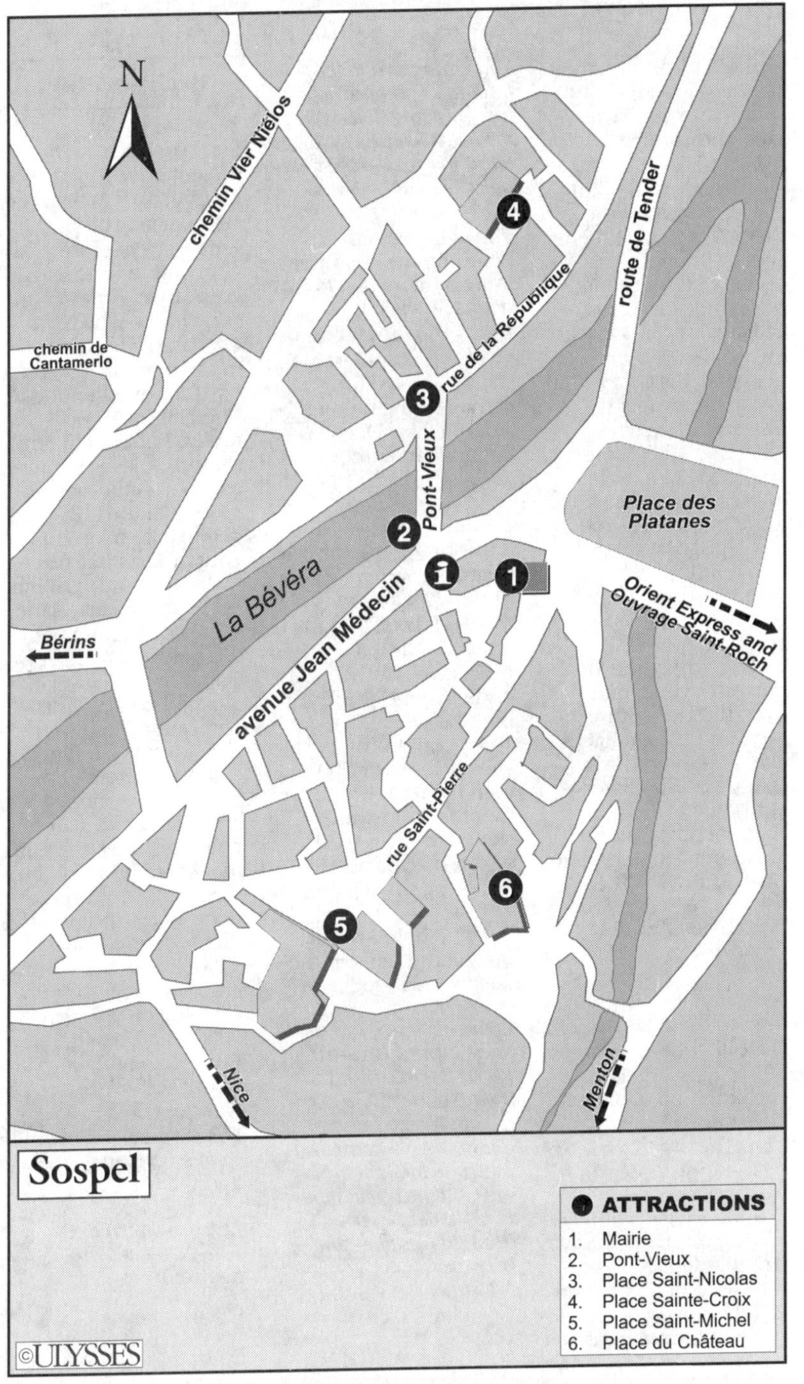
N
chemin Vier Niélos
route de Tender
rue de la République
chemin de Cantamerlo
Pont-Vieux
Place des Platanes
La Bévéra
avenue Jean Médecin
Orient Express and Ouvrage Saint-Roch
Bérins
rue Saint-Pierre
Nice
Menton
Sospel
ATTRACTIONS
1. Mairie
2. Pont-Vieux
3. Place Saint-Nicolas
4. Place Sainte-Croix
5. Place Saint-Michel
6. Place du Château
©ULYSSES

At the end of this street lies the most beautiful spot in Sospel: **Place Saint-Michel**. Paved with stones and lined by arcades from the Middle Ages and by the Chapelles des Pénitents Gris et Rouges, it is dominated by the imposing façade of the **Cathédrale Saint-Michel**. This cathedral, rebuilt between 1641 and 1720 in the baroque style, has nevertheless retained its 12th-century Lombard steeple. Its impressive size makes it the biggest church in the Alpes Maritimes. The interior harbours 19th-century Italian organs as well as several works of art, among which the Pieta triptych, which dates from the late 15th century, and the Immaculate Virgin reredos stand out. The latter is attributed to François Bréa, nephew of the illustrious painter from Nice, Ludovico Brea.

Head toward the Place du Château.

Narrow alleys lead up toward the **Place du Château**, whose vestiges of old ramparts bespeak the medieval villages' need for protection. The south wall's beautiful gate near the washhouse, and the leaning tower, with its arches, are particularly striking. On a promontory west of this tower stand the ivy-covered ruins of a Carmelite convent.

You can return to the itinerary's point of departure by going down one of the alleys leading to Rue Saint-Pierre and the town hall.

Those interested in boarding the old **Orient Express train** *(Mon to Sun noon to 6pm; ☎04.93.04.00.43)* can do so at the Sospel train station, where four carriages, including a stunning Art-Deco restaurant car, can be visited.

You can also tour an old fortress, the **Ouvrage Saint-Roch** *(summer, Tue to Sun 2pm to 6pm; ☎04.93.04.00.70)*, just outside of town on the D2204. In wartime, this underground fortress, built between 1930 and 1934, could provide shelter for over 200 men for up to three months, who were stationed there to watch out for possible attack by the Italians.

Finally, there are various hiking trails in the Sospel area (see p 380).

Upon leaving Sospel, continue toward Breil-sur-Roya (23km or 14.3mi away) on the D2204, which travels over the Col de Brouis. You can also return to Menton (15km or 9.3mi away) via the D2566, which goes through Castillon and over the Col de Castillon (707m or 2,320ft).

Breil-sur-Roya

Breil-sur-Roya marks the entrance to the glorious **Parc National du Mercantour**. The picturesque alleys of the old city, built on the Roya cove, follow the mountain slopes. The town's *trompe l'œil* façades and the remains of its ramparts are worth a look. The Saint-Jean bell tower, behind the train station, is also of interest, as it is the only vestige of an 11th-century Romanesque church. Another place certainly worth visiting is the **Église Santa Maria**, a historic monument on the Place de Brancion, opposite a pink arcaded palace. This baroque church in the Greek cross design is extended laterally by chapels. Among its artistic treasures are painted vaults depicting the Assumption of the Virgin Mary, a triptych dedicated to Saint-Pierre dating from 1400, lovely silverware and, finally, a magnificent organ case. Every year at the beginning of July, you can take part in the **Festival d'Art Baroque** ("les Basoquiales"), which stages concerts, opera and theatre.

Leave town via the E74–N204, toward Saorge.

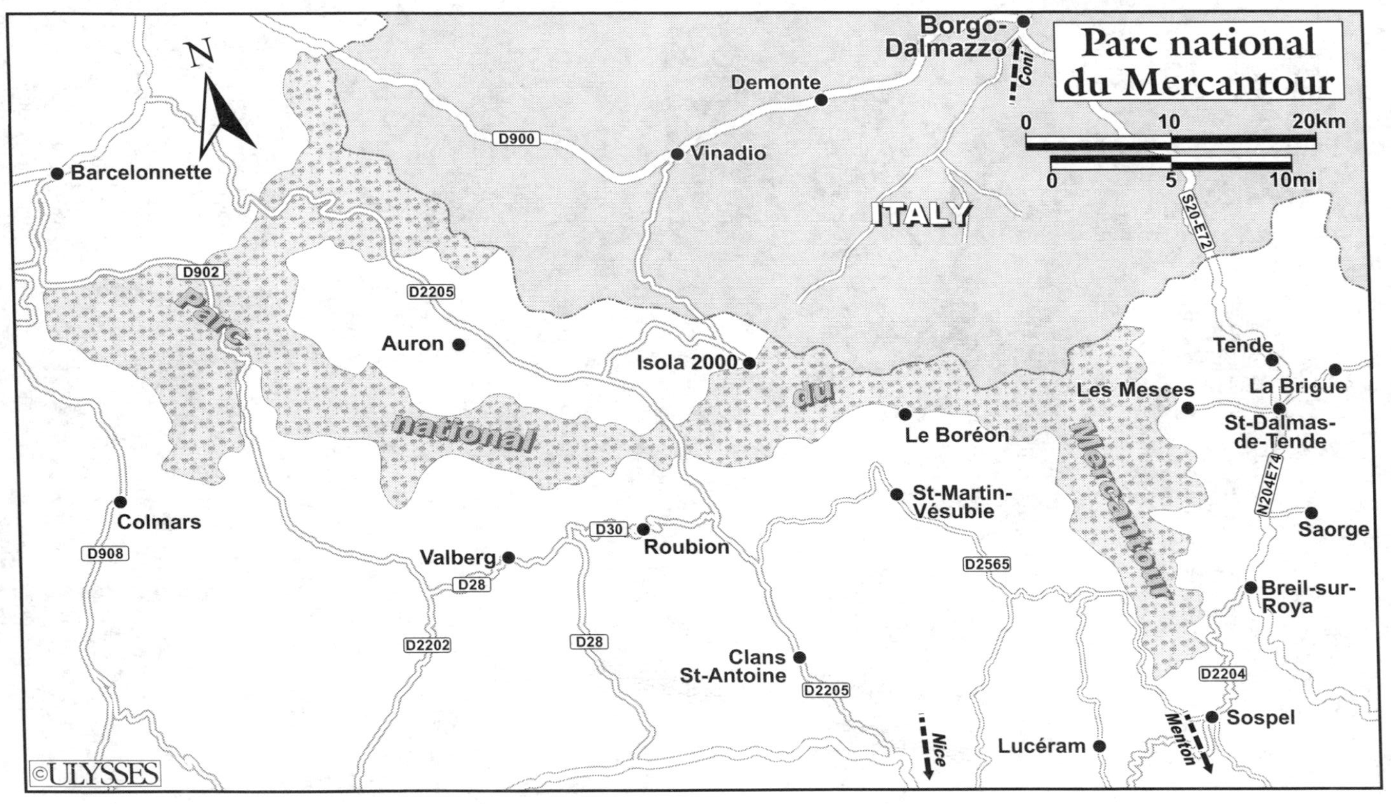

Parc national du Mercantour
0
10
20km
0
5
10mi
N
Borgo-Dalmazzo
Coni
Demonte
Vinadio
D900
ITALY
S20-E72
Barcelonnette
D902
D2205
Parc
national
du
Mercantour
Auron
Isola 2000
Tende
La Brigue
Les Mesces
St-Dalmas-de-Tende
Le Boréon
N204E74
St-Martin-Vésubie
Saorge
Colmars
D908
D30
Roubion
Valberg
D28
D2565
Breil-sur-Roya
D2202
D28
Clans
St-Antoine
D2205
D2204
Sospel
Nice
Lucéram
Menton
©ULYSSES

Saorge

While on the road from Breil, you will see this strange village, perched in the hills, and wonder how to reach it. A detour leading to the small D38 road, which runs to the village, is in order.

Clinging to a mountainside towering above the Roya gorges, this municipality, listed as a historic monument, looks like a Tibetan village. But it is truly a western medieval village and the site of many battles on account of its strategic geographical position. It was fortified early on by the Dukes of Savoie, who wanted to control the road from Nice to Turin.

The village is a maze of narrow streets, along which many 15th- and 16th-century houses succeed each other. Visiting the **Église Saint-Sauveur**, which was rebuilt in 1500 after a fire ravaged the village in 1465, is an absolute must. The vault, for its part, was redone in the early 18th century. The baroque style reaches its peak here with the *trompe l'œil* paintings. The retables date from the 17th century and the Italian organs, from the mid-19th century.

Below the village stands the **Chapelle de la Madone del Poggio**, a private property dating from the 11th century. Nothing remains of this era, but the chevet with three apses. This chapel is also noteworthy for its beautiful seven-story Romanesque steeple in the Lombard style.

Finally, at the end of the village, you will reach the **Couvent des Franciscains**, a monastery that dates back to the 17th century. Its restored baroque façade conceals a 17th-century carved wood retable. The monastery is adorned with frescoes depicting Saint-Francis.

Saorge experienced a sharp decline in the 19th century, which only worsened with the construction of the road through the valley in the 20th century. The village thus sustained steady depopulation. Some inhabitants even immigrated to Canada. These days, however, the region has recovered thanks to its established calling as a tourist attraction. As such, in extreme cases, a house purchased for 2,000F in the 1960s could now fetch around 300,000F.

The northbound E74–N204 leads to Saint-Dalmas-de-Tende, by skirting the Gorges de Bergue.

Saint-Dalmas-de-Tende

Considered French only since 1947, following a referendum, this village was of great importance in the 1930s. Indeed, at the time, it acted as a border station between France and Italy. Its impressive station with balusters attests to this.

Saint-Dalmas is the point of departure for the road to the Vallée des Merveilles (see p 380).

The Vallée des Merveilles is accessible on the D91, which leads to Les Mesches or Casterino. North of Saint-Dalmas lies Tende, this tour's ultimate destination; to the east, the D143 leads to La Brigue.

Tende

Tende creates a striking first impression, spread as it is on the mountainside. At the summit stand the ruins of the Lascaris castle, which dominated the village until the end of the 17th century. In the Middle Ages, Tende was of paramount importance, as it guarded an important pass into Piémont.

These days, the city is rather ordinary, and its tall houses roofed in *lauze* (a regional variant of slate), which seem to have a great deal of character when seen from afar, are a bit of a disappointment up close. That being the case, we were not even inclined to recommend a hotel, nor even a restaurant, to visitors.

Nonethless, Tende is worth a visit for its excellent **Musée de Tende** *(30F, children 5F; closed mid-Nov to Christmas, Wed to Mon 10:30am to 6pm, winter 5pm; on RN 204, ☎04.93.04.32.50)*. Built in 1996, the museum is closely associated with to Mont Bego, which was a sacred site devoted to the cult of a couple of primeval divinities consisting of the Taureau-Dieu (Bull-god, symbolizing lightning and rain) and the Déesse-Terre (Earth-goddess, symbolizing the earth's fertility). The museum contains traces of thousands of rock engravings (most of them plaster reproductions) dating to the agro-pastoral societies of the Copper and Bronze Ages. Three themes run through the superbly laid-out exhibition space: natural history, archaeology and the arts, and folk traditions. A video lets you experience the sacred rites of ancient times. Also worth noting: each year the museum hosts temporary international exhibits that tie in with the museum's themes.

La Brigue

This village, strongly pervaded with a medieval character, is situated in the Vallon de la Levense. Most of the houses in the old village are built of green shale from the Roya. The village has a rich religious heritage and there are many major architectural buildings of various styles.

On the square at the village entrance stands the **Collégiale Saint-Martin**. This collegiate church was built around 1500 in the Lombard- Romanesque style, with a heavy emphasis on the Gothic. Inside, the decor is enhanced by numerous paintings on wood. These works, including a crucifixion, the Sainte-Marthe triptych and, most especially, the nativity retable, attributed to Ludovico Brea, are of considerable artistic value.

There are two chapels around the collegiate church. The first, on the left, the **Chapelle de l'Annonciation**, boasts a stunning ellipsoidal shape. This chapel contains a collection of artifacts and priestly vestments. The other, the **Chapelle de l'Assomption**, on the large square on the right, conceals a Renaissance decor behind a baroque facade.

It is thus clear that La Brigue, a small village of only a few hundred inhabitants, has become the meeting point of Romanesque, Gothic, Renaissance and baroque art.

Finally, don't miss the **Chapelle Notre-Dame-des-Fontaines**, set deep in the country, near a waterway and surrounded by trees. To visit, contact the tourist office.

Chapelle Notre-Dame-des-Fontaines is situated 4km (2.5mi) from La Brigue, via the D43, then the D143, on the right.

Nicknamed the "Sistine Chapel of the Mediterranean Alps", and rightly so, this chapel has an abundance of frescoes painted in the latter half of the 15th century. Created for the most part, by Piedmontese painter Jean Canavesio, these frescoes, permeated with heavily anguished realism and violence, convey the political turmoil of the period.

Outdoor Activities

Hiking

The region is ideal for magnificent hikes, the

best of which lie in the Vallée des Merveilles (see below). Indeed, visitors can follow beautiful trails throughout the region from Levens, Coaraze, Lucéram, Sospel, Breil or Saorge.

We recommend the French guide *Au pays d'Azur*, published by Didier Richard, which describes 150 hikes between the l'Esterel massif and the Roya.

Sospel

Sospel is where a good half-dozen trails converge. Visitors can obtain a description of these trails in the *Itinéraires du Bureau de Recherches de Sentiers Touristiques du Canton de Sospel* publication, on sale at the Pont-Vieux tourist office *(☎04.93.04.00.09)*. Here is a sample:

The GR52, which links the Mediterranean to Holland, runs through Sospel, as does the GR52A, also called the "Panoramique du Mercantour" and the "GR des Huits Vallées" (GR of the eight valleys). Visitors can also take guided tours by calling ***☎04.93.04.04.72***.

Saorge

A very lovely hike from this perched village is something not to be missed. The 2hr tour begins behind the Couvent des Franciscains and allows visitors to see the Bendola canyon and its waterfalls, as well as the Sainte-Croix chapel.

La Brigue

There are magnificent strolls near this wonderful village. It is a fair distance from all the activity of the Vallée des Merveilles'. The GR52A (see above) runs through here. By heading north, you can climb up to Mont Bertrand. Finally, other, longer hikes lead to Italy after crossing mountains with altitudes ranging between 1,700 (5,577ft) and 2,200m (7,218ft).

★★★ The Vallée des Merveilles

Picture a mountain valley at a height of 2,000m (6,562ft): a place where trees are scarce because of the altitude, and where Italian wolves are starting to appear once again. This "marvellous" spot, as its name indicates in French, consists of rocks smoothed by the glaciers and lies at the foot of strangely named, imposing summits. In this exceptional setting, 4,000 years of human history are written on hundreds of shale slabs. The Vallée des Merveilles and the Val de Fontanalbe, both listed as historic monuments, are the only sites in the world where close to 30,000 rock engravings can be admired.

Some sensitive areas are only accessible if accompanied by a tour guide authorized by the Parc National du Mercantour. Moreover, these guided tours will allow you to better discover and understand the park's fauna, flora and engravings. It must be noted that the rock engravings throughout the territory are protected sites. Damaging the engravings in any way, be it by graffiti of any kind, destroying or walking on them, is strictly forbidden!

A place prized by all hiking enthusiasts, the Vallée des Merveilles is overcrowded during the months of July and August. It is best to visit the valley in June or September to fully appreciate its splendour and really commune with nature.

To reach the starting point of the hikes, take the D91 from St-Dalmas-de-Tende to Lac des Mesches or Casterino. You can also get there by bus from the St-Dalmas-de-Tende S.N.C.F. station.

A two-to three-day stay is recommended.

On the first day, you can head to the Refuge de la Fontanalbe. Good walkers will make it in an afternoon. Reservations are required, however, if you wish to spend the night in the hostel's common rooms. More athletic types can end the day with a climb to the Cime de la Charnassère (summit), passing by Lac Gelé.

The second day can be devoted to a walk to **Mont Bégo**, at 2,921m (9,583ft) in altitude, after passing along Lac Vert. Once you have reached your destination, you can either head back down toward the point of departure or spend an extra night in another hostel.

To climb back down, you can loop back toward Lac du Basto and then through the actual Vallée des Merveilles, on the GR52. Once you have crossed the valley, you will end up at the Refuge des Merveilles, surrounded by a many small lakes. You can spend the night here, of course, provided you have made reservations. Those who choose to continue should allow for two to 3hrs more to reach Lac des Mesches.

Those who wish to go for a longer hike can do so from Lac du Basto, heading northwest to the Nice hostel, where you can spend the night. This hostel is surrounded by three lakes: Lac Nire, Lac Long and Lac de la Fous. The third day will be dedicated to returning to the point of departure via the Mont des Merveilles and the myriad lakes clustered around the Refuge des Merveilles.

For addresses and phone numbers, consult the "Practical Information" section, p 372.

Horseback Riding

Sospel

The Auberge du Col de Braus offers excursions on horseback (*☎04.93.79.61.33*).

Mercantour
Dennis Longfellow
Le Boréon
☎04.93.03.30.23
This organization offers excursions with Merens horses. The outings last from a few hours to a few days (in summer).

La Brigue

Riding Club
Club équestre de La Brigue, Mrs. Vacarezza
☎04.93.04.66.59

Tennis

Sospel

You can play tennis here on three courts, two of which are lit (*☎04.93.04.04.37*).

Vallée de La Roya

There are three tennis courts in Breil *(reservations: ☎04.93.04.40.71)*.

Saorge

Two courts *(reservations at the town hall: ☎04.93.04.51.23)*.

Hunting and Fishing

Sospel

Inquire about hunting and fishing at the Pont-Vieux.

Swimming

Sospel

Sospel has both a local swimming pool *(500m or 1,640ft from the train station, on Route du Col de Castillon)* and a miniature golf *(La Guinguette du Gard, ☎04.93.04.10.90)*.

Vallée de La Roya

A lovely swimming pool awaits you in Breil *(Jun to Sep; ☎04.93.04.46.66)*.

Rock Climbing and Mountaineering

Vallées de La Roya–Béréra

The Roya has a great number of gneiss or limestone cliffs, ideal for practising such sports. Visitors can also enjoy rafting in the six different canyons in the region.

AET Nature
☎***04.93.04.47.64***

Association Renard
☎***04.93.04.77.73***

Bureau des Guides de la Béréra
(guide office)
☎***04.93.04.07.19***

Mountain Biking

All Regions

Destination Nature

☎***04.93.32.06.93***

Vallée de La Roya–Béréra

Many mountain trails, often with very rugged routes, straddle the French-Italian border. These are reserved for experienced cyclists.

Roya Evasion
☎***04.93.04.91.46***

Spelunking

Vallée de La Roya

The chasyms in the Massif du Marguareis are famous among spelunking buffs. This massif is very wild and not recommended for beginners.

Canoeing and Kayaking

Vallée de La Roya

With its quiet courses running toward Breil or very difficult ones rushing toward Saorge, the Roya is a valley particularly renowned for canoeing and kayaking. There are close to 9km (5.6mi) of navigable rivers, 6km (3.7mi) of which are open to all, awaiting to be discovered.

Ligue Côte d'Azur de Canoë Kayak
49 Boulevard Delfino, 06300 Nice, or Mr. Faloci
☎***04.93.04.91.46***

Base USTP
L'aigara, 06540 Breil-sur-Roya
☎***04.93.04.46.66***

Accommodations

Tourette-Levens

Auberge Chez Lucien
180F-220F, 1/2b 220F
ps, ss, tv, ℜ, K
Place de l'Église
☎***04.93.91.52.51***
Located at the entrance to this pretty medieval village, this little inn is run by a family whose son is unfortunately the only one who really knows how to welcome tourists. Still, its ambiance is not unpleasant. The rooms are clean and rather charming. Very good value for the price.

Sospel

Camping Le Domaine Sainte-Madeleine
Route du Moulinet
☎***04.93.04.10.48***
Camping Le Domaine Sainte-Madeleine offers spacious camp sites in a peaceful setting. The campground is a little outside of town: take the D2566, toward Turini-Moulinet, and follow the signs.

There are no quiet places to recommend in the village proper. On the other hand, those who venture just outside of town will be rewarded with two establishments, both excellent though very different:

Auberge Provençale
320F-440F, ½b 300F-480F
ps or pb, tv, ℜ, ℝ
Route du Col de Castillon
☎04.93.04.00.31
⇄04.93.04.24.54
aupro@aol.com
Overlooking the village, the Auberge Provençale is set in enchanting surroundings. Exceedingly well-kept by the welcoming owner, this hotel is a must-see! The bright and thoroughly charming dining room opens onto a lovely shaded garden. The fully renovated rooms are dazzlingly clean and very comfortable. In short, this place guarantees excellent value for your money. Finally, a footpath brings you to the village in just 10min.

La Lavina
440F for B&B and eveing meal, bkfst incl.
☎04.93.04.04.72
Nine kilometres (5.6mi) west of Sospel, on the D2204, a signpost marks the entrance to La Lavina. This is a farm-hotel where you can stay with locals on their farm. Those who appreciate the "real" countryside—complete with hens, roosters and small pigs—will be content with this utterly charming farm, which also acts as a mountain *gîte*. The owners, who are great nature lovers, are warm and welcoming, and enjoy sharing their love of nature with guests. Moreover, during the day, the owner organizes mountain hikes according to the clients' wishes.

Breil-sur-Roya

Castel-sur-Roya
410F-450F
ps or pb, ≈, ℜ
Route de Tende
☎04.93.04.43.66
⇄04.93.04.91.83
The hotel-restaurant Castel-sur-Roya is very well situated: on the outskirts of the village, and near the train station. It overlooks the river and occupies 2ha of property, in the middle of which is a patio and swimming pool. Guests here will be lulled by the constant murmur of the river. Hotel services are adequate. Its attractive setting will allow guests to relax or benefit from a host of outdoor activities in the vicinity. The restaurant has earned a good reputation.

Saint-Dalmas-de-Tende

Le Prieuré
305F-350F
pb, ℜ, *tv*
Rue Jean Médecin
☎04.93.04.75.70
⇄04.93.04.71.58
On the outskirts of the Vallée des Merveilles, Le Prieuré is a splendid hotel, located slightly below the village. It looks out over a small river, in an oasis of peacefulness. What sets this hotel apart from others is that it also serves as a youth rehabilitation work centre. Supervised and assisted by qualified staff, the young people who take part in this program provide all the hotel's services. The success of the program is clearly manifested by the impeccable state of the premises. The large rooms, some of which have vaulted ceilings, all have a view of the river. The welcome is exceptional. Highly recommended!

Casterino

Les Mélèzes
200F-320F
closed Dec, Tue pm and Wed (during the low season)
ps, tv
☎04.93.04.95.95
⇄04.93.04.95.96
Conveniently accessible to all the outdoor activities offered by the Vallée des Merveilles, Les Mélèzes, a hotel and restaurant, is a picturesque place to stop before going hiking, snowshoeing or skiing. The hotel has two sections: the older part contains simple rooms with sloped ceilings, which are rustic but not devoid of charm; the newer part is more comfortable but less appealing on the whole. Gay travellers can expect a warm welcome here. See restaurant description, p 385.

La Brigue

Hôtel-Restaurant Fleur des Alpes
185F-230F, ½b 195-220F
sink or ps, ℜ, tv
☎04.93.04.61.05
Situated by a small river, the Hôtel-Restaurant Fleur des Alpes is a modest but decent establishment. It is managed by the proprietress, while the proprietor attends to the kitchen. Seeing this *bon vivant* is enough to give you ample confidence in his talents! The rooms, be they in the front or rear, all afford lovely views. The place also has a trout pond. The restaurant is surrounded by large windows, providing a restful view of the wild little river. Very good value provided by charming hosts!

Hôtel-Restaurant Mirval
260F-320F, ½b 270F, obligatory in summer
closed Nov to Mar
ps or pb, ℜ, tv
☎04.93.04.63.71
⇌04.93.04.79.81
Located on the opposite side of a quaint little bridge, the Hôtel-Restaurant Mirval is excellently situated. Further attractions include a lovely terrace, a dining room with panoramic views and the option of hiking excursions. The rooms are decent and, surprisingly, the cheapest ones seemed the most interesting. Moreover, the meals are excellent!

Restaurants

It seems that the best restaurants in this region are located in the hotels or inns recommended in this section. What better way to get to know your hosts and learn about the region? However, listed below are a few additional possibilities.

Sospel

Auberge Provençale
$$-$$$
The restaurant of Auberge Provençale offers guests Provençal specialties. Located 1km (0.6mi) from the village exit as you head towards Menton. A friendly welcome awaits you.

Saorge

Restaurant Bellevue
$-$$
closed Wed
☎04.93.94.51.37
The Restaurant Bellevue is a superb establishment run by a friendly couple. Its chandeliers lend a charming baroque touch to the decor, and the view is spectacular. The new owners are no amateurs, since they previously owned a restaurant in the Var for quite some time. They serve regional cuisine adapted to what's available and in season. For instance, dishes featuring boar are served in winter. If not, we recommend you try the young pigeon with port and honey. Monsieur welcomes the guests and Madame makes the food.

Saint-Dalmas-de-Tende

Prieuré
$-$$
The Prieuré restaurant is flooded with light pouring in through the large windows. The place serves typical regional dishes, and a few others that have more eloquent names, like the *magret de canard au miel* or the *papillette de filets de truite à la porvençale.*

Tende

Auberge Tendasque
$-$$
65 Avenue du 16 Septembre 1947
☎04.93.04.62.26
Before or after visiting the Musée de Tende, enjoy the traditional cuisine prepared by the owner at the pleasant, quality Auberge Tendasque. You can sample the trout soufflée, duck filet with *cèpes* and other delicacies. The simple, rustic setting is nothing short of wonderful. The value is excellent for the price.

The slender silhouettes of boats are harmoniously aligned in the small fishing port of Vallon des Auffes. In Marseille, the sea is always close by...
- *C. Sappa*

rotected site, Porquerolles land is one of the Hyères Islands and fers attractive andy beaches and superb ews from the tops of cliffs at tower over a shimmering sea.
- *E. Luider*

At sunset, the houses in the lovely city of Menton are bathed in a warm light tha is evocative o nearby Italy.
- E. Luider

The harsh, beautiful landscape of the Alpes-de-Haute-Provence is perpetually snowbound. The region lies at the heart of the Varois backcountry, halfway between the Mediterranean and the Alps.
- C. Sappa

Casterino

Les Mélèzes
$-$$
The restaurant in the Hotel Les Mélèzes serves cuisine prepared by the owner, who is a native of these parts. In addition to regional specialties like home-made ravioli and roast rabbit stuffed with spinach, the menu includes fondues and raclettes, which go perfectly with the rustic mountain decor. See p 383.

Shopping

Coaraze

Located 20km (12.2mi) from Nice, this village is home to several artisans offering handicrafts made of leather or pewter, engravings, silk-screen prints and weaving.

At the beginning of June, the community organizes medieval days and a great arts-and-crafts market featuring dances, music, tricks, etc.

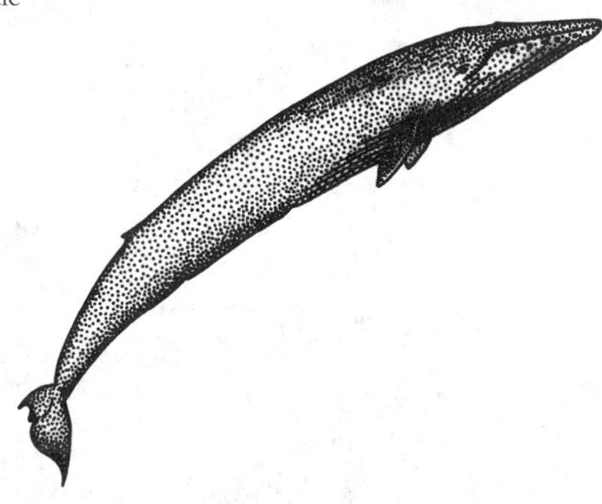

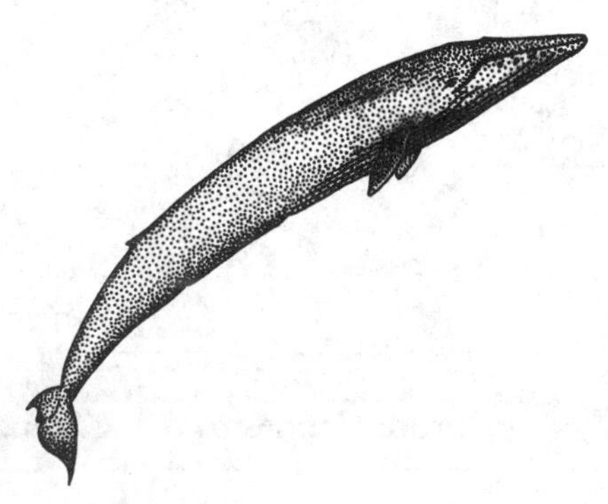

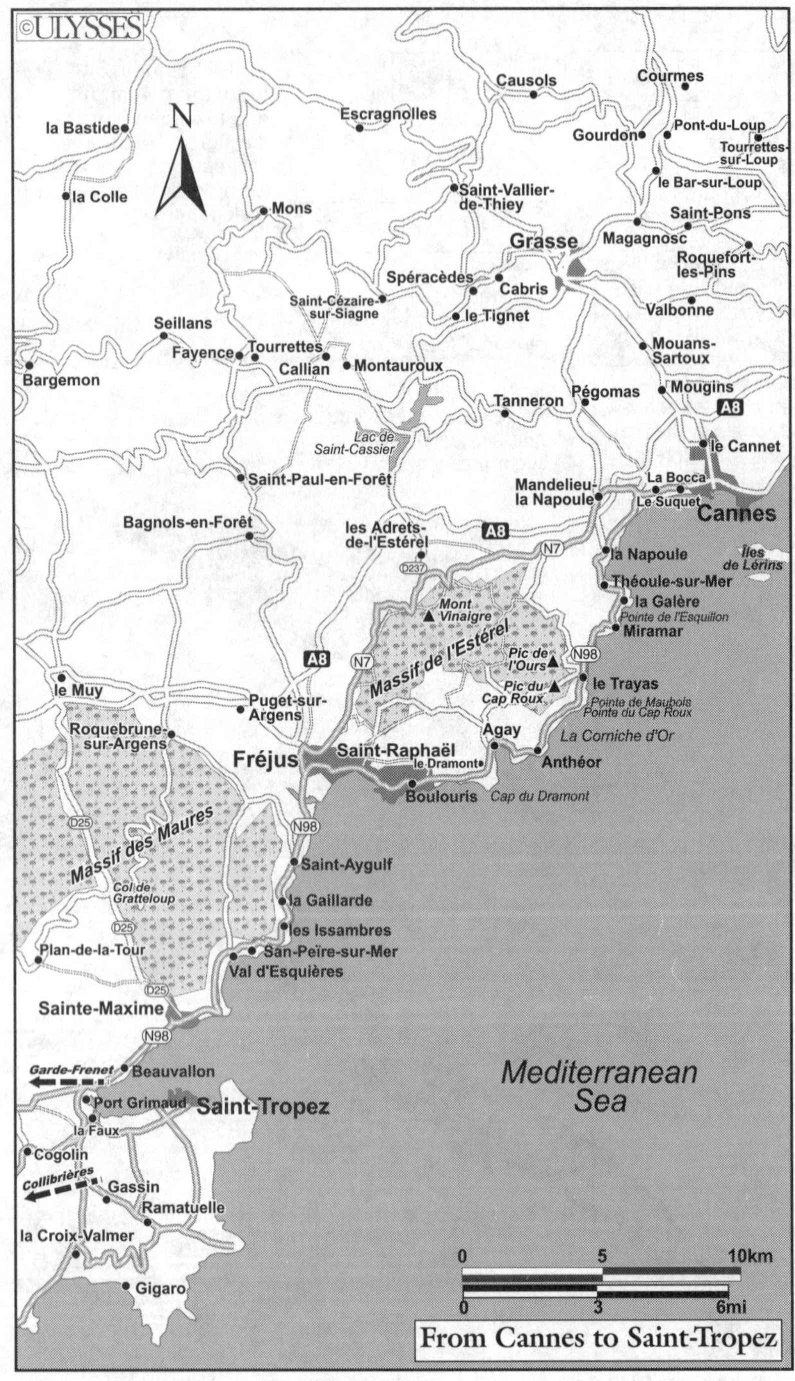

©ULYSSES
N
Causols
Courmes
Escragnolles
la Bastide
Gourdon
Pont-du-Loup
Tourrettes-sur-Loup
le Bar-sur-Loup
la Colle
Saint-Vallier-de-Thiey
Mons
Saint-Pons
Magagnosc
Grasse
Roquefort-les-Pins
Spéracèdes
Cabris
Saint-Cézaire-sur-Siagne
le Tignet
Valbonne
Seillans
Fayence
Tourrettes
Callian
Montauroux
Mouans-Sartoux
Bargemon
Mougins
Pégomas
Tanneron
A8
Lac de Saint-Cassier
le Cannet
Saint-Paul-en-Forêt
La Bocca
Mandelieu-la Napoule
Le Suquet
Cannes
Bagnols-en-Forêt
les Adrets-de-l'Estérel
A8
N7
D237
la Napoule
Îles de Lérins
Théoule-sur-Mer
la Galère
Mont Vinaigre
Pointe de l'Esquillon
Miramar
Massif de l'Estérel
Pic de l'Ours
N98
A8
N7
le Muy
Pic du Cap Roux
le Trayas
Pointe de Maubois
Pointe du Cap Roux
Puget-sur-Argens
Roquebrune-sur-Argens
Agay
La Corniche d'Or
Fréjus
Saint-Raphaël
le Dramont
Anthéor
Boulouris
Cap du Dramont
D25
N98
Massif des Maures
Saint-Aygulf
Col de Gratteloup
la Gaillarde
D25
les Issambres
Plan-de-la-Tour
San-Peïre-sur-Mer
Val d'Esquières
D25
Sainte-Maxime
N98
Garde-Frenet
Beauvallon
Mediterranean Sea
Port Grimaud
Saint-Tropez
la Faux
Cogolin
Collibrières
Gassin
Ramatuelle
la Croix-Valmer
0
5
10km
Gigaro
0
3
6mi
From Cannes to Saint-Tropez

From Cannes to Saint-Tropez

Fanatics of the sea, the beach, and stunning landscapes of rolling hills that are perfect for hiking will find exactly that in the magnificent region stretching from Cannes to Saint-Tropez.

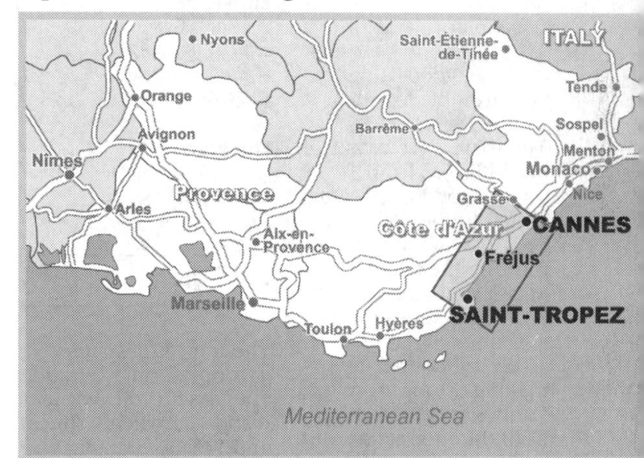

A multitude of seaside resorts are spread out along the coast and, behind them, the countryside awaits exploration—by car, by bicycle or on foot. Beyond the Massif de l'Estérel, which extends to Fréjus, are the Maures, a vast hilly area stretching to Hyères. Its highest peaks reach altitudes from 550 to 650m (1,804 to 2,133ft).

Unfortunately, the Côte d'Azur is becoming very developed. The hotspot of the area is unquestionably Saint-Tropez and its peninsula. Saint-Tropez is incredibly charming, but its charm is best appreciated outside of the peak summer season. Don't miss visiting the peninsula, where one sandy beach follows the next, and two lovely villages await: Ramatuelle and Gassin.

Finally, to complete your visit to the region, a picturesque tour through the Massif des Maures is suggested.

Finding Your Way Around

For those planning to spend most of their vacation in the Massif des Maures region or around the Îles d'Hyères, it would be better to land at the Toulon/Hyères airport rather than in Nice. However, there are coach connections to Fréjus/Saint-Raphaël and Saint-Tropez from the Nice airport.

By Car

The easiest way to see this beautiful corner of the world is by car. However, remember to avoid driving in rush hour between noon and 1pm, or in the early evening during peak season. Between 5pm and 8pm, the outskirts of Saint-Tropez are to be especially avoided, unless you are not in a rush.

There are two ways to get to Fréjus from Cannes: by Route N98, which follows the sea, or N7, which cuts through the spectacular Massif de l'Estérel. Both are very scenic roads and offer dazzling vistas. Of course, by making a loop from Cannes, you can see both the mountains and the sea in the same day. Hikers and walkers can and should stop while crossing l'Estérel by car for a quick stroll or a major hike.

From Fréjus, there is only one way to get to Saint-Tropez. Follow the coastline road N98 that passes through Sainte-Maxime and Port Grimaud. In fact, once past Fréjus, the other road, the **N7**, swings north and follows the highway.

If you want to cut down your travelling time between Cannes and Saint-Tropez, take the A8-E80. Exit at D25 (12km or 7.2mi past Fréjus), which will take you to Saint-Maxime and Saint-Tropez.

Car Rentals

Saint-Raphaël

Europcar
Place de la Gare
☎***04.94.95.56.87***

Fréjus

Europcar
308 Avenue de Verdun
☎***04.94.51.53.88***
≠***04.94.52.35.12***

By Train

The train is another good option if you limit your visit to the seaside resorts between Cannes and Fréjus, since the rail line follows the coastline beside the N98. However, from Fréjus, the train goes all the way north of the Massif des Maures and follows the highway (A8) to Toulon. The portion between Fréjus, Saint-Tropez and Le Lavandou cannot be reached by train, despite certain efforts that were made at the end of the last century. Of course, these cities are accessible by bus from Fréjus.

Train Station

Fréjus

Gare SNCF
123 Rue W.-Rousseau
☎***08.36.35.35.35***

By Bus

Several coach and bus services are available between this region's villages and towns, but they can prove to be long trips. On the other hand, there is a shuttle every hour between Cannes, Saint-Raphaël and Fréjus.

Information about the Toulon-Hyères airport summer-bus service from Saint-Tropez: ☎***04.94.97.45.21***.

Bus Stations

Fréjus

Square Régis (next to the SNCF train station)
☎***04.91.78.78.78***

Saint-Tropez

Avenue Général Leclerc
☎***04.94.65.21.00***
☎***04.94.97.41.21***

By Taxi

Taxi Stand

Fréjus

Avenue de Verdun
☎***04.94.51.51.12***

By Bicycle

Bike Rental

Saint-Tropez

Location Deux Roues
bicycle, mountain bike, and scooter rental
3 and 5 Rue Quaranta (near Place du XVe Corps)
☎*04.94.97.00.60*

Practical Information

Tourist Offices

Mandelieu-la-Napoule
Office de Tourisme et d'Animation
270 Rue Jean Monnet
☎*04.93.49.95.31*
⇄*04.92.97.99.57*

Agay
Tourist Office
Boulevard de la plage, B. P. 45
☎*04.94.82.01.85*
⇄*04.94.82.74.20*

Saint-Raphaël
Tourist Office
Rue J. Barbier, B.P. 210
☎*04.94.19.52.52*
www.saint-raphael.com

Fréjus
Office Municipal du Tourisme, de la Culture et de l'Animation
325 Rue Jean Jaurès
☎*04.94.51.83.83*
www.ville-frejus.fr

Sainte-Maxime
Tourist Office
Promenade Simon Lorière, B. P. 107
☎*04.94.55.75.55*
⇄*04.94.55.75.56*
www.ste-maxime.com

Grimaud
Bureau Municipal de Tourisme
at the entrance to the village
☎*04.94.43.26.98*
⇄*04.94.43.32.40*

Saint-Tropez
Tourist Office
Downtown
Quai Jean Jaurès
☎*04.94.97.45.21*
⇄*04.94.97.82.66*
www.nova.fr/saint-tropez

Maison du Tourisme Golfe de Saint-Tropez/Pays des Maures
Carrefour de la Foux, between Port-Grimaud and the entrance to Saint-Tropez
☎*04.94.43.42.10*
⇄*04.94.43.42.78*
www.franceplus.com/golfe.de.st-tropez
Thanks to the centralized reservations system of the Saint-Tropez tourist office, it's easy to find a place to stay in this area.

Ramatuelle
Tourist Office
Place de l'Orneau
☎*04.94.79.26.04*
⇄*04.94.79.12.66*

Cogolin
Tourist Office
Place de la République
☎*04.94.55.01.10*
⇄*04.94.55.01.11*

Emergencies

Fréjus
Police Station
Commissariat Central, Place Mangin
☎*04.94.17.66.00*

Saint-Tropez
Police Station
Gendarmerie
☎*04.94.97.26.25*

Hospital
☎*04.94.97.47.30*

Post Office

Fréjus
Post Office
8:30am to 7pm, Sat 8:30am to noon
Avenue Aristide-Briand
☎*04.94.17.60.80*

Exploring

From Cannes to Fréjus

From Cannes, we suggest a scenic tour, which can be done in a day and that leads back to Cannes. The road takes you full-circle, starting by the seaside road (N98) to Saint-Raphaël and Fréjus. To return to Cannes, cross the **Massif de l'Estérel** via the N7. If you like to view sunsets over the sea, start the tour in the opposite direction.

The Massif de l'Estérel

Between the Mediterranean Sea and the limestone of Provence is the Massif de l'Estérel, a volcanic massif of 32,000ha (79,072 acres), of which 13,000ha (32,123 acres) are protected. Consisting of sumptuous red rock, it features mountainous terrain and jagged landscapes that plunge abruptly into the sea.

Its history is very ancient, dating back almost 300 million years. Apparently, before the creation of the Mediterranean, the Estérel was attached to Africa. During the Tertiary era, part of the Estérel drifted and Corsica was born.

Its history has also been marked by all the civilizations that have criss-crossed the Mediterranean Basin, beginning as early as the Romans, who came here to quarry porphyry, the very hard rock of that makes up the Massif.

Today, the Massif is the scene of various activities. The Office National des Forêts (ONF) has many forest rangers who are happy to share their knowledge and love of this wild massif with visitors. Among its trails, there are 45km (27mi) for hiking, 100km (60mi) for mountain biking and 100km (60mi) for horseback riding. Pick up the map of the Massif published by the ONF on sale at the Saint-Raphaël Office de Tourisme for complete information.

While you are at the Saint-Raphaël Office de Tourisme, you can also find out about the various activities it organizes in conjunction with the ONF to promote this splendid area. You can take tours led by rangers or, better still, set off with them (on Tuesdays only) to investigate the local flora and fauna.

If you happen to be more sedentary, you can explore the Massif by joining one of the four-wheel-drive excursions organized by the sports club, JDC Loisirs et Découvertes *(☎06.09.09.73.90)*.

But the Massif also features all the splendours of the sea. Saint-Raphaël is a designated *Station Voile* (sailing area) a mark of quality awarded by the Féderation Française de Voile, and you can enjoy a multitude of water sports here.

The Saint-Raphaël district includes several yacht clubs, sailing schools and boating centres that offer diverse services to those of all ages or levels.

Moreover, diving has a place of honour here. Its shores have been at the centre of intensely active commercial routes since early antiquity. As a result, there are some 50 sunken ships off the coast of Saint-Raphaël. These underwater sites are accessible to snorkellers as well as scuba divers. Finally, you don't need to be an athlete to explore the sea floor, since tours can be taken in underwater-sightseeing boats.

Office de Tourisme de Saint-Raphaël
☎04.94.19.52.52
www.saint-raphaël.com

Office National des Forêts
www.onf.fr

Mandelieu-la-Napoule

Upon leaving Cannes, you will quickly reach Mandelieu-la-Napoule, renowned for its cultivation of mimosa. The municipality has a marina as well as an impressive **château** *(25F; afternoon guided tours; Feb to Nov, Wed to Mon; Boulevard Henry-Clews, ☎04.93.49.95.05)*, whose original construction dates from the 14th century. At the beginning of the 20th century, U.S. sculptor Henry Clews bought the place and renovated it, while his wife tended the gardens surrounding the château.

Finally, from the Mandelieu port, visitors can also take a ferry to the Iles de Lérins.

Théoule-sur-Mer

Théoule-sur-Mer is a small, peaceful seaside resort right next to Cannes. Its main attraction is the nearby Parc Forestier de la Pointe de l'Aiguille, in the Massif de l'Estérel. This park is particularly spectacular in that it stretches along the coast and offers magnificent views and possibilities for pleasant hikes (see p 407).

Next, the road goes through small villages that all allow easy access to l'Estérel by walking trails. From **Miramar**, you can make a quick climb towards l'Esquillon and enjoy spectacular views.

Commune de Saint-Raphaël

Le Trayas marks the beginning of the Commune de Saint-Raphaël, as well as the Département du Var. From Trayas, you can access other trails that feature several lookout points over l'Estérel and the sea. Finally, Trayas makes up the heart of the **Corniche d'Or**.

Not far from Trayas, near Pointe de Maubois, another trail leads towards **Pic du Cap Roux**. The climb to the peak can prove to be difficult for some, but is really worth the effort.

Visitors will then reach **Anthéor**, which stretches below Cap Roux. Right nearby, a forest road leads to Cap Roux. From Anthéor, the rock turns red and displays many signs of water erosion.

Agay

After the Pointe de Baumette, you will reach Agay, whose name is derived from the Greek *agathon* meaning "favourable." No doubt this is in reference to the village's enviable location, protected by the harbour. It was only after the arrival of the railway in 1860, however, that the village began to grow thanks to the construction of seaside villas.

Renowned author Saint-Exupéry was married here in 1932, and remained here until his death. He was killed an accident during an air mission in 1944.

The route continues toward **Le Dramont**— a place whose history dates back to 1500 BC. A menhir (listed as an historic monument) from this era attests to this. Visitors can go for a walk around the cape along a path skirting the coast.

Saint-Raphaël–Ville

The noteworthy beginnings of this seaside village go back to the 11th century, when its port became more important than that of Fréjus. However, its original settlement dates back even further. During the Roman era, Saint-Raphaël was already a residential suburb of Fréjus.

The **Église Saint-Pierre des Templiers** ★, which was set in the heart of the medieval village, is of the Romanesque-Provençal style. It served as a fortress and refuge for the population in case of attack. Its tower dates from the 13th century. Near the church is the **archaeological museum** ★ *(10am to noon and 2pm to 5pm; ☎04.94.19.25.75)*, housed in the 18th-century presbytery.

This museum is world-famous for submarine archaeology, thanks to its large collection of amphorae from sunken ships in the vicinity.

The city's attractions include seaside resorts, a casino and a marina. The resort was developed mostly during the 19th century, as evidenced by the few remaining villas that attracted artists and high society. The *belle époque* era did indeed bestow a certain charm upon tthis city.

★★
Fréjus

Though banal in appearance, Fréjus has many treasures such as fabulous historic monuments in its oldest part, and several streets with beautifully restored old houses.

While you're here, spend some time visiting the **old city** ★★. Its origins go back to Roman times, when the Forum Julii (Julius market), located on Voie Aurélienne, that links Rome and Arles, was an important stopping place for the Romans. From AD 374 onward, the town became an episcopal city and was fortified at the beginning of the 14th century.

Following this period of glory, Fréjus became a small, insignificant city until the beginning of the 20th century. At the end of the 19th century, Saint-Raphaël had been at the forefront of the evolving tourist industry. Only after World War II did this city begin to regain some of its stature, as development intensified, but the consequences of this are controversial.

This tour begins at the heart of the old city. Follow the many signs indicating the city centre. There is a parking lot nearby where you can leave your car.

Place Formigé is the site of the cathedral, baptistery, and cloister. It is named for the architect who directed major restoration work on the

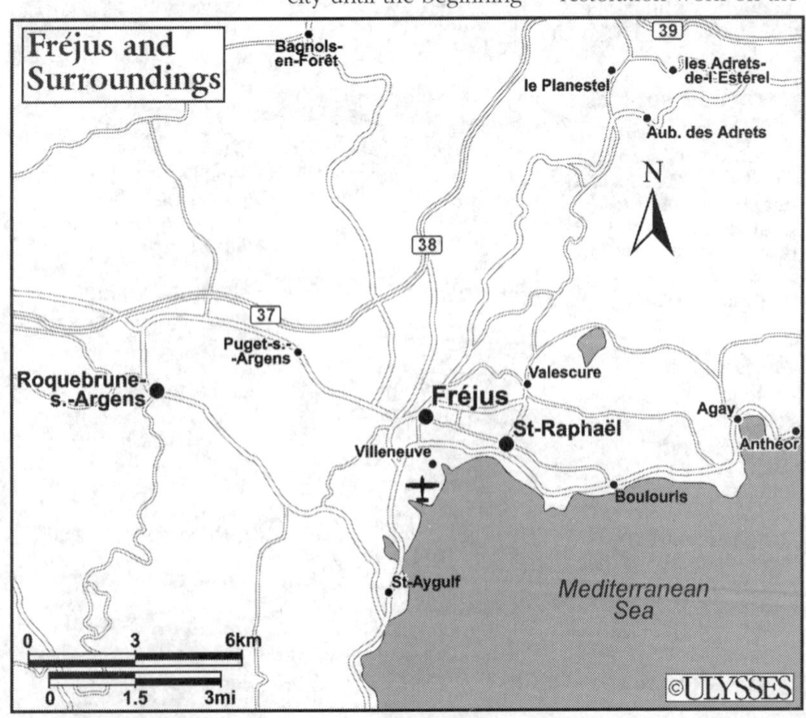

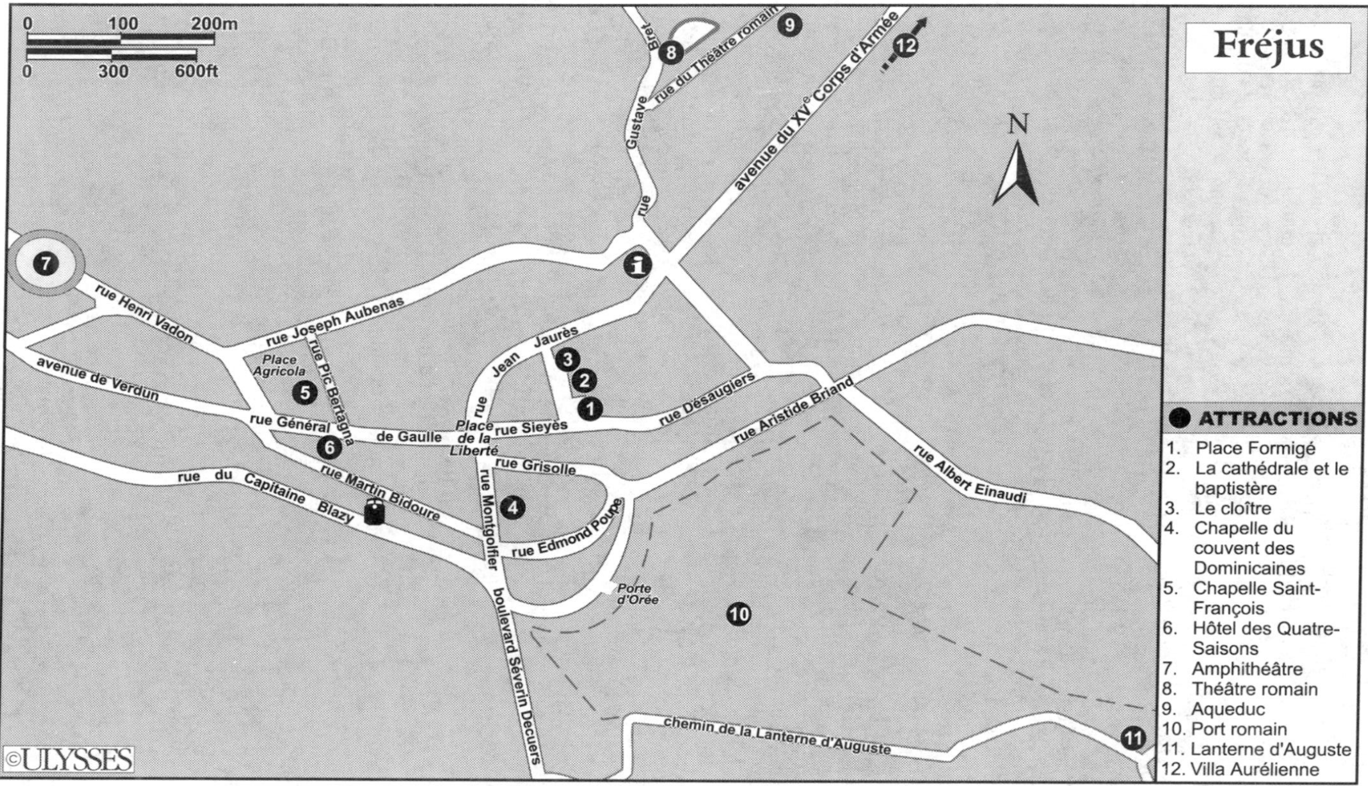
Fréjus
ATTRACTIONS
1. Place Formigé
2. La cathédrale et le baptistère
3. Le cloître
4. Chapelle du couvent des Dominicaines
5. Chapelle Saint-François
6. Hôtel des Quatre-Saisons
7. Amphithéâtre
8. Théâtre romain
9. Aqueduc
10. Port romain
11. Lanterne d'Auguste
12. Villa Aurélienne
0 100 200m
0 300 600ft
N
rue Henri Vadon
avenue de Verdun
rue Joseph Aubenas
Place Agricola
rue Pic Bertagna
rue Général de Gaulle
rue du Capitaine Blazy
rue Martin Bidoure
rue Jean Jaurès
Place de la Liberté
rue Sieyès
rue Désaugiers
rue Grisolle
rue Montgolfier
rue Edmond Poupe
boulevard Séverin Decuers
Porte d'Orée
rue Aristide Briand
rue Albert Einaudi
chemin de la Lanterne d'Auguste
rue Gustave Bret
rue du Théâtre romain
avenue du XVe Corps d'Armée
©ULYSSES

baptistery and the cloister between 1920 and 1930.

The **Cathédrale ★★** *(closed Mon, Apr to Sep 9am to 7pm, until 5pm the rest of the year; ☎04.94.51.26.30)*, built on the site of an ancient Roman temple, is Gothic, but nevertheless presents many Roman characteristics. It is composed of two naves. The main nave dates back to the 13th century. The other nave, which supports the bell tower, dates back to the 11th century but was only completed in the 12th century. Most noteworthy in this building are the exquisitely sculpted, wooden Renaissance-style doors.

We strongly recommend the guided tour of the baptistery and the cloister. You will learn a wealth of fascinating historical details.

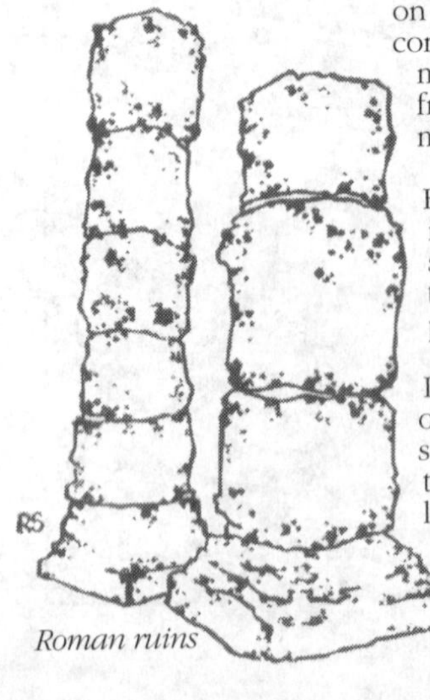
Roman ruins

The **Baptistère ★★**, dating back to the 5th century, is especially interesting since it is one of Gaul's oldest Christian monuments. Pillars and capitals from ancient Roman sites were used in the construction of this building with octagonal walls. It's interesting to note that the entrance to the baptistery is not the original doorway. Instead, there were originally two doors on either side: one small door, by which those to be baptised entered, and a large one by which they exited, since they had "grown" through their baptism.

The **Cloître ★★** also incorporates several elements from old Roman buildings. It opens up to two floors of galleries around a well in the centre. The wooden ceilings are painted with Apocalyptic scenes. The small archaeological museum, on the second floor, contains a magnificent mosaic that comes from an opulent Roman palace.

Finally, the city hall is also located in this square, housed in the old episcopal palace.

In the streets of the old city, there are several other architectural treasures, namely the **Chapelle du Couvent des Dominicains ★** on Rue Montgolfier, the **Chapelle Saint-François ★**, a Gothic church dating back to the early 16th century, and the **Hôtel des Quatre-Saisons ★**, on Rue du Général De Gaulle.

Visit the **Amphitheatre** *(free admission on Sun; 10am to noon and 2pm to 5:30pm; winter, until 4:30pm; Rue Henri Vaden, ☎04.94.51.34.31)*, slightly to the west of the city-centre, and be transported back to Roman times. The amphitheatre is actually an arena since it forms a complete circle. It dates back to the beginning of the first millennium and has fallen to ruins over the centuries, its materials having been used in other constructions. The site is now being restored and hosts outdoor shows.

The ruins of the **Théâtre Romain** *(same hours as the Amphitheatre)* can be found to the northeast of the city. Only vestiges of the stage and of the supporting walls of the stands remain.

Nearby, the ruins of the city walls, dating back to the first century BC, are visible. These walls once completely surrounded the city-centre. They stretched all the way to the amphitheatre, which was built outside of the walls.

Still on the same site, the **aqueduc,** also dating back to the 1st century BC, carried water to Fréjus from La Siagnole over an ap-

Shortcuts Across the Fields

The city of Fréjus has set up six thematic tours to optimize your explorations in the region and has extremely attractive brochures to describe them. What's more, each brochure includes a recipe from *cuisine de terroir*, (regional cuisine) based on local ingredients.

The Clay and Potters Route

These small roads introduce you to a region where, since time immemorial, clay has been the very basis of civilization. Earthenware, age-old, yet so current, decorates Provençal floors, wall and roofs. This route leads to Salernes, the Mecca of Provençal pottery. However, since the tour extends as far as Moustiers-Sainte-Marie, it requires a few days to complete. You can also use it as inspiration for your tour of the Var.

The Olive Tree and Grapevine Route

This tour leads you on small roads that cross the superb Provençal landscape where age-old fields of olive trees and grapevines bloom. Constantly gaining ground against the forest, these fields nestle at the heart of virgin, green hills that are as yet untouched by cultivation. Like the previous one, this tour takes several days. It essentially covers central Var, revolving around Draguignan. You can also take the opportunity to visit the many vineyards found in the environs of Arcs-sur-Argens.

The Scents and Fragrances Route

This tour will appeal to romantics. All your senses will be aroused by the fragrances and colours of flowers, especially mimosa, whose yellow globes brighten the February landscape, and broom that clothes the hills in June with an equally brilliant yellow. Not to mention the violet and lavender that spread across the fields and the unforgettable scents of the wild herbs, notably thyme and rosemary, that will fill your nostrils. What's more, the incredible light—which reaches the epitome of softness in December—adds its impressionistic touch to the fertile countryside of Provence. This tour essentially covers the Pays de Fayence and the Estérel but also includes Grasse, the city of every fragrance. It is accented with a number of pretty villages that are each associated with a particular fragrance: Fréjus (myrtle), Les Adrets de l'Estérel (oregano), Tanneron (mimosa), Grasse (jasmine), Saint-Vallier (thyme), Montauroux (rose), Callian (sage), Mons (rosemary), Fayence-Tourrettes (violet), Seillans (lavender), Saint-Paul-en-Forêt (savory) and Bagnols-en-Forêt (broom).

Fréjus's Creeks and Shoreline Route

This tour follows the Chemin des Douaniers or the Sentier du Littoral, so-named because it traces the curve of the sea. Dotted with fine-sand beaches, rocky creeks and little inlets, underwater diversity is close at hand. A face mask is all you'll need to

From Cannes: one day, about 40km (25mi)

Vallauris *(D803)*, Golfe-Juan, Juan-les-Pins, Antibes *(stop at the beach)*, Marineland-La Brague *(about 5km or 3.1mi from Antibes, in the direction of Cagnes-sur-Mer on the N98)*, return via highway A8.

Itinerary V: tour deep into the backcountry

Take in the **Gorges de la Vésubie**, Utelle, Madone d'Utelle, Lantosque, Saint-Martin-Vésubie, Saint-Dalmas, Saint-Sauveur-de-Tinée, Beuil, then descend through the **Gorges du Cians** ★★ or via Valberg and the **Gorges de Daluis** ★, ending up in **Entrevaux**.

proximate distance of 40km (24.9ft).

South of the old city is where the **Roman port** once stood. Now gone, the port was located by a pond rather than the sea. Still remaining is the **Lanterne d'Auguste**, the light which marked the entrance to the port. Over 10m (32.8ft) high, it was restored in the 19th century.

To fully appreciate all the historical value that lies hidden in Fréjus, be sure to get a map from the tourist office to help plan your stroll through the city.

You will notice signposts for the recently restored **Villa Aurélienne** *(Avenue de Général Calliès, ☎04.94.51.83.83)* on the N7 towards the A8. The Villa presents temporary photography exhibitions.

Finally, near the highway, you can stop and visit the wildcats and monkeys living at the **Parc Zoologique de Fréjus** *(10am to 6pm, until 5pm in winter; Capitou sector, ☎04.94.40.70.65)*.

Return to Cannes via highway A8 or, if you have the time, by N7, which passes through the beautiful landscape of Massif de l'Estérel. On the way, take D237 and stop in the charming little village of **Les Adrets-de-l'Estérel**, in the heart of the mountain range. This is an interesting place to stop for travellers seeking the tranquillity of the Provençal countryside, since it is home to several good hotels and restaurants.

Finally, if you have children and would like to offer them a special treat, take them to **Aquatica** *(125F, 100F children; Jun to Sep 10am to 6pm; Route N 98, ☎04 94 51 82 51)* before you leave Fréjus. The most elaborate water park on the Côte d'Azur, Aquatica has the largest wave pool in Europe, a tubing river, many water slides, an *aquatigolf* area(yes, you read it correctly!) and much more. In short, enough variety so that everyone in the family will want to get their feet wet.

From Fréjus to Saint-Tropez

The segment of the N 98 that runs along the sea between Fréjus and Saint-Tropez, via Sainte-Maxime and Port-Grimaud, offers fewer points of interest than the road between Cannes and Fréjus.

However, almost as soon as you leave Fréjus, you come to the **Étangs de Villepey** ★★, one of the rare series of ponds between Nice and Marseille. A protected area, the ponds cover 255ha (630 acres) in an extraordinary natural setting. The ocean lies on one side of the road, while the unspoiled, freshwater lagoons lie on the other. Magnificent! You can readily imagine the plants and wildlife they support. No fewer than

217 bird species have been observed on these ponds. Unfortunately, since these birds are very easily disturbed, few of them nest here. Their numbers peak early in the morning in March.

Finally, why not try out the separate, country-style cycling path which runs alongside the road?

Next, you'll come to **Les Issambres**, a great place to stop primarily for the wild landscape of its rocky inlets and beaches.

A little farther on, in Val d'Esquières, you will see a luxury hotel that was built in 1932 to attract a wealthy clientele. It is here that water-skiing was supposedly first practised in France, in 1935.

Those with ample time should leave Fréjus for **Roquebrune-sur-Argens**, dominated by its rock. This small village, on the edge of the **Massif des Maures** ★★★ (see p 403), contains a tight jumble of buildings known as *castrum*, composed of a church, a château and houses that recall the feudal period.

Set off toward the Col de Gratteloup to join the D25, which runs to Sainte-Maxime. The road between Roquebrune and Sainte-Maxime offers a number of beautiful views.

Sainte-Maxime

A seaside resort opposite Saint-Tropez, Sainte-Maxime extends up from a rather beautiful and sometimes very lively seafront. The place is ideal for pleasant strolls and all kinds of water sports.

Saint-Maxime's history follows that of the Golfe de Saint-Tropez due to its geography. First, the Phocaeans set up a post here, where wine, oil, olives and various kinds of ore were traded. After Roman occupation, the village fell into the hands of the Lérin monks in the 7th century. The monks gave the town its current name, in honour of a saint of their religious order, around the year 1000.

Built by the Lérin monks in the 16th century, the **Tour Seigneuriale**, or **Tour Carrée**, was put to many uses: seigneurial residence, prison, etc. Also situated here were cannons, which faced those of the **Tour du Portalet** in Saint-Tropez, thus ensuring the protection of the gulf's waters. Today, the Tour houses the **Musée Traditions Locales** *(closed Tue; ☎04.94.96.70.30)*, houses a small local museum.

In the 18th century, the small port of Sainte-Maxime saw another explosion of commercial activity: the wood, cork, oil and wine from the Maures region passed through here en route to Marseilles and Italy. This trade was, however, supplanted at the end of the 19th century by the tourist industry.

★ Port-Grimaud

A modern 20th-century "Venetian" city built on a marshy area, Port-Grimaud is the brainchild of architect François Spoerry. Canals spanned by bridges replace roads in this city. No cars are allowed, so visitors must leave their vehicles in the pay parking lot at the entrance to the village.

The market square and the Place du Sud are the two busiest centres of this town, whose charm is the product of clever design from the ground up. Fortunately, the passing years are managing to give a more authentic look to the architecture.

A visit to Port-Grimaud can be made more pleasant by exploring its **canals** *(every day 8am to 10:30pm, every 15min in summer, closed mid-Nov to mid-Dec; departure from Place du Marché, ☎04.94.56.21.13)*.

Port-Grimaud is nonetheless a financial success for the investors and speculators who took an interest in the project despite the increase in land prices since the village was created.

The village has an abundance of little restaurants and businesses of all kinds. At the bottom of the village, a large beach borders the sea.

A small **tourist train** *(30F; stops at Les Prairies de la Mer camping ground, at Port-Grimaud's main entrance and at Place de l'Église in Grimaud; information:* ☎*04.94.54.09.09)* links Port-Grimaud to the old village of Grimaud.

★

Grimaud

This typically Provençal village is worth taking the time to stroll through and explore. The ruins of the **château** ★ dominate the village. Built in the 11th century, the castle was surrounded by three walls. It was torn down in 1655 under the orders of Cardinal Mazarin.

Most of the village's narrow streets are for pedestrians only. The great variety of plants and flowers that adorn the houses and gardens makes this village one of the most picturesque in the region.

Along Rue des Templiers you'll find the **Maison des Templiers**, a Renaissance-style building which is also called the *Maison des Arcades*. It stands facing the **Église Saint-Michel** ★, which was built in the 11th century in a purely Romanesque style.

Towards the cemetery, you'll see the restored **Moulin de Grimaud**, a mill dating back to the 12th century, as well as an 11th-century chapel.

Finally, try, **Les Santons**, a restaurant whose gastronomical delights should not be missed (see p 419).

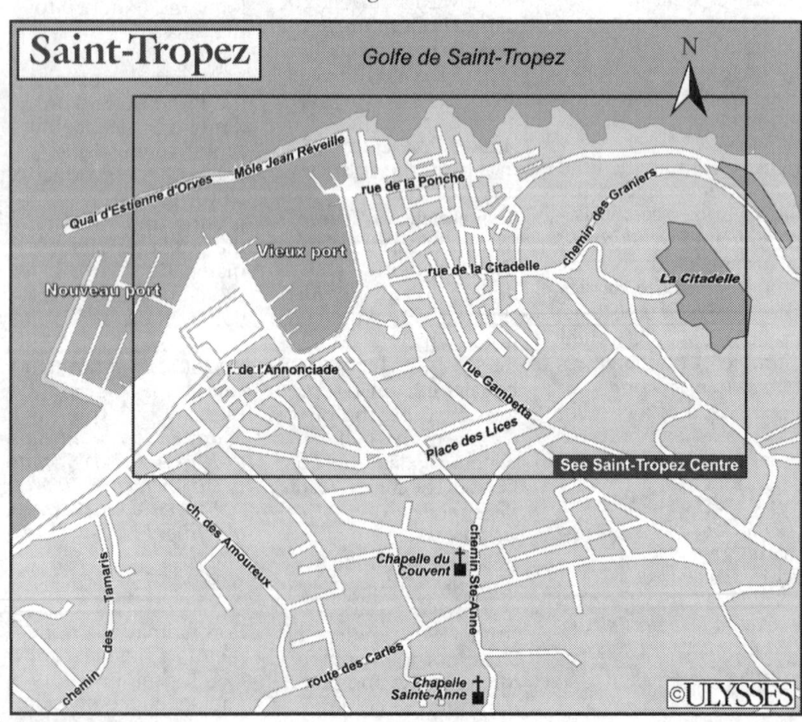

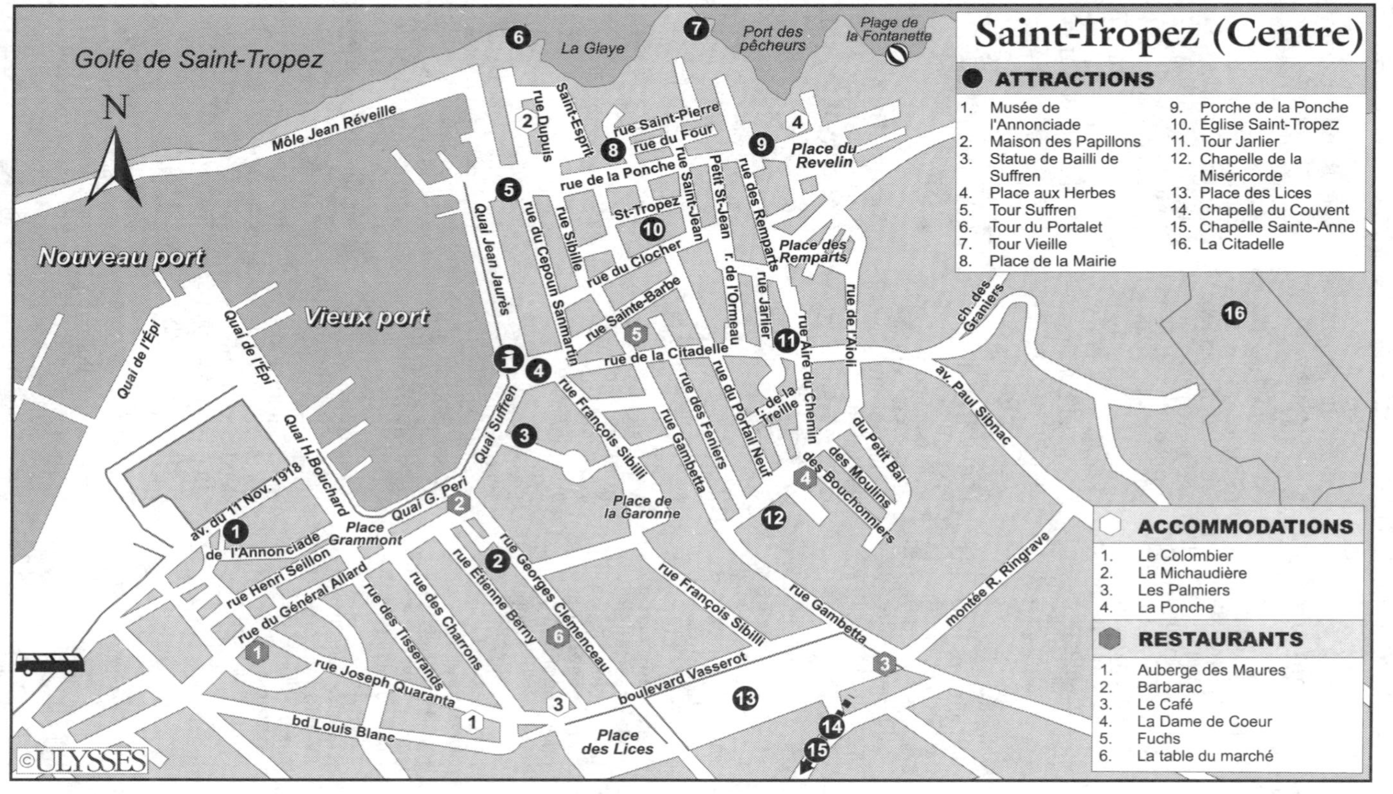
Saint-Tropez (Centre)
ATTRACTIONS
1. Musée de l'Annonciade
2. Maison des Papillons
3. Statue de Bailli de Suffren
4. Place aux Herbes
5. Tour Suffren
6. Tour du Portalet
7. Tour Vieille
8. Place de la Mairie
9. Porche de la Ponche
10. Église Saint-Tropez
11. Tour Jarlier
12. Chapelle de la Miséricorde
13. Place des Lices
14. Chapelle du Couvent
15. Chapelle Sainte-Anne
16. La Citadelle
ACCOMMODATIONS
1. Le Colombier
2. La Michaudière
3. Les Palmiers
4. La Ponche
RESTAURANTS
1. Auberge des Maures
2. Barbarac
3. Le Café
4. La Dame de Coeur
5. Fuchs
6. La table du marché
Golfe de Saint-Tropez
La Glaye
Port des pêcheurs
Plage de la Fontanette
N
Môle Jean Réveille
Nouveau port
Vieux port
Quai de l'Épi
Quai H.Bouchard
Quai Jean Jaurès
Quai Suffren
Quai G. Peri
Place Grammont
av. du 11 Nov. 1918
de l'Annonciade
rue Henri Seillon
rue du Général Allard
rue Joseph Quaranta
bd Louis Blanc
rue des Tisserands
rue des Charrons
rue Étienne Berny
rue Georges Clemenceau
boulevard Vasserot
Place des Lices
rue François Sibilli
rue Gambetta
montée R. Ringrave
Place de la Garonne
rue Dupuis
Saint-Esprit
rue Saint-Pierre
rue du Four
rue de la Ponche
rue du Cepoun Sanmartin
rue Sibille
St-Tropez
rue Saint-Jean
Petit St-Jean
rue des Remparts
Place du Revelin
Place des Remparts
rue du Clocher
rue Sainte-Barbe
rue de la Citadelle
r. de l'Ormeau
rue Jarlier
rue Aire du Chemin
rue de l'Aioli
r. de la Treille
rue des Feniers
rue du Portail Neuf
des Moulins
des Bouchonniers
du Petit Bal
ch. des Graniers
av. Paul Sibnac
©ULYSSES

★★★ Saint-Tropez

Despite all the clichés, Saint-Tropez really is one of the most beautiful and charming spots on the Côte d'Azur. It is situated on a magnificent bay, and its old town is authentically preserved thanks to careful renovations.

Is it any wonder that the Ligurians, the Celts, the Greeks and the Romans were attracted by the natural beauty of this little piece of paradise?

The city is named for a certain Torpès, a soldier in Nero's Roman army. This man was beheaded in Pisa after becoming a Christian. His remains, cast into a small boat, drifted to the village. It was only after the French Revolution that Saint-Torpès became Saint-Tropez.

Since AD 739, the history of Saint-Tropez has been punctuated by constant wars, destruction and pillaging that persisted for several centuries. The tower of Château Suffren, at the far end of the port, was constructed at the end of the 10th century. It stands as testimony of the village's defence.

In 1441, the city was established once and for all with the arrival of Genoese families, and subsequently became a small independent republic. It was Colbert, France's centralizer, that put an end to this special status in 1672.

In the centuries that followed, fishermen and merchants transformed the village into a flourishing commercial centre. The 19th century brought on the Industrial Era, and after this Saint-Tropez began to decline.

Fortunately, the development of the tourist industry near the end of the 19th century saved the city. Several artists settled here including Franz Liszt and Signac, followed by Matisse and Picabia. Writer Colette took up residence in a superb house near the Place aux Herbes, and later Anaïs Nin, Henry Miller's companion, came here to write the *Tahitian* chapter of her autobiography.

Every summer from 1950 onward, the great stars of Paris such as Greco, Sagan, Vian and Prévert moved to "Saint-Trop".

Saint-Tropez always brings to mind Brigitte Bardot. Since she moved here in the 1960s, the city has indeed become world-famous. Her reputation, even today, is one that nobody can remain indifferent to.

Despite the German bombings which destroyed the port in 1944, Saint-Tropez now shines in all its splendour thanks to some very well-planned reconstruction. The hoards of tourists that invade the streets in July are the price to be paid for all that glory. Unfortunately, as the city swells with all those people, much of the town loses its charm and its traditional appeal. Postpone your visit to the winter or spring, when the city's beauty is more radiant... it is truly spectacular!

Walking Tour of Saint-Tropez (see map of the city)

Leave your car in one of the parking lots next to the new port or on Place des Lices. It is futile to look for a parking spot near the old city, especially during the peak tourist season.

The tour begins at the southwest point of the Vieux-Port.

The old Notre-Dame de l'Annonciation chapel built in 1568, was transformed into a museum in 1955: the **Musée de l'Annonciade** ★★ *(admission charge; summer, Wed to Mon 10am to noon and 5pm to 7pm; rest of year, 10am to noon and 2pm to 6pm; closed Nov; Place Grammont, ☎04.94.97.04.01)*. The rooms are stunning. The museum contains, among other things, Georges Grammont's prestigious personal collection, which he bequeathed to the city in 1963.

The Musée de l'Annonciade is a dazzling reminder that Saint-Tropez was one of the most active centres of the artistic avant-garde at the beginning of 20th century, a status it owes mostly to the presence of neo-impressionist painter Paul Signac. Enchanted by the site and the exceptional quality of its light, he bought a house here at the end of the last century. Matisse, Derain and Marquet were likewise seduced. The collections housed here are remarkable as much for their quality as for their homogeneity. The artists, whose works are exhibited, were inspired by the light and colours they found, each rendering them in their own style while remaining faithful to the subject. The museum's collection includes works from several of the great artistic movements that marked the beginning of the century, including pointillism, fauvism and nabis.

Take Rue des Charrons from Place Grammont, take the first left and then the first right.

Maison des Papillons ★ *(same schedule as Musée de l'Annonciade; 9 Rue Étienne Berny, ☎04.94.97.63.45)* contains over 4,500 butterfly specimens, some of which are quite rare or on the verge of extinction.

Go back towards the port and walk along the docks.

Countless pleasure boats, some quite luxurious, are lined up along the docks. In front of Quai Suffren stands the **statue of Bailli de Suffren**. Nearby, an archway leads to the fish market.

Continue along the docks and you will soon come to the tourist office, which marks the beginning of Quai Jean Jaurès. Hidden behind it is the very picturesque **Place aux Herbes** ★ where lively fruit and vegetable markets fill the morning air with activity.

At the end of the dock, to the right, stands the **Tour Suffren** ★, dating back to the 10th century, and which played an important role in the city's history.

Rue Portalet leads to **Tour du Portalet** ★, which was built in the 15th century and was part of the fortifications. From this vantage point, there is a good view of the **Tour Vieille** ★, another 15th-century construction, which stands at one end of the fishing port of La Ponche.

Go back towards Tour Suffren to get to Quartier de La Ponche.

Place de la Mairie ★ features an amazing door which was sculpted, so they say, by natives from Zanzibar. It opens onto the lovely Rue de la Ponche, where there stands another 15th-century tower, the **Porche de la Ponche**. ★ Beyond this lies Place du Revelin. This square shelters the **Hôtel La Ponche** (see p 414). The hotel's restaurant terrace at the back overlooks the fishing port of La Ponche.

The old town is surrounded by fortifications, and the **Église Saint-Tropez** ★, inside the walls, was built in the 18th century. It contains the bust of Saint Torpès, which is paraded around the town during the processions of **La Bravade**, a celebration held in May since 1558. This holiday commemorates the arrival of the patron saint's body to the village in his boat.

To the south, there is a fourth 15th-century tower, the **Tour Jarlier** ★, which housed the prison.

By heading further south, you can visit the **Chapelle de la Miséricorde** ★, built in the 17th century. Rue de la Miséricorde passes through the chapel's flying buttresses. This gives it a very medieval look that is absolutely charming.

The **Place des Lices**, a very popular spot, is the site of a bustling market on Tuesday and Saturday mornings. It is a pleasant place to meet, with its café terraces offering wonderful views of the *pétanque* games.

Of the two churches—**Chapelle du Couvent** and **Chapelle Sainte-Anne** ★—located at the far south end of the village, the second makes for a more interesting visit. It is a designated historic monument that was built in 1618 by the people of Saint-Tropez to give thanks for having been spared from the Plague. Located on Sainte-Anne Hill, it offers remarkable views of the gulf.

Finally, top off your visit with a tour of the **Citadelle** ★. This 16th-century building overlooks the city and stands in the middle of a large nature park. For centuries, this was the most important element of defence between Antibes and Toulon. It remains one of the only monuments of its size on the Côte Varoise. The dungeon houses the **Musée Naval** *(Wed to Mon, 10am to 5pm; summer, until 8pm; closed from Nov. 15 to Dec. 15; ☎04.94.97.06.53)*, where the history of Saint-Tropez is recalled.

A pleasant walk on the top of the hill offers an exceptional view over the gulf and of Old Saint-Tropez. From this vantage point, visitors can appreciate how the city maintains its genuine cachet despite the throngs of tourists. The urban planners left enough natural growth so that you never feel "trapped" in a living museum.

Walkers might want to catch the **Sentier des Douaniers** trail down towards the sea by the naval cemetery. It follows the coastline of the peninsula to Cavalaire-sur-Mer, where bus transportation back to Saint-Tropez is available.

Saint-Tropez Peninsula

A never-ending paradise! Here you'll find the most beautiful beaches in the Côte d'Azur overlooked by

gorgeous hills that offer a magnificent view over the sea and the Maures. The two charming medieval villages of Ramatuelle and Gassin add to the undeniable beauty of the site.

Suggested Tour (50km or 31mi):

From Carrefour de la Foux (between Port-Grimaud and Saint-Tropez), take D559 and then D89 to Gassin.

Gassin ★

Here is a wonderful place to stop and relax, away from the hustle and bustle of Saint-Tropez. This medieval village, which is one of the most beautiful in all the country, offers a panoramic view of the Côte d'Azur that spans all the way to the Îles d'Hyères. A stroll through the narrow streets during afternoon siesta is a great way to soak in the calm, laid-back atmosphere.

From Gassin, go towards Ramatuelle and follow the signs for Moulins de Paillas. Keep going until you reach Ramatuelle.

Ramatuelle

Here rests the body of the great actor Gérard Philippe. Ramatuelle is also where you will find one of, if not the most beautiful beach on the Côte d'Azur: the Plage de Pampelonne. This village is surrounded by numerous vineyards and hosts a theatre festival every summer.

Leave the village and head towards the beaches.

One possibility is a visit to the lighthouse, the Phare du Cap Camarat. The D93 provides access to the many beaches strung one after the other all the way to Saint-Tropez. The most famous are the Pampelonne, Tahiti, des Salins and, finally, Canebiers beaches, site of La Madrague, Brigitte Bardot's estate.

★★★
Massif des Maures

The Massif des Maures spans over 60km (37.3mi) between Fréjus and Hyères, and is 30km (18.6mi) wide. Its peaks are nearly 800m (2,625ft) high. The mountain range is crossed by several roads and numerous walking trails offering spectacular views of a landscape that has remained virtually untouched.

We suggest an 85km (52.8mi)- drive starting from Saint-Tropez that will allow you to discover some of its charms.

Leave Saint-Tropez by D14 in the direction of Grimaud and Collobrières. Head toward Cogolin.

Cogolin ★

Cogolin is a name of Celtic-Ligurian origin that means "small hill." This village has an eventful history, beginning with Saracen raids in the Middle Ages and followed by conflicts sparked by the 16th-century Religious Wars.

Life was peaceful for villagers until the early 20th century, when a phylloxera epidemic attacked the vines, wreaking havoc. The village was also hard hit, of course, by the two world wars, the first in particular.

On a lighter note, Cogolin boasts the striking **Église Saint-Sauveur ★**, whose origins go back to the 11th century, though it was modified in the 16th century. Of particular note inside is its wooden triptych, dating from 1450 and listed as a historic monument.

In the village, you can also check out a small museum, **L'Espace Raimu** *(summer, 10am to noon and 4pm to 7pm, winter, 10am to noon and 3pm to 6pm; 18 Avenue G. Clemenceau, ☎04.94.54.18.00)*, devoted to the French actor who immortalized Provence in the thirties by playing the part of Caesar, as created by Marcel Pagnol.

The **Ville Haute ★**, or upper town, is worth a visit. Its streets recall medieval times and feature a few lovely houses, including the **Château Sellier**, on Rue Nationale. At the top of the hill stands the **Tour**

de l'Horloge, the clock tower, which is all that remains of the château, which was destroyed in the 14th century.

Lastly, Cogolin is particularly well-known for its crafts production. In fact, many Cogolin residents earn their livings by producing pipes, rugs, corks or reeds for clarinets.

The **Fabrique de Pipes Courrieu** *(every day 9am to noon and 2pm to 7pm; 42 Avenue Clémenceau, ☎04.94.54.63.82)* has been in existence for over two centuries and has a worldwide reputation. Here, pipes are made from aged briar, which actually comes from the roots of trees in the nearby Maures forest. Enthusiasts will want to visit the factory and then stop at the store to pick one out to bring home as a little souvenir. The store also sells beautifully handcrafted pepper mills and salad bowls.

The **Manufacture de Tapis de Cogolin** *(Mon to Fri; 10 Boulevard Louis-Blanc, ☎04.94.55.70.65)* welcomes visitors to its showroom. This factory was created in the 1920s by Armenian refugees. Carpets produced here decorate, among other places, the White House in the United States and one of the Aga Khan's palaces. Note, however, that the workshops are off limits to visitors.

Take the D48 to the D14, which leads to Collobrières.

About 5km (3.1mi) before Collobrières, don't miss the crossroad that leads to the **Chartreuse de la Verne** ★ *(30F; 10am to 6pm, closed Tue in Oct to Jun, closed Jan; ☎04.94.43.45.41)*. A designated historical building since 1921, la Chartreuse's history goes back to 1170. During the centuries that followed, it suffered a great deal of destruction, mainly as a result of forest fires. There are therefore few Roman vestiges that remain. Since 1982, la Chartreuse has been a monastery occupied by a group of nuns, the Sœurs de Bethléem. It is presently being restored.

Collobrières

Capital of the Maures, this village is one of the most picturesque and authentic in the Var area. The huge forests surrounding the village and the small wild river running through give it a tangibly rustic feeling. You should make a short stop, time enough to go to the **Confiserie Azuréenne** *(☎04.94.48.08.00)* to buy a few *marrons glacés*—these chestnuts are the hallmark of this little village.

Leave the village for Notre-Dame-des-Anges by taking the D39 (2km or 1.2mi from the village).

Perched on a hill overlooking Collobrières, **Notre-Dame-des-Anges** is an ancient chapel dating back to 517. The chapel was completely restored in the 19th century and has become a place of pilgrimage.

Continue toward Gonfaron and follow signposts for the Village des Tortues (on the D75).

The **Village des Tortues** *(admission fee; 9am to 7pm, summer until 8pm; closed Dec to late Mar; ☎04.94.78.26.41)* was created to ensure the perpetuation of the Hermann tortoise, which inhabits the Massif des Maures. This species has suffered greatly from the fires that have ravaged the Massif's forests. Corsica is the only other place where this species, over 50 million years old, can still be found.

Continue along the D75 toward La Garde-Freinet, then take the D558 toward Grimaud and Cogolin to quickly return to the tour's starting point.

If you have more time and want to further explore the Massif des Maures, head to **Les Mayons**. This small village essentially owes its livelihood to the chestnuts and cork oak (from which corks are made) that thrive in its surrounding forest. A small road leads from here to Cros-de-Mouton. Finally, La Garde-

Freinet is accessible via a magnificent forest road that travels up and down the Massif's summits.

Hikers should bring their walking shoes, for the GR9 trail runs through this area and also makes its way to La Garde-Freinet.

Outdoor Activities

Swimming

Commune de Saint-Raphaël

There are approximately 30 beaches in this sprawling administrative district. You're sure to find one that pleases you, since they're all so diverse. There are beaches that could be categorized as primitive, or unspoiled, found in the steep part of the Massif de l'Estérel. Small, or even tiny, they are nestled in little inlets and creeks formed by the red cliffs, and they are not necessarily sandy or supervised.

On the other hand, since they're less accessible to families, these beaches are quieter and offer more privacy than larger ones. Also, they feature extraordinary views that are enhanced by the contrast of the turquoise blue sea crashing against the surrounding, red, craggy rocks, before it finally subsides on the garnet-coloured gravel that lines the shore.

The longest beaches are found in the centre of Saint-Raphaël and in the Baie d'Agay. These are sandy beaches that normally include all the usual seaside services, including restaurants, mattress rentals and life guards. As you will have guessed, Saint-Raphaël is a perfect place for all water sports.

Saint-Aygulf

The Saint-Aygulf Beach is right in the middle of a natural park amid splendid landscapes. This long and wide sandy beach lies just across the road from the Étangs de Villepey (see p 396).

The Saint-Tropez Peninsula

The peninsula's beaches have long been famous. Each one leading into the next, these beaches are sandy and clean. The Canebiers Beach, renowned because of Brigitte Bardot, is attractively nestled in a pretty bay. However, since it's near the centre of Saint-Tropez, it quickly becomes crowded in summer.

It's definitely worthwhile to go past the Cape of Saint-Tropez, even as far down the peninsula as Pampelonne Beach. Certainly the most beautiful, it has the advantage of stretching over 5km (3mi), so it's possible to find a spot even when the crowds are at their peak. It also has many beach attendants who provide all the normal seaside amenities.

Golf

Saint-Raphaël

Golf 9 de Cap Estérel
nine holes: 120F, two rounds: 150F
B.P. 940, 83708 Saint-Raphaël
☎04.94.82.55.00
⇄04.94.82.58.73
The course offers spectacular views of the sea.

Golf de l'Estérel Maeva Latitudes
18 holes: 250F, weekends: 280F
Avenue du Golf, 83700 Saint-Raphäel
☎04.94.52.68.30
⇄04.94.52.68.31

Sainte-Maxime

Golf de Beauvallon
9 holes: 150F, 18 holes: 240F, 300F weekends
Boulevard Des Collines Beauvallon, 83120 Sainte-Maxime; on the route that leads to Grimaud
☎04.94.96.16.98

The Sentier du Littoral

The Sentier du Littoral was formerly called the Sentier des Douaniers or customs trail. As its name implies, it was created in the early 19th century so that customs officers could monitor and control the arrival of boats.

Today, it no longer serves this purpose; it has been recycled as a spectacular walking trail. Since the coast between Cannes and Saint-Tropez is often very steep and hard to access, the trail sometimes comes to a sudden end. Nevertheless, there are several well-established segments that are absolutely delightful. The following descriptions go from west to east, but the trails can be taken in either direction.

Commune de Saint-Raphaël

Distance: 8km (4.8mi)
Time: 2.5hrs
Route: the trail begins at the beach at the Long campground, at the eastern end of the Baie d'Agay, and ends at the Santa-Lucia port. You'll soon arrive at the Plage du Débarquement, named for the August 15, 1944 landing here of 20,000 United States soldiers. A stela on the esplanade in Dramont commemorates this event.

This walk allows you to admire the spectacular colours of the rock. Mostly red sandstone, it sometimes changes colours along the path. Just past the Plage du Débarquement, it becomes a more recent grey-blue volcanic rock, known locally as esterellite. But it can also be black, as is the case just before the beach at Aigue Bonne. These black rocks were formed by ash from a volcano that was active 230 million years ago.

Les Issambres

Distance: 11km (6.6mi)
Time: 3.5hrs
Route: the trail starts at the de la Gaillarde beach, past Saint-Aygulf, and ends in front of the Issambres city hall annex.
On this path you will encounter lovely creeks like Tardieu and Bonne Eau.

The Saint-Tropez Peninsula

Distance: 18km (10.8mi)
Time: 5hrs
Route: the trail begins at the Tour du Portalet in Saint-Tropez and leads to Cap Camarat.

This is an outstanding hike with remarkably pretty scenery, but its best feature is that it can be tailored to fit the time available. Starting from the Tour du Portalet, you'll reach Baie des Canebiers in 45min. Next, it takes 1hr 45min to reach the beach at Salins and 1hr more to get to the Tahiti beach.

Once you are at Cap Camarat where there is a lighthouse, it is possible to lengthen the hike. In fact, you can push on to Cavalaire-sur-Mer, adding 19km (11.4mi) and 6hrs of additional walking to your hike. Fortunately, it is possible to return to Saint-Tropez by bus. Check the schedule at the Office de Tourisme.

Golf de Sainte-Maxime
9 holes: 180F, 18 holes: 250F
Route du Débarquement, 83120 Sainte-Maxime
☎04.94.55.02.02
⇌04.94.55.02.03
The course winds through the mountain, offering superb panoramic views.

Roquebrune-sur-Argens

Golf de Roquebrune
220F
C.D. 7, 83520 Roquebrune-sur-Argens
☎04.94.19.60.35
⇌04.94.82.94.20
This course is located at the foot of Roquebrune's rock, in the backcountry.

Hiking

Fréjus–Saint-Raphaël

You can bask on the beaches or go on walking tours in the nearby **Massif de l'Estérel**. Here are a few suggestions for walking tours. However, it is best to get a good map that indicates the various walking trails. The tourist office *(☎04.94.19.52.52)* can certainly be of help here.

Note: Camping, fires and even smoking are prohibited in the Massif, as is picking plants. Make sure you bring drinking water.

The Office National des Forêts (O.N.F.) manages the forests. You'll see different coloured markings as you stroll through the woods. Beware! These markings are not necessarily direction indicators, and to follow them blindly could get you lost in the forest.

Finally, if you're leaving a car behind, don't tempt thieves by leaving things in it.

If you want to see the site of the old Malpasset dam, which tragically broke in 1959 killing more than 400 people, a trail starts where the old D37 stops. The elevation is not too high, only 300m (984.3ft). This hike takes at least 2hrs.

Mont Vinaigre ★★ looms over the Massif at an elevation of 614m (2,014ft). The view from the summit is dazzling. It can be reached from a trail that starts at Pont de l'Estérel on the N7. Allow at least 4 hours for this hike.

Pic de l'Ours and **Pic d'Aurelle ★** offer splendid views over the coastline. These can be accessed from the train station at Trayas, which is on the coast between Cannes and Saint-Raphaël. The elevation is almost 500m (1,640ft).

Finally, many other hiking trails are accessible from parking areas along the forest road that runs through the Massif. The paths can often be seen winding up hillsides. Short or long hikes are possible along these trails.

Horseback Riding

Saint-Raphaël

L'Estérel à Cheval
Domain du Grenouillet, Agay
☎06.85.42.51.50

Fréjus

Centre Équestre de Fréjus "La Tourrache"
☎04.94.51.29.49

Sainte-Maxime

Centre Hippique des Maures
Domaine du Bouchage
☎04.94.56.16.55
The stables of the Centre Hippique des Maures are in Beauvallon, situated on Route N98, about 5km (3.1mi) from the edge of town, toward Port-Grimaud. This horseback riding centre organizes trips to the Maures.

Water Sports

Saint-Raphaël

Saint-Raphaël is a designated *Station Voile* (sailing resort). Consequently, a multitude of water sports are available.

Wind Club d'Agay
☎04.94.82.08.08
The Wind Club d'Agay is recommended for fans of recreational sailing.

Club Nautique de Saint-Raphaël
☎04.94.95.11.66
Club Nautique de Saint-Raphaël offers diverse aquatic activities at all levels.

Péninsule de Saint-Tropez

Union Sportive Tropézienne
open year-round
Route des Salins, Baie des Canoubiers
☎04.94.97.73.07
Union Sportive Tropézienne has everything from catamarans to dinghies, and windsurfing boards to rowboats. It offers courses at all levels for people of every age.

It is possible to go **deep-sea fishing** (*☎04.94.54.40.61*) on the double-masted *Brigantine*. Equipment and bait are supplied.

Sailing School
Baies des Canebiers, road to des Salins, in the direction of Cap des Salins, east of the old city
☎04.94.97.73.07

Team Water Sports
Route de l'Épi, Plage de Pampelonne
☎04.94.79.82.41
Parasailing, jet skiing, water skiing, wind-surfing)

Scuba Diving

Saint-Raphaël

C.I.P Odyssée
Quay Albert 1
☎04.94.83.03.53
Located next to the harbour station, C.I.P Odyssée can take you to explore the most beautiful underwater sites in the region. Initiation, certification, shipwreck exploration and night diving are available here.

Club de Plongée d'Agay
☎04.94.82.02.03
Diving is also possible at the Club de Plongée d'Agay.

Saint-Tropez

Octopussy
parking at the port
☎04.94.56.53.10
This is a school for all levels.

Tennis

Saint-Raphaël

Centre Rolland Garros
every day
Boulevard de l'Aspé, Valescure
☎04.94.95.43.00
Centre Rolland Garros has 16 tennis courts, six of which are lit.

Saint-Tropez

Les Tennis de Saint-Tropez
Route des Salins
☎04.94.97.36.39
Clay, synthetic grass and concrete courts.

Aeronautical Sports

Saint-Tropez

H.S.C. Yachting
10 Rue du Portalet
☎04.94.97.73.86
⇄04.94.97.64.68
Seaplane excursions, flying jaunts, introductory lessons.

Accommodations

The region's many campgrounds fall into two categories: the usual, rather large type; and much smaller, rural campgrounds and natural areas. While the first category offers many more services and activities, the second one provides better communion with nature. For example, some of these campsites are located on farms.

Les Adrets-de-l'Estérel

If you prefer the tranquillity and beauty of nature, and the intimacy and simplicity of small villages, then this village is a must. It is located in the Massif de l'Estérel, between Cannes and Fréjus, near the N7 and Lac St-Cassien.

Les Philippons
Apr to Oct
s, ℜ, ≈
D237, Quartier Les Philippons
☎04.94.40.90.67
In the open wilderness, camping here is pleasant, especially since the site is not too big.

Hôtel de la Verrerie
290F-330F
closed Oct to Nov
ps, tv
Quartier de la Verrerie
☎04.94.40.93.51
Hôtel de la Verrerie is a small seven-room hotel in a large Provençal-style villa. It is perched on a hillside, slightly off the beaten path, but the way is clearly indicated. Guests can enjoy the tranquillity of nature and have breakfast in the garden while admiring magnificent views of l'Estérel. The clean rooms are spacious, modern and sunny. And the same goes for the bathrooms. This hotel is a very good value.

L'Estirado des Adrets
410F bkfst incl.
pb, ≈, *tv, P,* ℜ
☎04.94.40.90.64
⇄04.94.40.98.52
www.estirado.com
L'Estirado des Adrets is a family inn that has a panoramic view of the Massif de l'Estérel thanks to its slightly elevated location. The simple rooms are decorated in rustic fashion. There is also a small shop that sells handicrafts and a restaurant that serves *cuisine du terroir* (local adaptations of the regional cuisine, made with the freshest local products). Depending on the season, you can dine outdoors or at fireside.

Auberge des Adrets
990F-1,400F
pb, ≡, *tv, P,* ℜ
Route Nationale 7
☎04.94.82.11.82
⇄04.94.82.11.80
www.auberge-adrets.com
This 17th-century, former mail-coach inn was the scene of part of the romance between outlaw Gaspard de Besse and Dame Rose (rooms bear their names). It has been renovated superbly. The decor is tasteful, luxurious and refined. As you may have gathered, Auberge des Adrets provides first-rate services. For a description of the restaurant, see p 415.

Théoule-sur-Mer

Hôtel de la Corniche d'Or
570F-1200F, bkfst 60F
pb, ≈, *P*
mid-Mar to mid-Nov
10 Boulevard Esquillon
Miramar
☎04.93.75.40.12
⇄04.93.75.44.91
Situated below the road between the mountain and the sea, Hôtel de la Corniche d'Or, run by Germans, has an exceptional view. Both tranquillity and comfort are guaranteed here. The immense, airy reception area opens onto a sitting room whose large bay windows are perfect for relaxing while taking in the sea view. It goes without saying that the less expensive rooms face the mountain, rather than the sea.

Commune de Saint-Raphaël

Le Trayas

Auberge de Jeunesse
mid-Feb to Dec
9 Avenue de Véronèse
☎04.93.75.40.23
⇄04.93.75.43.45
This youth hostel with room for 110 guests has an ideal location, close to all the sports activities that the Massif de l'Estérel has to offer.

Camping Azur Rivage
Apr to Sep
ℜ, ≈
On Route Nationale 98 in Anthéor
☎04.94.44.83.12
⇄04.94.44.84.39
www.saint-raphael.com/azurivage
This small campground with 66 sites is advantageously located 30m (98ft) from the beach and is close to Cannes. Moreover, it provides all the necessary services to make your stay enjoyable.

Anthéor–Cap Roux

Auberge d'Anthéor
780F-1,070F bkfst incl.
closed Nov and Dec
pb, tv, K ≈, ⌂, ℜ
Boulevard Eugène Brieux
☎04.94.44.83.38
⇌ 94.44.84.20

Halfway between Cannes and Saint-Raphaël, on the edge of Massif de l'Estérel, you'll discover the Auberge d'Anthéor. This is a remarkable place, directly on the sea. Although the hotel has no beach, there is a small cement dock which literally extends out over the water and is furnished with deck chairs. You can dive into the sea or even dock a boat there. If that doesn't appeal to you, there is a beautiful sea-water swimming pool. This modern Provençal-style hotel is one of the Châteaux et Demeures Traditionel of France. All the rooms, with their rustic Provençale decor, are clean and possess all the modern comforts. In addition, they look out at the sea and some of them have big private terraces. There is also a restaurant on the premises (see p 416).

Agay

Hôtel Beau Site
260F-340F, studio 500F
pb or ps, tv
Camp Long, RN 98
☎04.04.82.00.45
⇌04.94.82.71.02

Located 30m (98.4ft) from the beach, on the Corniche d'Or, just before the centre, the Hôtel Beau Site is a simple but clean place with fairly spacious rooms, most of which have balconies. It also has a flower-decked terrace adjoining its restaurant.

Cap de l'Estérel
835F bkfst incl.
pb, tv, ℜ, ≈, ≡
☎04.94.82.51.00
⇌04.94.82.58.73

On a little hill overlooking the Baie d'Agay sits a very modern vacation complex built by the Pierre et Vacances organization, which includes residences that can be rented by the week as well as the Hotel Cap de l'Estérel. The view, which encompasses the Massif de l'Estérel as well as the sea, is superb. This is ideal for families and older people who prefer spending their vacation in one place. Everything is available on site including numerous restaurants, a vast swimming pool, tennis courts and a small golf course. A medical clinic, massage service and thalassotherapy are also available.

Saint-Raphaël–centre

Hôtel du Soleil
230F-340F
closed Nov through Mar
pb or ps, tv
47 Boulevard du Domaine du Soleil
☎04.94.83.10.00
⇌04.94.83.84.70

A 1920s villa in the Plaines quarter, the Hôtel du Soleil is removed from the action in Saint-Raphaël—which can be a big plus. And yet, it's just a 15min walk from the beaches and the downtown area. A charming place, it deserves high points for comfort, its peaceful atmosphere and its owners' warm hospitality. Furnished studios equipped with kitchenettes and private terraces are also available by the week *(1,400F and 2,600F depending on the season)*. Perfect for families with children.

Le Clocher
240F-330F bkfst incl.
Mar to Oct and by reservation from Nov to Febs
pb/sb
50 Rue de la République
☎04.94.19.06.96
leclocher@yahoo.fr

The only bed and breakfast in Saint-Raphaël, Le Clocher is run by a very likeable Italian couple. Located in the pedestrian zone in the heart of the old city, the premises of this very clean, bright, smoke-free establishment have been completely renovated.

Simply furnished, it offers a calm environment conveniently close to the train station and the beach. Moreover, breakfast is served as a buffet, so it's quite substantial. Note, however, that there are only three rooms, and only one of these has a private bathroom. Lastly, credit cards are not accepted.

Hôtel de Flore
380F-450F
closed Jan
pb, ≡, tv, ℜ, P
56 Rue de la Liberté
☎04.94.95.90.00
⇄04.94.83.75.57
Also in the heart of the old city, the Hôtel de Flore provides the same advantageous location as Le Clocher. However, it offers better quality services, commensurate to its rates. If you prefer an added touch of anonymity…

La Chêneraie
570F-750F bkfst incl.
closed Nov
pb, ℜ, ≈, P
167 Avenue des Gondins–Résidence Quercus
☎04.94.95.03.83
⇄04.94.19.49.23
Certainly one of our most exciting discoveries, this family-run hotel is set in a stunning, late 19th-century Victorian manor, which is slightly out of the way, and therefore enjoys complete tranquillity. The personalized service at La Chêneraie will make you feel truly at home. Laurence, the young owner, will take care of you in an exceptionally friendly fashion. Though the decor is refined, the atmosphere is relaxed. This is this ideal place to stop and rest for a while. It has a terraced garden with a pool where you can loaf to your heart's content. In fact, everything about the place is restful. The decor of the public areas is restrained and soothing. The fabrics for the curtains and furniture have been selected with care and hand-sewn. Lastly, it doesn't hurt at all that the food is heavenly (see p 417) and that all the breads, croissants and other breakfast rolls are homemade. A must!

Fréjus

On the Route des Commandants d'Afrique du Nord, which goes to Bagnols-en-Forêt, there's one campground after another: nine in all, four of which have more than 500 sites. Goodbye privacy! Generally open from April to October, all have facilities including restaurants, swimming pools, play areas for children, and more. The smallest one, **Le Dattier** *(☎04.94.40.88.93, ⇄04.94.40.89.01)* has 180 sites; the largest, **La Baume** *(☎04.94.19.88.88, ⇄04.94.19.83.50)* has 780 sites.

Auberge de Jeunesse
Feb to mid-Dec
Chemin du Counillier
☎04.94.53.18.75
⇄04.94.53.25.86
It's best to ask about the exact location of this 140-place youth hostel at the Fréjus tourist office, because the Fréjus administrative district is very spread-out.

Les Résidences du Colombier
380F
pb, ≡, tv, ≈, ℜ, P
On the road to Bagnols-en-Forêt
1239 Rue des Commandants d'Afrique du Nord
☎04.94.51.45.92
⇄04.94.53.82.85
Off the beaten path, this residential hotel offers weekly rates. The rooms are quite plain, are distributed among several small buildings, and have private terraces. There is also a swimming pool and a restaurant featuring a fixed-price menu at 100F, including wine.

Café Galerie du Monde
3,600F-4,000F/week
pb, tv, ≈
49 Place Formigé
☎04.94.17.01.07
The Café Galerie du Monde also rents large apartments that accommodate up to six people. Each apartment has a living room and a fully equipped kitchen. In winter and low season, there are more reasonable rates for longer stays, as low as 2,300F/week. Its advantages: calm location, nearby restaurants and shops, cleanliness and the fact that the owner

runs the café downstairs and lives within 100m (328ft) of the apartments.

Saint-Aygulf

L'Escale du Soleil
240F-350F
closed Nov to Feb
ps, tv, ≡, ℜ
75 Avenue Marius-Coulet
☎04.94.81.20.19

Saint-Aygulf is 6km (3.7mi) from Fréjus, on the N98 towards Saint-Maxime. There you will find L'Escale du Soleil. This is a small, pleasant hotel offering simple comforts. It is very clean and a good value. Located in a peaceful spot, 50m (164ft) from the sea, this hotel has a shaded terrace and parking space for the guests. Ask for a room on the top floor. The owners are very friendly.

Les Issambres

Villa Saint-Elme
1,750F-1,950F bkfst incl.
2,400F-4,600F for a suite
closed mid-Jan to end of Mar
pb, ≡, tv, ℝ, ≈, ⌂, ⊛, ℜ
Corniche des Issambres
☎04.94.49.52.52
⇒04.94.49.63.18

Those who can afford princely luxury should head down to the Villa Saint-Elme. This place is so close to the ocean, it is almost like living on a boat. The rooms are very tastefully decorated and the bathrooms are equipped with whirlpool baths. The less expensive rooms and suites are in the hotel's annex, on the other side of the street, but they are just as pleasant. Finally, guests also have access to a swimming pool filled with sea water, as well as to a sauna and Turkish baths. See p 418 for a description of its restaurant.

Sainte-Maxime

L'Ensoleillée
240F-350F-300F
closed Oct to Mar
ps or pb, tv, ℜ
29 Avenue Jean-Jaurès
☎04.94.96.02.27
⇒04.94.29.06.21

We found another peaceful hotel in the centre of this coastal village. L'Ensoleillée is a charming little Provençal-style hotel, only 50m (164ft) from the beach. This place is ideal for a night's stay, but not particularly recommended for an extended holiday, though the modest-sized rooms were flawless.

Royal Bon Repos
340F-530F
closed mid-Oct to Mar
ps
11 Rue Jean Aicard
☎04.94.96.08.74

Located just a bit above the heart of the village, the Royal Bon Repos offers peace and quiet just steps from the beaches. Don't be put off by the rather unattractive exterior, as the rooms are pleasant, quite spacious and very comfortable. Studios equipped with kitchenettes are also available by the week *(1,900F-4,000F)*; each has a terrace or a balcony and some offer views of the sea and of the Golfe de Saint-Tropez. Last but certainly not least, you can expect a charming welcome.

Port-Grimaud

Giraglia
990F-1,700F, 2,000 to 2,200F for a suite
pb, tv, ℝ, ≡, ≈
☎04.94.56.31.33
⇒04.94.56.33.77

There are few places to stay in this recently built-up village. The Giraglia is at some distance from the village's main attractions. The rooms are very comfortable and recently, the common areas and suites were attractively renovated. Also, guests have access to a private sandy beach and a pool with a whirlpool that opens directly onto the sea. The reception is slightly impersonal, but is still courteous. Finally, a permit issued by the hotel allows you to get there by car.

Grimaud (village)

In Saint-Pons Les Mûres there are two pleasant campgrounds with all the facilities: **Les Prairies de la Mer** *(☎04.94.79.09.09, ⇒04.94.79.09.10)* has tennis courts and **Domaine des Naïades**

(☎04.94.56.35.41) has a pool.

Domaine du Prignon
340F-380F bkfst incl.
pb, P
leave Grimaud on the D14 and follow the signs that say "chambres d'hôtes" (approximately 3.5km or 2.2mi).
☎04.94.43.34.84
At the foot of the Maures, the Domaine du Prignon is a guest house run by young wine growers Christelle and Paul. You will stay in a Provençal farmhouse in the centre of their vineyard. Moderately spacious and clean, the rooms have private entrances and separate terraces. Breakfast is served outside, weather permitting. Cash only.

Athénopolis
550F-660F
closed Nov to Mar
pb, tv, ℝ, ≈, P
Quartier Mouretti
☎04.94.43.24.24
⇄04.94.43.37.05
Approximately 3km (1.9mi) from Grimaud, on the road to La Garde-Freinet, is a very comfortable, indeed luxurious spot, the Athénopolis. The rooms, equipped with balconies or private terraces, overlook the swimming pool. What's more, the hotel has a restaurant that serves up market-fresh Provençale cuisine.

Le Verger
600F-1,200F
ps or pb, ≈, tv, P, ℜ
Route de Collobrières
☎04.94.43.25.93
⇄04.94.43.33.92
If La Boulangerie has no vacancies, try the hotel-restaurant Le Verger, on the same road. This is another *auberge* in the middle of a large park with a garden and swimming pool that will surely win you over. Certain rooms have been recently renovated. They are now very spacious and the bathrooms have been totally redone. Meals are served indoors or on the lovely terrace featuring a pastoral decor. Here, once again, tranquillity reigns.

La Boulangerie
680F-820F
1,580F for the suite
closed mid-Oct to Easter
pb, ℝ, tv on request, ≈, tennis, tv, P
☎04.94.43.23.16,
⇄04.94.43.38.27
Around 3km (1.9mi) west of the village, on the road to Collobrières, La Boulangerie is a small and charming hotel nestled in a very pretty garden. At the back, a swimming pool surrounded by a terrace offers views of the foothills of the Massif des Maures. It is an ideal place to spend a relaxing day or simply to have breakfast. Dinner is served in the evening for 160F. The hotel is a peaceful spot where you will feel like a guest at a large private villa. It offers great comfort and warm welcomes from the charming owner. You can enjoy a light lunchtime meal on Sundays.

Saint-Tropez

La Michaudière
320-520F
shared shower or pb for the most expensive room, K
8 Rue Portalet
☎04.94.97.18.67
At the heart of Vieux Saint-Tropez, on a small side-street at the end of the port (near Tour Suffren), visitors can stop at a small modest hotel with a roof-top terrace, La Michaudière. The owner, Monsieur Thomas, will only be too happy to share with you his vast knowledge of the village's history, customs, activities and restaurants. Note, however, that cheques and credit cards are not accepted.

Hôtel Le Colombier
350F-470F, suite 800F
closed Nov to Jan
pb, tv
Impasse des Conquettes
☎04.94.97.05.31
⇄04.94.97.32.57
At the end of a quiet, dead-end street near the city centre and the port, you'll walk through a garden full of flowers to reach the entrance of Hôtel Le Colombier. The immaculate, renovated rooms at this small hotel are decorated in pastel shades. The garden is certainly a plus and

having breakfast in it is a good way to start the day.

Hôtel Les Palmiers
430F-730F
pb, ≡, tv, ℝ
Place des Lices
24 Boulevard Vasserot
☎04.94.97.01.61
⇌04.94.97.10.02
More luxurious than the Hôtel Le Colombier, the Hôtel des Palmiers occupies a lovely house overlooking the Place des Lices which, shaded by large plane trees, is one of Saint-Tropez's truly magical places. It offers every modern convenience. Moreover, some of its gorgeous, clean rooms open onto the vibrant flower garden where breakfast is served.

La Ponche
1,100F-1,950F, 2,600F for a suite overlooking the sea
closed mid-Nov to Mar
pb, ℝ, *tv,* ℜ, ≡
3 Rue des Remparts, Port des Pêcheurs
☎04.94.97.02.53
⇌04.94.97.78.61
Can you imagine spending the night in a mythical place reminiscent of *And God Created Woman*, a place where Romy Schneider often stayed and where Françoise Sagan came to write? Then you must spend some time at La Ponche. The hotel is located in the heart of the old village; it is therefore best that a valet take care of your car when you arrive. The rooms are superbly decorated in soft, calm colours and are equipped with extravagant marble bathrooms. The room Françoise Sagan used to stay in is available for any visitor looking to tune in some artistic vibes. Its blue walls harbour many memories and the terrace is magnificent. Dispersed throughout the hotel are paintings by local artist, Jacques Cordier. The friendly reception is the epitome of excellence. One of the two owners, Madame Duckstein is a living history book. She will be happy to recount the thousand and one stories that make up the history of this establishment. There is also a restaurant; see p 419 for its despription.

Ramatuelle

Camping La Cigale
Apr to Oct
ℜ, ≈
on the L'Escalet Road
☎04.94.79.22.53
⇌04.94.79.12.05
Near one of the beaches on the Saint-Tropez Peninsula, this small campground with 75 sites has been kept to a human scale.

Les Tourterelles
400F-600F bkfst incl. 45F
closed Nov to Easter
pb, tv, ≈, K, ℝ, *P*
on the road to L'Escalet
☎04.94.79.22.84
⇌04.94.79.13.17
Near the beach at L'Escalet, but far enough from the main street to enjoy the tranquillity of nature, this well-kept, clean establishment has rooms and studios with kitchens and private terraces where you can enjoy a secluded meal. Some rooms have air conditioning. Relatively inexpensive for the Saint-Trop peninsula. No pets allowed and credit cards are not accepted.

La Ferme d'Augustin
620F-1,100F, 1,600F-1,800F for a suite
closed mid-Oct to mid-Mar
ps, salon, ℝ, *tv, ≈,* ℜ, ≡, *P*
Plage de Tahiti
☎04.94.97.23.83,
⇌04.94.97.40.30
Around 5min (by car) from Saint-Tropez and 300m (984ft) from the beach, we recommend La Ferme d'Augustin. This luxury farmhouse-style hotel is surrounded by a magnificent garden with a very beautiful swimming pool and tennis courts. It is only a few steps away from Saint-Tropez's fabulous beaches. In short, guests here can stay in a corner of paradise at a reasonable price. The subtle charm of this farm, furnished with Provençal antiques, won us over instantly. There is also a restaurant where you can dine outdoors. Small, simple meals and bar service are available as well.

Les Bouis
1,120F-1,200F
closed Nov to mid-Mar
pb, tv, ℝ, ≈, P, private terrace
Route des Plages, Pampelonne
☎04.94.79.87.61
⇌04.94.79.85.20
The hotel Les Bouis is located around 1km (0.6mi) from the sea and 6km (3.7mi) from Saint-Tropez. Surrounded by an umbrella-pine forest, this peaceful spot offers exceptional views. The hotel, built a few years ago in Provençal style, has everything you'll need for a most pleasant stay, including a large swimming pool.

Gassin

La Dame de Cœur
320F-400F
closed Dec to Feb
pb
☎04.94.56.14.17
La Dame de Cœur is a very pleasant, simple and affordable hotel. According to the business card, this is a hotel that reflects all your needs. In any case, two things are certain: you'll enjoy peace and quiet and a terrace with a view of the sea. In addition, you can obtain information about the best restaurants in the region. Credit cards not accepted.

Cogolin

Coq'hôtel
240F-480F
pb, tv, ℜ
Place de la Mairie
☎04.94.54.13.71
⇌04.94.54.03.06
This extremely charming little hotel in the heart of Cogolin is unusual in that its rooms vary considerably. Clean and well-maintained, the Coq'hôtel is attractive and invitingly decorated. Also, breakfast is served in a small courtyard. The most expensive rooms have air conditioning and rooms in the front have double windows to eliminate street noise. The hotel also has a pleasant little restaurant that serves traditional cuisine and features a terrace.

La Croix-Valmer

Le Souleias
630F-1,530F
closed Nov to Easter
pb, tv, ≡ in most rooms, ≈, ℜ
Plage de Gigaro
☎04.94.79.61.91
⇌04.94.55.10.55
There is a very beautiful neo-Provençal style hotel overlooking the sea from the top of a hill: Le Souleias. You will feel like you are on a small island in the middle of a very lovelyl park with a large swimming pool. Most of the rooms look directly onto the park, and others have balconies. They are very comfortable and most face south, towards the sea. The beach is 5min away by car or can be reached on foot via a path that slopes downward. Lastly, the hotel has a renowned gourmet restaurant. This large restaurant ***($$-$$$)*** offers a most refined cuisine in a decor that is complemented by natural lighting and a spectacular view. The prices are commensurately high. It is best to try it at lunchtime when there is a fixed-price menu at 190F.

Restaurants

In the Massif de l'Estérel

Les-Adrets-sur-l'Estérel

Auberge des Adrets
$$$-$$$$
closed Nov, Sun evenings and Mon, except in summer
Route Nationale 7
☎04.94.82.11.82
⇌04.94.82.11.80
If you make an excursion to the Massif de l'Estérel, plan to stop at this famous restaurant. In summer, the utterly refined and gorgeous dining room, decorated with antique furniture, is extended by a spacious terrace with a superb view of Cannes's bay. The menu offers carefully selected *cuisine du*

terroir. What would you say to sautéed *noix de Saint-Jacques* (scallops) with morels and aged-vermouth cream sauce, or *dos de cabillaud* (fresh cod) prepared à la *plancha* (sautéed) with salt cod purée and crispy Serrano ham?

Théoule-sur-Mer–Miramar

Restaurant Follies
$$
closed Mon
Port of Figuerette
☎04.93.75.03.97
⇌04.93.75.45.14

You'll have to look carefully for the sign at the entrance to this restaurant because the road is extremely sinuous in this area. Would it be easier to arrive by boat? Possibly! In any case, the emphasis here is on seafood, fish and grilled meats—simple but good. There is an attractive view of the sea and, as a final point of distinction, the meals are served at tables set up on the lawn.

Auberge du Père Pascal
$$-$$$
closed Wed evening and Thu except during the high season, closed Nov to Feb
on the waterfront road between Cannes and Saint-Raphael
☎04.93.75.40.11

The Auberge du Père Pascal is a chic place known for its fish and shellfish. Its huge outdoor seating area offers beautiful views of the sea. The speciality at this establishment is *fleur de courgette farcie au crabe*.

Anthéor

Auberge d'Anthéor
$$-$$$
closed Nov and Dec
Cap Roux, Anthéor
☎04.94.44.83.89

This restaurant certainly offers one of the most exceptional panoramic views in the Massif de l'Estérel. The terrace literally overhangs the ocean and red rocks. You'll never tire of gazing at the seascape, especially in the evening, since as night falls, the changing light transforms the entire scene. The menu is based on fish and seafood dishes. Some of the restaurant's specialties are combination platters that let you sample several different items within a given theme, such as a selection of beechwood–smoked fish or a variety of shellfish.

Saint-Raphaël–centre

Chez Pascal
$-$$
closed Jul to Aug, Wed and Thu at noon
144 Rue de la Garonne
☎04.94.95.54.14

Chez Pascal is a favourite with local residents because of its convivial atmosphere. This small restaurant stays on the cutting edge, creating a colourful and highly flavoured *cuisine du marché*. Two examples: *rillettes de rouget* (potted red mullet), and *tartare de canard en vinaigrette d'agrumes and marjolaine* (duck tartare made with marjoram–flavoured citrus vinaigrette). Despite its location on a small, quiet downtown street, from the minute you walk through the door you know this place is happening! Inexpensive, in view of its quality.

Le Sémillon
$$-$$$
closed Sun evening, Mon and Tue noon, except in Jul and Aug
21 Place Carnot
☎04.94.40.56.77

Highly recommended, Le Sémillon restaurant merits a special trip. First, the young owners Laurent and Sophie Loutz will provide you with friendly, unpretentious attention. Next, you'll be seduced by Madame's skilfully prepared regional specialties. Let yourself succumb to the *noisette de selle d'agneau* (saddle of lamb), *andouillettes d'agneau* (lamb chitterlings) or *loup poêlé aux tomates confites et olives picholines* (sea bass sauteed with tomato conserve and green olives), *carpaccio de thon et aubergines* (tuna and eggplant *carpaccio*). The desserts are pure delight. We recommend the chocolate and candied ginger *croquette* or the trilogy of *crème brûlée* (to be tasted according to the owner's instructions), which will stay fresh your memory for years to come! Note that there is a 95F lunch menu, wine included.

Restaurant Pastorel
$$$
closed Nov and the first two weeks of Feb
54 Rue de la Liberté
☎04.94.95.02.36
⇄04.94.95.64.07

Charles Floccia, the chef-owner of Restaurant Pastorel, is a member of the Association des Maîtres Restaurateurs Varois. This friendly *bon vivant* is a true Provençal. While he runs the kitchen, his wife attends to the dining room with an ever-ready smile. You'll dine in an arbour protected by a retractable awning from rainy or overly warm weather. The parade of flavours begins from the moment you're seated, with a delicious tapenade to help you wait. Do you like garlic? If so, you're in luck, the *aïoli* here is superb. The use of garlic doesn't stop here, however, as witnessed by two of the house specialties: tasty *salade de filets de rouget à l'anchoïade légère*, and the copious *bourride raphaëlloise* (fish stew). This *bourride* is striking in its generous use of saffron and is served with a *rouille* that is well-seasoned with garlic. The garlic-saffron combination works marvellously. Of course, there are other less pungent dishes from which to choose... if you must! Lastly, the desserts are not to be scorned; for example, the delicious *gratiné* of white peaches served with rosemary *sabayon* sauce. What flavour!

La Chêneraie
$$$-$$$$
lunch and dinner, closed Nov
167 Avenue des Gondins, in the Résidence Quercus
☎04.94.95.03.83

If you want to dine well in a refined, relaxing and pleasant setting, La Chêneraie is the place! In this family-run restaurant, the host Laurence's uncle reigns in the kitchen. After a delicious starter, why not let yourself be tempted by the *foie gras de canard des Landes maison aux raisin blonds confits au muscat de Beaumes-de-Venise à la canelle* (duck liver with grapes, wine and cinnamon)? Unless of course you would prefer something lighter, such as the *émincé de filet de thon au jus de vin blanc de Provence concassé d'olives* (tuna filet with wine and crushed olives), or perhaps the *queue de langoustine en lasagne au beurre d'orange* (prawn with orange-flavoured butter)? Whatever you choose, you'll be spoiled from beginning to end. The table settings are attractive, the plates are charming, and the most crucial element is in place: the food is delicious, refined, creative and above all, light. You will leave the table feeling full and satisfied, but without any disagreeable heaviness. Moreover, the wine list provides a good selection to enhance this masterful array of taste sensations. In short, the perfect meal! (See p 411.)

Fréjus

Café Galerie du Monde
$
49 Place Formigé
☎04.94.17.01.07

Just a stone's throw from the cathedral, Café Galerie du Monde opens onto the large pedestrian square. Whether you are seated on the terrace or in the originally decorated dining room, Françoise (the owner) or Michael (in charge of the kitchen) will happily serve you their African or South American specialties. Bagels and other light snacks are also available. Downstairs from the café, there is a shop and an art gallery that showcases temporary exhibitions (see p 411).

Le Poivrier
$$
closed Sun
52 Place Paul Albert Février
☎04.94.52.28.50

Some 100m (328ft)further on, to the west of the cathedral, you'll be warmly received at Le Poivrier. With Marie-Lou in the kitchen and Florence providing service, you can explore excellent dishes like *charret d'agneau* (lamb), *magret de canard* (fillet of duck breast) and *gambas* (Mediterranean prawns) *au pastis.* You can eat on the terrace or downstairs in the gorgeous dining room with a vaulted cellar that dates back to the15th century.

La Voûte
$$-$$$
19 Rue Désaugiers
☎04.94.53.89.89
For fish lovers, we recommend La Voûte, where chef José Parodi and his wife, who supervises the service, can guarantee excellent meals with a good quality to price ratio, in a location right next to the cathedral (Place Formigé). The house specialty *marmite de pêcheur* must be ordered a day in advance; it is guaranteed to be fresh.

Saint-Aygulf

Angelo
493 Boulevard de la Liberation
Do you have a craving for ice cream? Angelo's ice cream parlour is the place to go.

Le Jardin
$
583 Avenue de la Corniche d'Azur
☎04.94.81.17.81
Le Jardin offers tasty little dishes at reasonable prices, including grilled food, pizza and home-made ice cream. This little restaurant is located near l'Escale au Soleil (see p 412).

Les Issambres

La Réserve
$$-$$$
closed Oct to Apr and Tue evening and Wed
☎04.94.96.90.41
For a sumptuous meal, try La Réserve, a new little restaurant located 300m (984ft) from Villa St-Elme. The atmosphere is pleasant, and the service is friendly. Other than les marmites du pêcheur and les bourrides, the chef's speciality is tuna cooked in olive oil with fresh ginger.

Saint-Elme
$$$-$$$$
☎04.94.49.52.52
The very chic restaurant of the Saint-Elme hotel (see p 412) possesses a superb view of the Golfe de Saint-Tropez and two dining rooms. Aromatic regional specialities with mint, pistou and tapenade are served in a very chic decor.

Roquebrune-sur-Argens

Le Gaspacho
$-$$
closed Wed, Oct to Mar
21 Avenue de Général de Gaulle
☎04.94.45.49.59
Don't be misled by this restaurant's name, the menu at Le Gaspacho consists of regional specialties and grilled foods. This small, family-run establishment offers personalized service as well as cuisine. Guests have the choice of dining on the shady terrace or in the dining room with its attractive Provençal tablecloths.

Saint-Tropez

Chez Fuchs
$-$$
7 Rue des Commerçants
☎04.94.97.01.25
A very "in" spot in the city centre, Chez Fuchs offers Provençale cuisine in a cantina-like setting. Highly recommended by local connoisseurs who come here to enjoy a cigar while savouring a *pastis.*

Auberge des Maures
$$-$$$
closed Nov to Mar
evenings only
4 Rue Dr. Boutin
☎04.94.97.01.50
Auberge des Maures is a very nice out-of-the-way spot in a tiny side-street. Its large shaded terrace will delight you: it's an ideal place to take shelter from the summer heat and spend a relaxing moment while dining in the arbour. Moreover, the Provençal setting is refined. The food served is *cuisine du marché* with an emphasis on fresh fish.

Le Café
$$-$$$
at the end of Place des Lices
☎04.94.97.29.00
Le Café is famous for its Provençale cuisine.

La Table du Marché
$$-$$$
closed mid-Jan to Feb and mid-Nov to mid-Dec
38 Rue Georges Clemenceau
☎04.94.97.85.20
La Table du Marché is an upscale *traiteur* located on a small street that branches off Places des Lices. You can eat in or take out. Only delicious, high quality food is sold here. One glance at the display cases will be enough to convince you that everything must be good—but expensive. A number of packaged products are also available: honey, preserves and various kinds of oils, notably nut, almond and, of course, olive. Finally, the second floor houses a sushi bar (***$$***) that is less taxing on the wallet.

La Ponche
$$-$$$
The restaurant at the Hôtel La Ponche is really worth trying, whether you are staying at the hotel or not. In summer, meals are served on a very beautiful terrace that looks out onto a small busy square of the old village, near the old port. The meat and fish dishes are skilfully prepared and the desserts are divine. Moreover, the wine list features some good regional selections. The service is friendly and efficient. The owner, Madame Duckstein, will take your order and, if you wish, will introduce you to the illustrious history of this "almost sacred" spot. Picasso and many others have come for a drink here, in this establishment which originally was no more than a meeting place for local fishermen. Strongly recommended: the delicious *tulipe de fruits frais*. See p 414.

La Dame de Cœur
$$$
open in the evening only
2 Rue de la Miséricorde
☎04.94.97.23.16
Formerly in Gassin, La Dame de Cœur is a great spot. The menu *(200F)* changes daily according the mood of the owner-cum-chef.

Finally, in the port area there is an excellent ice cream stand, **Barbarac**, whose offerings are certain to tempt you.

Saint-Tropez Peninsula

L'Esquinade
$$
closed Dec to mid-Mar
Pampelonne Beach, on the Bonne Terrasse road
☎04.94.79.83.42
Right on the beach, this rustic (to say the least) "shack" is popular with locals. Fish dishes and salads are served here, and you can dine on the terrace with a view of the sea.

Chez Camille
$$-$$$
closed Nov to Mar and Tue, except in summer
Bonne Terrasse, near Cap Camarat
☎04.94.79.80.38
This restaurant has earned one of the best reputations on the peninsula. If you ask locals where they prefer to go for grilled fish, prawns or *bouillabaisse* (famous), they'll send you to Chez Camille.

Grimaud

Les Santons
$$$$
closed Wed and Nov to mid-Mar, except during the Christmas holidays
If you appreciate fine dining, don't miss Les Santons. Treat yourself for an evening! It starts with Mme. Girard's warm welcome, followed by Monsieur Girard's exquisite cuisine, served in the finest Provençale decor where each element has been tastefully selected. A mere glance at the menu tells you you're in for an evening of delights, and you won't be disappointed! As an appetiser, depending on the season, you may choose creamy lobster risotto, *ravioles de truffe*, or *saumon d'Écosse Label Rouge* (Red Label Scottish salmon). As an entrée, the *selle d'agneau de Sisteron* (saddle of lamb roasted with thyme) is a memorable choice and has had top billing on the menu for many years

now. There is a well-stocked wine cellar and the pleasant sommelier can offer excellent advice to make your wine choice easier. True, the prices are on the steep side, but the exceptional quality of the food and the impeccable service more than justify the expense. In short, an unforgettable experience. Simply divine!

Collobrières

La Petite Fontaine
$$-$$$
Place de la République
☎04.94.48.00.12
La Petite Fontaine is a wonderful place for lunch. You can eat outdoors on a peaceful terrace which overlooks a small shaded square with a fountain. The restaurant serves Provençal specialities. The portions are generous and the value is excellent. Note that credit cards are not accepted.

Entertainment

To find out about all the touristic and cultural activities taking place in this region, visit the Web site: ***www.cg83.fr***.

Saint-Raphaël

Festivals and Cultural Events

Compétition Internationale de Jazz de New Orleans
early July
A New Orleans-style jazz festival in the streets.

Festival du Cinéma Européen
late Oct
A European film festival.

Fête des Pêcheurs
one weekend in early August
At the port
A fishermen's festival with traditional celebrations, local music, competitions and dance.

Fête de Mimosa
late Feb

Casino

Grand Casino
slot machines 11am to 4am; gambling 8pm to 4am, in summer until 5am
Square de Gand
☎04.94.95.10.59

Coco Club
Port Santa Lucia
☎04.94.95.95.56
The Coco Club piano bar is a pleasant place to stop in for a drink.

Fréjus

La Playa
every day 11pm to sunrise, buffet Thu at 8:30pm, in season
☎04.94.52.22.98
La Playa is certainly the most popular nightspot in Fréjus. Since many styles of music are played, the club pleases a vast clientele. The dinner-dance on Thursdays in high season is the highlight of the week. Starting at 8:30pm, people dine (cold buffet, a hot dish and unlimited wine) and then dance. Very lively! A big plus: this nightclub is located right on the beach and has two open-air dance floors.

Les Nuits Auréliennes
late Jul
music concerts.

Festival d'Art Pyrotechnique
Jul and Aug
A fireworks festival.

Saint-Tropez

Bars and Nightclubs

Le Papagayo
with one drink included 100F
every night 11:30pm until dawn
Résidence du Port
☎06.87.80.83.64
Super atmosphere...

Les Caves du Roy
Hôtel Byblos
☎04.94.56.68.00
Les Caves du Roy is certainly the most yup pie nightclub on the Côte d'Azur and as such, it attracts stars. In the chic and expensive Hôtel Byblos.

Bravade de St-Tropez
mid-May
Festival celebrating the city's patron saint.

Salon des Peintres de Saint-Tropez
(Aug)
Exhibition featuring Saint-Tropez painters.

Nöel à Saint-Tropez
entire month of Dec
Christmas in Saint-Tropez.

Gay Bars

Le Pigeonnier
with one drink included 70F
every night 11pm
13 Rue de la Ponche
☎04.94.97.36.85
A mixed crowd comes here.

L'Esquinade
Fri and Sat only, except in summer, 11pm to 4am
Rue du Four, behind Place de la Mairie
☎04.94.97.38.09

Sainte-Maxime

Festival des Écoles de Musique
mid-July
A music festival that also includes theatre.

Festival d'Automne Chopin, George Sand et Leur Temps
early Oct
This festival celebrates the lives and times of Chopin and Sand.

Semaine du Gout et des Terroirs
mid-Oct
local products, wine and food.

Saint-Hilaire-de-la-Mer

Le Saint-Hilaire-de-la-Mer
Fri and Sat 11pm until dawn
Avenue Général Leclerc, on the seaside
☎04.94.96.19.20

Ramatuelle

Jazz at **Théâtre de Verdure**
mid-July

Temps Musicaux: Festival de Musique Classique
second half of July
Théâtre de Verdure
Classical music festival,.

Festival de Théâtre
first half of August
Théâtre de Verdure
Theatre festival.

Cogolin

Les Soirs d'Éte
July and August
Information at the Centre Culturel
☎04.94.55.01.10

Shopping

Saint-Raphaël

Salon "Marché de Provence"
Apr
Tourism, recreation and gastronomy show.

Salon du Palais Gourmand
late Nov
Exhibitors from all regions of France offer samples and sell their specialties.

Fréjus

Art Tendance Sud - Salon des Métiers d'Art
three days in the middle of May
Port Fréjus
Handicrafts exhibit.

Sainte-Maxime

Foire aux Antiquaires
last two weeks of May
Antique show at Place Jean Mermoz.

Saint-Tropez

Poterie Augier
22 Rue Clémenceau
☎04.94.97.12.55
This shop, located on a charming commercial street, sells an astonishing range of attractively coloured ceramics from eggcups to large serving platters.

There is another Augier shop as you enter the pretty village of Gassin.

La Tarte Topézienne is on the same street. It was in this pastry shop, in 1955, that a Polish chef created this famous tart, which is actually a cream-filled sponge cake.

Château Suffren
Place de la Mairie
☎***04.94.97.85.15***
You'll find some fine antique pieces and high-quality knick-knacks at Château Suffren.

Salon des Antiquaires
late August and early September
Antique show.

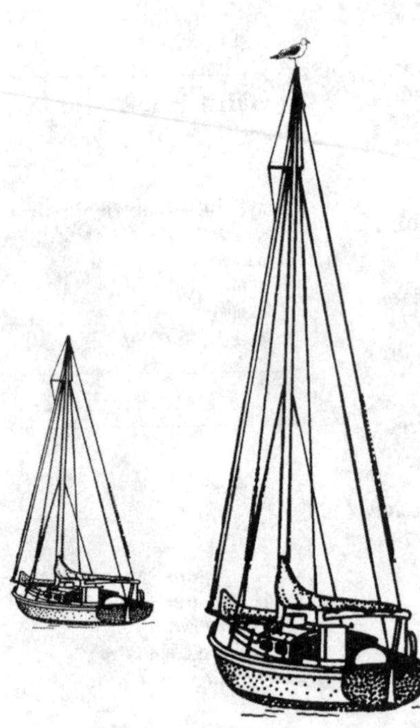

Between Saint-Tropez and Bandol

Heading west from Saint-Tropez, the glittering part of the Côte d'Azur that made this area one of the world's greatest resort destinations, soon fades.

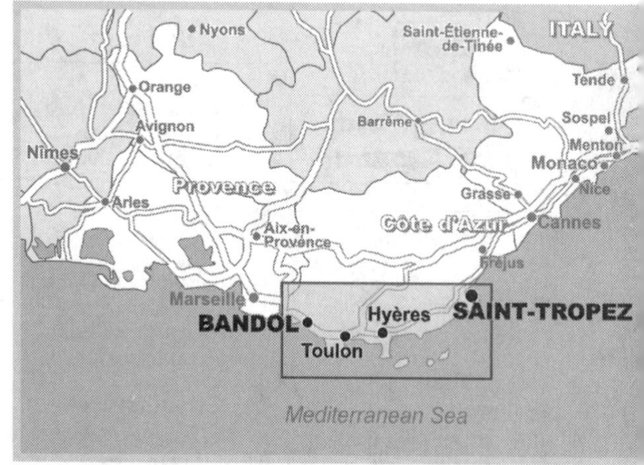

Yet, the name "Côte d'Azur" originates from Hyères. The social whirl is less pronounced here and the beaches are certainly not as well known, but this part of the coast still consists of a group of vacation resorts brimming with natural beauty. There is only one sour note in the region: Toulon. This, the largest city, offers very little of interest. It was heavily destroyed during World War II and rebuilt with buildings that are, quite frankly, ugly. The passage of time has not improved the city's allure either, which is a shame considering the wonderful natural location of its original site.

But to speak of its beauty, there is plenty to say: the Îles d'Hyères (Hyères islands); the magnificent hill range called the Massif des Maures; Bandol and the Île de Bendor opposite its port; and the delightful villages that are hidden back from the sea, La Cadière-d'Azur and Le Castellet for example, which possess undeniable charm.

Considering that the sea is so omnipresent, numerous water activities await visitors. The area inland, known collectively as the *arrière-pays*, or backcountry affords countless opportunities for gentle walks and serious hiking. Let's not forget that the area is a reputed wine-growing region, and thus the promise of relaxing evenings tasting local bottles is always a pleasant possibility... And last but not least, are the culinary wonders that await.

Note that the Comité Régional de Tourisme (CRT) du Var divides this region into three sectors. From west to east, we will go through **La Provence d'Azur**, **Toulon et sa Rade** (Toulon and its harbour) and **La Côte Provençale** (the Provençal Coast).

Finding Your Way Around

By Plane

The largest regional airport is located at Hyères, 18km (11.2mi) east of Toulon. Connections are made with all the major French cities. The passenger boarding pier for the Îles d'Hyères is just 5km (3.1mi) from the airport. International flights land at the airports of Marseille *(50km or 31mi) from west of Bandol)* or Nice *(100km or 62.1mi east of Toulon).*

By Train

The train network operates between Marseille and Toulon. From Toulon, the railroad follows the north side of the Massif des Maures and heads directly to Fréjus. Therefore, apart from a small line linking Toulon with the Hyères airport, there is no coastal train between Hyères and Fréjus. It is therefore impossible to reach Saint-Tropez by train.

SNCF Train Station Toulon
Place Europe
information and reservations
☎*08.36.35.35.35*

By Ferry

Boating plays an important role in this region, due to the importance of the many islands. Most of these boats are *vedettes* (modern launches) or smaller vessels which make regular trips between the islands and mainland.

Îles d'Hyères

Most departures can be made from the far end of Presqu'île de Giens at the Tour Fondue, situated south of Hyères and the Toulon-Hyères Airport. But the islands can also be reached from Toulon, from Hyères-Plage, from the Port-de-Miramar *(13km or 8.1mi east of Hyères)*, from Lavandou and from Cavalaire-sur-Mer *(18km or 11.2mi west of Saint-Tropez).*

Hyères

Landing Stage of Hyères Harbour
☎*04.94.57.44.07*
⇌*04.94.38.30.58*
Departures to Îles du Levant and Port-Cros.

TLV (Transport Littoral Varois)
☎*04.94.58.21.81*
⇌*04.94.58.91.73*
Shuttle service to the islands. Parking with admission charge is mandatory (between 20 and 25F per day).

Île de Porquerolles

Departures are from **Port de la Tour-Fondue** *(☎04.94.58.21.81)* at the far south end of the Presqu'île de Giens, since its the shortest distance. At least five return trips a day are made during low season, and 20 a day during July and August. Furthermore, in July and August, it is possible to tour the two islands, Porquerolles and Port-Cros.

Île du Levant and Île de Port-Cros

Departures are made most often from Lavandou (the shortest and least expensive), but also from Port-de-Miramar, from Port Saint-Pierre or from the Presqu'île de Giens. From Le Lavandou and the Port de la Tour Fondue, you can tour Île de Port-Cros and Île du Levant in the same day, from April to October.

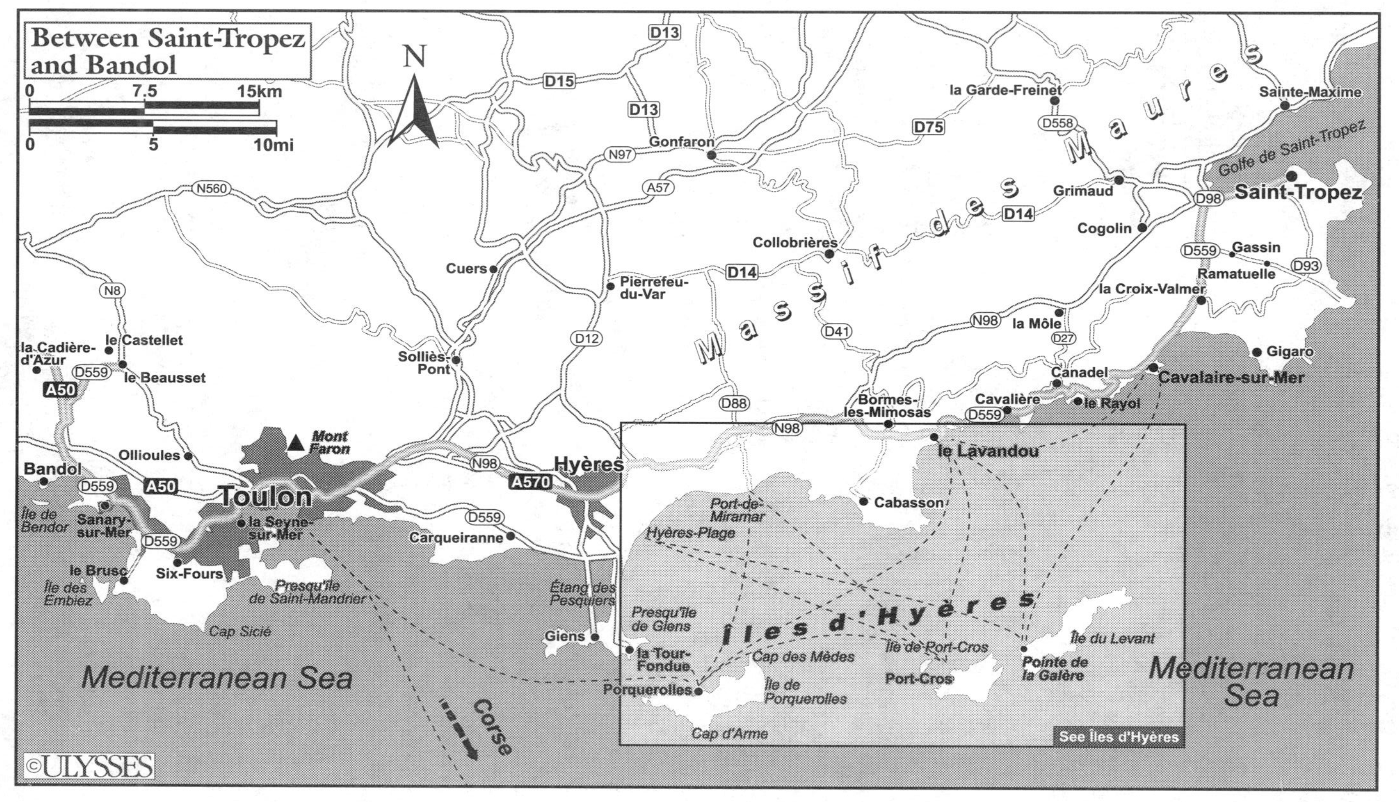

Between Saint-Tropez and Bandol
0
7.5
15km
0
5
10mi
N
Massif des Maures
Îles d'Hyères
Mediterranean Sea
Mediterranean Sea
Saint-Tropez
Sainte-Maxime
Golfe de Saint-Tropez
la Garde-Freinet
Grimaud
Cogolin
Gassin
Ramatuelle
la Croix-Valmer
Gigaro
Cavalaire-sur-Mer
le Rayol
Canadel
Cavalière
la Môle
Bormes-les-Mimosas
le Lavandou
Cabasson
Collobrières
Gonfaron
Pierrefeu-du-Var
Cuers
Solliès-Pont
Hyères
Carqueiranne
Étang des Pesquiers
Giens
Presqu'île de Giens
la Tour-Fondue
Porquerolles
Île de Porquerolles
Cap d'Arme
Cap des Mèdes
Hyères-Plage
Port-de-Miramar
Île de Port-Cros
Port-Cros
Île du Levant
Pointe de la Galère
See Îles d'Hyères
Toulon
Mont Faron
la Seyne-sur-Mer
Presqu'île de Saint-Mandrier
Cap Sicié
Six-Fours
le Brusc
Île des Embiez
Sanary-sur-Mer
Île de Bendor
Bandol
Ollioules
le Castellet
le Beausset
la Cadière-d'Azur
Corse
D13
D15
D13
D75
D558
D14
D14
D98
D559
D93
N98
D27
D41
D12
D88
D559
N98
N97
A57
N560
N8
D559
A50
A50
D559
D559
N98
A570
D559
©ULYSSES

Three Island Circuit

A circuit running in July and August two or three times a week allows passengers to visit the three islands in the same day. Departures are from Port de la Tour-Fondue. For less active types, this is an ideal way to see the area, for there is little time to visit the islands by foot.

Île des Embiez

From the Brusc port, the crossing takes 10min, with departures about every 30min during high season. Allow for about 25F per person for the return trip. Information: ☎04.94.74.93.00.

Île de Bendor

The crossing takes 7min. Crossings every 30min.

Toulon

Harbour Station
Port de Commerce
☎04.94.22.80.82
Departures to the islands and Corsica.

By Car

Due to the deficiencies in the rail network in this area, it is probably wisest to rent a car upon arrival.

The road network is well-developed. The A50 highway links Marseille, La Ciotat, Bandol, Toulon and Hyères. Leaving Toulon, the A57 rejoins the A8–E80 and continues eastwards towards Fréjus, Cannes and Nice.

The national and departmental roads are very well maintained and pass through some magnificent countryside. The two main routes are the D559, which follows the seaside, and the N98, which is farther north. The problem with this region is that it is almost always necessary to go through Toulon. Unfortunately, work on a hoped–for expressway across it had to be interrupted because of a mistake in planning. In short, for a long time now, crossing Toulon has been a real hassle!

Car Rental

Toulon

Europcar
Rd-Pt bir-Hakeim
☎04.94.41.09.07
⇌04.94.46.65.12

Taxi

Toulon

Taxi
24hrs/day
☎04.94.93.51.51

By Bus

A number of bus excursions are possible. Departures can be made from the majority of villages along the coast. Local tourist offices provide all the necessary information.

Practical Information

Tourist Offices

La Croix-Valmer
Maison du Tourisme La Provence d'Azur
☎04.94.01.84.30
⇌04.94.01.84.31
www.provence-azur.com
The Maison du Tourisme de La Provence d'Azur provides information on the region that stretches from Le Lavandou to Hyères, including the islands.

Le Lavandou
Tourist Office
Quay Gabriel Péri
☎04.94.00.40.50
⇌04.94.00.40.59
www.lelavandou.com
This tourist bureau deserves five stars for its service, since its personnel are so helpful and friendly.

Bormes-les-Mimosas
Tourist Office
One Place Gambetta
☎04.94.71.15.17
⇌04.94.64.79.57

Hyères–Les Palmiers
Tourist Office
Forum of the Casino
3 Avenue Ambroise Thomas
☎04.94.01.84.50
⇌04.94.04.84.51
www.ville-hyeres.fr

Îles d'Hyères
Bureau d'Information Porquerollais
☎*04.94.58.33.76*
⇌*04.94.58.36.39*
www.porquerolles.com

Bureau du Parc National de Port-Cros
☎*04.94.01.40.72*
⇌*04.94.01.40.71*

Bureau de Tourisme de l'Île du Levant
☎*04.94.05.93.52*

Toulon
Tourist Office
Place Raimu
☎*04.94.18.53.00*
⇌*04.94.18.53.09*
Guided walking tours are organized by the tourist office, Wednesday at 9:30am, only if arranged in advance.

Tourist Information Counters
Toulon-Hyères Airport
☎*04.94.22.81.60*

La Seyne-sur-Mer
Tourist Office
Corniche G. Pompidou
☎*04.98.00.25.70*
⇌*04.98.00.25.71*

Île des Embiez
www.ile-des-embiez

Sanary-sur-Mer
Tourist Office
Les Jardins de la Ville
☎*04.94.74.01.04*
www.sanarysurmer.com

Bandol
Tourist Office
Allée Viven
☎*04.94.29.41.35*
⇌*04.94.32.50.39*
www.bandol.org

La Cadière-d'Azur
Tourist Office
Place G. de Gaule
☎*04.94.90.12.56*
⇌*04.94.98.30.13*

Le Beausset
Tourist Office
Place Général de Gaulle
☎*04.94.90.55.10*
⇌*04.94.98.51.83*

Place Raimu

Post Office

Toulon

(city hall office)
Rue Jean-Bartolini
☎*04.94.01.51.20*

Miscellaneous

Le Lavandou

Motorboat Rentals
Vedettes Îles d'Or, Quai Gabriel Péri
☎*04.94.71.01.02*
⇌*04.94.71.78.95*

Exploring

We will start with the Corniche des Maures, which follows the shore between Saint-Tropez and Hyères. The Îles d'Hyères will follow, and the last section will cover the area between Toulon and Bandol, including the villages found inland.

Leave Saint-Tropez by the D559 towards La Croix-Valmer.

At the interstection of D93 and D559 stands the cross for which the village of **La Croix-Valmer** was named. It was only in 1935 that the Valmer designation was added to avoid any confusion with other villages.

The Beaches of Lavandou

The Le Lavandou administrative district stretches over several kilometres and contains several localities like Pramousquier, Cavalière and Aiguebelle. The coast changes often, creating many separate beaches, each with a different personality. Twelve in number, they all have nicknames suggestive of their characters. Something for every beach-lover!

Le Lavandou's beaches are safe, since they are supervised by expert-certified lifeguards. The sand is cleaned on a daily basis and the flag of "Le Pavillon Bleu" d'Europe, awarded by the Fondation de l'Éducation à l'Environnement, flies over Lavandou, underlining the quality of its waters and its environment.

Here is a list of the beaches from west to east:

Plage de l'Angladen–la Branchée
(the fashionable)
The first of the resort's beaches sets the tone.

Plage du Lavandou or Grande Plage–La Familiale (family)
The longest of the beaches, you will be charmed by its golden sand. It's very popular with families since its size permits them to take part in many activities.

Plage Saint-Clair–La Perle (the pearl)
A pleasant beach, shorter than the Lavandou, but overhanging pines trees provide it with a more natural setting. It gets plenty of sun.

Plage de la Fossette–La Souriante
(the welcoming)
Having carved out a niche for itself between two rocky outcrops, this tiny beach is has a slightly untamed aspect.

Plage d'Aiguebelle–La Charmeuse
(the charming)
The main attraction of Aiguebelle, which literally means "beautiful water", is the transparency of its water.

Plage Jean Blanc–L'Écrin d'Argent
(the jewel box)
This small, unspoiled beach materializes suddenly at the heart of an inlet. It remains fairly private because it is harder to access; however, the small effort of getting here is amply rewarded by the welcoming pines, sunshine and sea.

Plage de l'Éléphant–La Sauvage (the primitive)
Its nickname says it all. It is so untamed that you have to climb over rocks or come by sea to reach it... not a far cry from that desert isle that lovers long for.

Plage du Rossignol–l'Integrale
The name of this beach means "complete," perhaps in the sense of the complete, all-over tan you can get, since its privacy is conducive to taking off one's clothes...

Plage du Layet–L'Anse du Boucanier
(buccaneer's cove)
Entirely hidden from view, like the preceding one, it encourages naturalism.

Plage de Cavalière–La Sportive
(the sports-lover)
What would you like to do today... sail, jet ski, catamaran, pedal

boat, scuba dive, waterski, play badminton or volleyball? You've got it!

Plage Cap Nègre–La Paisible (the peaceful)
The ideal place to recapture some tranquillity after the overwhelming activity of the preceding one.

Plage de Pramousquier–La Mystérieuse
(the mysterious)
The mystery lies in the colour of its water which teasingly adopts myriad shades that are never precisely green, blue or turquoise.

Finally, all these beaches are accessible thanks to the ***Petit Train des Plages***, which goes from one end to the other. There are four departures in both directions each day, with the first at approximately 10am and the last at about 7pm. The complete route takes 50min.

Cavalaire-sur-Mer is a seaside resort somewhat popular with tourists—families in particular. Since the turn of the century, its long fine-sand beach has attracted many people, including Marie Curie.

Soon after leaving Cavalaire, you will reach the **Rayol**. Those with a passion for gardens won't want to miss the **Domaine du Rayol ★★** *(40F; guided tours mandatory; every half-hour; Jul to Aug, Tue to Sun 10am to 11am and 4pm to 6pm; otherwise Tue to Fri 3pm, Sat and Sun 10am and 3pm; closed in winter; avenue du Commandant Rigaud, ☎04.94.05.32.50)*. This magnificent 20ha (49.4 acre) estate comprises a splendid Art-Nouveau villa, with stairs descending to the ocean and huge gardens displaying over 400 exotic plant species. The site has been maintained and managed by the Conservatoire du Littoral, a public organization, since 1989.

If you are travelling as a family, your children will be thrilled with a visit to the **Parc Nautique Niagara ★** *(Route du Canadel, La Môle, ☎04.94.49.58.85)*. This water park has huge water slides, a swimming pool, whirlpools and aquatic rock-climbing walls. The park can be reached from Canadel on the D27 toward Môle. The roadsigns are well indicated.

Le Lavandou

This seaside resort in the shadow of the Massif des Maures contains kilometres and kilometres of fine-sand beaches. It is nicknamed "La Station aux 12 sables" (resort of 12 sands). The number 12 is important to Le Lavandou: its 12 beaches stretch over 12km (7mi). All different, they range from a vast, fine-sand beach to a small, wild inlet. But they have one thing in common: they are all extremely clean. Le Lavandou was awarded the Pavillon Bleu d'Europe for the quality of its waters and its environment.

The old city, while small, is truly charming. It has a multitude of inviting little restaurants with terraces that are pleasant places to linger for a while. In other respects, the city is usually very crowded during high season, since it is the main boarding point for the Îles du Levant and Île de Port-Cros (see p 424).

What makes this place worth visiting is that you can rent boats here to explore the numerous bays and magnificent capes along the coastline southwest of the village. These places can also be reached by bicycle. Moreover, Le Lavandou is an ideal starting point for wonderful bike rides into the .

Leave Le Lavandou via the D41 for Bormes-les-Mimosas.

Bormes-les-Mimosas

This village will enchant you with its old pink-tile houses built on different levels on the cliffside, its sloping roads, along with the remains of its fortress walls and imposing castle.

A Ligurian tribe from Italy called the Bormani first settled on the coast around 400 BC. For a long time they were fishermen, but in the 9th century they emigrated to the hills to defend themselves against incessent attacks by Saracens. The village wasn't built until the 12th century, and despite the construction of the ramparts, its inhabitants continued to suffer invasions.

In 1913, the community lost a great part of its territory and population when the Lavandou district separated in order to develop its maritime activity.

In 1968, a decree officially recognized the appellation Bormes-les-Mimosas, due to the presence of the flowering (January to March) mimosa tree, part of the acacia family. A festival attracting thousands of visitors occurs the third Sunday in February to celebrate this tree, the community's symbol. The highlight of this event is the parade of floral-decorated floats. Since 1970, Bormes-les-Mimosas obtained the distinction "*quatre fleurs*" (four flowers) for being one of the most flowery villages in France, the first village worthy of such an honour.

Take some time to stroll through the very pretty roads of the old village, where the charming houses are decorated with fresh flowers and plants. You will be ceaselessly amazed by the bougainvillea and wisteria that cling to the facades of houses everywhere.

At the top of the village, only the ruins of the **Château de Bormes** remain. Built between the 13th and 14th centuries, it burnt down in 1589. Today, it is private property and can not be visited. Nevertheless, this spot offers a panorama overlooking the plain and the sea.

The **Chapelle Saint-François-de-Paule ★** keeps alaive the memory of this saint who cured Bormes of the plague in 1481. The chapel has housed a 17th-century retable in praise of the village's protector since 1560.

Situated outside the medieval city's ramparts, the **Église Saint-Trophyme ★**, with three Romanesque-inspired naves, dates from the 18th century. The Latin text gracing the façade means "from the hour of the day to the hour of God". Inside, the pillars bear gilded reliquary busts, a Way of the Cross comprising 14 oil paintings by Alain Noon (1980), as well as a majestic painting depicting Saint-Trophyme, which dominates the nave.

Along the Rue Carnot in the old village the **Musée "Arts et Histoire" ★** *(closed Tue and Sun afternoon, 10am to noon and 3pm to 6pm, 5pm in winter)* is located in a magnificently restored 17th-century building that will amaze you with its splendid stone ceilings. While it formerly served as a prison and as a school for boys, since 1926 it has housed collections which retrace the history of Bormes, Collobrières, Brégançon and of the Chartreuse de la Verne. The paintings exhibited are from the 19th and 20th centuries.

Continue below the old village towards Cabasson.

By heading down from the old village toward

Cabasson, visitors will reach the **Fort de Brégançon ★**. Erected in the 16th century for François I, on the cape of the same name that separates the Hyères and Bormes harbours, the fort has been a presidential residence since 1968. It is only open to the public in September when several of France's historic monuments hold open houses.

Cabasson is an ideal spot to go walking or cycling. What's more, the village is not always accessible by car. This is the place for nature-lovers, as forests, vineyards and the sea surround the village.

The Corniche des Maures ends here. If you wish to return to Saint-Tropez, take the N98 toward **La Môle**. Those who would like to stop for something to eat will find a very good restaurant in this village (see p 455).

Head west to Hyères by the N98.

Hyères–Les Palmiers

This seaside resort is very spread-out, since in addition to its city centre, it includes a port (Port Saint-Pierre), several beaches, the Presqu'île de Giens and the Îles d'Hyères. Moreover, the only airport between Nice and Marseille, the Toulon–Hyères Airport, is also situated in its territory.

The glory days of this seaside resort occurred during the second half of the 19th century. It was visited by many artists and members of high society, most of whom were English. Among those who fell under Hyères' charms were Queen Victoria, the queen of Spain, Tolstoy and Victor Hugo.

Unfortunately, few traces of this glorious past are visible today. In the 20th century, Hyères lost its worldly status to Cannes and Nice. However, it has once again become a popular seaside resort in the past few years. An old villa now houses a **casino**. A glassed-in addition has been integrated into the original building, creating a rather original piece of architecture.

There is little to see, apart from the **vieille ville ★**, or old town. The covered passages and medieval houses confer a certain charm, and traces of the old ramparts can be spotted here and there.

You won't want to miss the **Collégiale Saint-Paul** *(2:30pm to 5pm; ☎04.94.65.83.30)*. The collegiate church features a monumental stairway leading to the entrance and sundry votive offerings inside.

Finally, once again, at the top end of the village stand the ruins of a château destroyed during the Religious Wars.

Admirers of 1930s architecture will enjoy the **Villa Noailles ★** *(Chateau Saint-Bernard, summer 9am to 7pm, otherwise 5pm; Montée de Noailles; ☎04.94.01.84.50)*. Located below the château ruins, this house was built by the famous architect Mallet-Stevens. The owners, wealthy patrons of the arts, entertained numerous cultural figures there, among them Man Ray, Giacometti, Bunuel and Cocteau.

To reach the landing stage for the Îles d'Hyères, pass through the Presqu'île de Giens. You will be strongly tempted to turn towards one of the beaches to enjoy a dip in the sea! There is a rather spectacular road, the D97, on the west side of the peninsula. This narrow road is delineated by the Salins des Pesquiers on one side, and the sea on the other.

Boats depart from La Tour-Fondue, at the tip of the peninsula, for Porquerolles only. However, the three islands may be reached from Port St-Pierre. See p 424.

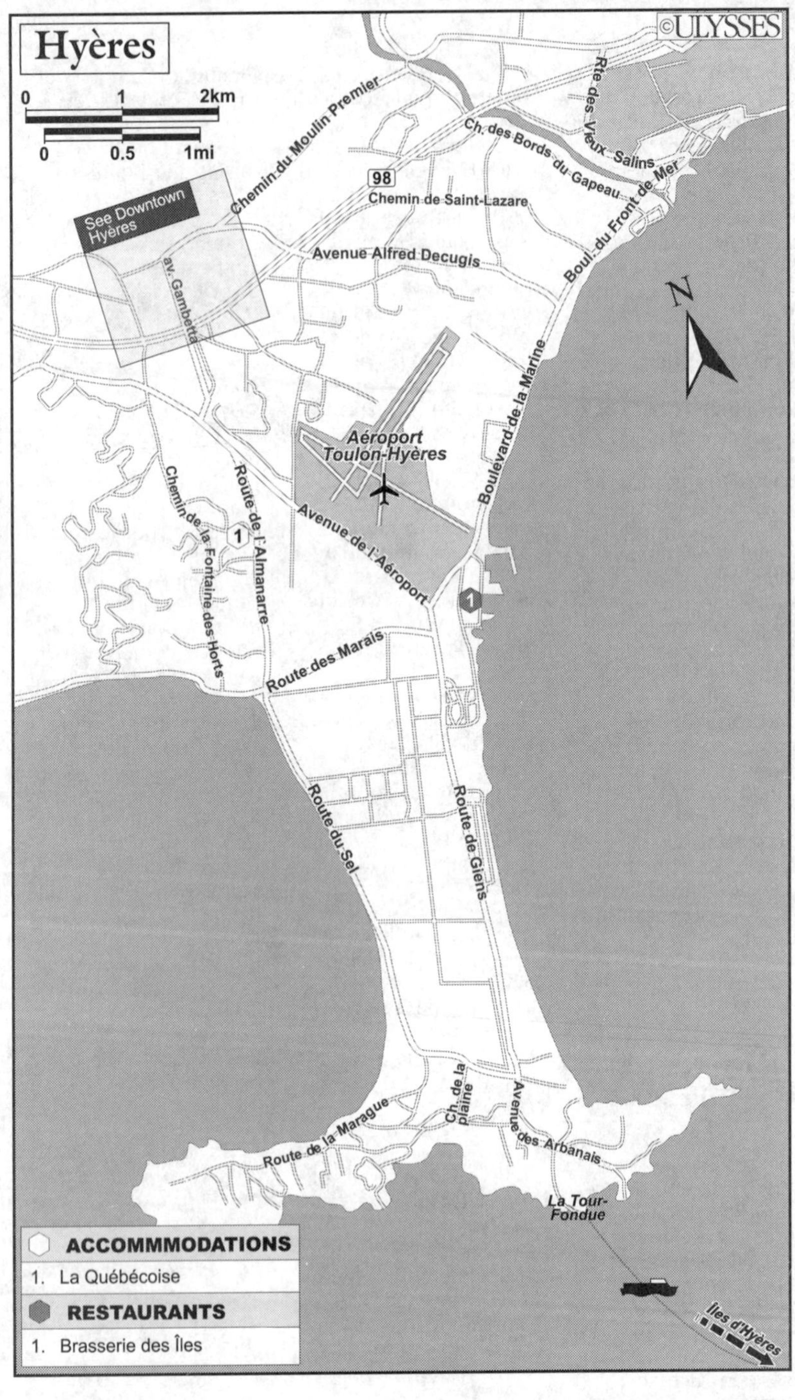
Hyères
©ULYSSES
0
1
2km
0
0.5
1mi
See Downtown Hyères
Chemin du Moulin Premier
98
Chemin de Saint-Lazare
Ch. des Bords du Gapeau
Rte des Vieux Salins
Boul. du Front de Mer
Avenue Alfred Decugis
av. Gambetta
Boulevard de la Marine
N
Aéroport Toulon-Hyères
Chemin de la Fontaine des Horts
Route de l'Almanarre
Avenue de l'Aéroport
Route des Marais
Route du Sel
Route de Giens
Ch. de la plaine
Avenue des Arbanais
Route de la Maraque
La Tour-Fondue
Îles d'Hyères
ACCOMMMODATIONS
1. La Québécoise
RESTAURANTS
1. Brasserie des Îles

Îles d'Hyères

These islands were called the "Îles d'Or" (islands of gold) during the Renaissance. But a more interesting legend exists about their creation. Many ages ago, the King Olbianus and his four beautiful and adventurous daughters lived in this land. The princesses adored swimming and their passion took them far and wide. But alas, one day, they were hunted down by pirate ships. Happily, the gods intervened and before the nasty pirates could catch them, the four water-princesses were transformed into the Îles d'Or! This explains the existence of the fourth island—the tiniest one facing Port-Cros, called Île de Bagaud.

More realistically, these islands have successively endured many influences: Ligurian, Etruscan, Greek and Roman, before being regularly ravaged by the Saracens. It seems like these islands continued to share the same fate as the legendary princesses...

Advice: To really appreciate the flora and fauna of these islands, it is preferable to visit in the spring or au-

Hyères
Downtown

0 250 500m
0 750 1,500ft

ATTRACTIONS
1. Casino
2. Collégiale Saint-Paul
3. Villa Noailles

ACCOMMODATIONS
1. Portalet
2. Soleil

RESTAURANTS
1. Le Bistrot de Marius
2. Le jardin
3. Les Jardins de Bacchus
4. Les oubliettes

tumn. Summer is not the best season, as the flowering vegetation is past its prime and most of the birds have migrated elsewhere.

★★★

Île de Porquerolles

In the beginning of the 19th century, this island, the largest of the three, was not at all known by tourists. It was primarily used as a convalescent centre for soldiers returning from colonial wars. It was at this point that the Génie Militaire, military engineers, decided to create the village.

At the turn of the 20th century, a rich businessman bought the whole island just to enchant his young bride. Imagine that! After his death, the French state purchased the land, except for a few properties which stayed in the hands of the descendants of this family. The owner of the chic hotel Le Mas du Langoustier is the granddaughter of that rich businessman.

Since 1988, the island has been officially recognized as a national historic site. With its attractive sandy beaches and superb viewing points along the southern cliffs that dominate the shimmering sea, Porquerolles is a favourite spot for walking and bicycling.

As the island is only around 8km (5mi) long and 2km (1.2mi) wide, it is recommended to rent a bicycle *(about 60F a day)*. They can be rented from a number of shops found at the port entrance.

Remember that smoking or even lighting a fire is prohibited outside the village. Moreover, nature must always be respected.

Upon disembarking at the port, you will immediately recognize the special island-vacation atmosphere of the place. One could just as well be in the Caribbean. In any case, you will recognize Europe as soon as you set foot in the central village square where the church is enshrined.

With a bicycle, you can roam all over the island. There are a few stops worth making along the way, however.

Fort Sainte-Agathe *(May to Sep 10am to noon and 2:30pm to 5:30pm; ☎04.94.12.30.40)* was constructed in the 16th century to defend the island. An exhibition on the national park as well as archaeological objects found underwater are presented. A panoramic view of the island is possible from the fort's tower.

The island also contains the **Conservatoire Botanique National** *(May to Sep, 9:30am to 12:30pm and 1:30pm to 6pm; ☎04.94.12.30.40)*. The gardens and orchards sheltering different types of fruit trees make for an enjoyable visit.

★★★

Île de Port-Cros

Upon reaching this island's harbour, you will be under the impression that you have travelled to a faraway place and are now entering the small port of a bygone French colony—in Africa! Indeed, there are very few buildings, many palm trees and a certain languidness in the air...

This entire island has been a national park, both terrestrial and marine, since 1963. Regrettably, for some thirty years now the coastal vegetation has been seriously ravaged by pollution from the ocean beds. It is said that "the earth is seasick". Numerous efforts are being made to remedy or at least improve the situation, but so far the results have been rather limited. You can find out more once on site, for the park is equipped with an information centre at the port, where qualified and friendly staff will answer any questions you may have.

Due to its classification in 1963 as a national park, this island has remained untouched by man. Lovely walks lead to **Fort de l'Estissac**, which holds small exhibitions in the summer.

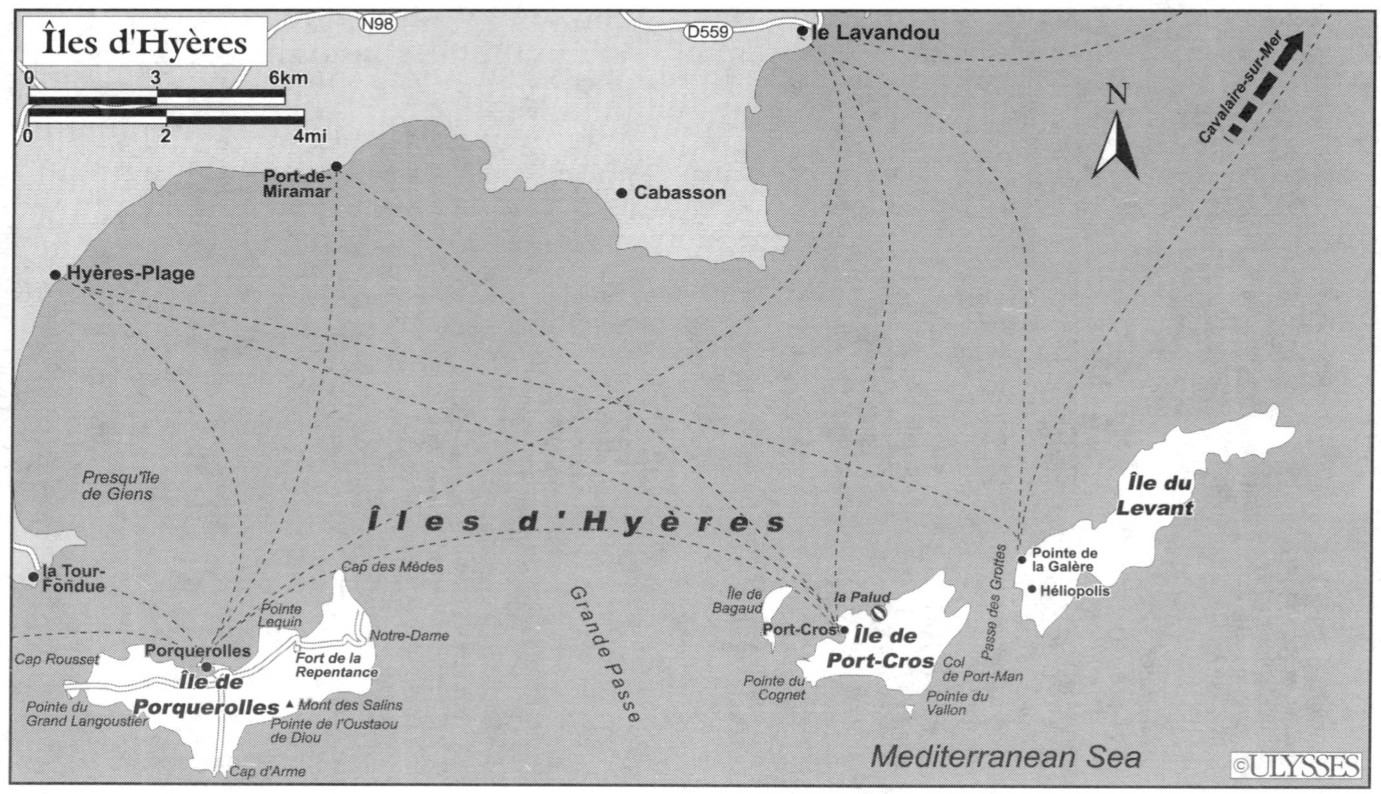

Îles d'Hyères
0 3 6km
0 2 4mi
N98
D559
le Lavandou
Cavalaire-sur-Mer
N
Port-de-Miramar
Cabasson
Hyères-Plage
Presqu'île de Giens
la Tour-Fondue
Îles d'Hyères
Cap des Mèdes
Pointe Lequin
Notre-Dame
Porquerolles
Fort de la Repentance
Cap Rousset
Île de Porquerolles
Mont des Salins
Pointe du Grand Langoustier
Pointe de l'Oustaou de Diou
Cap d'Arme
Grande Passe
Île de Bagaud
la Palud
Port-Cros
Île de Port-Cros
Pointe du Cognet
Col de Port-Man
Pointe du Vallon
Passe des Grottes
Pointe de la Galère
Héliopolis
Île du Levant
Mediterranean Sea
©ULYSSES

The **Sentier Botanique ★★**, a botanical trail, begins below the fort and leads to the **La Palud** Beach.

This beach is the site of an **underwater path ★★★** *(a mask and flippers usually available at desk, check first)*. This is truly something out of the ordinary: a path in shallow water (less than 5m deep) where guides help visitors discover the many beautiful types of fish and plant life. There is even a type of algae which, once calcified, ressembles coral. The experience encourages close encounters of the underwater kind, in our case a jelly-fish insisted on making contact with us...

★ Île du Levant

Île du Levant is particularly known for the **Héliopolis**, a small paradise for nudists, covering the southern part of the island. Small wild paths cross wooded spaces and run along the cliffside above the sea. However, the main occupant of the island is the Marine Nationale (navy). It uses 90% of the territory.

Beaches here are not ideal — there is only one which is sandy. Access to the water is possible by jumping from the rocks along the coast, but beware of sea urchins; there are loads of them.

The tour continues with Toulon. From Hyères, take the N98 then the A570 highway. If you are coming from Tour-Fondue, cross the Étang des Pesquiers dune, and follow the D559.

Toulon

The city has an exceptional geographical position between Mont Faron and a wide harbour which prides itself on being the prettiest in Europe. This was no doubt true some time ago!

It was occupied as of antiquity by Celto-Ligurian fishermen. In the 5th century, the city developped rapidly thanks to the establishment of a bishop's residence here. The inhabitants' livelihood was made from fishing, tanneries, the wine trade, salt and also... piracy.

Toulon became strategically important only after 1481 when the Count of Provence left Provence to the King of France in his legacy. In 1514, the Tour Royale was constructed to defend the harbour entrance, called La Petite Rade. In 1595, Henry IV created the Arsenal Maritime, whose main task was to build the royal fleet of galleys. The naval shipbuilding industry has developed ever since, making Toulon the number one military establishment in France.

Upon ascending to the throne, Louis XIV asked Vauban to build fortifications capable of defending Toulon by land and sea.

In the 18th century, Toulon reached the height of its maritime power and became the most important European port. After having been taken by the English and the Spanish in 1793, the port was reconquered by Bonaparte.

After years of decay, Toulon only regained its prosperity under the Second Empire. The opening of the Suez Canal in 1869 reinforced the city's strategic position.

Up until World War II, the navy was omnipresent. However, the city was half-destroyed during the war, and as a consequence, Toulon carries the scars of history and of its destiny as a strategic military port.

In 1974, after an interruption of 181 years, Toulon regained its position as the police headquarters for the entire Var department. Since the 1980s, the city has put a lot of effort into revitalising its image and it is currently making major changes in its infrastructure. These efforts seem to have paid off; the old town has been greatly enhanced and it is now a pleasant place to stroll about. Hopefully, more progress will be made in restoring the city itself. Its progress bears following, but in spite of these improvements the city still seems rather dreary.

Politically, Toulon represents a thorn in France's side: It is the largest city in France to have an extreme right-wing mayor.

City Tour

Leave your car in the public parking lot at Place d'Armes. Head towards the port.

You will soon reach the **Porte de l'Arsenal ★★**, which is registered as a historic monument. Its four columns support the statues of Mars, the god of War, of Minerva, the goddess of the Infantry, plus those of the Arts and of Intelligence. These are the works of Puget. The gate shelters the **Musée de la Marine ★** *(29F; Wed to Mon 9:30am to noon and 2pm to 6pm; Place Monsenergue, ☎04.94.02.02.01)* where more than two centuries of French maritime history are evoked through the use of models, maps, photos, paintings, etc.
A stroll along the piers is recommended. The Quai Stalingrad leads to a number of small restaurants with terraces.

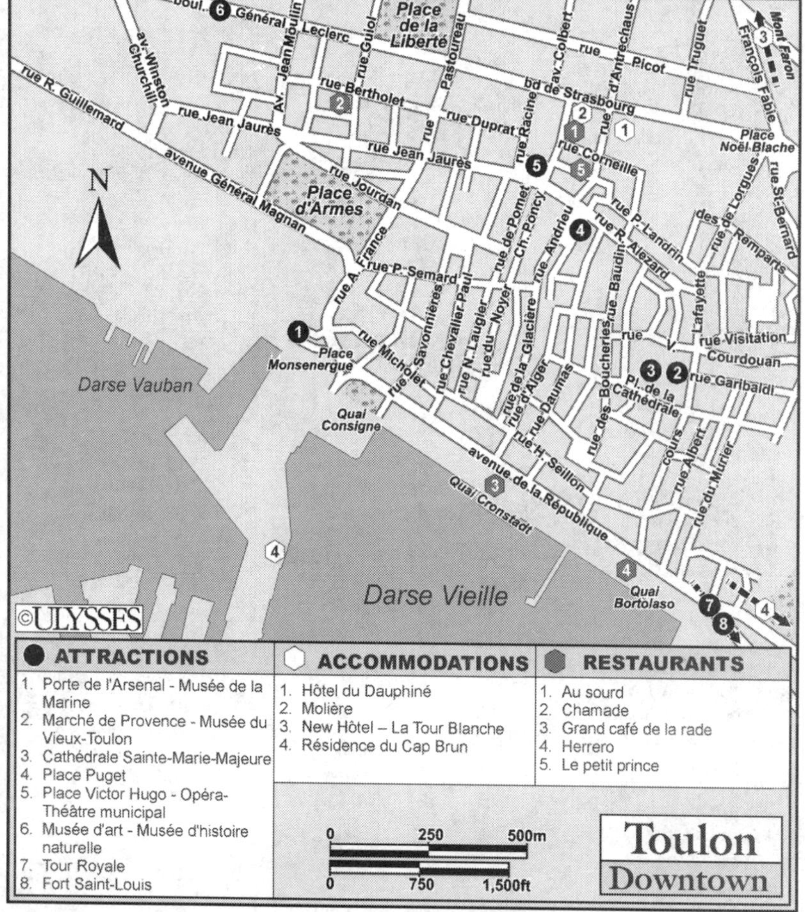

Note the **Atlantes de Puget**, which date from 1657 and grace the Mairie d'Honneur (civic hall).

Head towards Cours Lafayette in the old town.

The Provençal market is held on the **Cours Lafayette**, which is lined with plane trees. In addition, the local history museum is found here, the **Musée de Vieux Toulon** *(free admission; Mon to Sat 2pm to 6pm; ☎04.94.92.29.23).*

The old town still possesses several charming spots. Some old roads shelter medieval houses. The **Cathédrale Sainte-Marie-Majeure ★** is found on Place de la Cathédrale. This old Romanesque church dates from the 11th century and was enlarged in the 17th century. Behind the classical façade hides a fine baroque altar in stucco and marble, made by Veyrier (a student of Puget) and a number of paintings, including one by Puget.

Head northwest towards the opera house.

The Place Puget and its famous Fontaine des Trois-Dauphins are found here. Admirers of fountains may in fact follow a circuit which passes by a number of the city's finest. For more information, contact the Mairie d'Honneur in the port.

In the neighbouring streets, there are two or three pleasant hotels (see p 451).

A bit farther west, on the Place Victor-Hugo, lies the **Opéra-Théatre Municipal** *(☎04.94.92.70.78)*, a splendid structure built in 1862. The statues outside are the work of Toulonnais sculptors and represent, for the most part, the muses of the arts. This opera house is renowned for its fine acoustics. The interior is richly decorated with paintings, stucco effects and Napoléon III-style bronzes. Each year, between 12 and 15 operas and operettas are presented.

Head west along the Boulevard de Strasbourg, which is behind the opera house.

The **Musée des Beaux-Arts** *(free admission; 1pm to 7pm; 113 Boulevard Maréchal Leclerc, ☎04.94.93.15.54)* is a Renaissance-style structure, built in 1887. It houses a library, the second collection of French contemporary art (1960-1988) and some paintings from the Provençal school, covering the period between the 17th and 20th centuries. The building also houses the **Musée d'Histoire Naturelle** *(free admission; Mon to Sat 9:30am to noon and 2pm to 6pm; ☎04.94.93.15.54).*

Head south toward the naval dockyard, near the starting point.

Stretching over 10km (6.2mi), the **naval dockyard** employs a significant number of Toulon residents. The best way to see it is by climbing aboard one of the small motorboats criss-crossing the harbour. *(45F; mid-Apr to Oct; ☎04.94.64.41.14).*

You can end your visit of Toulon with the Mourillon district, to the east.

This is where the most popular and, consequently, the liveliest beach in Toulon is located. Lined with cafés and restaurants, Mourillon Beach offers all the usual vacation pleasures. This is also the beach where the Sentier du Littoral (beach trail) begins. It heads to the Anse du Méjean by way of Cap Brun, where the charming hotel, Résidence du Cap Brun, is peacefully located. (see p 452). At the tip of this headland stands the **Tour Royale**, which dates from 1514 and was built to protect the port. This tower was equipped with cannons and also served as a prison. A little farther west is the **Fort Saint-Louis**, built in 1692 to guard the entrance to the sizeable harbour. Neither one of these strategic structures is open to the public.

Mont Faron Excursion

If travelling by car, follow the directions towards Mont Faron, which appear upon leaving the SNCF train station. A winding road leads all the way to the top, where there are beautiful lookout points. The summit can also be reached by cable car *(Tue to Sun 9:30pm to noon and 2:30pm to 7pm; Boulevard Amiral-Vence, ☎04.94.92.68.25).* **Please note:** the cable car is not in service when there are high winds.

Ath the summit, at an altitude of 500m (1,640 ft), there is a wonderful view overlooking Toulon and its harbour. A magnificent wooded park is perfect for a relaxing stroll; there are well-kept pathways, picnic tables and children's play areas.

There is also a **Zoo** *(☎04.94.88.07.89)* dedicated to the raising of fawns and a **Mémorial** to the Débarquement en Provence, the historic landing of the Allied Forces in 1944 along the coast of Provence *(entry charge; Tue to Sat 9:30am to 11:30am and 2:30pm to 7pm; ☎04.94.88.08.09).*

Leave Toulon by the D559 in the direction of La Seyne-sur-Mer, which occupies the eastern part of Cap Sicié.

La Seyne-sur-Mer

Fort Balaguier *(Wed to Sun 10am to noon and 2pm to 6pm, Jul and Aug 3pm to 7pm; Boulevard Bonaparte, ☎04.94.94.84.72)*, was built in the 17th century to defend the small harbour because of its strategic position overlooking it. Today, it houses a small naval museum where exhibitions are held.

By skirting the coast, you will then reach Tamaris, one of La Seyne's districts, where you can visit **Fort Napoléon**, also built in the 17th century. Travelling modern art exhibitions are featured here during the summer, as well as festivals.

Those who wish to spend some time on the beach should head to Les Sablettes, a maritime station after which the beach is named. This district also marks the entrance to the Saint-Mandrier peninsula. In our opinion, however, this place is hardly worth the trip.

Head southwest instead, toward the Notre-Dame-du-Mai chapel. You will thus cross what is known as the "Corniche Varoise." The little road is delightful and will lead you to Le Brusc and Île des Embiez by cutting through the pretty Janas forest.

Six-Fours-les-Plages

Occupying the western part of Cap Sicié, this "Station Voile" invites you to experience life as it is lived between the forest and the sea. In addition to Île des Embiez, its territory includes 1000ha (2,471 acres) of forest reserve and 18km (12mi) of coastline where fine-sand beaches alternate with hidden, rocky inlets.

You'd be correct in assuming that sports lovers are in heaven here. In addition to water sports, there are many trails you can take along the Sentier du Littoral or through forests made up of mimosas, broom, lavender, eucalyptus and pines of all sorts.

You can also take the trail used by pilgrims to the **Chapelle Notre-Dame-du-Mai ★**, built in 1653 on the summit of Cap Sicié. Overhanging the cliffs, it offers an impressive view that stretches from the Presqu'île de Giens to the Toulon harbour. There is a viewpoint indicator to help you get your bearings. Call ☎04 94 34 54 93 to find out when you can visit.

A heritage building since 1967, the **Chapelle Notre-Dame de Pépiole** (3pm to 6pm) dates back to the sixth century. Predating the

Romanesque, it has three apses and three juxtaposed naves, enhanced by a bell tower and bell. Its most modern sections date from the 12th century.

Île des Embiez

Park your car in the small Brusc district and take the small shuttle boat *(25F return trip; 10 min trip, departures every 30 min; ☎04.94.74.99.00)*.

This charming little island is perfect for walks along the flower-lined paths or the rough seacoast which hides small inlets suitable for swimming. In addition, there is a small tourist train *(19F)* that guides visitors across the island.

The Fort Saint-Pierre houses the **Institut Océanographique Paul Ricard** ★ *(20F; 10am to noon and 1:30pm to 5:45pm; ☎04.94.34.02.49)* that includes a Mediterranean aquarium and library. Temporary exhibitions with conferences and films are presented for the public with the aim of increasing their awareness of marine issues.

A tourist attraction of the first order, the ***Aquascope*** *(75F; duration: 35min, departures every 45min; ☎04.94.34.02.49)* invites you to discover the ocean beds as well as take a boat trip. This glass-bottom boat allows passengers to admire lush vegetation, which is a veritable oasis of life and a refuge for scores of herbivorous fish.

Sanary-sur-Mer

This seaside resort is certainly not without charm, mainly on account of a few ancient buildings around the port. Particularly noteworthy is the **Chapelle Notre-Dame-de-Pitié**, which dates back to the 16th century and looms over the port, giving you a lovely panorama on the bay.

Several pre-eminent writers have stayed in this village, including Aldous Huxley, Joseph Kessel and Jean Anouilh. But the village is primarily recognized for having been the refuge of a number of famous German writers during Hitler's reign, notably Thomas Mann, Ernst Bloch, Arthur Koestler, Bertolt Brecht, Franz Werfel and Herbert Marcuse.

Sports-car buffs won't want to miss the **Musée de l'Automobile Sportive** *(summer 9am to noon and 2pm to 8pm, off-season only on weekends and holidays; ☎04.94.29.63.63)*. To reach the museum, follow the signs on Route D559. The museum is near the A50. On the other side of the highway, the **Jardin Exotique et Zoo de Sanary-Bandol** *(Mon to Sat 8am to noon and 2pm until dusk, Sun 2pm until dusk; ☎04.94.29.08.59)* is sure to delight children, who will feast their eyes on the many species of birds and exotic plants featured here.

Bandol

Bandol's history started in 1594 when Henry IV had a fort built here, opposite the Île de Bendor.

In the 19th century, the village was populated primarily by coopers, the barrel-makers who produced the famous Bandol wine. The port served as a loading centre. Unfortunately, the arrival of the train and the diseases which struck the vines dealt a devastating blow to this flourishing port.

Today, Bandol has become the most important seaside resort on this part of the coast. It likes to consider itself a little Saint-Tropez, although it really hasn't attained this status yet. Also, the welcome here is not overly friendly.

The village, however is not devoid of charm: behind the port some pretty, narrow streets lie hidden. On the tiny square where the market is set up is the

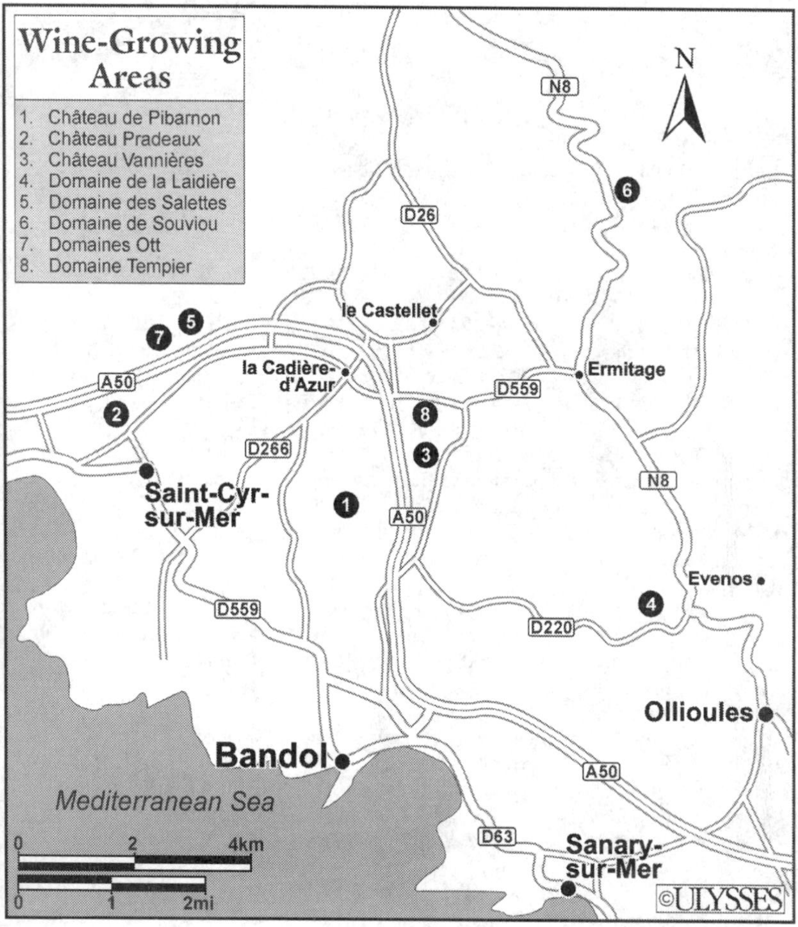

Wine-Growing Areas

1. Château de Pibarnon
2. Château Pradeaux
3. Château Vannières
4. Domaine de la Laidière
5. Domaine des Salettes
6. Domaine de Souviou
7. Domaines Ott
8. Domaine Tempier

N
N8
D26
le Castellet
la Cadière-d'Azur
Ermitage
A50
D559
D266
Saint-Cyr-sur-Mer
N8
A50
Evenos
D559
D220
Ollioules
Bandol
A50
Mediterranean Sea
0 2 4km
0 1 2mi
D63
Sanary-sur-Mer
©ULYSSES

Église Saint-François-de-Sales, built in the middle of the 18th century.

Lovely walks remain the primary interest in Bandol. By climbing the Allée Alfred Vivien, there is a very pretty view over the **Anse de Renecros**, a small bay with a beach which is found on the other side of the port. Up on the hill is also a very pretty hotel, the Ile Rousse (see p 453), which offers a splendid view over the bay as well as over Bandol's port.

Île de Bendor

Ferries every half-hour, every 15min in summer; last departures around midnight; car ferry weekdays between 8:30am and 11:30am.

Bendor was founded as long ago as the 12th century. In the 17th century, Count Robert, a thief and pirate, sought exile here. Later on, this little gem of an island was little more than a deserted rock.

This all changed in 1950, when Paul Richard purchased the island. It was then turned into a large garden, graced with multicoloured houses and a few superb hotels. Unfortunately, time has taken its toll on these

Bandol's Great Wines

Before Côtes de Provence wines gained recognition, Bandol wines were the only ones with a good reputation in the south of France. Today, one thing is still certain: some very great estates produce Bandol wines.

Bandol wines are essentially rosés or reds, but some whites are also produced. The reds are wines that must be kept in oak casks for a minimum of 18 months. They only reach full maturity after several years of aging.

There are three great estates truly worth visiting:

Le Domaine Tempier
9am to noon and 2pm to 6pm
Located a few minutes from Bandol on the road to Castellet, this esteemed estate has belonged to the same family since 1834 and produces a rosé wine as well as a very good red wine. You can taste and buy wine at the estate. It's always a pleasure to stop here because of the personalized and courteous service.

Le Château de Pibarnon
9am to noon and 2pm to 6pm
closed Sun
Comte de Saint-Victor
La-Cadière-d'Azur
☎04.94.90.12.73
⇌04.94.90.12.98
You have to follow a small winding road for several kilometres before arriving at the chateau. It may seem long, but it's worth it! The chateau is situated on an admirable site with a breathtaking view of the Var countryside. This is a first-rate establishment: the salesroom and tasting chamber are located in superb vaulted cellars that have been restored with great discrimination. With an unwavering reputation and highly praised by experts, the wines produced here measure up to the setting. The reds should be kept for a minimum of five years and are available in Québec.

Les Domaines Ott
Les Domaines Ott are three commonly owned estates, two of which produce *appellation contrôlée* Côtes de Provence wines and the third, *appellation contrôlée* Bandol wines. All three produce wines that have long been distinguished and never cease to amaze thanks to constant adherence to quality in their production. These are great wines (also more expensive) that are instantly recognizable by their striking unusually shaped bottles. These wines are always a pleasure to drink, in all of their varieties and colours!

Château Romassan (*appellation contrôlée* Bandol)
10am to 12:30pm and 2pm to 6pm (7pm in summer)
closed Sun
601 Route de Mourvèdes
Le Castellet
☎04.94.98.71.91
⇌04.94.98.65.44
The most recently opened of the estates (1956), Château Romassan has the greatest variety, offering six different vintages: three rosés, two reds and a white. The tasting chamber is located in very pretty, soberly restored, vaulted cellars. Wines produced here include a remarkable rosé, Coeur de Grain, and a highly prized red wine that improves over a long period.

Château de Selle (*appellation contrôllée* Côtes de Provence)
10am to noon and 2pm to 6pm
closed Sun
Route Départementale 73
Taradeau
☎***04.94.47.57.57***
⇌***94.94.47.57.58***
It was in Château de Selle, located in the centre of the Var near Lorgues, that Marcel Ott began operations in 1912. Four vintages were created here, two reds, a white and a rosé. Here, as at the Bandol estate, the Cœur de Grain rosé and the red wine aged for several years steal the laurels.

Clos Mireille
9am to noon and 2pm to 6pm (7:30 in summer)
closed Sun except in summer
Route de Brégançon
La Londe-Les-Maures
☎***04.94.98.71.91***
⇌***04.94.98.65.44***
Clos Mireille, the smallest of the estates, is located between Le Lavandou and Hyères. It only produces two white wines, one of which is the marvellous Blanc de Blancs, created in 1938. One of the great white wines, it's not to be outdone!

If you don't wish to tour the vineyards, there are two establishments on the same street as the tourist office that sell Bandol wines at estate prices and promote them through wine-tastings.

La Maison des Vins de Bandol
22 Allées Vivien
at the port
☎***04.94.29.45.03***
With exceptional kindness and lively enthusiasm, Michel will help you make finds among the producers who are members of the Syndicat des Domaines en Appellation Bandol Contrôlée. If, after tasting their wines, you would like to visit their vineyards, he can direct you thanks to the enormous map on the wall. A few suggestions: the rosé wines from the Domaines de La Laidière and Château Pradeaux, the white wine from Domaine des Salettes and the red wines from Château Vannière and Domaine de la Tour du Bon.

Le Caveau des Vins de Bandol
Allées Vivien
☎***04.94.29.60.45***
Practically next door, Le Caveau des Vins de Bandol offers a different selection of wines that come from wine-producers who are members of the Syndicat des Producteurs de Vins d'Appellation d'Origine Contrôlée Bandol.

buildings. Moreover, the island seems somewhat overbuilt. On the other hand, it does have a few lovely beaches—some sandy, some rocky—ideal for practising all kinds of water sports, as well as an international scuba-diving centre.

The Bandol Backcountry

Leave Bandol via the A50. Turn off the highway at Cadière-d'Azur. You can also opt for the more scenic D559.

A little farther north, is **Le Castellet ★**, a small, charming village whose lovely alleyways are worth exploring.

On the other side of the highway lies its twin town, La Cadière-d'Azur. What a lovely name!

La Cadière-d'Azur

Built high on a hill (144m or 472.4ft), La Cadière-d'Azur's construction dates from the Middle Ages, as the labyrinth of narrow streets attests. What's even more remarkable is that the village has been able to preserve its age-old charm.

Panoramic views can be had around the village. Under the exceptional light of Provence, the azur sky allows you to discover the luxuriant countryside of the Paluns plain and beyond towards the Sainte-Baume Massif. To the south, the Grand Vallat stream flows lazily through the plain and vineyards up to the Bandol Beach. Such luminosity, unhindered by fog and mist, has been immortalized by many famous painters, notably Van Gogh.

Finally, it would be a shame to visit La Cadière without stopping at the **Hostellerie Bérard** (see p 454 and 459). This exceptional place pairs culinary art with the beauty of Provence.

Take the D559 to Beausset.

Le Beausset is another little medieval village. On a little hillock right near the village stands the Chapelle du Beausset-Vieux, a Provençal, Romanesque-style, and rather sombre-looking chapel, the only trace of the original village. The hillock also affords a beautiful panorama of the surrounding area.

By heading back down towards the south, visitors will reach the village of **Évenos**, which has a lovely Romanesque church from the 13th century, dominated by the ruins of an old 16th-century chateau. From there, you can also take the 14km (8mi) return hike to the village of Sainte-Anne.

Farther south is **Ollioules**. It is primarily renowned for its **Gorges**, which were populated as early as prehistory and lie right nearby. The village was founded in the 10th century. Once again, there is both a feudal castle and a Romanesque–Provençal chapel here. Finally, Ollioules is also a starting point for pleasant walks in the area.

Cormorant

Outdoor Activities

Hiking

La Croix-Valmer

Park your car at the Gigaro beach.

A magnificent hike towards two capes situated southwest of the Presqu'île de Saint-Tropez, **Cap Lardier** and **Cap Cartay**, can be started from this spot. Small creeks and beaches can be discovered along the shoreline path. Allow about a half-day.

Hyères and its Islands

There are many opportunities for hiking in Hyères. First, there is the 17km (10mi.) tour of the Presqu'île de Giens, which takes approximately 5hrs. It begins at Madrague Beach and ends at Badine Beach. The best time of year to do this walk is mid-September, when some 1,500 pink flamingoes gather here.

It is also possible to circle the Île de Porquerolles on the Sentier du Littoral (28.5km or 17mi), which takes about 9.5hrs. While the northern part of the island is developed, the southern part is still wild and features spectacular settings.

Finally, the Sentier du Littoral that circles the Île de Port-Cros takes slightly less time. It takes approximately 5hrs to walk its 17km (10.6mi). Since Port-Cros is a national park, it constitutes a reserve for Mediterranean fauna and flora.

Toulon

Mont Faron is a marvellous place for hiking. The tourist office will give you a map of the trails at your request. The view from the summit is impressive. Looking towards the sea (south) it is not bad at all, but the north side is simply magical. It's so rugged and you can never tell when the mistral (wind) will begin to wail…

Bandol–Ile de Bendor

The tourist office in Bandol gives out maps of its backcountry trails, notably those that go to Cros Cerveau, the Massif de la Ste-Baume and the Gorges d'Ollioules.

Moreover, there is always the Sentier du Littoral—head from Anse de Renécros, in Bandol, to Lecques, located 11km (7mi) to the west. On your way you'll discover the port of Alon with its lovely creeks, and eventually you will reach **Pointe de la Fauconnière**, with its superb panorama of the Baie des Lecques, at the end of the walk. If you wish, you can take the bus from Lecques back to Bandol.

Also, the **Randonneurs Pédestres de Bandol** hiking club *(16 Rue Pons, ☎04.94.32.56.11)* organizes excursions every Friday throughout the year, except July and August. Registration takes place on Tuesday mornings between 9:30am and 11am at the Centre Nautique de Bandol. These excursions will better acquaint you with the region's charming inhabitants.

Finally, let's not forget the marked paths and trails officially designated "Grand Randonnées" (GR9, 90, 98, 99, 51 and 49). GR hiking guides, available in specialty bookshops, provide extensive details.

Bicycling

Le Lavandou

Many beautiful cycling or walking trips are possible in this area, around this seaside resort in the direction of Cap Bénat. Contact the tourist office for details.

Bicycle Rentals

Holiday Bikes
Avenue Vincent Auriol
☎04.94.15.19.99

Île de Porquerolles

This island was made for cycling. It's also a great way to reach the wonderful beaches and partake in various water sports, notably scuba diving and snorkeling. Bicycle rental is available at the landing site of the island:

Locavélo
☎04.94.58.33.03

Bandol–Île de Bendor

Bicycle Rentals

Holiday Bikes
127 Route de Marseille
☎04.94.32.21.89

Golf

Le Lavandou

Golf Club du Lavandou
Avenue de la Grande Bastide, Plaine du Batailler
☎04.94.71.88.28

La Garde (between Hyères and Toulon)

Golf de Valgarde
Les Castelles, Chemin de Rabasson
☎04.94.14.01.05

St-Cyr-sur-Mer

Golf de Frégate
slightly west of Bandol on Route D559
☎*04.94.29.38.00*
The Golf de Frégate is certainly one of the most beautiful golf courses in the region: the scenic views of the sea are extraordinary.

Scuba Diving

Îles d'Hyères is an extremely popular area for scuba diving because of the purity of the water and the variety of marine species found here.

Le Lavandou

Plongée C.I.P. Lavandou
Port of Lavando
Port parking lot, across from Lavandou Tourisme
☎*04.94.71.54.57*
⇄*04.94.15.13.09*
Plongée C.I.P. Lavandou offers initiation, shipwreck exploration and diving in the Îles d'Hyères.

Île de Porquerolles

Porquerolles Plongée
Carré du Port, Local 7
☎*04.98.04.62.22*
⇄*04.98.04.62.21*

Île de Embiez

Centre Plongée de l'Île des Embiez
☎*04.94.34.12.78*

Bandol–Île de Bendor

Centre International de Plongée Bendor
(international diving centre)
mid-Feb to mid-Dec
Île de Bandor
☎*04.94.29.55.12*

Centre de Plongée Bandolais
2 Boulevard Victor Hugo
☎*04.94.29.41.57*

Deep-Sea Fishing

Le Lavandou

ORCA
Quai Baptistin Pins
☎*04.94.71.69.07*
⇄*04.94.64.92.77*
You can fish for tuna, or simply enjoy a cruise on the *ORCA*.

Bandol

Hooker
19 Corniche Bonaparte
☎*04.94.29.46.93*
⇄*04.94.32.49.03*
Go fish for the big ones by renting a boat for the day *(4,500F-6,000F/pers.)*.

Sailing

Note that this region includes two areas labelled "Station Voile," guaranteeing ideal conditions for water sports.

Le Lavandou

École de Voile du Lavandou
Plage du Lavandou
☎*04.94.71.53.01*
☎*06.14.71.83.98*
The sailing school on the beach at Le Lavandou provides state-certified instructors for courses in windsurfing and sailing on dinghies or catamarans. Equipment rental on site.

Six-Fours-les-Plages (Station Voile)

La Cahute
23 Corniche du Cros
Le Brusc
☎*04.94.34.11.01*
La Cahute offers courses and rents equipment.

Bandol–Île de Bendor (Station Voile)

Société Nautique de Bandol
Port de Bandol
☎*04.94.29.42.26*
⇄*04.94.32.56.07*

Club Nautique de Bendor
Île de Bandor
☎*04.94.29.52.91*
Diving school.

Ecole de Voile L'Île du Fun
Île de Bandor
☎*04.94.32.46.56*
⇄*04.94.32.28.80*
Windsurfing boards are rented here.

Tennis

Le Lavandou

Tennis-Club du Lavandou
Avenue Vincent Auriol, 50m (164ft) from the beach
☎ ***04.94.64.83.79***

Bandol–Île de Bendor

Tennis Club de Bandol
every day 8am to 10pm
Avenue Albert 1er
☎ ***04.94.29.55.40***

Horseback Riding

Saint-Cyr-sur-Mer

Pian Cavale
Quartier de La Plaine–entre Bandol and Saint-Cyr
☎ ***04.94.26.69.32***
⇌ ***04.94.25.09.64***

Aeronautical Sports

Le Castellet

Aéro Club du Soleil
Aérodrome du Castellet
☎ ***04.94.90.70.50***

Race Track

Le Beausset

Circuit Paul Ricard
R.N.8
☎ ***04.94.90.74.27***
⇌ ***04.94.90.72.75***

Accommodations

Le Rayol-Canadel

Les Mimosas
250F-290F, ½b 360 F
ps, P
Route de la Môle
☎ ***04.94.05.61.06***
By taking the road toward La Môle, you will quickly reach Les Mimosas, a small and very quaint family-style hotel. Somewhat old-fashioned perhaps, but that's what makes it so charming! It is nonetheless very well-kept and clean. The bar and dining room (family-oriented and serving Provençale cuisine) are particularly French. Without being too far from the sea, you will still get a taste of the backcountry away the brash tourism of the Côte d'Azur. Please note: the hotel doesn't accepts credit cards.

Le Lavandou

Camping de Pramousquier
May to Sep
☎ ***04.94.05.83.95***
⇌ ***04.94.05.75.04***
Located 400m (1,313ft) from the easternmost of Le Lavandou's beaches, Camping de Pramousquier has 180 campsites, many of which are in the shade, and a restaurant as well. You can get to the city centre from here by taking the small *Plages* train which travels through the 12 beaches, departing from Pramousquier.

Le Lavandou–plage d'Aiguebelle

Le Grand Pavois
470F-550F, ½b 400F-450F wine included
pb, P, ℜ, ≈
Plage d'Aiguebelle
☎ ***04.94.05.81.38***
⇌ ***04.94.05.81.38***
The hotel Le Grand Pavois is run by a dynamic manager who has renovated it. The comfortable rooms are tastefully decorated and have balconies. Although the hotel doesn't directly overlook the sea, an underground passage links it to a sandy beach. This is well-appreciated by those visitors travelling with children. In any event, the small road in front of the hotel is a dead-end, so clients can enjoy relative tranquillity facing the sea. The Provençale meals are prepared by the owner himself.

Les Roches
2,200F-3,000F, 3,800F-6,200F suite or apt., bkfst incl.
closed mid-Oct to Easter
pb, tv, ℝ, ≡, ℜ, ≈
One Avenue des Trois Dauphins
☎ ***04.94.71.05.07***
⇌ ***04.94.71.08.40***
Les Roches is one of the Côte d'Azur's most luxurious hotels under the Relais et Châteaux banner. The establishment is right on the sea front, as is its swimming pool and magnifi-

cent dining room. Each room has a balcony or terrace and white bathrobes in the lavatories. Guests can also reach the hotel by boat. It coasts about 500F per person to dine here.

Le Lavandou–plage de Saint-Clair

Auberge de La Falaise
355F-385F/pers. ½b plan only
closed Nov and Dec
pb, tv, P, ℜ
at the beginning of the Saint-Clair Beach
☎04.94.71.01.35
≠04.94.71.79.48

With only a small road separating it from the sea, this simple, family-run inn offers personalized service as well as comfort. Some of the rooms at the Auberge de La Falaise have a view of the sea, as does the terrace where breakfast is served. Finally, the evening meal, served in a dining room with rustic decor and large picture windows, is inspired by Provençal, home-style cooking.

Hôtel Tamaris
450F-500F
from Easter to Oct
pb, tv, P
☎04.94.71.79.19
≠04.94.71.88.64

Hôtel Tamaris, in a higher category, is a large hotel complex. The two-storey buildings are typical of motels in Provence. Rooms on the main floor have small terraces, while those on the second floor have balconies. The rooms are clean and appropriately furnished, and there are two restaurants nearby.

Le Lavandou–Centre

L'Auberge Provençal
170F-300F
Closed Jan to mid-Feb
pb/sb, tv, ℜ
11 Rue Patron Ravello
☎04.94.71.00.44
≠04.94.15.02.25

This hotel is located in the heart of the pedestrian centre, in one of the oldest houses in Le Lavandou. This admittedly unpretentious hotel is maintained by a charming young man whose parents run the very pleasant restaurant, La Favouille (see p 455), in the street behind it. Since they have private bathrooms, the more expensive rooms are more comfortable. The main advantage of this hotel is that, though situated in the most attractive part of the city, it is still only minutes away from the beaches. The inn's restaurant serves regional specialties (*bourride, aïoli*), either on the terrace or in its inviting dining room.

L'Auberge de la Calanque
570F-800F
650F-1,200F with ½b
Mid-Mar to Oct
pb, ≡, tv, ℝ, *P,* ≈, ℜ
62 Avenue du Général de Gaulle
☎04.94.71.05.96
≠04.94.71.20.12

This grand hotel sails above the fray. When you arrive in the city centre by way of the seashore, L'Auberge de la Calanque is so imposing that it's hard to miss. The vast, airy lobby is followed by a series of lounges. Large picture windows open onto lush gardens where the swimming pool is located and also onto the sea, of course. What's more, it's undergone major alterations in recent years to meet new European standards. Martine Dalpossa, the charming owner, must be very happy to have the hassle of renovations behind her. We're anxious to see what the future holds for this magnificent hotel, now that it has been restored to its former glory, especially since it was already quite pleasant and comfortable. Lastly, the hotel includes a restaurant that specializes in seafood.

Bormes-les-Mimosas

Camping Clau Mar Jo
Apr to Sep
895 Chemin de Bénat
Bormes-Les-Mimosa
☎04.94.71.53.39

Located approximately 1km (0.6mi) from the beach, this campground has the advantage of being near Cap Bénat, an ideal place for bicycling or hiking. Although it's small, with only 71 campsites, it has a restaurant.

Grand Hotel
210F-400F
closed mid-Nov to mid-Dec
pb, P, ℜ, K, ℜ
167 Route du Baguier
☎04.94.71.23.72
⇌04.94.71.51.20
North of the village, perched up high, is the Grand Hotel. This establishment has been completely renovated and offers a very pretty view over the Côte d'Azur. Certain rooms even have a balcony. Just a few minutes from the village, an old-fashioned cosy atmosphere reigns in this haven of peace and calm. This hotel offers both good value and a warm welcome. There is also a restaurant on site *($; closed Sat).*

Villa Naïs
290F bkfst incl., ½b obligatory in Jul and Aug, 300F/pers.
≈, P, pb, ℜ
☎04.94.71.28.57
⇌04.94.71.64.39
Located on the N98, in the heart of the Massif des Maures, the Villa Naïs is a *table d'hôte*, or residence that rents out rooms. It is located in the backcountry, near Bormes-Les-Mimosas, so you're just a short distance from the sea, with the hills of the massif at your feet. Monsieur and Madame Devos guarantee a pleasant stay in this pretty villa, that has both a pool and a tennis court. Madame Devos cooks up delicious food. Upon request, Monsieur Devos, a fisherman, can take you tuna fishing. A good place to admire the wild beauty of the Maures in a pleasant setting.

Hyères

The most beautiful campgrounds are in the Hyères administrative district, since they're often located beside the sea and are the best equipped. Moreover, there are nearly 50 campgrounds in this area, so you'll have your pick. Alternatives can be found in the surroundings of Le Lavandou or Sanary-sur-Mer.

Presqu'île des Giens

Camping Le Pinède
Apr to Sep
268 Boulevard Alsace Lorraine
☎04.94.58.22.61
⇌04.94.65.39.42
Camping Le Pinède has 120 campsites that are only 150m (492ft) from the beach, a grocery store and a restaurant.

Camping International La Réserve
Apr to Sep
1737 Route de la Madrague
☎04.94.58.90.16
⇌04.94.58.90.50
In addition to 160 campsites, Camping International La Réserve has a grocery store, a restaurant and a bar. Some organized activities and entertainment are also offered.

Plage des Salins

Camping Port Ponthuau
Apr to mid-Oct
101 Chemin des Ourlèdes
☎04.94.66.41.17
⇌04.94.66.33.09
An immense campground with 380 sites, located 1km (0.6mi) from the beach, Camping Port Ponthuau offers a plethora of activities: miniature golf, tennis, pool, volleyball and movies. Grocery store and restaurant on the grounds.

Camping Rebout
Apr to mid-Oct
Clos Rose-Marie B.P. 30
☎04.94.66.41.21
⇌04.94.66.40.41
On a more modest scale than Camping Port Ponthuau, with only 54 campsites, Camping Rebout understandably offers fewer activities and less entertainment. Nevertheless, it has a grocery store, a pool and tennis courts.

Hôtel du Portalent
170F-280F
pb
4 Rue de Limans
☎04.94.65.39.40
⇌04.94.35.86.33
This small and modest hotel, found in the heart of the medieval district, is undergoing constant renovations to improve it. There is no restaurant, but they can guide you to the best addresses in the area.

Hostellerie Provençale la Québécoise
280F-410F, ½b obligatory in Jul and Aug 340F-385F
ps or pb, ≈, ℜ
20 Avenue de l'Amiral-Costebelle
☎04.94.57.69.24
⇄04.94.38.78.27

The most noticeable address in Hyères is the Hostellerie Provençale la Québécoise. It is located 3km (1.9mi) south of the city-centre, direction Almanarre, towards the D559. Half-way between Hyères and the sea, there is a sign marking the way to this lovely hideaway. The owner—no prizes for guessing that she's from Québec—greets guests with a warm welcome. Rooms are pretty and very clean. Meals are served on a large terrace next to a magnificent over-grown garden with a swimming pool and the sounds of birds singing. This is an ideal spot to relax for a few days. What's more, it is a good base from which to make excursions in the area, notably the Îles d'Hyères. Excellent value.

L'hôtel du Soleil
340F-390F
pb
Rue du Rempart
☎04.94.65.16.26
⇄04.94.35.46.00
soleil@hotel-du-soleil.fr

L'hôtel du Soleil is very close to the city-centre but in fact is quite peaceful due to its location on the hillside *(access from Place Clémenceau)*. Once settled in, you can reach the Massillon square by way of the crooked lanes behind it—lots more fun! The hotel is now under the aegis of new owners, friendly Belgians. Moreover, the hotel seems to reflect the dynamism of its new boss, who has become president of the Association des Hôteliers de Hyère since his arrival. This is a simple, charming place that offers a good quality to price ratio. Half-board is available for an additional 120F per person.

Îles d'Hyères

Île de Porquerolles

L'Augerge des Glycines
790F-890F/pers., ½b plan mandatory in summer
pb, tv, ≡, ℝ
Place d'Armes
☎04.94.58.30.36
⇄04.94.58.35.22
www.porquerolles.net

This inviting hotel is located next to the church on the Place d'Armes, the nerve centre of the island. The rooms are tastefully decorated in a refined Provençal style, and the modern bathrooms are well equipped. But L'Augerge des Glycines has a surprise in store for you—once inside it, you'll discover the pretty garden where meals are served (see p 456) in spring and summer. Moreover, since the establishment is located at the quieter end of the square, it offers true tranquillity. During low season, the hotel offers 5-night, half-board packages at a very attractive rate: 1390F per person.

Hôtel et Residence Les Mèdes
900F-950F
Closed Nov to Jan, except Christmas holidays
pb, tv, ≡, K, ℝ
Rue de la Douane
☎04.94.12.41.24
⇄04.94.58.32.49
www.hotel-les-medes.fr

The Hôtel et Residence Les Mèdes offers rooms of two types: normal hotel rooms and, at a slightly lower rate, residential ones (minimum two-night stay), which provide access to a kitchenette, but lack daily housekeeping service. Recently built, the rooms offer all the modern conveniences. Also, the very generous breakfast buffet is served on a sunny veranda. Other pluses are a children's playground and a garden with tables shaded by parasols, where you can relax.

Le Mas du Langoustier
1,100F-1,650F; 3,330F-4,485F for 5-day ½b package off-season
closed mid-Oct to Apr
pb, ℜ, ≡, tv
☎04.94.58.30.09
⇄04.94.58.36.02
www.langoustier.com

For those interested in the ultimate in luxury, head for Le Mas du Langoustier. This beautiful, entirely renovated establishment is located at the end of the island in an area where the beauty of the forest and

La Môle

Auberge de La Môle
$$-$$$
closed mid-Nov to mid-Mar
Place de l'Église
☎04.94.49.57.01
L'Auberge de La Môle has a very good reputation in the area. The restaurant features specialties from the southwest of France, such as *confit de canard* (conserve of duck), *cassoulet* (stew of beans, pork, goose, etc.). Please note: the restaurant doesn't accept credit cards.

Le Lavandou

La Favouille
$$
Mar to Oct
9 Rue Abbé Hélin
☎04.94.71.34.29
Françoise, the restaurateur at La Favouille, plies her trade with grace and *savoir-faire*. She greets you with a personal invitation into her home. There is nothing forced or selfish about her smile. It comes from the heart, but it also stems from confidence in her product. Wait until you taste her *anchoïade*, which is overflowing with fresh vegetables—enough to feed a regiment; but more importantly, the dressing tastes sublime! Apart from this, the menu features good grilled fish, a *marmite du pêcheur* and the traditional *aïoli*. In short Françoise is completely authentic. And what better quality could you ask for in a restaurateur?

Massif des Maures

The Route des Crêtes is a spectacular area to tour. Since you have to refuel from time to time, why not take advantage of the occasion to try a *real* table d'hôte, a convivial way to dine in a local's home? Most tables d'hôte are slightly out of the way, and reservations are required, since the majority of them function on demand. You should also know that the menu is predetermined and features fresh, natural, home-grown products. You can't get any closer to the land than that! Lastly, everyone usually eats together, seated communally around a large table. Here are the telephone numbers for two such establishments:

Clos Charlot
☎04.94.71.62.90

La Colline
☎04.94.64.82.87

Le Relais du Vieux Sauvaire
$$
Easter to Sep
Route des Crêtes
☎04.94.05.84.22
⇌04.94.15.21.02
If the conviviality of tables d'hôte doesn't appeal to you, or if you're travelling with children, Le Relais du Vieux Sauvaire is a good alternative. Its home-style cooking is simple and includes pizza as well as fish cooked in salt or *bouillabaisse*. Everyone in the family will be satisfied.

Bormes-les-Mimosas

Lou Cantoun de Mireïo
$
Place Gambetta
☎04.94.71.27.80
This is a small, pleasant *crêperie* where you can enjoy a crepe and salad meal that won't take too much time and can be eaten on the terrace. The restaurant's name, Lou Cantoun de Mireïo, indicates that the cook's first name is Mireille.

Lou Poulid Cantoun
$$
Apr to Sep
6 Place Lou Poulid Cantoun
☎04.94.71.15.59
How enchanting it is to eat in a garden in full bloom! This is exactly what you'll do at Lou Poulid Cantoun. A good place to eat in Bormes, it is located on one of the town's most inviting plazas.

Lou Portaou
$$-$$$
closed Nov to Feb except during Christmas holidays and Tue
One Rue Cubert des Poètes
☎04.94.64.86.37
⇌04.94.64.81.43
This restaurant is simply magical! First, there's the name of the street that it's situated

on: Cubert des Poètes. But the most sensational aspect is the fact that the terrace occupies a vaulted, stone passageway with a ceiling of exposed wooden beams and joists. This is a unique place that embodies all the charm of old Bormes. The place settings are attractive and the short menu of Provençal dishes is very appealing. Finally, just next door, the restaurant owners run a wonderful shop that sells antiques and decorative objects.

Hyères

Pastry Shop–Caterer
at the beginning of Avenue Gambetta, going towards the old city
☎04.94.01.46.46
This place comes highly recommended and you won't be disappointed! The quality is exceptional, whether you have a hankering for something sweet or savoury. So if you crave a wee bite to eat…

La Bergerie
$
16 Rue de Limans
☎04.94.65.57.97
For crepes and home-made ice cream: La Bergerie.

Le Bistrot de Marius
$$
closed Nov and Jan
One Place Massillon
☎04.94.35.88.38
In old Hyères, on a lovely square, is Le Bistrot de Marius, a quaint little restaurant worth trying. Why? Good food and good value for the money, especially the *lotte rôtie à l'ail* (garlic-roasted monkfish) with *confit de légumes*.

Le Jardin
$$
noon to midnight
19 Avenue Joseph Clotis
☎04.94.35.24.12
Located across from the city hall, this small restaurant has an adorable, shady terrace. Moreover, Le Jardin's extensive opening hours can be handy. Fish dishes and salads are served here, and wine is available by the glass.

La Brasserie des Îles
$$-$$$
☎04.94.57.49.75
On the harbour, a very pleasant place in the warm weather, you'll find La Brasserie des Îles, which was completely renovated. Now featuring a huge glassed-in area, it's the perfect spot to watch all the activity in the port and is very popular with the locals. The prices are fair, given the quality of the food and the cost of the renovation. The menu includes tasty fish dishes like a *loup* and mullet combo served with *langoustine* (a small variety of lobster) coulis; spit-roasted monkfish with a three-herb sauce and a thick piece of turbot *en bourride* (in aïoli sauce with spices and herbs).

Les Oubliettes
$$-$$$$
Carrefour Saint-Gervais, going towards Toulon
☎04.94.35.64.19
This restaurant qualifies as a tourist attraction, since its design was inspired by medieval prisons, called *oubliettes*. Admittedly, this is a theme restaurant, but the concept has been well executed. The atmosphere is in keeping with the theme and the food is grilled over wood fires and served on trenchers. One of a kind!

Les Jardins de Bacchus
$$$-$$$$
closed Sun night and Mon
32 Avenue Gambetta
☎04.94.65.77.63
Provençale cuisine served in a modern decor. Specialties include *galette de St-Jacques* with leek and *Rossini de pigeonneau* in truffle sauce, and *cappercino de raviole de homard aux truffes et parmesan*.

Îles d'Hyères

Île de Porquerolles

L'Auberge des Glycines
$$-$$$
Place d'Armes
☎04.94.58.30.36
The restaurant of this inn (see p 450) specializes in local Provençal cuisine, of which the *dorade farcie à la porquerollaise* (stuffed sea bream) is a good example. On the

whole, the menu emphasizes fish and seafood. We particularly enjoyed the fish soup and its *rouille*. Other suggested dishes make use of *pistou*, a Provençal delicacy, and you can have *tagliatelles*, or tuna enhanced by this marvellous condiment. Finally, the experience is enhanced by the pleasant garden where you can dine. Ah, summer!

Auberge L'Arche de Noé
$$-$$$
Apr to Oct
Place d'Armes
☎04.94.58.33.71
Place d'Armes, the nerve centre of Porquerolles, is bordered by a multitude of restaurants. Which should you choose? L'Arche de Noé is located next to a butcher's store–delicatessen. Specializing in grilled fish, *bouillabaisse* and other *bourrides*, this restaurant has a terrace that opens onto the square.

Le Mas du Langoustier
$$$$
May to mid-Oct
☎04.94.58.30.09
The restaurant of this deluxe hotel (see p 450) enjoys one the best reputations in the region. Justifiably so, for it offers fine dining in extremely pleasant surroundings: an enormous sunroom with its doors thrown open in summer. Of course, the service is of the high calibre found at most great restaurants. The chef is one of the modern generation of gourmet cooks who believe in combining foods that while light, are bursting with flavour. And, as always in this part of the country, fish holds the place of honour on the menu. So why not let yourself be tempted by one of the chef's combinations: sauteed red mullet (nothing is more emblematic of Provence!), almond puree and salad with tomato conserve and purslane!

Toulon

The old town has undergone a number of changes and has become quite pleasant—just like the warm welcome that awaits guests in the local establishments. We made two new finds near the opera house.

Le Petit Prince
$$
closed the first two weeks of Aug
10 Rue de l'Humilité
☎04.94.93.03.45
First of all, Le Petit Prince is one of the new arrivals on the Toulon scene. In a very tasteful, contemporary Provençal decor, the pretty young proprietress welcomes guest with an irresistible smile, while her husband prepares what will later appear on your plate. Undeniably alluring. They serve traditional cuisine like *fois gras* and *confit de canard maison*, as well as delicious homemade frozen nougat *coulis de fruits rouges*.

Au Sourd
$$-$$$
closed Sun and Mon
10 Rue Molière
☎04.94.92.28.52
Secondly, Au Sourd, is a local institution that prides itself on being the oldest restaurant in Toulon. The menu consists mainly of fresh fish caught by local fishes. The prices indicated are for 100-gram portions. Selections include *loup*, John Dory and a *bouillabaisse toulonnaise*.

La Chamade
$$$
closed Sun and the first half of Aug
25 Rue Denfert Rochereau
☎04.94.92.28.58
Madame Bonneau's welcome radiates charm, while Monsieur devotes himself to creating a memorable impression of La Chamade's food. The setting is classic but intimate.

Along the port, there are a number of restaurants which, while not outstanding, are nevertheless perfectly acceptable, especially considering their reasonable prices.

Le Grand Café de la Rade
$$
224 Avenue de la République, Carré du Port
☎04.94.24.87.02
One of these is the trendy Le Grand Café de la Rade. Everything is plentiful and filling, in the Alsatian tradition. Especially good is the

Flammenküche (one portion is ample for two!). Try the *choucroute alsacienne* (Alsatian sauerkraut). There is a large terrace over-looking the port and the service is efficient and courteous.

Herrero
$$
45 Quai de la Sinse
☎04.94.41.00.16
If you're in the mood for fish, Herrero is the place to go. 110F will get you some *parillada* (grilled fish), a tasty Spanish specialty. You can also have *bouillabaisse* and *bourride toulonnaise*.

Sanary-sur-Mer

Hôtel-Restaurant Bon Abri
$-$$
closed Jan and Mon, Oct to June
94 Rue Pasteur
☎04.94.74.02.81
≠04.94.74.30.01
At Hôtel-Restaurant Bon Abri, their chief concern is creating home-style cooking that uses as many local products as possible. So, in accordance with the region, the menu includes many fish dishes. The ace in the hole of this hotel restaurant (see p 453) is its terrace in a rear courtyard—utterly peaceful and shaded by 100-year-old plane and palm trees.

Hôtel-Restaurant Le Castel
$$$
closed the last two weeks of Oct and Jan
925 Chemin de la Canolle (between Sanary and Bandol)
☎04.94.29.82.98
≠04.94.32.53.32
What strikes you as you enter the restaurant at Hôtel Castel is the unusual country-style decor with orange-and-blue tablecloths. It's a change from the customary Provençal decor and is very pretty. This restaurant's regional, home-style cooking is so good it has kept the same clientele for years.

Bandol

Au Fin Gourmet
$-$$
16 Rue de la République
☎04.94.29.41.80
For fish and seafood, try Au Fin Gourmet. The midday menu includes two courses for 79F and *moules-frites* (mussels and fries) are 45F. The chef will even prepare bouillabaisse ($$$) if ordered ahead of time.

L'Oulivo
$ lunch, $$ dinner
closed Sun
19 Rue des Tonneliers
☎04.94.29.81.79
This restaurant is hidden away in the city-centre along a small side street, west of the Place de l'Église is L'Oulivo. A friendly ambience reigns in this pleasant bistro whose owner, Marc, does the cooking, while Véronique welcomes the guests. This is one spot to recommend to all those who would like to experience the charm of the Var people. It is well away from the touristy parts of town, and the prices offer good value.

Auberge du Port
$-$$$
9 Allée Jean Moulin
☎04.94.29.42.63
Auberge du Port overlooks the port. This spot is highly recommended by locals and by Bandol's culinary connaisseurs. Its cuisine is supervised by a chef from Île Rousse. The restaurant is known for its oysters, paellas and, of course, for its fish. The full-course menu is 120F.

Les Oliviers
$$-$$$$
☎04.94.29.33.00
Les Olivier, the restaurant in the Île Rousse Hotel is a shrine dedicated to fine dining and exceptional ambiance. Everything here is top-notch: the magnificent terrace overlooking the **Baie de Renécros** and the quality of the food. Sure it's more expensive, but the location is so spectacular that the prices are justified, especially since it is unusual to find a restaurant in a grand hotel that lives up to the quality of the accommodations. See p 453.

Those who appreciate creative vacations, take note!

The charming owner of this establishment, Madame Bérard, offers **Provençal cooking courses** *(package includes five nights accommodation with four days of classes; year-round)* with her husband-chef. Classes are held in a pretty cottage tastefully redone to preserve its old Provençal style. You can also stay here (four superb rooms are available). Ravishing! Students go to the port to meet fishers then pick your fish, visit the markets together, collect herbs on the hills and learn to prepare the authentic regional cuisine. A special course on cooking with truffles is offered in January. *(Information from: Hostellerie Bérard, 83740 La Cadière d'Azur, ☎04.94.90.11.43, ⇄04.94.90.01.94).*

La Cadière d'Azur

Hostellerie Bérard
$$$-$$$$
closed Mon midday only
☎04.94.90.11.43
If travelling inland between Toulon and Bandol, under no circumstances should visitors pass up the opportunity to enjoy a meal at the Hostellerie Bérard. The restaurant proposes four set-price menus: *"marché"*, *"saison"*, *"gourmand"* and "dégustation". René Bérard prepares light cuisine of the highest quality, where the flavours of only the finest ingredients reign. What's more, Danièle Bérard who reigns in the dining room, will help you choose wisely, since she's very knowledgeable about René's cooking. And, she's also very involved in his search for innovative combinations. She's definitely no slouch! So, it should come as no surprise that there are more new creations to be discovered every visit. Just consider the divine purple artichoke *millefeuille* and *foie gras au jus à la barigoule* or the steamed *fin St-Pierre* in zucchini flowers with *concassé de pomme d'amour* (tomatoes), served with vegetable tempura, drizzled with fresh coriander bouillon; or the rhubarb fritter accompanied by exquisite rose petal–flavoured *glacé*! What else is there to say about this place, except that it borders on addictive? If only all addiction was like this, how beautiful life would be! *Peuchère* (you can say that again!)!

Entertainment

To find out about all the touristic and cultural activities taking place in this region, visit the Web site: ***www.cg83.fr***.

Cavalaire-sur-Mer

Les Estivales
all summer
Concerts and shows held at the Esplanade du Port.

Rayol-Canadel
Soirées Musicales du Domaine du Rayol
Jul and Aug
Classical music.

Le Lavandou

Free shows and concerts take place in Lavandou from mid-July to mid-August.

Le Flamenco
with one drink 100F
every night 11pm to 5am
☎***04.94.71.13.37***
Boulevard du Front de Mer
Discotheque. Live entertainment starting around 1am is often presented.

Bormes-les-Mimosas

Mimosalia
Jan
Mimosa festival.

Grand Corso Fleuri
Feb
Parade with allegorical floats.

Soirées Musicales de Bormes
Jul
Information
☎***04.94.71.15.08***
Both classical music and jazz are featured.

Hyères

Coupe du Monde de Funboard
Mar
Funboard World Cup.

Festival de Jazz
last 15 days of Jul
Information
☎***04.94.35.90.81***
This jazz festival is held in the pine grove at the racecourse.

Bars and Casinos

The Night
every day 9pm to dawn
Avenue 1er Division Brosset
☎***04.94.65.54.21***
The Night has a dance floor with live music, as well as a piano bar, and holds theme nights.

Le Loft
In the beach complex at the Hyères port
☎***04.94.57.57.49***
Le Loft has a very attractive setting with an unbeatable view of the port. Musical variety and a diverse clientele.

Casino des Palmiers
every day noon to 4am
Avenue Ambroise Thomas
☎***04.94.12.80.80***
The Casino des Palmiers features a restaurant, a bar and a private club, as well as gambling.

The New Dream
every night 10pm to 4am off-season, Fri to Sun
Port de la Capte
☎***04.94.58.00.07***
Discotheque with theme nights and snack bar.

Toulon

Festival de Musique de Toulon
all summer
Music festival.

Jazz à Toulon
Jul
Jazz festival.

Danse à Châteauvallon
Jul
Dancing in Toulon's backcountry.

Salon des Beaux-arts
Oct
Art exhibition.

Salon des Antiquaires
Dec
Antiques.

Bars

Le Magot
every day until 5am
3261 Avenue de la Résistance, Cap Brun
☎***04.94.27.08.55***
Le Magot is a piano-bar with a giant tv screen. Karaoke.

Gay Bars

Le Boy's Paradise
every day 11pm to dawn
One Boulevard Pierre Toesca
☎***04.94.09.35.90***
Le Boy's Paradise is a cabaret and nightclub on two storeys. Show nights.

Le Pussycat
entry with one drink weekdays 50F, Sat 60F
11pm to dawn, closed Mon and Tue
655 Avenue de Claret
☎***04.94.92.76.91***
Popular club-discotheque for a lesbian clientele. Live entertainment.

La Seyne-sur-Mer

Fête de la Mer et des Pêcheurs
late Jun
Celebrates fishermen and the sea.

Festival des Arts et de la Poésie
Jun
Art and poetry.

Festival de Jazz
beginning of Aug; Fort Napoléon
inquiries at the tourist information centre

Le Joker
cover charge plus a drink: 80F, free cover Wed, Thu and Sun
every day 11pm to 5am
Les Sablettes
☎04.94.87.25.70
Discotheque. Activities on Fridays.

Six-Fours-les-Plages

Les Voix du Gaou
last two weeks of Jul
World music.

Sanary-sur-Mer

Floralies
May
This biennial flower show began in 1995.

La Fête des Pêcheurs
Jun
Fishermen's festival featuring terrific *bouillabaisse.*

Bandol

Printemps des Potiers
Easter weekend
☎04.94.29.37.35
Pottery.

Fête des Vins
first Sun in Dec
The year's vintage is celebrated with great pomp, featuring many organized events surrounding Bandol wine-tasting.

Casino
4pm to 4am
☎04.94.29.31.31
Roulette, black jack, craps and slot machines are available. Plus, two bars and a restaurant open at night and a club *(from 11pm).*

La Cadière-d'Azur

Fête des Vendages
Sep
Grape Harvest Festival.

Défilé de Santons
Dec
Procession with manger statues.

Shopping

Îles d'Hyères

Île de Porquerolles

Boucherie Traiteur
Place d'Armes
☎04.94.58.30.81
This small, inviting store is very lively. People crowd inside it to find something to snack on or ingredients for a meal. Choices range from take-out dishes and sandwiches to cold cuts, cheese and olives.

Bandol

Caves de la Poste
157 Avenue du 11 Novembre
☎04.94.29.45.27
⇌04.94.32.36.23
This is a place that wine-lovers will enjoy. Caves de la Poste sells the best vintages from all regions of France. Of course, you can also find good wines from Bandol here. The emphasis is on *can*, because the new vintages of Bandol wine are often sold in advance, and the remaining bottles sell out quickly. There are also Provençal products in Bandol style such as tapenade (delicious) or *anchoïdiade* made with wine from Bandol and Bandol wine conserve, a kind of alcoholized grape jelly. Hic!

Plan du Castellet

Domaine Tempier
9am to noon and 2pm to 6pm
☎04.94.98.70.21
⇌04.94.90.21.65
The wines of Bandol are renowned all over the world, and the region is abounding with wineries. One of our particular favourites is the Domaine Tempier. Located a few minutes from Bandol on the road to Castellet, this vineyard has belonged to the same family since 1834 and boasts an excellent reputation. They make very good red wine, as well as rosé. You can sample and purchase their products on the premises. The courteous, personalized service makes it a pleasure to stop by.

Le Beausset

Domaine de Souviou
closed Sun except in high season
Route National 8
☎04.94.90.57.63
⇌04.94.98.62.74
The exquisite oil produced by Domaine de

Souviou is used by the greatest restaurateurs, notably those of the Hostellerie Bérard and La Bastide de Moustier. There are 3,000 olive trees of six different varieties on the estate. Olive picking is done by hand between November and January. Souviou oil comes exclusively from the first cold pressing, so only the purest elements remain. With an acidity of less than 1%, it is an "extra virgin" oil. Of the three varieties of oil produced here, the "Olea Plinia" is excellent for salad dressings. The estate also produces good Bandol wines, in particular, a *rosé*.

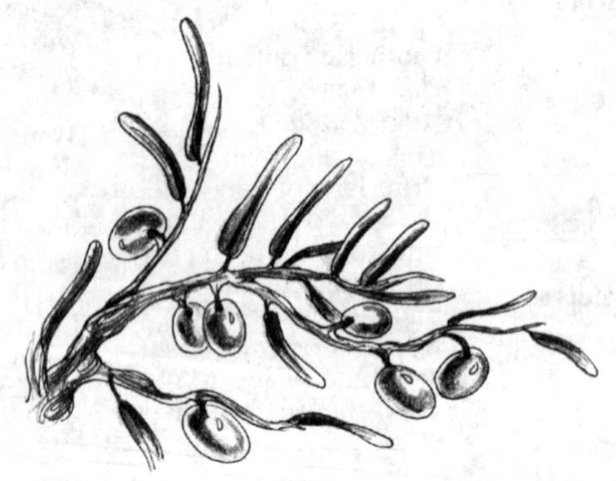

The Var Backcountry and the Gorges du Verdon

The Var covers a large part of the Côte d'Azur. Highway A8 is an east-west axis that cuts through the area, separating it into two equal parts.

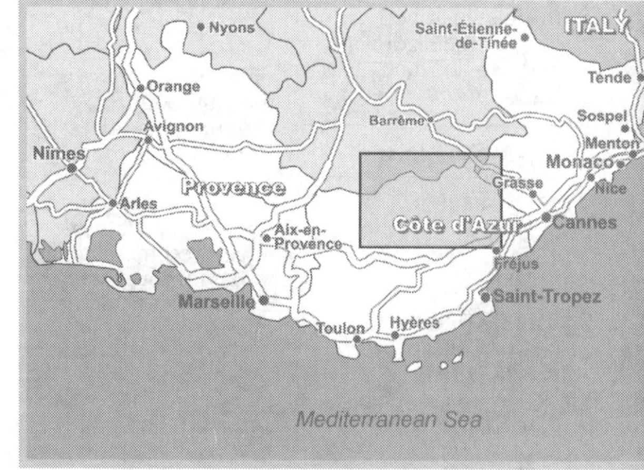

The Var backcountry is the Provençal countryside north of the highway, or Provence Varoise, characterized by the serenity of its cultural heritage sites, of which the Abbaye du Thoronet is undoubtedly the most important.

But the Var backcountry is also defined by the Verdon River, by the wild beauty of its gorges, Grand Canyon and impressive cliffs known as the Falaise des Cavaliers. The Verdon empties into a huge artificial lake whose brilliant colour wavers between emerald green and turquoise. An entire village was sacrificed to create this lake, which is actually a reservoir built to provide the region with a supply of potable water.

Finding Your Way Around

The train isn't the best way to get to this region. It stops in only two cities, Draguignan and Brignoles. The diversity and vast beauty offered in the Var can best be appreciated by car. Rentals are available in any large city on the Côte d'Azur (see the "Practical Information" section for each city).

There is, of course, bus service to link the villages; most of these busses leave from Draguignan or Brignoles. However, If you choose this option, you will be at the mercy of fixed bus schedules and limited to the routes available.

We propose a tour by car that covers the entire region. This tour, in the form of a loop, begins in the east, climbs north, traverses the Alpes-de-Haute-Provence from east to west and then descends southwards again. This tour will take about four days to complete, depending on how much time you wish to spend on outdoor activities when you get to the Verdon's gorges and Lac de Sainte-Croix.

By Train

There are only two SNCF train stations in the territory:

Gare SNCF de Draguignan
Avenue du Maréchal-Gallieni
☎***08.36.35.35.35***

Gare SNCF de Brignoles
Avenue de la Gare
☎***08.36.35.35.35***

By Car

The Var can be reached easily from anywhere in Provence or the Côte d'Azur. The A8 Highway crosses the entire territory and connects Menton to Aix-en-Provence. The suggested itinerary begins in the small village of Les Arcs, which has its own highway exit. From here, a multitude of small departmental roads lead to just about everywhere in the territory.

Draguignan

Emergency car repairs
24hrs a day
Var Dépannages
☎04.94.68.70.73

By Bus

The two main transfer points are at Draguignan and Brignoles. These two cities provide access to a vast network of routes, served by numerous companies. The only disadvantage is that, although Draguignan and Brignoles are the largest cities in the territory, they have little to offer. It can be somewhat tiresome having to pass through these cities to get to other places that are more interesting to visit.

In any case, get a **bus schedule**, called the *Indicateur des Lignes Routières Départmentales du Var,* which is available at the tourist office in any of the towns or villages that the bus serves. It contains all the information you need to plan your trip.

Finally, there are direct coach services from Draguignan to the Nice or Toulon airports *(for information in Draguignan: Comité Départemental du Tourisme, ☎04.94.50.55.50).*

Draguignan

Gare routière
parvis des Droits de l'Homme
☎***04.94.68.15.34***

Brignoles

Transvar (autocars)
☎***04.94.28.93.28***

Practical Information

Tourist Offices

Les Arcs-sur-Argens
21 Boulevard Gambetta
☎/⇄***04.94.73.37.30***
www.ville-lesarcs.com

Draguignan
Avenue Lazare Carnot
☎***04.98.10.51.05***
⇄***04.98.10.51.10***
www.ville_draguignan.fr
Here you can pick up all the information you need for your trip, including lots of pamphlets that cover the region as well as the whole country and beyond. The friendly, courteous staff know the city and the area very well, and are extremely helpful.

Fayence
☎***04.94.76.20.08***
⇄***04.94.84.71.86***
www.mairie-fayence.com

Castellane
B.P. 8 Route Nationale
☎***04.92.83.61.14***
⇄***04.92.83.76.89***
www.castellance.org

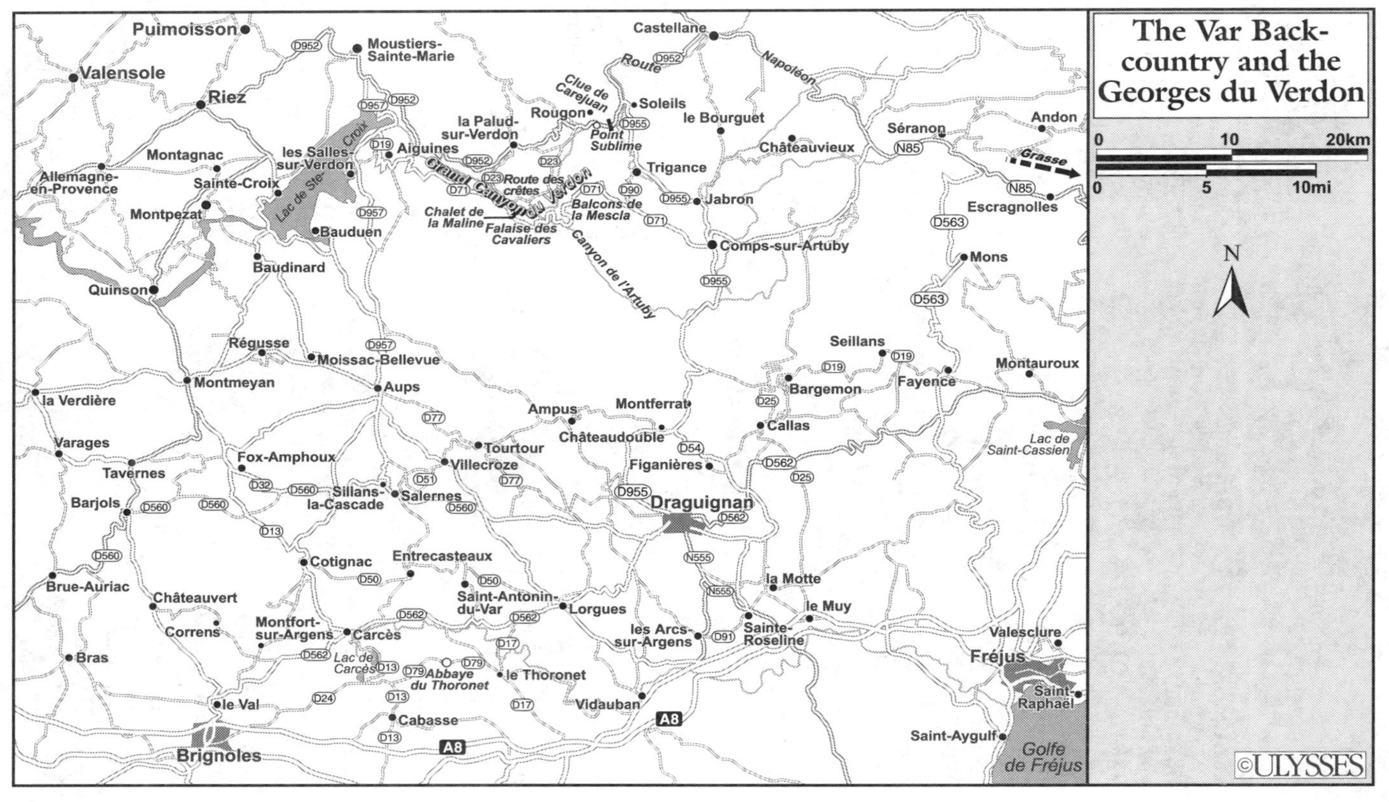
The Var Back-country and the Georges du Verdon
0
10
20km
0
5
10mi
N
©ULYSSES
Puimoisson
Valensole
Riez
Moustiers-Sainte-Marie
Montagnac
Allemagne-en-Provence
Sainte-Croix
Montpezat
les Salles-sur-Verdon
Lac de Ste-Croix
Aiguines
Bauduen
Baudinard
Quinson
la Palud-sur-Verdon
Rougon
Clue de Carejuan
Point Sublime
Grand Canyon du Verdon
Route des crêtes
Chalet de la Maline
Falaise des Cavaliers
Balcons de la Mescla
Canyon de l'Artuby
Castellane
Route Napoléon
Soleils
le Bourguet
Trigance
Jabron
Comps-sur-Artuby
Châteauvieux
Séranon
Andon
Grasse
Escragnolles
Mons
Seillans
Fayence
Montauroux
Bargemon
Callas
Lac de Saint-Cassien
Régusse
Moissac-Bellevue
Montmeyan
Aups
la Verdière
Varages
Tavernes
Barjols
Fox-Amphoux
Sillans-la-Cascade
Salernes
Villecroze
Tourtour
Ampus
Châteaudouble
Montferrat
Figanières
Draguignan
Cotignac
Entrecasteaux
Saint-Antonin-du-Var
Lorgues
Brue-Auriac
Châteauvert
Correns
Montfort-sur-Argens
Carcès
Lac de Carcès
Abbaye du Thoronet
le Thoronet
les Arcs-sur-Argens
Sainte-Roseline
la Motte
le Muy
Vidauban
Bras
le Val
Brignoles
Cabasse
Valescure
Fréjus
Saint-Raphaël
Saint-Aygulf
Golfe de Fréjus
D952
D957
D19
D23
D71
D90
D955
N85
D563
D25
D54
D562
N555
D91
D77
D51
D560
D32
D13
D50
D17
D79
D24
A8

Trigance
☎*04.94.76.91.01*
⇌*04.94.76.92.44*

Le Verdon
83630 Aiguines
☎*04.94.70.21.64*
⇌*04.94.84.23.59*
www.verdon-provence.com

04120 Castellane
☎*04.92.83.67.36*
⇌*04.92.83.73.11*

Moustiers-Sainte-Marie
June 15 to September 15 (morning and evening)
☎*04.92.74.67.84*
⇌*04.92.74.60.65*
www.ville.moustiers-sainte-marie.fr
Rest of the year, 2pm to 4pm
Town Hall
☎*04.92.74.66.19*

Aups
Place Frédéric Mistral
☎*04.94.70.00.80*
www.aups98.citeweb.net

Tourtour
Hôtel de Ville (city hall)
☎*04.94.70.57.20*
⇌*04.94.70.53.42*

Salernes
Place Gabriel Péri
☎*04.94.70.69.02*
⇌*04.94.70.73.34*

Barjols
Boulevard Grisolle
☎*04.94.77.20.01*

Cotignac
2 Rue Bonnaventure
☎*04.94.04.61.87*

Entrecasteaux
Syndicat d'Initiative
☎/⇌*04.94.04.40.50*

Lorgues
Place d'Antrechaus
☎*04.94.73.92.37*

Brignoles
Maison du Tourisme de La Provence Verte
Carrefour de l'Europe
Brignoles
☎*04.94.72.04.21*
⇌*04.94.72.04.22*

Tourist Office
Hôtel de Clavier
☎*04.94.69.27.51*

Emergencies

Draguignan

Emergency Medical Service in Draguignan
24 hrs
☎*04.94.67.01.01*

Local Police
Mairie (town hall) Annexe–Rue Notre-Dame-du-Peuple
☎*04.94.60.61.60*

Brignoles

Hospital
☎*04.94.72.66.00*

Post Office

Draguignan
Boulevard Maréchal Joffre
☎*04.94.50.57.35*

Exploring

This tour begins at the exit for "Les Arcs" on A8.

Les Arcs sur Argens

This quaint Provençal town is located between the Mediterranean and the Alps. The town lies in the shadow of the old medieval village, perched high upon its rocky peak. Traces of that medieval era still remain, including the surrounding wall and the old 12th-century castle with its impressive watchtower. Today, the old castle is a hotel with lots of character.

Explore the narrow streets and vaulted staircases of the old village, where there are many gorgeous houses. Fans of painter Ludovico Brea will find a Gothic reredos by this artist in **Église Saint-Jean-Baptiste**.

Leave the village by D91, towards Sainte-Roseline.

Sainte-Roseline

The **Château Sainte-Roseline** is a vineyard that produces Côtes-de-Provence wines. Wine-tastings are possible here.

The history of the château goes back to the 12th century, when it was an abbey. At the beginning of the 14th century and for about two centuries, it became the only Carthusian convent for women in the Var.

Only the **chapel** ★ *(Tue to Sun 2pm to 7pm, winter until 5pm; ☎04.94.99.50.30)*, listed as a historic monument in 1980, is open to visitors. It houses Sainte-Roseline's tomb, as well as, a baroque retable and the works of several artists, including a mosaic by Chagall, a bronze lectern by Giacometti and stained-glass windows by Raoul Ubac and Jean Bazaine.

Continue along D91 to N555, which leads to Draguignan.

Draguignan

This city's origins are said to date back as far as the 2nd century BC. In AD 843, Provence was annexed to the Holy Roman-German Empire, and Draguignan subsequently became a *cité comtale*. At the end of the Middle Ages, it acquired royal status after France took control of Provence.

Today, it is a rather unattractive town with little to offer visitors. The municipality has, however, set a huge rehabilitation program in motion meant to revitalize this old town. In summer, a host of activities are organized: festivals of all kinds, shows and other events.

The city itself is not so attractive, but it does have a nice museum. The **Musée des Arts et Traditions Populaires** ★ *(20F; Tue to Sun 9am to noon and 2pm to 6pm closed Sun am; 15 Rue Roumanille, ☎04.94.47.05.72)*, is dedicated to the arts and popular traditions of central Provence. It is located on an ancient religious site, and is dedicated to preserving the Provençal heritage. Regional history will unfold before your eyes when you see, among other things, the reproduction of an oil mill and of a Provençal kitchen.

The **Musée Municipal** *(Mon to Sat 9am to noon and 2pm to 6pm; 9 Rue de la République, ☎04.94.47.28.80)* lays claim to, among other things, a few paintings by Rembrandt and a beautiful marble statue by Camille Claudel.

Tour de l'Horloge

Finally, before setting off from Draguignan, take a stroll over to the **Tour de l'Horloge**, one of the most important vestiges of Draguignan's heritage. It was erected on a plateau, which affords interesting views of the surrounding area. Moreover, at the foot of the tower lies the **Théâtre de Verdure**, a peaceful garden area. Right next to it stands the Provençal, Romanesque-style **Chapelle Saint-Sauveur**, which, like the tower, dates from the 13th century.

Leave Draguignan via the D955 for Châteaudouble.

Châteaudouble

Those with a little time to spare should make a brief stop here. The road leading to the village is very pleasant. A veritable eyrie whose entrance is cut right out of the rock, the village overlooks the **Gorges de la Nartuby**, listed as a historic monument. Visitors can wander the streets at will, for no thoroughfare runs through the village. The houses were recently restored in order to preserve the medieval character of the village.

Also, the village has a few small squares with traditional Provençal fountains. One of these, Place Vieille, with a splendid view of the countryside, is home to a pleasant guest house with its own restaurant (see p 478).

Finally, lovers of the outdoors can make the most of the dozens of kilometres of trails that criss-cross the region and run all the way to the Gorges. You can also go rock-climbing, swimming or trout fishing in the Gorges.

Leave Châteaudouble to meet the road to Callas.

Église Notre-Dame-de-Montaigu

Callas

This quintessentially Provençal village was founded in the 11th century. Almost a thousand years old, it is composed of vines and olive trees; the Moulin de Callas produces very good oil (see p 494, "Shopping"). Provençal charm prevails here thanks to the tall, ancient houses, small flowered squares and surrounding hills covered in pine, olive and oak trees. Also worth a look here are the **ruins of the Pontevès nobility's old château**, which was torched by the villagers in 1579 during a revolt. The newly restored **Église Romanesque Notre-Dame** is also a pretty sight.

Take the D25 to Bargemon.

Bargemon

You can make a quick stop in this other little Provençal village to check out the vestiges of its medieval wall, whose two towers are still standing: the Tour de l'Horloge and Tour du Clos. Also worth seeing is the small **Église Notre-Dame-de-Montaigu**, which houses a beautiful gilded baroque-style altar.

Take the D19 toward Seillans.

Seillans

The road between Bargemon and Seillans is spectacular and leads to one of the most beautiful towns in France. An air of mystery surrounds this hillside town. It could be its picturesque streets lined with high narrow houses, its church or its castle that creates this impression of travelling back to the Middle Ages. The **Église Saint-Léger** and the castle date back to the 11th century, which is also when the first houses began to appear around the castle.

Notre-Dame-de l'Ormeau is an 11th-century chapel that was rebuilt in the 13th century in a very Spartan-Romanesque style. It is 1km (0.6mi) from Seillans, on Route de Fayence. Historians believe that the village was first set up here around this chapel in the 11th century. The chapel contains several works sure to be of interest to fans of religious art. Those interested in visiting the chapel should make inquiries at the village's tourist information centre.

Fayence

Fayence was home to the bishops of Fréjus from the 18th century up until the French Revolution, when they relinquished their seigneurial rights over the village. The old village is still a maze of narrow streets, leading up to the bishops' castle at the top of the hill. Below the village, a

13th-century fortified door called the **Porte Sarrasine** still stands.

Because of its geographical location overlooking the plain, Fayence became a paragliding centre after World War II. It now enjoys international fame.

For a short hike, head from Fayence towards its twin village **Tourettes**. Just before Tourettes is the **Église Saint-Jean-Baptiste**. This church, built in 1750, has a beautiful high altar of pink, grey and white marble. In Tourettes itself stands **Notre-Dame-des-Cyprès**, a pretty 13th-century Romanesque chapel.

Leave by the D563 towards Mons.

Mons

This is the Fayence region's most northern hillside village, with an elevation of 800m (2,625ft). It was completely repopulated by the Genoese after the plague of 1348 wiped out all its inhabitants.

An interesting thing to note: in Provençal villages, the street signs give the Provençal translation below the French name. In Mons, the order is reversed.

Église Notre-Dame was built in the 13th century beside the seigneurial castle, which was later destroyed. It's worth visiting this church to see its three reredos.

Place Saint-Sébastien, at one end of the village, offers a lovely panoramic view. Thanks to the viewpoint indicator found here, you can better visualize and understand your location in terms of the regional geography. This indicator also shows suggested short walks. Finally, the tourist office is just at hand.

Bargème

This 12th-century medieval village is ranked among the most beautiful villages in France. A heritage site, it also has the highest elevation of all the villages in Var (907m or 2,977ft). In fact, it is a typical Provençal village with all the region's characteristics: it is perched on a rocky peak for better protection against the enemy, fortified by walls (of which a few vestiges remain) and dominated by a castle and a church.

The **Château de Pontevès** was destroyed during the Religious Wars, but its silhouette can still be discerned thanks to the square dungeon and a few round towers which have survived.

The **Église Saint-Nicholas** is a 12th-century Romanesque church whose baptismal font dates back to the first century. It also contains a 16th-century retable.

The best way to appreciate this type of village is to stroll through it at a leisurely pace with no particular goal in mind, exploring whichever narrow streets and turnings that happen to catch your fancy.

Take the D563 northbound to Route Napoléon, or N85, which leads to Castellane.

The Route Napoleon is the road that Napoleon and his army travelled on foot to get from Golfe-Juan, on the Côte d'Azur to Grenoble, in the Isère. However, there are few points of interest along this segment of the road.

Castellane

This town is in the department of Alpes-de-Haute-Provence, halfway between the Mediterranean and the Alps. Castellane, a stone's throw from the Gorges du Verdon, is a typically Provençal village with its narrow streets, small squares, fountains and a main square shaded by century-old plane trees. The town is dominated by a gigantic rocky peak, from which the Notre-Dame chapel seems to keep a benevolent watch over the village. The sight is quite stunning. It is undoubtedly because of these features that Castellane is counted among the "Villages et Cités de Caractère."

The **Église Saint-Victor**, with its strikingly simple and modest façade, was built in the 12th century. The church's architecture is an interesting example of the transition between Romanesque and Gothic art. It was designated as a historic monument in 1944.

The rocky peak can be reached by a footpath that begins behind the church. The path is easier than it looks. It winds among the remains of the ancient fortification walls that surrounded Castellane in the 14th century and leads to **Chapelle Notre-Dame-du-Roc**, which has been a pilgrimage site since ancient times. Each year, on August 14th, the townspeople hold a Veillée aux Flambaux, a spectacular illuminated evening procession to the chapel.

Castellane is also characterized by the untamed nature that surrounds it and protects it from pollution and noise. There is nothing but fresh air, open spaces and sunlight. Hiking, horseback riding, hunting and fishing are only some of the activities that can be enjoyed.

Leave via D952 towards Gorges Du Verdon to Point Sublime on the north bank of Gorges du Verdon.

Point Sublime

Point Sublime offers a striking view of the entrance to Verdon's Grand Canyon. This site offers the most tourist facilities in the immediate area, including parking, telescopes, and documentation as well as an inn. From here you can get to the **Sentier Martel**, a trail considered the *grande classique* (great classic) of hikes. It is 14km (8.7mi) and about 8hrs on foot to the Chalet de la Maline. It's a good idea, however, to do it the other way around. For a shorter hike, try the **Sentier du Couloir Samson**, which goes down to the bottom of the Gorges and can be completed in 2hrs. This trail gives a good perspective of the Gorges.

Gorges du Verdon

The Gorges and their Grand Canyon are two of Europe's largest natural sites. They are definitely must-sees. There are trails on the right (north) and left (south) banks. No matter which side you choose, the view is equally spectacular and both trails end at Moustiers-Sainte-Marie. We recommend the left bank, even though it offers fewer spectacular vantage points, because it allows the possibility of visiting Trigance and Aiguines. Of course, you could always cover both sides by going full circle on the trails. This 130km (80.8mi)-trip takes an entire day and can even begin from Nice or Cannes, since the Gorges are only one and a half hours away by car.

For the right bank tour, go up to the D952.

The **right bank tour** starts at the Auberge du Point Sublime on D952. At the beginning of the tour, a secondary road leads to **Rougon**. The trip up to the village guarantees an exceptional view of the Verdon River. Back on D952, there is an intersection just before La Palud. Take this road, the D23, or Route des Crêtes. There are several lofty viewpoints in succession along this road, that forms a loop which ends at La Palud. This is an ancient supply-village with a few stores and hotels (see Restaurants and Accommodations sections in this chapter).The Refuge de la Maline, along this road is the suggested departure point for the hike along the Martel trail to Point Sublime.

To finish the tour, take D952 again; there are

panoramic views all the way to Moustiers.

End of the right bank tour.

The left bank tour starts with a tour of the village of Trigance. To get there, take D955 at Pont-de-Soleils, and then follow D90.

Trigance

This old village was built way up high on the rocky spur of a mountain at an elevation of 800m (2,625ft). It is dominated by a fortress that dates back to the 11th century, which is now a hotel belonging to the *Relais et Châteaux* association. Stroll through the village and discover its vaulted passageways, sculpted-stone lintels and 12th-century Romanesque church.

The ancient fortress is only open to guests who are staying there. Its terrace offers gorgeous views of the area. You can also eat in the castle's beautiful vaulted medieval dining room (see p 489). Of course, some may find it a bit expensive!

If plants and herbs interest you, you can meander along the fragrant path that starts at the city hall. Markers along it will introduce you to the scents of thyme, savory and lavender. It continues onto a botanical path, also marked, which is part of the Parc Naturel Régional de Verdon.

Trigance is a good place to stay overnight since both banks of the Gorges du Verdon can be easily reached from here.

Take D90 south to D71, which leads to the left bank of the Gorges.

The **left bank tour** is called the Sublime Corniche. It begins with the **Balcons de la Mescla**, where the Verdon and Artuby rivers meet. The view is spectacular. The road continues past a succession of magnificent lookouts culminating at the **Falaise des Cavaliers**, which is most impressive. The **Hôtel du Grand Canyon** (see p 482), has a captivating view over the Gorges, from the rooms as well as the restaurant. Several hiking trails on both the left and right banks can be reached from this point via a footbridge. You'll then reach the Refuge de la Maline and the trailhead of the famous Sentier Martel.

The trail follows the Gorges and ends at Aiguines. End of left bank tour.

Aiguines

At an elevation of over 800m (2,625ft), Aiguines offers a spectacular view of **Lac de Sainte-Croix**, the 3,000ha (7,413 acre)-artificial lake that provides Aix, Toulon and Marseilles with drinking water. The main attraction in this village, besides its church and private castle is the **Musée des Tourneurs sur Bois** (*☎04.94.70.20.89*), a lathe artisans' museum.

Take D19 towards Lac de Sainte-Croix, then D957 to D952 leading to Moustiers-Ste-Marie.

Lac de Sainte-Croix

Route D19 descends towards the lake and offers superb panoramic views. At the lake, the scenery becomes even more spectacular, especially where the Verdon empties. The water takes on every shade ranging from emerald to turquoise. A few resorts offering all kinds of water sports line the shore.

Moustiers-Sainte-Marie

Moustiers is also called the pearl of Provence and the doorway to the Gorges du Verdon. This village, famous for its earthenware, has a serene and remarkably vast landscape.

The village, divided in two by a rushing mountain stream, embraces the mountain on either side. The exposed rock of the mountain and the bridges that span the torrent as a constant reminder of the rushing water, make it an interesting place for a stroll. Most of the houses along the narrow village streets date back to the 18th century. There are also many restaurants and boutiques which sell, among other things, the village speciality: world-famous **Moustiers** earthenware. Pottery-lovers will want to visit the **Musée de la Faïence** (*Apr to Oct, Wed to Sun 9am to noon and 2pm to 6pm; in the crypt near the church, ☎04.92.74.61.64*), an earthenware museum.

In the village, **Église Notre-Dame** is worth seeing. It dates back for the most part to the 12th century. Its highlight is its Romanesque Lombard-style bell tower.

Those up for more of a challenge can walk up to the **Chapelle Notre-Dame-de-Beauvoir**. Overlooking the village, the chapel offers a magnificent view of the rooftops. It includes a Romanesque section with a single nave built in the 12th century, to which two Gothic bays were added in the 16th century.

On the weekend following Pentecost *(between mid-May and mid-Jun, depending on which date Easter falls)*, the village turns into a two-day international earthenware forum for the Fête de la Cité de la Faïence (earthenware city festival). Clad in 18th-century garb, the villagers go up the path leading to the Notre-Dame-de-Beauvoir chapel to attend high mass. For the entire weekend, the village revels and bustles with festivities of all kinds for young and old alike.

Les Salles-sur-Verdon

This village, the youngest in France, was founded in 1973 to replace the old village that was inundated when the lake was created. Fans of the great outdoors who come here for water sports are sure to enjoy themselves.

Continue southward on the D957. On the way to Aups, you can take a small detour to Bauduen, another resort by the lake.

Bauduen

This small village is particularly bright and sunny. Before the creation of the lake, the village lay 1km (0.6mi) from the Verdon River. It now lies at its base and came close to being engulfed. In Roman times, it was a stopping place on the Roman road that linked Fréjus to Riez, now "on the other side of the lake," since the lake's creation.

The narrow streets climbing up to the medieval church make this a typical Provençal village. The church affords a panoramic view of the Maures and the lake.

If you feel like taking a dip, you'll be happy to hear that the lake's water is even warmer than the Mediterranean's.

Return to the D957 and continue toward Aups.

Aups

Even though this town is located in the lower foothills of the Alps, Aups is only 60km (37.3mi) from the sea. This is a good place to stop a while and stroll through the old picturesque streets and discover many of the characteristic features of Provençal towns, such as the old wash house, fountains, plane trees, sundials, and the clock tower.

Art lovers should visit the **Collégiale Gothique Saint-Pancrace** *(summer, 9am to noon and 4pm to 6pm; off-season, 9am to noon and 3pm to 5pm; Rond-Point du Général-de-Gaulle, ☎04.94.70.00.53)*. This Provençal–Gothic church was established in 1489 and suffered some setbacks during the course of its history. This explains why its admirable original portal had to be redone and why it includes the Renaissance style. Also of interest here is the **Musée Simon Segal** *(summer; Avenue Albert 1er, ☎04.94.70.01.95)*, set up in the former Chapelle des Ursulines, which was built in 1629. The museum features works by different artists from Toulon, Paris and Bourges.

Gourmets shouldn't miss the **Marché aux Truffes Noires**, the truffle market held in Aups every Thursday morning between November and February. The truffles are sniffed out by well-trained dogs.

Leave the town by D7 towards Tourtour.

Tourtour

The road to Tourtour is splendid. From a rocky peak, the village (which is one of the most beautiful in the country) looks over a sea of hills. In the 12th century there was a castle, now in ruins, and like all medieval villages, a church. **Église Saint-Denis** replaced the medieval church and offers a superb view of the entire area, stretching all the way to the coast.

Tourtour is a nice place for a quiet walk, but offers no other points of interest. You can take a leisurely stroll and even relax on one of the terraces on the main square in the centre of the village.

Leave by D51 towards Villecroze.

Villecroze

This village is in the lower foothills of the Alpes de Provence at an elevation of 350m (1,247ft). Its narrow streets and picturesque archways preserve Villecroze's medieval character.

Overhanging a beautiful park are the **caves** ★, which are definitely worth a visit. The villagers used to take shelter here whenever there was an invasion. There is also a subterranean lake that provided them with water.

Continue on D51 towards Salernes, then take D560 towards Sillans-la-Cascade (famous for canoeing and rafting), and continue towards Fox-Amphoux, accessible via D32.

Salernes

This village is not particularly attractive. It is primarily known for its tiling industry, which began with the production of *tomettes*, small red hexagonal floor tiles commonly used in Provençal homes between the 17th century and 1945. These days, though the industry still exists, the tiles produced are really rather plain.

Leave via the D560 toward Sillans-la-Cascade.

The waterfall (*cascade*) is sure to captivate athletic types, who can enjoy canyoning here. Canyoning is a variant of rafting, where aficionados must work their way down the river with the help of a rope!

Continue along the D560 toward Fox-Amphoux, accessible via the D32.

Fox-Amphoux

This charming old village has remained virtually unchanged. Tucked high up on a ridge, it has been spared the usual invasion by the tourist industry. The little shaded square is truly adorable. It also has a hotel that offers a pleasant place to stop, as you can find absolute tranquillity here (see p 491).

The village's setting remains untamed and natural making it a nice spot to explore on foot.

Go back on D560 to get to Barjols.

Sillans-la-Cascade

This other medieval village is mainly renowned for its famous waterfall. It is easily accessible for the whole family by way of a bucolic, 800m (2,626ft)-long path which starts near the entrance to the village and is lined with enormous, 100-year-old plane trees. The 42m (138ft) **waterfall** ★ plunges into a small, bubbling, emerald–coloured lake.

Barjols

The name of this village comes from the words *barre* (hills) and *joulx* (beautiful). The village does not live up to its name; however, a few sites are worth visiting.

The **Collégiale Notre-Dame-de-l'Assomption** is a designated historic monument. Dating back to the 11th century, this church was built in a Gothic-Provençal style. Behind the Collégiale is the residence of the Pontevès, the entrance of which is marked by a **stone porch** (another historic monument), built in 1532. This town has no fewer than 30 fountains and 12 wash houses.

Each year, the village holds a leather fair *(Aug)* to commemorate the great prosperity brought here by this industry in the 18th century. Today, only a few abandoned tanneries remain.

Leave by D560 towards Cotignac.

Cotignac

Built at the foot of a cliff crowned by two towers, vestiges of the former 15th-century château, this village has lovely alleyways, fountains and a superb central square, pleasantly shaded by numerous plane trees.

You can enjoy a pleasant walk up toward the cliff, along an alley lined with ruined houses. Pierced with caves, the cliff once served as a shelter.

Take the D50 to Entrecasteaux.

Entrecasteaux

Entrecasteaux is an authentic Provençal town with a small river winding its way through the lush, gently rolling hills.

The imposing mass of a castle dominates the valley. Its origins date back to the 11th century, but it has been pillaged many times and undergone successive transformations over the centuries. Very dilapidated by time, it was purchased in 1974 by a wealthy British citizen who hoped to save it. This monstrously huge undertaking swallowed up his entire fortune. Today, it's been restored, although it would take considerably more money to get it back into good condition.

The brand-new owner hopes to do just that. For now, the castle is not open to the public, but it's possible that it will be, once the task of renovating it is completed. Ask at the Syndicat d'Intiative *(☎04.94.04.40.50)* before going. This tourist bureau also organizes guided tours of the village.

The château has a restaurant, and it will soon offer lodging.

The town, a designated historic site, is a beautiful little collection of old houses with high narrow façades, pretty 17th-century porches and vaulted passageways. The Saint-Sauveur fortress-church dates back to the 13th century.

For a walk in the refreshing country air, follow the marked trails.

Leave via D50 towards Lorgues.

studio apartments that have separate living rooms, kitchenettes and private terraces with tables for dining outdoors. These studio apartments accommodate up to four people and are rented by the week in July and August. The hotel also has a restaurant (see p 488).

Moulin de la Camandoule
600F-760F/pers. ½b mandatory except in low season
Chemin de Notre-Dame des Cyprès, between Fayence and Seillans
☎04.94.76.00.84
⇌04.94.76.10.40
Located in a restored former oil mill, in the heart of a peaceful 4ha (10 acre) park, this charming hotel will delight you with its character. All we can say is that you're guaranteed first-rate service in every respect. As a bonus, the hotel has two enchanting suites with loft bedrooms. In addition to the gourmet restaurant (see p 488), there is another that offers poolside dining.

Seillans

Hôtel-Restaurant des Deux Rocs
300F-600F
closed Nov
pb, ℜ
☎04.94.76.87.32
⇌04.94.76.88.68
Hôtel-Restaurant des Deux Rocs enjoys an exceptional view of the lush surrounding countryside. It occupies an old, middle-class house that, while a bit old-fashioned, is full of charm. Decorated with antique furniture, the rooms have character, especially those in the front that look out over the two rocks and the square, which is dominated by a pretty Provençal fountain. You can dine on the square (see p 488) by candlelight at tables set up under trees and around the fountain. Magical!

Montauroux

Hostellerie de Montauroux
500F
pb, ≡, tv, P, K, ≈, ℜ
7 Rue Eugène Second on the square in the city centre
☎04.94.39.12.00
⇌04.94.39.12.01
The Hostellerie de Montauroux offers studio apartments that are spacious, (45m² or 472 sq ft), bright, well equipped (VCR, stereo) and comfortably furnished. Also, as of summer 2001, the hotel plans to have a swimming pool. Some of the apartments have terraces with stunning views of the neighbouring hills. Ideal for longer stays, especially since it has a restaurant *($$)* on site.

Montferrat

La Bastide des Moines
280F-300F
pb, tv, ℜ, P
☎04.94.70.92.09
⇌04.94.70.92.41
Located on the road from Draguignan to the Gorges du Verdon, this hotel is set in a rustic, 12th-century home. Renovated in 1992, it offers all the comforts necessary for a pleasant stay.

Bargemon

Hôtel-Restaurant Auberge des Arcades
250F-300F
pb/sb, tv, P
Avenue Pasteur
☎04.94.76.60.36
⇌04.94.76.68.33
Hôtel-Restaurant Auberge des Arcades is the ideal place to stay in this small medieval village. The rooms are simple but comfortable. The hotel also has a restaurant *($$-$$$)* that serves truffles in season, and where you can dine on a shaded terrace in summer.

Comps-sur-Artuby

Grand Hôtel Bain
265F-415F
closed mid-Nov to Christmas
pb, P, ℜ
☎04.94.76.90.06
⇌04.94.76.92.24
This hotel has been in the Bain family for 260 years. Today, three descendants and their spouses carry on the tradition. The facade of the Grand Hôtel Bain is invitingly well-kept, as are the rooms. Also, in the bar, you can overhear discussions carried on by the regulars as they sip their drinks. In short, this is the sort of unpretentious, family-run hotel that exudes authenticity. And

Verdon is just next door. Since this establishment is beside the street, ask for a room in the back. It's also possible to dine here (see p 489).

Séranon (between Castellane and Grasse)

L'Aigle d'Argent
220F to 240F, ½b 480F-500F
closed Jan
La Clue, RN85
☎04.93.40.56.80
⇄04.93.60.35.15
In the middle of nowhere, this hotel on Route Napoléon, L'Aigle d'Argent will do for one night. The inn has decent rooms and a restaurant, but nothing more.

It must be added that there are many restaurant-inns on Route Napoléon, but all are subject to noisy traffic.

Mons

Petit Bonheur
140F-230F
ps or pb
Place Frédéric Mistral
☎04.94.76.38.09
For a quiet but not luxurious place to stay, stop at the Petit Bonheur. The hotel offers a Provençal atmosphere and beautiful views over the surrounding area. The village is charming and the hotel rates are quite reasonable. Also, the hotel has a restaurant *($$, closed Wed in low season)* with a pleasant terrace on the nearby square.

Castellane

There are no less than sixteen campgrounds in Castellane and the surrounding area. The region is very popular because of its proximity to the Gorges du Verdon. These are just a few of the campgrounds:

Castillon de Provence (nudist centre)
closed Oct to Mar
100 campsites
trailer rentals
s, ≈, ℜ
La Grande Terre, La Baume
☎04.92.83.64.24
This nudist camp is located 11km (6.6mi) from Castellane, near Lac de Castillon. It offers fishing and canoeing.

Camping Le Frédéric Mistral
60 campsites
s
Bd Frédéric Mistral, Castellane
☎04.92.83.62.27
⇄04.92.83.6879
This is the only campground that is open year-round. It is located only 100m (328.1ft) from the city centre, on Route Gorges du Verdon. However, it has few sports activities to offer. You can also stock up on supplies here.

Camping des Gorges du Verdon
closed Oct to Apr
235 campsites
bungalow and trailer home rentals
s, ℝ, tv, ≈
Route des Gorges du Verdon, Castellane
☎04.92.83.63.64
⇄04.92.83.74.72
This campground is located 9.5km from Castellane, towards Gorges du Verdon. A very pleasant and friendly place with coordinators who organize lots of sports activities. There is also a pool.

Camp du Verdon
closed Oct to Mar
500 sites
bungalows, trailers, studios and mobile homes for rent
shops, ℝ, tv, ≈
☎04.92.83.61.29
⇄04.92.83.69.37
This camp ground, the biggest and most extensive in the region, is located 1.2km (0.7mi) from Castellane when heading toward the Gorges du Verdon. Campers can partake in the many activities offered here and practise virtually every kind of summer sport (the only exception being tennis), including horseback riding. Highly recommended for families.

Camping International
200 sites
bungalows, trailers and mobile homes for rent
shops, ℝ, *tv,* ≈
Quartier de la Palud, Castellane
☎***04.92.83.66.67***

To reach the camp ground, take the N85 toward Digne. You can go horseback riding here, and there are many other activities as well. Ideal for families and definitely nicer than the previous camp since it's smaller.

Trigance

Le Vieil Amandier
290F-450F
½b 300F-370F/pers.
closed Nov to Feb
ps or pb, tv, ℜ, ≈
Montée Saint-Roch
☎***04.94.76.92.92***
⇄***04.94.85.68.65***

At the entrance to the village, you'll find Le Vieil Amandier. The owners, Monsieur and Madame Clap, are dynamic people (M. Clap is the village mayor) who are tirelessly devoted to improving their establishment. The rooms are comfortable, but those overlooking the pool are best, as they have small private terraces. Note: the owners prefer the half-board option since the restaurant is their main interest (see p 489).

Château de Trigance
600F-1,800F
½b 625F-775F/pers.
closed Nov to mid-Mar
pb, ℝ, *tv,* ℜ
☎***04.94.76.91.18***
⇄***04.94.85.68.99***

To experience the atmosphere of a medieval castle, stop at (or rather climb up to) the Château de Trigance. The owner, Guillaume Thomas welcomes you to this castle at the very top of the village that his parents completely renovated over the course of 30 years. And you'll no doubt run into Mr. Thomas, the father, as this cheerful fellow still putters about the area. The ancient 9th-century fortress was completely rebuilt and converted into a hotel about 30 years ago. Each room has a large bed with a medieval-style canopy, and is carefully and tastefully decorated with antique furniture that is often rearranged. This is a peaceful, restful site that offers a most spectacular panorama. Member of the Relais et Châteaux chain. See the description of the restaurant, p 489.

La Palud-sur-Verdon

This is a pleasant place to stop while visiting the Verdon gorges, since it's in the heart of nature but still offers a bit of action for those looking for a lively atmosphere. What's more, there is a slew of places to stay.

Auberge de Jeunesse
70F per person, bkfst incl.
sheets 17F
☎/⇄***04.92.77.38.72***

The Auberge de Jeunesse will suit travellers with simple needs. It has 65 beds, which are distributed among dormitories containing eight beds apiece (for a small surcharge, you can reserve one of two double rooms), and is run by some very friendly young people. There are sinks in the rooms, but the showers and bathrooms are shared. Twenty-five campsites are available as well *(27F, bkfst 19F)* and you can do your laundry for 25F.

Le Provence
235F-320F, ½b 225F-270F
closed Nov to Easter
pb, tv, P, ℜ
☎***04.92.77.38.88***
☎***04.92.77.36.50***
⇄***04.92.77.31.05***

Le Provence will sweep you off your feet. A small family hotel run by some truly friendly people, it has basic but comfortable rooms, especially #18, #19 and #20. These modern, adorable, little slope-roofed rooms also happen to be the least expensive. The food, which consists of regional specialties, is served buffet-style, and may be eaten in the little garden. At these prices, this place is an unbeatable deal! Moreover, the hotel has a restaurant (***$-$$***) that offers Provençale cuisine.

Hôtel des Gorges du Verdon
490F-540F/pers.
½b obligatory
closed Nov to Easter
pb, tv, P, ℜ, private terrace, ≈
☎04.92.77.38.26
⇌04.92.77.35.00
If you're looking for even more comfort and really want to be on top of things, so to speak, opt for the Hôtel des Gorges du Verdon. Overlooking the gorges and the village, this luxurious hotel, run by the same family for 25 years, was renovated during the winter of 1997-98. In fact, in order to keep the place up to snuff, the owners give it a complete overhaul every 10 years. This hotel is the perfect place to relax—you can take a swim in the heated pool (a new one to be reinstalled in 2001), enjoy a game of tennis or ping-pong or simply lounge about and admire the splendid scenery. Restaurant on site (***$-$$***).

Gorges du Verdon

Hôtel-Restaurant Du Grand Canyon
380F-460F, ½b 350F-390F
closed mid-Oct to Mar
pb, tv
Falaise des Cavaliers, D71
Aiguines
☎04.94.76.91.31
⇌04.94.76.92.29
The Hôtel-Restaurant Du Grand Canyon takes full advantage of the Gorges du Verdon, one of the Var's most magnificent sites. At an elevation of 800m (2,625ft), you can enjoy an exceptional panorama over the gorges from the restaurant or terrace. The hotel's greatest advantage is its proximity to the hiking trails that start right next to it. In addition, the rooms are quite comfortable. The owner will be glad to share his advice on hiking in the area. Always remember that nature reigns here. See the description of the restaurant , p 489.

Moustiers-Sainte-Marie

Le Relais
280F-480F, ½b 300F-380F
closed Dec and Jan
pb or ps, elevator, tv
☎04.92.74.66.10
⇌04.92.74.60.47
Le Relais stands right in the middle of town, by the waterfall that divides the village in two. You can expect a warm welcome and good service. The hotel is clean and comfortable (particularly the mattresses), and the location makes for a wonderful atmosphere. What's more, there are terrific views from the rooms; just wait until you wake up and open the shutters in the morning! Le Relais also has a pleasant restaurant that serves regional cuisine (see p 489).

Hôtel le Baldaquin
300F-450F
pb, tv
Place Clérissy
☎/⇌04.92.74.67.28
cell ***☎06.08.06.49.95***
Located in a middle-class, 17th-century house, on a small, quiet square, removed from the more commercial section of town, the Hôtel le Baldaquin is very appealing. The owners Monsieur and Madame Dumont are charming and ever-attentive to making your stay as enjoyable as possible. And they take care of everything themselves! The spacious rooms and modern bathrooms are spotless thanks to Madame, while Monsieur maintains the building, which he renovated himself.

La Bouscatière
750F-980F
bp
closed mid-Nov to mid-Dec and mid-Jan to mid-Mar
☎/⇌04.92.74.67.67
www.labouscatiere.com
This place lives up to its designation: guest residence. Build in 1765, it once served as a storage house for firewood (formerly called a *bouscatière* in French). This splendid and extremely original house, which once belonged to a potter, is built into the cliff. The common areas are wonderful, beginning with the cheerful and dazzling third-floor sitting room, that has a fireplace. But it's equally inviting to relax

in the small garden nestled between the house and the rock.

The rooms at La Bouscatière define refinement. For that matter, the owner, Tonia Peyot was responsible for decorating the rooms at the famous chef Alain Ducasse's **Bastide de Moustiers**, the description of which follows. The bathrooms here are spectacular. You can't imagine the ingenuity involved in the unique way that space has been utilized in this house, due to the way it has been built, clinging to the rock.

La Bastide de Moustiers
1,000F-1,750 F
pb, tv, ≡, ℜ, ℝ, ≈, *P*
Chemin de Quinson
☎04.92.70.47.47
⇌04.92.70.47.48
www.bastide-moustiers.i2m.fr
This hotel is set up in the former house of a master potter, and has been renovated and carefully refurbished by local artisans with the greatest respect for tradition. An integral part of chef Alain Ducasses's empire, La Bastide de Moustiers combines refinement and great comfort without the stuffiness so often found at luxury establishments. The location radiates tranquillity and offers gorgeous rustic views of the neighbouring countryside. It could be said that the concept is based on the principle of a secondary residence in the country. In this spirit, the rooms are equipped with everything necessary to put you at ease. For example, they supply you with a nightgown, bathrobe and slippers so you'll feel at home. Some rooms have fax machines, stereos or private terraces. What's more, if the pool and whirlpool aren't enough for you, you can always borrow a bicycle and go for a ride. They'll even arrange a picnic basket for you, should you so desire. In short, it's like a second home with valets and maids.

Les Salles-sur-Verdon

These two campgrounds are of similar size (approximately 100 campsites) and are located near a beach. They offer children's activities and have restaurants:

Camping Les Pins
Apr to Oct
☎04.94.70.20.80
⇌04.94.84.23.27

Camping La Source
Apr to Oct
☎04.94.70.20.40
⇌04.94.70.20.74

Gîtes de France
1,800F/2 ppl.; 2,300F/4 ppl. per week
pb, tv, ≡, *K, P*
8 Traverse St-Joseph
☎04.94.70.66.24
⇌04.94.70.79.84
In the vacation village of Lac de Sainte-Crois, Gîtes de France is owned by the daughter of Monsieur and Madame Bouillard of Tourtour (see p 484). The four comfortable furnished rooms have private terraces with barbecues and are only 500m (1641ft) from the lake. The first two, for two persons, measure 35m² (223 sq ft) and even have dishwashers and washing machines. The two others can each accommodate four people. They have air-conditioning, in addition to the same conveniences as the other rooms, and provide 55m² (589 sq ft) of space.

Bauduen

The Lac de Sainte-Croix region has several attractive areas for camping and taking advantage of available water sports.

Camping Les Vallons
Easter to Oct
☎04.94.70.09.13
⇌04.94.84.39.93
This small campground has 65 campsites near the lake. It features a pool, a restaurant, a store and activities for children.

Domaine de Majastre
380F bkfst incl.
pb, P, tv room, ≈
☎04.94.70.05.12
Located a few minutes from magnificent Lac de Sainte-Croix, the Domaine de Majastre is a guesthouse steeped in Provençal charm. The rooms are truly

inviting, with period furniture and parquet and Provençal-tile floors. What's more, there's a pool at the hotel, where you can pick up a snack.

Aups

L'Auberge de la Tour
260F-350F
closed Nov to Mar
ps or pb
☎04.94.70.00.30
⇄04.94.70.05.22
Located in a courtyard, set back from the road, L'Auberge de la Tour provides simple but decent rooms. The more expensive rooms, however, are likewise the more desirable. In the heart of the village, the hotel is next to numerous restaurants, bars and shops. This hotel seems to be the most peaceful in the village (see restaurant description, p 490).

Tourtour

Le Mas de l'Acacia
320F bkfst incl.
pb, tv, ≈
☎/⇄04.94.70.53.84
Le Mas de l'Acacia is a real find. At this guesthouse overlooking the surrounding plains, you can relax by the pool on a lovely terrace decked out with flowers. What really makes this place special, though, is the friendly hosts, Monsieur and Madame Bouillard, who go to great lengths to make sure that you have a pleasant stay. And then there are the comfortable, spotless rooms. This place is a real bargain, especially for Tourtour! A suite with communicating bedrooms and another with a private terrace (complete with a barbecue), a kitchen, a sitting room, a private bath and one or two bedrooms *(500F or 650F per day respectively)* are also available.

La Petite Auberge
490F-1,060F, ½b 490F-735F
pb, ℜ, tv, ℝ, ≈, ⌂
☎04.94.70.57.16
⇄04.94.70.54.52
La Petite Auberge belongs to the Relais du Silence chain. Located at the bottom of the village, on the hillside, it offers a lovely view over the surrounding countryside. The elegant rooms are generously proportioned, and were recently completely redecorated. They offer every modern convenience and are equipped with beautiful bathrooms with Italian tiles. It's as peaceful as you could wish, and you can relax beside the pool or in the sauna. For a description of the restaurant, see p 491.

L'Auberge St-Pierre
450F-530F
½b 425F-470F/pers.
closed mid-Oct to Mar
pb, shared tv lounge, ≈
☎04.94.70.57.17
⇄04.94.70.59.04
L'Auberge St-Pierre is located outside of the village, right in the countryside. This hotel, formerly a 16th-century residence, has been run by the same family for 40 years. The young owners are very proud of their Provençal roots. Paying particular attention to detail, they have created an authentic, rustic Provençal decor. The rooms provide all the necessary comforts, and some have terraces that open out onto the lovely swimming pool, which is kept covered until the weather is nice enough to permit swimming. The hotel grounds offer a pleasant place to take a stroll in a pastoral setting. See the description of the restaurant, p 491.

La Bastide de Tourtour
950F-1,500F
½b 770F-1,000F
pb, ℜ, tv, ℝ, ≈
☎04.98.10.54.20
⇄04.94.70.54.90
The Châteaux et Hôtels Indépendants chain has one hotel in this village, La Bastide de Tourtour, which is only a short walk from the small Saint-Denis church. This is an old, carefully tended Provençal country house where you will find tranquillity and fine dining in a luxurious decor. The rooms are well equipped, even the less expensive ones. Some have pretty terraces that look out onto a most peaceful panorama. Surrounding the hotel is a magnificent park perfect for a quiet walk. See the description of the restaurant, p 491.

Fox-Amphoux

Auberge du Vieux Fox
380F-530F
ps or pb, ℝ, tv
☎04.94.80.71.69
⇌04.94.80.78.38
The Auberge du Vieux Fox is shaded by the trees of a small square. This village has a population of... 15! Established in the old priory of a 12th-century Romanesque church, the eight rooms each have a different character and all were all redone in 1998. The bathrooms are modern, but the tile-work is in the Provençal style. See the description of the restaurant, p 491. To avoid disappointment, make your reservations early, especially during peak season.

Cotignac

Domaine de Nestuby
350F bkfst incl.
Mar to Oct
pb, P, ℜ
☎04.94.04.60.02
⇌04.94.04.79.22
Nathalie and Jean-François welcome you to this completely renovated 19th-century Provençal farmhouse in the heart of their vineyard. This guest house, lulled by the sound of cicadas, has been superbly redone. Breakfast (delicious home-made bread and preserves) or dinner (see p 492) is served in a vast dining room which was actually a stable when the house was first built. Also, the original tiling is magnificent. The exceptionally large rooms have modern bathrooms and are very comfortable. One of them can accommodate a family, since in addition to a double bed it has bunk-beds. And, of course, you can stock up on wine before you leave.

Entrecasteaux

Mamie Thérèse
230F-270F
closed Jan and Feb
ps, tv in the spacious lounge
Route de Carcès
☎04.94.73.84.00
An old country house that still has its stables, situated between Lorgues and Entrecasteaux, the Mamie Thérèse will welcome you at the heart of a shaded park. This site has lots of character with its blend of stone, wood and Provençal tilework. The inn's few rooms offer every comfort and are tastefully decorated. See the description of the restaurant, p 492.

Lorgues

Hôtel du Parc
170F-280F, ½b 160F-215F
closed mid-Nov to mid-Dec
ps or pb, tv
25 Boulevard Georges Clémenceau
☎04.94.73.70.01
With its shaded park and regional cuisine, the Hôtel du Parc promises a most pleasant stay. This hotel takes you back in time to the France of the 1950s and '60s. But most pleasant of all is the old-fashioned charm that permeates this simple hotel, and the rooms decorated with ancient furniture. Ask for room No. 7 or 8 (with sloping ceiling). They both have lovely views of the park. See the description of the restaurant, p 492.

La Celle

Hostellerie de l'Abbaye de la Celle
1,300F-1,900F
pb, tv, ≡, ℝ, ℜ, P, ≈
Place du Général de Gaulle
☎04.98.05.14.14
⇌04.98.05.14.15
www.abbaye-celle.com
This hotel consists of several buildings, of which the main one is a middle-class Provençal house dating from the 18th century. The Hostellerie de l'Abbaye de la Celle is the result of the collaborative efforts of Alain Ducasse and Bruno Clément, of the restaurant **Chez Bruno** (see p 492). In concept and spirit, it is a lot like **La Bastide de Moustiers** (see p 490). Calm and luxury are the order of the day: the rooms are spacious and well furnished, some with private terraces; sitting rooms and common areas have been spectacularly restored, as shown by the decorative woodwork and doors; the immense garden hides a pool; and finally, as all of this

would lead you to expect, the hotel has a first-class, gourmet restaurant (see p 493).

Restaurants

Les Arcs-sur-Argens

Le Logis du Guetteur
$$$-$$$$
Closed mid-Jan to Feb
☎04.94.99.51.10
⇌04.94.99.51.29
The restaurant at this hotel (see p 477) offers a cuisine that is full of Provençal flavours, a delight for the palate. As appetizers, if you can resist the batter–fried zucchini flowers with ricotta cheese, opt for the savoury crayfish, accompanied by its *gâteau de champignons.* Among chef-owner Max Callégari's other specialties are rack of lamb, encrusted with herbs and garlic and garnished with *petits farcis provençaux* (small stuffed vegetables). Incidentally, he places a lot of importance on the presentation of vegetables. Also deserving special mention is the strawberry *soupe* and its lavender–flavoured *sorbet*, a dessert like no other with a refined, delicate taste that suitably crowns the meal. Moreover, there is plenty of good wine to have with your meal, thanks to the excellent wine list established by Joël; this engaging and enthusiastic wine steward can also give you judicious advice about making your selecton.. All things considered, an unforgettable meal! In summer, this experience is even more agreeable, as your table will be located on the magnificent terrace where there is a charming view of the countryside.

Draguignan

La Mangeoire
$-$$
closed Sun
8 Rue Pierre Clément
La Mangeoire, is a little restaurant that serves Italian and Provençal specialties in a rustic and friendly setting. There are a few tables in a small enclave that opens onto the street. They offer a very affordable pitcher of wine (750 ml or 26.4 fl.oz), making an inexpensive complement to the meal.

Hostellerie du Moulin de la Foux
$-$$
closed Sun night
☎04.98.10.14.14
The restaurant of the Hostellerie du Moulin de la Foux serves, among other things, home-made foie gras and smoked salmon. Other specialties include *paillarde au basilic* (game), *gratin drocénois* and freshly caught trout. See the description of the rooms, p 477.

Châteaudouble

Le Restaurant du Château
$$$-$$$$
closed Tue, Tue and Wed (low season)
Place Vieille
☎04.94.70.90.05
Young chef Jean-Michel Bélin creates contemporary dishes in which French cuisine meets "fusion" cuisine. The menu offers *cuisine du marché*, which varies depending upon what has just arrived at the market. The chef does his shopping in Nice because, as he says, "The variety is incomparable!" One of his specialties consists of new versions of sauteed *foie gras.* In summer, meals are served outside on the square where tables are set up in front of an exceptional panorama of the Gorges de la Nartuby. And while you're here, why not spend the night (see p 478)?

Flayosc

Hôtel-Restaurant La Vieille Bastide
$$-$$$$
closed the first three weeks of Nov and the three last weeks of Jan and Sun and Mon (low season)
226 Rue du Peyron
☎04.98.10.62.62
⇌04.94.84.61.23
It's a thoroughly enjoyable experience to eat on a vast terrace shaded by 100-year-old chestnut trees. What's more, as night falls,

small lights attached to the trees create a magical atmosphere that is enhanced by soft classical music and impeccable service. So much for form! Let's move on to the substance—the food. Chefs Marie and Frédéric Guigoni believe they complement each other well as a twosome. Indeed they do, for they offer us a marriage of *savoir faire* that creates unforgettable flavours. Just consider the *noix de St-Jacques*, *queues de gambas* and *Sot-l'y-laisse* of free-range chicken, cooked in chicken broth with saffron pistils—an appetizer so generous it could substitute for a main course! If your mouth is already watering, note that the entire menu, from beginning to end, is equally inspiring.

Ampus

La Fontaine
$$-$$$
closed Feb and Oct and Mon and Tue (noon only Jul and Aug)
Place de la Fontaine
☎04.94.76.07.59
What a gem! You'll receive an unpretentious welcome from Alexandra, who will make you feel right at home. The chef, Marco, has a single goal: to pamper your taste buds. And he succeeds—especially since the restaurant was awarded a star in the Michelin guide. And the patrons are the ones who reap the rewards, the cost of the meal is set at 198F for dinner and 120F for lunch. These prices are unbelievable considering the category in which it ranks. What's more, La Fontaine earned its star for all the right reasons: the cuisine is interesting, creative and flavourful while the service is attentive and cheerful (Alexandra enjoys her work!). Guests are spared the heavy, pompous decorum so often found in top-notch restaurants. Marco and Alexandra are young and have a refreshing approach that is reflected in their restaurant: fresh, sophisticated cuisine served in a friendly manner so that guests can focus on enjoying their meal. It would be a crime to pass through this area without stopping here!

Callas

Gorges de Pennafort
$$$-$$$$
closed Sun evening and Mon off-season
☎04.94.76.66.51
This renowned restaurant is considered one of the best in the region. The chef creates Provençal cuisine with flavours that complement each other marvellously.

Fayence

Here are a few restaurants that were recommended by the locals:

L'Entracte
$
L'Entracte is a creperie, (they also offer pizza) that is ideal for small, simple meals anytime of the day.

Restaurant des Arts
$-$$
closed Wed except in summer
One Rue Font de Vins
☎04.94.76.00.20
Magali and Bernard Baranco run this simple, convivial restaurant on one of the town's steep, narrow streets. Magali, vibrant and Provençal to her fingertips, is also an actor and regularly organizes dinner-theatre evenings. The 250-year-old dwelling that houses the restaurant is charming, with vaulted ceilings and exposed wooden beams. Guests can enjoy good Provencal cooking here without spending a fortune. In summer meals are served on the attractive little square.

Le Patin Couffin
$$
closed Mon
Place de l'Olivier
☎04.94.76.29.96
Le Patin Couffin, gets its name from a Provençal expression that means "to skip from one subject to another." This restaurant has a very special atmosphere, and it is a meeting place for many of the locals, who put this quaint expression into practice. This restaurant offers a good quality to price ratio and also has a small

terrace in the front which allows you to catch all the goings on. Credit cards not accepted.

Auberge Fleurie
$$
Quartier Saint-Éloi
☎04.94.84.76.64
The Auberge Fleurie is situated below the village. The house specialties are fish, oysters and seafood. The mussels are excellent (50F *moules frites*), but the real highlight is the delicious shellfish fricassee. The *gratin de fruits rouges* is a tempting choice for dessert.

Auberge des Pins
$$
Domaine Le Chevalier
Tourrettes
☎04.94.76.06.36
⇌04.94.76.27.50
In this establishment located in a village near Fayence, grilled fish and meats are among the specialties. Otherwise, the menu includes Provençal specialities with market-fresh flavours: *aïoli*, *anchoïade* and, in summer, *petits farcis niçois*. If ordered 48hrs in advance, *bouillabaisse* is also available. In winter, the food becomes slightly heavier, featuring game and terrines of homemade *foie gras*. In any case, the climax is still the red–berry *tiramisu* drizzled with raspberry liqueur. Completely fresh and delectable!

Moulin de la Camandoule
$$$-$$$$
Chemin de Notre-Dame des Cyprès, between Fayence and Seillans
☎04.94.76.00.84
⇌04.94.76.10.40
Moulin de la Camandoule is a gourmet restaurant with a refined ambiance. You can opt for the poolside restaurant ***($$)*** which features grilled foods, or the more sophisticated restaurant ***($$$-$$$$)*** that also serves on the terrace in summer. Its menu features innovative *cuisine du marché*, as evidenced by the *marbré de langoustines royales et mangues à la pulpe d'avocat, vinaigrette d'agrumes* (prawns with mangoes, avocado pulp and citrus dressing), served as an appetizer.

Le Temps des Cerises
$$$-$$$$
closed last three weeks of Nov and last two weeks of Jan, also Tue night in summer only
Place de la République
☎04.94.76.01.19
It's hard to miss this new restaurant dominating the village main street. Especially since its decor and name are so attractive. The owner, originally from Holland, demolished everything to create the dining room and kitchen of his dreams. His fellow citizens would call it "top nickel," meaning spotless! For now, the food is still traditional French cuisine, but small exotic touches are beginning to appear on the menu. His intention is to eventually change to "fusion" cuisine, so that the fresh, top-quality products he uses can really soar.

Seillans

Hôtel-Restaurant des Deux Rocs
$$-$$$
Apr to Oct, closed Tue in low season
☎04.94.76.87.32
This restaurant is certainly one of the most magical places to eat on summer evenings. Candle-lit tables are set up under trees around the Provençal fountain that crowns the middle of the square in front of the hotel (see p 479). The Hôtel-Restaurant des Deux Rocs serves traditional French specialties and Provençal *cuisine du marché*. Brunch is also served on Sundays.

Montferrat

La Bastide des Moines
$$
☎04.94.70.92.09
⇌04.94.70.92.41
Located on the road between Draguignan and the Gorges du Verdon, La Bastide des Moines features buffet service for appetizers and desserts. The selection is varied and generous, and breads and breakfast rolls are baked on the premises. Meats cooked on a spit over a wood fire are a specialty, and unlimited, local wine is

considered part of the meal.

Mons

La Pierre sur le Toit
$
closed Nov to May and Mon
☎04.94.76.39.89
The pizzeria La Pierre sur le Toit also serves small, simple meals that will satisfy the whole family. Its terrace opens onto the Place Saint-Sébastien.

L'Auberge Provençale
$-$$
closed Nov and Tue
☎04.94.76.38.33
The major attraction of this little restaurant, located near the Place Saint-Sébastien, is its setting, perched high on the hillside. The picture windows in it's dining room literally overhang the landscape. What's more, its terrace encircles it completely. People often speak of panoramic views: this time, that's an understatement—the view is truly spectacular! You can stop here for a simple meal or for a snack, since it doubles as a tearoom.

Comps-sur-Artuby

Grand Hôtel Bain
$-$$$
closed mid-Nov to Christmas holidays
☎04.94.76.90.06
≠04.94.76.92.24
The confident, home–style cooking of each generation of the Bain family fits in perfectly with pure Provençal tradition: *soupe au pistou, pigeon farci* (stuffed squab), seasonal truffles menu, and delicious lavender–flavoured *glacé*. All are served on the terrace. Why not?!

Trigance

Vieil Amandier
closed Nov to Feb
Montée Saint-Roch
☎04.94.76.92.92
≠04.94.85.68.65
The dining room of the Vieil Amandier, with its sobre yet elegant decor, will delight you with its cuisine from the south of France ***($$-$$$)***. You can even savour a plate of truffles ***($$$$)*** that come from the area. Believe it or not, every dish on this menu contains truffles, even the dessert, which is a *crème brulé aux truffes*. While Madame see that everything goes smoothly in the dining room, smiling warmly here and there, Monsieur mans the stoves. His specialties include filet of red mullet as an appetizer and rack of lamb as a main course.

Château de Trigance
$-$$
The restaurant of the Château de Trigance (see p 481) serves fine gastronomic cuisine. One of its specialties is the *agneau faciaux pistaches encrôute de miel et fleur de Hym*. The dining room is spectacular. It is nestled in a stone vault, lending it a truly medieval atmosphere. But if you prefer to eat by daylight, you can also choose the terrace (10 tables only). The view is lovely.

Gorges du Verdon

Hôtel-Restaurant Du Grand Canyon
$$
The Hôtel-Restaurant Du Grand Canyon (see p 482) offers cuisine that ranges from simple to elaborate. The *soupe au pistou* (vegetable soup with basil and garlic) is recommended.

Moustiers-Sainte-Marie

Le Bellevue
$$
closed Tue off-season and Nov and Dec
☎04.92.74.66.06
Le Bellevue, has a particularly interesting terrace, which gives the impression of floating on an island. The interior, however, is rather dull. The restaurant serves Provençale specialties and game meats in season.

Le Relais
$$-$$$
closed Dec and Jan, and on Fri
Place du Couvent
≠04.92.74.60.47
The restaurant in the Hotel Le Relais serves good market cuisine that makes use of fresh regional products. Furthermore, the ser-

vice is pleasant and efficient. One appetizer was particularly impressive: the eggplant caviar with tomato coulis. Also worth mentioning is the cheese selection, which includes a large number of fresh local cheeses as well as some more traditional offerings. Finally, the wine chosen by the owner is both satisfying and affordable.

Les Santons
$$$$
closed mid-Nov to mid-Dec, Jan and Tue (Mon and Tue in low season)
☎04.92.74.66.48
≠04.92.74.63.67
www.les-santons.com
After a good meal at Les Santons, it's clear that the owner Monsieur Abert is a man of impeccable taste. Of course the beautiful Moustiers china adds to the pleasure of eating here; but the experience is enhanced even further, since you dine under an arbour on a small, flower–filled terrace overlooking the stream that runs through the village. On arrival, you're offered a delicious tapenade, served with *gressins* (slender toasted bread), by way of a welcome. Among the house specialties is an appetizer of delicious *ragoût d'escargot "petits gris" de la robine comme en bourrides* with croutons and potatoes. This is followed by rack of Sisteron lamb (famous), roasted with herbs and served with stuffed squash (remarkable), *panisses* and dried tomatoes. Next, the selections for the cheese platter proved to be rapturous, as did the lavender–flavoured *crème brûlée*. The menu states that its products are selected from the best suppliers. This isn't just hot air; it's a guarantee!

La Bastide de Moustiers
$$$$
Chemin de Quinson
☎04.92.70.47.47
≠04.92.70.47.48
www.bastide-moustiers.i2m.fr
The decor is nothing less than sumptuous at this restaurant whose flavours will make your day. Divided into several rooms, the dining room at La Bastide de Moustiers is magnificent, and the authenticity of the decor is displayed in the marquetry, decorative woodwork and fireplaces. The splendid custom-made lamps, created by a master artisan, add a slightly more contemporary touch, transcending the whole. But let's talk about the food! What can we say about the *bouillon de haricot coco* (green bean–based bouillon with egg) with its hint of vinegar, *caillé de brebis* (fresh curd cheese made from sheep's milk) and *aceto balsamico* (balsamic vinegar)? Ah! Meat and a squab with summer truffles, chanterelle mushrooms and giblet broth would be more to your liking? Done! Lastly, to enhance your pleasure, take a table on the shaded garden terrace that opens onto the countryside or, to prolong the experience, why not stay for the night (see p 485)?

Bauduen

Domaine de Majastre
$$
☎04.94.70.05.12
Located a few minutes from magnificent Lac de Sainte-Croix, the simple restaurant of the Domaine de Majastre offers a 120F table-d'hôte during the summer complete with apéritif. Wine is also available. *Soupe au pistou* is a house specialty. Finally, from December to March, a 300F truffle menu is available upon request

Aups

Auberge de la Tour
$-$$
closed Nov to late Mar
Auberge de la Tour offers reasonable prices. Copious meals are served in a lovely garden, away from all the ruckus of the town (see p 484). Regional market-fresh cuisine.

Chez Catherine
$$
closed Mon evenings and Tue in off-season
☎04.94.70.12.11
The locals also recommended Chez Catherine, located next to Place Général Girard. Behind the restaurant there is a lovely

shaded, flowering garden where it's wonderful to eat in summer. Also a delicatessen, this restaurant sells local products: oils, tapenades, honey, wine and preserves.

Restaurant l'Aiguière
$$-$$$
Closed Tue and Wed in low season
6 Place Maréchal Joffre
☎04.94.70.12.40
There's been a change of name and administration at this inviting little restaurant that stands out in Aups. Apart from the warm setting found inside, it offers a pretty shaded terrace in front. Michèle Boyer and Luc Dahot offer cuisine with Provençal flavours (*cannellonis de saumon* in a *coulis de favouille fraîche*) as well as *foie gras*, game, or dishes based on truffles, according to the rhythm of the seasons.

Tourtour

L'Alechou
$
closed Dec to Jan
☎04.94.70.54.76
For a simple, light lunch away from the action of the village's main square, stop at L'Alechou for crepes and salad in an intimate setting. There are several tables on the little terrace. A very good selection of delicious salads is available. The only disadvantage is that the restaurant is right next to the road. It can be noisy in summer at the height of tourist season.

Les Girandolles
$$
☎04.94.70.54.29
This restaurant–caterer below the church square sells top-quality groceries, notably preserves, as well as take-out meals.

L'Amandier
$$-$$$
Place des Ormeaux
☎04.94.70.56.64
Young chef Gouabault has studied under "greats" like Ducasse. He now runs a restaurant on the large, lively village square, where he serves traditional *cuisine du marché*.

Auberge St-Pierre
$$-$$$
closed Wed and mid-Oct to Mar
The restaurant of the Auberge St-Pierre (see p 484) takes pride in only using products that contribute to its healthy, natural appeal. The specialties are, of course, traditionally Provençale.

La Petite Auberge
$$$
closed mid-Nov to Feb
☎04.94.70.57.16
≠04.94.70.54.52
The restaurant at this charming hotel serves regional cooking that uses only the freshest of ingredients. In winter, patrons dine near the fireplace, while in summer, they're seated on the lovely, flower–decorated terrace. Among La Petite Auberge's specialties are: the sauteed scampi with seasonal fresh mushrooms, served with asparagus; and Provençal ravioli with cream sauce, flavoured with mild garlic and *pistou*. In summer, you can have a simple meal at poolside, thanks to the grill that's set up there.

La Bastide de Tourtour
$$$$
The restaurant of La Bastide de Tourtour offers a reasonable lunch menu *(weekends only, 160F)* considering the high quality of the establishment. Fine regional cuisine. See the description of the rooms, p 484.

Fox-Amphoux

Auberge du Vieux Fox
$$-$$$
The restaurant of l'Auberge du Vieux Fox offers simple regional cuisine. In keeping with traditional recipes, the *galette du berger*, an original lamb specialty, is worth mentioning. The dining room opens out onto the garden where guests can dine peacefully in warm weather. The dining room that opens out onto the back of the hotel offers a splendid view over the surrounding countryside. A noticeable detail: the dishes are all garnished with a delicious, oven-roasted clove of unpeeled garlic. See the description of the rooms, p 485.

Cotignac

Domaine de Nestuby
$$
Mar to Oct, closed Sat and Sun
☎04.94.04.60.02
⇄04.94.04.79.22
This guest house (see p 485) is also a *table d'hôte*. Guests and the family eat together at an immense table enthroned in the middle of the dining room. The ambiance is very festive, and allows you to learn a bit more about the lives of your hosts who, in this case, are wine-growers. The food is family–style Provençal cooking, and the wine, included in the price, flows in torrents.

Entrecasteaux

Auberge de Mamie Thèrese
$$
closed Feb, Sun evening and Mon
on the road towards Lorgues
☎04.94.73.84.00
The dining room of the Auberge de Mamie Thèrese serves Provençal specialties on the garden terrace, during the summer. In winter, the fireplace adds warmth to the already cosy, rustic atmosphere. Here you'll find both good value and a warm welcome. See the description of the rooms, p 485.

La Fourchette
$$-$$$
closed Jan and Feb, Sun evening and Mon
☎04.94.04.42.78
⇄04.94.04.40.91
Located next to the château at the top of the small hill, La Fourchette is typical of restaurants found at small family inns. You can dine in tranquillity on the beautiful terrace while admiring the Provençal countryside spread out before you. The owners, Pierre and Léa Nicolas, are a charming, unpretentious couple. Léa, a bilingual American, greets her guests warmly, while Pierre takes care of the kitchen. In addition to preparing truffles (*cassolette de St-Jacques aux truffes et feuilletage*, for example) that they find themselves with the help of their dog, Pierre concocts an absolutely divine dish of which he says people never tire. No wonder! His cannelloni with *foie gras* and smoked duck breast is absolutely exquisite and certainly leaves you with a memory that will last for a long, long time! Among the suggested menus is an interesting one at 200F that features the famous cannelloni and includes a glass of wine with each course. Well worth visiting!

Lorgues

Chez Doumè
$-$$
closed Mon during the high season, from Sun to Wed during the low season and from mid-Nov to mid-Dec
Place Clemenceau
☎04.94.67.68.97
Chez Doumè is a simple little restaurant that faces onto a pretty square. A few tables are set up outside during the warm weather. A delightful place for lunch.

Hôtel du Parc
$$-$$$
closed Sun evenings in off-season
The restaurant of the Hôtel du Parc, with its garden terrace, specializes in game meats, namely wild boar and rabbit, and truffles in season. This hotel is a very pleasant place to stop. See the description of the rooms, p 485.

Chez Bruno
$$$$
closed Sun pm and Mon
on the road from Logues to Les Arcs
☎04.94.85.93.93
⇄04.94.73.78.11
Chez Bruno, a typically Provençal farmhouse hidden away in the Varois countryside, is a veritable institution. People come from all over to savour Bruno's truffles. Guests can enjoy their meal outside at one of the numerous tables attractively set up on the flower-decked terrace.

The setting and food are no doubt too bourgeois, but the patrons certainly seem satisfied.

La Celle

Hostellerie de l'Abbaye de la Celle
$$$$
Place du Général de Gaulle
☎04.98.05.14.14
≠04.98.05.14.15
www.abbaye-celle.com
What can be said about this inn (see p 485), enshrined in a historical site? The great care applied to the preparation of meals is both echoed by the service and matched by the ravishing decor. Lastly, none of this ever becomes pretentious.

Entertainment

To find out about all the touristic and cultural activities taking place in the Var, visit the Web site: ***www.cg83.fr***.

Les-Arcs-sur-Argens

Les Médiévales
Jul, in years that end in even numbers
Re-enactments, parades and period costumes.

Draguignan

Foire de l'Olive
late Jun
Ten days of festivities linking tradition and entertainment.

Draguifolies
free
mid-July to mid-Aug
☎04.98.10.51.05
Various shows, jazz, rock, classical, and traditional music.

L'Eté Contemporain
Aug to Sep
☎04.98.10.51.05
Shows, exhibitions, and events in 14 different locations throughout the city.

Festival de Jazz
Oct
Jazz festival.

Callas

Festival de Musique Ancienne
last two weeks of Jul
Medieval music.

Fayence

Championnat du Monde de Voltige et de Vol à Voile
Sep
Gliding and acrobatics world championships.

Festival "Musique en Pays de Fayence"
late Oct
☎04.94.47.75.90
Gothic, Romanesque and baroque churches of the villages in the district of Fayence become the backdrop for chamber music concerts.

Bargème

Festival de Musique Ancienne
mid-Jul to mid-Aug
Medieval music.

Aups

Journée de la Truffe Noir
Jan
Black Truffle Day.

Fête de l'Olive
Mar
Olive Festival.

Les Nuits Musicales
Jul
Concerts.

Entrecasteaux

Festival International de Musique de Chambre
late Aug to early Sep
information:
☎04.94.04.40.50
Chamber music festival.

Lorgues

A l'Écoute des Jeunes Artistes
early Aug
☎04.94.67.67.62
Five concerts in five days, featuring young performers.

Le Thoronet

Rencontres de Musique Médiédale du Thoronet
mid-Jul
Week–long medieval music conference.

Brignoles

Piano Var
first week to the end of Jul
☎*04.94.69.41.70*
Piano festival.

Festival de Jazz
Aug
☎*04.94.69.30.19*
Jazz festival.

La Celle

Soirée Musicales de l'Abbaye de La Celle
mid-Jul to mid-Aug
Evenings of classical music.

Shopping

Draguignan

Marché de Noël
before Christmas to Dec 31
Place du Marché
☎*04.94.47.07.47*
Local products, arts-and-crafts and *santons.*

Châteaudouble

Bastide de Fonteye
☎*04.94.70.90.00*
Open to the public, the Bastide de Fonteye is a goat, cow and sheep farm, which produces traditional cheeses that are sold on the premises.

Callas

Le Moulin de Callas
8am to noon and 2pm to 6pm, closed Sun morning
Quartier les Ferrages
☎*04.94.76.68.05*
Since 1928, the Bérenguier family has run this mill. Very high quality oil is produced here. Hand-crafted salad bowls and other home-made products (preserves, honey, soaps) are also on sale here.

Fayence

Marché Paysan de la Ferme du Laquet
closed Mon, Tue to Sun 8am to 12:30pm, Fri and Sat 4pm to 7:30pm
Between Fayence and Callian
☎*04.94.47.68.07*
Producers in the canton of Fayence bring their fresh produce to the farmers market at the Ferme du Laquet.

Fayence Tissu
closed Jan and Sun
24 Place Léon Roux
☎*04.94.76.10.61*
Fayence Tissu are specialists in making Provençal fabric and offer 400 swatches to choose from. Three full-time seamstresses will have your napkins, towels, bedspreads or cushions ready before the end of the day.

La Faïencerie
closed Jan and Sun
Placette de l'Olivier
☎*04.94.76.03.79*
This store sells authentic Provençal glazed earthenware, as well as glasses and ovenware from other areas in the region.

Trigance

Le Moulin de Soleils
☎*04.94.85.66.17*
⇌*04.94.76.91.89*
Monsieur Amoros is one of a rare breed: a miller! In fact, he is passionately involved in running the last working traditional flour mill. This imposing, hand-crafted water–powered mill produces organic flour of a kind that is no longer available. The miller then uses it to make enormous loaves of old-fashioned bread. His reputation is beginning to spread. Famous restaurant owners, having heard about his bread, are starting to buy their supplies from him. Since Le Moulin de Soleils is a small, family-run, hands-on operation, it's hard for him to distribute his product, despite the demand. So it's best to go directly to him. Apart from bread, soaps and honeys from Verdon are also sold here. Lastly, his wife runs a small *crêperie* which serves crepes made from his flour and organic fruit juices.

Moustiers-Sainte-Marie

You simply cannot leave this magnificent village without browsing through the many shops that sell locally produced earthenware.

Le Cloître
on one of the village lanes
☎04.92.74.62.03
⎙04.92.74.62.15
Many people in Moustiers make their living in the glazed–earthenware industry. Traditional Moustiers china is very standard: pastel patterns on a white background. While most stores sell this pottery, Le Cloître features glazed earthenware made by artists. The shapes are more original and the colours are different (the green is incredible!). Moreover, the kind owner packages these creations flawlessly, so you need not worry.

Aups

The beautiful **Atmosphère** store offers a wide variety of Provençal products: wine, dried flowers, cosmetics, soaps, dishes, fabric, etc.

Le Mille Morceaux
Place Gauthier
☎04.94.84.02.32
Yveline Gatau of Le Mille Morceaux makes and sells incredible mosaics. She uses pieces of Salernes tiling to create lamps, tables and astonishing decorative obects. This isn't kitsch, it's art. Her work is truly striking and creative. No wonder she sells it all over the world!

Brocante la Déniche
in the pedestrian centre
☎06.80.22.81.28
The Brocante la Déniche is the place to go if you'd like to bring home beautiful, old-fashioned embroidered sheets or an embroidered lace nightgown.

Tourtour

Fol Avoine
Courtyard of the Raphaelis Château
☎04.94.70.55.19
This pretty shop sells Jacquard tablecloths, top quality decorative objects, china settings and soaps. Fol Avoine also has a whole range of interesting educational products, toys and accessories for children.

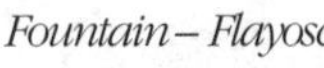
Fountain – Flayosc

L'Estoffe
☎04.94.70.59.13
L'Estoffe sells Provençal fabric as well as napkins, towels and clothing that are made from it. The owner is a tailor and, with advance notice, can make whatever you would like.

Barjols

This little village with few tourist attractions is primarily renowned for the making of various **leather goods**. A leather fair takes place here in August.

Lorgues

Sharing space with the restaurant Chez Bruno, **La Truffe et le Vin** is a specialty food shop that sells foie gras, oils and carafes, as well as truffles and wine, as you would expect.

Le Thoronet
Monastère de Bethléem
next to the Abbaye du Thoronet
☎04.94.85.92.05
The monks and nuns at the Bethléem monastery make beautiful hand-crafted objects, including glazed earthenware, hand-painted icons, wooden sculptures and greeting cards. They also make plant–based health and hygiene products.

English-French Glossary

Greetings

Hi (casual)	*Salut*
How are you?	*Comment ça va?*
I'm fine	*Ça va bien*
Hello (during the day)	*Bonjour*
Good evening/night	*Bonsoir*
Goodbye, See you later	*Bonjour, Au revoir, à la prochaine*
Yes	*Oui*
No	*Non*
Maybe	*Peut-être*
Please	*S'il vous plaît*
Thank you	*Merci*
You're welcome	*De rien, Bienvenue*
Excuse me	*Excusez-moi*
I am a tourist.	*Je suis touriste*
I am American (m/f)	*Je suis Américain(e)*
I am Canadian (m/f)	*Je suis Canadien(ne)*
I am British	*Je suis Britannique*
I am German (m/f)	*Je suis Allemand(e)*
I am Italian (male/female)	*Je suis Italien(ne)*
I am Belgian	*Je suis Belge*
I am Swiss	*Je suis Suisse*
I am sorry, I don't speak French	*Je suis désolé(e), je ne parle pas français*
Do you speak English?	*Parlez-vous anglais ?*
What is your name?	*Quel est votre nom?*
My name is...	*Je m'appelle...*
friend (m/f)	*ami(e)*
single (m/f)	*celibataire*
married (m/f)	*marié(e)*
divorced (m/f)	*divorcé(e)*
widower/widow	*veuf(ve)*

Directions

Is there a tourism office near here?	*Est-ce qu'il y a un bureau de tourisme près d'ici?*
Where is...?	*Où est le/la ... ?*
straight ahead	*tout droit*
to the right	*à droite*
to the left	*à gauche*
beside	*à côté de*
near	*près de*
here	*ici*
there, over there	*là, là-bas*
into, inside	*à l'intérieur*
outside	*à l'extérieur*
in front of	*devant*
behind	*derrière*

Getting Around

airport	*aéroport*
on time	*à l'heure*
late	*en retard*
cancelled	*annulé*

plane	*l'avion*
car	*la voiture*
train	*le train*
boat	*le bateau*
bicycle	*la bicyclette, le vélo*
bus	*l'autobus*
train station	*la gare*
bus stop	*un arrêt d'autobus*
corner	*coin*
neighbourhood	*quartier*
square	*place*
tourist office	*bureau de tourisme*
bridge	*pont*
building	*immeuble*
safe	*sécuritaire*
fast	*rapide*
baggage	*bagages*
schedule	*horaire*
one way ticket	*aller simple*
return ticket	*aller retour*
arrival	*arrivée*
return	*retour*
departure	*départ*
north	*nord*
south	*sud*
east	*est*
west	*ouest*

Cars

for rent	*à louer*
a stop	*un arrêt*
highway	*autoroute*
no passing	*défense de doubler*
no parking	*stationnement interdit*
no exit	*impasse*
parking	*stationnement*
pedestrians	*piétons*
gas	*essence*
traffic light	*feu de circulation*
service station	*station-service*
speed limit	*limite de vitesse*

Money

bank	*banque*
credit union	*caisse populaire*
exchange	*change*
money	*argent*
I don't have any money	*je n'ai pas d'argent*
credit card	*carte de crédit*
traveller's cheques	*chèques de voyage*
The bill please	*l'addition, s'il vous plaît*
receipt	*reçu*

Accommodation

inn	*auberge*
youth hostel	*auberge de jeunesse*
bed and breakfast	*gîte*
hot water	*eau chaude*
air conditioning	*climatisation*
accommodation	*logement, hébergement*
elevator	*ascenseur*
bathroom	*toilettes, salle de bain*
bed	*lit*
breakfast	*déjeuner*
bedroom	*chambre*
pool	*piscine*
floor (first, second...)	*étage*
high season	*haute saison*
off season	*basse saison*
fan	*ventilateur*

Shopping

open	*ouvert(e)*
closed	*fermé(e)*
How much is this?	*C'est combien?*
I need...	*J'ai besoin de...*
a store	*un magasin*
a department store	*un magasin à rayons*
the market	*le marché*
salesperson (m/f)	*vendeur(se)*
the customer (m/f)	*le / la client(e)*
to buy	*acheter*
to sell	*vendre*
skirt	*une jupe*
shirt	*une chemise*
pants	*des pantalons*
jacket	*un blouson*
blouse	*une blouse*
shoes	*des souliers*
sandals	*des sandales*
hat	*un chapeau*
eyeglasses	*des lunettes*
handbag	*un sac*
gifts	*cadeaux*
local crafts	*artisanat local*
sun protection products	*crèmes solaires*
cosmetics and perfumes	*cosmétiques et parfums*
camera	*appareil photo*
film	*pellicule*
records, cassettes	*disques, cassettes*
newspapers	*journaux*
magazines	*revues, magazines*
batteries	*piles*
watches	*montres*
jewellery	*bijouterie*
gold	*or*
silver	*argent*
wool	*laine*
cotton	*coton*
leather	*cuir*

Miscellaneous

big, tall (person)	*grand(e)*
small, short (person)	*petit(e)*
short (length)	*court(e)*
low	*bas(se)*
fat (person)	*gros(se)*
slim, skinny (person)	*mince*
a little	*peu*
a lot	*beaucoup*
something	*quelque chose*
nothing	*rien*
good	*bon*
bad	*mauvais*
more	*plus*
less	*moins*
big	*grand*
small	*petit*
hot	*chaud*
cold	*froid*
I am ill	*je suis malade*
pharmacy, drugstore	*pharmacie*
I am hungry	*j'ai faim*
I am thirsty	*j'ai soif*
What is this?	*Qu'est-ce que c'est?*
Where?	*Où?*

Weather

rain	*pluie*
clouds	*nuages*
sun	*soleil*
It is hot out	*Il fait chaud*
It is cold out	*Il fait froid*

Time

When?	*Quand?*
What time is it?	*Quelle heure est-il?*
minute	*minute*
hour	*heure*
day	*jour*
week	*semaine*
month	*mois*
year	*année*
yesterday	*hier*
today	*aujourd'hui*
tomorrow	*demain*
morning	*le matin*
afternoon	*l'après-midi*
evening	*le soir*
night	*la nuit*
now	*maintenant*
never	*jamais*
Sunday	*dimanche*
Monday	*lundi*
Tuesday	*mardi*
Wednesday	*mercredi*
Thursday	*jeudi*
Friday	*vendredi*

Saturday	*samedi*
January	*janvier*
February	*février*
March	*mars*
April	*avril*
May	*mai*
June	*juin*
July	*juillet*
August	*août*
September	*septembre*
October	*octobre*
November	*novembre*
December	*décembre*

Communication

post office	*bureau de poste*
air mail	*par avion*
stamps	*timbres*
envelope	*enveloppe*
telephone book	*bottin téléphonique*
long distance call	*appel outre-mer*
collect call	*appel collecte*
fax	*télécopieur, fax*
telegram	*télégramme*

Activities

swimming	*la baignade*
beach	*plage*
scuba diving	*la plongée sous-marine*
snorkelling	*la plongée-tuba*
fishing	*la pêche*
sailing	*navigation de plaisance*
windsurfing	*la planche à voile*
bicycling	*faire du vélo*
mountain bike	*vélo tout-terrain (VTT)*
horseback riding	*équitation*
hiking	*la randonnée pédestre*
museum or gallery	*musée*
cultural centre	*centre culturel*
cinema	*cinéma*

Touring

river	*fleuve, rivière*
waterfalls	*chutes*
viewpoint	*belvedère*
hill	*colline*
garden	*jardin*
wildlife reserve	*réserve faunique*
peninsula	*péninsule, presqu'île*
south/north shore	*côte sud/nord*
town or city hall	*hôtel de ville*
court house	*palais de justice*
church	*église*
house	*maison*
manor	*manoir*
bridge	*pont*
dam	*barrage*

workshop	*atelier*
historic site	*lieu historique*
train station	*gare*
stables	*écuries*
convent	*couvent*
door, archway, gate	*porte*
customs house	*douane*
locks	*écluses*
market	*marché*
canal	*canal*
seaway	*voie maritime*
museum	*musée*
cemetery	*cimitière*
mill	*moulin*
windmill	*moulin à vent*
hospital	*Hôtel Dieu*
lighthouse	*phare*
barn	*grange*
waterfall(s)	*chute(s)*
sandbank	*batture*
neighbourhood, region	*faubourg*

NUMBERS

1	*un*
2	*deux*
3	*trois*
4	*quatre*
5	*cinq*
6	*six*
7	*sept*
8	*huit*
9	*neuf*
10	*dix*
11	*onze*
12	*douze*
13	*treize*
14	*quatorze*
15	*quinze*
16	*seize*
17	*dix-sept*
18	*dix-huit*
19	*dix-neuf*
20	*vingt*
21	*vingt-et-un*
30	*trente*
40	*quarante*
50	*cinquante*
60	*soixante*
70	*soixante-dix*
80	*quatre-vingt*
90	*quatre-vingt-dix*
100	*cent*
200	*deux cents*
1,000	*mille*
10,000	*dix mille*
1,000,000	*un million*

Index

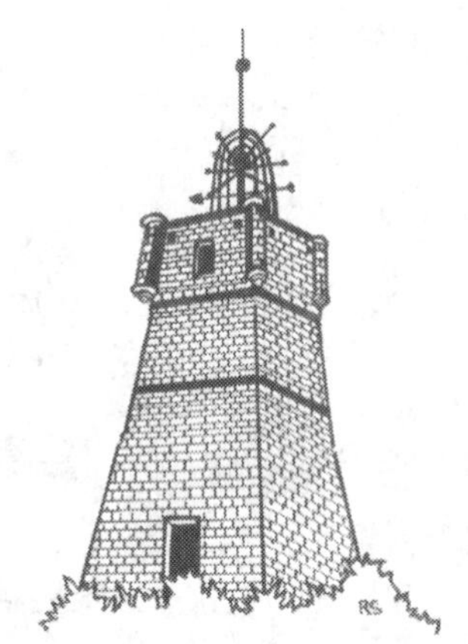

Order Form

Ulysses Travel Guides

- ☐ Atlantic Canada .... $24.95 CAN / $17.95 US
- ☐ Bahamas .... $24.95 CAN / $17.95 US
- ☐ Beaches of Maine .... $12.95 CAN / $9.95 US
- ☐ Bed & Breakfasts in Québec .... $14.95 CAN / $10.95 US
- ☐ Belize .... $16.95 CAN / $12.95 US
- ☐ Calgary .... $17.95 CAN / $12.95 US
- ☐ Canada .... $29.95 CAN / $21.95 US
- ☐ Chicago .... $19.95 CAN / $14.95 US
- ☐ Chile .... $27.95 CAN / $17.95 US
- ☐ Colombia .... $29.95 CAN / $21.95 US
- ☐ Costa Rica .... $27.95 CAN / $19.95 US
- ☐ Cuba .... $24.95 CAN / $17.95 US
- ☐ Dominican Republic .... $24.95 CAN / $17.95 US
- ☐ Ecuador and Galápagos Islands .... $24.95 CAN / $17.95 US
- ☐ El Salvador .... $22.95 CAN / $14.95 US
- ☐ Guadeloupe .... $24.95 CAN / $17.95 US
- ☐ Guatemala .... $24.95 CAN / $17.95 US
- ☐ Hawaii .... $29.95 CAN / $21.95 US
- ☐ Honduras .... $24.95 CAN / $17.95 US
- ☐ Islands of the Bahamas .... $24.95 CAN / $17.95 US
- ☐ Las Vegas .... $17.95 / $12.95
- ☐ Lisbon .... $18.95 CAN / $13.95 US
- ☐ Louisiana .... $29.95 CAN / $21.95 US
- ☐ Martinique .... $24.95 CAN / $17.95 US
- ☐ Montréal .... $19.95 CAN / $14.95 US
- ☐ New Orleans .... $17.95 CAN / $12.95 US
- ☐ New York City .... $19.95 CAN / $14.95 US
- ☐ Nicaragua .... $24.95 CAN / $16.95 US
- ☐ Ontario's Best Hotels and Restaurants .... $16.95 CAN / $12.95US
- ☐ Ontario .... $27.95 CAN / $19.95US
- ☐ Ottawa .... $17.95 CAN / $12.95 US
- ☐ Panamá .... $24.95 CAN / $17.95 US
- ☐ Peru .... $27.95 CAN / $19.95 US
- ☐ Phoenix .... $16.95 CAN / $12.95 US
- ☐ Portugal .... $24.95 CAN / $16.95 US
- ☐ Provence - Côte d'Azur .... $29.95 CAN / $21.95US
- ☐ Puerto Rico .... $24.95 CAN / $17.95 US
- ☐ Québec .... $29.95 CAN / $21.95 US
- ☐ Québec City .... $17.95 CAN / $12.95 US
- ☐ Québec and Ontario with Via .... $9.95 CAN / $7.95 US
- ☐ Seattle .... $17.95 CAN / $12.95 US
- ☐ Toronto .... $18.95 CAN / $13.95 US
- ☐ Tunisia .... $27.95 CAN / $19.95 US
- ☐ Vancouver .... $17.95 CAN / $12.95 US
- ☐ Washington D.C. .... $18.95 CAN / $13.95 US
- ☐ Western Canada .... $29.95 CAN / $21.95 US

Ulysses Due South

- ☐ Acapulco .... $14.95 CAN / $9.95 US
- ☐ Belize .... $16.95 CAN / $12.95 US
- ☐ Cartagena (Colombia) .... $12.95 CAN / $9.95 US
- ☐ Cancun Cozumel .... $17.95 CAN / $12.95 US
- ☐ Huatulco - Puerto Escondido .... $17.95 CAN / $12.95 US

☐ Los Cabos and La Paz .... $14.95 CAN
$7.99 US

☐ Puerto Plata - Sosua ..... $14.95 CAN
$9.95 US

☐ Puerto Vallarta .... $14.95 CAN
$9.95 US

☐ St. Martin and St. Barts .... $16.95 CAN
$12.95 US

Ulysses Travel Journals

☐ Ulysses Travel Journal .. $9.95 CAN
(Blue, Red, Green, Yellow, Sextant)
$7.95 US

☐ Ulysses Travel Journal ... $14.95 CAN
(80 Days)
$9.95 US

Ulysses Green Escapes

☐ Cycling in France .... $22.95 CAN
$16.95 US

☐ Cycling in Ontario ...... $22.95 CAN
$16.95 US

☐ Hiking in the Northeastern U.S. .... $19.95 CAN
$13.95 US

☐ Hiking in Québec .... $19.95 CAN
$13.95 US

Ulysses Conversation Guides

☐ French for Better Travel .. $9.95 CAN
$6.50 US

☐ Spanish for Better Travel in Latin America .. $9.95 CAN
$6.50 US

Title	Qty	Price	Total

Name:	Subtotal	
	Shipping	$4 CAN $3 US
Address:	Subtotal	
	GST in Canada 7%	
	Total	

Tel: Fax:

E-mail:

Payment: ☐ Cheque ☐ Visa ☐ MasterCard

Card number________________________ Expiry date______________

Signature____

ULYSSES TRAVEL GUIDES

4176 St-Denis,
Montréal, Québec, H2W 2M5
(514) 843-9447
fax (514) 843-9448

305 Madison Avenue,
Suite 1166,
New York, NY 10165
Toll free: 1-877-542-7247

www.ulyssesguides.com
info@ulysses.ca